The Practical Guide to Humanitarian Law

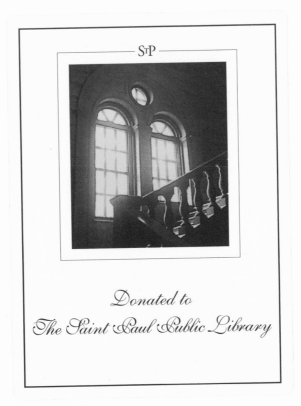

The Practical Guide to Humanitarian Law

First English Language Edition

Françoise Bouchet-Saulnier

Edited and Translated by Laura Brav

ROWMAN & LITTLEFIELD PUBLISHERS, INC.
Lanham • Boulder • New York • Oxford

ROWMAN & LITTLEFIELD PUBLISHERS, INC.

Published in the United States of America
by Rowman & Littlefield Publishers, Inc.
4720 Boston Way, Lanham, Maryland 20706
www.rowmanlittlefield.com

12 Hid's Copse Road
Cumnor Hill, Oxford OX2 9JJ, England

British Cataloguing-in-Publication Information Available

Library of Congress Cataloging-in-Publication Data

Bouchet-Saulnier, Françoise.
  [Dictionnaire pratique de droit humanitaire. English]
  The practical guide to humanitarian law / Françoise Bouchet-Saulnier.—1st English language ed.
    p. cm.
  Includes index.
  ISBN 0-7425-1062-X (cloth : alk. paper)—ISBN 0-7425-1063-8 (pbk. : alk. paper)
  1. Humanitarian law—Dictionaries. 2. Human rights—Dictionaries. 3. Treaties—Ratification—Indexes.
 I. Title.

KZ6471.B6813   2002
341.4'81'03—dc21   2001016227

Printed in the United States of America

∞™ The paper used in this publication meets the minimum requirements of American
National Standard for Information Sciences—Permanence of Paper for Printed Library
Materials, ANSI/NISO Z.39.48-1992.

To Christian, Martin, Jean, and Clémence

This book is dedicated to all those who confront violence and human destruction,
whether in their hearts or on their television screens;
to all those who suffer violence;
and to all those who fight it.

Contents

Acknowledgments

I would like to thank Médecins Sans Frontières (without whose support, trust, and encouragement this work would never have been possible) and all volunteers everywhere who fight to defend human dignity through their relief work.

I would first like to thank Laura Brav for her tireless commitment to the production of the English edition of this book.

I would like to thank Fabien Dubuet, in particular, for his invaluable and unremitting collaboration in the preparation of the book.

I would like to thank Jacqueline Schuchman for the thoroughness and precision of her work in defining the structure of the guide.

I would like to thank Roselyne Boisseau for her work in preparing the new edition, and Chrystel Battistella and Natacha Carrelet for their work in updating the index.

I would like to thank Dominique Borde for his financial support toward the English translation of this book.

I would also like to thank the following people, both for their meticulous proofreading of the text and for the invaluable advice they have given me:

- Louise Doswald-Beck and the Legal Division of the International Committee of the Red Cross;
- Stéphanie Jaquemet, legal adviser at the United Nations High Commissioner for Refugees;
- Brigitte Stern, professor of International Public Law at the University of Paris-I Panthéon-Sorbonne.

Abbreviations

GENEVA CONVENTIONS AND PROTOCOLS

GCI	Geneva Convention for the Amelioration of the Condition of the Wounded and Sick in Armed Forces in the Field, August 12, 1949
GCII	Geneva Convention for the Amelioration of the Condition of the Wounded, Sick, and Shipwrecked Members of Armed Forces at Sea, August 12, 1949
GCIII	Geneva Convention Relative to the Treatment of Prisoners of War, August 12, 1949
GCIV	Geneva Convention Relative to the Protection of Civilians in Time of War, August 12, 1949
PI	Protocol Additional to the Geneva Conventions of 12 August 1949, and Relating to the Protection of Victims of International Armed Conflicts, June 8, 1977
PII	Protocol Additional to the Geneva Conventions of 12 August 1949, and Relating to the Protection of Victims of Non-International Armed Conflicts, June 8, 1977

INTERNATIONAL ORGANIZATIONS AND AGENCIES
(SEE INDEX FOR ADDITIONAL ABBREVIATIONS)

ECOSOC	Economic and Social Council of the UN
FAO	Food and Agricultural Organization
GA	General Assembly of the UN
ICC	International Criminal Court
ICRC	International Committee of the Red Cross
ICTR-Y	International Criminal Tribunals for Rwanda and former Yugoslavia
NATO	North-Atlantic Treaty Organization
NGO	Nongovernmental organization
OAS	Organization of American States
OAU	Organization of African Unity
OCHA	UN Office for the Coordination of Humanitarian Affairs

OSCE	Organization for Security and Cooperation in Europe
UN	United Nations
UNDP	UN Development Program
UNHCHR	UN High Commissioner for Human Rights
UNHCR	UN High Commissioner for Refugees
UNICEF	UN Children's Fund
UNIFEM	UN Development Fund for Women
WEU	Western European Union
WFP	World Food Program
WHO	World Health Organization

Legend

What follows are some general guidelines for reading and interpreting the entries, specifically addressing the individual features that recur throughout the *Guide:*

- Boxed, screened text with a pointing hand: summary of key points addressed in entry
- Boxed, unscreened text with headlines: additional important points
- → cross-references to related topics covered in the *Guide;* cross-references at the end of a paragraph refer only to that paragraph, those directly below a paragraph only to that section, and those at the end of an entry to the entire entry
- 📖 further reading on the topic
- ✎ the address of the organization or agency referred to in the entry

Introduction

The international law of armed conflict, known as humanitarian law, is a law that is argued and defended through action. It belongs neither to lawyers nor specialists, and it must be understood and defended by a great number of actors.

This guide is for those who may never read the Geneva Conventions (the main texts regulating humanitarian law) but who strive to defend spaces of humanity through concrete relief actions. It is for those who try to understand the acts played out before them in the international arena and who wonder what is the purpose of law when there is no justice. It is also for lawyers, who may feel disoriented when faced with international humanitarian law meant to regulate relations between parties as unequal as states and armies, on one side, and individuals and relief organizations, on the other.

Finally, it is for each and every one of us, potential victims of the violence of armed conflicts, to help us resist and survive crimes against humanity and to make the emerging global society a little more humane.

This book strives to give back precise meaning and content to all the words that have invaded the media's language of tragedy, when all the while we have forgotten that these terms carry legal weight. Its aim is to introduce its readers to the international legal standards that regulate situations of crisis and conflict, to acquaint them with the laws meant to enable individuals to withstand times of inhumanity chaos and insanity.

This is not an academic work; there are already many scholarly books on humanitarian law. However, those are written mostly by lawyers for other lawyers, whereas most humanitarian actors have no legal background. Furthermore, they often explain the rules from the point of view of the dominant and most powerful actors: states and armed forces.

This book presents humanitarian law in a new light: from the perspective of relief action carried out for the benefit of victims. It sets forth an interpretation of the rules that defends the interests of the weakest.

It aims to convey, in clear and simple terms, the entire set of rules protecting the victims, and conferring rights and duties upon relief organizations.

From A to Z, it enumerates the rights of victims and humanitarian organizations in times of conflict, tension, and crises. It defines the responsibilities of the different actors in these situations and their margin of action. It highlights the traps that await relief action and can turn such responses into illusions that conceal dehumanization or extermination. Finally, it lists the legal arguments that will enable humanitarian actors to define and defend relevant relief initiatives in each specific context.

This book is a practical guide to the different ways in which international law can be used for relief actions. As such, it covers both humanitarian law in the strict sense and other applicable branches of international law, as well as certain aspects of international relations.

The main provisions of the Geneva Conventions and their Additional Protocols, relating to protection and assistance for victims of conflicts, are explained throughout the text. The reader will also find the key elements of other legal instruments likely to be applicable to situations in which the protection offered by humanitarian law cannot be applied or is rejected by certain actors. These instruments include refugee law; conventions on torture, genocide, the rights of the child, and human rights; international criminal law; as well as the rules governing peacekeeping and the interstate solidarity mechanism organized within the UN.

Humanitarian actors are rarely lawyers. If they are to defend relevant notions of humanitarian law through their daily acts, they must understand the key elements of this law. These are elements that enable them to define, identify, and label the various situations of danger; the populations and individuals who must be protected; the rights, duties, and responsibilities of the different national, international, and nongovernmental actors; the crimes set forth by humanitarian law and the recourses it provides.

Today, international human rights and humanitarian laws outline, on paper, the legal protection foreseen for civilians in situations of crisis or armed conflict. Similarly, humanitarian action has never been so widespread or so well regarded. Yet, in many countries, entire populations are faltering under scourges created by humankind, and the rights of individuals are disintegrating under the rule of the most powerful. Why is there such a gap between laws and reality?

We cannot help but notice that the defense of victims' rights rarely echoes across a courtroom floor, nor is it reflected in experts' opinions. Although international law establishes mechanisms of implementation, control, defense, and sanction, states are rarely willing to implement them. Apparently for diplomatic reasons, states and the United Nations clearly seem reluctant to acknowledge a situation as one of armed conflict. This is even more true in the case of internal conflict. Hiding behind soft vocabulary can help ease diplomatic tensions and can also appease feelings of failure on the side of international organizations, such as the UN, whose aim is to preserve peace. But it leads to the terrible result of depriving individuals of their legal status of war victims. The debate about the protection of internally displaced persons illustrates this reluctance to recognize them as victims of an armed conflict.

Perhaps worse still, the supposed victims' defenders—whether organizations or individuals, lawyers or nonlawyers—still know too little about the minimum standards of protection for humanity.

When individuals are in danger because the community can no longer defend them, or no longer wants to, international law establishes minimum rights to international assistance and protection for every person and authorizes humanitarian relief actions.

We forget too often that the front lines of humanitarian law are not defended before courts but through concrete relief actions. Acts that protect populations during life-threatening emergencies cannot wait long enough for the time required by justice, yet they must be rooted in law.

Law in general, and humanitarian law in particular, result from rigorous definitions and wording that describe facts and situations. Therefore, all it takes is a simple semantic spin to turn a situation regulated by law into one that entails no legal obligations. All it takes is calling a genocide a "humanitarian crisis," and the entire set of legal obligations to which states are beholden vanishes.

ONE WAR BEHIND

Wars often end with a legal victory: the adoption of new texts meant to provide more protection and to prevent similar suffering from ever happening again. Paradoxically, if these new laws are not later interpreted in a way adapted to new forms of danger and threats to individuals, they will always be one war behind.

In 1949, after World War II caused thirty-eight million deaths, political and military leaders of all states drafted international conventions. Four conventions, signed in Geneva on August 12, 1949, are mainly pragmatic: they establish clear limits on the destruction and killing that are allowed during armed conflicts. They set forth precise obligations to provide protection and relief for the most vulnerable categories of the population. They define the essential difference between acts of war, war crimes, and crimes against humanity.

To protect the principles of humanity in situations of armed conflict, these conventions do not rely mainly on condemnations under justice—which are unlikely to occur and too slow to save lives. Instead, they are based mainly on the quality of relief actions and on the precise definition of each actor's spheres of responsibility. Humanitarian law defines specific rights and duties depending on the different responsibilities of each actor: states, armed forces, aid organizations, victims.

In adopting humanitarian law, states recognized their inability to be both judges and parties when it comes to protecting civilians in armed conflicts. They thus conferred this important duty on the International Committee of the Red Cross (ICRC), as well as on other impartial humanitarian organizations. This law grants legal guarantees for protection and assistance to victims of war under the condition that they be implemented by independent and impartial organizations. This is a way for warring parties to ensure, among themselves, that humanitarian actions will not be diverted for other purposes.

The responsibility of humanitarian organizations is thus to act independently, to link assistance and protection, and to report on states that are unable to fulfill their responsibilities, so as to guarantee that the basic rights of victims are respected. The responsibility of states is to act unilaterally and collectively to enforce the law and take action in case of grave violations. This pattern of responsibility tends to become blurred when states enter the field of assistance, under a very vague legal framework.

The Geneva Conventions are an exhaustive and lucid monument of law, inspired by victims and lessons of past crimes. However, most humanitarian organizations have little or no knowledge of this complete and complex law, which too often remains the domain of the Red Cross.

Today, the word *humanitarian* is a label that tends to be used for a wide variety of activities undertaken by actors who do not meet the humanitarian law concept of an "impartial humanitarian organization," such as states, interstate organizations, even government-financed private voluntary organizations, operating under very different forms and legal conditions.

Although everyone makes references to humanitarian principles, there is a great difference between activities undertaken under humanitarian law, peacekeeping or peace enforcement law, human rights law, refugee law, and the law of interstate cooperation and assistance.

The confusion created by the so-called "integrated response to complex humanitarian emergencies" most often results in the rules that are the least favorable to victims and the least constraining to states being applied. The term *humanitarian law,* long reserved for situations of armed conflict, has not resulted, so far, in a coherent legal discipline that allows the most favorable laws to be applied to individuals when their lives are threatened.

The post–Cold War world is far from being peaceful. Conflicts multiply. So do crimes against humanity. Armies having become too powerful to confront one another directly, it is now civilians who fall by the thousands in the conflicts of a new world order—conflicts that now have less to do with national border issues than with questions of human societies' identity and roots. In twentieth-century conflicts, 90 percent of all victims were civilian.

Humanitarian action spreads over increasingly complex battlefields, as a sign of resistance and protest against the international social order. Its label covers actors and organizations with widely varied goals, means, and responsibilities. However, in a reflection of its helplessness, it sometimes seeks to appease the emotions of public opinion more than to defend the fundamental rights of victims. All the images of aid convoys must not allow us to forget that most suffering is not caused by scarcity but by violence.

International humanitarian law includes provisions for assistance and protection in times of war. Its starting point is the recognition of the specific vulnerability of civilians, due to the nature of violence and conditions of war.

Humanitarian action is much more than the simple delivery of technical or material assistance. To be protective, it must apply to civilians' specific needs and vulnerabilities. It must also perpetually analyze the violence and conditions of war, as they affect the status and well-being of the most vulnerable. Such conditions may include the deliberate targeting, deprivation, and suffering of civilians in order to increase the flow, manipulation, or diversion of aid or to achieve some strategic advantage or political objective. It is crucial that humanitarian organizations insist on the respect for the status of individuals in times of war and resist acts such as forced displacement, regroupment, or deliberate starvation. The humanitarian actor must be able to monitor and respond to the specific violence or conditions that threaten individuals.

Almost invariably, the causes and conditions of a conflict are political. They must be viewed separately from their humanitarian consequences. The central task for those seeking a solution to the conflict is to define the problems and solutions clearly, rather than to settle for vague problem definitions that mask political causes and responsibilities, or to settle for imperfect but feasible solutions. This will clarify the political causes that create humanitarian needs and will lift the humanitarian veil that often hides political inaction. Humanitarian action, by itself, cannot solve the problem of the populations' suffering, which exists in a political and military framework. Pouring assistance blindly into such contexts can neither improve the quality of politicians' work nor decrease the weight of military actors' influence. If not bound by strict operational principles, humanitarian assistance can actually be a fuel for war economy and risks prolonging the war and strengthening the power of criminal leaders.

Written after Auschwitz, the 1949 Geneva Conventions took into account the main dilemmas that relief actions encounter in situations of violence and conflict. Nonetheless, more than fifty years later, a large majority of individuals and humanitarian organizations continue to be unaware and ignorant of the exact content of the rights and duties toward humanity that the conventions set forth. Relief actions continue to refer only to vague and well-intentioned humanitarian principles, which shatter when they come into contact with the real world's constraints.

THE DECEPTIVE REVIVAL OF HUMANITARIAN ACTION

Humanitarian action currently seems to be a societal phenomenon with a new scope. Yet it is an ancient activity, indivisible from the human condition and life in society, and underscored by important political, religious, and philosophical currents.

The development of the welfare state, in the West, reinforced the notion of the "social contract," a term coined by Jean-Jacques Rousseau, and relegated humanitarian action to exceptional situations such as wars. The progressive affirmation of human rights reflects this contractual relationship, which emancipates individuals with relation to power. People became subjects of rights rather than being simple objects of charity. On other continents, namely in developing countries, humanitarian action has long taken on various forms (including international ones), beginning with missionary aid and followed by development aid and cooperation organized among states or within the United Nations.

Humanitarian action has evolved within the flaws, ruptures, and weaknesses of the social contract. Its goal is to protect human life and dignity when, for diverse reasons, society is no longer capable or desirous of ensuring the survival of some of its members.

Today, humanitarian action faces a new challenge. While human rights have been recognized at a universal level, it is now states and societies that are collapsing, exploding, or tearing apart, throughout most of the world, leaving individuals defenseless, without direction, helpless victims of violence and destruction.

At the national level, the state's loss of resources and power has accelerated the weakening of numerous social services. In many industrialized states, important sectors related to national solidarity have now been privatized, neglected, or abandoned. Some examples are the impoverishment of public health services, the reduction of public assistance to the poor or vulnerable families and children, and a decrease in care for people in prison. Today, while waiting for new adjustments, these sectors are partially covered by humanitarian action.

At the same time, the individualist concept of human rights is suffering from the same crisis as is the institution of the state. Despite their universal nature, human rights are actually closely tied to notions of nationality and citizenship. Paradoxically, without a state that protects these rights and liberties, the notion of human rights is more vulnerable than ever.

Thus, invoking these rights is useless in a society that is not in a position to protect its own citizens or that has decided to exclude or exterminate some of them. For those fleeing their state or for those whom the state has failed, only the relief of international humanitarian law now remains.

Humanitarian action is apolitical (in the sense that it does not have its own plans for society and does not claim to substitute for the political power to organize life in society). However, it does maintain complementary relations with the political power, as well as a position of protest, because it is a way to challenge the established order by revealing its failure to include and dignify certain categories of people. Humanitarian action is also of a temporary nature. Its purpose is to help excluded individuals and populations in danger survive until they are once again partners in the social and political organization.

This action therefore takes on diverse forms, depending on the context. It expresses individuals' pacific attempts to defend spaces of humanity themselves, at the heart of increasingly complex societies. It reflects the capability and responsibility of each individual to repair, in his or her own way, injustices perpetrated against other human beings.

More than an act of generosity, humanitarian action aims to restore spaces of normality in "abnormal" situations. Much more than simple material aid, it aims to reestablish minimum rights and human dignity for individuals at the heart of a community.

Thus, the current crisis of the welfare state, the collapse of certain states, and the chaotic construction of an international society are all new causes for the increase in humanitarian action. Epidemics, famine, conflict, exodus, populations marginalized or abandoned within a state, forgotten countries (on the path to disintegration or collapse), the forsaken of the society of nations—humanitarian action occupies the space left vacant or not yet filled by the established powers.

This reality upsets not only the forms but also the means and the meaning of humanitarian action. Whereas it used to be the deed of individuals protesting the established order, humanitarian action appears today as a mode of minimal government adopted by international organizations such as the United Nations (UN), the European Union (EU), and certain states.

In the past, there was a clear distinction between development aid, actions of solidarity in cases of disasters, and humanitarian action in times of conflict. Today, we seem to have entered a period of chronic crisis and conflict in which emergency humanitarian action has become the only available form of political expression. The variety of humanitarian actors and the scope of their actions produce an illusion of consensus and a reassuring spectacle of action, yet it leads to a loss in the significance of the word *humanitarian*.

Humanitarian action designates a gesture whose only end is humankind. By definition, no political power established at a national or international level can be reduced to this single interest. Humanitarian law clearly defines the difference between the obligations conferred upon states and those entrusted to impartial humanitarian organizations, as neutral intermediaries in conflicts.

This impartiality is not synonymous with confidentiality. The experience of World War II demonstrated the dangers of a "silent humanitarian action." Since then, humanitarian law has clarified the responsibilities of humanitarian organizations, thus providing a legitimate framework for them to speak out.

Considering the lessons-learned "process" launched, following the past years' tragedies in the former Yugoslavia and Rwanda, it is striking to see how little responsibility nongovernmental organizations (NGOs) and other humanitarian actors accept to take on. Speeches on accountability remain limited to technical issues regarding assistance, yet they include no discussion on protection. For example, few humanitarian organizations have reconsidered the silent advocacy strategies they use to inform the UN and member states about a humanitarian situation, even after having learned that states were fully aware of the 1994 genocide in Rwanda.

From the moment that humanitarian action is carried out by states or intergovernmental organizations, such as the UN or the EU, it loses its essential dynamic component. It no longer expresses a social protest against the established order but becomes an acceptance of political paucity, which is even more dangerous for the safety of threatened individuals.

Whatever governments' intentions in this arena may be, their action can result in a dangerous confusion. In fact, it positions humanitarian action at the center of diplomatic negotiation, thereby making a negotiation element out of something that should be nonnegotiable: the right of survival.

Although the humanitarian nature of some UN agencies is asserted, it remains difficult for them to enjoy the absolute political freedom required to be called "independent and impartial." This difficulty is aggravated when other branches of the UN are engaged in measures such as sanctions, peacekeeping, or peace enforcement operations. This is also the case when a country is run by unrecognized authorities, when the state itself has collapsed, when the UN refuses to recognize or deal with a given faction for various reasons, or when the UN imposes sanctions on a given group. Numerous such situations have occurred. Furthermore, UN security regulations often limit UN staff's ability to function effectively in such conditions.

This challenge is further complicated by the current trend at the UN to integrate humanitarian activities into global and strategic frameworks related to peace and security, and to link the delivery of humanitarian assistance to political objectives such as restoring peace, democracy, and the rule of law. Using humanitarian assistance to influence a given military confrontation may indeed offer levers to affect positive changes in a country. Yet, while this might be politically efficient or expedient, it jeopardizes the necessary political independence of humanitarian action.

The unacceptable result is that humanitarian activities are de facto subordinated to high-level and honorable concerns that are other than humanitarian. This in itself distorts the very meaning of these actions and imperils the presence of humanitarian actors in the field by blurring their image and the respect due to their work and intentions.

The recent lessons learned from the international use of armed force wrapped in a humanitarian cloak show that the protection of civilians will continue to rest on the initiatives and activities of humanitarian organizations rather than on occasional international military intervention. This potential should be protected and respected.

Another consequence of these flourishing state humanitarian actions is that, in the end, they marginalize humanitarian law. The legal framework within which the UN, regional organizations, or states undertake humanitarian actions refers first and foremost to the laws of interstate cooperation. It only invokes the respect for human rights in a generic manner, and it rests on a system of diplomatic immunities and administrative procedures specific to these actors.

We would be justified in expecting that the many private organizations that exist would make better defenders of victims. This is only too rarely the case. They function at the margins of the law, from where they defend the mandate they have granted themselves, based on their moral requirements, or even more often on their technical capabilities. They stand by their good intentions and hold themselves accountable only to how much they have given, rather than to whether they succeeded in reaching the most vulnerable.

The ethics of relief action therefore vary greatly, depending on the organization and the situation, and because there are numerous practical constraints. The aid personnel and material come from a given country, cross borders, and enter in contact with governments that may or may not be recognized as such, with armed groups, with international organizations, and with donors. At each of these steps, relief action encounters the laws of others: national sovereignty, international and national laws, contracts of all kinds. At each of these steps, the actors have to obtain rights so that victims can also benefit from them.

The scope of relief action most often results in each humanitarian participant choosing a technical specialization in response to a specific kind of suffering. Most of the time these actors concentrate on their own rights and mandate and know very little about the rights of the victims. The multiplication of these actors leads to a scattering of responsibilities. Thus, the gap between humanitarian law and the right of humanitarian action grows. The technical response to situations of crisis may seem adequate, but without referring to legal norms, one is unable to counterbalance the power struggles that characterize conflicts, to tilt it in favor of victims.

THE LAWS OF WAR: FOR WHOM AND FOR WHAT?

By definition, war is a transitional state. Therefore, it must be conducted in a way that will not make a return to peace impossible and will not cause irreparable damage.

One of the bases of most societies is the fact that individuals are prohibited from killing or making their own justice. Yet, in times of conflict, states restore the right to kill. Of course, this restitution is limited, ritualized, and regulated, to prevent the destruction of society itself.

The laws of war are at the crossroads between realpolitik and metaphysics because, in addition to accepting violence and regulating the means and methods of warfare, they address concepts of humankind and society. Humanitarian law developed slowly over the course of time, on the basis of both pragmatic and religious grounds. It evolved, paradoxically, to apply to the very situations in which laws have disappeared: wars, conflicts, major crises.

The four 1949 Geneva Conventions, ratified by virtually all states, and the two Additional Protocols thereto, of 1977, summarize and codify this legal heritage and adapt it to the weapons and models of violence encountered in more recent wars. They establish specific prohibitions on different methods of warfare and set the minimum standards of treatment of individuals. However, unlike human rights law, humanitarian law does not establish universal rights applicable to all individuals. Instead, it defines categories of persons and situations, so as to offer the most adapted protection in regard to the risks incurred by each category of person in each different situation. The efficiency of such a regime of protection rests on vigilance, since a failure or refusal to define the status of an individual or the nature of a situation may paralyze the law's implementation.

The implementation of humanitarian law depends on achieving a balance between acting and punishing. The Conventions precisely define the crimes that are qualified as "war crimes" and "crimes against humanity." They foresee bold mechanisms to file complaints, to investigate, prosecute, and punish.

The populations in danger have the right to appeal to relief organizations. States confer a right of initiative upon impartial humanitarian organizations when they implement their relief actions. The Geneva Conventions thus recognize the specific role of nongovernmental actors in situations of conflict. They further clarify that these initiatives cannot be considered as interference.

However, humanitarian law faces a challenge new in the history of humanity: it must reconcile the growing tensions that result from a universal concept of humanity and human society's global dimension.

Humanitarian Law: A Manual

Law is a tool that regulates human, social, and international relations. With or without courts, law is first and foremost a set of norms and procedures. It offers not only a standard of reference but also the time and the arguments that are necessary to replace relations based on power struggles with ones based on the power of words. Laws do not spare us from conflicts, but they enable each actor to turn to clear definitions of what is just or unjust, normal or abnormal, behavior that is legitimate or unacceptable. The only means of pressure at the disposal of humanitarian actors are pacific means, and humanitarian law is one of the main instruments.

It is true that, in times of crisis or conflict, the fate of individuals weighs little in comparison to issues of collective security or defense that are at stake. Since the latter issues are entrusted to states and armies, the voice of victims usually fades long before justice can hear it.

In the absence of an impartial system of justice, the only way to protect victims is by negotiating concrete relief actions. This can only take place if victims can find advocates, within relief organizations, who are capable and willing to defend their rights. These advocates are rarely lawyers, and they work in situations of vital emergency, which leave little room for legal contemplation, let alone scholarly debates.

It is only fair to point out that the cleavage between realists and idealists is often reversed in times of crisis. Governments do not have sole claim to realism: relief organizations, directly confronted with the consequences of suffering, often take a realist stance.

Definitions are the first step toward giving or denying a person's rights. Rights and obligations always result from a precise definition of the relevant persons, situations, or objects. During the genocide in Rwanda, states talked about a "humanitarian crisis," thus avoiding their own obligations under such circumstances both to act and to punish. The ability to recognize a person or an objective as civilian or military, an attack as proportionate or indiscriminate, a facility as being of a medical nature, a repatriation as voluntary or forced, is a practical element that delineates the limit between a legitimate use of force and a crime. The actors directly involved in a situation must know that, in each case, their choice of words will determine whether rights are granted or denied.

Laws must never be interpreted unilaterally. Even if the rules of international law were drafted by states, this does not mean that they are free to interpret them as they choose. They are under the obligation to interpret them in good faith, in conformity with the spirit of the conventions in question. The legal world is full of rules with different and sometimes contradictory values and meanings. Furthermore, the rules do not all have the same force of law or the same level of precision. The provisions of international law are superior to those of domestic law.

These elements provide the instruments that frame a genuine space for discussion and negotiation, in which the different interests represented can be heard and respected.

International law in general, and humanitarian law in particular, is imperfect, lacking independent courts, judges, and police. Recognizing this fact, states adopted the statute for a permanent International Criminal Court (ICC) on July 17, 1998. This is a revolution in international law, though it defers to states or the UN Security Council as a reflection of the fact that the act of prosecuting perpetrators of the most serious crimes (genocide, crimes against humanity, and war crimes) remains largely at the mercy of political decisions.

Yet, humanitarian law is constantly invoked by state actors trying to justify their behavior and give legitimacy to their power. While this law is not universally respected, no state officially admits to violating its rules. This space of legitimacy can be defended in practice by humanitarian organizations during negotiations concerning relief actions.

It is crucial that each actor acknowledge his or her responsibilities in such circumstances, because, although imperfect, international law is a law that is constantly changing, evolving. Each action undertaken plays a direct role in the evolution of laws, whether in the name of "custom" or "precedent." Paradoxically, humanitarian action can also weaken humanitarian law and increase the danger to victims. Each time a right is defended successfully during a negotiation, it can later be invoked when faced with similar demands. On the other hand, if relief organizations accept, without protesting, that their free access to victims be denied or that in a given situation they are prevented from providing assistance indiscriminately, then they renounce their rights, in both the present and the future.

Law, unlike other treasures, fades and wastes away only when it is not used.

Actions that provide assistance and combat inhumanity must be established on legal, intellectual, and material bases in order to resist the power struggles that surround them, and to achieve their humanitarian objectives. We hope that the following pages will help clarify and simplify these choices. The future functioning of an International Criminal Court will increase the challenge surrounding humanitarian organizations' responsibility to prevent and testify on war crimes and crimes against humanity.

Relief workers and citizens must learn the keys and traps to the use of humanitarian law. This is the way to break through a power struggle and use law as a tool of humanitarian negotiation.

We wish to transmit this humanitarian approach to using law to new and future defenders of humanity.

■ ADOPTION

Both domestic and international laws exist concerning adoption, to protect the interests of children and guarantee the respect for families. In times of peace or in situations of internal disturbances, the principles that regulate adoption are clearly set forth in Article 21 of the Convention on the Rights of the Child (CRC) and in the 1993 Hague Convention on the Protection of Children and Cooperation in Respect of Intercountry Adoption. During international armed conflicts, these guarantees are supplemented by rules that restrict the evacuation of children, so as to defend the family unit and diminish the risk of adoption fraud and trafficking of children (PI Article 78). These rules can serve as a framework or as guidelines for the work of relief organizations, including in noninternational armed conflicts. ➔ **Internal disturbances and tensions; Noninternational armed conflict**

I. IN TIMES OF PEACE OR SITUATIONS OF INTERNAL DISTURBANCES AND TENSIONS

1. Article 21 of the Convention on the Rights of the Child

"States Parties that recognize and/or permit the system of adoption shall ensure that the best interests of the child shall be the paramount consideration and they shall:

(a) ensure that the adoption of a child is authorized only by competent authorities who determine, in accordance with applicable law and procedures and on the basis of all pertinent and reliable information, that the adoption is permissible in view of the child's status concerning parents, relatives and legal guardians and that, if required, the persons concerned have given their informed consent to the adoption on the basis of such counseling as may be necessary;
(b) recognize that inter-country adoption may be considered as an alternative means of child's care, if the child cannot be placed in a foster or an adoptive family or cannot in any suitable manner be cared for in the child's country of origin;

(c) ensure that the child concerned by inter-country adoption enjoys safeguards and standards equivalent to those existing in the case of national adoption;

(d) take all appropriate measures to ensure that, in inter-country adoption, the placement does not result in improper financial gain for those involved in it;

(e) promote, where appropriate, the objectives of the present article by concluding bilateral or multilateral arrangements or agreements, and endeavour, within this framework, to ensure that the placement of the child in another country is carried out by competent authorities or organs."

2. The 1993 Hague Convention on the Protection of Children and Cooperation in Respect of Intercountry Adoption

The Convention on Intercountry Adoption was adopted on May 29, 1993, following the Hague Conference on International Private Law, which sixty-six states attended. Over half of these countries have now signed the Convention, and forty-one have ratified or acceded to it. The states that have ratified or acceded to, and are therefore bound by, the Convention are Albania, Andorra, Australia, Austria, Brazil, Burkina Faso, Burundi, Canada, Chile, Colombia, Costa Rica, Cyprus, Czech Republic, Denmark, Ecuador, El Salvador, Finland, France, Georgia, Iceland, Israel, Italy, Lithuania, Mauritius, Mexico, Moldova, Monaco, Mongolia, Netherlands, New Zealand, Norway, Panama, Paraguay, Peru, Philippines, Poland, Romania, Spain, Sri Lanka, Sweden, and Venezuela.

The aim of the Convention is to combat the trafficking of children. Among other provisions, it establishes that

- the competent authorities of the country of origin must verify that the child is "adoptable" and not the victim of commercial trafficking;
- the receiving state must verify that the prospective adoptive parents are eligible and suited to adopt and must ensure the legality of the child's arrival upon its territory;
- each state party to the Convention must create a Central Authority in charge of receiving and examining adoption requests. The aim of the screening done by this Authority is mainly to reduce the number of steps that individuals have to take, such as the "rounds" made by prospective adopters, going from one orphanage to the next, in search of a child. Prospective adopters who are in states parties must file their request with the Central Authority, which then contacts the Central Authority of the preferred state of origin of the child. In France, for instance, the Central Authority confers this responsibility on the international adoption mission of the Ministry of Foreign Affairs.

II. PROVISIONS IN CASE OF EVACUATION, IN TIMES OF INTERNATIONAL ARMED CONFLICT

☞ No party to a conflict may arrange for the evacuation to a foreign country of children who are not its own nationals, except in the case of a temporary evacuation caused by compelling reasons such as the health, medical treatment, or (except in occupied territory) the safety of the children (PI Article 78.1).

> ☞ In order to facilitate the return of evacuated children to their families, the authorities of the party to the conflict that is arranging the evacuation must issue a standard identity card, with specific information concerning the child, and send it to the Central Tracing Agency of the International Committee of the Red Cross (PI Article 78.3).

If the parents or legal guardians can be found, their written consent to the evacuation of children to a foreign country is required. If not, the written consent of the persons who by law or custom are primarily responsible for the guardianship of the children is required. Any such evacuation must be supervised by the Protecting Power in agreement with the parties concerned—namely, the party arranging for the evacuation, the party receiving the children, and any parties whose nationals are being evacuated (PI Article 78.1).

Whenever an evacuation does occur, each child's education, including his or her religious and moral education (as desired by the parents), shall be provided with the greatest possible continuity (PI Article 78.2).

→ **Central Tracing Agency; Children; Evacuation; Family; Family reunification; Protecting Powers**

📖 **For Additional Information:**

Katz, Lisa M. "A Modest Proposal? The Convention on Protection of Children and Cooperation in Respect of Intercountry Adoption." *Emory International Law Review* (Spring 1995): 9.

■ THE AFRICAN COMMISSION FOR HUMAN AND PEOPLE'S RIGHTS

The African Commission for Human and People's Rights was established per Article 30 of the African Charter on Human and People's Rights, which was adopted by the Organization of African Unity (OAU) on June 27, 1981, and entered into force on October 21, 1986. The Commission is responsible for promoting and monitoring the implementation of the Charter. Its headquarters are in Banjul, Gambia.

A protocol to the Charter was adopted on June 9, 1998, in Burkina Faso. It foresees the establishment of an African Court of Human Rights, which will enter into force when fifteen states have ratified the protocol. As of December 1999, only two states had done so (Senegal and Burkina Faso).

1. Structure

The Commission's eleven members are independent experts, elected by the Assembly of Heads of State and Government, to six-year terms. They can be reelected once.

The Commission meets twice a year. It is supposed to meet for two-week sessions, but, since 1991, has had to reduce the sessions to eight days for budgetary reasons. At each session, the Commission presents an activity report to the Assembly of Heads of State and Government.

2. Mandate

The Commission's mandate is set forth in Article 45 of the African Charter. It includes

- interpreting the Charter's provisions;
- promoting human and people's rights (Article 45.1 specifies some of the ways in which Commission can implement this goal: collecting and preparing legal documents relating to human

rights; centralizing documentation, research, studies; disseminating information and raising awareness; cooperating with other African and competent international institutions; formulating and laying down principles and rules aimed at solving legal human rights problems; etc.);
- ensuring the protection of human and peoples' rights.

3. State Communications

If a state party to the African Charter on Human and People's Rights believes that another state party has violated the provision of the Charter, it may draw the attention of that state to the matter, by written communication (Article 47). If, within three months, no mutually satisfactory solution has been found, either party to the dispute can submit the matter to the Commission.

The state alleging the human rights violation also has the option to refer the case directly to the Commission. Whether the case is referred directly or not, the Commission will only examine a case if all local remedies have been exhausted, "if they exist" and "unless it is obvious to the Commission that the procedure of achieving these remedies would be unduly prolonged" (Article 50). This is the main criteria for admissibility.

Once the Commission is considering a matter, its aim is not to pronounce a judgment but to search for an amicable solution, in light of the written and oral explanations submitted by the concerned states. In case this fails, it sends a report on the findings to the states party to the dispute and to the Assembly of Heads of State and Government. The report can include nonbinding recommendations (Articles 52 and 53).

The entire procedure remains confidential. However, if the Assembly of Heads of State and Government so decide, the report may be published.

4. Other Communications

"Other communications" designates all complaints transmitted by other sources (such as individuals or NGOs).

> ☞ In addition to states, individuals and NGOs can submit communication to the African Commission for Human and People's Rights, which is competent with regard to all states parties to the African Charter on Human and People's Rights (currently forty-nine states). Nevertheless, such communications are subject to various admissibility conditions.

The Commission does not automatically consider all cases. Before each session, the list of communications is transmitted to the Commission's members. The Commission then considers a complaint on the request of a simple majority of its members.

The communications are then subject to seven conditions of admissibility (Article 56). They must not be anonymous (i.e., they must indicate the authors, even if they later request anonymity), written in disparaging or insulting language, or based exclusively on news from the mass media, and they must not deal with cases that have already been settled by the states involved in accordance with the principles of the UN Charter, the OAU Charter, or the African Charter on Human and People's Rights. On the other hand, the communication must be compatible with the African Charter, be sent to the Commission after local remedies were exhausted (unless such procedure is unduly prolonged), and be submitted within a reasonable period.

After this examination of the admissibility of the case, the Commission begins the examination of its merits and notifies the accused state. If one or more of the communications appear to "reveal the existence of a series of serious or massive violations of human and peoples' rights," the Commission informs the Assembly of Heads of State and Government (Article 58). In case of emergency, it may submit the information directly to the chair of the Assembly, who may request an in-depth study from the Commission. This will result in a report, including recommendations. All measures taken within the procedure remain confidential, unless the Assembly decides otherwise.

➔   **Human rights; Individual recourse**
➔   **List of states party to international human rights and humanitarian conventions (No. 10)**

✎   African Commission for Human and People's Rights
    Kairaba Avenue
    PO Box 673
    Banjul, The Gambia
    Tel.: (220) 39 29 62
    Fax: (220) 39 27 64

■ AGGRESSION

Although international law has not clearly codified the notion of "aggression," it is generally recognized as describing "the use of armed force by a state against the sovereignty, territorial integrity, or political independence of another state" (UN General Assembly Resolution 3314 (XXIX) of December 14, 1974). Such acts are forbidden in international law, which specifically establishes that the only legitimate use of force in international relations is when defending oneself against aggression.

Therefore, to justify their own behavior on the grounds of self-defense, many states have tried, and continue to try, to expand the definition of aggression to include other kinds of "violence," which does not involve the use of armed force. These include, for instance, certain economic or financial acts that directly affect certain states, such as blockades.

In striving to maintain international peace and security, the first article of the UN Charter posits that one of the main purposes of the organization is to suppress acts of aggression. The Charter further establishes that the threat or use of force is prohibited in relations between member states of the UN (Article 2.4 of UN Charter). The Security Council—in the context of its "responsibility for the maintenance of international peace and security" (Article 24.1 of UN Charter)—has a unique role in determining the existence of acts of aggression.

In certain situations, however, the use of force against another state may be tolerated:

- a state that is the victim of an act of aggression has the right to use force in self-defense (Article 51 of UN Charter);
- force may be used in the context of collective measures of security adopted by the UN Security Council (Article 42 of UN Charter).

☞ A precise definition of aggression—and therefore the ability to incontestably qualify an act as such—continues to elude lawyers and diplomats.

Acts carried out in the context of a people's exercise of their right to self-determination or of a struggle against colonial domination, foreign occupation, or racist regimes, are

(continues)

(*continued*)

not considered acts of aggression (GA Resolution 3314 [XXIX] of December 14, 1974; PI Article 1).

The statute of a permanent International Criminal Court (ICC), adopted in July 1998, establishes that the ICC will eventually have jurisdiction over the crime of aggression (Article 5 of ICC statute). However, the Court cannot undertake any action with regard to this crime until a precise definition of the term has been drafted and adopted by the states parties to the statute. This will take place during a later process of amendment or revision of the statute.

→ **Collective security; International Criminal Court; Methods (and means) of warfare; Public order; Sanctions (diplomatic, economic, or military); Security Council of the UN; Self-defense; War**

For Additional Information:

Dinstein, Yoram. *War, Aggression and Self-defense*. The Hague: Grotius, 1988.
Rifaat, A. M. *International Aggression*. Stockholm: Almqvist & Wiksell International; Atlantic Highlands, N.J.: Humanities Press, 1979.

■ AMNESTIES

An amnesty is a decree enacted by the authorities of a state that prescribes official disregard for one or more categories of offenses and cancels any penal consequences that would normally result from such acts.

In the case of a noninternational armed conflict, international law encourages the granting of amnesties at the end of hostilities, stating that "the authorities in power shall endeavour to grant the broadest possible amnesty to persons who have participated in the armed conflict, or those deprived of their liberty for reasons related to the armed conflict" (PII Article 6.5).

At the same time that humanitarian law sets forth amnesties as a measure of clemency—with the goal of favoring national reconciliation and a return to peace—it grants a central position to the importance of justice and the prosecution and punishment of certain serious crimes committed in the context of these conflicts. It forbids the application of amnesties to grave breaches of humanitarian law and establishes rules to combat impunity for the perpetrators of these crimes, who are often persons of high political or military ranking or who acted on the orders of their superiors.

☞ The 1949 Geneva Conventions forbid states from absolving themselves or other states of any liability incurred with respect to grave breaches of humanitarian law (GCI Article 51, GCII Article 52, GCIII Article 131, and GCIV Article 148). Furthermore, since states party to the Conventions have undertaken to penalize such breaches, they may not grant amnesties for these crimes, whether by enacting national laws or in the context of negotiating peace accords.

States are under the obligation to enforce effective penal sanctions for war crimes committed during a conflict, no matter who the perpetrators were (GCI Article 49, GCII Article 50, GCIII Article 129, and GCIV Article 146), and many of these crimes are not subject to any statute of limitation. The fact that an individual committed a crime pursuant to an order issued by a superior in no way relieves the perpetrator of his or her individual criminal responsibility. Superiors are also criminally accountable if they fail to take measures to prevent or punish the commission of these crimes by persons under their authority.

This obligation to prevent and punish individuals accused of certain crimes is also entrenched in certain conventions applicable in times of peace, such as in the case of torture and genocide.

Amnesties are national measures that do not preclude other states from initiating legal procedures against the alleged perpetrators of crimes that are considered of an international nature.

➜ **Impunity; Judicial guarantees; Nonapplicability of statutory limitations; Responsibility; Universal jurisdiction; War crimes/Crimes against humanity**

■ ANNEXATION

Annexation is the act of one state claiming sovereignty over all or part of the territory of another state. It is forbidden by international law. Nonetheless, in case annexation does take place, the laws of the Occupying Power may not be imposed in their entirety. Civilians in the occupied territories remain protected by humanitarian law (GCIV Article 47).

➜ **Judicial guarantees; Methods (and means) of warfare; Occupied territories; War**

■ APARTHEID

The International Convention on the Suppression and Punishment of the Crime of Apartheid defines "the crime of apartheid" as "inhuman acts committed for the purpose of establishing and maintaining domination by one racial group of persons over any other racial group of persons and systematically oppressing them" (Article 2 of Apartheid Convention). This Convention was adopted on November 30, 1973, by the General Assembly of the UN, entered into force in 1976, and today binds 101 states parties.

Individuals, members of organizations, and representatives of the state, regardless of their motives and their country of residence, are held criminally responsible under international law, if they

- commit, participate in, directly incite, or conspire in the commission of acts of apartheid;
- directly abet, cooperate with, or encourage the commission of the crime of apartheid.

The practice of apartheid, and any other inhuman and degrading practices based on racial discrimination and involving outrages on personal dignity, are considered war crimes if they are committed during an international armed conflict (PI Article 85.4). Apartheid is also considered a crime against humanity, as set forth in the statute of the International Criminal Court, which was adopted in July 1998.

➜ **Discrimination; International Criminal Court; War crimes/Crimes against humanity**
➜ **List of states party to the International Convention on the Suppression and Punishment of the Crime of Apartheid (No. 25)**

📖 **For Additional Information:**

Lemon, Anthony, ed. *The Geography of Change in South Africa.* Chichester: Wiley, 1995.
Slye, Ronald C. "Apartheid as a Crime against Humanity: A Submission to the South African Truth and Reconciliation Commission." *Michigan Journal of International Law* (Winter 1999): 267.

■ ARBITRATION

The different parties to a dispute may agree expressly to refer or submit their dispute to an authority whose powers to settle an argument are not drawn from a national or international institution. This form of dispute settlement is called *arbitration*. It differs from conciliation in that it results in a legally binding settlement.

In many cases, each party to the dispute designates an independent arbitrator, and the two arbitrators select a third one. This is a common practice in business matters, and it also plays an important role in international relations between states. When used between states, it is seen as a means of pacific settlement of disputes: states themselves choose the judges, either establishing an ad hoc arbitral body or in the framework of an existing mechanism, who then pronounce a binding ruling on the basis of law. A Permanent Court of Arbitration was created in 1907, based on the Arbitration Convention established by The Hague Convention (I) for the Pacific Settlement of International Disputes (July 29, 1899).

States are under no obligation to use this method to settle their disputes. If they do so, as mentioned before, they choose their own "judges" (the arbitrators), as well as the procedure and, in some cases, the applicable law. The arbitration itself is based on principles of law but also at times on notions of fairness. Hence, this procedure meets the requirements imposed by the notion of state sovereignty, since it leaves states at liberty to decide when and under what conditions to accept a limitation on their own powers for the sake of settling a dispute.

The UN Security Council may also contribute to the peaceful settlement of disputes by inviting parties to submit disputes that are of a legal nature to arbitration or to action by the International Court of Justice (Articles 33 and 36 of the UN Charter).

→ **International Court of Justice; UN Security Council**

📖 **For Additional Information:**

Brownlie, Ian, and Surya Prakash Sinha. "The Peaceful Settlement of International Disputes in Practice: Blaine Sloan Lecture." *Pace International Law Review* (Spring 1995): 257.

■ ASSISTANCE

The 1949 Geneva Conventions use the word *assistance* to designate the overall aid (in terms of food, medicine, clothing, etc.) that must be provided for victims of conflicts, in accordance with humanitarian law. It covers the goods essential to their survival. In the Geneva Conventions, material assistance is linked to a specific legal framework that defines the status of the different categories of protected persons whom the law seeks to protect. → **Protected persons**

The status of the protected persons is what determines the specific rights and obligations of the various authorities to ensure the survival of the populations in their power. This status also determines the right of initiative and the responsibility of relief organizations, as well as the means and conditions for the distribution of aid, based on the needs of the different categories of persons at risk.

Humanitarian law thus establishes different rights to receive assistance depending on the different categories of protected persons—civilians, populations in occupied territory, detainees, women, children, the elderly, and the wounded and sick—and the different kinds of conflicts—international and internal (GCIII Articles 25–32; GCIV Articles 50, 55–63 89, 92; PI Articles 68–71, 81; PII Articles 4, 5, 7, 17 and 18). ➔ **Children; Civilians; Detention; Occupied territories; Prisoners of war; Relief; Women; Wounded and sick persons**

Humanitarian law also establishes different rights for relief organizations, depending on the situation. ➔ **Humanitarian and relief personnel; Medical services; Relief; Right of access; Right of initiative**

In the 1951 Convention Relating to the Status of Refugees, the link between assistance and protection is equally emphasized. Based on this convention, UNHCR takes on the function both of protecting and of providing material assistance to refugees, in an indivisible manner. UNHCR undertakes to assist refugees while they wait to be granted the appropriate legal status and to defend their right to receive this status.

☞ Assistance and protection must always be provided together. Thus linked, they form genuine relief operations, as foreseen by humanitarian law.

The objective of providing assistance is to enable individuals to enjoy their rights and regain their individual autonomy, which is the only guarantee for their survival.

In international law, assistance is always seen as a temporary phase, which must be tied to the recognition of the legal status and rights of individuals in danger. In practice, this recognition must be incorporated into relief actions.

The content and format of assistance are explained in the entry on ➔ **relief.**

➔   **Children; Detention; Humanitarian and relief personnel; Protected objects and property; Protected persons; Protection; Relief; Women; Wounded and sick persons**

📖 **For Additional Information:**

Anderson, Mary B. "'You Save My Life Today, but for What Tomorrow?' Some Moral Dilemmas of Humanitarian Aid." In *Hard Choices: Moral Dilemmas in Humanitarian Intervention*, ed. Jonathan Moore. Lanham, Md.: Rowman & Littlefield, 1998, 137–56.

Law in Humanitarian Crises: Access to Victims: Right to Intervene or Right to Receive Humanitarian Assistance? Luxembourg: European Commission, 1995.

Plattner, Denise. "Assistance to the Civilian Population: The Development and Present State of International Humanitarian Law." *International Review of the Red Cross* 288 (May–June 1992): 249–63.

■ ASYLUM

A place of asylum is where an individual can take refuge to protect him- or herself from danger. The right of asylum is a fundamental human right, as set forth in the Universal Declaration of Human Rights.

Freedom of movement includes the right of all individuals to flee their country and seek asylum in another state. However, this right is limited by the fact that there is no reciprocal obligation for states to grant asylum.

According to the UNHCR, the European Union received almost 390,000 asylum applications in 2000. These were mostly sumitted by citizens of the former Yugoslavia (42,300), Iraq (34,700), and Afghanistan (28,000). The principal countries that received those applications were the United Kingdom (22 percent of the European total), Germany (17 percent), the Netherlands (10 percent), Belgium (7.6 percent), and France (6.6 percent). The United States welcomed 44,221 asylum seekers.

There were 984,000 asylum seekers throughout the world in 2000. Approximately 26 percent were granted refugee status.

The Rights of Asylum and Flight

Article 14 of the 1948 Universal Declaration of Human Rights establishes that:
"everyone has the right to seek and to enjoy in other countries asylum from persecution.

This right may not be invoked in the case of prosecutions genuinely arising from non-political crimes or from acts contrary to the purposes and principles of the United Nations."

The 1951 Convention Relating to the Status of Refugees (Refugee Convention) and the UNHCR Statute attempt to guarantee and protect the right of asylum for all individuals who fear persecution in their country (Article 8.a and 8.d of UNHCR Statute; Articles 1, 31–33 of Refugee Convention).

The right of asylum is defended concretely by the following provisions:

- States may not expel or return *(refouler)* an individual seeking asylum to a territory where his or her life or freedom would be threatened, even if he or she entered this state illegally (Articles 32 and 33 of Refugee Convention).
- States shall not impose penalties on refugees who entered or are present illegally on its territory if they arrive directly from a territory where their life or freedom was threatened. This provision applies as long as the refugees present themselves without delay to the authorities and show good cause for their illegal entry or presence (Article 31 of Refugee Convention).
- Temporary asylum: in case of a large-scale influx of asylum seekers, the state where the exodus stops (generally a neighboring country) is under the obligation to provide this population with temporary asylum. This assistance is to be given with the collaboration of the entire international community, through UNHCR, until a durable solution is found (Conclusion 22 of April 24, 1981, UNHCR Executive Committee XXXII session).
- National authorities must grant refugee status to all individuals who meet the qualifications defined by the Refugee Convention.

The right to flee one's country does not mean refugees have the right to choose their country of asylum. The term *first country of asylum* or *safe country* illustrates this notion by indicating that while fleeing his or her own country the asylum seeker crossed another territory, whether he or she stayed there or only passed through, in which he or she could have sought the protection foreseen by the Refugee Convention.

Many states refuse to examine individuals' request for refugee status if such a country of first asylum exists and the asylum seeker can be sent back there. In Europe, this prerogative is expressly recognized by

- a 1992 resolution adopted by the Council of Ministers of the European Union concerning a harmonized approach to questions concerning the safe third country—this text establishes the criteria for such a state;
- the Schengen Convention of June 14, 1985 (regulating the movement of asylum seekers within the states party to the Convention);
- the Dublin Convention of June 15, 1990 (determining the state responsible for examining asylum applications).

These treaties apportion the responsibilities with regard to asylum seekers among the member states of the European Union. Other states have domestic laws, acts, and regulations that regulate the procedure for parties granting asylum.

In its Conclusion 58 (XL session, 1989), the UNHCR Executive Committee recommends that an individual be sent back to a "safe third country" only if he or she will be treated in accordance with basic humanitarian norms—in other words, with respect for the civil rights set forth by the Refugee Convention and the Universal Declaration on Human Rights.

→ **Displaced persons; Population displacement; *Refoulement* (forced return) and expulsion; Refugees; Repatriation; UNHCR**

📖 **For Additional Information:**

Plaut, W. Gunther. *Asylum: A Moral Dilemma*. Westport, Conn.: Praeger, 1995.
Sinha, S. Prakash. *Asylum and International Law.* The Hague: Martinus Nijhoff, 1971.
UNHCR. "The Asylum Dilemma." In *The State of the World's Refugees, 1997–1998: A Humanitarian Agenda*. Oxford: Oxford University Press, 1997, 183–224.

■ ATTACKS

Humanitarian law defines *attacks* as acts of violence against the adversary, whether carried out in offense or in defense, and in whatever territory conducted (PI Article 49.1).

☞ The basic rule governing attacks is that the parties to a conflict must at all times distinguish between the civilian population and combatants, and between civilian objects and military objectives. The parties to the conflict may direct their operations only against military objectives (PI Article 48). Attacks that are indiscriminate are therefore prohibited at all times.

Humanitarian law establishes that military commanders are under the obligation to take precautionary measures when preparing and carrying out attacks, so as to limit their possible detrimental effects and to ensure that they are not indiscriminate (PI Articles 57 and 58).
→ **Duty of commanders; Military objectives**

I. PROHIBITED ATTACKS

1. Protected Persons and Objects

International humanitarian law clearly defines the persons and objects who must be protected in times of conflict, both international and internal. It forbids intentionally launching attacks and reprisals against them, including the following:

- Attacks against the civilian population as such, and acts or threats of violence the primary purpose of which is to spread terror among the civilian population (PI Article 51.2 and PII Article 13).
- Attacks against civilians by way of reprisals (PI Article 51.6). The corollary to this is that parties to the conflict may not direct the movement of civilians in order to attempt to shield military objectives from attacks or to protect military operations, nor may they use the presence of a protected person to render certain points immune from military operations (GCIV Article 28 and PI Article 51.7).
- Attacks against civilian and cultural objects and property, places of worship, objects indispensable to the survival of the civilian population, and works or installations containing dangerous forces that may cause damage to the natural environment and hence prejudice the health or survival of the population (PI Articles 52 to 56, PII Articles 14 and 15). Humanitarian law defines the distinctive emblems and signs that must be used to signal the presence of such protected objects.
- Medical units and personnel must never be the object of attacks (GCI Article 19, GCII Article 23, GCIV Article 18, PI Article 12, and PII Article 11).
- Attacks on demilitarized or neutral zones and undefended places are prohibited (GCIV Article 15 and PI Article 60).
- → **Civilian population; Distinctive (or protective) emblems, signs, and signals; Human shields; Humanitarian and relief personnel; Medical personnel; Protected objects and property; Protected persons**

The statute of the new International Criminal Court, adopted on July 17, 1998, reaffirms that such attacks are war crimes, whether committed during international or internal armed conflicts (Article 8 of ICC statute). Furthermore, it states that a specific set of crimes, "when committed as part of a widespread or systematic attack directed against any civilian population," are crimes against humanity (Article 7 of ICC statute). These crimes will fall under its jurisdiction once it is operational, though this may take a number of years since sixty states must ratify its statute before it enters into force. → **International Criminal Court; War crimes/Crimes against humanity**

2. Indiscriminate Attacks

Humanitarian law also prohibits any kind of indiscriminate attacks. Such attacks do not distinguish between military objectives and civilian persons or property. Such attacks are clearly defined and prohibited in detail in Article 51 of the 1977 Additional Protocol I to the Geneva Conventions:

- attacks that are not directed at a specific military objective;
- attacks that employ a method or means of combat that cannot be directed at a specific military objective;

- attacks that employ a method or means of combat whose effects cannot be limited;
- attacks by bombardment, by any methods or means, that treat as a single military objective a number of clearly separated and distinct military objectives located in a city, town, village, or other area containing a similar concentration of civilians or civilian objects;
- attacks that may be expected to cause incidental loss of civilian life, injury to civilians, damage to civilian objects, or a combination thereof and that would be excessive in relation to the concrete and direct military advantage anticipated.

This last prohibition introduces the notion of "proportionality" that must be respected: any attack must be in proportion to the threat that is faced, and any reprisal must be proportionate to the attack suffered. If this proportionality requirement is not followed, humanitarian law considers the attack to be indiscriminate.

→   **Bombardment; Methods (and means) of warfare; Proportionality; Reprisals; War**

II. PRECAUTIONS IN ATTACK

Humanitarian law defines the precautionary measures that must be taken in the conduct of military operations so as to spare civilians and civilian objects.

> ☞ If military and civilian objectives are near one another, a certain number of specific precautions must be taken in carrying out an attack so as to limit any detrimental effects that civilians might incur (PI Articles 57 and 58).

It is the responsibility of combatants, and in particular of commanders, to respect certain precautions during military attacks. Two articles establish the measures that must be applied to ensure that this principle is effective in practice. These rules are in Protocol I and are therefore mandatory only in international armed conflicts. However, they may serve as a guide to illustrate measures that can be applied to the general principles of precaution that are set forth for internal armed conflicts.

1. Precautionary Measures

- "With respect to attacks, the following precautions shall be taken:
  (a) those who plan or decide upon an attack shall:
    (i) do everything feasible to verify that the objectives to be attacked are neither civilians nor civilian objects and are not subject to special protection but are military objectives (. . .)
    (ii) take all feasible precautions in the choice of means and methods of attack with a view to avoiding, and in any event to minimizing, incidental loss or civilian life, injury to civilians and damage to civilian objects;
    (iii) refrain from deciding to launch any attack which may be expected to cause incidental loss of civilian life, injury to civilians, damage to civilian objects, or a combination thereof, which would be excessive in relation to the concrete and direct military advantage anticipated.

(b) an attack shall be cancelled or suspended if it becomes apparent that the objective is not a military one or is subject to special protection or that the attack may be expected to cause incidental loss of civilian life, injury to civilians, damage to civilian objects, or a combination thereof, which would be excessive in relation to the concrete and direct military advantage anticipated.

(c) effective advance warning shall be given of attacks which may affect the civilian population, unless circumstances do not permit" (PI Article 57.2).

- When a choice is possible between several military objectives that would result in a similar military advantage, the attack selected shall be the one that may be expected to cause the least danger to civilian lives and to civilian objects (PI Article 57.3).
- "No provision of this article may be construed as authorizing any attacks against the civilian population, civilians or civilian objects" (PI Article 57.5).

2. Duty of Commanders

The commanders have the obligation to respect the precautionary measures described here. Furthermore, they must see to it that their subordinates also respect these rules. They therefore have the duty to ensure that members of the armed forces under their command, as well as other persons under their control, are aware of their obligations under the Geneva Conventions and Protocols and respect them. If members of the armed forces violate humanitarian law, the commanders must take the necessary measures to end such acts and to initiate the disciplinary or penal action that are necessary against the perpetrators of such violations.

➔ **Distinctive (or protective) emblems, signs, and signals; Duty of commanders; International humanitarian law; Methods (and means) of warfare; Proportionality; Protected objects and property; Protected persons; Reprisals; War**

📖 **For Additional Information:**

ICRC. "Protection of Civilian Persons and Populations in Time of War." In *Basic Rules of the Geneva Conventions and Their Additional Protocols.* Geneva: ICRC, 1995, chapter 4.

Mulinen, Frederic de. "Conduct of Attack." *Handbook on the Law of War for Armed Forces.* Geneva: ICRC, 1989, 102–04.

B

■ BELLIGERENT

The term *belligerent* was used until the end of World War II to refer to

- the states taking part in a war or
- the individuals authorized to use armed force.

This term no longer has a precise legal definition. Instead, the term *party to the conflict* is now used to define both state and nonstate actors participating in an armed conflict.

However, the term *belligerent* continued to be used until 1977 to refer to individual insurgents who, in a civil war, actually controlled part of the territory of a state. So as to ensure a more cohesive system of protection and to simplify the distinction between the civilian population and those fighting in an international armed conflict, the term *combatant* is now used in humanitarian law (PI Articles 43, 44, 48). The word *belligerent* is still used in everyday language.

→ **Combatant; Geneva Conventions; High contracting party; Party to the conflict; War**

📖 **For Additional Information:**

Basic Bibliography of International Humanitarian Law. Geneva: Henry Dunant Institute, 1985.

■ BLOCKADE

A blockade is a military operation that blocks all maritime movement to or from a port or coast. Blockades may also be aerial. A military operation carried out on land that isolates or encircles an area is called a *siege*.

A blockade is an act of war that is regulated by international law—namely, by the 1856 Paris Declaration Respecting Maritime Law, and Articles 1 to 22 of the 1909 London Declaration concerning the Laws of Naval War. It is important to distinguish between the terms *blockade* and *embargo*. An embargo is a type of economic sanction that may be adopted under the aegis of the UN or another international organization, to try to force a state to comply with a decision.

24

Regardless of whether the situation is a blockade or an embargo, humanitarian law clearly posits that states are under the obligation to allow the free passage of relief that is of an exclusively humanitarian and impartial nature and is indispensable to the survival of the civilian population (GCIV Article 23, PI Article 70, and PII Article 18.2).

→ **Embargoes; Methods (and means) of warfare; Protected objects and property; Relief; Sanctions (diplomatic, economic, or military); Sanctions Committees; Siege; War**

For Additional Information:

Heintschel von Heinegg, Wolff. "The Law of Armed Conflicts at Sea." In *The Handbook of Humanitarian Law in Armed Conflicts*. Oxford: Oxford University Press, 1995, 470–73.
"San Remo Manual on International Law Applicable to Armed Conflict at Sea." *International Review of the Red Cross* 309: 595–637.

■ BOAT PEOPLE

The problems raised by the category of asylum seekers known as "boat people" (or refugees at sea) are more complex than for other kinds of asylum seekers because rescues at sea are carried out in conformity with the laws and customs of the sea. This means that several states are usually concerned by the fate of boat people: the people's state of origin, the flag state (the state where the ship is registered and whose flag it is flying), the state where the ship makes its first stop after the rescue, and, if the case arises, the state offering to let the boat people resettle in its territory.

This plurality encourages states to adopt restrictive practices. These include, in particular, the refusal to admit the asylum seekers into the territory of the state they were trying to reach once they had been picked up.

Some of the most recent examples of boat people include the hundreds of Somali and Ethiopian refugees who crossed the Gulf of Aden to reach Yemen in 1998, the refugees who fled the Democratic Republic of Congo by boat for Tanzania in the fall of 1998 (according to UNHCR, sixteen thousand people reached Tanzania that way), and the Sierra Leonean refugees who fled across the water toward Guinea in January 1999.

There are certain clear principles of applicable law, described in the following sections.

1. The Legal Status of Boat People

Not every clandestine passenger or "boat person" is considered a refugee at sea under international law. To be considered as such, the individual must meet the criteria established in Article 1.A of the 1951 Convention Relating to the Status of Refugees (also reflected in the 1969 OAU Convention Governing the Specific Aspects of Refugee Problems in Africa). In other words, he or she must fear persecution on the basis of his or her race, religion, nationality, membership in a particular social group, or political opinion. According to UNHCR, less than 10 percent of clandestine passengers come under this definition.

2. The State Responsible for Refugees at Sea

Refugees at sea are under the protection offered by the flag state. The situation will therefore be different for boat people, who are likely to be on a ship belonging to their country of origin, or for clandestine passengers, who are more likely to be on a ship flying the flag of a different state.

Refugees fleeing in their own makeshift boat cannot benefit from the protection of their flag state, since that state's power is precisely what they are seeking to escape. Their boat's fragility may lead to the problem being addressed from the point of view of the obligation to provide assistance to ships in distress and the rules governing rescues at sea.

The 1980 Brussels Convention reaffirms that a captain who fails to go to the aid of any person lost at sea—as long as he or she can do so without endangering his or her own ship, crew, or passengers—even if the person belongs to an adverse power, can be fined or imprisoned. This makes the rescue of asylum seekers in distress at sea mandatory; however, it does not posit that they can choose their port of disembarkation.

An earlier Convention, signed in Brussels in 1957, seemed to solve the question of the status of clandestine passengers by imposing the obligation to receive such persons upon the state of the first port of call instead of on the flag state. However, this Convention never entered into force, as states refused to take on such a clear human obligation toward clandestine passengers.

☞ There is no law accepted by states that determines with certainty which state—the flag state or the state of first port of call—is under the obligation to allow individuals rescued at sea to disembark on its territory.

Clandestine passengers face the same dilemma when they embark on a boat stopping in their state, in the hope of disembarking in a foreign state. The responsibility of the flag state and the state of first port of call is not clearly established by international law, in the case of receiving clandestine passengers. This only makes the responsibility of captains all the greater and more uncomfortable.

---

3. Legal Obligations

From a practical point of view, only the obligations to rescue people at sea are clearly set forth in international law. This is the basis from which to protect boat people, in a first phase and as best as possible, because the absence of any solution to the disembarkation question results in more or less automatic or characteristic refusals to carry out such rescues. Today, it seems that being shipwrecked and cast ashore is the only legal way for boat people to "disembark."

UNHCR can play an important role in solving this dilemma, by suggesting resettlement procedures in a second state, in the state of the first port of call, or in the state that agrees to receive the refugees.

📖 For Additional Information:

UNCHR. *The State of the World's Refugees: In Search of Solutions.* Oxford: Oxford University Press, 1995, Box 5.4.

Zarjevski, Yefime. *A Future Preserved: International Assistance to Refugees.* Oxford: Pergamon, 1988.

■ BOMBARDMENT

Bombardment is an accepted method of warfare; however, there are rules limiting its use. These rules are enumerated clearly in Protocol I, which elaborates on provisions in the Geneva Conventions stating that "extensive destruction . . . not justified by military necessity and carried out unlawfully and wantonly" (GCI Article 50, GCII Article 51, GCIII Article 130, and GCIV Article 147) constitutes a grave breach of the Convention. Protocol I clearly prohibits bombardments and attacks on certain specific targets.

Indiscriminate bombardment and that whose primary purpose is to spread terror among the civilian population are also specifically prohibited (PI Article 51). International law considers that a bombardment is indiscriminate if it "treats as a single military objective a number of clearly separated and distinct military objectives located in a city, town, village or other area containing a similar concentration of civilians or civilian objects" (PI Article 51.5.a).

Attacks on the following targets are prohibited:

- the civilian population as such (PI Article 51 and PII Article 13);
- medical units (GCI Article 19, GCII Article 23, GCIV Article 18, PI Article 12, and PII Article 11);
- cultural objects and places of worship (PI Article 53);
- objects indispensable to the survival of the civilian population (PI Article 54);
- works and installations containing dangerous forces (PI Article 56);
- nondefended localities and demilitarized zones (GCIV Article 15 and PI Articles 59 and 60).

Furthermore, camps for prisoners of war and places of internment must have shelters against air bombardments and other hazards of war (GCIII Article 23 and GCIV Article 88).

The statute of the new International Criminal Court, adopted on July 17, 1998, reaffirms that such attacks are war crimes that will fall under its jurisdiction, once its statute enters into force. This will apply whether these crimes are committed in international or internal armed conflicts, though the statute only specifically uses the word *bombardment* in relation to international conflicts (Articles 8.2.b.v of ICC statute).

→ **Attacks; Methods (and means) of warfare; Protected objects and property; Protected persons; War; Weapons**

For Additional Information:

Mulinen, Frederic de. *Handbook on the Law of War for Armed Forces*. Geneva: ICRC, 1989.

C

■ CAMPS

The term *camp* is used to describe a place where people are gathered. Different kinds of camps are addressed by international law, and the protection that must be granted to the individuals gathered in these places varies depending on the rules of law that are applicable to each kind.

I. REFUGEE CAMPS

When there are mass flows of people seeking asylum (e.g., individuals who leave their home countries to flee a conflict), camps are organized under the responsibility of the host country's government, in cooperation with UNHCR. These camps must be located at a reasonable distance from the fighting—in other words, at a reasonable distance from the border with their country of origin (1969 Convention Governing the Specific Aspects of Refugee Problems in Africa, Article 2.6)—and must not serve as a base from which to run military operations. The UN Security Council used this notion to frame its defense of the "civilian and humanitarian character of refugee camps and settlements" in Resolution 1208 (1998), adopted on November 19, 1998.

The term *refugees* is used to designate the individuals in these camps, although they do not actually enjoy individual refugee status in the sense of the 1951 Convention Relating to the Status of Refugees. In certain circumstances, because of the number of people involved and the situation of emergency, an entire group of people may be qualified as refugees (a qualification accorded only to individuals under the 1951 Refugee Convention), without going through individual interviews. Within the camps, these refugees benefit from assistance provided by the host country or the international community through UNHCR activities. They remain under the physical protection of the territorial authorities. Sometimes, UNHCR may distribute individual refugee cards. In most cases, this document serves as the refugees' identity card and entitles them to the assistance distributed in the camps and to a certain amount of freedom of movement.

UNHCR makes sure that refugees are not returned to their country by force (*refoulés*). It also ensures that they have access to the procedure for requesting asylum, on an individual basis, if they do not want to be repatriated or if their collective refugee status is withdrawn during a repatriation operation.

→ *Refoulement* **(forced return) and expulsion; Refugees; Repatriation; UNHCR**

II. CAMPS FOR INTERNALLY DISPLACED PERSONS IN TIMES OF PEACE

Even in times of peace, individuals may be displaced within their own country, for diverse reasons. Although they may gather in a camp and may receive aid from the international community, they are still under the authority of their government and the domestic laws of the country. The international assistance that is provided takes place within the national institutional framework and norms.

No international agency has a specific mandate to protect displaced persons, and no international laws establish specific provisions to protect them. However, general international human rights standards may be invoked in such cases.

Internally displaced persons are only entitled to UNHCR's protection if they are "returnees." These are individuals who were refugees or sought refuge outside their country and were then repatriated to their state but not to the exact place where they used to live. Even in such cases, individuals are only protected if UNHCR and the state of origin negotiated an agreement concerning the repatriation, and it also depends on the content of the negotiation.

→ **Internally displaced persons; Repatriation**

III. CAMPS FOR INTERNALLY DISPLACED PERSONS IN TIMES OF WAR

In times of armed conflict, internally displaced persons are entitled to protection under international humanitarian law. In such situations, gathering them together may facilitate their protection, but it may also increase their exposure to the dangers of the conflict.

1. Camps Regulated by the Law of Armed Conflict

Humanitarian law sets forth provisions allowing a limited right to gather populations together. It expressly allows two kinds of camps:

- Camps for prisoners of war: captured combatants are prisoners of war and they may be gathered into camps regulated by the Third Geneva Convention.
  → **Prisoners of war**
- Camps for civilian internees: in international armed conflicts, a party to the conflict can intern civilians residing in its territory who are nationals of the enemy party. Foreigners who reside on the territory of a party to a conflict may also request voluntary internment (GCIV Articles 41–43 and 79–141).
  → **Internment**

Humanitarian law also allows gathering places that provide shelter for vulnerable populations from fighting. These are nondefended localities, hospital zones and localities, hospital and safety zones, and neutralized zones.

→ **Protected areas and zones**

2. Camps Forbidden by the Law of Armed Conflict

Certain camps are forbidden under international law, though they still occur in practice. These include

- concentration camps,
- forced regroupment camps,
- forced labor and reeducation camps, and
- extermination camps.

Parties to a conflict often justify the creation of such camps by saying they need to use the land for extensive military operations. Another justification may be the need to separate certain individuals from the civilian population, either because they doubt their loyalty or because they fear that the adversary may manipulate them for economic or military reasons. Sometimes, such forced gathering of civilians is organized in order to cut off any support from the society to a guerilla movement. Mandatory or forced gatherings are forbidden under international humanitarian law.

In practice, when such camps are forcibly established, people often have to work, not only to ensure their own survival but also to help sustain the military presence and the "security" operations carried out, in and around the camp.

At first, gathering individuals into these camps may enable the authorities to better protect them from the effects of the war. However, it also makes these people much more vulnerable: they risk either becoming a target for military activities or, more passively, being weakened through their loss of autonomy, means, and their ability to subsist or survive.

Deprived of any autonomy and a legal framework within which to defend themselves, the population is left to endure the laws of violence and arbitrariness that always threaten to transform a concentration camp into an extermination camp.

Practices explicitly forbidden by international humanitarian law include the following:

- Civilians must not be displaced by force. In internal conflicts, forced population movements are prohibited by the Additional Protocol II to the Geneva Conventions. Hence, the "displacement of the civilian population shall not be ordered for reasons related to the conflict unless the security of the civilians involved or imperative military reasons so demand. Should such displacements have to be carried out, all possible measures shall be taken in order that the civilian population may be received under satisfactory conditions of shelter, hygiene, health, safety and nutrition" (PII Article 17).
- Any authority that imposes population gatherings must ensure their means of subsistence. In any situation of conflict, military authorities are directly responsible for ensuring the well-being of any population interned or gathered together. The aim of this provision is to prevent armed forces from making a profit from population gatherings. Relief operations must not favor population regroupments.

In other situations, such as large-scale refugee flows or natural disasters, governments can always appeal for international assistance to help them provide aid to the population in distress. Such assistance can be provided on a bilateral basis or through intergovernmental organizations such as UNHCR, UNDP, OCHA, and so on.

→ **Displaced persons; Internment; Population displacement; Prisoners of war; Refugees; Repatriation**

📖 **For Additional Information:**

Brauman, Rony. "Refugee Camps, Population Transfers, and NGOs." In *Hard Choices: Moral Dilemmas in Humanitarian Intervention*, ed. Jonathan Moore. Lanham, Md.: Rowman & Littlefield, 1998, 177–94.
Levi, Primo. *The Drowned and the Saved*. New York: Summit Books, 1988.
Todorov, Tzvetan. *Facing the Extreme*. New York: Metropolitan, 1996.

■ CEASE-FIRE

A cease-fire is an agreement that regulates the cessation of all military activity for a given length of time, in a given area. It may be declared unilaterally, or it may be negotiated between parties to a conflict.

The term *armistice* is sometimes used, although it has a slightly different meaning: an armistice is a military convention, the primary purpose of which is to suspend hostilities over the whole theater of war, usually for an indefinite period of time. An armistice or a cease-fire do not represent an end to hostilities, only a truce (a temporary suspension of hostilities). Furthermore, they do not reflect a juridical end to the state of war. In this respect, they must not be confused with peace agreements, which do reflect an end to a conflict.

Humanitarian law requires that "whenever circumstances permit, an armistice or a suspension of fire shall be arranged, or local arrangements made, to permit the removal, exchange and transport of those who are wounded or sick as a result of combat" (GCI Article 15). However, the principal aim of a cease-fire is not to enable humanitarian actions. It is a military decision that responds to strategic objectives: gathering forces, evaluating the opponent's authority and chain of command, or carrying out negotiations.

☞ There is always a risk that relief operations negotiated in the context of a cease-fire may be used as a "bargaining chip" by the parties to the conflict, so as to obtain political or military compromises or to test the good faith of the adverse party or its ability to control its own troops or a given territory. Relief organizations must be aware of this risk and evaluate the danger that they may incur in the field because of this. Humanitarian assistance must not be conditional.

→ **Peace; War**

■ CENTRAL TRACING AGENCY (CTA)

The CTA is a division of the ICRC, based in Geneva, that acts as an intermediary between separated persons to help them find each other and to renew or maintain contact with their family when they can no longer communicate directly because of situations such as conflicts, internal disturbances and tensions, or natural disasters.

Humanitarian law affirms the principle of family unity, the right to family correspondence, and the rights of individuals to know the fate of their family members. Thus, the Geneva Conventions provide for a system of National Information Bureaus (NIB) and a Central Information Agency to collect information and transmit it to families. The role of the Central Information Agency has been taken over by the ICRC's Central Tracing Agency.

In times of conflict, the CTA acts as a liaison, working in coordination with the NIBs that the parties to a conflict are under the obligation to set up (GCI Article 16, GCII Article 19, GCIII Articles 122 and 123, and GCIV Articles 136–140). If there is no NIB or official auxiliary agency, the National Societies of the Red Cross and Red Crescent must fill this important role.

At all other times, the CTA may still offer its services, by virtue of the ICRC's right of initiative and its position as a neutral intermediary.

In all circumstances, the CTA's tasks succeed thanks to the network that the National Societies make up.

☞ Humanitarian organizations—interceding in situations in which individuals face difficulties in communicating with their relatives and close friends—can be useful in distributing the appropriate standard forms and in providing individuals with information concerning the different possibilities for renewing contact with their family members: exchange of correspondence, tracing requests, requests for other information, and family reunification.

For each of these requests, standard forms should be used. These are available though National Red Cross and Red Crescent Societies or the ICRC.

The CTA carries out five principal activities, with the assistance of the National Societies, each described in the following sections:

1. Exchange of Correspondence

This service enables the exchange of family information to be maintained or restored when normal channels of communication are obstructed or blocked because of conflicts, internal disturbances, or natural disasters.

The CTA sets up a special system of correspondence, if and for as long as there is not another way to deliver family correspondence. This "Red Cross mail" is mainly set up for families but can be extended to others in situations of emergency.

The CTA uses standard forms, in conformity with the Geneva Conventions:

- The Red Cross Message (RCM), or Family Message, is the best known. It gives the complete address of the sender and the addressee and can contain a maximum of twenty-five words. The information included must be of a strictly personal or family nature, without political, economic, military, or discriminatory references. The message is not confidential. Civilian or military officials of the state from which the message is being sent, or from the recipient state, may therefore censor it. National Societies may only censor these messages if they contain information that is not personal and family related.
- The "Anxious for News" form is used in certain emergency situations in the hope of receiving a reply rapidly. As with the Family Message, the most recent complete address of the addressee must be given by the sender. However, the message reads "urgent, send news" only.
- The "In good health" card is used for victims of serious events to inform their relatives that they are in good health.

2. Information Consolidation

The CTA receives, collects, and keeps track of information concerning a person or group who may be the subject of a tracing request or a request for family reunification at a later date.

Such persons include civilian internees, prisoners of war, unaccompanied children, and sick persons.

The sources of information concerning the whereabouts of such persons vary depending on the country and situation. It may come from civilians, military or religious officials, NGOs, UN agencies, the victims themselves, or their families. It is important that the different sources transmit information that is complete and precise, as delineated by the different standard forms. This is crucial to the efficient management of the database in which the information is consolidated.

Therefore, though the information may arrive in any form—letters, faxes, phone calls, tapes—it must contain the following elements:

- Personal identification information: complete name, sex, and date of birth. The nationality or country of origin, name of the mother, father, spouse, married status, profession, and so forth, may also be added, if appropriate.
- Information concerning the event: the description of the event (conflict, disaster, national or international crisis) and, if possible, what happened to the person (when he or she left, was separated from others, etc).
- The date and source of the document from which the information came.

No matter what form the information arrives in, it is then transcribed onto a standard individual identification form, which are kept in the same computerized database as the tracing requests (described in the next section), so as to establish matches between people looking for each other. This information is kept for one hundred years when it concerns individuals protected by humanitarian law, so that approximately three generations can take advantage of this information. It may also be used as the basis for later affidavits, so that former captives or their families can claim retirement, reparations, or retirement pensions.

3. Tracing Requests

People who are worried about the fate of their close family and friends because of a situation of emergency (whether armed conflict, natural disaster, etc.) may file a tracing request with the Red Cross. The CTA and National Societies of the Red Cross and Red Crescent carry out these searches.

Requests by family members are given priority. However, those filed by friends may be looked into if they are spurred by humanitarian concerns. As with the individual identification forms, there are standard forms for tracing requests, though the original request may arrive in any form, such as letters. These data are then transcribed into the same computerized database as the consolidated information.

☞ Hiding may be a way to protect oneself, therefore certain precautions must be taken to ensure that the traced person is not imperiled by the search. Therefore, once they are found, they are informed that someone is looking for them. The identity of the requesting person is then provided, and the address of the traced person is only transmitted with their permission.

4. Family Reunification

Once the tracing or information requests have been successful, they usually result in requests for family reunification. The role of the CTA and National Societies then consists of counseling the persons concerned and helping them collect the necessary documentation and meet the required traveling formalities (authorizations for departure and entry, etc.).

It is up to the individuals concerned to decide where they would like to be reunited. Once again, there are standard forms for family reunification requests. A distinction is made between different degrees of family reunification:

- *First-degree family reunification:* the head of family and family members who are directly dependent on, or related to, the head of family, such as the spouse, children who are minors, elderly parents.
- *Second-degree family reunification:* the head of family and family members who do not directly depend on him or her because they can provide for themselves.

If the sociocultural context provides a broader definition of "the family," it is possible to widen the concept.

5. ICRC Travel Documents

Established in 1945, the ICRC travel document is given free of charge to displaced persons, stateless persons, and refugees who cannot return their country of origin or residence or go to a country willing to receive them, because they are missing the necessary papers. The document is delivered only under certain circumstances (absence of valid passport or any other form of travel document; commitment to deliver a visa on the part of the state to which the person wishes to go). Once the journey has been completed, the document must be given back to the ICRC.

➔   **Adoption; Children; Evacuation; Family; Family reunification; Internal disturbances and tensions; International armed conflicts; Prisoners of war; Red Cross; War**

📖 **For Additional Information:**

Djurovic, Gradimir. *The Central Tracing Agency of the ICRC*. Geneva: Henry Dunant Institute, 1986.

✎   Central Tracing Agency
International Committee of the Red Cross (ICRC)
19, avenue de la Paix
CH 1202 Geneva, Switzerland
Tel.: (41) 22 734 6001
Fax: (41) 22 733 2057

■ CHILDREN

A child is a person who does not have an individual juridical personality (meaning he or she is not recognized as an independent person before the law). The child's protection must therefore be provided by the family or, in the absence of a family, by society. A child is an individual who has specific needs so as to be able to develop normally, both physically and mentally. International and national law devotes part of its guarantees to protecting children's regular development, within the context of family and society.

Children are greatly affected by situations of conflict, as well as situations of extreme poverty that frustrate many governments' social programs. In such situations, UNICEF and nongovernmental humanitarian actors play an important role in elaborating concrete relief actions. Such actions should not take place in a legal vacuum that risks increasing children's vulnerability to different kinds of abuse. Instead, relief actions should seek to restore or reinforce a minimum legal framework of protection.

☞ Children make up 40 percent of the civilian victims in conflicts and 50 percent of the refugees and internally displaced persons. According to UNICEF, two million children died because of wars since 1991.

The protection of children cannot be ensured by increasing their self-sufficiency, as is the case with adults. Instead, external systems of protection must be developed that protect the child from violations he or she might suffer because of the social or family environment.

All actors in society are hence directly responsible for ensuring the protection of children. In cases of emergency or exclusion, this includes humanitarian actors.

Minor and *child* are not synonymous legal terms. National laws take into account that the needs of children vary depending on their age, and they set a different minimum legal age for purposes such as employment, marriage, testifying in court, criminal liability, and imprisonment.

Most provisions of international law refer to "children" under a specific age, instead of "minors." In general, international law considers children to be persons under eighteen; however, it provides certain specific provisions for other ages. For instance, it is expressly forbidden to recruit children under the age of fifteen into the armed forces.

In times of conflict, international humanitarian law gives children both general protection, as civilian persons taking no part in hostilities, and special protection, as particularly vulnerable and unarmed individuals. They have the right to specific material assistance and to strengthened protection. Humanitarian law usually does not speak of "minors" because the age at which a child reaches legal majority varies from one country to the next. The Geneva Conventions generally consider children to be all persons under the age of eighteen; however, it enumerates additional specific rights and guarantees for newborn infants and children under twelve and under fifteen. Humanitarian organizations often pay additional attention to children under five, through targeted medical or nutritional programs. ➔ **Minors**

The Convention on the Rights of the Child (CRC)—adopted November 20, 1989, by the General Assembly of the UN—defines and aims to protect the rights of children at all other times, when humanitarian law is not directly applicable (in times of peace, situations of internal disturbances and tensions). The CRC defines children as "every human being below the age of eighteen years unless under the law applicable to the child, majority is attained earlier" (Article 1). It entered into force in 1990 and currently has 191 states parties. This Convention may not be used directly by children, but it establishes norms that are meant to be incorporated into national legislation. Its Article 38 provides for protection in times of armed conflict by referring states parties to humanitarian law, which they undertake to respect.

On May 25, 2000, the UN General Assembly adopted two Optional Protocols to the Convention on the Rights of the Child (A/RES/54/263), one on the involvement of children in armed conflicts and one on the sale of children, child prostitution, and child pornography. These will enter into force when ten states have ratified them. As of March 2001, seventy states have signed the Protocol on children in armed conflict, but only Bangladesh, Canada, and Sri Lanka have ratified it. Seventy-five have signed the other Protocol, but only Bangladesh and Panama have ratified it.

I. Protecting Children in Times of Conflict: The Geneva Conventions and Protocols

The 1949 Geneva Conventions and Protocols establish that "children shall be the object of special respect and shall be protected against any form of indecent assault. The parties to the conflict shall provide them with the care and aid they require" (PI Article 77). They center the provisions for the protection of children around several main objectives—namely, sheltering them from hostilities, maintaining family unity, and ensuring the necessary care, relief, or protection, for those caught in hostilities. The rules established for international armed conflict are more detailed than for internal conflicts, but nothing prevents relief agencies from using the former as a framework for their work in situations of internal conflict. These rules are derived mostly from the Fourth Geneva Convention (Relative to the Protection of Civilians in Time of War) and the two Protocols Additional (Relating to the Protection of Victims of International and Non-International Armed Conflicts).

1. Sheltering Children from Hostilities

As soon as hostilities break out, parties to a conflict may establish hospitals and safety zones and localities to protect wounded, sick and aged persons, children under fifteen, pregnant women, and mothers of children under seven (GCIV Article 14). ➔ **Protected areas and zones**

In case foreign persons are present on the territory of a party to the conflict, those under the age of fifteen, pregnant women, and mothers of children under seven must benefit from the same preferential treatment as the nationals of the state concerned (GCIV Article 38.5).

a. Occupied Territories

In an occupied territory, the Occupying Power must facilitate the proper working of all institutions devoted to the care and education of children. It may not, under any circumstances, change their personal status or enlist them in formations or organizations subordinate to it. Should the local institutions be inadequate for the purpose, the Occupying Power shall make arrangements for the care and education of children who are orphaned or separated from their parents, if possible by persons of their own nationality, language, and religion.

The Occupying Power may not hinder the application of any preferential measures with regard to food, medical care, and protection from the effects of war for children under fifteen, expectant mothers, and mothers of children under seven (GCIV Article 50).

b. Evacuation

The Conventions and Protocols contain provisions for the temporary evacuation of children if compelling security reasons exist. This includes removing them from besieged or encircled areas. Such evacuation must follow precise organizational and security rules and methods so as not to jeopardize the children's future in any way. ➔ **Evacuation**

c. Other provisions specifically relating to the protection of children in armed conflict

- In the case of unaccompanied children (UAC) and orphans under the age of fifteen, the parties to the conflict must endeavor to send them to protection in a neutral country (GCIV Article 17).

- An Occupying Power may not compel individuals under the age of eighteen to work (GCIV Article 51).
- Children have a right, overall, to the protection of their cultural environment, their education, and the exercise of their religion (GCIV Articles 24 and 50).
- Specific rules have been established to regulate all conditions of adoption or evacuation of children, so as to avoid the kind of fraud and abuse that may occur in situations as disruptive as wars (PI Article 78). Though these rules legally apply legally only to international armed conflict, nothing prevents relief agencies from using them as a framework for their work in situations of noninternational armed conflict.

→ **Adoption**

2. Maintaining the Family Unit

States are under the obligation to facilitate the exchange of family correspondence, including for dispersed families. In any case, states party to a conflict must never hinder such correspondence. All persons in the territory of a party to the conflict, or in an occupied territory, shall be enabled to give news of a strictly personal nature to members of their families, wherever they may be, and to receive news from them.

If, as a result of circumstances, it becomes difficult or impossible to exchange family correspondence, the parties to the conflict concerned shall apply to a neutral intermediary, such as the ICRC's Central Tracing Agency, to determine the best way to permit families to communicate amongst themselves. If the parties to the conflict consider it necessary to restrict family correspondence, they may at most restrict such communication to the use of standard forms containing twenty-five freely chosen words and limit the number sent to one each month (GCIV Article 25).

The parties to the conflict must facilitate the reunion of dispersed families, and they must encourage the work of organizations engaged in this task (GCIV Article 26, PI Article 74, and PII Article 4.3.b). They also commit to establishing their Information Bureaus and Agencies (GCIV Article 136). → **Central Tracing Agency; Family; Family reunification**

In case of detention or internment, the family unit must be maintained whenever possible, by lodging the family members together (GCIV Article 82 and PI Article 75.5). → **Detention; Internment**

3. Specific Care and Relief for Children in Times of Conflict

- Children shall be the object of special respect and shall be protected against any form of indecent assault. The parties to the conflict must provide them with the care and aid they require, whether because of their age or for any other reason (PI Article 77.1).
- Pregnant women and newborn babies come under the category of "wounded persons" and hence benefit from the same protection provided for the wounded and sick under humanitarian law (PI Article 8).
- In the distribution of relief supplies, priority shall be given to persons who must be accorded privileged treatment or special protection, such as children, expectant mothers, maternity cases, and nursing mothers (GCIV Articles 38.5 and 50; PI Article 70.1).
- In besieged areas or occupied territories, the states party to the Conventions must permit the free passage of all supplies of essential foodstuffs, clothing, and tonics intended for children under fifteen and expectant and nursing mothers (GCIV Article 23).

- Children held in detention: The Detaining Power must ensure that they are
  — lodged with their family, in the same place of internment (GCIV Article 82 and PI Article 75.5);
  — given additional food, in proportion to their physiological needs (GCIV Article 89);
  — allowed to attend school, either within the place of internment or outside (GCIV Article 94);
  — released in priority, if possible even before the end of hostilities (GCIV Article 132).

4. Children in Armed Forces

a. *General Prohibition on Recruitment of Children*

Children under the age of fifteen may not be recruited into armed forces (PI Article 77.2 and CRC Article 38.3). If parties to the conflict do incorporate juveniles between the ages of fifteen and eighteen into their armed forces, they must give priority to the oldest. The perpetration of war crimes by child soldiers poses serious problems in terms of criminal responsibility.

An Optional Protocol to the Convention on the Rights of the Child on the involvement of children in armed conflicts, adopted by the UN General Assembly on May 25, 2000, but needing ten states to ratify it so as to enter into force, raises the age at which participation in armed conflicts is permitted from fifteen to eighteen, and it establishes a ban on compulsory recruitment below eighteen years. It also requires states to make a declaration, upon ratification, regarding the age at which national forces will permit voluntary recruitment, as well as the steps that states will take to ensure that such recruitment is never forced or coerced.

The statute of the International Criminal Court (ICC) adopted on July 17, 1998, specifies that, in both international and internal armed conflicts, "conscripting or enlisting children under the age of fifteen years into armed forces or groups or using them to participate actively in hostilities" is a war crime (Articles 8.2.b.xxvi and 8.2.e.vii of the ICC statute). Under certain conditions, and once its statute has entered into force, the Court will be able to prosecute the perpetrators of such crimes.

b. *Provisions for Child Soldiers Who Are Prisoners of War*

If, nonetheless, children under fifteen do participate in hostilities and fall into the power of an adverse party, they must continue to benefit from the special protection foreseen for children (PI Article 77), whether they are recognized as prisoners of war or not.

5. Judicial Guarantees for Children in International Armed Conflicts

Children arrested, detained, or interned for reasons related to the armed conflict must benefit from special guarantees due to their age, their specific psychological and physiological needs, and the fact that they may not—in general criminal law—be held responsible for their crimes. These guarantees are protected in humanitarian law by the following provisions:

- Even in the case of detention, priority shall be given to children (and other persons in need of special protection) in the distribution of relief supplies (GCIV Articles 23 and 50; PI Article 70).
- The treatment of accused or detained persons shall take into consideration the special treatment to which children are entitled (GCIV Article 76). Article 50 of the Fourth Geneva Con-

vention establishes the general regime of protection for children. Other provisions forbid recruiting children into groups dependent on the Detaining Power and establish that they must be given the necessary material care and education. States are also under the obligation to provide them with the privileged treatment foreseen for them with regard to the distribution of food, medical care, and shelter from the effects of war.

- If arrested, detained or interned for reasons related to the armed conflict, children shall be held in quarters separate from those of adults, except where families are accommodated together (PI Article 77.4).
- The death penalty may not be applied to children who were under the age of eighteen at the time the offense was committed (GCIV Article 68 and PI Article 77.5). ➜ **Death penalty**

6. Guarantees for Children in Noninternational Armed Conflicts

In situations of internal armed conflict, a minimum set of rights exists that must be protected for children. These are derived from Article 3, common to the four Geneva Conventions (known as common Article 3), and the provisions relating to children in Additional Protocol II of 1977:

- Common Article 3 establishes that, as persons taking no part in the hostilities, children must "in all circumstances be treated humanely, without any adverse distinction founded on race, colour, religion or faith, sex, birth or wealth, or any other similar criteria." To this end, certain acts remain prohibited at any time and in any place whatsoever. These include violence to life and person, cruel treatment and torture, outrages on personal dignity such as humiliating and degrading treatment, the taking of hostages, and the passing of sentences without previous judgment pronounced by a regularly constituted court. ➜ **Fundamental guarantees**
- Article 4.3 of Protocol II posits that:

    "Children shall be provided with the care and aid they require, and in particular:
    - (a) they shall receive an education, including religious and moral education, in keeping with the wishes of their parents, or in the absence of parents, of those responsible for their care;
    - (b) all appropriate steps shall be taken to facilitate the reunion of families temporarily separated;
    - (c) children who have not attained the age of fifteen years shall neither be recruited in the armed forces or groups nor allowed to take part in hostilities;
    - (d) the special protection provided by this Article to children who have not attained the age of fifteen years shall remain applicable to them if they take a direct part in hostilities despite the provisions of subparagraph (c) and are captured;
    - (e) measures shall be taken, if necessary, and whenever possible with the consent of their parents or persons who by law or custom are primarily responsible for their care, to remove children temporarily from the area in which hostilities are taking place to a safer area within the country and ensure that they are accompanied by persons responsible for their safety and well-being."

- Furthermore, the death penalty shall not be pronounced on persons who were under the age of eighteen years at the time of the offense and shall not be carried out on pregnant women or mothers of young children (PII Article 6.4). ➜ **Death penalty**

II. Situations Other Than Armed Conflict

1. The Convention on the Rights of the Child

In times other than during armed conflicts (either peace or internal tensions), the Convention on the Rights of the Child (CRC) establishes the overall rights of children recognized by the 191 states party to the Convention. The government on which the child depends is responsible for ensuring the respect for these rights. Their implementation depends on the government adopting legislation in conformity with the Convention.

A Committee on the Rights of the Child was created, per Articles 43 to 45 of the CRC. It is made up of ten experts—elected to four-year terms by the states parties—and promotes and monitors government initiatives with respect to their obligations under the Convention.

States parties undertake to submit reports, every five years, on the measures they have adopted to enact the Convention. When it examines the reports, the Committee may invite UNICEF and any other competent bodies to provide expert advice on the implementation of the CRC in specific areas (Article 45.a). This provision enables NGOs to participate in the debate on the rights of the child in a given country. → **Committee on the Rights of the Child**

Throughout its fifty-four articles, the CRC specifies the principal rules and standards that must be followed or respected in order to protect the rights of children:

- the best interests of the child must be the primary consideration driving all decisions and actions concerning children (Article 3);
- states are under the obligation to adopt all legislative, administrative, and other measures for the implementation of the rights recognized in the Convention (Article 4);
- the right to life, and to the survival and development of the child (Article 6);
- the right to an identity and a nationality, registered and recognized before the law (Articles 7 and 8);
- respect for the family environment (Articles 9–11);
- freedom of expression—in particular before judicial and administrative institutions—as well as freedom of thought, conscience, religion, and association (Articles 12–15);
- respect for the parents as having primary responsibility for the upbringing of each child, with his or her best interests as their main concern (Article 18);
- protection from any form of maltreatment—including all forms of physical or mental violence, abuse, exploitation, or neglect—and states parties undertake to implement all appropriate legislative, administrative, social, and educational measures to this effect (Article 19);
- rights in case of adoption (Article 21); → **Adoption**
- rights of child refugees (Article 22); → **Refugees**
- rights of mentally or physically disabled children (Article 23);
- the right to the enjoyment of the highest attainable standard of health and the duties of states to make the necessary provisions (Articles 23 and 24);
- the right to the periodic review of a child's placement for his or her treatment (Article 25);
- rights related to education (Articles 28–31);
- protection from economic exploitation or any work that may be detrimental to the child's education or health (Article 32);
- protection from the illicit use and trafficking of drugs (Article 33);
- protection from sexual exploitation (Article 34);
- protection from the abduction, sale, or traffic of children or any form of prejudicial exploitation (Articles 35 and 36);

- protection from torture or other cruel, inhuman, or degrading treatment or punishment (Article 37);
- rights of children deprived of liberty and other due process guarantees (Articles 37, 40, and 41); ➔ **Detention; Judicial guarantees**
- protection in case of armed conflict: states parties undertake to respect the rules of international humanitarian law (Article 38).

As mentioned earlier, two Optional Protocols were adopted on May 25, 2000, on children in armed conflicts and on the sale of children, child prostitution, and child pornography, but they have yet to enter into force.

2. Standards Regarding Children Deprived of Their Liberty

The General Assembly of the UN adopted a resolution on the Standard Minimum Rules for the Administration of Juvenile Justice (known as the "Beijing rules," GA Resolution 40/33 of November 29, 1985) to further enumerate and develop a set of minimum rules and standards concerning the administration of justice for children. This text establishes the principles that must be respected relating to the criminal responsibility of children, the measures for sanctioning them, the standards for their education, and other guarantees for children in conflict with the law. In 1990, it was reinforced by the UN Rules for the Protection of Juveniles Deprived of Their Liberty (adopted by the General Assembly Resolution 45/113 on December 14, 1990). ➔ **Detention**

3. Regional and National Protection

There have also been some efforts made at the regional level to reinforce protection for the rights of children, such as the adoption in 1990 of the African Charter on the Rights and Welfare of the Child (CAB/LEG/24.9/49) by the Organization of African Unity. This Convention has not yet entered into force. Among the human rights obligations, the states parties undertake to respect and ensure respect for rules of international humanitarian law applicable in armed conflicts, including situations of internal armed conflicts and tension that concern children, and to take all feasible measures to ensure the protection and care of children who are affected by armed conflicts, including refugees.

Some countries have special national laws that enable the prosecution of persons who, while in a different country, committed sexual crimes against minors. Such trials may be carried out before the courts of the state of which the accused is a national, or before the courts of the state where the acts were committed. Such laws are adopted in the context of the fight against pedophilia and sex tourism. ➔ **Rape**

➔ **Adoption; Central Tracing Agency; Committee on the Rights of the Child; Detention; Evacuation; Family; Family reunification; International Criminal Court; Internment; Judicial guarantees; Minors; Protected persons; Rape; Red Cross; UNICEF; Women**

For Additional Information:

Campbell, Tom D. "The Rights of the Minor: As Person, as Child, as Juvenile, as Future Adult." In *Children's Rights and the Law*, ed. Philip Alston, Stephen Parkes, and John Seymour. Oxford: Clarendon, 1992.

Dutli, Maria Teresa. "Captured Child Combatants." *International Review of the Red Cross* 278 (September–October 1990): 421–34.

Jeannet, Stephane, and Joel Mermet. "The Involvement of Children in Armed Conflict." *International Review of the Red Cross* 322 (March 1998): 105–25.

Kuper, Jenny. *International Law Concerning Child Civilians in Armed Conflict.* Oxford: Clarendon, 1997.

■ CIVIL DEFENSE

When there are natural disasters, crises caused by accidents, or armed conflicts, "civil defense" measures and services—organized by the civilian and military authorities of a country—are implemented to guarantee the relief operations necessary for the protection of the civilian population and the maintenance of public order. The principal goal is to protect civilians, mainly by trying to limit the damage that may be suffered by civilian populations or objects. Civil defense includes preventive actions, such as preparing and training the civilian population and relief personnel, installing warning systems (e.g., fire alarms), and preparing and planning of emergency assistance or evacuation.

The Geneva Conventions define civil defense as "the performance of some or all of the undermentioned humanitarian tasks intended to protect the civilian population against the dangers, and to help it to recover from the immediate effects, of hostilities or disasters and also to provide the conditions necessary for its survival. These tasks are:

- warning;
- evacuation;
- management of shelters;
- management of blackout measures;
- rescue;
- medical services, including first aid, and religious assistance;
- fire-fighting;
- detection and marking of danger areas;
- decontamination and similar protective measures;
- provision of emergency accommodation and supplies;
- emergency assistance in the restoration and maintenance of order in distressed areas;
- emergency repair of indispensable public utilities;
- emergency disposal of the dead;
- assistance in the preservation of objects essential for survival;
- complementary activities necessary to carry out any of the tasks mentioned above, including, but not limited to, planning and organization" (PI Article 61).

International humanitarian law establishes specific provisions for the protection of civil defense personnel, as well as for the installations, equipment, and supplies they use (PI Articles 61–67). Because of the close links between civil defense services and military authorities (which help organize them), the personnel and organizations involved in such activities are protected by international humanitarian law, when they are assigned exclusively to the performance of the tasks listed earlier (PI Article 61):

- Civil defense organizations and persons must not be the target of attacks or reprisals (PI Articles 62–65).

- Civil defense organizations, their personnel, and their matériel, must be identified by a distinctive sign: a blue triangle on an orange background (PI Article 66; PI annex I Article 15).

→ **Disaster; Humanitarian and relief personnel; Medical services; Public order**

📖 **For Additional Information:**

Gasser, Hans-Peter. "Protection of the Civilian Population: Civil Defence." In *The Handbook of Humanitarian Law in Armed Conflicts*, ed. Dieter Fleck. Oxford: Oxford University Press, 1995, 234–39.

■ CIVILIANS

The civilian population is made up of individual civilians, in other words, individuals who do not belong to any of the various categories of combatants.

Under humanitarian law, civilians in general are granted protection from the dangers of military operations, and certain categories of civilians are entitled to reinforced protection.

I. DEFINITION

The civilian is defined in opposition to the combatant. Literally, a "civilian person" is any individual who is not a member of armed forces. The term *armed forces* has a broad definition, which confers equal protection on all those who take up arms. Therefore, a civilian is any individual who is not a member of one of the following groups:

- the regular armed forces, even one that professes allegiance to a government or authority not recognized by the adverse power;
- the armed forces of a party to the conflict, as well as militias or volunteer corps forming part of such armed forces;
- all organized groups and units, as long as these groups and units are under a command that is responsible for the conduct of its subordinates, even if the party to the conflict to which it responds is represented by a government or authority not recognized by an adverse party. This last category includes organized resistance movements and other small armed groups (GCIII Article 4.a.1-3 and 4.a.6; PI Articles 43 and 50).

In certain situations, it is difficult to distinguish between civilians and combatants:

- In the context of an international armed conflict, civilians may participate in resistance movements, in particular in occupied territories.
- In an internal armed conflict, guerrilla movements may be in close contact with the civilian populations. In such cases, humanitarian law acknowledges that it may be difficult for combatants to distinguish themselves from the civilian population in accordance with the rules. The two 1977 Protocols Additional to the Geneva Conventions take into account the evolution of various methods of warfare so as to offer better protection to both combatants and civilians.

☞ The "civilian population" includes all civilians. The presence, within the civilian population, of isolated individuals who do not come under the definition of civilians shall not deprive the population as a whole of its civilian character or of the protection to which it is entitled (PI Article 50).

At times, civilians may take part in hostilities without formally belonging to any regular armed force. This may happen, most notably, in the context of spontaneous uprisings in occupied territories. It may also occur in the context of internal armed conflicts in which the distinction between civilians and combatants becomes more difficult. Civilians who take part directly in hostilities temporarily lose the protection provided for civilians—for the duration of their direct participation (PI Article 51.3; PII Article 13.3). In such cases, if they are captured, they benefit from the status of prisoner of war.

In case of doubt concerning the status of an individual, he or she must be considered a civilian (PI Article 50).

➔ **Combatants**

II. PROTECTION OF THE CIVILIAN POPULATION

The law of armed conflict only recently accorded specific protection to civilians. Before 1949, the main international conventions only regulated the conduct of hostilities and the fate of wounded, sick, or shipwrecked combatants or prisoners of war. The protection granted to civilians was only an indirect result of the general obligation to attack only military objectives and the specific obligation of combatants to wear a military uniform and to conduct military operations openly.

Since 1949, the Fourth Geneva Convention specifically protects the civilian population. It is aimed particularly at protecting civilians from acts carried out by the adverse party to the conflict. In this respect, humanitarian law establishes a general system of protection for civilians, and it reinforces this protection in certain specific situations—such as in occupied territories or in cases of internment or evacuation—or for certain specific categories of persons, considered more vulnerable—such as children, sick and wounded persons, or detainees (all of GCIV, PI Articles 48–56; PII Articles 13–18).

In 1977, Additional Protocol I to the Geneva Conventions reinforced the protection foreseen for the overall civilian population in the context of international armed conflicts. Additional Protocol II to the Geneva Conventions extended this protection to civilians in noninternational armed conflicts, in which they are particularly exposed to danger because of the increased difficulty of distinguishing between combatants and civilians in such conflicts.

Finally, the two Protocols set forth minimum guarantees of protection for all persons who do not benefit from a more favorable system of protection. ➔ **Fundamental guarantees; Protected persons; Situations and persons not expressly covered by humanitarian law**

1. Protection of Civilians in International Armed Conflicts

a. General Protection of the Population against Attacks

The respect for and protection of the civilian population and civilian objects rests on the obligation of the parties to the conflict to distinguish between the civilian population and combatants, on one hand, and between civilian objects and military objectives, on the other (PI Article 48). This obligation is one of the foundations of humanitarian law.

All civilians, without any adverse distinction and in all situations, must be protected from the effects of military operations (GCIV Article 13). Hence, they may not be the target of fighting or attacks, and they have the right to receive the necessary assistance.

This general system of protection is defined in Article 51 of Protocol I. Articles 52 to 56 protect civilian objects, including those indispensable to the survival of the civilian population (PI Article 54). These provisions are reinforced by precise rules and definitions relating to the concept of attacks (PI Articles 49–51) and by the specific precautions that must be taken during attacks (PI Article 57):

- The civilian population, as such, must not be the object of attacks. Acts or threats of violence, the primary purpose of which is to spread terror among the civilian population, are prohibited (PI Article 51.2).
- Attacks that may hit military objectives and civilians or civilian objects indiscriminately are prohibited. "Indiscriminate attacks" are defined as those not directed at a specific military objective, those that employ a method or means of combat that cannot be directed at a specific military objective, or those that employ a method or means of combat the effects of which cannot be limited (PI Article 51.4).
- Attacks in the form of reprisals may not be aimed at the civilian population (PI Article 51.6).
- Civilians must not be used to shield military objectives or operations or to render them immune from attacks (PI Article 51.7). → **Attacks (III. Precautions in Attacks)**
- Such protection also covers civilian objects, which also must not be the object of acts of violence, direct or indiscriminate attacks, or reprisals (PI Article 52). This protection also specifically concerns objects indispensable to the survival of the population (which may not be attacked, destroyed, removed, or made the object of reprisals; PI Article 54), cultural objects and places of worship (Article 53), the natural environment (Article 55), and works and installations containing dangerous forces (Article 56). → **Protected objects and property**

b. The Right to Receive Assistance

The system of protection regulates the humanitarian assistance to which civilians are entitled if they do not have sufficient food, medical supplies, clothing, bedding, means of shelter, and other supplies essential to their survival. The relief actions foreseen in Protocol I address the specific case of civilians in occupied territory, but they also apply to all other cases in which the civilian population is affected by a situation of armed conflict (PI Articles 69–70).

c. Additional Protection for Specific Categories of Protected Persons

Humanitarian law specifies that civilians in the power of a party to the conflict—in particular, a party of which they are not a national—must be granted reinforced protection, as established by the Fourth Geneva Convention and Protocol I. These categories of protected persons are

- civilian populations in occupied territories (GCIV Articles 47–77; PI Articles 68–71);
- civilian detainees in occupied territories (GCIV Articles 64–77);
- civilians in the power of a party to the conflict (PI Articles 72–75);
- civilian internees (GCIV Articles 79–135);

- foreigners, refugees, and stateless persons (GCIV Articles 35–46);
- women and children (PI Articles 76–78);
- wounded and sick persons (GCIV Articles 13–26—Part II; PI Articles 8–31; PII Articles 7–9), who must be cared for without adverse discrimination or delay;
- medical personnel, installations, and means of transportation, which must be respected and must be able to carry out their work despite any hostilities;
- pregnant women, newborn infants, and infirm persons, who are included in the humanitarian law definition of "wounded and sick," in order to better ensure their protection (PI Article 8);
- relief and humanitarian personnel, who are always protected as civilians (PI Article 71).
  → **Protected persons**

d. Fundamental guarantees for all individuals, regardless of their status

All individuals must be treated in conformity with the fundamental guarantees set forth by humanitarian law (PI Article 75). → **Children; Detention; Fundamental guarantees; Internment; Medical duties; Relief; Protection; Women; Wounded and sick persons**

2. Protection of Civilians in Noninternational Armed Conflicts

The distinction between combatants and civilians tends to be less straightforward during internal armed conflicts; therefore, Protocol II does not establish a clear definition of combatants on one hand and civilians on the other. Instead, it only distinguishes between those who are fighting and those who are not, or no longer, fighting.

> ☞ In noninternational armed conflicts, humanitarian law establishes that individuals may belong to the category of civilians yet participate directly in hostilities at certain times. Protocol II establishes that such individuals shall benefit from the protection granted to civilians. This protection may be suspended only for the duration of their direct participation in hostilities.

Protocol II hence assumes that the entire population is civilian and therefore must be granted the protection established by humanitarian law, "unless and for such time as they take a direct part in hostilities" (PII Article 13.3).

a. General Protection of the Civilian Population

Articles 13 to 18 of Protocol II define the protection and means of protection that must be adopted for the benefit of the civilians.

- "The civilian population and individual civilians shall enjoy general protection against the dangers arising from military operations." To this effect, they must never be the object of attacks or of any acts or threats of violence the primary purpose of which is to spread terror (PII Article 13).
- Starvation of civilians as a method of combat is prohibited. It is therefore prohibited to attack, destroy, or remove objects indispensable to the survival of the civilian population (PII Article 14).

- Works or installations containing dangerous forces—namely, dams, dykes, nuclear plants, and electrical generating stations—must never be the target of an attack if such an attack may cause the release of dangerous forces and consequently cause severe losses among the civilian population (PII Article 15).
- Cultural objects and places of worship that constitute the cultural or spiritual heritage of peoples must never be attacked or used in support of the military effort (PII Article 16).
- "The displacement of the civilian population shall not be ordered for reasons related to the conflict, unless the security of the civilians involved or imperative military reasons so demand" (PII Article 17). Thus, it must respect strict conditions. → **Population displacement**

b. The Right to Receive Assistance

- Exclusively humanitarian and impartial relief actions must be undertaken for the civilian population if it is suffering undue hardship owing to a lack of the supplies essential for its survival, such as food and medical supplies (PII Article 18).→ **Relief, Right of access**

c. Additional Protection for Specific Categories of Protected Persons

Special provisions reinforce the protection, in noninternational armed conflicts, for

- persons deprived of their liberty (detainees) for reasons related to the conflict (PII Article 5); → **Detention**
- wounded, sick, and shipwrecked persons (GCIV Article 3; PII Article 7); → **Wounded and sick persons**
- medical and religious personnel (PII Article 9); → **Medical personnel**

d. Fundamental Guarantees for All Individuals, Regardless of Their Status

All individuals must be treated in conformity with the fundamental guarantees set forth by humanitarian law (PII Article 4). → **Fundamental guarantees**

→ **Attacks; Combatants; Fundamental guarantees; Human shields; International humanitarian law; Methods (and means) of warfare; Military objectives; Noncombatants; Protected persons; Protected objects and property; Protection; Reprisals; Situations and persons not expressly covered by humanitarian law**

⬚ For Additional Information:

Gasser, Hans-Peter. "Protection of the Civilian Population." In *The Handbook of Humanitarian Law in Armed Conflicts*, ed. Dieter Fleck. Oxford: Oxford University Press, 1995, 209–92.

Plattner, Denise. "Assistance to the Civilian Population: The Development and Present State of International Humanitarian Law." *International Review of the Red Cross* 288 (May–June 1992): 249–63.

■ COLLECTIVE PUNISHMENT

International law posits that no person may be punished for acts that he or she did not commit. It ensures that the collective punishment of a group of persons for a crime committed by an individual is also forbidden, whether in the case of prisoners of war or of any other individuals

(GCIII Article 87; PI Article 75.2.d; PII Article 4.2.b). This is one of the fundamental guarantees established by the Geneva Conventions and their protocols. This guarantee is applicable not only to protected persons but to all individuals, no matter what their status, or to what category of persons they belong, as defined by the Geneva Conventions (GIV Article 33).

> ☞ Collective punishment is prohibited, based on the fact that criminal responsibility can be attributed only to individuals. Respect for this principle can be ensured solely by establishing guarantees that protect judicial procedures.
>   This principle must also be monitored in the context of disciplinary sanctions procedures.

→   **Judicial guarantees; Prisoners of war; Protected persons; Responsibility**

📖 **For Additional Information:**

Jeschek, Hans-Heinrich. "Collective Punishment." In *Encyclopedia of Public International Law*, ed. R. Bernhardt. Amsterdam: North-Holland, 1982, vol. 3: 103–04.

■ COLLECTIVE SECURITY

The notion of collective security refers to a system in which states agree not to use force unilaterally. Instead, they agree to participate in, and defend, a system of collective security. The UN Charter governs this system for the entire international community, based on the need to defend the international public order defined by the Charter. It is meant to be implemented through the Security Council of the UN.

One of the primary objectives of the UN is to "maintain international peace and security, and to that end: to take effective collective measures for the prevention and removal of threats . . . or breaches of the peace" (Article 1 of the UN Charter). With this consideration, the UN system of collective security includes mechanisms for the pacific settlement of disputes—using arbitration and conciliation—as well as options for international peacekeeping or peacemaking action.

The system prohibits states from using or threatening to use force in their interstate relations, except in cases of self-defense (Articles 2.4 and 51). However, the Charter establishes a two-step method for collective response, and it entrusts the Security Council with the principal responsibility for it (Article 24):

- *Step 1: Pacific Settlement of Disputes (Chapter VI of UN Charter)*
  In the initial phase, the Council must strive to facilitate the pacific settlement of disputes among the concerned states. This is the preventive stage. States are under the obligation to seek peaceful solutions to their disputes, whether through negotiation, inquiry, mediation, conciliation, or arbitration (Article 33). However, the Security Council may expressly call on the parties to do so, if it deems it necessary. It may also investigate any dispute to determine whether its continuation threatens international peace and security (Article 34). In any case and at any stage in the dispute, the Council may recommend procedures or methods of adjustment that it considers appropriate. In particular, it may suggest that the states refer legal disputes to the International Court of Justice (Article 36).

If the perpetuation of the dispute is likely to endanger international peace and security, states are under the obligation to submit their disputes to the Security Council. The Council may also consider a case and make recommendations if all states party to the dispute request it.

- *Step 2: Responses to Breaches of the Peace and Acts of Aggression (Chapter VII of UN Charter)*

In cases of threats to the peace, breaches of the peace, and acts of aggression, if all preventive actions fail, the Security Council may have recourse to more forceful measures such as sanctions, including military ones. It is up to the Council to determine the existence of a "threat to international peace and security." It examines each situation referred to it individually and decides whether the public international order is in danger. The reasons set forth by the Council vary from one situation to another. In particular, the Council may decide to adopt provisional measures that are without prejudice to the rights of the parties concerned (Article 40). These measures are binding on all states. To ensure that its decisions are respected, the Council may apply various kinds of diplomatic or economic sanctions. Should it consider that such measures have proven inadequate, it may eventually employ international armed forces to restore order.

☞ In determining whether a threat or breach of the peace exists, the Security Council examines various criteria. Since those on which it bases its final decisions—further influenced by the possible veto of the permanent members of the Council—vary from case to case, it is very difficult, in practice, to determine what situation might trigger that reaction.

Other systems of collective security exist at the regional level, especially in Europe. They often function according to principles similar to those set by the UN, and in any case they have the duty to respect the global system. The Security Council may subcontract missions to regional organizations responsible for these regional mechanisms (e.g., NATO, OSCE, WEU, OAU), in accordance with Chapter VIII of the UN Charter. However, in such cases, the Council remains responsible for monitoring—and therefore retains the authority over—the use of force carried out on its behalf (Articles 53 and 54).

→ **Intervention; Peacekeeping; Public order; Sanctions (diplomatic, economic, or military); Security Council of the UN; Self-defense; United Nations**

📖 **For Additional Information:**

Koskenniemi, Martti. "The Place of Law in Collective Security." *Michigan Journal of International Law* 17 (1996): 455.

Roberts, Adam, and Benedict Kingsbury, eds. *United Nations, Divided World: The UN's Roles in International Relations*. New York: Oxford University Press, 1993, 63–103.

Weiss, Thomas G., David P. Forsythe, and Roger A. Coate. *The United Nations and Changing World Politics*. Boulder, Colo.: Westview, 1997, 21–122.

■ COMBATANTS

Combatants are all the members of the armed forces of a party to a conflict, except for the medical and religious personnel belonging to these forces (PI Article 43).

☞ The definition of a combatant is crucial because, in the context of international armed conflicts, the implementation of humanitarian law rests on the distinction between civilians and combatants. The latter are bound by the law of armed conflict to respect specific obligations. This law was also written to protect them, for instance, if they are prisoners of war.

In the context of internal armed conflicts, humanitarian law does not use the term *combatant* because it is harder to determine or define clearly who is or is not participating in the hostilities. Instead, it establishes a distinction between the persons taking part in hostilities and those who are not (or no longer), granting them—under the appropriate circumstances—the protection to which either prisoners of war, the wounded and sick, or civilians are entitled.

Combatants are persons who are authorized to use force. As long as their use of force is in conformity with the provisions of the laws of war, they may not be subject to criminal pursuit. The use of force may not occur as a result of individual initiative but must take place under a clear chain of responsible command, within the framework of respect for the rules of the law of armed conflict. It is this authorization to use force that distinguishes combatants from civilians. The status of combatant gives rise to a special regime of protection, established by the Third Geneva Convention, which regulates the treatment of prisoners of war.

The notion of "members of the armed forces" is broadly defined by the Geneva Conventions and their Additional Protocol I. It covers the diverse methods of warfare that may exist and provides equal protection and responsibilities for all those who take up arms.

I. DEFINITIONS

1. Armed Forces

As defined by the Third Geneva Convention and Protocol I, the armed forces of a party to a conflict consist of all the organized armed forces, groups, and units placed under a command that is responsible for the conduct of its subordinates. These forces, groups, and units make up the armed forces of a party even if that party is represented by a government or an authority that is not recognized by the adverse party. Armed forces must be subject to an internal disciplinary system that, among other obligations, enforces compliance with the law of armed conflict (PI Articles 43 and 50; GCIII Article 4.a, paragraphs 1, 2, 3, and 6).

2. Combatants

Combatants are

- members of the armed forces of a party to the conflict, as well as members of militias or volunteer corps forming part of such armed forces; or
- members of regular armed forces, even those which profess allegiance to a government or authority not recognized by the adverse power; or
- members of all organized armed groups and units, as long as these groups and units are under a command that is responsible for the conduct of its subordinates, even if the party to the conflict to which it responds is represented by a government or authority not recognized by an adverse party (GCIII Article 4.a.1–3; PI Articles 43 and 50).

Hence, persons who are members of "guerrilla" forces or small armed groups may have the status of combatants or of members of armed forces, as long as they follow certain conditions. These include carrying arms openly during confrontations, being commanded by a person responsible for his or her subordinates, and following an internal disciplinary system that—among other obligations—enforces compliance with the rules of international law applicable in armed conflict.

The fact that one party to a conflict may not recognize the legitimacy of the government or authority of the adverse party shall not deprive combatants of the status of prisoner of war (GCIII Article 4.a.1; PI Article 43.1). ➔ **Prisoners of war**

☞ At times, civilians may take part in hostilities without formally belonging to any regular armed force. This may happen, most notably, in the context of spontaneous uprisings in occupied territories. It may also occur in the context of internal armed conflicts where the distinction between civilians and combatants becomes more difficult. Civilians who directly take part in hostilities temporarily lose the protection provided for civilians—for the duration of their participation (PI Article 51.3; PII Article 13.3). In such cases, if captured, they benefit from the status of prisoner of war.

In case of doubt concerning the status of an individual, he or she must be considered a civilian (PI Article 50).

II. Rights and Obligations

1. Obligations toward Prisoners of War

Any combatant who falls into the power of an adverse party shall have the status of prisoner of war (PI Article 44.1). In case of a dispute concerning a person's status, there are two possible approaches:

1. The Third Geneva Convention establishes a detailed (and therefore strict) definition of who may be considered a prisoner of war and benefit from that status. This definition is broader than that of combatants in the strict sense of the term (GCIII Articles 4.1 and 4.5).
2. Protocol I, on the other hand, establishes that any person participating in hostilities—not clearly a combatant—who falls into the power of an adverse party shall be presumed to be a prisoner of war (PI Article 45.1).

Spies do not have the right to the status of prisoner of war (PI Article 46). Mercenaries do not have the right to the status of combatant or of prisoner of war (PI Article 47). They are entitled to the fundamental guarantees.

➔ **Espionage; Fundamental guarantees; Mercenaries; Prisoners of war**

2. Obligations of Combatants

First and foremost, combatants are under obligation to comply with the rules of humanitarian law (PI Articles 43.1 and 44.1). The Geneva Conventions define which acts are considered war crimes. Combatants who commit such crimes are individually responsible, even if they acted under the orders of a superior. The military commander or other hierarchical superior will also be held criminally responsible for the acts of their subordinates, whom they are under the obligation to stop or prevent.

Nevertheless, the fact that a combatant may have violated humanitarian law shall not deprive him or her of the right to the status of combatant or of prisoner of war should he or she fall into the power of an adverse party (PI Article 44.2).

➔ **Duty of commanders; Methods (and means) of warfare; Responsibility; War; War crimes/Crimes against humanity**

Furthermore, to make the protection of civilians possible, combatants are under the obligation to distinguish themselves from the civilian population. This is of particular importance while the combatants are engaged in an attack or a military operation in preparation for an attack. However, the Geneva Conventions recognize that there are situations in armed conflicts in which, owing to the nature of the hostilities, armed combatants cannot distinguish themselves in such a manner. In such cases, they will retain their status as combatants as long as they carry their weapons openly during each military engagement (PI Articles 44.3 and 48).

➔ **Attack; Civilians**

3. Recruitment of Children into Armed Forces

It is forbidden to recruit children under the age of fifteen into the armed forces (PI Article 77).

➔ **Children**

4. Internal Armed Conflicts

The status of combatant and that of prisoner of war may be also applied by parties to internal armed conflicts. If such a status is not applied, combatants who are detained by the adversary must at a minimum benefit from the guarantees established for persons who have been deprived of their liberty for reasons related to the armed conflict, as provided for in the Geneva Conventions and Protocol II (PII Articles 4 and 5). ➔ **Fundamental guarantees; Detention; Prisoners of war**

➔ **Attacks; Children; Duty of commanders; Fundamental guarantees; Insurgents; Mercenaries; Methods (and means) of warfare; Noncombatants; Prisoners of war; Responsibility; War; War crimes/Crimes against humanity**

📖 **For Additional Information:**

Ipsen, Kurt. "Combatants and Non-Combatants." In *The Handbook of Humanitarian Law in Armed Conflicts*, ed. Dieter Fleck. Oxford: Oxford University Press, 1995, 65–80.
Meron, Theodor, and Allan Rosas. "Current Development: A Declaration of Minimum Humanitarian Standards." *American Journal of International Law* (April 1991): 85.

■ COMMISSION (AND SUB-COMMISSION) ON HUMAN RIGHTS

The UN Economic and Social Council (ECOSOC) set up the Commission on Human Rights pursuant to Article 68 of the UN Charter, which entrusts the Commission with the promotion of human rights within the organization. The Commission therefore has jurisdiction over all member states of the UN, whether or not they have ratified international human rights conventions.

When ECOSOC defined the Commission's statute, in Resolutions 5.1 and 9.2 (of February 16, 1946, and June 21, 1946, respectively), it added protection to the Commission's mandate.

I. COMPOSITION AND STRUCTURE

ECOSOC selects the fifty-four states that will be represented at the Commission for two years, taking equitable geographic representation into consideration. Each state then nominates its representative, after consultation with the UN Secretary-General.

The Commission meets in Geneva once each year, for six weeks (usually around March–April).

☞ Unlike for most international human rights organs (whether courts or committees), the members of the Commission on Human Rights are not independent experts; they are diplomats representing their government. The debates maintain a political scope. The experts on its Sub-Commission have more independence.

The Commission has the authority to create subsidiary organs. In 1947, it created the Sub-Commission on Prevention of Discrimination and Protection of Minorities. In 1999, ECOSOC renamed this body the UN Sub-Commission on the Promotion and Protection of Human Rights. This Sub-Commission consists of twenty-six experts, elected by the Commission, upon nomination by their governments and on the basis of equitable geographic representation. It serves mainly as an antechamber for the Commission, preparing the latter's sessions. It has also been known to act as a pressure group vis-à-vis the more political Commission.

The Sub-Commission meets in Geneva once each year, for three weeks (usually in August), preceded by various Working Groups, which are the first to review communications. It can also meet in emergency situations, if the majority of member states so decide. This was done to address the situation in the former Yugoslavia in 1992 and 1993, Rwanda in 1994, and East Timor in 1999.

II. MANDATE

1. Human Rights Promotion

The Commission's main vocation is the formulation of international legal texts. It was originally created to draft an international Bill of Rights and is thus at the origin of the 1948 Universal Declaration of Human Rights and the two 1966 International Covenants, on Civil and Political Rights, and on Economic, Social, and Cultural Rights.

The Commission's mandate therefore includes carrying out studies, making recommendations, and preparing drafts of human rights conventions. It also develops technical assistance programs by nominating "independent experts" to carry out country studies on legal issues and to suggest means of assistance.

2. Human Rights Protection

From 1946 to 1967, the Commission did not really respond to human rights violations, mainly because it lacked the mechanisms to do so. In the 1960s and 1970s, ECOSOC broadened its mandate to include improving the UN's capacity to put a stop to human rights violations wherever they might occur. Nevertheless, the Commission is not a judicial monitoring body. Its overall philosophy is not to sanction or try to obtain reparation for violations committed. Rather, its aim is to apply international pressure on the governments concerned during the examination of the human rights situations in their countries.

In 1967 and 1970, ECOSOC adopted Resolutions 1235 (June 6, 1967) and 1503 (May 27, 1970), which established two special procedures (known under the names of the resolutions that adopted them) to examine human rights situations.

a. The 1235 Procedure

This procedure enables the Commission to decide, on its own initiative, to address situations of massive, flagrant, and systematic human rights violations (by referring such cases to itself). This procedure is public and leads to an issue's examination, which may result in the Commission adopting a resolution that condemns the state in question, as well as issuing a public report.

The Commission may also decide to establish an ad hoc monitoring or information mechanism for a specific country or topic, such as a Special Rapporteur, a Working Group, or a Group of Experts. The 1235 Procedure is hard to use because political or other alliances between state representatives often block resolutions that the Commission might otherwise adopt.

b. The 1503 Procedure

This procedures authorizes the Commission to "consider all communications . . . which appear to reveal a consistent pattern of gross and reliably attested violation of human rights and fundamental freedoms." This includes communications from NGOs and individuals. For such a communication to be admissible, certain criteria must be met: it must not be anonymous or abusive, all available means at the national level must have been resorted to and exhausted, and the situation must not be being dealt with under other international procedures. Most of the communications come from NGOs, which transmit their information via the Office of the UN High Commissioner for Human Rights.

These communications are first filtered by a Working Group, which consists of no more than five of the Sub-Commission's members, with due regard to geographic distribution. The Working Group decides whether a matter comes under the mandate of procedure 1503. The second screening is more political, carried out by the Sub-Commission, which decides what communications it will transmit to the Commission.

The 1503 Procedure is confidential. There are four possible options at the end of a review of the 1503 situations: the Commission can decide to keep a case under review, in the hopes that more evidence will be received the following year; it may decide to gather more information; an ad hoc committee can be appointed to carry out a confidential, on-site investigation, with the consent of the state concerned; if the state shows a lack of goodwill and the violations are serious, it may transfer the case to the 1235 Procedure, thereby making it public.

☞ All NGOs can refer matters to the Commission, but only those that have consultative status recognized by ECOSOC can participate in the Commission's and Sub-Commission's annual sessions, as observers. They can make written and oral presentations.

Many political obstacles hinder the Commission's procedures and do not always make it possible to protect the confidentiality of NGOs sources of information.

→ **ECOSOC; Human Rights; Individual recourse; Special Rapporteur; United Nations High Commissioner for Human Rights**

✎ Commission on Human Rights
Office of the High Commissioner for Human Rights (OHCHR)
52 rue Paquis
1202 Geneva, Switzerland
Tel.: (00 41) 22 917 92 39
Fax: (00 41) 22 917 90 12

■ COMMITTEE AGAINST TORTURE (CAT)

The Committee against Torture is the body established pursuant to Article 17 of the Convention against Torture and Other Cruel, Inhuman, or Degrading Treatment or Punishment, adopted by the UN General Assembly on December 10, 1984 (known as the Torture Convention), to monitor the implementation of the Convention by the states parties (of which there are currently 118).

The Committee began operating in 1987 and meets twice a year. It submits an annual report to the UN General Assembly and to all states parties to the Torture Convention. Its ten members are "experts of high moral standing and recognized competence in the field of human rights" (Article 17 of Torture Convention). They are elected for four years, with consideration being given to equitable geographic distribution, from a list of persons nominated by states parties. They can be reelected once.

> ☞ The mandate of the Committee against Torture is that of a conventional treaty-monitoring body: its jurisdiction is restricted to the states that have ratified the convention. Furthermore, states that do ratify the treaty may make reservations that restrict some of the CAT's activities. Beyond this, the Torture Convention allows victims of torture to submit their cases to the national courts of any country, provided the perpetrator of the crime is on the territory of the state in question.

The Torture Convention sets forth four different kinds of control that the CAT may exercise, although most of these mechanisms are dependent on the prior consent of the state concerned.

1. Country Reports

Article 19 of the Torture Convention establishes that each party must submit an initial report to the CAT, on the measures undertaken to implement the Convention, one year after it ratifies the Convention, and thereafter every four years. The CAT may make "general comments," which are transmitted to the state concerned, and may decide to include such comments—along with any responses received—in its annual report.

This mechanism is mandatory for all 123 states that have ratified the Convention (as of March 2001).

2. Information Gathering and Confidential Inquiries

☞ Article 20 authorizes the Committee to receive information from states, intergovernmental organizations, NGOs, and individuals. If it appears from "reliable information" and "well-founded indication" that torture is being systematically practiced, the Committee may ask the accused state for explanations. It may also designate one or more of its members to make an inquiry (which can include a visit to the territory, with the state's consent) and report back to the CAT urgently. These inquiries are confidential, and their findings are transmitted to the state concerned with any appropriate comments or suggestions.

The CAT's authority to carry out such inquiries is meant to be mandatory; however, certain states have rejected this competence by making a reservation against part or all of Article 20 upon ratifying the Convention. As of July 1999, the CAT had authority over 106 states. The following had made reservations: Afghanistan, Bahrain, Belarus, Bulgaria, China, Kuwait, Israel, Morocco, Poland, Saudi Arabia, and Ukraine.

3. State Communications

If a state party considers that another state party is not fulfilling its obligations under the Convention, it may, by written communication, bring the matter to the attention of that state party (Article 21). If the two states do not reach a mutually satisfactory solution within six months, either state has the right to refer the matter to the CAT. The Committee can then make its good offices available with a view to finding a friendly solution, and it may, when appropriate, set up an ad hoc Conciliation Commission.

For a period of twelve months, the Committee can receive oral and/or written explanations. After this period, it submits a report to the parties concerned.

However, the CAT's ability to carry out this mandate is dependent on two cumulative conditions:

- Both states concerned must have declared that they recognize "the competence of the Committee [under Article 21 of the Torture Convention] to receive and consider communications to the effect that a State Party claims that another State Party is not fulfilling its obligations under this Convention." Forty-six states parties have currently accepted CAT's competence on this issue (discussed later).
- The CAT must ascertain that the victim has exhausted all available domestic remedies unless these remedies appear to be unreasonably prolonged or are unlikely to bring effective relief to the victim.

4. Individual Communications

This mechanism, established by Article 22, enables individuals (victims, members of their families, or their legal representatives) to submit complaints to the CAT. However, once again, this possibility is only available to individuals in states that have expressly recognized the CAT's competence to receive and consider communications from or on behalf of victims (there are forty-three such states).

The Committee will not consider any communications that are anonymous or that it considers to be an abuse of the right of submission of such communications or to be incompatible with the provisions of the Convention. Furthermore, the Committee shall not consider any communications unless it has ascertained that the same matter is not being examined under another international investigation procedure and that the individual has exhausted all available domestic remedies (again, this shall not be the case if the remedies are unreasonably prolonged or unlikely to bring effective relief).

The background investigation is confidential and lasts six months, during which time the state under examination must submit written explanations or statements to the Committee, clarifying the matter and the remedies, if any, that it has taken. The CAT makes its decisions on the basis of this information. The views of the Committee are then forwarded to the state concerned and to the individual. These decisions have no mandatory force.

The following forty-two states have recognized the competence of the Committee under Articles 21 and 22: Algeria, Argentina, Australia, Austria, Belgium, Bulgaria, Canada, Croatia, Cyprus, Czech Republic, Denmark, Ecuador, Finland, France, Greece, Hungary, Iceland, Italy, Japan, Liechtenstein, Luxembourg, Malta, Monaco, Netherlands, New Zealand, Norway, Poland, Portugal, Russian Federation, Senegal, Slovak Republic, Slovenia, South Africa, Spain, Sweden, Switzerland, Togo, Tunisia, Turkey, Uruguay, Venezuela, and Yugoslavia.

In addition, the United Kingdom and the United States have recognized the competence of the Committee under Article 21 only.

→   **Human rights; Individual recourse; Torture**
→   **List of states party to international human rights and humanitarian conventions (No. 12)**

✎   Committee against Torture
    Office of the High Commissioner for Human Rights (OHCHR)
    52 rue Paquis
    1202 Geneva, Switzerland
    Tel.: (00 41) 22 917 92 39
    Fax: (00 41) 22 917 90 12

■ COMMITTEE ON ECONOMIC, SOCIAL, AND CULTURAL RIGHTS

The Committee on Economic, Social, and Cultural Rights was established by the Economic and Social Council (ECOSOC) under the International Covenant on Economic, Social, and Cultural Rights (which was adopted by the General Assembly on December 16, 1966, and entered into force on January 3, 1976). It monitors the implementation of the Covenant, which has been ratified by 142 countries.

I. COMPOSITION

The Committee has eighteen members, elected by secret ballot by ECOSOC for a term of four years, from a list of persons nominated by states party to the Covenant. The members are experts with recognized competence in human rights, serving in their personal capacity. Due consideration is given to equitable geographic distribution and to the representation of different forms of social and legal systems.

II. MANDATE

The human rights which the Covenant seeks to promote and protect are of three kinds: the right to work in just and favorable conditions; the right to social protection, to an adequate standard of living, and to the highest attainable standards of physical and mental well-being; and the right to education and the enjoyment of benefits of cultural freedom and scientific progress. The Covenant provides for the realization of these rights without discrimination of any kind.

The states parties submit periodic reports to the Committee on how they have been implementing the Covenant's provisions. The Committee studies these reports and discusses them with representatives of the governments concerned. Its comments on the Covenant aim to help states in their task of implementation, as well as to bring to their attention deficiencies in reports and procedures. The Committee submits to ECOSOC a report on its activities that contains observations relating to each state party's report, in order to help ECOSOC fulfill its responsibilities under Articles 21 and 22 of the Covenant. The Committee meets two times a year in Geneva for a period of up to three weeks.

NGOs in consultative status with ECOSOC are permitted to submit to the Committee written statements that might contribute to full and universal realization of the rights set forth in the Covenant (ECOSOC Resolution 1988/4).

➜   **Human rights; Individual recourse**
➜   **List of states party to international human rights and humanitarian conventions (No. 4)**

✎   Committee on Economic, Social, and Cultural Rights
    Office of the High Commissioner for Human Rights (OHCHR)
    52 rue Paquis
    1202 Geneva, Switzerland
    Tel.: (00 41) 22 917 92 39
    Fax: (00 41) 22 917 90 12

■ COMMITTEE ON THE ELIMINATION OF DISCRIMINATION AGAINST WOMEN

The Committee on the Elimination of Discrimination against Women was created according to Article 17 of the 1979 Convention on the Elimination of All Forms of Discrimination against Women (CEDAW) adopted by the UN General Assembly. It is responsible for monitoring and overseeing the implementation of CEDAW by the Convention's states parties.

The Committee is made up of twenty-three independent experts, elected by states parties. They are elected for four years, on the basis of equitable geographic distribution and with regard for representation of the principal legal systems of the world.

1. Procedure

The Committee follows a similar procedure to that of other UN human rights treaty bodies: it makes recommendations based on its examination of country reports, though these suggestions are not binding on the concerned state.

The states party to the Convention must submit a report to the Committee one year after the treaty enters into force for that country and then "at least every four years" (Article 18.2 of CEDAW).

The Committee meets only once a year for "a period of not more than two weeks" (Article 20 of CEDAW). To complete the work necessary to examine the reports, the Committee established a presessional working group that prepares a list of issues and questions, which are sent in advance to the reporting states. It also has two standing working groups, which meet during the regular sessions and study ways to expedite and reinforce the work of the Committee. Every year, the Committee submits a report of its activities to the UN General Assembly, through the Economic and Social Council.

Article 22 of CEDAW states that the specialized agencies of the UN are entitled to be present at the consideration of the reports, and the Committee "may invite the specialized agencies to submit reports on the implementation of the Convention in areas falling within the scope of their activities." No reference is made to a direct role for NGOs; however, the Committee has recommended that governments cooperate with NGOs in preparing their reports, and, in practice, information received from NGOs and independent agencies is an important factor in the Committee's assessment of the condition of women in the different states.

2. The Mandatory Country Reports

The Committee carries control that is of a nonjudicial nature. It is responsible for monitoring the implementation of the Convention. Its mandate is binding on states parties, which are under the obligation to comply with its procedures (Article 18.1 of CEDAW).

The country reports submitted by the member states parties inform the Committee of the measures each state has taken to incorporate the provisions of the Convention into its laws and customs and the possible difficulties encountered.

The "suggestions and general recommendations" made by the Committee after the meetings—generally held in public—are included in the Committee's report to the General Assembly, along with any comments from states parties.

➔ **Human rights; Individual recourse; Women**

➔ **List of states party to international human rights and humanitarian conventions (No. 24)**

✎ Committee on the Elimination of Discrimination against Women
Office of the High Commissioner for Human Rights (OHCHR)
52 rue Paquis
1202 Geneva, Switzerland
Tel.: (00 41) 22 917 92 39
Fax: (00 41) 22 917 90 12

■ COMMITTEE ON THE ELIMINATION OF RACIAL DISCRIMINATION

The Committee on the Elimination of Racial Discrimination is the body responsible for monitoring the implementation of the International Convention on the Elimination of All Forms of Racial Discrimination (CERD). This convention was adopted on December 21, 1965, and entered into force in 1969. It currently has 157 member states.

The Committee, established pursuant to Article 8 of the Convention, was the first body established by the United Nations to examine the application of a human rights treaty. It opened the path to the establishment of similar treaty-based monitoring committees. ➔ **Committee on**

the Elimination of Discrimination against Women; Committee on the Rights of the Child; Committee against Torture; Human Rights Committee

The Committee holds two annual two- to three-week sessions, generally in March and August. Following UN General Assembly Resolution 53/131, the 1999 and 2000 summer sessions were expanded to four weeks. The Convention foresees that the meetings will be held at the UN headquarters in New York (Article 10.4 of CERD), but they usually take place in Geneva.

The Committee is made up of eighteen independent experts, elected for four years by the states party to the Convention. Equitable geographic distribution and the representation of the "different forms of civilization" and of the principal legal systems are taken into consideration.

Four different procedures are used to examine the Convention's implementation, each of which is described in the following sections.

1. Country Reports

States parties must present country reports on the legislative, judicial, administrative or other measures which they have adopted in order to give effect to the provisions of the Convention (Article 9 of CERD). Usually, a representative of the state presents the report and answers the Committee's questions. The Committee may request additional information. It then presents its recommendations, which are not mandatory.

Originally, the states were to present an initial report, one year after the Convention's entry into force, and then a report every two years. However, in 1988, the Committee decided to request that states provide a detailed report every four years, with an intermediate report every two years. The Committee can also ask states to present a special report at any moment, when it considers that the situation in the country in question so demands.

If a state has not presented a report in five years or more, the Committee will automatically exercise its control and require the state's accountability.

NGOs may also transmit information to the Committee to assist the examination of the report.

2. State Communications

Under Article 11 of the Convention, if a state party considers that another state party is not adequately implementing the provisions of the Convention or is violating them, it may bring this to the Committee's attention. As of March 2001, this procedure had never been used: states rarely choose to accuse one another of violating human rights. The Committee examines the communication according to a procedure described in Articles 11 to 13 of the Convention, which aims to achieve an amicable solution between the two states. The Committee transmits the complaint to the state concerned, which then has three months to submit written explanations or statements clarifying the matter and any remedy that may have been taken.

Once the Committee has gathered and studied all the information, it establishes an ad hoc Conciliation Commission made up of five members appointed with the consent of the parties to the dispute. The members are independent and cannot be nationals of the states party to the dispute or of a state not party to the Convention. They do not have to be members of the Committee. The Conciliation Commission makes its good offices available to the states concerned with a view to reaching an amicable solution, on the basis of respect for the Convention. When the Commission has fully considered the matter, it submits a report to the Committee with its findings on all questions of fact relevant to the issue and any recommendations. The Committee communicates the report to the states party to the dispute, which have three months to inform the Committee of their decision to accept the recommendations or not.

3. Individual Communications

Article 14 of the Convention establishes a procedure that allows individuals or groups of persons who claim to be victims of a violation of the Convention by their state to transmit communications to the Committee. This recourse is only available to them if the state in question has recognized the competence of the Committee to receive individual communications. Only twenty-nine states have accepted this competence: Algeria, Australia, Bulgaria, Chile, Costa Rica, Cyprus, Denmark, Ecuador, Finland, France, Hungary, Iceland, Italy, Luxembourg, Macedonia, Malta, Netherlands, Norway, Peru, Poland, Republic of Korea, Russian Federation, Senegal, Slovakia, Spain, South Africa, Sweden, Ukraine, and Uruguay.

These communications are subject to two conditions: they must not be anonymous, and the individual or group of individuals must have exhausted all local remedies, except where the application of the remedies has been unreasonably prolonged.

The Committee began examining individual communications in 1982, after ten states had agreed to submit to this optional competence, per Article 14.9. The procedure for examining such communications is established in Articles 14.6 to 14.8 of the Convention.

The Committee refers the communication to the state party alleged to be violating the Convention, without revealing the identity of the individual or groups of individuals concerned. The state then has three months to submit written explanations or statements clarifying the matter and any remedy taken. The Committee then considers the communication in light of the information made available by the state and the petitioner. Finally, it transmits its suggestions and recommendations, if any, to them.

4. Prevention of Racial Discrimination, Early Warning, and Emergency Procedure

The Committee can decide on an ad hoc basis to monitor any situation that presents a risk of racial discrimination or in which the provisions of the Convention are being violated. Within this framework, NGOs can usefully transmit information to the Committee.

The Committee can then request that the state in question submit a special report, or it can invite this state to send a representative to its session to explain the situation and answer its questions.

→ **Apartheid; Discrimination; Human rights; Individual recourse; Protection; Special Rapporteurs**

→ **List of states party to international human rights and humanitarian conventions (No. 23)**

✎ Committee on the Elimination of All Forms of Racial Discrimination
Office of the High Commissioner for Human Rights (OHCHR)
52 rue Paquis
1202 Geneva, Switzerland
Tel.: (00 41) 22 917 92 39
Fax: (00 41) 22 917 90 12

■ COMMITTEE ON THE RIGHTS OF THE CHILD

The Committee on the Rights of the Child was created per Article 43 of the 1989 Convention on the Rights of the Child (CRC) and began operating in February 1991.

☞ The Committee is responsible for monitoring the implementation of the Convention on the Rights of the Child by all states party to the Convention.

To carry out its mandate, the Committee must follow a set procedure: it examines the mandatory periodic reports submitted by states. It has no mandate to address emergency situations.

There is no procedure for children or their representatives to file individual complaints. However, the Committee can apply a certain degree of pressure on a given state party, by requesting that it provide "further information relevant to the implementation of the Convention" on specific issues or cases of concern (Article 44.4 of CRC).

NGOs may submit information to the Committee at any time, including that on individual cases.

This procedure does not enable the Committee to take urgent situations or cases into account, since the country reports and examinations thereof only take place every five years.

I. STRUCTURE AND FUNCTIONS

The Committee is made up of ten independent experts, elected by the states party to the Convention. They are elected for four years and eligible for one reelection, on the basis of equitable geographic distribution and regard for representation of the principal legal systems of the world. An amendment, which has not yet gone into effect, was adopted in December 1995 to increase the number of experts to eighteen.

☞ The Committee is responsible for monitoring the implementation of the Convention on the Rights of the Child. This is done mainly by examining country reports that the states party to the Convention must submit: an initial report two years after the treaty enters into force for that country, and then a report every five years.

When studying country reports, the Committee may request and receive information or recommendations from any competent UN organ or other organizations, such as NGOs, "in order to foster the effective implementation of the Convention and to encourage international cooperation" (Article 45 of CRC). It may also request additional information from states, as explained further later.

The examination procedure is public, and it has both an oral and a written phase. Following the examination of the country reports, the Committee may make suggestions and general recommendations, although these are not binding on the concerned state.

The Committee holds three sessions a year, each of which lasts four weeks. At its first session, held in October 1991, it adopted its own rules of procedure, as well as guidelines structuring the state reports. Every two years, it submits a report of its activities to the UN General Assembly, through the Economic and Social Council.

II. MANDATE

The Convention confers a double mandate on the Committee: to protect and promote the rights of the child.

1. Protection: The Use of Mandatory Country Reports

The Committee is an entity of nonjudicial control, responsible for monitoring the implementation of the Convention on the Rights of the Child. Its mandate is binding on states party to the Convention, which must comply with its procedures (Article 44 of CRC). This kind of binding obligation is particular to such treaty-monitoring bodies and is exceptional among instruments set up to defend human rights.

The states' main obligation is the submission of country reports. These inform the Committee of the measures each state has taken to incorporate the provisions of the Convention into its laws and customs and the possible difficulties encountered.

Two to three months before the Committee sessions, a presessional working group meets to begin the preliminary examination of the reports and to identify the problems that might merit an in-depth discussion during the Committee's official session. During these months, NGOs have an important role to play because they are often invited to participate in the working group. This is also the only time throughout the procedure that NGOs are authorized to take the floor.

The Committee may request additional information from states, often sending them a "list of issues," and invites them to respond in writing before the official session. One of the questions asked by the Committee is that states provide the definition of a child provided in their laws and regulations. This is important in understanding the age of responsibility determined for different crimes and therefore the recourses that may be available. → **Minors**

Although it is not mandatory, each state usually sends a representative to answer the Committee's questions during the discussion of the report. At the end of the process, states must publish the initial country report, the summary of the preliminary examination, and the concluding observations of the Committee, according to Article 44.6 of the Convention.

This report-based monitoring began in 1993, and one hundred and sixty-two states had submitted initial reports as of April 2000. Forty-six submitted periodic reports. The Committee's methods for studying the country reports vary from session to session, in particular with regard to certain issues such as

- the participation of NGOs in the examination of the reports,
- the time allowed for states to respond to the "list of issues,"
- the form this response must take (oral or written), and
- the amount of time devoted to studying each report.

2. Promotion of the Rights of the Child

The Committee can organize thematic discussions, request commission studies on the rights of the child, carry out informal visits, and pursue other such activities to ensure that the principles of the Convention are being disseminated and to stimulate international cooperation on the issue of children's rights.

→ **Children; Human rights; Individual recourse; Minors**
→ **List of states party to international human rights and humanitarian conventions (No. 11)**

Committee on the Rights of the Child
Office of the High Commissioner for Human Rights (OHCHR)
52 rue Paquis
1202 Geneva, Switzerland
Tel.: (00 41) 22 917 92 39
Fax: (00 41) 22 917 90 12

■ CORPORAL PUNISHMENT

It is prohibited under international law to inflict corporal punishment on any protected person, including prisoners of war (GCIII Article 87, GCIV Article 32, PI Article 75.2.a, and PII Article 4.2.a).

Firmly abolished in most "Western" states, corporal punishment—which may include sentences as serious as the amputation of body parts—is still accepted as a penal sanction in certain countries. Even where legal, these sanctions may not be pronounced until after a fair trial has been held, one that respects basic norms of judicial guarantees. Such guarantees are defined in international conventions, which must then be ratified by states and incorporated into domestic laws.

→ **Ill treatment; Judicial guarantees; Torture**

▢ **For Additional Information:**

Bahrampour, Firouzeh. "Note and Comment: The Caning of Michael Fay: Can Singapore's Punishment Withstand the Scrutiny of International Law?" *American University Journal of International Law & Policy* 10 (Spring 1995): 1075.

■ CUSTOMARY INTERNATIONAL LAW

Customary international law reflects certain practices that states follow in a repeated and consistent manner and that they accept as law (*opinio juris*). Defined by the International Court of Justice (ICJ) as "evidence of a general practice accepted as law" (Article 38.1 of ICJ statute), customary law is one of the oldest sources of international law. In the international arena, states create legal norms not only by expressly stating their will through international conventions but also through their conduct. Written law represents only a small part of international law. Certain behavior, accepted and recognized by states as legitimate and beneficial, is gaining legal authority. Failure to respect such custom is therefore a violation of law.

1. Customary Law Is a Right of Action

> ☞ Customary international law originates from standards of behavior, recognized and accepted as legitimate and beneficial. This conduct makes up the "precedents" that can be invoked as proof of such law. Conversely, repeated acts violating the law may result in the progressive erosion of international law, if they are not denounced openly.
>
> In the realm of humanitarian action, the conduct of state actors—as well as, increasingly, that of nonstate actors—may therefore result in either the strengthening or weakening of international law and humanitarian principles. It is the duty of humanitarian actors to defend humanitarian customs through their actions and to denounce any failure to respect them.

Customary law often precedes written law. It may later be codified—for instance, in the form of a convention or a formal resolution adopted by the General Assembly of the UN or by the International Law Commission. This approach stands in contrast to the tradition of written law followed by most of the judicial systems based on Roman law, and it gives significant weight to the conduct followed by each actor in the international arena.

2. Customary Law Is Binding on All States

Customary law plays an important role in filling the voids left by written law, whether because it does not exist or because it cannot be applied—for instance, owing to the complex procedure of signing, ratifying, and possibly issuing reservations to an international convention. In fact, it is the second source of law to which the International Court of Justice refers (Article 38.1 of ICJ statute). → **Hierarchy of norms**

In humanitarian law it is particularly important to avoid cases in which a person could be left without protection or assistance. This can happen if the relevant convention has no provisions for the situation in which the person finds him- or herself or if it is not in force in the country in question. The 1949 Geneva Conventions reiterate the fact that persons and situations not covered by the Conventions nonetheless remain covered by international customary law. This principle is found in all four Conventions and their first Protocol Additional. Commonly known as the "Martens clause," it states that "in cases not covered by the [Conventions or Protocol I] or by other international agreements, civilians and combatants remain under the protection and authority of the principles of international law derived from established custom, from the principles of humanity and from the dictates of public conscience" (PI Article 1.2, GCI Article 63, GCII Article 62, GCIII Article 142, and GCIV Article 158).

☞ International customary law is as binding on states as the international conventions to which they are parties (as evidenced by Article 38 of the International Court of Justice). The fact that a state has not signed an international convention has no bearing on its obligations under customary law.

Today, the four 1949 Geneva Conventions have gained the status of customary international law. This means that even states that have not ratified them may be held accountable to their rules.

The International Law Commission recognized in 1980 that the Geneva Conventions reflected the general principles that are the basis of humanitarian law. The Secretary-General of the UN reiterated this in his report on the establishment of the International Criminal Tribunal for the former Yugoslavia (S/25704 of May 3, 1993). The Security Council approved this report in its Resolution 827 (May 5, 1993).

→ **Fundamental guarantees; Hierarchy of norms; International conventions; International humanitarian law; International law; Methods (and means) of warfare; Natural law and positive law; Situations and persons not expressly covered by humanitarian law; War**

📖 **For Additional Information:**

Bruderlein, Claude. "Custom in International Humanitarian Law." *International Review of the Red Cross* 285 (November–December 1991): 579–95.

Meron, Theodor. "The Continuing Role of Custom in the Formation of International Humanitarian Law." *American Journal of International Law* 90 (1996): 238.

———. *Human Rights and Humanitarian Norms as Customary Law.* Oxford: Clarendon, 1989.

D

■ DEATH PENALTY

The death penalty is not forbidden under international law if the criminal laws of a state provide for it as a form of punishment for the most serious crimes. In all cases, it may be pronounced only as the result of a final judgment, rendered by a competent court established by law and in conformity with due process rules and norms (Article 6 of the International Covenant on Civil and Political Rights).

→ **Judicial guarantees**

☞ The death penalty should not be confused with extrajudicial executions. An extrajudicial or summary execution is when a person is arbitrarily deprived of his or her life without a judgment by a competent and independent court or any recourse to processes of law; it is strictly prohibited by international law, whether during peace or war. A Special Rapporteur appointed to the UN Commission on Human Rights is in charge of monitoring and reporting on such executions. It is currently Ms. Asma Jahangir, from Pakistan.

→ **Special Rapporteurs**

Several international human rights conventions are available for states that wish to renounce the death penalty as a criminal sentence. These texts can mostly be found in the form of optional protocols to existing conventions, which establish provisions for the elimination of the death penalty:

- The Second Optional Protocol to the International Covenant on Civil and Political Rights, Aiming at the Abolition of the Death Penalty, was adopted under the aegis of the UN in 1989 and entered into force in 1991 (forty-three states parties).
- The Sixth Protocol to the European Convention for the Protection of Human Rights and Fundamental Freedoms, Concerning the Abolition of the Death Penalty, was adopted by the Council of Europe in 1983 and entered into force in 1985 (thirty-nine states parties).

■ The Protocol to the American Convention on Human Rights, to Abolish the Death Penalty, was adopted by the Organization of American States in 1990 and entered into force in 1991 (six states parties).

These protocols, and the restrictions imposed on the use of the death penalty in human rights treaties and declarations, reflect the fact that the general trend in international law is to encourage states to abolish the use of capital punishment.

None of the International Criminal Tribunals that have jurisdiction over individuals—the two ad hoc International Criminal Tribunals for the former Yugoslavia and Rwanda, established in 1993 and 1994, respectively, and the permanent International Criminal Court, the statute of which was adopted on July 17, 1998—include the death penalty among their penalties.

The strongest witness to this trend is the fact that, in order to join the European Union, states are under the obligation to abolish the death penalty, in both law and practice. The American Convention on Human Rights also establishes that "the death penalty shall not be reestablished in states that have abolished it" (Article 4.3 of the ACHR). Finally, on August 24, 1999, the UN Sub-Commission on Human Rights called for the elimination of the death penalty for criminals who were under the age of eighteen at the time that they committed their crime. It also asked states that do still have provisions for the death penalty within their laws to hold a moratorium on executions during 2000.

The principal states and territories that still maintain the death penalty, in both law and practice, are just under half of the countries in the world: Afghanistan, Algeria, Antigua and Barbuda, Armenia, Bahamas, Bahrain, Bangladesh, Barbados, Belarus, Belize, Benin, Botswana, Bulgaria, Burkina Faso, Burundi, Cameroon, Chad, Chile, China, Comoros, Cuba, Democratic Republic of Congo, Dominica, Egypt, Equatorial Guinea, Eritrea, Ethiopia, Gabon, Ghana, Guinea, Guatemala, Guyana, India, Indonesia, Iran, Iraq, Jamaica, Japan, Jordan, Kazakhstan, Kenya, Kuwait, Kyrgystan, Lao People's Democratic Republic, Latvia, Lebanon, Lesotho, Liberia, Libyan Arab Jamahiriya, Lithuania, Malawi, Malaysia, Morocco, Myanmar, Nigeria, North Korea, Oman, Pakistan, Palestinian Authority, Qatar, Russian Federation, Saint Kitts and Nevis, Saint Lucia, Saint Vincent and the Grenadines, Saudi Arabia, Sierra Leone, Singapore, Somalia, South Korea, Sudan, Swaziland, Syrian Arab Republic, Taiwan, Tajikistan, Tanzania, Thailand, Trinidad and Tobago, Tunisia, Turkmenistan, Uganda, Ukraine, United Arab Emirates, United States of America, Uzbekistan, Vietnam, Yemen, Yugoslavia (Serbia and Montenegro), Zambia, and Zimbabwe.

The Death Penalty in Times of Conflict

The international law of armed conflict restricts or prohibits the use of the death penalty against certain categories of persons:

Persons under eighteen years of age, pregnant women, and mothers of young children:

In both international and internal armed conflicts, the Protocols to the Geneva Conventions include in their judicial guarantees that "the death penalty shall not be pronounced on persons who were under the age of eighteen years at the time of the offence and shall not be carried out on pregnant women or mothers of young children" (PI Articles 76.3 and 77.5; PII Article 6.4).

(continues)

(continued)

The civilian population of occupied territories:

The Fourth Geneva Convention establishes specific restrictions on the use of the death penalty in occupied territories:

- The death penalty may only be imposed in cases of espionage, serious acts of sabotage against the military installations of the Occupying Power, or intentional offenses that have caused the death of one or more persons, provided that such offenses were punishable by death under the law of the occupied territory in force before the occupation began (GCIV Article 68);
- in all cases, the death penalty may not be pronounced unless the court has taken into account the fact that the accused, not being a national of the Occupying Power, is not bound to it by any duty of allegiance (GCIV Article 68);
- under no circumstance may the death penalty be pronounced against a protected person who was under eighteen years of age at the time of the offense (GCIV Article 68);
- persons condemned to death shall always have the right to petition for pardon, reprieve, or appeal (GCIV Article 75);
- no death sentence shall be carried out until at least six months after the date at which the Protecting Power was informed of the final judgment confirming the death penalty (GCIV Article 75).

Prisoners of war:

- Prisoners of war and the Protecting Powers shall be informed as soon as possible of the offenses that are punishable by the death sentence under the laws of the Detaining Power (GCIII Article 100);
- the death sentence cannot be pronounced on a prisoner of war unless the court has taken into account the fact that, since the accused is not a national of the Detaining Power, he or she is not bound to it by any duty of allegiance and is a prisoner as the result of circumstances independent of his or her own will (GCIII Article 100);
- if the death penalty is pronounced on a prisoner of war, the sentence shall not be executed before at least six months after the date at which the Protecting Power was informed of the decision (GCIII Article 101).

→   **Children; Human rights; International Criminal Court; International Criminal Tribunals; Judicial guarantees; Women**

📖 **For Additional Information:**

Amnesty International. *When the State Kills: The Death Penalty v. Human Rights*. London: Author, 1989.
Manchesi, A. "The Death Penalty in Wartime." *International Review of Penal Law,* no. 1–2 (Paris: Cujas, 1996): 319–31.

■ DEPORTATION

Deportation is a phenomenon that affects the population of a territory under occupation or conquest. *Deportation* refers to the forced transfer of civilians (or other persons protected by the

Geneva Conventions) from the territory where they reside to the territory of the Occupying Power or to any other territory, whether occupied or not. It is different from "population transfer," which describes a forced movement of population that takes place within the national territory. ➔ **Population displacement**

> ☞ Individual or mass deportations are prohibited, regardless of their motive, by the Fourth Geneva Convention (Article 49).
>
> The Occupying Power is also prohibited from deporting or transferring part of its own civilian population into the territory it occupies (GCIV Article 49).
>
> Such acts are war crimes (GCIV Article 147). Furthermore, they contribute toward the commission of crimes such as ethnic cleansing and genocide.
>
> The statute of the International Criminal Court, adopted in July 1998, defines deportation and transfer both as war crimes and crimes against humanity (Articles 8.2.a.vii, 8.2.b.viii, and 7.1.d of ICC statute). The transfer by the Occupying Power of its own civilian population into occupied territory is also a war crime (Article 8.2.b.viii). Once the statute enters into force, the ICC will be able to judge authors of such crimes, under certain conditions.

Article 49 of the Fourth Geneva Convention tolerates the total or partial evacuation of the civilian population from a given area, under very specific and restrictive conditions, such as cases in which the security of the population or imperative military reasons require it. Such an evacuation can only be temporary, and the population must be allowed to return as soon as possible. ➔ **Evacuation**

In such cases:

- the Occupying Power may only evacuate individuals to another area within the bounds of the occupied territory;
- it must inform the Protecting Power that is responsible for this population of any transfer and evacuation as soon as it has taken place;
- the transfer may not take place toward an area exposed to the dangers of war; and
- the Occupying Power undertaking such transfer or evacuation must ensure that proper accommodation is provided to receive the protected persons; that the transportation meets satisfactory conditions of hygiene, health, safety and nutrition; and that family members are not separated from each other.

Deportation may also occur in the broader context of population displacement.

➔ **Camps; Civilians; Displaced persons; Evacuation; International Criminal Court; Internment; Population displacement; Protected persons; Refugees**

▪ DETENTION

International law makes a distinction between *detention* and *internment*. Detention is a measure that deprives an individual of his or her freedom and is enacted pursuant to a decision taken by a judicial body.

The internment of individuals, on the other hand, results from an administrative decision. It may also take place in times of armed conflict, when the military authorities of parties to a conflict adopt measures of internment, affecting either civilians or prisoners of war. Such measures are explained in the entry on ➔ **internment**

However, humanitarian law establishes the same guarantees of protection for detainees and internees, in times of internal armed conflict.

In situations of conflict, the Geneva Conventions give the International Committee of the Red Cross (ICRC) the right to have access to all detention sites where protected persons are being held and the right to meet with them. This applies to both civilians (GCIV Article 143) and prisoners of war (GCIII Article 126). So as not to weaken the responsibilities with regard to protection that humanitarian law gives the ICRC, the presence of any other humanitarian organizations working with detained individuals should be absolutely transparent, and their actions should occur with full knowledge and respect for the rules of law applicable to such situations.

☞ Individuals deprived of liberty often find themselves in environments that are conducive to ill treatment. They risk being subjected to various forms of pressure, abuse, deprivation, and violence, without any defense or possibility of escape. As a result, deprivation of liberty may have serious consequences on the health of those detained, as well as on the very notion of medical practice.

In many countries, the judicial system is paralyzed by the lack of public funds, and prisons become a place where people stay for a long time while awaiting a judgment. Many of them do not even survive their conditions of detention. Delinquents and criminals mix with individuals who are victims of abusive denunciations or who are considered members of an "undesirable" group from a social point of view (e.g., street children, poor or marginalized persons, the sick, etc.).

In a prison context, marked by scarcity and violence, any humanitarian action must be grounded in a precise set of rights and operational principles in order to assist the individuals who need it.

We will explain here that specific judicial guarantees must frame arrests and detention (Section I). Other standards establish a framework to regulate the minimum material conditions that must exist, including the medical services (Section II). Finally, humanitarian law sets forth specific standards that must be respected in times of armed conflict (Section III).

Detainees (a term used mainly in the Geneva Conventions) are individuals who have been incarcerated as a result of a conviction. They are also called "imprisoned" or "convicted" persons. "Accused" (or "indicted") persons are those awaiting judgment. The terms *detained persons* or *untried prisoners* also refer to those deprived of liberty for reasons other than a conviction for an offense ("Body of Principles for the Protection of All Persons under Any Form of Detention or Imprisonment, Resolution of the UN General Assembly, 43/173, 1988).

I. JUDICIAL GUARANTEES RELATING TO THE ARREST AND DETENTION OF INDIVIDUALS

Under normal circumstances, individuals are detained on the basis of legal decisions.

1. Prohibition on Arbitrary Detention

Detaining an individual without judgment is prohibited by all international human rights texts, as well as the criminal laws of most states. This point is set forth clearly in Article 9 of the 1948 Universal Declaration of Human Rights, and it is echoed and expanded by Article 9 of the 1966 International Covenant on Civil and Political Rights (ICCPR).

- All individuals have the right to liberty and security of person. No one shall be subjected to arbitrary arrest or detention, or deprived of his or her liberty, except on such grounds and in accordance with such procedures as are established by law.
- Any individual who is arrested must be informed, at the time of arrest, of the reasons for the arrest, and must be promptly informed of any charges against him or her.
- Any individual arrested or detained on a criminal charge must be brought promptly before a judge or other officer authorized by law to exercise judicial power. The individual must be tried within a reasonable amount of time or must be released. Detaining people in custody while awaiting trial should be the exception, not the rule. The release of persons being held may be conditional upon certain guarantees, such as their appearing for trial and other parts of the proceedings.
- A release may also be requested if the investigation is completed and there is no risk that the accused will hinder the trial proceedings.
- All individuals deprived of liberty, by arrest or detention, are entitled to take proceedings before a court, in order that the court may decide without delay on the lawfulness of their detention and order their release if the detention is unlawful.
- Any person who has been the victim of unlawful arrest or detention has an enforceable right to compensation.

2. Limits to Provisional Detention

Most states provide the possibility of provisional or preventive detention for individuals suspected of having committed a crime for which they have not yet been judged. This decision should be taken by the judicial authority whose role it is to facilitate the inquiry or prevent the individuals from fleeing.

Specific time frames are established by the criminal laws of the country in question. At the end of the legislated time, the detained person must be released automatically, unless an official decision was taken to prolong the period of provisional detention.

> ☞ In many countries, the paralysis of the judicial system means that individuals may be held in detention for prolonged periods of time while awaiting judgment, long after the official period of provisional detention has expired.
>
> It is possible to take action on a case-by-case basis by examining the individual files of detained persons, on the basis of the standards established by domestic laws.

II. MINIMUM STANDARDS REGULATING THE CONDITIONS OF DETENTION

In addition to the judicial guarantees regulating arrest and detention, there are international norms regulating the minimum conditions of detention, so as to protect the respect for the dignity of human beings in such circumstances.

1. Minimum Material Conditions of Detention

Article 10 of the ICCPR states:

1. All persons deprived of their liberty shall be treated with humanity and with respect for the inherent dignity of the human person.

2. (a) Accused persons shall, save in exceptional circumstances, be segregated from convicted persons and shall be subject to separate treatment appropriate to their status as unconvicted persons;

   (b) Accused juvenile persons shall be separated from adults and brought as speedily as possible for adjudication.

3. The penitentiary system shall comprise treatment of prisoners the essential aim of which shall be their reformation and social rehabilitation.

☞ Prisoners are often environments of violence, coercion, and hardship, in which individuals are victims of ill treatment.

International texts establish rules relating to the standard minimum rules for the treatment of prisoners in order to ensure that

- prisoners' conditions of detention do not constitute any form of torture or other cruel, inhuman, or degrading treatment; and
- they are given the necessary means of survival, such as vital space, food, medical care, air, light, and physical activities.

The set of regulations for the Standard Minimum Rules for the Treatment of Prisoners are set forth in Resolution 2076 of the UN Economic and Social Council, which completes and expands Article 10 of the ICCPR, although its rules are not binding on states since they are only presented in a UN resolution. Hence, from a legal point of view, it would be feasible for national authorities to challenge these standards. In practice, however, such a challenge would be highly questionable since the standards set forth do not present an ideal set of rules but rather the minimum behavior that should be accepted or rejected.

These principles were reiterated, in similar form, in the 1988 "Body of Principles for the Protection of All Persons under Any Form of Detention or Imprisonment" (UN General Assembly Resolution 43/173, of December 9, 1988) and in the 1990 "Basic Principles for the Treatment of Prisoners" (UN General Assembly Resolution 45/111), by which we can conclude that these norms have become customary and are therefore binding upon all states. They must therefore serve as a standard of reference and be defended through concrete relief or advocacy actions.

The minimum conditions established by ECOSOC Resolution 2076, which must be respected in times of crisis, emergency, or conflict, as well as during times of peace, are the following:

- *Rule 7—Holding a register:* In every place where persons are imprisoned, a bound registration book with numbered pages must be kept, indicating for each prisoner his or her identity; the reasons for his or her detention and the authority that decided it; and the day and hour of his or her admission and release. No person shall be received in an institution without a valid commitment (or detention) order, the details of which shall have been previously entered in the register.
- *Rule 8—Separation of categories of prisoners:* The different categories of prisoners must be held in separate institutions or parts of institutions. For instance, young prisoners shall be separate from adults; untried prisoners shall be separate from convicted prisoners; men and women must be detained in separate institutions, or at least in entirely separate premises; and the reason for the detention should be taken into account.
- *Rules 9 to 14—Accommodation:* All accommodation provided, in particular sleeping accommodations, must meet the health requirements, including air, minimum floor space, lighting, heating, ventilation, and the necessary sanitary equipment and installations to ensure a decent and dignified life.

- *Rules 15 to 20—Living conditions:* Prisoners must be able to maintain their self-respect, and must therefore be able to wash themselves, wear clean clothes, have individual underclothing, eat food in sufficient quantity, and be able to exercise.
- *Rules 21 to 26—Medical services:* See section 3: medical services in prison settings.
- *Rules 27 to 32—Discipline and punishment:* Order and discipline may be maintained inside detention institutions, but must always be enforced according to written laws or internal regulations that clearly set forth which conduct constitutes a disciplinary offense, the types and duration of punishment that may be inflicted, and the authority competent to impose such punishment. Corporal punishment and all cruel, inhuman, or degrading punishment, are prohibited as punishment for disciplinary offenses. Punishment by close confinement or a reduction of diet shall never be inflicted unless the medical officer has examined the prisoner and certified in writing that he or she is fit to sustain it. The medical officer shall visit prisoners undergoing disciplinary punishment every day.
- *Rules 33 and 34—Instruments of restraint*
- *Rules 35 and 36—Information for, and complaints by, prisoners*
- *Rules 37 to 39—Contact with the outside world*
- *Rules 40 to 42—Books and religion*
- *Rule 43—Retention of prisoners' property*
- *Rules 44 and 45—Notification of death, illness, transfer, etc.*
- *Rules 46 to 55—Personnel working for the detention institution and inspection*

2. Special Conditions of Detention

Additional rules are applicable to specific categories of detainees or to especially vulnerable individuals such as children, mentally or physically ill persons, or pregnant women. These rules are also included in the rules for the Standard Minimum Rules for the Treatment of Prisoners (Resolution 2076 of the Economic and Social Council).

- *Sentenced prisoners—Rules 56 to 81:* These rules serve as a reminder that being deprived of liberty is their punishment, the purpose and justification of which are to allow the offender to improve themselves. The means of detention must not create new suffering and should enable the individual to reinsert him- or herself into society. The rules suggest concrete measures to put these principles into practice, in terms of treatment of the detainees, their work, education, and social relations.
- *Insane and mentally abnormal prisoners—Rules 82 and 83:* Persons who are found to be insane shall not be detained in prisons and should be taken to mental institutions as soon as possible. The medical or psychiatric service of the penal institutions shall provide for the psychiatric treatment of all other prisoners who are in need of such treatment.
- *Prisoners under arrest or awaiting trial—Rules 84 to 93—and persons arrested or detained without charge—Rule 95:* All persons who have not yet been convicted must be presumed innocent and treated as such. Untried prisoners shall be kept separate from convicted prisoners, and young untried prisoners shall be kept separate from adults. Untried prisoners shall be allowed to keep their own clothing. If they wear prison dress, it shall be different from that supplied to convicted prisoners. They must be offered the opportunity to work, but are not required to do so. If they work, they shall be paid for it.

   An untried prisoner shall be allowed to inform his or her family and lawyer immediately and shall be given all reasonable facilities to communicate with them, including for

communicating confidentially with his or her lawyer. No measures of reeducation or rehabilitation may be imposed on persons not convicted of a criminal offense.

- *Civil prisoners—Rule 94:* In countries where the law allows individuals to be imprisoned for
  debt, persons so imprisoned shall be treated no less favorably than untried prisoners, with the
  exception that they may be required to work to pay off their debts.
- *Women—Rules 8a, 53, and 23:* Women and men must be detained in separate institutions, as
  far as possible. In an institution that houses both men and women, the whole of the premises
  allocated to women shall be entirely separate and shall be under the authority of a responsible
  woman officer.

   Women prisoners shall be attended and supervised only by women officers. This does not,
   however, preclude male members of the staff, particularly doctors and teachers, from carrying
   out their professional duties in institutions or parts of institutions set aside for women.

   In women's institutions there shall be special accommodation for all necessary pre- and
   postnatal care and treatment. Arrangements shall be made, wherever possible, for children to
   be born in a civilian hospital. If a child is born in prison, this fact shall not be mentioned in the
   birth certificate.
- *Children:* The principle according to which young prisoners shall be kept separate from adults
  is reaffirmed in all relevant legal documents, such as rules 8.d and 85 of the Standard Minimum Rules for the Treatment of Prisoners (Resolution 2076 of the Economic and Social Council), and Article 10.2.b of the ICCPR.

   The 1989 International Convention on the Rights of the Child (CRC) adds several important elements to this rule:

   (a) No child shall be subjected to torture or other cruel, inhuman or degrading treatment or punish-
       ment. Neither capital punishment nor life imprisonment without possibility of release shall be im-
       posed for offences committed by persons below eighteen years of age;
   (b) No child shall be deprived of his or her liberty unlawfully or arbitrarily. The arrest, detention or
       imprisonment of a child shall be in conformity with the law and shall be used only as a measure
       of last resort and for the shortest appropriate period of time;
   (c) Every child deprived of liberty shall be treated with humanity and respect for the inherent dignity
       of the human person, and in a manner which takes into account the needs of persons of his or her
       age [namely, in terms of food and education]. In particular, every child deprived of liberty shall
       be separated from adults unless it is considered in the child's best interest not to do so and shall
       have the right to maintain contact with his or her family through correspondence and visits, save
       in exceptional circumstances;
   (d) Every child deprived of his or her liberty shall have the right to prompt access to legal and other
       appropriate assistance, as well as the right to challenge the legality of the deprivation of his or
       her liberty before a court or other competent, independent and impartial authority, and to a
       prompt decision on any such action (Article 37 of CRC).

- On November 29, 1985, the UN General Assembly adopted the UN Standard Minimum Rules
  for the Administration of Juvenile Justice (known as the "Beijing Rules," UN GA Res. 40/33),
  which further elaborates on the principles relating to criminal responsibility of minors and the
  principles governing sanctions enacted against them. These guidelines were complemented
  with the adoption of the UN Rules for the Protection of Juveniles Deprived of their Liberty
  (UN General Assembly Resolution 45/113, of December 14, 1990).

3. Medical Services and Medical Ethics in Prison Settings

Various rules set the framework for carrying out medical services in detention centers or prisons.
Deprivation of liberty sometimes has grave consequences on the health of detainees, as well as

on the very notion of medical practice. The rules that the medical personnel must follow are guided by the respect for medical ethics and by the standards imposed on medical services in prison settings.

The "Principles of Medical Ethics Relevant to the Role of Health Personnel, Particularly Physicians, in the Protection of Prisoners and Detainees against Torture and Other Cruel, Inhuman or Degrading Treatment or Punishment" (Resolution 37/194), was adopted by the UN General Assembly on December 18, 1982:

- These principles establish that health personnel charged with the medical care of prisoners and detainees have a duty to provide them with treatment and care of the same quality and standard as is afforded to those who are not imprisoned or detained (principle 1).
- They provide a broad definition of medical ethics and therefore of the responsibility of physicians since they establish that "it is a gross contravention of medical ethics, as well as an offence under applicable international instruments, for health personnel, particularly physicians, to engage, actively or passively, in acts that constitute participation in, complicity in, incitement to or attempts to commit torture or other cruel, inhuman or degrading treatment or punishment" (principle 2). This text indicates that a physician's presence in a place of detention may place him or her in the position of a passive accomplice of inhuman acts committed against the detainees. Medical personnel can only break with this passive complicity by taking concrete measures of alertness and prevention, in addition to the normal medical procedures.

Other organizations, such as the World Health Organization (WHO) and the World Medical Association (WMA, the international association of national medical associations), also adopt guidelines and declarations relating to specific aspects of practicing medicine in prison settings (concerning, e.g., mandatory AIDS testing). States are not bound by these texts; however, humanitarian organizations may use them as standards of reference for their field operations.

Finally, the Standard Minimum Rules for the Treatment of Prisoners (ECOSOC Resolution 2076), presented earlier, sets forth the rights and duties governing medical services in places of detention:

- *Rule 22:* At every penitentiary institution, at least one qualified medical officer shall be available. In the absence of a physician certified by the penitentiary administration, it is important that the substitute medical personnel have knowledge of the responsibilities, beyond straightforward care, to which physicians are beholden in prison settings.
- *Rule 23* concerns care for women; see section 2, earlier.
- *Rules 24 and 25.1:* The medical officer must examine every prisoner as soon as he or she is admitted and, being responsible for the physical and mental health of the prisoners, shall see all sick prisoners every day, as well as all those complaining of illness, and any to whom his or her attention is specially directed.
- *Rule 25.2:* The medical officer shall report to the director whenever he or she considers that a prisoner's physical or mental health has been, or will be, injuriously affected by continued imprisonment or by any condition of imprisonment.
- *Rule 26:* The medical officer shall regularly inspect and advise the director on issues of food, hygiene, and other issues of sanitation, such as heating, lighting, and ventilation, the quality and cleanliness of the bedding. The prison director must take the reports and advice of the medical officer into consideration, as prescribed under Articles 25 and 26.
- *Rule 32:* The medical officer must examine any prisoner who is going to undergo punishment and must certify in writing that he or she is fit to sustain it. The medical officer must also visit

prisoners undergoing such punishments daily and advise the director if the punishment should be terminated or altered on grounds of physical or mental health.

- The specific rules that protect medical services and ethics in times of armed conflict, addressing medical care both for prisoners of war and for the population as a whole, are detailed in the entries on ➔ **prisoners of war; wounded and sick persons.**

III. RULES APPLICABLE DURING ARMED CONFLICTS

The minimum rules for the treatment of prisoners, listed earlier, constitute standards of reference that remain applicable even in times of conflict, since they set forth "minimum rules," specifically. Persons whose detention is not related to the conflict must definitely continue to be granted the protection provided by these rules.

Humanitarian law establishes specific rules to protect individuals deprived of liberty for reasons related to the armed conflict. This is important because, in times of armed conflict, the normal judicial guarantees are mostly inefficient. The risks of abuse increase owing to the fact that the authorities who have control over the detainees often belong to the adverse party to the conflict. Hence, the guarantees established by humanitarian law to control the fate of the detainees go beyond the common basic principles, and they include concrete rules that are mandatory for states.

1. International Armed Conflicts

> ☞ Humanitarian law is applicable to two main categories of persons who may be detained for reasons related to the conflict: combatants and civilians.
>
> Combatants who fall into the hands of an adverse party are usually protected by the status of prisoners of war. The 143 articles of the Third Geneva Convention regulate the treatment of prisoners of war.
>
> Civilians deprived of liberty for reasons related to the conflict are protected by the specific rules that regulate detention and internment. Humanitarian law takes into account the issue of the administration of justice and the conditions of detention in territories occupied by the enemy, and it imposes precise regulations.
>
> ➔ **Internment; Prisoners of war**

a. General Protection

The 1977 Additional Protocol I to the Geneva Conventions sets forth the general provisions for the protection of civilians.

- Any person arrested, detained, or interned for actions related to the armed conflict shall be informed promptly, in a language he or she understands, of the reasons for these measures being taken. Except in cases of arrest or detention for criminal offenses, such persons shall be released with the minimum delay possible, and in any event as soon as the circumstances justifying the arrest, detention, or internment have ceased to exist (PI Article 75.3).
- No sentence may be passed and no penalty be executed on a person found guilty of a penal offense related to the armed conflict, except pursuant to a conviction pronounced by an impartial and regularly constituted court (PI Article 75.4).

- Any person arrested, detained, or interned for reasons related to the conflict shall benefit from the full judicial guarantees set forth by Article 75, and in particular 75.4, of Protocol I, as elaborated upon in the entry on ➔ **judicial guarantees.**
- Women whose liberty has been restricted for reasons related to the armed conflict shall be held in quarters separated from men's quarters. They shall be under the immediate supervision of women. However, in cases in which families are detained or interned, they shall, whenever possible, be held in the same place and accommodated as family units (PI Article 75.5).

b. Detention of Civilians in Occupied Territories

In cases where a territory is occupied by an enemy power, the Fourth Geneva Convention sets forth clear rules to protect the normal functioning of systems of justice and detention.

- "The Occupying Power may not alter the status of public officials or judges in the occupied territories, or in any way apply sanctions to or take any measures of coercion or discrimination against them" (GCIV Article 54).
- The penal laws of the occupied territory shall remain in force (GCIV Article 64).
- The Occupying Power can enact new regulations governing its conditions of occupation and defining new violations against the occupying authority, within the restrictions imposed by the Convention. These laws can never be retroactive (GCIV Articles 65 and 67).
- The Convention restricts the cases in which the Occupying Power can decide to impose the death penalty—namely, in the case of offenses against the Occupying Power's forces or administration (GCIV Article 68).
- Articles 71 to 74 describe the judicial guarantees and the rights of defense in case of trials before the courts of the Occupying Power.
- Protected persons who are accused or convicted must be detained in the occupied country. They must enjoy conditions of food and hygiene sufficient to keep them in good health and that will be at least equal to those obtained in prisons in the occupied country. They shall receive the medical attention required by their state of health. Women shall be confined in separate quarters and shall be under the direct supervision of women. Proper regard shall be paid to the special treatment due to minors (see above, special protection for children). Protected persons shall have the right to receive at least one relief parcel monthly (GCIV Article 76).
- Protected persons shall have the right to receive the visits of representatives or delegates of the Protecting Powers or the ICRC, who will be allowed to interview them without witnesses. The duration and frequency of these visits may not be restricted (GCIV Article 143).
- Protected persons who have been accused or convicted by the courts in the occupied territory must be handed over, at the end of occupation, with the records concerning them, to the authorities of the liberated territory (GCIV Article 77).

c. Internment of Civilians

A party to a conflict may decide to enact measures depriving certain persons of liberty, such as foreigners or nationals of the adverse party to the conflict who are on their territory or territory they occupy. Humanitarian law refers to such acts as "internment" or "placing in assigned residence."

Such measures may be ordered only for imperative reasons of security. Under specific conditions, the Occupying Power may also intern civilians who are protected by the Geneva Conventions, if they constitute a threat to occupying authority (GCIV Articles 41–43, 68, and 78).

All internment measures must follow the rules established in the Fourth Geneva Convention (GCIV Articles 79–141). → **Internment**

d. Specific Guarantees for Detained Children

Children arrested, detained, or interned for reasons related to the armed conflict must benefit from special guarantees due to their age, their specific psychological and physiological needs, and the fact that they may not—in general criminal law—be held responsible for their crimes. These guarantees are protected in humanitarian law by the following provisions:

- Children must be given priority in the distribution of relief supplies (GCIV Articles 23 and 50; PI Article 70).
- Children held in detention must be held in the same place of internment as—and lodged with—their family (GCIV Article 82); receive additional food, in proportion to their physiological needs (GCIV Article 89); allowed to attend school, either within the place of internment or outside (GCIV Article 94); released in priority, if possible even before the end of hostilities (GCIV Article 132).
- Article 50 of the Fourth Geneva Convention establishes that the treatment of accused or detained persons must take into consideration the special treatment to which children are entitled (GCIV Article 76). This system of special protection includes provisions forbidding the recruitment of children into groups dependent on the Detaining Power and establishes states' obligations to provide children with the necessary material care and education, as well as with the privileged treatment foreseen for them in terms of food, medical care, and shelter from the effects of war.
- If children are arrested, detained, or interned for reasons related to the armed conflict, they must be held in quarters separate from those of adults, except where families are accommodated together, in which case the family must be held together and accommodated as a family unit (PI Articles 77.4 and 75.5). → **Children**

e. Specific Guarantees for Detained Women

Humanitarian law specifies certain additional guarantees for women, especially pregnant women and mothers of young children:

- "Women whose liberty has been restricted for reasons related to the armed conflict shall be held in quarters separated from men's quarters. They shall be under the immediate supervision of women. Nevertheless, in cases where families are detained or interned, they shall, whenever possible, be held in the same place and accommodated as family units" (PI Article 75.5; GCIV Article 82).
- Pregnant women and mothers having dependent infants who are arrested, detained, or interned for reasons related to the armed conflict shall have their cases considered with the utmost priority (PI Article 76.2). In particular, in addition to children, expectant mothers, maternity cases, and nursing mothers must be given priority in the distribution of relief supplies (GCIV Articles 23 and 50; PI Article 70), and they must be given additional food in proportion to their physiological needs (GCIV Article 89).
- Pregnant women and mothers with infants and young children must be released in priority, if possible even before the end of hostilities (GCIV Article 132).

- Article 50 of the Fourth Geneva Convention establishes that the treatment of accused or detained persons must take into consideration the special treatment to which women, particularly expectant mothers and mothers of children under seven years, are entitled (GCIV Article 76).
→ **Women**

f. Specific Guarantees for Detained Prisoners of War

Wounded or sick prisoners of war who have certain serious injuries or diseases are entitled to special measures of protection under humanitarian law. These provisions take into account the vulnerability of such seriously ill or injured persons and the advantages that may be gained by treating them in a peaceful and safe environment (GCIII Articles 109–117). The Geneva Conventions and their Protocols establish the conditions under which seriously sick or wounded prisoners of war may be evacuated or hospitalized in a neutral state, rather than continuing to treat them in the hospitals of the Detaining Power and to consider them prisoners of war. Such measures may also be implemented for civilian internees who are seriously ill or injured (GCIV Article 132). → **Prisoners of war**

☞ The authorities are responsible for the health and physical integrity of the persons in their power. If they refuse to provide the necessary care to a person under their authority, or if they deliberately risk the health of the person, they are guilty of war crimes.

The Additional Protocol I to the Geneva Conventions reinforces the protection that must be provided to victims of conflict, in general, and the wounded and sick, in particular. It states that "the physical or mental health and integrity of persons who are in the power of the adverse Party or who are interned, detained or otherwise deprived of liberty as a result of a [conflict] shall not be endangered by any unjustified act or omission." Any such act or omission constitutes a war crime (PI Article 11).

This provision emphasizes the responsibility of humanitarian and medical organizations in terms of monitoring the state of health of the civilian population and alerting the appropriate authorities.

→ **Medical ethics; Prisoners of war; Wounded and sick persons**

---

2. Internal Armed Conflicts

The distinction between civilians and combatants is more complex during noninternational armed conflicts. The 1977 Additional Protocol to the Geneva Conventions Relating to the Protection of Victims of Non-International Armed Conflicts (Protocol II) does not define different categories of detained persons when setting forth the guarantees that must be respected. Instead, it applies consistently to "persons deprived of their liberty for reasons related to the armed conflict" (PII Article 5.1).

The rights it protects are applicable to both detained and interned persons and are coupled with obligations that the Detaining Powers must respect.

Detained individuals who come under the category of combatants may be able to benefit from the status of prisoners of war and the guarantees attached to that status, according to the Third Geneva Convention (GCIII Articles 4.A.1–3 and 4.A.6), following specific conditions of reciprocity and according to special agreements signed between the parties to the conflict. This status is thus not granted automatically. It is the result of a reciprocal agreement signed between the parties to the internal conflict.

→   **Combatants; Prisoners of war**

a. Minimum Guarantees

- Article 3 common to the four 1949 Geneva Conventions (known as common Article 3) foresees certain minimum guarantees during noninternational armed conflicts for individuals taking no active part in the hostilities, including members of the armed forces who have laid down their weapons and persons placed *hors de combat* by sickness, wounds, detention, or any other cause.

    It forbids torture and other cruel, inhuman, or degrading treatment or punishment.

    It also prohibits, at any time and in any place whatsoever, "the passing of sentences and the carrying out of executions without previous judgment pronounced by a regularly constituted court, affording all the judicial guarantees which are recognized as indispensable by civilized peoples" (common Article 3.1.d).

- Article 5.1 of Protocol II extends these provisions. It adds the following provisions that must be respected as a minimum with regard to persons deprived of their liberty for reasons related to the armed conflict, whether they are interned or detained:

    a. The wounded and the sick, whether or not they have taken part in the armed conflict, shall be respected and protected. They shall be treated humanely and shall receive, to the fullest extent practicable and with the least possible delay, the medical care and attention required by their condition. No distinction shall be made among them on any grounds other than medical ones (from PII Article 7).

    b. These persons shall, to the same extent as the local civilian population, be provided with food and drinking water and be given the necessary safeguards with regards to health, hygiene, and protection against the rigors of the climate and the dangers of the armed conflict.

    c. They shall be allowed to receive individual or collective relief.

    d. They shall be allowed to practice their religion and, if requested, to receive spiritual assistance.

    e. If made to work, they shall enjoy working conditions and safeguards similar to those enjoyed by the local civilian population.

    Individuals who are not detained but whose liberty is restricted for reasons related to the armed conflict shall enjoy the same rights.

b. Obligations and Responsibilities of the Detaining Powers (PII Article 5.2)

- Those who are responsible for the internment or detention of the persons [deprived of their liberty for reasons related to the armed conflict] shall also, within the limits of their capabilities, respect the following provisions relating to such persons:

    (a) except when men and women of a family are accommodated together, women shall be held in quarters separated from those of men and shall be under the immediate supervision of women;

    (b) they shall be allowed to send and receive letters and cards [. . .];

    (c) places of internment and detention shall not be located close to the combat zone. The persons [deprived of their liberty for reasons related to the armed conflict] shall be evacuated when the places where they are interned or detained become particularly exposed to danger arising out of the armed conflict, if their evacuation can be carried out under adequate conditions of safety;

    (d) they shall have the benefit of medical examinations;

(e) their physical or mental health and integrity shall not be endangered by any unjustified act or omission [. . .].

    If the authorities decide to release persons deprived of their liberty, they must take the necessary measures to ensure their safety (PII Article 5.4).

→   **Children; Fundamental guarantees; Ill treatment; Internment; Judicial guarantees; Medical ethics; Prisoners of war; Safety; Women**

📖 **For Additional Information:**

ICRC. "Visiting People Deprived of Their Freedom: An Introduction." Geneva: Author, August 1998.
Reyes, Hernan, and Remi Russbach. "The Role of the Doctor in ICRC Visits to Prisoners." *International Review of the Red Cross* 284 (September–October 1991): 469–82.

■ DISASTERS (NATURAL OR HUMANITARIAN)

A disaster is an unexpected event, by definition. The responses to disasters—which may be natural (climatic, seismic, or other natural causes) or human (accidental or voluntary)—must therefore employ exceptional measures. International law does not establish any legal protection for individuals in such situations. On the contrary, it gives national authorities extended powers to deal with disasters, which may include the momentary suspension of certain human rights.

    National civil defense services are responsible for providing relief to the affected population and maintaining public order. Nevertheless, states often cooperate in such situations.

    For humanitarian law to be applicable, the disaster must be the result of a conflict situation. It is therefore crucial to make a distinction between natural disasters and ones caused by humankind. To ensure that humanitarian law can be applied, it is also important to avoid terms such as *humanitarian disaster* or *crisis* when a more precise term can be used, since these terms describe a situation but do not invoke or create any rights for victims or relief organizations.

Humanitarian Disasters and Crises

To determine which rules of international law may be applicable in a given situation, it is important to look at the cause of a disaster—natural or conflict related—not its scope or the extent of the needs of those affected. Therefore, to be able to apply humanitarian law, it is crucial to qualify each situation precisely, since this qualification determines the rights and obligations of the different actors involved. Humanitarian law applies only in the case of a conflict.

    The words *humanitarian disaster* or *crisis* are nonlegal terms, which may be used in good or bad faith to describe circumstances of suffering without indicating their causes. When such terms are used, they allow states and other actors to avoid the specific obligations that result from the exact qualification of a situation, and the response can be restricted to sending relief supplies.

    For instance, the genocide that took place in Rwanda in 1994 was called a "humanitarian crisis" for several months before the word *genocide* was used. States parties to the 1948 Convention on the Prevention and Punishment of the Crime of Genocide are under the obligation to intervene to stop such acts, and recognizing that a genocide was

(continues)

(continued)

occuring would have required states to take action. Hence, the UN Security Council Resolution 929—adopted in June 1994, in the middle of the genocide and despite its own reference in earlier texts (S/RES/925 of June 8, 1994)—determined that "the magnitude of the humanitarian crisis in Rwanda constitutes a threat to peace and security in the region" (S/RES/929 of June 22, 1994).

One aim of humanitarian law is to prevent wars from causing natural disasters. Attacks against the natural environment, against objects indispensable to the survival of the civilian population, and against works or installations containing dangerous forces (which may cause damage to the natural environment and hence prejudice the health or survival of the population) are therefore prohibited. Such installations include dams, nuclear or chemical installations, and other such works likely to cause widespread disasters and population displacement. Any such attack is a war crime. ➔ **Protected objects and property**

The law of armed conflict also foresees the role of government organizations in terms of civil defense, working in cooperation with relief organizations to protect civilians, to help them recover from the immediate effects of disasters, and to provide the conditions necessary for their survival (PI Article 61).

➔ **Civil defense; Collective security; Fundamental guarantees; International humanitarian law; Protection; Relief; Responsibility**

📖 **For Additional Information:**

Brauman, Rony. *L'Action humanitaire.* Paris: Dominos-Flammarion, 1995.
Perrin, Pierre. "Strategy for Medical Assistance in Disaster Situations." *International Review of the Red Cross* 284 (September–October 1991): 494–504.

■ DISCRIMINATION

The principle of nondiscrimination is the pillar of the system of protection for individuals. Individuals may be protected in two ways. The first is to define specific rights and guarantees for them; the second is to ensure—at the very least—that all persons are treated equally. Nondiscrimination is therefore one of the most basic tenets of protection.

When a government adopts legislation that discriminates negatively against certain individuals or groups of individuals, this is often the first step—in the legal domain—toward a singling out and isolation of these persons that may eventually lead to persecution or other crimes, perhaps as serious as genocide.

It is important to distinguish between adverse discrimination (or adverse distinction), which is illegal, and positive forms of discrimination or distinction, which are aimed at improving the conditions of one group of persons or compensating them for inequality, rather than oppressing another. Such acts or legislation occur at both domestic and international levels, and are not illegal. The Convention on the Elimination of All Forms of Discrimination against Women (CEDAW), for instance, establishes that the "adoption by States Parties of temporary special measures aimed at accelerating *de facto* equality between men and women shall not be considered discrimination as defined in the present Convention, but shall in no way entail as a consequence the maintenance of unequal or separate standards" (Article 4 of CEDAW).

1. In Times of Conflict

In addressing the treatment of individuals or peoples in situations of conflict, humanitarian law forbids any adverse distinction to be made on the basis of "race, color, sex, language, religion or belief, political or other opinion, national or social origin, wealth, birth or other status, or on any other similar criteria" (PI Article 9, PII Article 2, GCI–IV common Article 3, GCI and GCII Article 12, GIII Article 16, and GCIV Article 13). The statute of the International Criminal Court (adopted July 17, 1998) further details the list by adding "age" and "ethnic origin" and replacing "sex" with "gender" (Article 21.3 of ICC statute).

In addition to this nondiscrimination clause, the articles of the Conventions and Protocols give certain specific instructions on the prohibition of any form of discrimination for specific situations:

- The provisions of the Conventions aimed at alleviating the suffering of civilians caused by war must be applied equally for all individuals (GCIV Article 13).
- In occupied territories, supplies must be distributed to civilian populations without adverse distinction between individuals (PI Article 69).
- This also applies to relief actions for the civilian population, whether carried out in occupied territories or other situations, especially in the case of medical care and attention (GCIV Article 16; PI Articles 10 and 11; PII Articles 7.2 and 9.2), and when providing other essential supplies (PI Articles 69 and 70; PII Article 18.2).
- Humanitarian law clearly states that the principle of nondiscrimination must be applied to prisoners of war (GCIII Article 16). It contains multiple provisions establishing that prisoners of war must be treated under conditions as favorable as those for the forces and civilian population of the Detaining Power. This applies to living conditions (GCIII Article 25), transfers (Article 46), working conditions (Article 51), and penal and disciplinary sanctions (Articles 82, 84, 88, 102, and 106).
- If internees commit offenses that are not punishable if committed by persons who are not internees, they may only incur disciplinary punishments, not penal sanctions (GCIV Article 117).

> ☞ It is always possible to relax the general rules in order to grant more favorable treatment to one category of individuals, justified by their condition or vulnerability (e.g., children, pregnant women, the wounded and sick).

2. In Times of Peace

Discrimination is also forbidden in times of peace. It violates one of the most basic principles guiding society: that all individuals are equal before the law. The practice of discrimination can fall under different categories, and several conventions and declarations forbid it:

- International Convention on the Elimination of All Forms of Racial Discrimination (GA Resolution 2106 [XX] of December 21, 1965);
- International Convention on the Suppression and Punishment of the Crime of Apartheid (GA Resolution 3068 [XXVIII] of November 30, 1973);
- Convention on the Elimination of All Forms of Discrimination against Women (GA Resolution 34/180 of December 18, 1979);
- Convention against Discrimination in Education, adopted under the aegis of UNESCO at its Eleventh Session on December 14, 1960;

- Convention (No. 100) Concerning Equal Remuneration for Men and Women Workers for Work of Equal Value, adopted under the aegis of the International Labor Organization (ILO) at its Thirty-fourth Session on June 29, 1951;
- Declaration on the Elimination of All Forms of Intolerance and of Discrimination Based on Religion or Belief (GA Resolution 36/55 of November 25, 1981).

3. The Rights of Individual Complaint

The Committee on the Elimination of Racial Discrimination

A Committee on the Elimination of Racial Discrimination was established per Article 8 of the International Convention on the Elimination of All Forms of Racial Discrimination, which had 157 states parties as of March 2001. Under Article 11, if a state party considers that another state party is not adequately implementing the provisions of the Convention, it may bring this to the attention of the Committee.

Article 14 of Convention establishes an optional procedure by which a state party can recognize the competence of the Committee to receive communications from individuals or groups of persons who claim to be victims of a violation of the Convention by their state. The twenty-nine states that have recognized this competence are Algeria, Australia, Bulgaria, Chile, Costa Rica, Cyprus, Denmark, Ecuador, Finland, France, Hungary, Iceland, Italy, Luxembourg, Macedonia, Malta, Netherlands, Norway, Peru, Poland, Republic of Korea, Russian Federation, Senegal, Slovakia, South Africa, Spain, Sweden, Ukraine, and Uruguay.

Other Mechanisms

Discrimination is strictly forbidden by most human rights conventions. Under certain conditions, it is therefore also possible to refer cases to human rights monitoring bodies.

→   **Apartheid; Committee on the Elimination of Discrimination against Women; Human rights; Individual recourse; Protection; Women**

→   **List of states party to international human rights and humanitarian conventions (Nos. 23, 24, 25)**

✎   Committee on the Elimination of All Forms of Racial Discrimination
Office of the High Commissioner for Human Rights (OHCHR)
52 rue Paquis
1202 Geneva, Switzerland
Tel.: (00 41) 22 917 92 39
Fax: (00 41) 22 917 90 12

■ DISTINCTIVE (OR PROTECTIVE) EMBLEMS, SIGNS, AND SIGNALS

Emblems and signs may be used to identify and protect certain humanitarian or peaceful activities, persons, or locations. The Geneva Conventions and their Additional Protocols list these distinctive signs, which indicate that the persons or objects wearing or carrying the signs benefit from specific international protection and must not be the target of any attack or act of violence (GCI Articles 24, 33, 35, 38–44, Annex I; GCII Articles 41–45; GCIV Articles 18–22; PI Articles 18, 37–39, 85, Annex I).

1. The Different Distinctive Emblems

Annex I to the first 1977 Additional Protocol to the Geneva Conventions provides a list and explains the protective role of the distinctive emblems:

- The red cross (or red crescent) on a white background protects all medical services, such as medical and religious personnel, medical units, and means of transportation.
- Oblique red stripes on a white background designate medical and safety zones and localities.
- A shield, consisting of a royal blue square and triangle, and two white triangles designate cultural objects and property.
- An equilateral blue triangle on an orange background protects civil defense personnel, installations, and material.
- A group of three bright orange circles of equal size, placed along the same axis and with the distance between each circle being one radius, protects works and installations containing dangerous forces.
- A white flag is the flag of truce and is reserved for *parlementaires* (persons authorized to negotiate directly with the adverse party).
- The letters *IC* (for internment camp), *PW,* or *PG* (for prisoners of war or *prisonniers de guerre*) designate internment camps for civilian internees and for prisoners of war.

2. The Red Cross and Red Crescent Emblems

The conditions governing the use of the red cross and red crescent emblems differ in times of war and of peace. When the emblems are used as indications (small size), whether in times of peace or of war, they show that a person or a place has a link with the International Red Cross and Red Crescent Movement. In times of war, they serve as a means to ensure protection (large emblems). Their use indicates that the medical personnel, services, installations, or material wearing the emblem enjoy protection provided by humanitarian law (GCI Articles 38–44, 53–54; GCII Articles 41–43; PI Article 18). Any deliberate attack on persons or objects carrying the emblems is a war crime under the Geneva Conventions and under the Statute of the International Criminal Court.

Hence, though this protective emblem belongs to the Red Cross Movement, it may also be used by other organizations to protect medical activities. The ICRC can use the emblem at all times, for both protective and indicative reasons. National Red Cross Societies' use of the protective emblem in times of war, however, is restricted by a set of rules adopted by the ICRC in 1991, which specify the condition under which they may use the emblem.

3. General Conditions Governing the Use of Distinctive or Protective Emblems

The Geneva Conventions and their Protocols further regulate the general use of all distinctive or protective emblems and signs recognized and protected by the Conventions. In particular, they clearly specify when it is forbidden to use them:

- It is prohibited to feign intent to negotiate under a flag of truce or of surrender (PI Article 37).
- It is prohibited to make improper use of the distinctive emblem of the red cross, red crescent, red lion and sun, or any other emblems, signs, or signals provided for by the Conventions or by Protocol I (PI Article 38).
- It is also prohibited to misuse deliberately other internationally recognized protective emblems, signs, or signals in an armed conflict, including the flag of truce and the protective emblem of cultural property (PI Article 38).

- It is prohibited to make use of the distinctive emblem of the United Nations, except as authorized by that organization (PI Article 38).
- It is prohibited, in an armed conflict, to use the flags or military emblems, insignia, or uniforms of neutral or other states not party to the conflict (PI Article 39).
- It is prohibited to make use of the flags or military emblems, insignia, or uniforms of adverse parties, whether during attacks or in order to shield, favor, protect, or impede military operations (PI Article 39).

4. Penalties

The perfidious use of the distinctive emblem of the red cross, red crescent, red lion and sun, or other protective signs recognized by the Geneva Conventions and Protocols constitutes a grave breach of the laws of war. In other words, it is a war crime covered by the principle of universal jurisdiction (PI Article 85).

As for the red cross and red crescent emblems (the only two signs currently used by the Red Cross Movement), states party to the Geneva Conventions have the obligation to adopt laws and sanctions to be enforced before national courts, which prevent and punish the perfidious use of these emblems in times of peace or of war. To implement such measures, domestic laws must be adapted to integrate the protection of these emblems.

→ **Medical personnel; Medical services; Perfidy; Protected objects; Protected persons; Protection; Universal jurisdiction; War crimes/Crimes against humanity**

📖 **For Additional Information:**

Bugnion, François. "The Red Cross and Red Crescent Emblems." *International Review of the Red Cross* 272 (September–October 1989): 408–19.
Cauderay, Gérald. *Means of Identification for Protected Medical Transports*. Geneva: ICRC, 1994.
Eberlin, Philippe. *Protective Signs*. Geneva: ICRC, 1983.
Sommaruga, Cornelio. "Unity and Plurality of the Emblems." *International Review of the Red Cross* 289 (July–August 1992): 333–38.

■ DUTY OF COMMANDERS

States party to the 1949 Geneva Conventions and Additional Protocol I of 1977 (Protocol I) are under the obligation to respect and enforce the respect for humanitarian law in situations of armed conflict (GCI–IV common Article 1; PI Articles 1 and 80.2). They must also punish individuals who violate such laws (GCI Articles 49–52; GCII Articles 50–53, 129–132; GCIV Articles 146–149; PI Article 86.1).

> ☞ The principle of authority is always coupled with that of responsibility.
>
> In situations of international armed conflict, humanitarian law clearly and precisely establishes the duties and responsibilities of commanders (PI Article 87):
>
> - Commanders must ensure that members of the armed forces under their command are aware of their obligations under the Geneva Conventions and Protocol I.
> - Military commanders must prevent members of the armed forces under their command and other persons under their control from committing breaches of the Conventions and
>
> *(continues)*

> (*continued*)
>
> Protocol I. When necessary, they must punish and report perpetrators of such breaches to competent authorities.
> - Any commander who is aware that subordinates or other persons under his or her control are going to commit, or have committed, a breach of the Conventions or Protocol I must initiate such steps as are necessary to prevent such violations and, where appropriate, initiate disciplinary or penal action against the individuals who committed such violations.

To ensure that these obligations are respected, humanitarian law imposes a precise definition of "armed forces" on states that allows commanders to control combatants through a system of internal hierarchy, organization, and discipline. This chain of command helps determine the different levels of responsibility and culpability of combatants and different ranks of military command. → **Combatants; Responsibility**

Other provisions of humanitarian law also emphasize the specific responsibility of military commanders in international armed conflicts, including on a criminal level:

- Commanders must do everything feasible to spare civilian persons and objects when planning or authorizing attacks (PI Article 57).
- The penal or disciplinary responsibility of a superior officer is not alleviated by the fact that a violation of humanitarian law was committed by a subordinate, if the superior knew—or had information at the time that should have enabled him or her to conclude—that the subordinate was committing or was going to commit such a breach and did not take all feasible measures within his or her power to prevent or repress the breach (PI Article 86.2).
- If a situation is not specifically foreseen or referred to in the Geneva Conventions, or if details of implementation or execution are not provided, a commander in chief may not use such absence of a direct reference to justify complete freedom of action. In such cases, the parties to the conflict, acting through their commander in chief, have the responsibility to make decisions on unforeseen cases, in conformity with the general principles of the Conventions (GCI Article 45; GCII Article 46).

The provisions governing the duty of commanders in situations of internal armed conflicts are not as explicit. However, Protocol II posits that all parties to a conflict are under the obligation to respect humanitarian law, and the armed group involved must be "under responsible command [which is able] to implement this Protocol" (PII Article 1.1). The provisions governing the duty of commanders, included in Protocol II, can thus always be interpreted according to the rules governing armed international conflicts.

→ **Attacks; Combatants; Penal sanctions in humanitarian law; Proportionality; Responsibility; War crimes/Crimes against humanity**

📖 **For Additional Information:**

Aubert, Maurice. "The Question of Superior Orders and the Responsibility of Commanding Officers in the Protocol Additional to the Geneva Conventions of 12 August 1949, and Relating to the Protection of Victims of International Armed Conflicts (Protocol I), of 8 June 1977." *International Review of the Red Cross* 263 (March–April 1988): 105–20.

Mulinen, Frederic de. "Command Responsibility." In *Handbook on the Law of War for Armed Forces.* Geneva: ICRC, 1989, 61–78.

■ THE ECONOMIC AND SOCIAL COUNCIL OF THE UN (ECOSOC)

One of the six principal organs of the UN, the Economic and Social Council (ECOSOC) is the central UN forum for international economic and social issues. The Council coordinates the economic and social work of the UN system, which engages 70 percent of the system's human and financial resources. All of the UN specialized agencies (e.g., the World Health Organization and the Food and Agriculture Organization), as well as all of the UN programs and funds (e.g., UNICEF and the World Food Programme), report to ECOSOC.

Established under Chapter X of the UN Charter, ECOSOC is the primary organ for promoting higher standards of living, full employment, and economic and social progress; solutions of international economic, social, health, and related problems; international cultural and educational cooperation; and universal respect for human rights and fundamental freedoms.

The Council is the principal UN forum for discussing economic and social issues and for formulating policy recommendations. It plays a key role in fostering international cooperation for development and in setting the priorities for action. It also offers NGOs the opportunity to bring their expertise to the UN, through the consultative status that it grants them (Article 71 of UN Charter), thereby maintaining a vital link between the UN and civil society.

The Council has fifty-four member countries, elected by the General Assembly for three-year terms. Voting is by simple majority; each country has one vote (Article 61 of UN Charter). It meets for one month each year, alternating its session between New York and Geneva. A special meeting of ministers discusses the most pressing economic and social issues. Beginning in 1998, the Council expanded its discussions to include humanitarian matters. The year-round work of the Council is carried out in its subsidiary bodies, which meet regularly and report back to the Council.

The Council's current program of work focuses on poverty alleviation, development of Africa, the effects of globalization, and enhanced working relations with the World Bank and the International Monetary Fund.

→ **Commission on Human Rights; NGOs; United Nations**

■ EMBARGO

The aim of an embargo is to force a state to change its behavior or comply with a decision. Embargoes can be applied to all means of transportation (they were originally meant for ships) or to any category of merchandise or products—in particular, weapons or other strategic products or petroleum products. When a state imposes an embargo, either it directly blocks all transportation going to, or destined for, the state on which the embargo has been declared, or it prohibits any exports to the state it wants to pressure. Exports from the targeted state toward the one imposing the embargo are also blocked.

It is important to distinguish between embargoes and acts of war such as blockades or sieges. An embargo can be enacted collectively against a country, by member states of the UN. Collective embargoes are generally decided by the UN Security Council, acting under Chapter VII of the UN charter, when faced with threats to the peace, breaches of the peace, and acts of aggression (Article 41 of UN Charter). Regional intergovernmental organizations can also impose embargoes.

☞ Humanitarian relief is always exempt from embargoes, even in the case of "total embargoes" on all forms of economic trade. In practice, the UN or the regional organization imposing the embargo sets up a Sanctions Committee to monitor the implementation and effects of the embargo or sanctions. This Committee decides whether a product is exempt from the embargo, taking into consideration the commercial or humanitarian nature of the transaction or the goods in question.

Certain goods are considered humanitarian by nature or destination, such as medicine, medical material, and food. The relevant Sanctions Committee gives these goods partial exemptions from the embargo.

The principle established by the Geneva Conventions and their Protocols posits that states are under the obligation to allow the free passage of relief supplies that are of an "exclusively humanitarian and impartial nature" (GCIV Article 23, PI Article 70, and PII Article 18.2). This list is much broader than the goods automatically considered humanitarian by the Sanctions Committees: it includes clothes, shelter, and construction material. This higher level of tolerance is based on the fact that international humanitarian law foresees that humanitarian organizations carry out the distribution of relief.

→ **Protected objects and property; Relief; Sanctions (diplomatic, economic, or military); Sanctions Committees; Supplies**

📖 **For Additional Information:**

Braunmülch, C. Von, and M. Kulessa. *The Impact of UN Sanctions on Humanitarian Assistance Activities.* Report on a study commissioned by the UN Department of Humanitarian Affairs. New York: United Nations, December 1995.

Palwanker, Umesh. "Measures Available to States for Fulfilling Their Obligation to Ensure Respect for International Humanitarian Law." *International Review of the Red Cross* 298 (February 1994): 9–25.

Scharf, Michael P., and Joshua L. Dorosin. "Interpreting UN Sanctions: The Rulings and Role of the Yugoslavia Sanctions Committee." *Brookings Journal of International Law* 19 (1993): 771, 807–10.

■ ESPIONAGE

Under international law, the act of spying, or espionage, describes an act of information gathering that is clandestine or takes place under false pretenses (PI Article 46).

International humanitarian law makes a distinction between *intelligence activities* and *espionage*. *Intelligence activities* describes the collection of information carried out by members of the armed forces in uniform, in order to assess the situation and determine the options open to the opponent.

A spy caught in the act is assimilated into the category of saboteurs and cannot benefit from the status of prisoner of war. The spy must nevertheless be treated with humanity and must not be punished without a fair and regular trial (GCIII Article 5).

➔   **Fundamental guarantees; Situations and persons not expressly covered by humanitarian law**

■ ETHNIC CLEANSING

The practice of "ethnic cleansing," used most notably in the former Yugoslavia, aims to artificially create geographic zones (usually using violent methods) in which the population is composed exclusively of persons of the same nationality or ethnicity. Such policies violate the rules of legitimate governance as foreseen and accepted by the international community.

States have adopted resolutions, decisions, and conventions prohibiting racial or any other form of discrimination. The UN based itself on this rationale to impose economic and diplomatic sanctions in protest against the policies of apartheid carried out by the South African government. Individuals who perpetrated acts of ethnic cleansing in the former Yugoslavia can be prosecuted by the International Tribunal for the former Yugoslavia, which was set up in 1993 and has jurisdiction over grave violations of the laws of war, crimes against humanity, and crimes of genocide that were committed in the former Yugoslavia since January 1, 1991.

☞ In times of conflict, the acts of violence that make up the practice of ethnic cleansing are war crimes. For instance, international humanitarian law prohibits

- methods of warfare whose primary purpose is to spread terror among the civilian population and
- forced displacement of populations and deportation.

Perpetrators of such acts are subject to the penal sanctions foreseen by humanitarian law.

The statute of the new International Criminal Court, adopted in July 1998, provides precise definitions of crimes against humanity and war crimes. ➔ **War crimes/Crimes against humanity**. These include the main elements that make up the practice of ethnic cleansing, such as widespread and systematic killings, disappearances, population transfers, rape, persecution, and other similarly inhumane acts. Following certain preconditions, the ICC will be able to judge the authors of such crimes, whether during international or internal armed conflicts, or in times of peace in the case of crimes against humanity.

→   **Apartheid; Discrimination; Genocide; International Criminal Court; International Criminal Tribunals; Methods (and means) of warfare; Penal sanctions of humanitarian law; Population displacement; War; War crimes/Crimes against humanity**

📖 **For Additional Information:**

Hassner, Pierre. *Violence and Peace: From the Atomic Bomb to Ethnic Cleansing.* Budapest: Central European University Press, 1997.

Human Rights Watch. *Bosnia and Hercegovina, "A Closed, Dark Place": Past and Present Human Rights Abuses in Foca.* New York: Author, July 1998.

Quigley, John. "State Responsibility for Ethnic Cleansing." *U.C. Davis Law Review* 32 (1999): 341.

■ EUROPEAN COMMITTEE FOR THE PREVENTION OF TORTURE (CPT)

The European Committee for the Prevention of Torture and Inhuman or Degrading Treatment or Punishment (CPT) is the body set up to monitor the implementation of the 1987 European Convention for the Prevention of Torture and Inhuman or Degrading Treatment or Punishment (referred to as the European Torture Convention).

The CPT was created in November 1989, in accordance with Article 1 of the European Torture Convention. Its role is to "examine the treatment of persons deprived of their liberty with a view to strengthening, if necessary, the protection of such persons from torture and from inhuman or degrading treatment or punishment" (Article 1 of European Torture Convention).

☞ The European Committee for the Prevention of Torture is an integral part of the European system of human rights protection. Its monitoring is mandatory for all states that ratify the European Torture Convention.

The Committee is a nonjudicial mechanism with the aim of preventing torture. It complements the judicial control carried out by the European Court of Human Rights, which has jurisdiction over crimes of torture committed in Europe by virtue of the 1950 European Convention for the Protection of Human Rights and Fundamental Freedoms, which prohibits such practices.

The CPT carries out its examinations by means of periodic or ad hoc visits. These are generally carried out by two of the Committee's members in "any place within its jurisdiction where persons are deprived of their liberty by a public authority" (Article 2 of the European Torture Convention). Its mandate is thus relatively broad, extending to any place where individuals are being held, whether by administrative, judicial, or military authorities.

NGOs and individuals can transmit information relating to suspicions of torture to the CPT.

1. Composition

The Committee has as many members as there are parties to the European Torture Convention (currently forty-one). They are elected by the Committee of Ministers of the Council of Europe by an absolute majority of votes, from a list of names drawn up by the Consultative Assembly. The members, "persons of high moral and character," must be independent and impartial, and no two members of the Committee may be nationals of the same state. They are elected for four years and may be reelected once (Articles 3 and 4 of the European Torture Convention).

2. Mandate: Visits and Reports

The Convention gives the Committee only a mission to prevent torture. It cannot render judgments or punishment if the European laws against torture are violated. → **European Court of Human Rights**

The CPT carries out periodic visits to places of detention in the states parties. It can also organize other ad hoc or surprise visits if the circumstances seem to warrant them (Article 7). It may request the assistance of experts, such as doctors, during these visits.

Theoretically, the Committee enjoys relatively extended powers in the exercise of its functions. Article 8 of the European Torture Convention establishes that the CPT must have or be given

- access to states parties' territory and the right to travel without restriction;
- full information on the place where persons deprived of their liberty are being held;
- unlimited access to any place where persons are deprived of their liberty, including the right to move inside such places without restriction;
- any other information available to the state party that is necessary for the Committee to carry out its tasks;
- the opportunity to interview persons deprived of their liberty, in private; and
- the opportunity to communicate freely with any person whom it believes can supply relevant information.

After each visit, the Committee draws up a confidential report accompanied by any recommendations it considers necessary, although they have no mandatory force on states. However, if the state "fails to cooperate or refuses to improve the situation in the light of the Committee's recommendations," the Committee may decide to make a public statement on the matter (Article 10). It may also publish its report, with any of the concerned state's comments, whenever requested to do so by that state. However, no personal data shall be published without the express consent of the person concerned (Article 11).

Since its creation, the CPT has carried out more than 110 visits. For instance, Turkey was the subject of two public statements—in 1992 and 1996—concerning the treatment of individuals detained by the police.

Subject to the rules of confidentiality, the Committee submits a general annual report to the European Committee of Ministers, which transmits it to the Consultative Assembly before it is made public.

3. Jurisdiction

The CPT's competence is mandatory for all parties to the European Torture Convention, at all times (peace, war, or public emergency). However, in times of conflict, its jurisdiction is subsidiary to that of the ICRC. In such situations, the Geneva Conventions prevail, and "the Committee shall not visit places which representatives or delegates of Protecting Powers or the International Committee of the Red Cross effectively visit on a regular basis by virtue of the Geneva Conventions of 12 August 1949 and the Additional Protocols of 8 June 1977 thereto" (Article 17.3 of the European Torture Convention).

→ **European Court of Human Rights; Individual recourse; Torture**
→ **List of states party to international human rights and humanitarian conventions (No. 13)**

✎ European Committee for the Prevention of Torture
   Council of Europe
   67075 Strasbourg Cedex, France
   Tel.: (33) (0)3 88 41 32 54
   Fax: (33) (0)3 88 41 27 72

■ EUROPEAN COURT OF HUMAN RIGHTS

1. Jurisdiction

The European Court of Human Rights, based in Strasbourg, France, is responsible for defending the respect for human rights and punishing member states of the Council of Europe for violations of the 1950 European Convention on Human Rights (Articles 32, 33, and 34 of ECHR).

Until November 1, 1998, this responsibility was entrusted to two organs: the European Commission and Court of Human Rights. On that date, Protocol No. 11 (which amended the 1950 text) entered into force, reforming the entire European system of human rights protection into a completely legalized structure. The Commission was eliminated and the Court became a single and permanent institution. The Court has mandatory jurisdiction over all members of the Council of Europe. It can receive complaints from both states and nonstate entities (whether individuals, NGOs, or other groups of individuals).

The purpose of this reform is to maintain and strengthen the effectiveness of the European system of human rights protection. It follows an important increase in the number of requests before the Court and the growth in the number of Council of Europe members.

In addition to its contentious jurisdiction, the Court has an advisory mandate (Articles 32 and 47 of the ECHR). On the request of the Committee of Ministers of the Council of Europe, it may give advisory opinions on questions of interpretation of the European Convention on Human Rights and its Protocols.

2. Composition of the Court

The Court is composed of as many judges as there are states party to the Convention (forty-one as of March 2001). They are elected by the Parliamentary Assembly of the Council of Europe, from a list of three individuals put forth by each member state.

The judges are independent (meaning they sit on the Court in their individual capacity and do not represent any state) and have a six-year mandate that can be renewed once. They elect the Court's president, two vice presidents (who are also presidents of Section), two presidents of Section, four vice presidents of Section, the registrar, and two adjunct registrars. They draft the rules of procedure. A new set of rules was adopted following the reform of the system of human rights protection.

The Court is made up of four Sections and a Grand Chamber. The composition of each Section is fixed for three years and is based on criteria of equitable representation so as to be geographically and gender balanced and to take into account the different legal systems of the member states of the Council of Europe. Within each Section, Committees of three judges are set up (for twelve-month periods) and Chambers of seven members are constituted (on a rotating basis).

The Grand Chamber consists of seventeen judges elected for three years. In addition to the ex officio members (the Court's president, two vice presidents, and the two other Section presidents), the Grand Chamber is composed of judges from two groups who rotate every nine months. Once again, these groups take into account the equitable representation in terms of geography, gender, and legal system.

The Grand Chamber is responsible for examining the requests for advisory opinions on questions of interpretation of the European Convention. It can intervene, exceptionally, in contentious cases.

Key Characteristics of the European Court of Human Rights

- All members states of the Council of Europe are automatically and obligatorily subject to the Court's jurisdiction.
- Any state member of the Council of Europe may bring a claim before the Court, if it alleges that another state member violate the European Convention on Human Rights (state applications, as foreseen in Article 33 of the ECHR). However, it is very rare for one state to file a complaint against another.
- Claims may also be referred to the Court by individuals (citizens of a state party to the European Convention, refugees, stateless persons, and minors prevented from doing so domestically because of national laws), NGOs, or groups of individuals alleging that they were victim of a violation of the rights defended by the European Convention (individual applications, as foreseen in Article 34 of the ECHR).
- Member states of the Council of Europe are under the obligation "not to hinder in any way the effective exercise" of the right to submit individual applications (Article 34).
- Individual applicants may submit complaints themselves, using a form available at the Court's Registry. However, once the application has been filed, it is recommended that they take legal representation. The Court has set up a system of legal aid for applicants who lack sufficient means pay for such representation.
- Individual applications are subject to conditions of admissibility, which are always interpreted in favor of the victim. Thus, the criteria requiring that the remedies under domestic law have been exhausted can be rejected by the Court for various reasons: when it is not possible—in practice—to have access to such recourse; if there has been unwarranted delay in the national proceedings; or if the state only initiated such proceedings when the case was referred to the Court, in an attempt to avoid coming under its jurisdiction.

---

3. Contentious Cases

a. Admissibility Procedures

State applications are not subject to admissibility procedures.

Individual applications must meet several conditions of admissibility (Article 35 of ECHR). In addition to having exhausted all local legal remedies, the applications must not be anonymous, must not be incompatible with the provisions of the European Convention on Human Rights in any way, and must not be clearly ill founded or an abuse of the right of application. The application submitted cannot be the same as another examined previously by the Court or also submitted to another international organ of inquiry or dispute settlement, unless it contains new information.

Either a Committee with three judges or a Chamber with seven judges rules on the case's admissibility. If it is a three-judge Committee deciding, and if it declares the application admissible, it transmits the application to a Chamber.

The Chamber may relinquish jurisdiction in favor of the Grand Chamber if a case raises a serious question affecting the interpretation of the Convention, or if it might have a result inconsistent with a judgment previously delivered by the Court (Article 30 of ECHR). The parties to the dispute can object to this relinquishment, within one month of notification of the intention to relinquish.

b. Procedure on the Merits

The procedure to examine the individual and state applications, carried out by the Court and the parties' representatives, is adversarial and public. The Chamber or Grand Chamber may decide to carry out an investigation. All concerned states are under the obligation to cooperate with such an investigation (Article 38.1.a of ECHR).

Throughout the procedure on the merits, the registrar can conduct confidential negotiations, with the aim of reaching a friendly settlement to the dispute.

The Court's judgments are final and binding on the states concerned (Article 46). They may include compensation for the victim (Article 41). The Committee of Ministers of the Council of Europe is responsible for supervising the execution of judgments. The state that was found to be in violation of the Convention must take adequate measures to remedy the violation, but it is not obliged to modify its laws. However, in these situations, states usually do modify their legislation so as to avoid being sentenced again.

If a case raises serious questions of interpretation or application of the Convention or its Protocols or other serious issues of general importance, any party to a dispute may request that the case be referred to the Grand Chamber, within three months of the delivery of a Chamber's initial judgment (Article 43). A Grand Chamber panel of five judges examines the admissibility of such a request and decides whether it is admissible.

→ **Human rights; Individual recourse; Torture**
→ **List of states party to international human rights and humanitarian conventions (No. 8)**

✎ European Court of Human Rights
Council of Europe
67075 Strasbourg Cedex, France
Tel.: (33-3) 88 41 20 18
Fax: (33-3) 88 41 27 30.
@ European Court of Human Rights: www.dhcour.coe.fr

■ EVACUATION

The term *evacuation* describes the act of transferring populations or individuals. In situations of conflict, humanitarian law prohibits the forced displacement of populations. Military or medical evacuations are permitted, but only in exceptional circumstances and respecting strict and precise conditions.

I. MILITARY EVACUATIONS

Military forces may impose certain kinds of evacuations on noncombatants.

1. The Rule

Humanitarian law insists on the principle according to which "the displacement of the civilian population shall not be ordered for reasons related to the conflict" (GCIV Article 49; PII Article 17). The transfer of a population, as well as the use of terror to force its displacement, is forbidden as a method of warfare. This rule is applicable to both international and internal conflicts, when the drive to control territory and population might incite belligerents to adopt such methods (e.g., the practice of population displacement contributes to ethnic cleansing).

Furthermore, regardless of the motive, humanitarian law prohibits individual or mass forcible transfer or deportation of protected persons, from the occupied territory to the territory of the Occupying Power or of any other country, occupied or not (GCIV Article 49). It also forbids the Occupying Power from transferring part of its own civilian population to the occupied territory.

2. Exceptions to the Rule

> ☞ Military evacuation is possible under strictly limited conditions. These conditions must be interpreted restrictively: the Commentaries written on the Protocols Additional to the Geneva Conventions explain that the evacuation of populations may never be used as a combat strategy and may never be carried out simply because of its practical efficiency in attaining a military objective. The term *imperative military reason* (discussed later) assumes that no military alternative to evacuation exists.

The circumstances in which military evacuations are allowed are the following (GCIV Article 49):

- The evacuation of a given area is possible if the safety of the population or imperative military reasons require it.
- Such evacuations must be temporary. Persons thus evacuated must be transferred back to their homes as soon as hostilities in the area in question have ceased.
- Such evacuations may not involve the displacement of protected persons outside the bounds of the occupied territory, except when it is impossible to avoid such displacement for material reasons.
- Such evacuations must be carried out with respect for the interests of the civilian population. They may not be evacuated to a region that is exposed to the dangers of war; the authorities undertaking these evacuations must ensure that the individuals are received in proper accommodation and are transported in satisfactory conditions of hygiene, health, safety, and nutrition; and family members must not be separated.
- The Protecting Power or its substitute, the ICRC, must be informed of any evacuations as soon as they have taken place.

In noninternational conflicts, the term *evacuation* is not used, but the provisions prohibiting forced population displacements, or regulating the exceptions, use parallel language (PII Article 17.1).
→ Population displacement

II. MEDICAL EVACUATIONS

Medical evacuations concern wounded, sick, and shipwrecked individuals who need medical attention. Such evacuations may also concern children and other vulnerable persons who, in certain circumstances, are covered by the same protection offered to the sick and wounded under humanitarian law.

In encircled or besieged areas, the parties to the conflict must "endeavor to conclude local agreements for the removal of wounded, sick, infirm, and aged persons, children and maternity cases, and for the passage of ministers of all religions, medical personnel and medical equipment on their way to such areas" (GCIV Article 17). Such persons are usually evacuated toward hospitals or appropriate medical structures.

If there is no such written agreement, humanitarian law establishes that, as far as military considerations allow, each party to the conflict shall facilitate measures undertaken to search for the dead, sick, and wounded and to evacuate them to a location where they can be cared for (GCIV Articles 16 and 17).

All of these operations, carried out by medical personnel, units, and transport, must be accomplished under the protective emblem of the red cross (or red crescent) and with respect for the same guarantees as those provided for military evacuations (GCIV Article 49). → **Medical services; Wounded and sick persons**

To better protect the medical installations to which the persons are being evacuated, the parties to the conflict may set up hospital and safety zones, at the onset of hostilities, as well as neutralized zones in which to shelter the vulnerable persons (GCIV Articles 14 and 15).

The persons concerned by these medical zones and localities are wounded, sick, infirm, and aged persons; children under fifteen; expectant mothers; and mothers of children under seven. The establishment and functioning of these zones are dependent on the authorities and relief organizations concluding special agreements that allow the appropriate entities to search for the individuals in danger and transport them to the hospital zones.

☞ Humanitarian organizations have an important role to play in the case of an evacuation, especially in negotiating the establishment of hospital and safety zones. In particular, they must draw up nominative lists of all evacuated persons and ascertain that their medical responsibilities prevail over any police or military decisions, so as to ensure the protection of these persons during the evacuation.

Given the risks incurred by individuals who are evacuated and then gathered together in hospital zones, the parties to the conflict must sign written agreements to regulate the operation of these zones (GCIV Articles 14 and 15). In particular, these agreements must define the different responsibilities in terms of protecting the populations in these zones.

The massacres committed in the past several years in security zones set up under the aegis of the UN should make each actor realize the importance of establishing clear responsibilities.

Evacuations must take place in a way that does not prevent the return home of the evacuees and does not hinder family reunification. Special measures must be taken for the identification of each person. These measures are particularly strict with regard to children.

→ **Protected areas and zones**

III. SPECIFIC MEDICAL EVACUATIONS

1. Evacuation of Children

If necessary, measures must be taken to "remove children temporarily from the area in which hostilities are taking place to a safer area within the country, and ensure that they are accompanied by persons responsible for their safety and well-being," in both international and internal conflicts (PII Article 4.3.e; PI Article 78). Whenever possible, this must be done with the consent of their parents or persons responsible for their care.

In case of an international conflict, children may not be evacuated to a foreign country, unless they are being evacuated by the party to the conflict of which they are nationals.

When children are evacuated, humanitarian law establishes many restrictions. The aim of such regulations is to protect the interests of the children, particularly to facilitate their return to their families and to prevent the development of practices such as illegal adoptions (PI Article 78).

The authorities arranging for the evacuation of children, or those of the country receiving them, must establish a card for each child and send it to the Central Tracing Agency of the Red Cross.

Each card must bear, whenever possible and whenever it involves no risk to the child, the following information: last and first name; gender; place and date of birth; father's and mother's first and last names; next of kin; nationality; the child's native language and any other languages he or she speaks; family's address; any identification number that might have been given to the child; state of health and blood type; any distinguishing features; the date and place where the child was found; the date and place from which the child left the country; the child's religion, if any; and the child's address in the receiving country. If the child should die before his or her return, the date, place, and circumstances of death and place of burial must also be noted (PI Article 78).

➔   **Adoption; Central Tracing Agency; Children**

2. Evacuation of Wounded Combatants

Humanitarian law prohibits any distinction being made between wounded civilians and wounded military personnel. They have the same rights to be collected, evacuated, and cared for.

However, wounded and sick members of a belligerent party who fall into enemy hands are considered prisoners of war (GCI Article 14). As such, they benefit from the rights established by the Third Geneva Convention and must be evacuated from the combat zone to an internment camp for prisoners of war situated away from the danger zones (GCIII Article 19). The evacuation must be carried out humanely and in conditions similar to those for the forces of the Detaining Power in their changes of station. In particular, they must be given food, drinking water, clothing, and any necessary medical attention (GCIII Article 20).

Prisoners of war who suffer from certain illnesses or wounds may not be kept in captivity or be cared for in the territory of the Detaining Power. Humanitarian law establishes that they should be transferred to the hospitals of neutral states or repatriated directly to their own country. The kinds of wounds and diseases to which these conditions apply are enumerated in Article 110 of the Third Geneva Convention and are further detailed in the entry on ➔ **prisoners of war**. Annex I of the Third Geneva Convention provides a model agreement concerning the direct repatriation and/or hospitalization in neutral countries of wounded and sick prisoners of war.

➔   **Blockade; Children; Deportation; Population displacement; Prisoners of war; Protected areas and zones; Siege; Wounded and sick persons**

📖 **For Additional Information:**

Stavropoulou, Maria. "The Right Not to Be Displaced." *American Journal of International Law and Policy* 9 (1994): 689.

▪ EXTERMINATION

Extermination is the intentional and massive homicide of an entire group of persons. The international law of armed conflict specifically establishes that it is forbidden to attack civilians (GCIV Article 32, PI Article 51.2, and PII Article 13); to murder or exterminate the wounded or sick, shipwrecked, prisoners of war, and civilians (GCI and GCII Article 12, GCIII Article 13, GCIV Article 32, PI Article 10, and PII Article 7); and to order that there shall be no survivors (PI Article 40).

The statute of the International Criminal Court, adopted in July 1998, includes extermination in the crimes against humanity over which it will have jurisdiction. It defines *extermination* as "includ[ing] the intentional infliction of conditions of life, *inter alia* the deprivation of access to food and medicine, calculated to bring about the destruction of part of a population" (Article 7.2.b).

Extermination may also fall under the qualification of genocide if the group in question is being targeted on the basis of national, ethnic, racial or religious grounds.

➔ **Ethnic cleansing; Genocide; International Criminal Court; International Criminal Tribunals; Persecution; War crimes/Crimes against humanity**

F

■ FAMILY

1. In Times of Armed Conflict

As a general rule, all protected persons are entitled to respect for their family rights, at all times during armed conflicts (GCIV Article 27). In addition to this provision, humanitarian law does refer to certain specific provisions for the protection of families. These specific rules aim to do the following:

- Maintain family unity in case of evacuation (GCIV Article 49.3), detention, or internment (GCIV Article 82, PI Article 75.5 and 77.4, and PII Article 5.2.a).
- Enable the reunion of families dispersed because of the war and facilitate the work of organizations engaged in this task (GCIV Article 26, PI Article 74, and PII Article 4.3.b).
- Permit the exchange of family correspondence, either directly or through a neutral intermediary, such as the Central Tracing Agency (CTA) of the International Committee of the Red Cross (GCIV Articles 25, 26, and 107). If the parties to the conflict consider it necessary to restrict family correspondence, they may at most restrict such communication to the use of standard forms containing twenty-five freely chosen words and limit the number sent to one each month (GCIV Article 25). For internees, this limit may not be less than two letters and four cards each month (GCIV Article 107).
- Inform members of dispersed families of the fate of their relatives (PI Article 32).

2. In Times of Peace or of Internal Disturbances

Family rights are fundamental, tied to the respect for each person's privacy. They are protected by international human rights conventions and other texts, particularly the Convention on the Rights of the Child (CRC). The main rights and freedoms are

- the right to family reunification (to be found in CRC Articles 9, 10, and 22 and through the principle of family unity endorsed by the UN Conference of Plenipotentiaries on the Status of Refugees and Stateless Persons, GA IV B, July 28, 1951); and

- the right to the protection of privacy and the right to live as a family (Article 16 of Universal Declaration of Human Rights; Articles 17, 23, and 24 of the International Covenant on Civil and Political Rights; Article 10 of the International Covenant on Economic, Social and Cultural Rights; Articles 9 and 16 of the CRC).

Several actors participate in the protection and implementation of these rights, particularly in times of conflict or tension. It is first and foremost the responsibility of the ICRC and its CTA, often with the cooperation of UN agencies (UNICEF, UNHCR, etc.) and NGOs. In cases that do not come directly under humanitarian law (e.g., in situations of tension that have not reached the level recognized as armed conflict) and that fall outside the ICRC's area of competence (or if it is absent), UN agencies and NGOs may also establish methods and procedures to search for the families of unaccompanied children.

☞ Family disintegration can be noted in many countries. It is sometimes a direct consequence of war and violence that is specifically and deliberately perpetrated against civilians. The term *unaccompanied children* (UAC)—which appeared after the genocide committed in Rwanda in 1994—illustrates the scope of the phenomenon. Family disintegration can also be the result of socioeconomic strain.

Whatever the cause, it makes children or groups of children extremely vulnerable. The assistance provided to children in such situations must take this point into consideration and ensure that they are not aggravating the solutions by encouraging families to "leave their children." On the contrary, they must work to reestablish family ties and must also provide relief to families.

→ **Central Tracing Agency; Children; Family reunification; Red Cross**

📖 **For Additional Information:**

ICRC. "Protection of Civilian Persons and Populations in Times of War." In *Basic Rules of the Geneva Conventions and Their Additional Protocols*. Geneva: Author, September 1995, chap. 4, sect. II.
Plattner, Denise. "Preserving the Family Unit in Situations of Armed Conflict." *International Review of the Red Cross* (November 1994).

■ FAMILY REUNIFICATION

Families form a natural protective environment for all persons, especially in precarious situations. For this reason, international humanitarian law provides for the protection of family rights in times of conflict and begins by trying to prevent the dispersion of families. → **Family**

However, should a family become separated as a result of the conflict or flight, humanitarian law establishes special measures that must be implemented to enable its reunification and to facilitate the work of humanitarian organizations engaged in this task (GCIV Article 26, PI Article 74, and PII Article 4.3.b). The Central Tracing Agency of the International Committee of the Red Cross (ICRC) and the international Red Cross and Red Crescent movement have a mandate that specifically includes searching for family members and assisting in their reunification. Other humanitarian organizations may also develop programs of a similar nature (e.g., UNICEF and Save the Children).

The right to family reunification is an issue that is particularly relevant to refugees. In fleeing their country, many people are forced to leave their families behind or are separated from them along the way. Refugee status is accorded to individuals and therefore may not always be granted to all members of a persecuted person's family. However, a refugee may later apply for family reunification (based on the principle of family unity endorsed by the UN Conference of Plenipotentiaries on the Status of Refugees and Stateless Persons, GA IV B, July 28, 1951). Such an application must be filed with the appropriate government entity in the country where the refugee is located. UNHCR, ICRC, or National Red Cross Societies may assist the refugee in this process.

The right to family reunification, as a corollary to the principle of family unity, is also established and protected by the Convention on the Rights of the Child (Articles 9, 10, and 22), the International Covenant on Civil and Political Rights (Article 23.1), and the International Covenant on Economic, Social and Cultural Rights (Article 10.1).

➔   **Central Tracing Agency; Children; Family; Red Cross; Refugees; UNHCR**

📖 **For Additional Information:**

Draper, G. I. A. D. "The Reunion of Families in Time of Armed Conflict." *International Review of the Red Cross* 191 (February–March 1977): 57–65.
ICRC. *Help Us Find Our Families—Rwanda: Unaccompanied Children.* Geneva: Author, 1995.

■ FAMINE

Famine is a severe shortage of food that stretches over a long period of time and leads to the death of the populations concerned. It is distinct from malnutrition, which may be endemic or chronic. However, certain medical indicators related to malnutrition can be used to evaluate the severity of the situation with regard to the entire population.

Medical Indicators for Malnutrition

Two indicators are commonly used to measure the level of malnutrition that a child is suffering:

- The measurement of the middle upper arm circumference (MUAC or brachial perimeter), measured with a bracelet. For a child under five years old, when the MUAC is less than 110 millimeters, the child suffers from severe acute malnutrition. If it is from 110 to 124 millimeters, he or she suffers from moderate acute malnutrition.
- The height/weight index. Normally, this index should be about 100 percent. If it is below 70 percent, the child is severely malnourished. For instance, a child who is three years old, 97 centimeters tall, and weighs 8.5 kilograms has a height/weight ratio of 57 percent and therefore suffers from acute severe malnutrition.

Famine is also measured using other indicators, such as agricultural yields and the cost and availability of food products in a given place. It can be linked to natural phenomena or caused by a conflict.

Systems of early warning and of international assistance and information have been set up by UN agencies, namely within the FAO (Food and Agricultural Organization) and the WFP (World Food Program).

1. The Causes of Famine

Contrary to many notions set forth, famine does not belong to the category of natural disasters. Rather, its origins are political and social. Often, the causes of famine cannot be summarized as a general problem of food availability. Many studies on situations of famine have demonstrated that the famine was the result not of a general shortage but of political and social problems that affect the distribution and sharing of existing foodstuffs inside a country. The work of Amartya Sen, recipient of the 1998 Nobel Prize for Economics, has shown that the nondemocratic nature of a political regime and the existence of a state of conflict are also factors that affect the evolution of famine.

Thus, famine is not a fatality tied to natural scourges or climatic conditions. It draws attention to the weakness or failure of social or national solidarity. In the framework of a conflict, it may also highlight political or military will to weaken part of a population and their leaders. In such contexts, relief action and international solidarity cannot be satisfied with a quantitative approach or with a delivery system that goes through national authorities. They must also develop mechanisms that make it possible to guarantee victims' access to food aid, and they must analyze the causes of a famine closely.

2. Humanitarian Law Provisions That Prohibit Famine

In situations of conflict, international humanitarian law prohibits the starvation of civilians as a method of warfare (PI Article 54; PII Article 14). It is prohibited to attack or destroy food products; agricultural areas intended for the production of foodstuffs, crops, livestock, drinking water installations, and supplies; and irrigation works. These goods are considered protected objects, because they are indispensable to the survival of the civilian population (PI Articles 54.2 and 54.4; PII Article 14). The statute of the International Criminal Court establishes that starvation of civilians constitutes a war crime when committed in international armed conflicts. In other situations, it can be a crime against humanity, under the definition of "extermination" (Articles 8.2.b.xxv and 7.2.b of ICC statute).

Starvation remains an authorized method of warfare only against combatants.

Special rules are applicable to besieged locations. The parties to a conflict must ensure the "free passage of all consignments of essential foodstuffs, clothing and tonics intended for children under fifteen, expectant mothers and maternity cases" (GCIV Article 23).

In internal or international armed conflicts, humanitarian law authorizes relief actions that are of an exclusively humanitarian and impartial nature, if civilians are suffering undue hardship owing to a scarcity of supplies essential for their survival, such as foodstuffs and medical supplies (PII Article 18.2; GCIV Articles 17, 23, and 59; PI Article 70).

➔ **Food; Food and Agriculture Organization; International Criminal Court; Protected objects and property; Relief; Supplies; World Food Program**

📖 **For Additional Information:**

Action against Hunger. *Geopolitics of Hunger: Using Hunger as a Weapon*. Paris: Presses Universitaires de France, 1999.

Macalister-Smith, Peter. "Protection of the Civilian Population and the Prohibition of Starvation as a Method of Warfare." *International Review of the Red Cross* 284 (September–October 1991) 440–59.
Sen, Amartya. *Poverty and Famines: An Essay on Entitlement and Deprivation.* Oxford: Oxford University Press, 1984.

■ FOOD

The right to food is protected by national laws, which establish obligations between members of the same family and more general obligations of national solidarity, guaranteed by the State. This right is also defended in different forms in many international texts, as an integral part of ensuring "a standard of living adequate for the health and well-being" of individuals and their families (Article 25 of Universal Declaration of Human Rights).

1. In Times of Peace or Unrest

States have organized an international solidarity system to supply food, under the aegis of the UN. The Food and Agriculture Organization (FAO) is the UN Specialized Agency that promotes cooperation and assistance between states to improve agricultural techniques and crop previsions. It has set up a warning system in case of food shortages.

At the same time, the World Food Program (WFP), established by the UN and FAO, is responsible for international assistance programs, in case a food shortage occurs in one part of the world, by using excess production and reserves that are available on a global scale.

Nutritional Requirements for Human Rights

WFP evaluates the nutritional requirements of a human being to be 2,100 kilocalories per day. However, different organizations have different estimates: Médecins sans Frontières (MSF) agrees with the WFP, for instance, while the ICRC sets the figure at 2,400 kilocalories. Furthermore, the needs vary depending on the age of the individual. Vulnerable individuals, such as children and pregnant women, have increased needs, yet they are often unable to fulfill these needs in times of hardship and competition for resources.

Food rations must be well balanced. They should contain the following products: cereals, fats, sugars, salt, and leguminous plants (e.g., peas, lentils, etc.). In all cases, they must contain 10 percent protein and 10 percent lipids.

In terms of water, each individual needs twenty liters per day (5.2 gallons):

- five liters (1.3 gallons) of drinkable water (for drinking, cooking, etc.) and
- fifteen liters (3.9 gallons) for other needs (cleaning clothes, hygiene, etc.).

---

2. In Times of Conflict

International humanitarian law takes into consideration the fact that food can become a weapon; therefore, it precisely regulates its use and posits the obligation to provide aid for civilians. It prohibits

- the use of famine or starvation of civilians as a method of warfare;
- the destruction of crops and goods essential to the survival of the population;
- the requisition of objects indispensable to the survival of the civilian population.

It imposes

- the free passage of relief supplies to besieged zones, in particular for women, children, and the elderly;
- the free passage of food when the population is suffering from unnecessary or excessive shortages or deprivations, as well as the control of distribution by impartial humanitarian organizations so as to ensure that the food is not diverted by one of the parties to the conflict or other groups;
- the obligation to provide adequate food supplies for interned or detained persons.

There are no international or national texts establishing a "right to water." In times of conflict, the Geneva Conventions and their Additional Protocols do not expressly mention this right; however, water is included de facto under the system of food and relief supplies. Hence, water benefits from the same protection as that established by humanitarian law for food and other goods indispensable to the survival of the civilian population. → **Protected objects and property**

→   **Children; Detention; Famine; Food and Agricultural Organization; Internment; Methods (and means) of warfare; Protected objects and property; Relief; Requisition; Supplies; Women; World Food Program**

📖 **For Additional Information:**

Action against Hunger. *Geopolitics of Hunger: Using Hunger as a Weapon*. Paris: Presses Universitaires de France, 1999.

Macalister-Smith, Peter. "Protection of the Civilian Population and the Prohibition of Starvation as a Method of Warfare." *International Review of the Red Cross* 284 (September–October 1991): 440–59.

Tomasevski, K. *The Right to Food: Guide through Applicable International Law*. The Hague: Martinus Nijhoff, 1987.

■ FOOD AND AGRICULTURE ORGANIZATION OF THE UNITED NATIONS (FAO)

The Food and Agriculture Organization of the United Nations (FAO) was founded in 1945 and currently has 180 member states plus the European Union (member organization). It is one of the Specialized Agencies of the UN, and its headquarters are in Rome.

1. Mandate

The FAO's mandate is to "free humanity from hunger" and to work toward providing "access for all people at all times to the food they need to lead an active and healthy lifestyle." Its aim is to increase the quantity and improve the quality of available food around the world. Its activities range from agricultural development to fisheries, forestry, and nutrition. It also monitors the economic aspect of food production and distribution.

The FAO has four principal functions: to offer technical assistance, to collect and analyze statistical data, to make recommendations to governments on agricultural policies, and to act as an international technical forum where states and international organizations can debate food and agricultural issues.

In case of scarcity or conflict, the FAO usually does not intervene directly with food relief operations. Within the UN system, these activities are generally entrusted to the World Food Program.

2. Structure

The Conference of Member Nations meets every two years. It elects a Council of forty-nine member states—elected for a period of three years—and a director-general—elected for six years (currently Jacques Diouf, 2000–06). The Council meets once during the year when the Conference does not meet and three times during the year when it does. Conferences relating to local issues are held in one of the five regional offices (Africa, Asia and the Pacific, Europe, Latin America and the Caribbean, and the Near East).

The organization is made up of eight departments: administration and finance, general affairs and information, economic and social policy, technical cooperation, agriculture, fisheries, forestry, and sustainable development. It employs approximately 2,300 headquarters staff and 2,000 field personnel.

3. Means

The FAO's biennial budget was set at $650 million for 2000–01. Member states finance the budget for the "regular program" (65 percent) through fixed contributions set by the Conference. This covers the cost of the secretariat and operations decided on in the conference. The "field programs" (35 percent) are financed through voluntary contributions from member states, plus contributions from UNDP and the regular FAO budget. These are specific aid projects for a location or region, established under the auspices of the FAO and the country in question.

The FAO has set up a system of information gathering that monitors the agricultural situation around the world. The Committee on World Food Security runs the Global Information and Early Warning System, which collects data on crops, worldwide commodity trends, and production capacity, so as to detect emerging food shortages and assess possible emergency food requirements. It also collaborates with the relevant bodies in the UN system—for instance, in ensuring coordination in the humanitarian domain. It is one of the lead agencies in the Inter-Agency Standing Committee (IASC), run by the Office for the Coordination of Humanitarian Affairs (OCHA).

→   **Famine; Nutrition; Relief; World Health Organization**

✎   Food and Agriculture Organization
     Via delle Terme di Caracalla
     I 00100 Rome, Italy
     Tel.: (39) 06 57 051
     Fax: (39) 06 57 0531/06 57 0551/55
@   Food and Agriculture Organization: **www.fao.org**

■ FORCE MAJEURE

Whether proclaimed by a state or an individual, a *force majeure* describes unexpected and unavoidable circumstances that prevent that government or person from keeping or implementing a written commitment (e.g., a treaty, a contract, etc.). Sometimes referred to as an "act of God," a *force majeure* is an outside event that is unpredictable and beyond the control of those invoking it. This notion may be applied to commitments undertaken by individuals.

War is often pronounced as a *force majeure* with regard to numerous obligations relating to contracts or conventions. It results in the limitation or suspension of many rights and freedoms.

> ☞ States may not invoke war as a *force majeure* to dodge obligations that result from international conventions relating to the laws of war. These are established specifically to apply in such extreme circumstances.

→ **Fundamental guarantees; Human rights; International humanitarian law**

■ FUNDAMENTAL GUARANTEES

The term *fundamental guarantees* describes the rules governing the minimum standards of protection for individuals that remain applicable in all circumstances. These guarantees are reflected and defined in international conventions related to human rights law, as well as in those regulating humanitarian law, and straddle both branches of international law.

1. In Times of Peace

In times of peace, the protection of human rights and fundamental freedoms is regulated at an international level by a large number of Conventions (which are generally not applicable in their entirety in periods of conflict). These Conventions are established for the protection of all persons, no matter what their nationality or status, and are binding on all states that have formally adhered to their principles. After a state has ratified these instruments, it must incorporate their provisions into its domestic law.

2. In Situations of Internal Disturbances and Tensions

Only parts of human rights conventions continue to be applicable in situations of tension. National legislation adopted in a state of emergency, siege, or other exceptional circumstances may restrict human rights and freedoms.

However, international human rights conventions establish that there are certain fundamental rights from which no derogation is allowed, no matter what the internal condition of a state may be. Such peremptory norms of international law must be respected and protected for all individuals, in all circumstances. Also known as *jus cogens* or nonderogable rights (see Section I of this entry, later), these rights are "recognized by the international community of states as a whole as a norm from which no derogation is permitted" (as defined by Article 53 of the 1969 Vienna Convention on the Law of Treaties).

Although human rights conventions are no longer applicable in their entirety in such situations, humanitarian law is not yet applicable if the clashes or confrontations have not reached the level of intensity qualified as armed conflict. Until such a level is reached, general humanitarian law cannot be enforced as such. However, certain principles—namely, those listed in common Article 3 of the Geneva Conventions (see Section II of this entry)—may be invoked, particularly by humanitarian organizations.

3. During Armed Conflicts

Humanitarian law establishes fundamental guarantees for the protection of individuals, which cover different categories of protected persons. These were codified in the four 1949 Geneva Conventions, and the two Additional Protocols to the Geneva Conventions, adopted in 1977, clarify and reinforce these guarantees, in situations of both international and noninternational armed conflict.

The nonderogable rights established in human rights conventions remain applicable at all times, to all individuals.

I. NONDEROGABLE HUMAN RIGHTS

☞ Certain rights and freedoms established by human rights conventions can never be infringed on or amended by states, even during times of crisis, states of emergency or armed conflict, or other exceptional circumstances. These rights are known as *nonderogable rights,* or peremptory norms of international law. They constitute the absolute minimum standard that must be respected at all times. → **Inalienability of rights; Inviolability of rights**

The rules of humanitarian law, applicable mainly in times of armed conflict, are more precise. It is therefore preferable, in the context of hostilities that can be qualified as "armed conflicts," to rely on the Geneva Conventions and their Protocols. In situations straddling the blurry line between the absence of peace and the absence of full-blown war, it is important to utilize the complementary aspects of human rights and humanitarian law.

Although they are embodied in international conventions, these specific rights must be respected and protected in all circumstances. They are mainly considered customary norms—part of what is considered customary international law. The important point is that these rules are applicable even in countries that have not ratified the relevant international conventions.

→ **Customary international law; International law; Natural law**

Nonderogable rights must be enforced at all times, for all individuals.

At an international level, these are defined, for instance, in the International Covenant on Civil and Political Rights (ICCPR), adopted December 16, 1966, by the General Assembly of the UN (GA Resolution 2200 A [XXI]). Article 4 of the ICCPR establishes the rights and freedoms from which no derogation is permitted. No state may suspend its protection of these rights, no matter what the circumstances may be. These rights are the ones listed in Articles 6, 7, 8.1 and 8.2, 11, 15, 16, and 18:

- Article 6 establishes the right to life and the right not to be deprived of one's life. There is one exception. In countries that have not abolished the death penalty, a person may be deprived of his or her life, but only pursuant to a judgment rendered by a competent court. Extrajudicial executions are forbidden in all situations.
- Article 7 prohibits torture or cruel, inhuman, or degrading treatment or punishment. It also prohibits subjecting a person to medical or scientific experimentation without his or her free consent.
- Article 8 prohibits slavery, slave trade, and servitude.

- Article 11 states that no one shall be imprisoned merely because of inability to fulfill a contractual obligation.
- Article 15 prohibits the application of a criminal law to acts that were committed before the law was enacted.
- Article 16 establishes the right for everyone, everywhere, to be recognized as a person before the law (the right to juridical personality).
- Article 18 provides that everyone shall have the right to freedom of thought, conscience, and religion, including the right to manifest one's religion or beliefs. It prohibits any coercion that would impair a person's freedom to have or to adopt a religion or belief of his or her choice.

The same rights are repeated and further developed in regional conventions such as the American Convention on Human Rights (adopted by the Organization of American States on November 22, 1969) and the European Convention for the Protection of Human Rights and Fundamental Freedoms (adopted by the Council of Europe on November 4, 1950).

- The American Convention permits no derogation from the following rights, as per Article 27: right to juridical personality (Article 3), right to life (Article 4), right to humane treatment (5), freedom from slavery (6), freedom from retroactive laws (9), freedom of conscience and religion (12), rights of the family (17), right to a name (18), rights of the child (19), right to nationality (20), right to participate in government (23), and "the judicial guarantees essential for the protection of such rights" (27).
- The European Convention permits no derogation from the following rights, as per Article 15: the right to life (Article 2), right to humane treatment (Article 3), freedom from slavery (4.1), and freedom from retroactive laws (7).

II. Article 3 Common to the Four 1949 Geneva Conventions

This article establishes the most fundamental guarantees that must be provided to all persons who are not or are no longer taking part in hostilities. Though the specificity of Article 3, common to all four 1949 Geneva Conventions (known as common Article 3) is that it was one of the first to establish fundamental legal principles regulating noninternational armed conflicts, the Conventions clearly establish that these are minimum norms to be respected in all situations of conflict. The application of humanitarian law to conflicts that are not of an international nature has evolved since 1977, and the principles of common Article 3 are now recognized as also applying to internal disturbances and tensions.

Common Article 3 states that

each Party to the conflict shall be bound to apply, as a minimum, the following provisions:
  (1) Persons taking no active part in the hostilities, including members of armed forces who have laid down their arms and those placed *hors de combat* by sickness, wounds, detention, or any other cause, shall in all circumstances be treated humanely, without any adverse distinction founded on race, colour, religion or faith, sex, birth or wealth, or any other similar criteria.
    To this end, the following acts are and shall remain prohibited at any time and in any place whatsoever with respect to the above-mentioned persons:
    (a) violence to life and person, in particular murder of all kinds, mutilation, cruel treatment and torture;
    (b) taking of hostages;
    (c) outrages upon personal dignity, in particular humiliating and degrading treatment;

(d) the passing of sentences and the carrying out of executions without previous judgment pronounced by a regularly constituted court, affording all the judicial guarantees that are recognized as indispensable by civilized peoples.

(2) The wounded and sick shall be collected and cared for.

An impartial humanitarian body, such as the International Committee of the Red Cross, may offer its services to the Parties to the conflict.

(*See also* ➔ **International humanitarian law, Section III.2,** for the full text of common Article 3.)

III. Fundamental Guarantees in Humanitarian Law

The specificity of the four Geneva Conventions is that each one applies to a category of protected persons, defining the minimum standard of treatment that must be respected for each category. The fundamental guarantees differ slightly depending on whether they relate to the protection of persons who are wounded, sick, shipwrecked, prisoners of war, or civilians. These standards are clearly established norms that states must respect in their treatment of nationals of the opposing party to the conflict.

The strength of this approach is that it lists specific rights, carefully adapted to protect individuals in these categories from the specific risks that they may incur as a result of their status or the nature of the situation. Its weakness is that if the Conventions are applied in bad faith, this can lead to a refusal or a delay in providing the necessary protection, as the concerned parties debate the specific definition or status of the protected person or of the situation. In practice, it is therefore crucial to start from the minimum standards that apply to all persons, at all times, without prejudice to more protective provisions and measures to which they may be entitled.

More specific guarantees applicable to different categories of persons are explained in the relevant entries on ➔ **children; detention; judicial guarantees; prisoners of war; women; wounded and sick.**

Basing themselves on the fundamental guarantees foreseen in common Article 3 (see above), the two Additional Protocols to the Conventions, adopted in 1977, further clarified the rights that must be guaranteed for victims of internal and international conflicts.

1. Fundamental Guarantees for the Victims of International Armed Conflicts

Additional Protocol I of the 1949 Geneva Conventions (Protocol I) is applicable to victims of international armed conflicts. In particular, it reinforces the protection that one party to the conflict must provide for the nationals of the adverse party. Its aim is to standardize the set of minimum rights that must be guaranteed for all victims of international conflicts. However, these minimum standards are applicable only if more favorable measures for the protection of these individuals do not exist under other provisions in Protocol I or in the Geneva Conventions.

In comparison with the Geneva Conventions, Protocol I adds to the number of acts that remain absolutely prohibited in all circumstances. For instance, it broadens the definition of torture to clearly include mental torture and adds a reference to sexual offenses. Furthermore, it elaborates detailed rules for judicial guarantees of due process. ➔ **Judicial guarantees**

Protocol I, Article 75: Fundamental Guarantees

1. In so far as they are affected by a situation [of international armed conflict], persons who are in the power of a Party to the conflict and who do not benefit from more favourable treatment under the Conventions or under this Protocol shall be treated humanely in all circumstances and shall enjoy, as a minimum, the protection provided by this Article without any adverse distinction based upon race, colour, sex, language, religion or belief, political or other opinion, national or social origin, wealth, birth or other status, or on any other similar criteria. Each Party shall respect the person, honour, convictions and religious practices of all such persons.
2. The following acts are and shall remain prohibited at any time and in any place whatsoever, whether committed by civilian or by military agents:
   (a) violence to the life, health, or physical or mental well-being of persons, in particular:
       (i) murder;
       (ii) torture of all kinds, whether physical or mental;
       (iii) corporal punishment; and
       (iv) mutilation;
   (b) outrages upon personal dignity, in particular humiliating and degrading treatment, enforced prostitution and any form of indecent assault;
   (c) the taking of hostages;
   (d) collective punishments; and
   (e) threats to commit any of the foregoing acts.
3. Any person arrested, detained or interned for actions related to the armed conflict shall be informed promptly, in a language he understands, of the reasons why these measures have been taken. Except in cases of arrest or detention for penal offenses, such persons shall be released with the minimum delay possible and in any event as soon as the circumstances justifying the arrest, detention or internment have ceased to exist.

2. Fundamental Guarantees for the Victims of Internal Armed Conflicts

Additional Protocol II of the Geneva Conventions (Protocol II) develops and supplements the guarantees for the protection of victims of noninternational armed conflicts, foreseen in common Article 3.

As its first article explains, Protocol II addresses the protection of victims of armed conflicts that "take place in the territory of a High Contracting Party between its armed forces and dissident armed forces or other organized armed groups which, under responsible command, exercise such control over a part of its territory as to enable them to carry out sustained and concerted military operations and to implement this Protocol" (PII Article 1.1).

Protocol II does not apply to situations of internal disturbances and tensions, such as riots, isolated and sporadic acts of violence, and other acts of a similar nature, because these are not qualified as armed conflicts (PII Article 1.2).

It establishes the rights and freedoms that a state caught up in an internal armed conflict must guarantee its nationals. Among other guarantees added to those in the Geneva Conventions, it reinforces the fundamental rights of children and the right to protection from gender violence and from slavery.

Protocol II, Article 4: Fundamental Guarantees

1. All persons who do not take a direct part or who have ceased to take part in hostilities, whether or not their liberty has been restricted, are entitled to respect for their person, honour and convictions and religious practices. They shall in all circumstances be treated humanely, without any adverse distinction. It is prohibited to order that there shall be no survivors.

2. Without prejudice to the generality of the foregoing, the following acts against the persons referred to in paragraph I are and shall remain prohibited at any time and in any place whatsoever:
   (a) violence to the life, health and physical or mental well-being of persons, in particular murder as well as cruel treatment such as torture, mutilation or any form of corporal punishment;
   (b) collective punishments;
   (c) taking of hostages;
   (d) acts of terrorism;
   (e) outrages upon personal dignity, in particular humiliating and degrading treatment, rape, enforced prostitution and any form of indecent assault;
   (f) slavery and the slave trade in all their forms;
   (g) pillage;
   (h) threats to commit any of the foregoing acts.
3. Children shall be provided with the care and aid they require, and in particular:
   (a) they shall receive an education, including religious and moral education, in keeping with the wishes of their parents, or in the absence of parents, of those responsible for their care;
   (b) all appropriate steps shall be taken to facilitate the reunion of families temporarily separated;
   (c) children who have not attained the age of fifteen years shall neither be recruited in the armed forces or groups nor allowed to take part in hostilities;
   (d) the special protection provided by this Article to children who have not attained the age of fifteen years shall remain applicable to them if they take a direct part in hostilities despite the provisions of subparagraph (c) and are captured;
   (e) measures shall be taken, if necessary, and whenever possible with the consent of their parents or persons who by law or custom are primarily responsible for their care, to remove children temporarily from the area in which hostilities are taking place to a safer area within the country and ensure that they are accompanied by persons responsible for their safety and well-being.

- Article 5 adds provisions that must be respected, as a minimum, with regard to persons who are deprived of liberty for reasons related to the armed conflict, whether they are interned or detained. ➔ **Detention**
- The fundamental guarantees foreseen for the protection of the wounded, sick and shipwrecked are established in Articles 7 to 12. ➔ **Medical duties**
- Those for the protection of the civilian population in general are in Articles 13 to 18. ➔ **Civilians**
- Judicial guarantees are established in Article 6, to ensure respect for due process. ➔ **Judicial guarantees**

➔ **Children; Civilian population; Detention; Inalienability of rights; International law; Internment; Inviolability of rights; Judicial guarantees; Natural law; Nonprotected persons and situations; Occupied territory**

📖 For Additional Information:

ICRC, Commission on Human Rights. "Fundamental Standards of Humanity." Geneva: Author, April 2000.

Kosirnik, Rene. "The 1977 Protocols: A Landmark in the Development of International Humanitarian Law." *International Review of the Red Cross* 320 (1997): 483–505.

Oraa, Jaime. *Human Rights in States of Emergency in International Law.* Oxford: Clarendon, 1992, 87–139.

■ GENERAL ASSEMBLY OF THE UN (GA)

Established under Chapter IV of the UN Charter, the General Assembly (GA) is the plenary body of the UN—the main organ for discussion and voting. All member states are represented at the General Assembly, under the principle of universal democracy, whereby all states are equal and respect the equal rights of all peoples. Each member state therefore has one vote (Article 18.1 of the UN Charter).

I. FUNCTIONS AND POWERS OF THE GA

The GA has multiple responsibilities. First, it has a general mandate over the entire sphere of activity of the organization (Article 10 of the UN Charter). It shares certain duties with other UN organs, such as the Security Council, with which it shares the responsibility of "discuss[ing] any questions relating to the maintenance of international peace and security" (Article 11). On these matters, however, it must give priority to the Security Council's specific functions and powers: the GA may not undertake any action or make any recommendation regarding a dispute or situation that is being dealt with by the Security Council (Article 12).

The GA's powers make it the main organ for discussion within the UN. It receives reports from other UN organs (Article 15); studies the general principles of cooperation in the maintenance of peace, particularly those concerning disarmament; promotes the development of international cooperation in the political, economic, social, and cultural fields and in human rights protection (Article 13); and contributes to the development of international law. Finally, its most significant function concerns financial and budgetary matters. Each year, the GA votes on the UN's overall budget (Article 17.1).

To accomplish its mission, the UN has a biannual regular budget, made up of membership fees divided among the member states in proportion to their national income. In 1998 and 1999, this budget was approximately $2.5 billion. For 1999 and 2000, the main assessed contributors were the United States (25 percent), Japan (17.98 percent), Germany (9.63 percent), France (6.49 percent), Italy (5.39 percent), and the United Kingdom (5.07 percent).

In addition to the regular budget, there are several special funds and budgets, consisting of voluntary or mandatory contributions. These are designated for Specialized Agencies to implement specific actions. The GA does not control these funds, but it does examine the administrative budgets and makes recommendations to the specialized agencies concerned (Article 17.3).

A number of important countries do not pay their dues regularly. As of September 2000, member states owed $3 billion to the UN. Much of this debt consists of the United States's unpaid arrears, which added up to $1.9 billion.

According to the Charter, a member state that does not pay its dues for more than two years "shall have no vote in the General Assembly," unless the GA authorizes it because it is "satisfied that the failure to pay is due to conditions beyond the control of the member" (Article 19). Given the severe financial difficulties the UN has faced in the past several years, the Secretary-General often uses the threat of a suspension of voting rights with the defaulting countries, which are led by the United States.

II. VOTING PROCEDURE

The GA meets annually in regular plenary session, where it adopts resolutions that have received a majority of votes of those present and voting. The vote must be carried by a two-thirds majority for important questions, which include recommendations concerning the maintenance of international peace and security, the election of nonpermanent members of the Security Council, the admission of new member states to the UN, and budgetary questions (Article 18.2).

The nature of a given resolution adopted by the GA determines whether it is binding on member states:

- *Binding decisions*: The GA may only make decisions binding on states in the following domains: approval of the UN's regular budget, election of nonpermanent members of the Security Council, election of the members of the Economic and Social Council, admission of new member states, and the suspension or expulsion of current members.
- *Recommendations*: GA resolutions concerning any other issues have only the strength of recommendations, and they can be adopted by a simple majority vote. However, to give more authority to these recommendations, these texts are often adopted by consensus, without a formal vote. A text submitted for adoption represents a careful compromise reached by the international community of states, which no one would risk upsetting by openly contesting it (if no one is opposed to a text, it means that everyone is in favor of it). The president of the session simply notes the absence of any objection on the part of a state or group of states on consideration of the text. This method generates significant amounts of preparatory work at the level of the GA's specialized committees and subcommittees.

➔   **Soft law**

III. GENERAL ASSEMBLY'S STRUCTURE

While the GA is not meeting, the UN's work is carried out under the aegis of six main committees:

1st Committee: disarmament and international security issues
2nd Committee: economic and financial issues

3rd Committee: social, humanitarian and cultural issues
4th Committee: special political and decolonization issues
5th Committee: administrative and budgetary issues
6th Committee: legal issues

These Committees are subdivided into Subcommittees, which act as working groups on specific questions and appoint experts and Special Rapporteurs. This creates a very complex organizational chart, but this is necessary given the range of issues covered and their technicality. The common use of the system of consensus voting implies that the organization's Committees are expected to spend considerable time preparing and drafting texts that will be acceptable to all.

➔ **Economic and Social Council of the UN; International Court of Justice; Secretariat/Secretary General of the UN; Security Council of the UN; United Nations**

■ GENEVA CONVENTIONS OF 1949 AND ADDITIONAL PROTOCOLS I AND II OF 1977

The Geneva Conventions of 1949 and their Additional Protocols constitute the heart of international humanitarian law. Adopted in reaction to the horror of World War II, they clarify and codify the many rules of the laws of armed conflict that had been established in earlier treaties. These Conventions have reached near-universal ratification. In 1977, two Protocols were adopted to provide additional protection for victims of armed conflict. These Protocols are optional; nevertheless, nearly three-quarters of the countries of the world have ratified them.

An artificial distinction is often made between two sectors of humanitarian law: the rules regulating warfare (Hague Conventions) and those providing for relief activities in times of conflict (Geneva Conventions).

Hence, the Geneva Conventions and their Protocols do more than simply codify the rules for the assistance and protection of civilians. They establish the right of relief, as well as the rules of conduct during hostilities, since they regulate certain methods of warfare and establish the responsibilities of the parties to the conflict. ➔ **The Hague Conventions; International humanitarian law; Methods (and means) of warfare**

The Geneva Conventions of August 12, 1949

- Geneva Convention for the Amelioration of the Condition of the Wounded and Sick in Armed Forces in the Field (GCI)
- Geneva Convention for the Amelioration of the Condition of the Wounded, Sick, and Shipwrecked Members of Armed Forces at Sea (GCII)
- Geneva Convention Relative to the Treatment of Prisoners of War (GCIII)
- Geneva Convention Relative to the Protection of Civilians in Time of War (GCIV)

One hundred eighty-eight states are party to the four Geneva Conventions.

(*continues*)

> (continued)
>
> ### *The Protocols Additional of 1977*
>
> - Protocol I: Protocol Additional to the Geneva Conventions of August 12, 1949, and Relating to the Protection of Victims of International Armed Conflicts (PI)
>
> One hundred fifty-four states are party to Protocol I.
>
> - Protocol II: Protocol Additional to the Geneva Conventions of August 12, 1949, and Relating to the Protection of Victims of Non-International Armed Conflicts (PII)
>
> One hundred forty-seven states are party to Protocol II.

The Geneva Conventions hence simultaneously codify the laws of war and the rules governing relief. The Conventions proceed by category, each one establishing the rules of relief in situations of conflict for a specific category of persons.

The first three Conventions set the rules for the treatment of combatants who are wounded, shipwrecked, or prisoners of war, in situations of international armed conflict. Only the fourth Convention establishes provisions for the protection of the civilian population, also in times of international armed conflict.

The two Protocols strengthen the protection of victims of conflicts. Protocol I reinforces the Fourth Geneva Convention, to the benefit of victims of international armed conflicts.

Protocol II completes Article 3, common to all four Geneva Conventions (known as common Article 3), relating to the protection of victims of noninternational armed conflicts. Details on common Article 3 are provided under the entry on ➔ **fundamental guarantees.**

The specific contents of these Conventions and Protocols are introduced under the entry on ➔ **international humanitarian law**.

➔   **Fundamental guarantees; The Hague Conventions; International conventions; International humanitarian law; Judicial guarantees; Methods (and means) of warfare**

■ GENOCIDE

Genocide is forbidden, in times of peace as in times of war, by the 1948 Convention on the Prevention and Punishment of the Crime of Genocide (known as the Genocide Convention).

> ### Definition
>
> Article 2 of the Genocide Convention defines *genocide* as
>> any of the following acts committed with intent to destroy, in whole or in part, a national, ethnical, racial or religious group, as such:
>>> (a) Killing members of the group;
>>> (b) Causing serious bodily or mental harm to members of the group;
>>> (c) Deliberately inflicting on the group conditions of life calculated to bring about its physical destruction, in whole or in part;
>>> (d) Imposing measures intended to prevent births within the group;
>>> (e) Forcibly transferring children of the group to another group.

The Genocide Convention was adopted by the General Assembly of the UN on December 9, 1948 (GA Resolution 260 A [III]) and entered into force in 1951. As of March 2001, 132 states had ratified the treaty. However, the provisions of the Convention are applicable even to states that have not ratified it, following a ruling by the International Court of Justice that recognized the Genocide Convention as codifying customary international law (Advisory Opinion of May 28, 1951), which is binding on all states. This was reinforced by the report of the Secretary-General of the UN on the establishment of the International Criminal Tribunal for the former Yugoslavia, in which he recalled that the Convention was part of customary law (report S/25704 of May 3, 1993). This was reaffirmed by the Security Council, which approved the report in its Resolution 827 (May 5, 1993).

Enforcement Provisions in the 1948 Genocide Convention

- The prohibition on genocide is to be enforced at all times, whether during peace or war.
- The Convention provides for not only the act of genocide to be punished but also any conspiracy, direct and public incitement, attempt to commit, or complicity in committing genocide (Article 3 of the Genocide Convention).
- All persons who commit such acts must be punished, whether they are "constitutionally responsible rulers, public officials or private individuals" (Article 4). No matter what a person's official position may be, he or she cannot benefit from any form of immunity.
- The states parties undertake to enact legislation instituting effective penalties for the individuals who commit these crimes and enabling the extradition of the accused toward the requesting countries (Articles 5 and 7).
- They further undertake to "call upon the competent organs of the UN to take such action as they consider appropriate for the prevention and suppression of [such acts]" (Article 8).
- The courts that have jurisdiction over the crime are those cited in Article 6—namely, a competent tribunal of the state on whose territory the act was committed or an international criminal court.

However, history has shown that domestic courts are unlikely to punish such crimes, the very nature of which implies the involvement of national authorities. The provisions for punishment in the 1948 Convention are thus not adapted to reality, since courts of countries in which the crime of genocide is committed are unlikely to prevent or punish these acts within any reasonable time frame. This explains why genocide usually goes unpunished and why the Convention has never been enforced by national courts, whether in Cambodia in 1975 or in Rwanda in 1994.

As for the notion of an international criminal court, it took states fifty years after this convention was adopted to agree to create such a court.

Other Existing Enforcement Mechanisms

Because of the historical failure of any national courts to punish individuals who commit acts of genocide, it was crucial that the statutes of the ad hoc International Criminal Tribunals for the Former Yugoslavia (ICTY) and for Rwanda (ICTR), as well as the recently adopted statute of a permanent International Criminal Court (ICC), included the crime of genocide in the list of crimes over which they have jurisdiction (Article 4 of ICTY statute, Article 2 of ICTR statute, and Article 6 of ICC statute). They retained the definition of genocide from the 1948 Convention, which does not include any reference to extermination of political groups.

> ☞ In 1998, the ICTR set a new legal precedent, in the judgment rendered against Jean-Paul
> Akayesu (ICTR-96-4-T, delivered on September 2, 1998). It was the first judgment rendered
> by an international tribunal that finds an individual guilty of genocide.
> → **International Criminal Tribunals**

The statute of the ICC was adopted on July 17, 1998, but will enter into force only after sixty states have ratified it. It took states fifty years after the adoption of the Genocide Convention to agree on the terms of the ICC, and—given the time needed for most states to ratify an international convention—it will be several years before the Court is fully functional.

Once the ICC is operational, it will have the authority to prosecute cases of genocide (as well as war crimes and crimes against humanity), but only if the crime was committed on the territory of, or by a national of, a state that has ratified the statute. If neither the state where the crime was committed nor that of the nationality of the accused has ratified the statute, only the Security Council can trigger the ICC's exercise of jurisdiction. If the relevant states have accepted the court's jurisdiction, the ICC can be seized of such a case in three ways: referral of a situation to the Court by any state party; by the Prosecutor him- or herself, based on information concerning acts of genocide received from any reliable source; or by the Security Council, acting under Chapter VII of the UN Charter (actions undertaken with respect to threats or breaches of the peace).

→ **International Criminal Court**

Finally, in times of conflict, the extermination of protected persons is considered a grave breach of humanitarian law. If genocide is committed in the context of a conflict, it can therefore be punished under the principle of universal jurisdiction, established by the 1949 Geneva Conventions. As mentioned earlier, this principle gives states the authority to prosecute the authors of certain serious crimes, defined as all grave breaches of the Geneva Conventions, even in cases in which the states have no significant links to the accused or to the acts committed.

→ **Universal jurisdiction**

> ☞ The crime of genocide, whether committed in time of peace or war, is not subject to any
> statute of limitation, as established by the 1968 Convention on the Non-Applicability of
> Statutory Limitations to War Crimes and Crimes against Humanity. Judicial proceedings can
> therefore be initiated no matter how much time has passed since the crime was committed.

→ **Immunity; International Criminal Court; International Criminal Tribunals; Nonap-
    plicability of statutory limitations; Universal jurisdiction; War crimes/Crimes against
    humanity**

📖 **For Additional Information:**

Dallaire, Romeo. "The End of Innocence: Rwanda 1994." In *Hard Choices: Moral Dilemmas in Humanitarian Intervention,* ed. Jonathan Moore. Lanham, Md.: Rowman & Littlefield, 1998, 71–86.

Des Forges, Alison. *Leave None to Tell the Story: Genocide in Rwanda.* New York: Human Rights Watch, 1999.

Martin, Ian. "Hard Choices after Genocide: Human Rights and Political Failures in Rwanda." In *Hard Choices: Moral Dilemmas in Humanitarian Intervention,* ed. Jonathan Moore. Lanham, Md.: Rowman & Littlefield, 1998, 157–76.

Neier, Aryeh. *War Crimes: Genocide, Terror and the Struggle for Justice.* New York: Times Books, 1998.

■ THE HAGUE CONVENTIONS OF 1899 AND 1907

These treaties are known as "The Hague Conventions" because they were adopted at the Peace Conferences that were held in The Hague, Netherlands, in 1899 and 1907. They establish the laws and customs of war in the strict sense, by defining the rules that belligerents must follow during hostilities. These rules are elaborated on in the entry on ➔ **methods (and means) of warfare**.

This branch of international humanitarian law defines the laws of war, as opposed to those governing the right to receive relief, as defined in the Geneva Conventions that establish the rules of relief in times of conflict.

The Conventions and Declarations adopted at The Hague on July 29, 1899, concerned issues such as the pacific settlement of international disputes and the laws and customs of war, which were strengthened in the 1907 Conventions. They also concern

- the prohibition on the use of projectiles that disperse asphyxiating gas and
- the prohibition on the use of bullets that expand or flatten easily in the human body.

The Hague Conventions of October 18, 1907, address

- the pacific settlement of disputes (based on The Hague Convention I, of 1899);
- the opening of hostilities (The Hague Convention III);
- the laws and customs of war (Convention IV, with annexes and regulations, based on Convention II, of 1899);
- the rights and duties of neutral powers in case of war on land (V);
- the status of merchant ships at the outbreak of hostilities (VI);
- the conversion of merchant ships into war ships (VII);
- the laying of automatic submarine contact mines (VIII);
- the bombardment by naval forces in time of war (IX);
- the adaptation to maritime war of the principles of the Geneva Convention of 1906 (X);
- restrictions with regard to the exercise of the right of capture in naval war (XI);

- the establishment of an international prize court (XII);
- the rights and duties of neutral powers in naval war (XIII).

Other treaties regulate the rules for the use or prohibition of certain weapons.

→ **Geneva Conventions; International humanitarian law; Methods (and means) of warfare; Mines; War; Weapons**

■ HIERARCHY OF NORMS

"Law" is made up of a set of rules of unequal weight. The force of law of these rules follows the principle that a hierarchy of norms exists. Therefore, in applying a law, one must make sure that a given rule does not contradict a principle of law that is superior to it.

1. Domestic Law

The hierarchy of norms in each country depends on the legal authority of the body that adopted the norm. The types of law and their hierarchy vary depending on the legal system; thus, it is difficult to try to establish a general hierarchy. For instance, in the United States, in written law, statutes are higher than regulations, and federal laws are above state laws. In France, ordinances are superior to decrees. But there are other kinds of norms, increasing the complexity of the comparison. Furthermore, in countries whose judicial system is based on the common law, such as the United States, judicial precedents (*stare decisis*) also carry significant weight. In the United Kingdom, the fountainhead of common law jurisprudence, much of the legal system is based on court rulings.

One possible generalization, at least in the domestic legislation of civil and common law states, is that a country's constitution has a higher authority than any other law. However, this is not true of all judicial systems. For instance, some systems do not separate religion and the state, and religious law has a privileged position in the hierarchy of laws. In Islamic law, the Koran is the highest authority.

Most legal systems admit that international law prevails over domestic law because governments commit to ensuring that their domestic laws are in conformity with conventions they ratify (which often means they must adapt their national legislation). The key, when faced with implementing or conforming oneself to specific legislation, is to make sure that the law in question is not in contradiction with one that has more authority—that it does not infringe on the exercise of a right or freedom protected by a principle that is superior in the hierarchy of laws.

2. International Law

Several interpretations of the doctrine of international law are possible. One of these posits that there is no hierarchy of norms at an international level because states are the sole source of international law. In other words, since all norms of international law supposedly represent the "general will" of states, they are of equal standing. This argument fails to recognize several contradictions:

- International society includes a variety of nonstate actors who contribute to, and participate in the development of, international rights and obligations. The term *soft law* is often used to refer to norms derived from rules, resolutions, decisions, and so on, adopted by intergovernmental organizations (on behalf of member states, but without the direct input of many states of the world, or at least without their formal commitment in the form of a signature or of legally binding obligations).

■ International law recognizes a set of rules of law whose authority is so strong that it can be imposed on all states. These are often defined as *jus cogens*, or peremptory norms of general international law. All states are under obligation to respect these rules, no matter what the conditions are in a country, and whether or not they have signed any international conventions. Furthermore, all states, having adhered to the UN Charter, accept that their obligations under the UN Charter prevail over those under any other international agreement (Article 103 of UN Charter). **→ Fundamental guarantees; International law**

a. The Different Norms and Their Hierarchy

International legal norms take different forms, and they may be written or not. They include, in decreasing order of authoritativeness:

■ *jus cogens*, or peremptory norms of general international law;
■ the UN Charter;
■ international conventions and customary international law;
■ Security Council resolutions adopted under Chapter VII of the UN Charter;
■ international contracts or operational mandates of international forces or institutions; and
■ soft law and other resolutions, declarations, and decisions of international organizations.

In practice, international law is a set of rules that links certain states and not others, and it is applied irregularly. The growth and diversity of international texts force lawmakers to seek ways to reconcile norms that may be contradictory.

b. The Hierarchy

The International Court of Justice (ICJ) has defined its own hierarchy of norms, to be applied when ruling on a dispute. That hierarchy is as follows:

1. international conventions;
2. international custom, as evidence of a general practice accepted as law;
3. general principles of law derived from legal systems of the world; and
4. judicial decisions and teachings, as subsidiary means for the determination of the rules of law (Article 38.1 of ICJ statute).

The future International Criminal Court will first apply its own statute and then "the established principles of the international law of armed conflict . . . and principles and rules of law as interpreted in its previous decisions" (Article 21 of ICC statute).

As a general rule, it is important to know how to interpret the value and meaning of rules of law. The provisions of later treaties prevail over earlier ones on the same subject (unless otherwise specified), and more specific provisions prevail over vague or more general rules (Article 30 of Vienna Convention on the Law of Treaties).

3. Monitoring the Implementation of the Hierarchy of Norms

In practice, the existing mechanisms to facilitate the reconciliation of contradictory norms, monitor the respect for their hierarchy, or ensure their compliance with superior norms are insufficient.

a. Domestic Mechanisms

Some states have an institution that examines the constitutionality of their laws and any international conventions they intend to ratify. In principle, this ensures that no law is adopted that is in contradiction with the country's constitution. Also, it is often the legislative body of a state that ratifies international conventions signed by the executive branch, which is meant to ensure that the government does not enter into international commitments that are incompatible with its domestic laws.

The only other way that the implementation of the hierarchy of norms can be monitored is directly through court rulings. However, in some legal systems, this application and control of norms takes place only in the context of a specific controversy, and in many jurisdictions such rulings only apply to the case in question.

b. International Level

The absence of a fully efficient global judicial system limits the possibilities of regulating the compliance with the hierarchy of norms.

If states or intergovernmental organizations have doubts concerning the conformity of a law with international standards or the proper hierarchy to be followed, they can refer questions of legal interpretation to the ICJ. The ICJ can only issue advisory opinions on these questions (as is the case for most judicial organs of the UN) and states must voluntarily submit such questions to it.

Within the framework of the UN, various committees were created to monitor the implementation of international conventions relating to human rights. They carry out periodic examinations of national laws and make sure that the national legislation has incorporated the provisions of the relevant international convention. Individuals do have some recourse before such nonjudicial bodies.

Certain regional judicial organs, on the other hand, have the authority to judge whether a domestic law is in compliance with international law. The European and Inter-American courts of human rights, for instance, can issue binding decisions on such matters. However, recourse to such bodies is often limited to the parties directly involved in the specific case, and there are many restrictions in submitting a case to such a body.

→   **Individual recourse**

☞   Actors in the humanitarian field must make sure that the decisions taken by states and international organizations do not contradict the principles and obligations of international humanitarian law.

NGOs must make it their responsibility to ensure that these humanitarian laws and principles are mentioned and respected within the context of every relief operation or operational agreement and prevail over national legislation with less legal authority.

→   **Customary international law; European Court and Commission of Human Rights; Individual Recourse; Inter-American Court and Commission of Human Rights; International conventions; International Court of Justice; International Criminal Court; International law; Natural law; Soft law**

■ HIGH CONTRACTING PARTIES

The Geneva Conventions employ this term to refer to the states that are party to the Conventions. *High Contracting Parties* is generally preferred to *state* or *government,* which could cause problems of legal recognition in the case of certain armed conflicts, since humanitarian law remains applicable even in situations in which one or more parties to a conflict may not be represented among the states party to the Conventions. This is the case namely when one of the parties represents a nonstate entity or an authority that the other party does not recognize.

The implementation of humanitarian law does not affect the legal status of the parties to the conflict (GCI–IV common Article 3; PI Article 4). In fact, it encourages the signing of special agreements between the adversaries or with relief agencies, the aim of which is to ensure that its application is not limited to individual states party to the Conventions.

☞ The duty to enforce international humanitarian law is not tied to obligations of reciprocity. A High Contracting Party is held to its humanitarian obligations even if the other party to the conflict is not bound by the Geneva Conventions or is not respecting them (GCI–GCIV common Articles 1 and 2; PI Article 1.1; GCI Article 63; GCII Article 62; GCIII Article 142; GCIV Article 158; PI Article 99).

→   **International conventions; International humanitarian law; Legal status of the parties to the conflict; Respect for international humanitarian law; Special agreement; War**

■ HOSTAGES

Taking hostages and executing hostages are acts that are strictly prohibited by various international conventions.

The taking of hostages may occur for various reasons. If the motivations are political, the objective may be to pressure the political authorities of a country—for instance, to get them to grant recognition to an armed opposition group, to free members of the group who are detained, and so on. Hostage taking may also be based purely on economic needs, in which case the only objective is to obtain a ransom. On a large scale, economically motivated hostage taking sometimes becomes a veritable industry, aimed at financing the activities of hostage takers.

Hostage taking may take place in times of conflict, peace, or internal tension.

1. In Times of Conflict

Humanitarian law prohibits taking and executing hostages. Such acts are considered war crimes (GCI–IV common Article 3; GCIV Articles 34 and 147; PI Article 75) and can be tried before any national court, under the principle of universal jurisdiction. This is possible as long as the state in question has incorporated this obligation (derived from the Geneva Conventions) into its domestic laws. **→ Universal jurisdiction**

The statute of the Nuremberg Military Tribunal, set up after World War II, also asserts that such acts are war crimes, as do its judgments (as established by the UN International Law Commission, in June 1950). This is reinforced by the statute of the International Criminal Court (ICC), adopted July 17, 1998. The ICC statute defines taking hostages in an international or internal conflict as a war crime, which will come under the Court's jurisdiction (Articles 8.2.a.viii and 8.2.c.iii of the ICC statute). Hence, following certain conditions governing the Court's operations, the ICC will be able to judge hostage takers. Humanitarian law also forbids the use of the human shield.

2. In Times of Peace or Internal Disturbances and Tension

The International Convention against the Taking of Hostages was adopted on December 17, 1979, by the UN General Assembly (Resolution 34/146). The Convention entered into force in 1983 and currently has eighty-five states parties.

Article 12 of the Convention expressly states that its provisions do not apply in times of armed conflict, in which case humanitarian law is applicable.

The Convention defines a hostage taker as "any person who seizes or detains and threatens to kill, to injure or to continue to detain another person (. . . 'hostage') in order to compel a third party, namely a State, an international inter-governmental organisation, a natural or juridical person, or a group of persons, to do or to abstain from doing any act as an explicit or implicit condition for the release of the hostage commits the offence of taking hostages ('hostage taking')" (Article 1 of Hostage Convention).

The Convention further specifies that not only those who commit such an act but also any person who attempts to commit or who participates as an accomplice in such an act or attempt is accountable and must be punished. The states party to the Convention undertake to punish such offenses (Article 2). They must therefore adapt their domestic legislation and take

such measures as may be necessary to establish [their] jurisdiction over any of the offences set forth in Article 1 which are committed:
   (a) in its territory or on board a ship or aircraft registered in that state;
   (b) by any of its nationals or, if that State considers it appropriate, by those stateless persons who have their habitual residence in its territory;
   (c) in order to compel that state to do or abstain from doing any act; or
   (d) with respect to a hostage who is a national of that State, if that State considers it appropriate. (Article 5)

In case an alleged offender is on the territory of a participant state and the state does not extradite him or her, the state is under the obligation, without exception whatsoever and whether or not the offense was committed in its territory, to judge that person (Article 8).

→ **Human shields; Mutual assistance in criminal matters; War crimes/Crimes against humanity**

📖 **For Additional Information:**

Salinas Burgos, Hernan. "The Taking of Hostages in International Humanitarian Law." *International Review of the Red Cross* 270 (May–June 1989): 196–216.
Wayne, E. H. "Hostages or Prisoners of War: War Crimes at Dinner." *Military Law Review* 149 (1995): 241–74.

■ HUMAN RIGHTS

The term *human rights* covers the rights possessed by all individuals by virtue of being human. It represents the legal recognition of human dignity and equality among all individuals. The enjoyment of these rights is an indispensable aspect of human development. Human rights are considered indivisible, inalienable, and universal. Nevertheless, some may be restricted in times of disturbance or conflict, but there are certain minimum standards of protection that may never be infringed upon. These standards are generally referred to as "nonderogable rights" or "fundamental guarantees." ➔ **Fundamental guarantees; Inalienability of rights; Inviolability of rights**

Human rights conventions establish the rights that governments must respect or defend for their citizens. They are applicable mainly in times of peace, but international human rights conventions clearly set forth which rights may never be infringed on, no matter what the circumstances may be. The category of "fundamental guarantees" also exists in international humanitarian law (the law of armed conflict) and overlaps with international human rights law to ensure a minimum standard of protection for individuals in all circumstances. In case of internal disturbances and tensions, for instance, it is necessary to resort to the complementarity between human rights and humanitarian law. ➔ **Internal disturbances and tensions; Situations and persons not expressly covered by humanitarian law**

Numerous international and regional conventions list the rights and fundamental freedoms recognized by the international community. Some are universal in nature while others have a thematic approach, either to protect certain categories of persons or to regulate or prohibit specific behavior.

I. FUNDAMENTAL RIGHTS AND FREEDOMS

1. International Conventions

The general framework of internationally recognized human rights is established in the 1948 Universal Declaration of Human Rights (UDHR). ➔ **Universal Declaration of Human Rights**

The UDHR is complemented by the two Covenants: the International Covenant on Civil and Political Rights (ICCPR) and the International Covenant on Economic, Social and Cultural Rights (ICESCR), which were adopted by the UN General Assembly on September 16, 1966, and entered into force in 1976. These three texts are known as the International Bill of Human Rights.

- The ICCPR has 148 states parties, as of March 2001. The rights enumerated in this convention protect the principal civil rights and freedoms of individuals from any violation or infringements by the authorities.
- The ICESCR has 143 states parties. The rights enumerated in this convention require that states take concrete measures to ensure the well-being of each person.

A distinction is sometimes made between rights known as "positive rights" and "negative rights." The former imply that states have an obligation to act in order for such rights to be enjoyed (which is the case for most economic rights, e.g.), while the latter imply a duty to abstain from interfering (as is the case for most civil liberties).

Some of the principal civil and political rights are

- the right to physical and mental well-being;
- freedom of movement, assembly, and association, including to form trade unions;
- freedom of thought, conscience, and expression;
- the right to equality, in general and before the law;
- the right to own property and to accomplish one's goals; and
- the right to participate in the political affairs of the country.

Some of the principal economic, social, and cultural rights are

- the right to work, under favorable conditions;
- the right to social security, including social insurance;
- the right to an adequate standard of living and of physical and mental health;
- the right to education; and
- the right to participate in the cultural life of the community.

2. Regional Conventions

- The European Convention for the Protection of Human Rights and Fundamental Freedoms was adopted on November 4, 1950, and entered into force in 1953. It has forty-one states parties, as of March 2001.
- The American Convention on Human Rights was adopted on November 22, 1969, and entered into force in 1978. It has twenty-five states parties.
- The African Charter on Human and Peoples' Rights was adopted on June 27, 1981, and entered into force in 1986. It has forty-nine states parties.
- → **African Commission on Human and People's Rights; European Court (and Commission) of Human Rights; Inter-American Court of (and Commission on) Human Rights**

II. THEMATIC CONVENTIONS

Numerous international or regional thematic conventions have been adopted to protect certain specific rights and prohibit certain acts or behavior:

- Convention on the Prevention and Punishment of the Crime of Genocide (Genocide Convention), adopted by the UN General Assembly on December 9, 1948, and entered into force in 1951. It has 132 states parties, as of March 2001.
- Convention on the Abolition of Slavery, the Slave Trade, and Institutions and Practices Similar to Slavery (Supplementary to the 1927 Slavery Convention), adopted by the UN General Assembly on September 7, 1956, and entered into force in 1957. It has 118 states parties.
- International Convention on the Elimination of All Forms of Racial Discrimination (Discrimination Convention), adopted by the UN General Assembly on December 21, 1965, and entered into force in 1969. It has 157 states parties.
- International Convention on the Suppression and Punishment of the Crime of Apartheid, adopted on November 30, 1973, by the General Assembly of the UN, and entered into force in 1976. It has 101 states parties.

- Convention on the Elimination of All Forms of Discrimination against Women (CEDAW), adopted by the UN General Assembly on December 18, 1979, and entered into force in 1981. It has 167 states parties.
- Convention Relating to the Status of Refugees, adopted by the UN General Assembly on July 28, 1951, and entered into force in 1954. It has 137 states parties.
- Convention against Torture and Other Cruel, Inhuman or Degrading Treatment or Punishment (Torture Convention), adopted by the UN General Assembly on December 10, 1984, and entered into force in 1987. It has 123 states parties.
- Convention on the Rights of the Child (CRC), adopted by the UN General Assembly on November 20, 1989, and entered into force in 1990. It has 193 states parties.

  Regional Conventions include

- Inter-American Convention to Prevent and Punish Torture, adopted by the Organization of American States on December 9, 1985, and entered into force in 1987. It has sixteen states parties.
- European Convention for the Prevention of Torture and Inhuman or Degrading Treatment or Punishment, adopted by the Council of Europe on November 26, 1987, and entered into force in 1989. It has forty-one states parties.
- Inter-American Convention on Forced Disappearance of Persons, adopted by the Organization of American States on June 9, 1994, and entered into force in 1991. It has four states parties.

➔ **Apartheid; Children; Discrimination; Genocide; Refugees; Torture; Women**

III. Weaknesses of Human Rights Conventions

Different problems may arise in implementing the provisions of these conventions.

1. States Do Not Always Have Specific Obligations

Many conventions enumerate general rights but do not establish precise obligations or concrete measures that authorities have to enact in order to protect or enforce these rights. The practical efficiency of these treaties is therefore often limited, but they serve an essential purpose: they clearly set forth the standards that should be achieved, the boundary between lawful and unlawful behavior. Domestic laws must then be written in conformity with these international norms.

It is important to note, however, that a government's consistent and repeated failure to try cases of human rights violations can itself be considered a human rights violation.

2. Certain Rights May Be Restricted in Times of Tension or Conflict

As explained earlier, human rights conventions are more easily implemented in times of peace. There are situations in which states have trouble implementing these conventions, especially in times of disturbances or conflicts. In such circumstances, national laws may limit or suspend the exercise of a great number of human rights, even though it is precisely in such times that individuals need reinforced protection.

Furthermore, in times of internal disturbances and tensions, the protection guaranteed by the law of armed conflict does not yet apply because the level of violence has not yet reached a level of intensity that qualifies the situation as an armed conflict. It is therefore crucial that the fundamental rights and guarantees be identified, as well as which ones may be subject to limitations. This is when the fundamental guarantees established by human rights and humanitarian law must be enforced.

→ **Fundamental guarantees**

3. The Weakness of Sanctioning Mechanisms in Case of Violations of Human Rights

Many human rights conventions lack an international mechanism for punishment. Only the Convention against Torture and the Geneva Conventions, on the law of armed conflict, have integrated a system that defines the grave breaches to the conventions and the penal sanctions to punish such violations. → **Penal sanctions in humanitarian law; Torture**

One of the most blatant examples of such a lacuna can be found in the Genocide Convention, which defines and prohibits the crime of genocide but does not establish a concrete mechanism to qualify, prevent, or sanction such acts. This gap should be filled by the establishment of a permanent International Criminal Court (the statute of which was adopted on July 17, 1998), which will have jurisdiction over crimes of genocide, crimes against humanity, and war crimes, once it begins operating. → **Genocide**

IV. MONITORING BODIES

Some of the conventions do establish monitoring bodies, to which states, individuals, and organizations (especially NGOs), can refer cases. These are usually diplomatic mechanisms (mostly treaty-monitoring bodies) rather than legal structures and usually exist more to determine the existence of violations than to prevent them. There are six different kinds of procedures, depending on the treaty that created them, which are applicable to the states that have ratified the relevant convention. The procedures may be initiated by different actors, and they may be mandatory or optional. If they are optional, states must specifically declare that they accept the Committee in question's competence to receive such communications.

1. Nonjudicial Monitoring Procedures

a. Periodic Country Reports

States must submit reports on the human rights situation in their country, every few years, to a given treaty-monitoring body, to which individuals and NGOs can submit information. This system of periodic reviews does not provide the possibility of an urgent response to violations, as they are being committed. Such a procedure is mandatory before

- the Human Rights Committee (Article 40 of ICCPR),
- the Committee against Torture—periodically as well as on an ad hoc basis (Articles 19 and 20 of Torture Convention),
- the Committee on the Rights of the Child (Article 44 of CRC),
- the Committee on the Elimination of Discrimination against Women (Article 18 of CEDAW), and
- the Committee on the Elimination of Racial Discrimination (Article 9 of Discrimination Convention).

b. State Communications

A state party to a human rights convention may issue a communication to the effect that another state party is violating its obligations. Such a procedure is mandatory before

- the European Commission of Human Rights (Article 24 of European Human Rights Convention),
- the African Commission on Human and People's Rights (Article 47 of African Human Rights Charter), and
- the Committee on the Elimination of Racial Discrimination (Article 11 of Discrimination Convention).

Such a procedure is optional before

- the Human Rights Committee (Article 41 of ICCPR),
- the Committee against Torture (Article 21 of Torture Convention), and
- the Inter-American Commission on Human Rights (Article 45 of American Human Rights Convention).

c. Individual Petitions

An individual may file a petition or communication in case of human rights violations by a state party. Such a procedure is mandatory before

- the African Commission on Human and People's Rights (Article 55 of African Charter),
- the Inter-American Commission on Human Rights (Article 44 of American Convention), and
- the Human Rights Committee (for states that have ratified the first Optional Protocol to the ICCPR, whose aim is specifically to accept this competence on the part of the HRC).

Such a procedure is optional before

- the European Commission of Human Rights (Article 25 of European Convention),
- the Committee against Torture (Article 22 of Torture Convention), and
- the Committee on the Elimination of Racial Discrimination (Article 14 of Discrimination Convention).

d. NGO Communications

An NGO may file a petition or communication in case of human rights violations by a state party. Such a procedure is mandatory before

- the African Commission on Human and People's Rights (Article 55 of African Charter) and
- the Inter-American Commission on Human Rights (Article 44 of American Convention).

Such a procedure is optional before

- the European Commission of Human Rights (Article 25 of European Convention).

2. Judicial Monitoring Procedures

a. Individual Claims

An individual may file a complaint before an international organ in case of human rights violations by a state party. Such a procedure is mandatory before

- the European Court of Human Rights (Article 34 of European Convention, as amended by Protocol 11).

b. NGO Claims

An NGO may file a complaint before an international organ in case of human rights violations by a state party. Such a procedure is mandatory before

- the European Court of Human Rights (Article 34 of European Convention, as amended by Protocol 11).

c. State Claims

A state party may file a complaint against another in case of human rights violations. Such a procedure is mandatory before

- the European Court of Human Rights (Article 33 of European Convention, as amended by Protocol 11).

Such a procedure is optional before

- the Inter-American Court of Human Rights (Article 62 of American Convention).

☞ In war-related situations, it is preferable to refer to violations of humanitarian law than to human rights violations. International humanitarian law provides more specific rights to individuals, including the right to assistance. It precisely defines the content of violations that come under the various categories of war crimes, crimes against humanity, and so on. It also offers types of judicial and nonjudicial recourse that are not available through the human rights mechanisms. In the case of torture, for instance, the Torture Convention specifically provides for judicial recourse under the principle of universal jurisdiction.

In situations in which human rights violations are not isolated acts but committed in the context of a policy of genocide, crimes against humanity, or war crimes, the statute of the International Criminal Court (which as of March 2001 has not yet entered into force) establishes that cases can be referred to it by states parties or by the Security Council. The Prosecutor may also initiate investigations and prosecutions, under certain conditions, based on information received directly from victims, NGOs, or any other source. Victims have the right to legal representation before the ICC and to obtain reparation (Articles 68 and 75 of ICC statute).

→ **Individual Recourse; International Criminal Court; Penal sanctions in humanitarian law; Torture; Universal jurisdiction**

3. Other UN Bodies

Other organs for the protection of human rights are not established by a specific treaty, such as the UN Commission and Sub-Commission on Human Rights, and the Special Rapporteurs who are in charge of examining the human rights situation in specific countries or under a specific theme. They have no legal functions. Their authority in cases of human rights violations mainly allows them to establish reports. As a last resort, they can make them public. As part of the UN system, these entities are useful to draw the international community's attention to a specific situation and gain its recognition.

In all situations of conflict or tension, it is important to have recourse to the complementarity between human rights and humanitarian law.

Reparations for Victims of Human Rights Violations

In general, international law mechanisms do not provide for victims of human rights and humanitarian law violations to receive reparations, except for the Inter-American Court of Human Rights, which has a relatively narrow jurisdiction, and the ICC, which is not yet operational. Victims and their families therefore continue to depend on the rulings of domestic courts or, for certain human rights violations, on ad hoc UN funds.

In fact, there are currently only two such funds, set up by the UN General Assembly: the fund for victims of torture, created in 1982, and the fund for victims of contemporary forms of slavery, created in 1991. These are mainly funded by states' voluntary contributions but are also open to NGOs, individuals, and actors in the private sector. They are severely underfunded.

The funds are run by the Office of the High Commissioner for Human Rights and a Board of Directors made up of five people, nominated by the Secretary-General of the UN for three-year renewable mandates. The Board strives to obtain funds, after studying the different projects submitted by NGOs working with victims of torture or slavery. NGOs are the mandatory vector through which all aid allotted by the donors must pass, since the Funds never give money directly to the victims.

The statute of the new International Criminal Court provides for the possibility of awarding reparations to victims of crimes of genocide, crimes against humanity, or war crimes (Article 73 of ICC statute).

In 1998, the Commission on Human Rights nominated an independent expert on the right to restitution, compensation, and rehabilitation for victims of grave violations of human rights and fundamental freedoms whose mandate ended in 2000. Following his final report, the Commission on Human Rights adopted a resolution (E/CN.4/2000/62) requesting that the UN Secretary-General circulate to all member states the text of the "Basic principles and guidelines on the right to a remedy and reparation for victims of violations of international human rights and humanitarian law."

→ **African Commission on Human and People's Rights; Apartheid; Children; Commission on Human Rights; Committee against Torture; Committee on the Elimination of Discrimination against Women; Committee on the Rights of the Child; Discrimination; European Court of Human Rights; Fundamental guarantees; Genocide; Human Rights Committee; Inalienability of rights; Individual recourse; Inter-American Court of (and Commission on) Human Rights; International Criminal Court; Inviolability of rights; Nationality; Special Rapporteurs; Torture; Universal Declaration of Human Rights; War; War crimes/Crimes against humanity; Women**

→ **List of states party to international human rights and humanitarian conventions (Nos. 4–14, 20, 23–25)**

📖 **For Additional Information:**

Diller, Janelle M. *Handbook on Human Rights in Situations of Conflict*. Minneapolis: Minnesota Advocates for Human Rights, 1997.

Hannum, Hurst. *Guide to International Human Rights Practice,* edited for the Procedural Aspects of International Law Institute in collaboration with the International Human Rights Law Group. Philadelphia: University of Pennsylvania Press, 1992.

Henkin, Louis. *The Age of Rights*. New York: Columbia University Press, 1990.

Oraa, Jaime. *Human Rights in States of Emergency in International Law*. Oxford: Clarendon, 1992.

■ HUMAN RIGHTS COMMITTEE

The Human Rights Committee (HRC) was established per Articles 28 to 39 of the International Covenant on Civil and Political Rights (ICCPR), which was adopted by the UN General Assembly on December 16, 1966, and entered into force on March 23, 1976. It monitors the implementation of the ICCPR.

I. COMPOSITION

The Committee has eighteen members elected by the states party to the ICCPR, from a list of persons of "high moral character and recognized competence" (Article 38 of ICCPR). Each state can nominate two persons. The terms are four years long, renewable once. The Committee may not include more than one national of the same state, and consideration must be given to equitable geographic distribution of membership and to the representation of "the different forms of civilization and of the principal legal systems" (Article 40).

The HRC's headquarters are in Geneva, and its members meet three times a year. It submits an annual report to the UN General Assembly and to the UN Economic and Social Council, which is made public.

The Committee's mandate is restricted to states party to the Covenant (148 states as of March 2001) and is optional for states in many cases (unlike the activities of the UN Commission on Human Rights, e.g., which concern all member states of the UN).

II. MANDATE

☞ The Human Rights Committee has three mechanisms that allow it to monitor the ICCPR's implementation:

■ It examines periodic country reports submitted by states parties, which present the national efforts that states have taken to promote the respect for human rights and the Covenant in general. These reports are mandatory for all states.

(continues)

(*continued*)

- Under optional Article 41 of the ICCPR, the HRC can receive and consider complaints from parties alleging that another state party is not fulfilling its obligations under the Covenant—as long as both the alleging party and the alleged violator have declared that they recognize the HRC's competence with regard to such complaints.
- In the case of states having ratified the first Optional Protocol to the ICCPR, the HRC can also receive and consider communications from individuals who claim to be victims of a violation by the participant state under whose jurisdiction they are.

1. Country Reports

Country reports are the foundation of the UN system of human rights protection. States that are party to the ICCPR "undertake to submit reports on the measures they have adopted which give effect to the rights" set forth in the ICCPR. They must submit such reports one year after the entry into force of the Covenant for that state, and then every five years.

The reports are submitted to the UN Secretary-General, who transmits them to the Committee for consideration. The Secretary-General may also, after consultation with the Committee, transmit copies of relevant parts of the reports to the specialized agencies of the UN whose field of competence covers given parts. After the Committee has studied the reports, it hears the states concerned, through both written and oral observations made by the state, explaining the measures it has taken as well as any difficulties and delays in the implementation of the ICCPR.

Unlike the other two mechanisms used by the HRC, country reports are mandatory for all 144 states party to the Covenant.

☞ NGOs can submit written documents to the Committee and may go to its public meetings. The questions that the Committee asks the states during the public hearings may be based on information received from nongovernmental sources.

2. State Communications

A state party may file a written communication alleging that another state party is violating its human rights obligations under the Covenant. This article (Article 41) is optional, meaning that it only applies to states parties that have expressly recognized the Committee's competence to receive and consider state communications.

For the Committee to consider such a communication, two conditions must be met: both the state submitting the communication and the one allegedly committing the violations must have made the declaration accepting the Committee's competence with regard to such communications; and the injured persons must have exhausted all available domestic remedies. However, in the case of the latter condition, this "shall not be the rule where the application of the remedies is unreasonably prolonged" (Article 41.1.c). Furthermore, the Committee will only begin to examine a state communication if the matter is not "adjusted to the satisfaction of both States Parties concerned," within six months after the state that is the object of the communication received the complaint (Article 41.1.b).

The Committee must make its good offices available, with a view to finding a friendly solution. After twelve months, during which time it can receive written and oral explanation from the states concerned, the HRC submits a report to the states concerned. The report either contains a brief statement presenting the facts and the solution that was reached or, if no solution was reached, a brief statement including the written and oral submissions made by the states concerned.

Finally, if a matter is not resolved to the satisfaction of the states concerned, the Committee may, with the states' prior consent, appoint an ad hoc Conciliation Commission, which continues the work begun by the Committee (Article 42). When it has fully considered the matter, and in any event no later than twelve months after having been seized of the matter, the Conciliation Commission submits a report for communication to the states concerned.

The state complaint mechanism does not work very well and is particularly limited, because only the following forty-seven states have accepted the Committee's competence to receive and consider state complaints: Algeria, Argentina, Australia, Austria, Belarus, Belgium, Bosnia-Herzegovina, Bulgaria, Canada, Chile, Congo, Croatia, Czech Republic, Denmark, Ecuador, Finland, Gambia, Germany, Guyana, Hungary, Iceland, Ireland, Italy, Liechtenstein, Luxembourg, Malta, New Zealand, Netherlands, Norway, Peru, Philippines, Poland, Republic of Korea, Russian Federation, Senegal, Slovakia, Slovenia, South Africa, Spain, Sri Lanka, Sweden, Switzerland, Tunisia, Ukraine, United Kingdom, United States, and Zimbabwe.

3. Individual Communications

This is the possibility for individuals (or their legal representatives, but not juridical persons such as members of NGOs) to transmit communications to the HRC with regard to violations of the rights under the ICCPR by their state party. However, the HRC's competence to receive individual petitions is limited to the ninety-eight states that have ratified the first Optional Protocol to the ICCPR—which was adopted and entered into force along with the Covenant—establishing this option. → **List of states party to international human rights and humanitarian conventions (No. 6: First Optional Protocol to the ICCPR)**

Several conditions must be met before the Committee can consider an individual communication:

- the victim must be a national of a state party to the Protocol;
- the victim must have exhausted all available domestic remedies (Articles 2 and 5 of Protocol I to ICCPR);
- the communication must not be anonymous, must not abuse the right of submission of such communications, and must not be incompatible with the provisions of the Covenant (Article 4); and
- the matter must not be under investigation under another procedure of international investigation or settlement (Article 5 of Protocol I to the ICCPR).

The procedure takes six months: the HRC first examines the complaint and then requests explanations from the state concerned. The response is transmitted to the victim. Following this exchange, the Committee forwards its "views" to the state concerned and the individual (Article 5.4 of Protocol I to the ICCPR). This decision has no mandatory force of law.

The HRC is also responsible for monitoring the Second Optional Protocol to the ICCPR, aiming at the Abolition of the Death Penalty. This Protocol was adopted by the UN General Assembly on December 15, 1989, and entered into force on July 11, 1991. It currently has forty-three states parties.

The states that have ratified the first Optional Protocol to the ICCPR, allowing individuals to send communications directly to the Committee, are Algeria, Angola, Argentina, Armenia,

Australia, Austria, Barbados, Belarus, Belgium, Benin, Bolivia, Bosnia-Herzegovina, Bulgaria, Burkina Faso, Cameroon, Canada, Central African Republic, Chad, Chile, Colombia, Congo (Brazzaville), Congo (Democratic Republic of), Costa Rica, Croatia, Cyprus, Czech Republic, Denmark, Dominican Republic, Ecuador, El Salvador, Equatorial Guinea, Estonia, Finland, France, Gambia, Georgia, Germany, Ghana, Greece, Guinea, Guyana, Hungary, Iceland, Ireland, Italy, Ivory Coast, Korea (Republic of), Kyrgyzstan, Latvia, Libya, Liechtenstein, Lithuania, Luxembourg, Macedonia, Madagascar, Malawi, Malta, Mauritius, Mongolia, Namibia, Nepal, Netherlands, New Zealand, Nicaragua, Niger, Norway, Panama, Paraguay, Peru, Philippines, Poland, Portugal, Romania, Russian Federation, Saint Vincent and the Grenadines, San Marino, Senegal, Seychelles, Sierra Leone, Slovakia, Slovenia, Somalia, Spain, Sri Lanka, Suriname, Sweden, Tajikistan, Togo, Trinidad and Tobago, Turkmenistan, Uganda, Ukraine, Uruguay, Uzbekistan, Venezuela, Yugoslavia, and Zambia.

→ **Death penalty; Human rights; Individual recourse**
→ **List of states party to international human rights and humanitarian conventions (Nos. 5, 6, 7)**

✎ Human Rights Committee
Office of the High Commissioner for Human Rights (OHCHR)
52 rue Paquis
1202 Geneva, Switzerland
Tel.: (00 41) 22 917 91 59
Fax: (00 41) 22 917 90 12

■ HUMAN SHIELDS

It is prohibited to seize or to use the presence of persons protected by the Geneva Conventions as human shields to render military sites immune from enemy attacks or to prevent reprisals during an offensive (GCIV Articles 28 and 49; PI Article 51.7; PII Article 5.2.c). It is hence prohibited to direct the movement of protected persons in order to attempt to shield military objectives or operations. Many categories of persons are specifically protected by humanitarian law, such as civilians, the wounded and sick, prisoners of war, and medical personnel.

Such acts are clearly established as war crimes under international humanitarian law. This is also reflected in the statute of the International Criminal Court (ICC), which includes the use of a civilian or other protected person as a shield for military operations in its definition of war crimes, when committed during an international armed conflict (Article 8.2.b.xxiii of ICC statute).

→ **Hostages; International Criminal Court; Methods (and means) of warfare; Population movement; Protected persons; War crimes/Crimes against humanity**

📖 **For Additional Information:**

ICRC. "Final Declaration of the International Conference for the Protection of War Victims." *International Review of the Red Cross* 310 (February 1996): 55–130.

■ HUMANITARIAN AND RELIEF PERSONNEL

In the context of armed conflicts, humanitarian action carried out for the relief and protection of populations in danger is supplemented by a variety of humanitarian actors The legal protection to which the personnel involved is entitled varies depending on personnel's status. In any given situation, relief personnel may have very different standings. For instance, volunteers working for international or local NGOs may find themselves working alongside the International Committee of the Red Cross (ICRC) personnel or staff from one of the UN Agencies. They all, in turn, work with local staff, who are nationals of the states party to the conflict.

The Growing Threat Against Humanitarian Personnel

Attacks against humanitarian personnel are on the increase around the world. Staff of the ICRC, UN agencies, and humanitarian organizations have been particularly affected.

Between 1992 and 2000, just within the UN system, 184 civilian staff were killed. Hundreds of hostages have been taken as well. When twelve UN civilian personnel were killed in 1998, the number of civilian staff killed in the line of duty exceeded that of UN military personnel for the first time in UN history. The fate of others—some of them detained or missing since the 1970s—remains unknown.

Condemning such attacks, the Security Council has recalled that the responsibility for the safety of UN missions rests with host countries and parties to the conflict. On December 9, 1994, the UN General Assembly adopted the Convention on the Safety of the United Nations and Associated Personnel.

I. MEDICAL PERSONNEL

The Geneva Conventions establish a special system of protection for medical personnel, in both internal and international armed conflicts. First, such persons must be protected at all times. To help identify them—so as to facilitate this protection—they are authorized to wear a specific protective emblem (PI Articles 8 and 15; PII Article 9). ➔ **Distinctive (or protective) emblems, signs or signals; Medical personnel**

☞ Humanitarian law does not offer special immunity to relief and medical personnel. Immunity is designed to protect diplomatic activities, not humanitarian ones.

However, the 1949 Geneva Conventions and their Additional Protocols recognize several categories of personnel involved in relief actions and grant them both general protection (that to which all civilians are entitled) and specific rights in function of their mission. For instance, to protect medical services, members of medical personnel are authorized to use the protective emblem of the red cross or red crescent, and a combatant's failure to respect such emblems is a war crime.

With regard to persons involved in UN humanitarian operations, several conventions exist with respect to the privileges and immunities of UN personnel, but their coverage is restricted to certain UN employees and is not comprehensive. Furthermore, their provisions are inadequate to address the characteristics of recent UN operations, which combine both military and humanitarian components. ➔ **Immunity**

(continues)

> *(continued)*
>
> The statute of the International Criminal Court (ICC), adopted on July 17, 1998, in Rome, recently expanded the definition of the categories of personnel engaged in humanitarian or peacekeeping operations against whom a deliberate attack is considered a war crime. These categories are
>
> - medical personnel and persons using the distinctive emblem of the red cross and
> - personnel involved in humanitarian assistance or peacekeeping missions, as long as their mandate entitles them to the protection given to civilians under the international law of armed conflict.
>
> The authors of any such attack, whether the act was carried out during an international or internal armed conflict, may be prosecuted by either national courts or the ICC (Articles 8.2.b.iii, 8.2.b.xxiv, 8.2.e.ii, and 8.2.e.iii of the ICC statute).

II. PERSONNEL QUALIFIED TO CARRY OUT THE PROTECTING POWER'S MISSION

The implementation of humanitarian law depends on a specific system meant to monitor the obligations of each party to a conflict. This responsibility is entrusted to a Protecting Power, whose representatives are individuals (known in law as "natural persons"), who have a right of access to, and authorization to visit, protected persons and populations threatened by an armed conflict. If the parties to a conflict cannot agree on who to designate as the Protecting Power, the ICRC has a mandate to act as the substitute body and take on these responsibilities.

States are under the obligation to train qualified personnel to facilitate the application of the Conventions and to participate in the activities of the Protecting Powers (PI Article 6). The Geneva Conventions specify that these persons are subject to the approval of the government authorities on whose territory they are to carry out their duties. The parties to the conflict must facilitate the tasks of these representatives who may not, in any case, exceed their mission. In particular, these representatives must take into account the "imperative necessities of security of the State wherein they carry out their duties" (GCIV Article 9).

The personnel of the Protecting Power is made up of representatives of other states not party to the conflict, who enjoy the status of diplomat. In practice, these functions are taken on by the delegates of the ICRC.

→ **Protecting Powers**

III. CIVIL DEFENSE PERSONNEL

The "personnel" of civil defense organizations, in situations of conflict, refers to the members of national civil defense organizations who are assigned exclusively to humanitarian tasks intended to protect the civilian population against possible dangers, to help it recover from the immediate effects of hostilities or disasters, and to provide the conditions necessary for its survival. It includes the persons assigned—by the competent authority of the party concerned—exclusively to the administration of these organizations (PI Article 61).

The members of civil defense personnel of such missions therefore belong to one of the parties to the conflict. It is possible, however, for personnel of civil defense organizations from neutral states, states not parties to the conflict, or international coordinating organizations to carry out a civil defense mission, with the consent and under the control of a party to the conflict (PI Article 64). Such personnel must be respected and protected (PI Article 62). In occupied territories, the Occupying Power may disarm the members of civil defense personnel but may in no way divert their mission or compel, coerce, or induce such organizations to perform their tasks in any manner prejudicial to the civilian population (PI Articles 63 and 64).

→   **Civil defense**

IV. RELIEF PERSONNEL

1. International Armed Conflicts

Relief actions are foreseen by the Geneva Conventions and their Additional Protocols for the benefit of civilians who are not adequately provided with the supplies and foodstuff essential to their survival (GCIV Articles 23, 55, and 59; PI Articles 69–71).

When the parties to the conflict give their permission for relief actions, they may make it conditional on the requirement that the distribution of this assistance be made under the local supervision of a Protecting Power or substitute thereof (PI Article 70).

In practice, the absence of any Protecting Power in most relief operations puts an additional burden of responsibility on relief personnel. They must be able to perform certain protection and monitoring duties, in their role as substitute Protecting Power. This includes, for example, the responsibility of ensuring that the relief is distributed in a humane and impartial manner and for the sole benefit of the civilian population. Without this guarantee, the relevant party to the conflict could refuse relief shipments.

☞ The High Contracting Parties must allow and facilitate rapid and unimpeded passage of all relief supplies and personnel, even if such assistance is destined for the civilian population of the adverse party (PI Article 70).

- Where necessary, relief personnel and equipment may form part of the assistance provided in a relief action, in addition to the actual relief supplies. Such persons are mainly in charge of the transportation and distribution of these supplies. Their participation is subject to the approval of the party on whose territory the duties will be carried out.
- Such personnel must be respected and protected (PI Article 71).
- Relief personnel may not exceed the terms of their mission, under any circumstances. In particular, they must take into account the security requirements of the party in whose territory they are carrying out their duties. Any personnel that does not respect these conditions may see its mission terminated (GCIV Article 9; PI Article 71).

---

2. Internal Armed Conflicts

Protocol II additional to the Geneva Conventions establishes only that Relief Societies may offer their services to carry out their traditional functions in relation to the victims of armed conflict. It also sets forth that the civilian population may, of its own initiative, care for the wounded and sick (PII Article 18).

This Protocol hence does not give a specific status to any clearly identified personnel, except by asserting expressly that medical personnel must be protected in internal conflicts (PII Article 9). However, it does posit that relief actions—in particular, medical ones—may in no way be regarded as hostile acts or acts in support of the adverse party. This is especially important in internal armed conflicts, when the distinction between combatant and civilian is sometimes difficult to make and which, for this very reason, tend to become all-encompassing wars in which even relief actions are considered acts of treason or disloyalty.

V. UNITED NATIONS PERSONNEL INVOLVED IN RELIEF ACTION

The field staff working for the different UN humanitarian agencies consists mostly of employees who do not benefit from the status and immunities provided for diplomats by the Vienna Convention on Diplomatic Relations of April 18, 1961. They also generally do not benefit from the immunities provided for the officials and experts of the UN that are set forth in the Convention on the Privileges and Immunities of the United Nations of February 13, 1946. The aim of the 1946 Convention is to protect UN personnel from national pressures and thereby enforce respect for the "exclusively international character" of the organization's mission, per Article 100 of the UN Charter. However, it does not provide any means of ensuring the protection and security of this personnel from dangers it may incur in the course of its relief actions.

On December 9, 1994, the UN General Assembly adopted the text for a Convention on the Safety of United Nations and Associated Personnel (A/RES/49/59). This Convention entered into force on January 15, 1999, and has thirty-three states parties as of March 2001. The issue confronted by this new set of rules is how to address attacks against UN and NGO personnel, from a legal perspective, and how to prevent such attacks. One problem posed by the Convention is that the same text is meant to protect both military personnel engaged in UN peacekeeping operations and humanitarian personnel engaged in relief operations. Currently, this ambiguity can only be circumvented by referring to the statuses granted to different categories of relief personnel under humanitarian law, which also provides for concrete but separate protection for combatants that can be applied to military personnel involved in UN operations. **→ Combatants**

Furthermore, this Convention does not cover any coercive activities in which the UN might engage. The text indicates that humanitarian law is applicable to military personnel deployed in the context of operations authorized by the UN Security Council acting under Chapter VII of the Charter. Hence, the Convention only concerns peacekeeping operations in the strictest sense of the term. **→ Peacekeeping; Security Council**

The statute of the new permanent International Criminal Court (ICC), adopted in July 1998, posits that persons participating in peacekeeping operations must enjoy certain guarantees, though they may only benefit from such protection if they are "entitled to the protection given to civilians" under humanitarian law (meaning that they are not considered combatants). If these conditions are met, directing intentional attacks against such persons is a war crime that can be judged by national courts or, failing that, by the ICC, once its statute enters into force. This applies to both internal and international conflicts (Articles 8.2.b.iii and 8.2.e.iii of ICC Statute).

→ **Distinctive (or protective) emblems, signs, or signals; Immunity; International Criminal Court; Medical personnel; Peacekeeping; Safety, Protection**

📖 **For Additional Information:**

Baccino-Astrada, Alma. *Manual on the Rights and Duties of Medical Personnel in Armed Conflicts.* Geneva: ICRC/League, 1982.

Moore, Jonathan, ed. *Hard Choices: Moral Dilemmas in Humanitarian Intervention*. Lanham, Md.: Rowman & Littlefield, 1998.

■ HUMANITARIAN PRINCIPLES

The International Red Cross and Red Crescent Movement codified the humanitarian principles on which it bases its action. The Movement's seven Fundamental Principles are humanity, impartiality, neutrality, independence, voluntary service, unity, and universality. ➔ **Red Cross**

To a large extent, however, humanitarian action has evolved outside the Red Cross Movement, and the humanitarian principles have been the subject of many critical debates and different interpretations aimed at improving the effectiveness of humanitarian relief action. This is particularly true of the principle of neutrality. Certain humanitarian actors felt that the strict interpretation of this principle, combined with the respect for absolute confidentiality, was an obstacle to the effective protection of victims of conflicts.

The silence that the International Red Cross imposed on itself during World War II is at the heart of the controversy over this principle. An organization such as Médecins sans Frontières, by refusing to subject its relief actions to absolute confidentiality, developed the notion of "bearing witness" (*témoignage*) to the plight of victims, as an additional measure of protection.

Modern humanitarian action is thus based on a more limited number of concepts—namely, humanity, independence, impartiality, and neutrality—which are interpreted in relation to their operational effectiveness. Neutrality is no longer an absolute tenet of humanitarian action but is rather a means, the value of which can be questioned in certain situations.

The debate surrounding the neutrality of humanitarian action reflects a key question: whether there is a principle of responsibility to which humanitarian organizations are accountable when faced with situations of extreme violence against populations. ➔ **Responsibility**

Humanitarian law itself only refers to two principles. The Geneva Conventions require that relief organizations be humanitarian and impartial. The Conventions also establish various operational principles related to the concrete relief or protection activities carried out by such organizations.

1. Principle of Humanity

According to the International Red Cross and Red Crescent Movement definition, the aim of this principle is to ensure that individuals are treated humanely in all circumstances. It is the justification for all medical and social action. To guarantee the humanitarian nature of an aid organization or a relief activity, it must be possible to prove that humanity is the only concern taken into consideration. This principle implies that each relief organization must be independent from any constraints other than humanitarian ones.

2. Principle of Independence

Humanitarian action must be independent from any political, financial, or military pressures. Its only limit, its only constraint, and its only goal must be the defense of the human being. Relief organizations must therefore be capable of proving that they are independent from any outside constraints, and the relief activities must also be independent from any military, political, ideological, or economic pressures.

This principle reflects the key concept that differentiates humanitarian acts carried out by states from those undertaken by private organizations. However, the private nonprofit nature of an organization is not enough to prove its independence. Factors such as the overall funding of the organization, its founding principles, and the transparency of its activities must also be taken into account.

3. Principle of Impartiality

The Geneva Conventions uses the term *impartial* to define humanitarian relief action. This crucial principle qualifies humanitarian action carried out without adverse discrimination. It reminds us that all individuals are equal in their suffering. No one can be deprived of the assistance he or she needs.

> ☞ Impartiality must not be confused with a mathematical neutrality that would consist of providing equal aid to each party present, under the pretext of not favoring any one. Impartiality actually requires that relief be given in priority to those who most need it, regardless of their affiliation.

This principle, the key to humanitarian assistance, has two aspects:

- the distribution of aid and the humane treatment of all victims must be carried out without any adverse distinction based on grounds such as race, religion, or political opinion;
- in providing assistance, including medical assistance, priority must be given to those who most need it.

4. Principle of Neutrality

To be neutral means not taking sides in a conflict, whether directly or by allying oneself with one or another party to the conflict. This notion is tied to international politics: certain states developed the concept of neutrality so as to be able to stay outside of military alliances and conflicts in which their neighbors engaged. When extending this concept to humanitarian organizations, it has to be approached and interpreted differently.

- States' neutrality obeys a specific regime established by the laws of war. A neutral state agrees to not take sides in hostilities and to abstain from committing any hostile act or any act that could give a military advantage to one party to the conflict.
- Humanitarian neutrality consists of getting the parties to the conflict to accept that, by nature, relief actions are not hostile acts, nor are they de facto contributions to the war efforts of one of the belligerents.

From its origin, this principle helped shelter members of relief societies from hostilities. It is one of the Fundamental Principles of the International Red Cross and Red Crescent Movement, which, in order to continue to enjoy the confidence of all sides, not only refrains from taking sides in hostilities but also refuses to engage in controversies of a political, racial, religious, or ideological nature, at all times.

In addition to the four 1949 Geneva Conventions and Protocol I of 1977, various other international conventions address the issue of neutrality:

- the 1856 Paris Declaration Respecting Maritime Law;
- the 1907 Hague Convention (IV) in respect to the Laws and Customs of War on Land and its annex: Regulations concerning the Laws and Customs of War on Land;
- the 1907 Hague Convention (VIII) relative to the Laying of Automatic Submarine Contact Mines;
- the 1907 Hague Convention (X) for the Adaptation to Maritime Warfare of the Principles of the Geneva Convention;
- the 1907 Convention (XI) relative to certain Restrictions with regard to the Exercise of the Right of Capture in Naval War;
- the 1907 Convention (XIII) concerning the Rights and Duties of Neutral Powers in Naval War;
- the 1909 London Declaration concerning the Laws of Naval War;
- the 1936 London Procès-verbal relating to the Rules of Submarine Warfare set forth in Part IV of the Treaty of London of April 22, 1930.

The principle of neutrality was the subject of great controversy revolving around the International Committee of the Red Cross's silence during World War II. The framework of the principle has since been revised.

Operational Principles

- The humanitarian principles must be translated into practice within the relief operations, because it is the respect for these principles that grants humanitarian organizations their right to be present in the field in times of armed conflict under the Geneva Conventions.
- Only two of the Red Cross's seven Fundamental Principles appear in the Geneva Conventions (and their two Protocols) to identify humanitarian action. These are the principles of humanity and impartiality, which the International Court of Justice has also elevated as the criteria to qualify all humanitarian action—in the case of Military and Paramilitary Activities in and against Nicaragua (*Nicaragua v. USA*), 1986.
- The Conventions foresee a general right of humanitarian initiative for impartial and humanitarian relief organizations. This right of initiative is completed by specific rights established by the Geneva Conventions and their Additional Protocols for the concrete relief operations foreseen. These define the operational standards.

In order to ensure that relief activities benefit the most vulnerable rather than fuel the war economy, every impartial humanitarian organization is entitled to:

- free access to victims in situations of conflict, especially to the wounded and sick;
- the right to freely evaluate the humanitarian needs of the victims;
- the right to undertake relief actions when the civilian population is suffering undue hardship owing to a lack of supplies essential to its survival;
- the duty to monitor that such assistance is supplied without any discrimination, except for that based on needs, and that it reaches the most vulnerable;
- the right to treat the sick at all times and in all places in conformity with the principles of medical ethics.

(continues)

> (*continued*)
>
> Relief organizations must respect and defend these operational standards through their daily actions.
>
> These standards can be invoked in all situations of conflict. They must be referred to in agreements signed between humanitarian organizations and national authorities or other actors. By doing so, relief agencies participate in consolidating and strengthening the international custom of humanitarian action. Failing this, they risk, on the contrary, weakening the principles of international humanitarian law.

- Neutrality is no longer presented as an intangible principle guiding humanitarian action but as an operational principle. This means it is only respected to the degree to which it is efficient within relief action. It has been recognized that taking a public position on an issue does not necessarily contradict this principle. Neutrality is not synonymous with obligations of silence or absolute confidentiality. There are different variations depending on the situation and the type of relief activity being carried out. This notion is not in opposition to careful communication that takes into consideration the victims' overall interest and that is respectful of the sensitive nature of certain information.

The International Red Cross and Red Crescent Movement has actually entrenched the fact that it now makes public denunciations of grave and repeated violations of humanitarian law, notably during the conflict in the former Yugoslavia. Humanitarian law itself establishes that such denunciations must be addressed to states and to the UN (PI Article 89). Obviously, public opinion and the media have an important role to play in this chain of recourses. **→ War crimes/ Crimes against humanity**

5. Principle of Humanitarian Responsibility

This set of principles, in particular the operational ones, raises the question of what relief organizations' responsibility should be when the principles are not respected. The implementation of humanitarian law is not only up to belligerents. It also depends on the rights and initiatives of relief organizations. It is impossible to ignore the responsibility of these organizations: they are key actors in certain situations in which the assistance they provide is not enough to protect the safety and life of the populations (e.g., in cases when the aid is diverted by belligerents or used to trap or to commit acts of violence against a given populations). Finally, the responsibility of these organizations is engaged when a member of their personnel directly witnesses crimes or other grave violations of humanitarian law. Other aspects of this issue are developed in the entry on **→ responsibility**.

→ International humanitarian law; NGOs; Protection; Red Cross; Relief; Responsibility; Right of access; Right of humanitarian initiative

📖 For Additional Information:

Blondel, Jean-Luc. "Fundamental Principles of the Red Cross and Red Crescent: Their Origin and Development." *International Review of the Red Cross* 283 (July–August 1991): 349–57.

Kalshoven, Frits. "Impartiality and Neutrality in Humanitarian Law and Practice." *International Review of the Red Cross* 273 (November–December 1989): 516–35.

Moore, Jonathan, ed. *Hard Choices: Moral Dilemmas in Humanitarian Intervention*. Lanham, Md.: Rowman & Littlefield, 1998.

I

▪ ILL TREATMENT

"Ill treatment" is a much broader legal category than "torture and other cruel, inhuman or degrading treatment or punishment." Ill treatment is prohibited by Article 3 common to the four 1949 Geneva Conventions and by various human rights conventions. These texts also set forth the fundamental guarantees accorded to individuals. ➔ **Fundamental guarantees; International humanitarian law (Section II.2); Torture**

The Geneva Conventions do not define "ill treatment" as such, but they list examples of forbidden behavior with regard to protected persons. They do specify that, in times of conflict, states party to the Geneva Conventions are under the obligation to treat all protected persons humanely. This obligation concerns the treatment of the sick and wounded (GCI Article 15), shipwrecked (GCII Article 18), prisoners of war (GCIII Article 13), and civilians (GCIV Article 27). The prohibition on ill treatment of these persons is reinforced by obligations to enact concrete measures to protect them.

Obligations

States party to the Geneva Convention are under the following obligations:

- Wounded, sick, shipwrecked, prisoners of war, and civilians must be respected and protected in all circumstances. They must be treated humanely, without any adverse distinction founded on race, color, religion or faith, sex, birth, or wealth, or any other similar criteria (GCI–IV common Article 3).
- Parties to the conflict must take all possible measures to protect the wounded and sick from pillage and ill treatment and ensure their adequate care (GCI Article 15; GCII Article 18).
- Women must be especially protected from any attack against their honor—in particular, from rape, enforced prostitution, or any form of indecent assault (GCIV Article 27).

(continues)

(continued)

This protection from sexual assault or abuse was extended to individuals of both sexes by the two Additional Protocols to the Geneva Conventions (PII Article 4; PI Article 75.2, 76).

Strictly prohibited acts

The following acts, in particular, are and remain strictly prohibited at any time and in any place whatsoever with respect to protected persons (GCI Article 12; GCII Article 12; GCIII Articles 13 and 17; GCIV Articles 27, 31, and 32):

- any attempt on their life, in particular violence to their person, murder, extermination, as well as willfully leaving them without medical assistance and care, exposing them to contagion or infection created to that effect or subjecting them to torture, medical, biological, or scientific experiments not necessitated by the medical treatment of a protected person;
- any other measures of brutality whether applied by civilian or military agents;
- any physical or moral coercion exercised against protected persons, particularly to obtain information from them or from third parties.

When ill treatment can be qualified as torture or inhuman treatment, it is considered a grave breach of the Geneva Conventions and therefore a war crime (GCI Article 50, GCII Article 51, GCIII Article 130, and GCIV Article 147).

Other acts enumerated in the Geneva Conventions or their Protocols as ill treatment include any form of corporal punishment; collective punishments; taking of hostages; acts of terrorism; outrages on personal dignity—in particular, humiliating and degrading treatment, rape, enforced prostitution and any form of indecent assault; slavery and the slave trade in all their forms; pillage; or threats to commit any of these acts (PII Article 4).

Detention and Internment

In situations of detention or internment, the Geneva Conventions further clarify the notion of ill treatment and establish additional obligations in terms of protection (GCIV Articles 100–118):

- The disciplinary regime in places of internment must be consistent with humanitarian principles and shall in no circumstances include regulations imposing any physical exertion on internees that might be dangerous to their health or involving physical or moral victimization (GCIV Article 100).
- The following acts are expressly prohibited: tattooing or imprinting signs or markings on the body for the sake of identification, prolonged standing and roll calls, punishment drills, military drills and maneuvers, and the reduction of food rations (GCIV Article 100), as well as imprisonment in premises without daylight, and, "in general, all forms of cruelty without exception" (GCIV Article 118).

→ **Corporal punishment; Discrimination; Fundamental guarantees; Persecution; Rape; Torture; War crimes/Crimes against humanity**

■ IMMUNITY

Immunity is a privilege enjoyed by certain persons that enables them to exercise their functions free from outside constraints or pressures, including legal ones. Individuals entitled to immunity from jurisdiction can thus avoid legal pursuit. This immunity exists mainly for diplomats, United Nations personnel, and parliamentarians, as well as government members and heads of state or of government. This immunity is never absolute and is generally restricted to acts committed in the exercise of official functions, during the time the person holds that official position. Immunity may be lifted in case of grave violations by the political or legal entities that control the various official functions.

Contrary to popular belief, members of humanitarian and relief personnel do not benefit from any form of immunity in the strict sense. There is no such thing as "humanitarian immunity." Such persons come under a protection regime established by international humanitarian law, which covers civilians, relief and medical personnel, and relief actions.

Deliberate attacks on such personnel may constitute a war crime, punishable under international or national law.

→   **Humanitarian and relief personnel; Medical personnel; War crimes/Crimes against humanity**

1. The Excuse of Official Functions

There are no international treaties that specifically establish immunity for heads of state and government. At an international level, the immunity of heads of state is the result of custom and is similar to diplomatic immunity. By definition, this custom is always susceptible to amendments, as proved in 1999 by various judgments rendered by the British and Spanish judicial authorities in the case of the former president of Chile, Augusto Pinochet, as well as by the indictment of the Yugoslav head of state, Slobodan Milosevic, by the International Criminal Tribunal for the former Yugoslavia.

On the other hand, the national laws of each state often clearly establish systems regulating immunities and criminal responsibilities of heads of state (generally in the constitution). However, these national provisions cannot take precedent over international law; therefore, they cannot shield such individuals from international legal procedures initiated against them, in cases limited to the most serious crimes of international law, such as crimes against humanity, genocide, war crimes, and torture.

In fact, in the case of such grave crimes, international law expressly establishes that no immunity can be invoked to shield an individual from justice.

Article 27 of the statute of the International Criminal Court (which will have jurisdiction over individuals accused of war crimes, crimes against humanity, and genocide, once it begins to operate) stipulates that the Court will have jurisdiction over "all persons without any distinction based on official capacity. In particular, official capacity as a Head of State or Government, a member of a Government or parliament, an elected representative or a government official shall in no case exempt a person from criminal responsibility under this Statute, nor shall it, in and of itself, constitute a ground for reduction of sentence."

This article confirms the principles previously set forth in the jurisprudence of the Nuremberg Tribunal and the International Criminal Tribunals for the former Yugoslavia and for Rwanda, thus giving them a permanent and mandatory legal status. It also confirms the provisions already foreseen in several specific conventions—namely:

- the Geneva Conventions' provisions concerning perpetrators of grave violations of humanitarian law;
- the Genocide Convention's provisions concerning the perpetrators of crimes of genocide;
- the Torture Convention's provisions concerning the punishment of this specific crime.

With regard to armed conflicts, humanitarian law takes into consideration the fact that it would be incoherent to engage the responsibility of individuals if their hierarchical superiors and others exercising their official functions were exonerated. Humanitarian law thus emphasizes the criminal responsibility of hierarchical superiors in cases of war crimes, unless they can prove that they did not give the order or that they took all feasible measures to prevent or stop the violations. Humanitarian law thus sets forth the duty to disobey unjust orders.

☞ International law establishes that, in the case of war crimes, crimes against humanity, genocide, and torture, no one may use their official status to claim immunity in an attempt to avoid facing justice. This provision is set forth in

- the 1948 Convention on the Prevention and Punishment of the Crime of Genocide (Article 4),
- the 1984 Convention against Torture and Other Cruel, Inhuman or Degrading Treatment or Punishment,
- the 1949 Geneva Conventions (GCI Article 49, GCII Article 50, GCIII Article 129, and GCIV Article 146),
- the statue of the Nuremberg Tribunal (Article 7),
- the statute of the International Criminal Tribunals for the former Yugoslavia and for Rwanda (Article 7.2 of the ITCY statute and Article 6.2 of the ICTR statute), and
- the statute of the International Criminal Court (Article 27).

---

2. Diplomatic Immunity

This form of immunity is established by the Vienna Convention on Diplomatic Relations, adopted on April 18, 1961, and entered into force in 1964 (it currently has 179 states parties). The many immunities that protect diplomats include the following:

- Immunity from any form of arrest or detention (Article 29): This means that "the person of a diplomatic agent shall be inviolable." He or she cannot be arrested or detained.
- Immunity from jurisdiction or from legal process (Article 31): A diplomat may not be prosecuted by any court of the state in which he or she is posted. This guarantee is applicable regardless of the seriousness of the alleged crime (felony or misdemeanor) and whether or not the acts were committed in the exercise of the diplomat's functions. Article 31 further specifies that a diplomatic agent is not obliged to give evidence as a witness. However, the diplomat's home state may waive the immunity from jurisdiction.

One tenet of the principle of immunity asserts that immunity from jurisdiction does not extend to the most serious crimes—crimes against the peace, war crimes, and crimes against humanity. Conversely, the 1961 Vienna Convention (as well as the 1946 UN Convention, explained later) determines that immunity is general.

- Inviolability of the residence and property (Article 30): The protection enjoyed by such objects is similar to that enjoyed by the premises of the diplomatic mission. Searches or seizures carried out in the diplomat's residence are prohibited. This inviolability also applies to the diplomat's papers, correspondence, and property. The term *property* covers diverse elements, such as luggage, a car, salary, and so on.

These prerogatives are granted to the diplomat when he or she is accredited with the host state (meaning that the diplomat's name appears on the list of individuals registered and therefore effectively considered as diplomats by the host state).

3. Immunities of UN Personnel

The Convention on the Privileges and Immunities of the United Nations was adopted on February 13, 1946; as of March 2001 it has 141 states parties. Its aim is to shelter members of UN personnel from national pressures and to ensure the "exclusively international character" of their mission, in conformity with Article 100 of the UN Charter.

Its provisions are applicable only to individuals who are officials and experts of the UN in the strictest sense. Personnel working in the field for humanitarian agencies of the UN are mostly under contract and are therefore not covered by the 1946 Convention. Persons working for UN specialized agencies come under a specific protection regime regulated by the Convention on the Privileges and Immunities of the Specialized Agencies, adopted by the General Assembly of the UN on November 21, 1947 (which currently has 104 states parties).

The 1946 Convention grants the following immunities:

- UN officials enjoy, inter alia, immunity from jurisdiction (or legal process), but only for acts committed in their official capacity (Article 5, section 18). They also enjoy immunity from arrest or detention, but this was not established in the 1946 Convention. This gap was filled by the Convention on the Prevention and Punishment of Crimes against Internationally Protected Persons, including Diplomatic Agents (adopted on December 14, 1973, and entered into force in 1977; it currently has 102 states parties).
- UN experts enjoy immunity from arrest and detention during the period of their mission and immunity from jurisdiction for acts accomplished in the performance of their mission. This immunity from legal process continues even after the mission is over (Article 6, section 22).
- In addition to the immunities and privileges specified in this Convention, the Secretary-General and all Assistant Secretaries-General of the UN are granted the same immunities, exemptions and facilities as those accorded to diplomatic envoys, in accordance with international law (Article 5, section 19).

4. Immunities of Members of Peacekeeping Forces

The immunities foreseen for members of peacekeeping forces depend on their status, which is determined by the agreement signed between the UN and the country in which the operation will take place. The model agreements regulating the status of peacekeeping forces establish several different regimes:

- the special representative, the commander of the military branch of the peacekeeping operation, the chief of the civilian police, and the high-level officials cooperating with the special representative and the commander enjoy full diplomatic immunity;

- military observers, members of the UN civilian police, and civilian agents who are not civil servants enjoy the immunities foreseen for UN experts;
- the military personnel of national contingents assigned to the military branch of the peacekeeping operation enjoy immunity from jurisdiction for acts carried out in the exercise of their functions. This immunity remains in force, even after they are no longer members of the operation.

☞ The Secretary-General of the UN has the authority to waive the immunity of any official or expert. He has the right and the duty to do so in any case in which, in his opinion, the immunity would impede the course of justice and can be waived without prejudice to the interests of the United Nations. The Security Council of the UN has the right to waive the Secretary-General's immunity (Article 5, section 20, and Article 6, section 23, of 1946 Convention).

This point is particularly important given that, in numerous peacekeeping operations, military personnel fall under the double responsibility of the UN and their own national military hierarchy. This situation makes it more complicated to determine which mechanisms must be used to clarify their responsibility in cases in which crimes are committed against individuals that they had a mission to protect.

→ **Duty of commanders; Humanitarian and relief personnel; Impunity; Peacekeeping; Protection; Responsibility; Secretariat of the UN; War crimes/Crimes against humanity**

■ IMPUNITY

This term refers to situations in which there are no effective measures to penalize violations or when such measures are not enforced. Impunity may result from a political decision and amnesty regulation or from a judicial system that functions poorly or is disintegrating.

In international law, impunity most often results from the absence of judicial mechanisms that are capable of judging a failure to comply with established rules. The enforcement of penalties for crimes committed is most frequently carried out by domestic courts. It is therefore especially difficult to render justice on war crimes or crimes against humanity that were committed by government actors or people under their command in times of armed conflict.

The Fight against Impunity

To fight impunity, international and national criminal law establishes that certain crimes are not subject to any statute of limitations. This means that legal proceedings cannot be limited in time and can be initiated even if the acts remain unpunished for years.

Humanitarian law imposes on all states the obligation to pursue the perpetrators of grave violations of the Geneva Conventions (war crimes) and to prosecute them no matter what their nationality. This is the concept of universal jurisdiction.

Furthermore, for such serious crimes, humanitarian law forbids that amnesties be granted at the time of negotiation of peace accords or under any other circumstance.

(continues)

> *(continued)*
>
> Two ad hoc tribunals were established in 1993 and 1994 by the UN Security Council. They have jurisdiction over the crimes committed in the former Yugoslavia and Rwanda.
>
> The statute of a permanent International Criminal Court (ICC) was adopted in Rome in July 1998, as the result of a diplomatic conference organized under the aegis of the UN. The Court will be responsible for prosecuting individuals accused of the crime of genocide, war crimes, crimes against humanity, and aggression. It will function when states are unable or unwilling to carry out the investigation or prosecution. In this respect, the ICC will be at the forefront of the fight against impunity for these crimes. However, given the time needed for most states to ratify an international convention, it seems likely that the ICC will not be operational for several years.

→ **Amnesties; Genocide; Immunity; International Criminal Court; International Criminal Tribunals; Nonapplicability of statutory limitations; Penal sanctions under humanitarian law; Responsibility; Torture; Universal jurisdiction; War crimes/Crimes against humanity**

📖 **For Additional Information:**

Bassiouni, Cherif, ed. *Reining in Impunity for International Crimes and Serious Violations of Fundamental Human Rights: Proceedings of the Siracusa Conference, 17–21 September 1998.* Toulouse: Eres, 1998.
Roht-Arriaza, Naomi. *Impunity and Human Rights in International Law and Practice.* New York: Oxford University Press, 1995.

■ INALIENABILITY OF RIGHTS

Certain rights—namely, those in the category of human rights—are inalienable, or nonrenunciable. This means that a person cannot willingly renounce these rights. This principle also applies to humanitarian law. Persons protected by the Geneva Conventions may not, under any circumstance, renounce the rights secured for them by these Conventions, in part or in their entirety (common Article 7 of GCI, GCII, GCIII, and Article 8 of GCIV).

Human rights conventions establish lists of "nonderogable" rights that may not be infringed on in any manner.

→ **Fundamental guarantees**.

☞ Any document, no matter what kind, that contains a renunciation of an individual's fundamental rights is invalid.

→ **Fundamental guarantees; Human rights; Inviolability of rights; Natural law and positive law; Protected persons**

■ INDIVIDUAL RECOURSE

Individuals do not have an "international legal personality" that is recognized under international law, which was written to regulate the actions of states or certain international entities. However, international law does confer an international legal status on individuals, which grants them rights or serves to protects them. ➔ **Protection (international legal status of individuals)**

However, these rights—established by international humanitarian and human rights laws and conventions—can be invoked before very few international institutions or courts, though it is nonetheless possible, in certain situations, to submit cases to various international bodies.

➔ **Human rights**

Available Recourses in Case of Grave Breaches of Humanitarian Law and Torture

- Victims of war crimes may in principle bring cases before any national court on the basis of universal jurisdiction, as established by the four 1949 Geneva Conventions and the Convention against Torture. However, such complaints can only succeed if the state in question has brought its legislation into conformity with this international obligation.
- Victims of events that took place in the former Yugoslavia or in Rwanda cannot file complaints directly with the two ad hoc International Criminal Tribunals, but they can submit information to the Prosecutor. They do not benefit from the status of "victim" before these Tribunals but from that of "witness."
- Victims may not directly seize the International Fact-Finding Commission, which is responsible for investigating alleged grave breaches and serious violations of humanitarian law. They must address themselves to states parties, which alone may request that the Commission initiate an inquiry.
- Victims of war crimes, crimes against humanity, and acts of genocide will not be able to bring cases directly to the future International Criminal Court (ICC). However, victims, as well as witnesses and NGOs, will be able to transmit information to the Prosecutor of the ICC who, following certain conditions, can launch an investigation on his or her own initiative. The procedure will provide victims and witnesses with special protection. Furthermore, victims may be present during the trials, and they or their family may be awarded reparations. The ICC statute was adopted in July 1998 and will enter into force when sixty states have ratified it.
- For victims of certain human rights violations, there are some international or regional bodies to which they can have recourse.
- Victims of torture or victims of grave breaches of humanitarian law may also bring cases before any national court on the basis of universal jurisdiction, as established by the 1949 Geneva Conventions and the 1984 Torture Convention. Once again, however, such complaints can only succeed if the state in question has brought its legislation into conformity with this international obligation.

➔ **Human rights; International Fact-Finding Commission; Torture; War crimes/Crimes against humanity**

International law makes few provisions to award reparations to victims of violations of humanitarian law. Usually it refers cases to national courts' rulings or to voluntary ad hoc funds. In terms of human rights protection, there are more opportunities for individuals to have recourse to an international organ, whether judicial or not. Several such entities, usually treaty-monitoring bodies (listed later), accept claims or petitions filed by individuals. ➔ **Human rights; International Criminal Court**

1. Individual Recourse to Judicial Bodies

At an international level, there is no mechanism that can provide universal protection of human rights or punishment for violations thereof. There is no international court that has a mandate to receive complaints from individuals concerning human rights violations. Once in force, the International Criminal Court (ICC) will be able to receive information from individuals on allegations of crimes of genocide, war crimes, and crimes against humanity. However, such complaints will not automatically trigger a prosecution on the part of the ICC, unless the Prosecutor so decides and certain preconditions to the Court's exercise of jurisdiction have been met.

At the regional level, the only two judicial organs that exist are the Inter-American and the European Courts of Human Rights, and only the latter offers the possibility for individuals to bring cases directly before the Court. Since the European Convention's Protocol 11 entered into force in November 1998, all states party to the Convention (forty-one as of March 2001) must accept the Court's competence to receive individual applications (Article 34 of European Convention).

2. Individual Recourse before Nonjudicial Bodies

A network of regional and international institutions (commissions and committees) has been set up to protect and enforce respect for human rights. Some of these organs allow individuals to file communications or petitions. However, the obligation of states to accept individuals' right of petition depends on whether the act of ratifying the relevant treaty—to which the mechanism is attached (be it a convention or a statute)—makes such an acceptance mandatory or optional.

- Optional mechanisms that allow individual recourse only if the state has explicitly made a declaration to that effect:
  —the Committee against Torture (Article 22 of the Convention against Torture);
  —the European Commission on Human Rights (Article 25 of the European Convention on Human Rights); and
  —the Committee on the Elimination of Racial Discrimination (Article 14 of the Convention on the Elimination of Racial Discrimination).
- Mandatory mechanisms that allow individuals to file complaints against all states that have ratified the treaty in question:
  —Human Rights Committee (First Optional Protocol to the International Covenant on Civil and Political Rights);
  —African Commission on Human Rights (African Charter on Human and Peoples' Rights);
  —Inter-American Commission on Human Rights (American Convention on Human Rights);
  —In times of armed conflict, ICRC is mandated by the 1949 Geneva Conventions to receive individual claims concerning humanitarian law violations.

☞ In practice, the efficiency of the mechanisms that can receive communications from individuals remains limited because their competence to receive such complaints is often optional—dependent on states' explicit consent—and the procedures are subject to multiple admissibility conditions. Furthermore, only rulings by judicial organs (in other words, the European Court of Human Rights) are truly binding on the accused states.

3. Other Mechanisms

Other kinds of complaint mechanisms exist that can be triggered by states or NGOs. These are presented under the entries on ➔ **human rights; war crimes/crimes against humanity.**

➔ **African Charter on Human Rights; Commission on Human Rights; Committee against Torture; Committee on the Elimination of Racial Discrimination; Committee on the Rights of the Child; European Committee for the Prevention of Torture; European Court and Commission of Human Rights; Human rights; Human Rights Committee; Inter-American Court and Commission on Human Rights; International Criminal Court; International Criminal Tribunals; International Fact-Finding Commission; Penal sanctions in humanitarian law; Universal jurisdiction; War crimes/Crimes against humanity**

➔ **List of states party to international human rights and humanitarian conventions**

📖 **For Additional Information:**

Shelton, Dinah. *Remedies in International Human Rights Law.* Oxford: Oxford University Press, 1999.

■ INSURGENTS

The term *insurgents* describes a group of people who reject the authority of their state's government. As a result of their activities, the government may enact exceptional measures to preserve public order. In such circumstances, the unrest is not yet defined as an "armed conflict"; therefore, humanitarian law is not yet applicable. Nonetheless, certain human rights and fundamental freedoms must always be guaranteed. Humanitarian rules of the law of noninternational armed conflict can be enforced if the activities of the insurgents translate into acts of war of a certain intensity and duration, especially if they trigger military retaliation on the part of the official authorities.

To gain the status of "combatants," insurgents must meet the requirements established by humanitarian law in defining organized armed forces. In other words, they must have a command structure that is responsible for the group's conduct.

➔ **Combatants; Fundamental guarantees; Internal disturbances and tensions; International humanitarian law; Parties to the conflict; Prisoners of war**

■ INTER-AMERICAN COURT OF, AND COMMISSION ON, HUMAN RIGHTS

The American Convention on Human Rights (ACHR) was adopted on November 22, 1969, by the Organization of American States (OAS) and entered into force on July 18, 1978. The Convention formalizes the Inter-American system of human rights protection, resting on the Inter-American Commission on Human Rights and the Inter-American Court of Human Rights, per Article 33 of the ACHR. In general, cases are first brought before the Commission, which may then decide to refer them to the Court.

The Commission has competence over all states parties to the ACHR: twenty-five states have ratified the Convention, out of thirty-five that are currently members of the OAS. The Court only has jurisdiction over the states party to the Convention that have expressly accepted its jurisdiction, currently only seventeen (see the list of states at the end of this entry).

I. INTER-AMERICAN COMMISSION ON HUMAN RIGHTS

The Commission is based in Washington, D.C. It is composed of seven independent members, elected by the OAS General Assembly from a list of candidates proposed by the member states. Their terms last four years, and they can be reelected once. The Commission holds at least three sessions a year, usually in Washington, but they can be held elsewhere. It submits annual activity reports to the OAS General Assembly.

The Commission was actually established prior to the 1969 ACHR. It was created in 1959 on the basis of the American Declaration of the Rights and Duties of Man, adopted in Bogotá, Colombia, in 1948. However, the ACHR entrusts it with a mission to defend and promote human rights in the Americas (Articles 34–51 of the ACHR).

Its functions of protection are based on its mandate to receive, analyze, and investigate "petitions" from NGOs and individuals, or "communications" from states parties, concerning human rights violations by one of the states parties (Articles 44 and 45).

1. Admissibility

☞ The Commission's competence to examine individual and NGO petitions is automatic and therefore mandatory for all states party to the American Convention on Human Rights. This is an important difference from most other international human rights mechanisms, which make it optional for states to accept individual communications. These petitions may be filed by an individual or group of persons or an NGO.

The Commission's jurisdiction over state communications, however, is optional. This means that such communications are only admissible if both the state alleging the violations and the state accused of the violations have declared that they recognize the Commission's competence to receive such communications (Article 45 of ACHR). Only ten states have currently made such declarations (see the end of Section I).

For communications and petitions to be admissible, there are requirements, which are established by Article 46 of the ACHR: they must not be anonymous; the subject of the petition or communication must not be pending before another international body; domestic legal remedies must have been pursued and exhausted; and the petition or communication must be lodged within six months of the date the final judgment from the local remedy has been pronounced. The last two requirements are not applicable if "the domestic legislation of the state concerned does not afford due process of law for the protection of the right or rights that have allegedly been violated; the party alleging violation of his [or her] rights has been denied access to the remedies under domestic law or has been prevented from exhausting them; or there has been unwarranted delay in rendering a final judgment under the aforementioned remedies" (Article 46.2 of ACHR).

Any individual, group of individuals, or NGO can file a petition or complaint. States can do so only if both they and the accused state have expressly recognized the Commission's competence to receive such communications (Article 45 of ACHR).

2. Procedure

The Commission's purpose is not to issue a judgment or sentence, since it is not a judicial organ. Instead, it seeks to reach friendly settlements in light of written and oral information transmitted, on the Commission's request, by the state concerned by the complaints. In "serious and urgent cases," the Commission may conduct on-site investigations, with the prior consent of the state in whose territory a violation was allegedly committed. In other situations, on-site visits to countries remain an instrument that the Commission can use to engage in more in-depth analysis of the situation, but they are the result of prior examination of the matter (Article 48 of ACHR).

If a friendly settlement is reached, the Commission draws up a report, transmits it to the petitioner and to all states party to the Convention, and submits it for publication to the OAS Secretary-General, including a brief statement of the facts and the solution reached (Article 49).

If no settlement is reached, the Commission draws up a report setting forth the facts and its conclusions, including any proposals and recommendations it sees as appropriate. This report is not public. If, within three months, the case has not been settled or submitted to the Inter-American Court of Human Rights by the Commission or one of the parties to the dispute, the Commission may continue its examination and investigation of the case. In such cases, it prepares a second report, which also generally contains conclusions and recommendations, and again grants the state a period of time to resolve the situation and comply with the Commission's recommendations. At the end of this second period of time, the Commission decides whether the state has taken the appropriate measures and whether to publish its report.

Instead of preparing a second report, the Commission may decide to take the case to the Inter-American Court, which it must do within three months of the date at which it transmits its initial report to the State concerned. The Commission appears before the Court for all cases.

The states that have currently recognized the Commission's competence to receive state communications are Argentina, Bolivia, Chile, Colombia, Costa Rica, Ecuador, Jamaica, Peru, Uruguay, Venezuela.

3. Other Functions of the Commission

Under its mandate to "promote respect for and defense of human rights," the Commission also

- observes the general human rights situation in the member states and publishes special reports when it considers it appropriate;
- promotes public awareness regarding human rights in the Americas, including publishing studies on subjects such as the independence of the judiciary, activities of irregular armed groups, and human rights conditions of children, women, and indigenous peoples;
- recommends to the OAS member states that they adopt certain measures that would contribute to human rights protection;
- responds to states parties' inquiries on matters related to human rights;
- requests that the Court order "provisional measures" in urgent cases that involve danger to persons, even where a case has not yet been submitted to the Court;
- requests advisory opinions from the Court, on the interpretation of the ACHR (Article 41).

II. INTER-AMERICAN COURT OF HUMAN RIGHTS

The Court, based in San José, Costa Rica, is the judicial organ of the Inter-American system of human rights protection. It was established by the 1969 American Convention on Human Rights but was actually set up in 1979, after the Convention entered into force. It is composed of seven independent judges, elected to six-year terms (they can be reelected once) by the states party to the American Convention on Human Rights.

The judges hold two regular sessions per year, but they may also meet in special sessions. They elect their president and vice president to two-year terms (they can also be reelected once). They appoint their secretary, whose staff is appointed by the Secretary-General of the OAS, in consultation with the secretary. The Court adopted its Rules of Procedure in 1980 and revised them in 1991 and 1993.

1. Advisory and Contentious Jurisdiction

At the request of OAS member states, the Court is competent to issue advisory opinions regarding the interpretation of the ACHR and other treaties concerning the protection of human rights in the Americas and any question relating to the jurisdiction of OAS organs. In particular, it may give opinions on the compatibility of domestic laws with these human rights instruments to requesting states.

It also has contentious jurisdiction over alleged violations of the ACHR, and it monitors states' application of the Convention. However, the Court's jurisdiction is not automatically binding on states, except for the seventeen states that have expressly accepted its jurisdiction (see the end of Section II).

☞ The Court's jurisdiction over cases of violations is optional for states party to the ACHR (Article 62 of ACHR). This means that states can either accept the Court's jurisdiction as binding, ipso facto (as seventeen states have now done, under Article 62.1 of the ACHR), or recognize its competence for a specified period of time or for specific cases, on the condition of reciprocity (as per Article 62.2. of the ACHR).

Only the Commission and states party to the ACHR can refer cases to the Court. Individuals or NGOs can only have access to the Court by lodging petitions with the Commission and waiting for the Commission's procedure to be completed.

The complaints that the Commission refers to the Court are those for which the Commission found no friendly settlement and for which the states in question accept the Court's jurisdiction. The Commission's screening of cases is actually part of the admissibility test of a case.

The judgments rendered by the Inter-American Court of Human Rights can include compensation for the injured party. International human rights mechanisms rarely provide such a possibility.

---

2. Judgments

If the Court finds that there has been a violation of a right or freedom protected by the ACHR, it rules that "the injured party be ensured the enjoyment" of the right or freedom that was violated. It may also rule that the measure or situation that constituted or resulted in the breach be remedied, and that fair compensation be paid to the injured party (Article 63.1 of ACHR). The Court's judgments are final and not subject to appeal. The OAS General Assembly is responsible for monitoring the implementation of these rulings (Article 67).

In extremely serious and urgent cases, the Court may adopt provisional measures to protect individuals in matters under its consideration. It may also do so on request of the Commission for cases that have not yet been submitted to it (Article 63.2).

The Court submits an annual report to the General Assembly of the OAS. In particular, it must specify the cases in which a state has not complied with the Court's judgments and make any pertinent recommendations (Article 65). The OAS may choose to signal which states failed to comply with these decisions.

The states that have accepted the Court's contentious jurisdiction ipso facto are Argentina, Bolivia, Chile, Colombia, Costa Rica, Ecuador, El Salvador, Guatemala, Honduras, Nicaragua, Panama, Paraguay, Peru, Suriname, Trinidad and Tobago, Uruguay, and Venezuela.

→   **Human rights; Individual recourse**
→   **List of states party to international human rights and humanitarian conventions (No. 9)**

✎   Inter-American Commission on Human Rights
      Organization of American States (OAS)
      1889 F St., NW
      Washington, D.C. 20006 U.S.A.
      Tel.: (1) 202 458-6002
      Fax: (1) 202 458-3992
      Secretariat of the Inter-American Court of Human Rights
      PO Box 6906-1000
      San José, Costa Rica
      Tel.: (506) 234-0581
      Fax: (506) 234-0584
@   Organization of American States: www.oas.org
      Inter-American Commission of Human Rights: www.cidh.oas.org

■ INTERNAL DISTURBANCES AND TENSIONS

Situations described in international law as "internal disturbances and tensions" are those in which the level of violence has not yet reached an intensity qualifying the situation as an armed conflict. This means that the law of armed conflict—humanitarian law—is not applicable. Situations of internal disturbances and tensions describe acts such as riots and isolated and sporadic acts of violence (PII Article 1.2).

☞ Humanitarian law is not applicable in situations where isolated and sporadic acts of violence and riots present a level of violence that is below the level that qualifies as a "conflict" and where such acts are not committed by organized armed groups capable of carrying out sustained and concerted operations.

In such situations, it may become difficult to protect all the rights of the population since the government may adopt exceptional measures that allow it to derogate from certain responsibilities and that constrain public liberties.

Certain fundamental guarantees remain enforceable, however, and continue to protect individuals. These are the human rights considered to be nonderogable and the principles contained in common Article 3 of the four 1949 Geneva Conventions.

→   **Fundamental guarantees; Situations and persons not expressly covered by humanitarian law**

1. Internal Disturbances

Internal disturbances are situations in which there is serious or lasting internal confrontation. In such situations, which do not necessarily escalate into open struggle, the authorities may use large police forces and even the armed forces to restore order within the country. They may also adopt exceptional legislative measures that give more authority to police and armed forces.

Internal disturbances differ from situations characterized as internal armed conflict because no dissident armed forces or other organized armed groups have formed, which carry out sustained and concerted operations (PII Article 1.1), though dissident groups may exist that are organized and visible. Humanitarian law is therefore not applicable, except for the principles established in Article 3, common to all four 1949 Geneva Conventions (known as common Article 3).

The protection of human rights may suffer many derogations due to exceptional legislative measures. However, certain fundamental rights and freedoms, known as nonderogable or inviolable rights, may not be derogated from under any circumstances.

2. Internal Tensions

"Internal tensions" are considered less serious than internal disturbances. Such situations are mostly characterized by high levels of tension (e.g., political, religious, racial, ethnic, social, economic). Such situations often precede or follow periods of conflict.

In times of internal tension, any force employed by the authorities must be of a preventive nature only. Such times may be characterized by

- a large number of arrests,
- a large number of political prisoners,
- probable ill treatment of detained persons,
- allegations concerning disappearances, and
- the declaration of a state of emergency.

In such situations, unlike in internal disturbances, the opposition to the regime is rarely organized in a visible manner.

There are certain human rights from which no derogation is allowed, no matter what the internal condition of the state may be and what exceptional measures the government may have implemented. Even though the level of violence is not intense enough to trigger the implementation of humanitarian law (PII Article 1.2)—except for common Article 3—these nonderogable rights must be protected.

→ **Fundamental guarantees; Insurgents; Parties to the conflict; Resistance movements; Situations and persons not expressly covered by humanitarian law; State of emergency/State of siege**

📖 **For Additional Information:**

Gasser, Hans-Peter. "Humanitarian Standards for Internal Strife: A Brief Review of Developments." *International Review of the Red Cross* 294 (May–June 1993): 221–26.

■ INTERNALLY DISPLACED PERSONS

Conflicts and other situations of political or economic tension often cause population movements as they flee persecution or violence. The applicable law varies depending on whether the individuals in question crossed an international border. If they do, they become refugees and are covered by international refugee law. If not, they become "internally displaced persons" (IDPs). There is no specific protection for IDPs foreseen under international law, but if they are displaced due to a conflict, they are covered under humanitariam law, as civilians.

☞ Individuals who have crossed an international border are refugees or immigrants. They are then covered by international refugee and national immigration laws.

If individuals become displaced inside their country of origin, they are called "internally displaced persons" (IDPs). According to the Special Representative of the UN Secretary-General on displaced persons, there are approximately twenty to twenty-five million IDPs in more than forty countries.

IDPs do not constitute a distinct legal category and therefore do not benefit from any specific protection under international law. In principle, they are still under the protection of their national laws, but the state itself may be the source of their displacement.

There is a legal framework, however, within which their protection should be undertaken:

- in times of peace, they remain under the protection of their national laws and human rights conventions.
- in times of conflict, they are protected by humanitarian law, as civilians.
→ **Fundamental guarantees**

Most states tend to do everything they can to avoid large-scale flows of individuals across their borders, whether due to a conflict or other situations. The UN Security Council qualified the mass exodus of Kurdish people who tried to flee from Iraq to Turkey in 1991 and remained stuck in the Kurd mountains as a threat to the peace and security of the region. The same occurred in the former Yugoslavia in 1993 and in Rwanda in 1994. Hence, individuals now most often move within the borders of their own country in an attempt to flee the consequences of conflicts or tensions.

1. Insufficient International Responsibility for Internally Displaced Persons

While refugees come under the mandate of UNHCR, there is no international institution with a general mandate, or one with the overall means, to protect and provide concrete assistance to individuals displaced within their own state. Yet, many of them face the same needs of assistance and protection as refugees.

The mandate of UNHCR was expanded several times by the UN General Assembly, to enable it to take charge of situations concerning IDPs. With the government's agreement, UNHCR can set up material assistance programs for IDPs; however, there is no permanent legal instrument aimed at protecting individuals in such situations. UNHCR's protective role therefore depends entirely on the negotiation and content of the ad hoc agreements that must be signed with the government concerned. This means that UNHCR's actions, and any form of protection aimed at such populations, are largely dependent on the goodwill of states.

In 1992, a Special Representative to the UN Secretary-General was nominated specifically to follow the issue of IDPs. The mandate, currently held by Francis Deng, consists of examining IDPs' conditions and suggesting a normative and institutional framework to stimulate action in their favor. He compiled humanitarian law, human rights, and refugee law rules that are applicable to IDPs. He also studied the rules prohibiting arbitrary displacement of populations and, at the 1998 session of the UN Commission on Human Rights, presented a set of Guiding Principles on Internal Displacement, aimed at clarifying and consolidating displaced persons' rights.

His mandate is limited, since Special Representatives have no direct protection or assistance functions toward the IDPs. Nevertheless, NGOs can transmit information concerning human rights and humanitarian law violations committed against IDPs to him.

In 1998, a Senior Adviser on IDPs was also appointed at the Office for Coordination of Humanitarian Affairs of the UN (OCHA), currently Dennis McNamara.

☞ Currently, internally displaced persons receive assistance as the result of simultaneous actions by several agencies, which are able to divide up the responsibilities in organizing relief actions. However, this has led to a dilution of the responsibilities taken in terms of protecting this population.

Worse yet, the multiplication of agencies present on the ground in situations involving many IDPs tends to lend a sense of normalcy to the situation, from a diplomatic point of view, which hinders the official recognition of an actual state of war. Such recognition would trigger the application of humanitarian law and hence formally open the right to assistance and protection to which IDPs—as civilians in a conflict—are entitled.

The apparent normalization of a situation can be dangerous since the protection of IDPs depends on the definition of their rights and of the different humanitarian actors' responsibilities with regard to the specific protection needs faced by these populations. In practice, the recognition of a state of conflict is what enables humanitarian law to be the basis for their protection. The agencies and relief organizations working with the displaced persons can contribute to the recognition of such a situation.

The massacre that took place in a camp of IDPs in Kibeho, Rwanda, in April 1995 is an example of the potential danger that can result from the inadequate determination of responsibilities. When the Rwandan army committed the massacre, the mandate for protection over this group was scattered among too many actors: the UN military forces (UNAMIR—the UN Assistance Mission for Rwanda) oversaw the physical protection of the camps (which did not necessarily include the individuals inside them); UNHCR's authority was only recognized for refugees returning to Rwanda, not for displaced persons who had never left the territory; the UN human rights observers only had a mission to observe, not protect. Above all, it was declared that the country was not in a situation of conflict, the ICRC was absent, and the government did not consider itself under any obligation vis-à-vis this population.

In certain cases, IDPs are gathered into specific zones or areas, whether spontaneously or as the result of international or national pressure, where they are meant to be protected. Depending on the status given to these zones, they may either come under the protection of humanitarian law or, conversely, find themselves more exposed to the dangers of war.

→ **Camps; Protected areas and zones**

2. In Times of Peace or Unrest

In times of peace, of internal disturbances or tensions, or if the authorities concerned have not formally recognized a conflict situation, individuals remain under the sole protection of their domestic laws and of human rights conventions. However, for various reasons, international human rights norms do not constitute a sufficient legal framework to protect persons displaced within their own country:

- Except for the fundamental guarantees (or "nonderogable" rights and freedoms), states can suspend the application of a majority of human rights in times of internal disturbances.
- Human rights conventions do not set forth concrete relief measures to assist such persons, nor do they posit any rights for humanitarian organizations or personnel.
- Any issue related to large-scale use of force (e.g., means and methods of warfare) is not covered by human rights regulations.
- Human rights rules apply only to state authorities, whereas humanitarian law applies to all belligerents, regardless of their status or nature.
- There are very few control mechanisms in the field of human rights, and those that exist are set up to determine the existence of violations more than to prevent them. Nevertheless, at all times, including situations of unrest that do not qualify as actual armed conflicts, IDPs are protected by the fundamental guarantees set forth by humanitarian law and the nonderogable rights established in human rights conventions.

→ **Fundamental guarantees; Human rights**

3. In Times of Conflict

If IDPs are victims of a situation of conflict, they can benefit from the protection of humanitarian law by virtue of their civilian status. → **Civilians; Protected persons; Protection**

The laws of international and internal armed conflict take into consideration the fact that armed combat may cause significant population movements. However, the displacement of certain minority communities may be a deliberate policy or military objective, in and of itself, which is why humanitarian law decrees specific rules to protect the fate of IDPs:

- it prohibits forced population displacement;
- it prohibits methods of warfare the primary purpose of which is to spread terror among the civilian population;
- it regulates the conduct of hostilities to prevent military harassment of the civilian population in general, or of certain groups in particular, from causing an exodus or wanderings;
- it authorizes and regulates the provision of relief supplies for civilians so that they will not need to flee because of a shortage of goods essential to their survival;
- finally, it establishes that, at any time and in any place, internally displaced persons must enjoy the fundamental guarantees of humanitarian law. IDPs can thus benefit from the right to international assistance and protection.

These rules, drawn from the Geneva Conventions and their Protocols, are expressly meant to be applied by the ICRC; however, they should be defended by all agencies and organizations present in such situations. The government in question cannot refuse the presence of the ICRC or NGOs.

➜ **Assistance; Camps; Fundamental guarantees; Human rights; International humanitarian law; Population displacement; Protected areas and zones; Protected persons; Protection; Refugees; Relief; Special Rapporteurs**

📖 **For Additional Information:**

Deng, Francis M. *Internally Displaced Persons: Report of the Representative of the Secretary General, Compilation and Analysis of Legal Norms*. Geneva: UNHCR, 1995.

Haroff-Tavel, Marion. "Action Taken by the ICRC in Situations of Violence." *International Review of the Red Cross* 294 (May–June 1993): 195–220.

Herczegh, Geza. "State of Emergency and Humanitarian Law—On Article 75 of Additional Protocol I." *International Review of the Red Cross* 242 (September–October 1984): 263–73.

Kalin, Walter. "Protection in International Human Rights Law." In *Internally Displaced Persons Symposium, 23–25 October 1995,* ed. Jean-Philippe Lavoyer. Geneva: ICRC, 1996, 15–25.

Lavoyer, Jean-Philippe. "Protection under International Humanitarian Law." In *Internally Displaced Persons Symposium, 23–25 October 1995*, ed. Jean-Philippe Lavoyer. Geneva: ICRC, 1996, 26–36.

———. "Refugees and Internally Displaced Persons. International Humanitarian Law and the Role of the ICRC." *International Review of the Red Cross* 305 (March–April): 162–80.

UNHCR. *The State of the World's Refugees, 1997–98: A Humanitarian Agenda*. New York: Oxford University Press, 1997, 99–142.

■ INTERNATIONAL ARMED CONFLICT

This term describes armed conflicts between two or more states (GCI–IV common Article 2). Wars of national liberation in which a people is fighting against colonial domination, foreign occupation, or racist regimes are also defined as international armed conflicts. In general, this is also the case for wars resulting from people's attempts to exercise their right to self-determination (PI Article 1).

The rules of humanitarian law were developed mainly in the context of international armed conflict. Today, the regulations for these conflicts are still the most detailed, establishing limitations on the means and methods of warfare and imposing obligations on the parties to the conflict in terms of relief and protection of civilian populations. They regulate the rights of humanitarian organization and the punishment of war crimes.

> ☞ The definition and recognition of an international armed conflict are crucial because they enable the implementation and enforcement of the rules of humanitarian law for such conflicts.
>
> An internal armed conflict may also become internationalized if a multinational peacekeeping force becomes involved on the territory.

The rules applicable in situations of international armed conflict are based mainly on the four Geneva Conventions of 1949 and Additional Protocol I of 1977.

➜ **Geneva Conventions of 1949 and Protocols Additional I and II of 1977; International humanitarian law; Legal status of the parties to the conflict; Noninternational armed conflict; Situations and persons not expressly covered by humanitarian law; Special agreement**

■ INTERNATIONAL CONVENTIONS

An *international convention* is a written agreement between two or more states, establishing their obligations and rights in a specific domain. Various other terms can be used as well, such as *treaty, agreement,* and so on. National governments choose the content of conventions, since they decide whether to adopt them, with one important restriction: the provisions of a convention must not contradict the *jus cogens* or peremptory norms that bind all states. Furthermore, all states, having adhered to the UN Charter, accept that the UN Charter prevails over any other international agreement (Article 103 of UN Charter). → **Hierarchy of norms; International law**

International conventions pertain to the body of "hard law," which is made up of the rules and regulations developed and adopted with the participation and explicit consent of the states or other actors who will be bound by these rules. It stands in contrast with "soft law," which embodies the kinds of international agreements that are called *declarations* or *recommendations,* for instance. One of the main differences between hard law and soft law is that the conventions that fall under the first category require that states ratify them, which makes them binding on the states.

In general, the rules governing the application of international conventions are codified in the Vienna Convention on the Law of Treaties, adopted in Vienna on May 23, 1969, and entered into force on January 27, 1980.

1. Ratification

After a treaty has been negotiated, drafted, and signed, states must ratify it in order to become parties to it. The act of ratification (which may also take the form of accession or succession) represents the approval of the relevant national organs. In most cases, ratification procedures involve the head of state, often with the authorization of the parliament or senate. The act of ratification binds the state internationally to its obligations because it reflects its consent to be bound by the treaty in question. Most conventions enter into force only after a specific number of states—determined in the convention itself—have ratified it, though in some cases it may enter into force immediately for each state as it ratifies the convention.

Even once a convention has entered into force, it does not always immediately have an impact on the internal order. At the time of ratification, states have the obligation to incorporate the provisions of the treaty into their domestic legislation or to modify their laws so as to bring them into conformity with the commitments contracted by ratifying, unless their laws are already in compliance with their obligations under the convention. The only exception to having to adapt the national laws is if the convention is "self-executing" and the country's legislation provides for the automatic incorporation of such conventions into its body of law.

Self-Executing and Non-Self-Executing Treaties

- States are under the obligation to ensure that their national laws are in conformity with international law. When a state ratifies a treaty, the treaty may either immediately become part of the domestic laws, through a system known as *automatic incorporation,* or it may have to be enacted into legislation, through the system of *legislative incorporation.*
- Treaties (or some of their provisions) can sometimes be "self-executing." This means that their provisions are precise enough to be implemented directly, without

(continues)

(*continued*)

interpretation. In states with legislation or a constitution allowing automatic incorporation of international norms, the provisions of self-executing treaties are enforceable in
the domestic courts of the state as soon as it ratifies the convention. An individual may
therefore invoke these treaties before national courts even if there has been no implementing legislation.

On the other hand, conventions or their provisions can be (and generally are) "non-
self-executing," even in states with automatic incorporation, because they require interpretation. In such cases, national legislation must be adapted or enacted to integrate the
international norms into the domestic laws.

---

2. Legal Status of International Conventions

The provisions of international conventions are binding on states parties.

The "rank" assigned to international law in relation to national law varies from state to state.
However, states must be consistent with their international commitments and integrate the provisions of international conventions into domestic legislation. As a consequence, most states consider
that international laws are superior to national laws (except, perhaps, for their constitution). This is
important to ensure that states can meet their international obligations without being hindered by
domestic laws in contradiction with the principle of the international conventions in question.

It is crucial to take the hierarchy of norms into account, particularly if one set of rules seems
to violate the spirit of a higher norm. ➔ **Hierarchy of norms**

3. Reciprocity

The implementation of international agreements usually rests on the reciprocal engagements
taken by states. If one state violates its obligations, the other states parties may invoke this failure to respect the law in order to dispense themselves of these same obligations vis-à-vis the
party that committed the violation.

Conventions relating to human rights and humanitarian law make an exception to this rule. In
fact, the 1969 Vienna Convention establishes special rules for "provisions relating to the protection
of the human person contained in treaties of a humanitarian character." In such cases, a state may
not justify its own failure to respect its obligations by invoking another state's violations of the law.

This specificity is derived from the fact that human rights and humanitarian law conventions
establish objective rights for individuals and other nonstate entities, as well as for states. As a
consequence, states cannot bargain with the respect or nonrespect of these rights. For instance,
a state may never carry out a reprisal against a state or party to a conflict if that reprisal constitutes a violation of humanitarian law, even if the adverse party violated the same law. In other
words, the duty to enforce humanitarian law is not tied to obligations of reciprocity, and all parties to a conflict are held to their humanitarian obligations even if the adversary is not bound by
the Geneva Conventions or is not respecting them.

Humanitarian law establishes certain specific provisions to this effect:

- The 1949 Geneva Conventions and their 1977 Protocols establish that states "undertake to respect and to ensure respect for" humanitarian law in all circumstances (GCI–IV common Ar-

ticle 1; PI Article 1.1). This formulation clearly indicates that the obligation to respect these conventions is mandatory and is not subject to conditions of reciprocity.

- The fact that a party to a conflict denounces the Conventions and renounces its obligations thereunder does not relieve any other party to the conflict of its obligation to respect humanitarian law (GCI Article 63; GCII Article 62; GCIII Article 142; GCIV Article 158; PI Article 99).
- The High Contracting Parties to the Geneva Conventions are internationally recognized states. In practice, however, parties to a conflict may not be states. This is particularly true of civil war situations, in which a government faces a rebellion. The fact that a party to the conflict has not ratified the relevant conventions of humanitarian law (whether because it is not a state actor or because it has not ratified the Conventions) must not in any way limit the application of such law. The Geneva Conventions are hence applicable to all parties to the conflict, regardless of their legal status, and without in any way affecting their legal status (GCI–IV common Article 3; PI Article 1.1).
- The Geneva Conventions also apply this principle of nonreciprocity to issues of criminal responsibility. "No High Contracting Party shall be allowed to absolve itself or any other High Contracting Party of any liability incurred by itself or by another High Contracting Party" with respect to alleged grave breaches of humanitarian law (GCIV Article 148).

➔ **High Contracting Parties; Legal status of the parties to the conflict; Parties to the conflict; Reprisals; Respect for international humanitarian law**

4. Reservations

A *reservation* is a unilateral statement made by a state, whereby it purports to exclude or modify the legal effect of certain provisions of a convention on that state. States may make reservations concerning entire articles of a convention or words, sentences, and so on.

Restrictions on reservations are clearly determined in the conventions themselves. The general rules governing such restrictions were codified by the 1969 Vienna Convention (Article 19):

- the treaty may prohibit reservations;
- the treaty may establish that only specified reservations may be made;
- reservations that are incompatible with the object and purpose of the treaty in question are prohibited.

When a state formulates a reservation, the legal consequences of the reservation depend on the acceptance or objection of other states:

- If the reservation is accepted, it is applicable only to the state that formulated the reservation (the "reserving state"). If the reservation was made with regard to a specific article, the treaty enters into force for the reserving state and is in force between that state and states parties that have accepted the reservation without the article in question.
- If another state makes a simple objection to the reservation, it does not prevent the treaty from entering into force for the reserving state. However, the provisions to which the reservation relates do not apply between the two states, and a compromise acceptable to both will have to be found.
- If a state makes an explicit objection to a reservation, it prevents the entire treaty from entering into force between itself and the reserving state, hence precluding any link between the two states via this convention.

Allowing reservations sometimes helps encourage more states to ratify a treaty but, conversely, may threaten the very nature of the treaty. Furthermore, it means that the actual content and obligations defined in a treaty are not the same for all states.

To limit the extent to which reservations may be used, humanitarian and human rights conventions prefer to use a system of optional articles or protocols. These usually involve issues concerning complaints, investigations, or treaty-monitoring procedures. Hence, states may become parties to conventions without having to adhere to such mechanisms.

5. Interpretation of Conventions

A convention, like any legal text, is subject to interpretation when it is implemented. Often, each adverse party tries to use the law to its advantage and may reach contradictory interpretations. It is therefore important that rules of interpretation be established by states with regard to each convention.

a. Rules for Interpreting Treaties

The Vienna Convention establishes the following principle (Article 31):

- A treaty must be interpreted in good faith, in the light of its object and purpose.
- A treaty must also be interpreted on the basis of the intention of the drafters. It is therefore important to refer to the spirit and context in which the rules were formulated.

The provisions of a convention that establishes rules for the protection of individuals must never be interpreted in a way that infringes on or limits this protection. The 1949 Geneva Conventions take the precaution of referring to this principle (GCI–III Article 9, GCIV Article 10, and PI Article 75.8).

In practice, it is useful for nongovernmental actors to know these principles of interpretation so as to be able to contest interpretations that states may make in order to justify their behavior. It is simply "easier" for a state to ignore the existence of an obligation by making a biased interpretation of the law than to admit and assume a violation thereof.

> ☞ The Vienna Convention on the Law of Treaties—adopted in Vienna on May 23, 1969, and entered into force on January 27, 1980—sets forth the general rules that govern international treaties, including the manner in which they should be interpreted. The Convention thus limits the risk of each state giving a different interpretation to a treaty and the obligations to which it has committed. It is an important tool to counter cynicism and bad faith in the interpretation of international law, and it can also be used in negotiations concerning humanitarian action.

b. Interpretive bodies

In international law, states both make the laws and interpret them. There is no centralized and compulsory organ responsible for interpreting treaties or ruling on the law to be applied, but several options are possible.

- States may agree to submit their disputes concerning the interpretation of international treaties to the International Court of Justice (Article 36.2.a of ICJ statute).
- Certain international human rights conventions provide specific mechanisms of interpretation that states are free to accept or not:
  — the European Court of Human Rights is competent to interpret the European Convention for the Protection of Human Rights and Fundamental Freedoms (Article 45 of the European Convention);
  — the Inter-American Court of Human Rights is competent to interpret the American Convention on Human Rights "and other treaties concerning the protection of human rights in the American states" (Article 64 of American Convention);
  — the African Commission on Human and People's Rights is competent to interpret the African Charter on Human and Peoples' Rights (Article 45 of African Charter).
- The Geneva Conventions entrust the ICRC with a certain responsibility in terms of interpreting the Conventions: they establish that, if parties to a conflict disagree on the interpretation of the provisions of the Conventions, the Protecting Powers must lend their good offices with a view to settling the dispute, in the interest of the protected persons (GCI–III Article 11 and GCIV Article 12). In the absence of a Protecting Power, the Conventions establish that the International Committee of the Red Cross will act as substitute Protecting Power and take on its functions.

➔ **African Commission on Human and People's Rights; European Court (and Commission) of Human Rights; Inter-American Court of (and Commission on) Human Rights; International Court of Justice; International law; Protecting Powers**

6. Monitoring the Implementation of Conventions

Some conventions create an organ responsible for monitoring their implementation. Depending on the convention, states, individuals, or organizations may refer complaints to these organs in case of violations of the treaty. Such monitoring bodies may be judicial, in which case they may render a ruling on the violation and sanction it, or nonjudicial (more frequently in the area of human rights and humanitarian law), in which case the procedures are generally of a recommendatory nature.

The available recourses in case of violations of humanitarian law and human rights are elaborated in the entries on ➔ **human rights; individual recourse** and under the headings of the different courts, commissions, and committees in this domain.

➔ **African Commission on Human and People's Rights; Commission on Human Rights; Committee against Torture; Committee on the Elimination of Discrimination against Women; Committee on the Elimination of Racial Discrimination; Committee on the Rights of the Child; European Committee for the Prevention of Torture; European Court of Human Rights; Human rights; Human Rights Committee; Individual recourse; Inter-American Court of (and Commission on) Human Rights; International Court of Justice; International Criminal Court; International Fact-Finding Commission**

📖 **For Additional Information:**

Brownlie, Ian. *Principles of Public International Law*, 4th ed. Oxford: Clarendon, 1990, 603–34.

■ INTERNATIONAL COURT OF JUSTICE (ICJ)

Established under Chapter XIV of the UN Charter, the International Court of Justice (ICJ) is the judicial organ of the UN, set up to settle disputes between states that have accepted its jurisdiction. The seat of the Court is at The Hague.

The ICJ applies rules of international law but may also, if the parties to the dispute agree, base its judgment on broader notions of "fairness" (Article 38 of ICJ statute). Its ruling then resembles an arbitration more than a judgment.

The decisions of the ICJ are binding on the states party to the dispute. The Security Council has the authority to implement measures to enforce a judgment rendered by the ICJ (Article 94 of UN Charter).

☞ Individuals and nonstate entities may not refer matters to the ICJ and may not be judged by it. (The ICJ should not be confused with the International Criminal Court, which can receive information from such entities.)

- The ICJ renders decisions on disputes between states, as long as the states concerned have accepted its jurisdiction.
- For states, the jurisdiction of the Court is not compulsory, although if they accept to submit a case to it, its decisions are binding.
- In addition to rulings on disputes, the ICJ may give advisory opinions on the interpretation of treaties or any other question of international law (Article 36.2.a and b of ICJ statute).

I. COMPOSITION

The ICJ is composed of fifteen judges elected for nine years by the General Assembly and the Security Council of the UN. The composition of the judges should endeavor to ensure that the principal legal systems of the world are represented (Articles 3, 4.1, and 9 of ICJ statute).

II. JURISDICTION

1. Contentious Cases between States

All member states of the UN are ipso facto parties to statute of the ICJ (Article 93.1 of UN Charter); however, acceptance of the ICJ's jurisdiction remains optional. This means that states must specifically agree to refer questions of law or fact over which they are in dispute with other states to the Court and then submit to its decision on that case. States can accept the jurisdiction of the ICJ in different ways:

- Permanent jurisdiction: at any time, states may make a formal declaration that they recognize ipso facto the jurisdiction of the Court as compulsory, with regard to all disputes and without reference to any dispute in particular. In so doing, they agree to submit to the Court all legal disputes with any other state that accepts the same obligation. The Court then has jurisdiction to rule on all legal matters concerning the interpretation of a treaty, any question of international law, the existence of any fact that, if established, would constitute a breach of an international obligation, and the nature or extent of reparations to be made for such a breach (Article 36.2 of ICJ statute).

- Case-by-case jurisdiction: in the case of a dispute, the states concerned may also agree to submit that particular case to the jurisdiction of the court (Article 36.1 of ICJ statute).
- More than three hundred international treaties include provisions to refer state disputes or questions of interpretation to the ICJ.

2. Referrals and Advisory Opinions

If, when investigating solutions for the pacific settlement of a dispute, the Security Council finds a matter to be of a mostly legal nature, it may recommend that the parties to the dispute refer their case to the ICJ (Article 36.2 of ICJ statute; Articles 33 and 36.3 of UN Charter).

The General Assembly and the Security Council of the UN may request an advisory opinion on any legal question. Other UN organs and its specialized agencies may do so as well, after authorization by the General Assembly (Article 96 of UN Charter). Today, there are twenty-one such UN bodies.

Under no circumstance is the court available to individuals or NGOs. In the case of judgments on contentious cases and decisions over disputes, only states may have recourse to the court (Article 34.1 of ICJ statute). The Court may give advisory opinions on any legal questions to authorized international organizations (Article 65.1 of ICJ statute).

Other tribunals or recourses exist for the enforcement of specific international conventions. Most recently, two ad hoc International Criminal Tribunals were established by the Security Council of the UN to prosecute individuals accused of crimes committed in the former Yugoslavia and in Rwanda, and, in July 1998, the statute of a permanent International Criminal Court was adopted in Rome.

→ **Arbitration; Economic and Social Council of the UN; European Court of Human Rights; General Assembly of the UN; Hierarchy of norms; Individual recourse; Inter-American Court and Commission of Human Rights; International conventions; International Criminal Court; International Criminal Tribunals; International Fact-Finding Commission; Penal sanctions in humanitarian law; Secretariat/Secretary-General of the UN; Security Council of the UN; United Nations; Universal jurisdiction; War crimes/Crimes against humanity**

For Additional Information:

Elias, Taslim Olawale. *The International Court of Justice and Some Contemporary Problems: Essays on International Law*. The Hague: Martinus Nijhoff, 1983.
Rosenne, Shabtai. *The World Court: What It Is and How It Works*. The Hague: Martinus Nijhoff, 1995.

✎ International Court of Justice
   Palais de la Paix
   NL 2517 KJ The Hague, Netherlands
   Tel.: (31) 70 302 23 23
   Fax: (31) 70 364 99 28
@ International Court of Justice: www.icj-cij.org

■ INTERNATIONAL CRIMINAL COURT (ICC)

I. BACKGROUND

The statute of the International Criminal Court (ICC) was adopted in Rome on July 17, 1998, as the result of an international diplomatic conference organized under the aegis of the UN. The Court will effectively begin operating after sixty states have ratified its statute. Although 139 states had signed the statute by February 2001, only twenty-nine had ratified it (Algeria, Argentina, Austria, Belgium, Belize, Botswana, Canada, Fiji, Finland, France, Gabon, Germany, Ghana, Iceland, Italy, Lesotho, Luxembourg, Mali, Marshall Islands, New Zealand, Norway, San Marino, Senegal, Sierra Leone, South Africa, Spain, Tajikistan, Trinidad and Tobago, and Venezuela). This suggests that it may be several years before the Court begins its operations.

The ICC fills a void in the ability of the international community to punish the perpetrators of the most serious crimes of international concern. Its statute was adopted with the goal of expanding on the work of the ad hoc International Criminal Tribunals established for the former Yugoslavia (ICTY) and for Rwanda (ICTR). The ICC will have jurisdiction, when certain conditions have been met, over individuals accused of the crime of genocide, war crimes, crimes against humanity, and the crime of aggression (Article 5 of the ICC statute).

However, one aspect of the ICC that limits its international scope is the fact that, contrary to the ICTY and ICTR, the ICC does not have primacy over national criminal jurisdictions but rather is complimentary to the national systems. The ICC will initiate proceedings only if the state in question is "unwilling or unable genuinely to carry out the prosecution or investigation" (Article 17). This means that if a national legal entity is carrying out such proceedings, the ICC may not act unless it can prove that the proceedings are not being carried out in good faith (explained further in Section IV). The aim of this approach is to encourage states to carry out their own prosecutions whenever possible.

Another compromise that was reached in establishing the Court actually subordinates the exercise of the ICC's jurisdiction to the prior consent of states. Whether a case concerns genocide, war crimes, or crimes against humanity, the Court may only investigate the crimes if either the state of nationality of the person accused or the state on whose territory the crime was committed has accepted the ICC's jurisdiction (Article 12). The absence of any reference to the state of nationality of the victim or of the state where the accused is located has doomed the most realistic scenarios under which investigations might have been triggered. Today, 90 percent of conflicts are internal; therefore, the state of nationality of the criminal and the state where the crime was committed are often the same. Finally, the statute includes a provision allowing states to refuse the Court's jurisdiction over war crimes for seven years after the statute's entry into force for the state concerned (Article 124).

The Security Council of the UN will have the highest level of authority. It is the only body that can bypass the requirement of state consent when it refers a case to the Court. It also has the power to prevent the ICC from acting. By adopting a resolution under Chapter VII of the UN Charter, it can prohibit an investigation or prosecution from being started or proceeded with, for one year, renewable indefinitely (Article 16).

Nevertheless, the ICC represents progress in the realm of international criminal law. The idea of a permanent international criminal court was first considered after the Nuremberg Tribunal, but states failed to agree until 1998. States also had never agreed on an acceptable definition of the crimes in question. Furthermore, its statute represents an important step in combining different legal systems of the world. For instance, in comparison with the existing ad hoc tribunals, for the former Yugoslavia and Rwanda (which were predominantly influenced by the common law system), the establishment of a Pre-Trial Chamber as a check on the Prosecutor and the possibility for victims to claim damages represent additions that are derived from civil law systems.

Yet, despite the positive aspects of the Court—the establishment of an independent prosecutor, the formalization of some interesting innovations in the definition of crimes, and the recognition of the right of victims to reparations—the Court will function, at least in its early stages, as a judicial body under political guardianship.

II. Structure and Organization of the ICC

The ICC is made up of several principal organs: the Office of the Prosecutor, the judicial Divisions and Chambers, the Registry, and the Presidency (Article 34 of the ICC statute).

There will also be an Assembly of States Parties (Article 112), in which each state party will have one representative. It is this Assembly, and not the Court itself, that is responsible for adopting the Rules of Procedure and Evidence; for providing management oversight to the Presidency, Prosecutor, and the Registry, regarding the administration of the Court; for considering and deciding the budget of the Court; and for examining any question relating to noncooperation on the part of states.

The ICC's funding will come from fixed contributions made by states parties, funds provided by the UN, and voluntary contributions from governments, international organizations, individuals, corporations, and other entities in accordance with specific criteria (Article 115 and 116).

1. Office of the Prosecutor

This office is "responsible for receiving referrals and any substantiated information on crimes within the jurisdiction of the court, for examining them, and for conducting investigations and prosecutions before the Court" (Article 42).

The Prosecutor is elected for an unrenewable nine-year term by an absolute majority of the members of the Assembly of States Parties. He or she may be assisted by one or more Deputy Prosecutors, who are elected in the same way from a list of candidates provided by the Prosecutor. The Prosecutor and the Deputy (or Deputies) are fully independent and must all be of different nationalities. They must be persons of high moral character, be highly competent, and have extensive experience with criminal matters. They may not engage in any other professional occupation.

The Prosecutor can nominate the personnel necessary to his or her work, such as advisers and investigators.

Under certain circumstances, the Prosecutor can launch an investigation on his or her own initiative (*proprio motu*), on the basis of information received from diverse sources, concerning crimes within the jurisdiction of the Court. He or she may "seek additional information from states, organs of the UN, intergovernmental or non-governmental organizations, or other reliable sources that he or she deems appropriate, and may receive written or oral testimony" (Article 15.2).

If the Prosecutor concludes that there is a reasonable basis to proceed with an investigation, he or she must request authorization from the Pre-Trial Chamber. Pending its ruling, the

Prosecutor may "on an exceptional basis, seek authority from the Pre-Trial Chamber to pursue necessary investigative steps for the purpose of preserving evidence," if there is an opportunity to obtain important evidence, or if there is a risk that it may not be available subsequently (Article 18.6).

2. The Chambers and Judges

The judicial organ of the ICC is composed of eighteen judges, divided into the different Chambers. The judges are elected by the Assembly of States Parties from the list of candidates presented by the states parties (Article 36). They are chosen from among persons of high moral character, impartiality, and integrity, who possess the qualifications required in their respective states for appointment to the highest judicial offices. They must be competent in relevant areas of international law, such as humanitarian law or human rights law, and have the necessary relevant experience in criminal law and procedure.

In selecting the judges, the states parties must take into account the need for the representation of the principal legal systems of the world, equitable geographic representation, and fair gender representation. Judges will hold office for a term of nine years, and they may not be reelected. They may not engage in any other professional occupation.

The judges are divided into three divisions, whose judicial functions are carried out by three Chambers (Article 39):

- The Appeals Division is composed of the President and four judges; the Appeals Chamber is composed of all the judges in the Division.
- The Trial Division is composed of no less than six judges; the Trial Chamber is composed of three of the judges from this Division.
- The Pre-Trial Division is composed of no less than six judges; the composition of the Pre-Trial Chamber will be decided in the Rules of Procedure and Evidence.

The statute provides for the possibility of having more than one Trial or Pre-Trial Chambers operating simultaneously when the Court's workload so requires.

3. The Registry

The Registry is the administrative organ of the ICC. It is responsible for the nonjudicial aspects of the administration and servicing of the Court (Article 43). The Registrar will be elected by an absolute majority of the judges for a five-year term, open for reelection once. He or she may have a Deputy Registrar, if needed, who will be elected in the same manner. The Registrar will exercise his or her functions under the authority of the President of the Court. The Registrar's responsibilities include the establishment of a Victims and Witnesses Unit (Article 43.6) that is in charge of assisting victims and witnesses who appear before the Court and others who are at risk on account of testimony given by such witnesses—namely, their families. The Unit provides for protective measures, security arrangements, counseling, and other appropriate assistance.

4. The Presidency

Three judges will be elected by an absolute majority of judges to the offices of President and First and Second Vice Presidents, for three-year terms. They can be reelected once. The Presidency is responsible for the proper administration of the Court and any other function conferred on it in accordance with the statute (Article 38).

III. JURISDICTION

1. Exercise of Jurisdiction

The statute establishes that the exercise of jurisdiction of the Court can be triggered if a state party (Article 14) or the UN Security Council (Article 13) refers a situation to the Prosecutor. The Prosecutor may also trigger the ICC's jurisdiction, on his or her own initiative, subject to control by the Pre-Trial Chamber (Article 15). However, as explained, if a state party or the Prosecutor refers a situation to the ICC, there is a precondition to the Court's exercise of jurisdiction: either the state of nationality of the accused or the state where the crime was committed must be a party to the statute. Only a referral by the Security Council overrides this constraint (Article 13). It is also possible for a state that is not a party to the statute, but is either the state of nationality of the accused or the state where the crime was committed, to accept the jurisdiction of the ICC with respect to a case, on an ad hoc basis, in which case it must also agree to cooperate fully with the Court (Article 12).

Furthermore, even if the court's jurisdiction is being exercised, the Security Council can interrupt or prevent the Court from investigating or prosecuting a situation, by adopting a resolution to that effect under Chapter VII of the UN Charter. This deferral lasts twelve months and can be renewed indefinitely (Article 16).

Summary of the Rules Governing the ICC's Exercise of Jurisdiction

- The ICC can only exercise its jurisdiction over a crime if either the state of which the person accused is a national or the state on whose territory the crime was committed has accepted the jurisdiction of the court for this crime by ratifying the ICC statute (Article 12 of the ICC Statute). This option is further restricted if the state of nationality of the accused and the state where the crime was committed are the same. In today's conflicts, this is most often the case.
- This restriction is not applicable if a situation is referred by the UN Security Council acting under Chapter VII of the UN Charter (Article 12.2).
- Upon ratifying the ICC statute, states may choose to refuse the Court's jurisdiction over war crimes for a period of seven years (Article 124).
- The Court's jurisdiction may not be exercised if a case is being investigated or prosecuted by a state that has jurisdiction over the case. This may be overruled if the Court can prove that the proceedings were undertaken for the purpose of shielding the accused from criminal responsibility before the ICC, if there was unjustified delay in the national proceedings, or if these were not conducted independently and impartially (Articles 17 and 20).
- The Court may also exercise its jurisdiction if it proves that the state is unable to carry out the investigation or prosecution—for instance, due to a total or substantial collapse or unavailability of its national judicial system (Article 17.3).

2. Subject Matter Jurisdiction (Jurisdiction *Ratione Materiae*)

Article 5 lists the crimes within the jurisdiction of the Court:

- *The crime of genocide* (defined in Article 6). For the purpose of the statute, the term *genocide* means

    any of the following acts committed with intent to destroy, in whole or in part, a national, ethnical, racial or religious group, as such:
    - (a) Killing members of the group;
    - (b) Causing serious bodily or mental harm to members of the group;
    - (c) Deliberately inflicting on the group conditions of life calculated to bring about its physical destruction, in whole or in part;
    - (d) Imposing measures intended to prevent births within the group;
    - (e) Forcibly transferring children of the group to another group.

    This definition is taken from the 1948 Convention on the Prevention and Punishment of the Crime of Genocide.
    → **Genocide**

- *Crimes against humanity* (defined in Article 7). → **War crimes/Crimes against humanity**
- *War crimes* (defined in Article 8). → **War crimes/Crimes against humanity**
    However, upon ratifying the ICC statute, states may choose to refuse the Court's jurisdiction over war crimes for seven years (Article 124).
- *Aggression.* The statute only gives the ICC jurisdiction over this crime in principle (Article 5). It provides that the definition of the crime and the conditions under which the Court will exercise jurisdiction with respect to this crime, will be adopted at a later date, as provided for under the revision procedures in Articles 121 and 123.

3. Personal Jurisdiction (Jurisdiction *Ratione Personae*)

The Court has jurisdiction over any individual accused of a crime within the jurisdiction of the ICC, except for any person who was under the age of eighteen at the time of the alleged commission of the crime (Article 26).

The Statute of the ICC expressly foresees that immunity can never be invoked with regard to the crimes over which it has jurisdiction.

Article 27 stipulates that the Court will have jurisdiction over "all persons without any distinction based on official capacity. In particular, official capacity as a Head of State or Government, a member of a Government or parliament, an elected representative or a government official shall in no case exempt a person from criminal responsibility under this Statute, nor shall it, in and of itself, constitute a ground for reduction of sentence."

This article confirms the principles emanating from the precedent established by the Nuremberg Tribunal and the two International Criminal Tribunals for the former Yugoslavia and Rwanda, and it gives them a permanent and mandatory legal status. It also reaffirms provisions already adopted to this effect in several international conventions.
→ **Immunity**

4. Temporal Jurisdiction (Jurisdiction *Ratione Temporis*)

The ICC has jurisdiction only over crimes committed after the entry into force of the ICC statute for the state concerned (Article 11). This is derived from the well-established legal principle of nonretroactivity of criminal laws, according to which a law may not be applied to acts committed before the law was enacted.

→ **Nonretroactivity**

5. Penalties

The Court may impose penalties of imprisonment for up to thirty years or, at most, a term of life imprisonment. It may also order fines and confiscation of proceeds, property, and assets derived directly or indirectly from that crime (Article 77). It will be the only international institution that will be able to impose such penalties on individuals.

The sentence of imprisonment will be served in a state chosen by the Court from a list of states that have indicated their willingness to accept sentenced persons (Article 103). The ICC will supervise the implementation of the sentences, but the conditions of imprisonment will be governed by the law of the state responsible for its implementation (Article 106). Only the Court has the right to decide any application for appeal and revision (Article 105).

IV. RELATIONSHIP BETWEEN STATES AND THE ICC

1. Relationship between the ICC and National Jurisdictions

In contrast to the ad hoc Tribunals, the ICC does not have primacy over national criminal jurisdictions. Its jurisdiction is complementary to domestic systems, meaning that the Court's jurisdiction may not be exercised if a case is being investigated or prosecuted by a state that has jurisdiction over the case. This may be overruled if the Court can prove that the proceedings were undertaken for the purpose of shielding the accused from criminal responsibility before the ICC, if there was unjustified delay in the national proceedings, or if these were not conducted independently and impartially (Articles 17 and 20). The Court may also exercise its jurisdiction if the state in question is unable to carry out the investigation or prosecution—for instance, due to total or substantial collapse or unavailability of its national judicial system (Article 17.3).

2. *Ne Bis in Idem*

This is a firmly established principle of law—in both general criminal and international law—according to which one person may not be judged twice for the same crime (also known as protection from double jeopardy). It is one of the main due process guarantees and is reflected in Article 20 of the ICC statute.

An individual tried before the ICC thus cannot be tried again before a national court for the same crime. By the same token, the ICC may not rule on an act for which a person was already tried by a national court. However, there are exceptions: the ICC may subsequently try the person if the proceedings in the other court were carried out "for the purpose of shielding the person concerned from criminal responsibility for crimes within the jurisdiction of the Court; or otherwise were not conducted independently or impartially in accordance with the norms of due process recognized by international law and were conducted in a manner that, in the circumstances, was inconsistent with an intent to bring the person concerned to justice" (Article 20.3).

3. Obligations of State Cooperation and Mutual Judicial Assistance

The ICC statute establishes that states have a general obligation to cooperate fully with the Court (Article 86). However, if a state fails to cooperate, there is no provision to penalize it. Article 87, paragraphs 5 and 7, establishes the only recourse for the Court: it can notify the Assembly of States Parties (which has no powers to penalize a state), or, if the UN Security Council referred the matter to the ICC, it can notify the Council.

The obligation to cooperate is applicable to all requests made by the Court in the context of its investigations and prosecutions. The requests may be related to the arrest and surrender of persons to the Court, the production of documents or evidence, the identification and whereabouts of a person, the execution of searches and seizures, and other types of assistance.

If the disclosure of information or documents would, in the opinion of a state, prejudice its national security interests, it may deny the Court's request. In that case, the Court and the state must take all reasonable steps to find a solution enabling the documents to be used without posing a threat to the national security of the state. If the state considers that there are no means or conditions under which it would authorize the disclosure of the information, it must so notify the Court, which then has no recourse other than those from Article 87, mentioned earlier.

V. STATUS OF VICTIMS AND WITNESSES

1. Reparations for Victims

Contrary to the current practice in the ad hoc international tribunals currently in operation, victims can be represented as such before the ICC and can be awarded reparations. This is an important step in bringing justice to victims of the egregious crimes over which the ICC has jurisdiction. The Court therefore makes a distinction between the status of victims and that of witnesses, in accordance with the prevailing approach in the civil law system.

The statute authorizes victims to be represented before the Court by attorneys if their personal interests are affected (Article 68.3). Article 75 establishes the principles relating to the different forms of reparation to be given to—or with respect to—the victims, including restitution, compensation, and rehabilitation. In its final decision, the Court may, "either upon request or on its own motion in exceptional circumstances," determine the scope and extent of any damage, loss, and injury to—or with respect to—the victims.

A trust fund will be set up for the benefit of victims and their families. It will be managed according to criteria to be determined by the Assembly of States Parties. The Court may order money and other property collected through fines or forfeiture to be transferred to the Trust Fund (Article 79).

2. Protection of Victims and Witnesses

Provisions have also been adopted to provide for the security, physical and psychological well-being, dignity, and privacy of victims and witnesses (Article 68). Provisions include the possibility of conducting any part of the proceedings *in camera* or presenting evidence by electronic means. A Victims and Witnesses Unit, attached to the Registry of the ICC, has been established to implement these protective measures.

➜ **Children; Genocide; Human rights; Individual recourse; International Criminal Tribunals; Nonapplicability of statutory limitations; Nonretroactivity; Penal sanctions in humanitarian law; Rape; Security Council of the UN; War crimes/Crimes against humanity; Women**

➜ **List of states party to the ICC Statute (No. 27)**

📖 **For Additional Information:**

Beigbeder, Yves. *Judging War Criminals: The Politics of International Justice*. London: Macmillan, and
    New York: St. Martin's, 1999, 186–99.
Human Rights Watch. *Justice in the Balance: Recommendations for an Independent and Effective Interna-
    tional Criminal Court*. New York: Human Rights Watch Report, June 1998.
Lee, Roy S., ed. *The International Criminal Court: The Making of the Rome Statute—Issues, Negotiations,
    Results*. The Hague: Kluwer Law International, 1999.
Yee, Lionel. "Not Just a War Crimes Court: The Penal Regime Established by the Rome Statute of the
    ICC." *Singapore Academy of Law Journal* 10, no. 321(1998).

@   www.un.org/law/icc/index.htm or www.iccnow.org

■ INTERNATIONAL CRIMINAL TRIBUNALS FOR THE FORMER YUGOSLAVIA (ICTY) AND RWANDA (ICTR)

I. BACKGROUND

After the conflicts in Rwanda and in the former Yugoslavia, and in the absence of a permanent
international criminal court, the international community chose to establish two ad hoc International Criminal Tribunals to prosecute individuals responsible for war crimes, crimes against humanity, and acts of genocide in these two specific situations. The International Criminal Tribunal
for the Former Yugoslavia (ICTY) was established in 1993, and the International Criminal Tribunal for Rwanda (ICTR) in 1994, to investigate and punish the perpetrators of the egregious
crimes committed during those conflicts.

The UN Security Council set up both Tribunals through resolutions adopted under Chapter
VII of the UN Charter. Such resolutions are binding on all states, and the Tribunals were established in this manner so as to impose their jurisdiction directly on all states. The other method
would have been to adopt a treaty creating such a body, which would have required states' consent and then ratification. → **International Conventions; Security Council**

Since then, on July 17, 1998, states adopted the statute of a permanent International Criminal
Court (ICC), which will be responsible for bringing to justice persons accused of genocide, war
crimes, and crimes against humanity. The ICC's jurisdiction will be subject to certain preconditions,
and it will operate only when the concerned state or states are unwilling or unable to carry out the
necessary investigations and prosecutions. The UN Security Council, however, can impose the
ICC's jurisdiction on a given state by adopting a resolution under Chapter VII of the UN Charter.
Given the time needed for most states to ratify an international convention, it will probably be several years for the Court's statute enters into force.
→   **International Criminal Court**

1. Legal Basis of the Tribunals: International Law, Civil Law, and Common Law

The ICTY was established by Security Council Resolutions 808 of February 22, 1993, and 827
of May 25, 1993. It is based in The Hague, Netherlands. The ICTR was established by Security
Council Resolution 955 of November 8, 1994, and is based in Arusha, Tanzania. The statutes of
the Tribunals are annexed to these resolutions.

Since there is no international code of criminal procedure, the Tribunals established their own Rules of Procedure and Evidence—adopted on February 11, 1994, for the ICTY, and June 29, 1995, for the ICTR. The ICTR adopted rules very similar to those of the ICTY. The Rules were largely inspired by the system of common law, which governs most Anglo-Saxon states, as opposed to civil law. The common law system is often labeled as having an accusatorial (or adversarial) approach, while the civil law one is considered to be inquisitorial.

In this respect, civil law proponents have noted certain significant differences incurred by this approach, detailed in the following sections.

a. Role of the Victim

One important contrast is the role of the victim. In common law, the victim in a criminal case is generally treated as a witness. This means two main things:

- The victim can usually not claim damages in a criminal case (compensation is usually awarded in civil cases, tried before civil or magistrates' courts), whereas, in civil law, plaintiffs may claim damages in criminal cases ("*se porter partie civile*").

    In the ICTY and ICTR, this is reflected in the fact that, once the Registrar has transmitted the guilty verdict to the competent authorities, the victims or persons bringing claims for them must take action before a national court or other competent body in order to obtain compensation (Rule 106 of the Rules of Procedure and Evidence of the Tribunals).
- The accusatory system may expose the victims and witnesses to harrowing cross-examination carried out by the defense.

    The Rules of Procedure and Evidence of the Tribunals include provisions to implement special measures for the protection and privacy of victims and witnesses. However, these provisions are only guaranteed while they are testifying. Their fate upon their return to their place of origin, as well as that of their family, is not taken into account.

    In certain circumstances, it is possible to submit information to the Prosecutor on condition that he or she not disclose the information and its source to the defense of the accused without the consent of the entity or person who provided it (ICTY Rules of Procedure and Evidence, Rule 70B).

b. *Trials* in Abstentia

Another difference between the common law and civil law systems reflected in the procedure of the Tribunals is the fact that they do not allow trials *in absentia* (in the absence of the accused). Such trials are considered a potential violation of the due process rights of the accused under common law systems (though sentences for certain minor crimes may be pronounced in the absence of the accused if he or she deliberately failed to attend the trial or has fled). Civil law systems are technically more open to carrying out "procedures by default," although these are actually meant to encourage the accused to present him- or herself, since a completely new trial must be initiated if the accused contests the judgment of the first one.

c. Role of the Prosecutor

In the common law system, the head prosecutor or attorney is responsible for both the investigation and prosecution, while in civil law, the investigation is carried out by examining magistrates and most of the interrogations during the trial are conducted by judges. This lightens the pressure of interrogation of victims and witnesses during the trial. In this respect, the structure of the Tribunals, explained later, also shows the influence of the accusatory system, mainly reflected in the dominant authority given to the Prosecutor.

The statute of the International Criminal Court (ICC), adopted in July 1998, comes closer to combining the two legal systems: it institutes a Pre-Trial Chamber that must authorize any investigations initiated by the Prosecutor, and it allows the ICC to order reparations to be made to (or with respect to) victims. Reparations may include restitution, compensation, or rehabilitation and may be paid either directly by the convicted person or through a Trust Fund set up by the Court's statute (Articles 75 and 79 of ICC statute).

→   **Hierarchy of norms; International Criminal Court**

II. STRUCTURE AND ORGANIZATION

The ICTY and ICTR, though independent, have organizational ties that ensure a unity and coherence in their judicial operations and increase the effectiveness of the resources allocated to them. They are made up of the judicial organ, the office of the prosecutor, and the administrative organ. The Tribunals share the Prosecutor and appellate judges but have separate trial judges, as well as separate administrative organs and budgets.

1. The Judicial Organ

The judicial organ has fourteen judges who must be of different nationalities. It was originally created with one Trial Chamber for each Tribunal (three judges each) and a common Appeals Chamber (five judges). However, two new resolutions adopted by the Security Council, aimed at accelerating the pursuit of justice (Resolutions 1165 of April 30, 1998, and 1166 of May 13, 1998), added a Trial Chamber for each Tribunal.

- The judges are elected by the General Assembly of the UN, which, as is the case with the International Court of Justice and the future ICC, must take into account the need for equitable geographic distribution and the representation of the principal legal systems of the world. The judges are elected for four years and can be reelected. They are chosen from a list of twenty-two names selected by the Security Council.
- The fourteen judges then elect the President of the Tribunal, who also presides directly over the Appeals Chamber, appointing them to the different Chambers. The Trial Chambers, once established, also elect their own Presidents.

2. The Office of the Prosecutor

The Tribunals share the office of the Prosecutor. The Prosecutor is appointed by the Security Council, upon nomination by the Secretary-General of the UN, for a four-year term, renewable once. He or she holds the rank of Assistant Secretary-General. In October 1996, Richard Goldstone of South Africa was replaced by Louise Arbour of Canada, who in September 1999 was succeeded by Carla Del Ponte of Switzerland. The staff in this office is nominated by the Secretary-General upon recommendation of the Prosecutor, who is also assisted by two Deputy Prosecutors (one for each Tribunal).

3. The Administrative Organ

The administrative organ is the Registry, run by a Registrar. Each Tribunal has its own Registry, responsible for the administration and servicing of the Tribunal. The Registrars are nominated to four-year, renewable terms by the Secretary-General of the UN after consultation with the President of the Tribunal. The Registrar has a staff that is also nominated by the Secretary-General, after consultation with the Registrar.

The 1999 regular budgets of the Tribunals, approved by the General Assembly of the UN, amount to $94 million for the ICTY and $68 million for the ICTR, to be drawn from the regular budget of the UN. The Tribunals also operate partly thanks to voluntary contributions made by states. This means that they frequently suffer from serious funding problems that hinder their activities. This is especially a problem for the ICTR.

III. Jurisdiction and Sentencing

1. Subject Matter Jurisdiction (Jurisdiction *Ratione Materiae*)

Both Tribunals have the power to "prosecute persons responsible for serious violations of international humanitarian law" (Article 1 of both statutes). The specific crimes over which they have jurisdiction are defined in detail in each of the statutes (Articles 2–5 of ICTY statute; Articles 2–4 of ICTR statute). These crimes fall under the categories of acts of genocide, war crimes, and crimes against humanity, for both Tribunals. Within this framework, each Tribunal has added a specific type of crime to its jurisdiction, in comparison with narrower past interpretations of international law:

- The ICTY raises the legal status of the crime of rape, as such, to that of a crime against humanity. This is a new judicial specificity. To this effect, the ICTY's Rules of Procedure and Evidence provide measures requiring a lighter burden of proof in cases of sexual assault (Rule 96).
- The ICTR extends the notion of grave breaches of international humanitarian law to include situations of internal armed conflict. It bases accusations on violations of Article 3 of Protocol II of 1977 (Article 4 of ICTR statute).

☞ The ICTR has set two very important legal precedents, on rape and genocide, in the judgment rendered against Jean-Paul Akayesu (ICTR-96-4-T, delivered on September 2, 1998). It is the first judgment rendered by an international tribunal that finds an individual guilty of genocide and rape, using legal definitions of rape and genocide, on the one hand, and of serious violations of Additional Protocol II of the Geneva Conventions, on the other.

In addition to the guilty ruling, the ICTR also set an important legal precedent by stating that rape can be an act of genocide. More details concerning the judgment are provided in the entry on ➔ **rape.**

---

2. Personal Jurisdiction (Jurisdiction *Ratione Personae*)

The two statutes rest on the principle of individual criminal responsibility (Article 7 of ICTY statute; Article 6 of ICTR statute). Under current international law, this principle only applies to "natural persons" (individual human beings), and the statutes insist on the fact that their jurisdiction is only over such persons (Article 6 of ICTY statute; Article 5 of ICTR statute). States, therefore, cannot be judged.

The Tribunals have the power to prosecute any individual accused of serious violations of international humanitarian law (Article 1 of both statutes), regardless of their level of responsibility. The statutes draw from the provisions of the Nuremberg Tribunal.

- Any person who planned, instigated, ordered, committed, or otherwise aided and abetted in the planning, preparation, or execution of a crime under jurisdiction of the Tribunals—whether a government official, military commander, or subordinate—is individually responsible for the crime and may be prosecuted (Article 7.1 of ICTY statute; Article 6.1 of ICTR statute).
- Neither the official rank of an accused nor the fact that he or she may have acted under superior orders are grounds for excluding criminal responsibility.
  - In the case of persons of superior rank—whether a head of state or government or a high civil servant—their official position neither relieves them of their criminal responsibility nor mitigates their punishment (Article 7.2 of ICTY statute; Article 6.2 of ICTR statute).
  - In the case of subordinates, the fact that they were following superior orders does not relieve them of criminal responsibility. However, superior orders may be considered a reason to mitigate their punishment, but only in cases in which these orders allowed them no freedom of action or judgment (Article 7.4 of ICTY statute; Article 6.4 of ICTR statute).
  - Furthermore, a superior will be held responsible for a crime committed by a subordinate, if the superior knew or had reasons to know that the subordinate was about to commit such acts or had done so, and the superior failed to take the necessary and reasonable measures to prevent such acts or punish the perpetrators (Article 7.3 of ICTY statute; Article 6.3 of ICTR statute). In this respect, the statutes reflect the provisions concerning the duty of commanders from the 1977 Protocol I of the Geneva Conventions (PI Article 87).

3. Territorial and Temporal Jurisdiction (Jurisdiction *Ratione Loci* and *Ratione Temporis*)

- The jurisdiction of the ICTY covers the territory of the former Socialist Federal Republic of Yugoslavia. Its temporal jurisdiction covers all crimes committed since January 1, 1991—the date that marked the beginning of the hostilities, according to the UN Security Council. The Tribunal's jurisdiction will end when the ICTY considers that the hostilities have ended.
- The jurisdiction of the ICTR covers the territory of Rwanda and of its neighboring states, while its temporal jurisdiction covers only a one-year period, from January 1 to December 31, 1994.

4. Penalties

Persons found guilty of grave violations of humanitarian law shall be sentenced to terms of imprisonment. The Tribunals do not apply the death sentence. Since there is no international criminal code, international law has no standard sentence determined for a given crime. The Tribunals are therefore subject to the general scales of prison sentences that exist in former Yugoslavia and in Rwanda (Article 24 of ICTY statute; Article 23 of ICTR statute).

Once a sentence has been pronounced, the term of imprisonment is served in a country designated by the Tribunal from a list of states that have indicated to the UN Security Council their willingness to accept sentenced persons (Article 27 of ICTY statute). The ICTR adds the possibility of serving out the sentence in Rwanda (Article 26 of ICTR statute).

As of March 2001, the ICTY had issued indictments for ninety-nine suspects, thirty-seven of whom were behind bars in the Netherlands. The ICTY also has a secret list of suspects, known only to the office of the Prosecutor so as to facilitate their arrest. It had rendered nine judgments.

The ICTR, for its part, had issued indictments against fifty-three people, forty-three of whom were being held in Tanzania. It had rendered seven judgments against eight individuals.

☞ The ICTY and ICTR have a scope of jurisdiction that is limited in time and space: the jurisdiction of the ICTY covers the territory of the former Socialist Federal Republic of Yugoslavia for crimes committed since January 1, 1991, and that of the ICTR concerns the territory of Rwanda and its neighboring states and covers only the time period from January 1 to December 31, 1994.

- The Tribunals have the authority to judge individuals accused of criminal acts, not states.
- The Tribunals operate in parallel with national courts but may request that the latter defer certain cases under investigation or prosecution to the Tribunals for judgment. This means that states remain under the obligation to search for and prosecute authors of these crimes.
- Victims and states may not bring complaints directly before these Tribunals.
- The Prosecutor alone can decide to open an investigation, either on his or her own initiative or based on information received. NGOs, victims, witnesses, intergovernmental organizations, and states may all submit information to the Prosecutor.
- The Tribunals adopted their own definitions of war crimes and crimes against humanity, which merge the definitions from the statute of the 1945 Nuremberg Military Tribunal and those contained in the 1949 Geneva Conventions and their 1977 Protocols.
- Neither the excuse of the official function of an accused nor that of following superior orders can serve as grounds for excluding criminal responsibility.
- Penalties are limited to prison sentences.
- The Tribunals depend on the judicial cooperation of states to ensure their effectiveness, which in turn requires that each state adapt its laws to be in conformity with the provisions of the statutes and their rules.

IV. State Cooperation

The existence of ad hoc tribunals does not relieve states of their obligation to search for and prosecute the perpetrators of grave violations of humanitarian law, as established in the 1949 Geneva Conventions. The Tribunals can only function properly if the national systems of justice are effective and cooperate with one another in criminal matters.

Even though the statutes of the Tribunals were adopted through UN Security Council resolutions, which are binding on all states, the judicial cooperation that is necessary between the Tribunals and the national authorities is only possible if each country has adapted its laws to legislate this cooperation.

1. Relationship between the Tribunals and National Jurisdictions

This relationship is founded on three principles:

a. Concurrent Jurisdiction

The Tribunals and national courts have concurrent jurisdiction to prosecute persons presumed guilty of serious violations of international humanitarian law (Article 9.1 of ICTY statute; Article 8.1 of ICTR statute). This is particularly important for victims. As has been explained, only the Prosecutor can initiate an investigation or prosecution, and victims cannot claim damages before the Tribunals. Hence, individuals and NGOs can only file complaints or ask for compensation—and victims can only receive reparations for the injuries suffered—before domestic courts. In this respect, national judges play an integral part in the exercise of international jurisdiction.

b. Primacy of International Tribunals

Although the jurisdiction is concurrent, both statutes clearly establish that the Tribunals have primacy over national courts (Article 9.2 of ICTY statute; Article 8.2 of ICTR statute). This means that, at any stage in the judicial proceedings, the Tribunals may formally request that national courts defer to the competence of the International Tribunal. The Rules of Procedure and Evidence set out the details of the deferral procedures.

This principle of primacy is an exception in international law and was not included in the statute of the new permanent International Criminal Court.

c. Ne Bis in Idem

This is a firmly established principle of law, both in general criminal and in international law, according to which one person may not be judged twice for the same crime (also known as protection from double jeopardy). It is one of the main due process guarantees, as provided for in the International Covenant on Civil and Political Rights (Article 14.7 of ICCPR). This fundamental right is reflected in the two Tribunal statutes (Article 10 of ICTY statute; Article 9 of ICTR statute).

An individual tried before one of the International Tribunals thus cannot be tried again before a national court for the same crime. By the same token, the Tribunals may not rule on an act for which a person was already tried by a national court. However, there are exceptions: the Tribunals may subsequently try the person if "the act was characterized as an ordinary crime [in the domestic trial]; or the national court proceedings were not impartial or independent, or were designed to shield the accused from international criminal responsibility; or if the case was not diligently prosecuted" (Article 10.2 of ICTY statute; Article 9.2 of ICTR statute).

2. Obligations of State Cooperation and Mutual Judicial Assistance

All states are under the obligation to cooperate with the two Tribunals, at all stages in the process of investigating and prosecuting a person (Article 29 of ICTY statute; Article 28 of ICTR statute). Such obligations include compliance, "without undue delay," with requests for assistance in gathering evidence; taking the testimony of witnesses, suspects, and experts;

identifying and locating persons; and serving documents. States must also carry out the requests of the trial chambers, such as summonses, subpoenas, arrest warrants, and transfer orders.

To facilitate the transfer of an accused by a state, the Tribunals have set up an arrangement between the Tribunal and the state in question that bypasses the legal impediments that often result from extradition proceedings.

These obligations include the duty to contribute to the budget, to make personnel available, and especially to adopt concrete judicial and legislative measures into domestic laws, so as to be able to implement the provisions in the statutes of the Tribunals and the resolutions that created them. The goodwill of states is hence a crucial element in ensuring that the Tribunals function smoothly. This is particularly important since the Tribunals, contrary to domestic courts, have no enforcement mechanism to back them up and no concrete provisions to punish a state that fails to cooperate with the Tribunals or does not amend its national legislation to incorporate the obligations derived from the statutes.

The stabilization force deployed by NATO in former Yugoslavia (SFOR), for instance, does not have the mandate of a police force responsible for searching for war criminals. Instead, its mandate establishes that the troops may arrest persons indicted for war crimes, if they encounter them in the context of their activities. However, several commando operations that were launched for the sole purpose of arresting indicted persons seem to indicate that the interpretation of this mandate remains in flux.

→   **Genocide; International Criminal Court; Judicial guarantees; Mutual assistance in criminal matters; Peacekeeping; Rape; Responsibility; Security Council of the UN; Universal jurisdiction; War crimes/Crimes against humanity**

📖 **For Additional Information:**

Bassiouni, M. Cherif, and Peter Manikas. *The Law of the International Criminal Tribunal for the Former Yugoslavia*. Irvington-on-Hudson, N.Y.: Transnational, 1996.

Beigbeder, Yves. *Judging War Criminals: The Politics of International Justice*. London: Macmillan and New York: St. Martin's, 1999, 146–85.

Graefrath, G. "Universal Jurisdiction and an International Court." *European Journal of International Law* (1990): 67–88.

Lescure, Karine. *International Justice for Former Yugoslavia: The Working of the International Criminal Tribunal of the Hague*. The Hague: Kluwer Law International, 1996.

Morris, Virginia, and Michael P. Scharf. *Insider's Guide to the International Criminal Tribunal for the Former Yugoslavia: A Documentary History and Analysis*. Irvington-on-Hudson, N.Y.: Transnational, 1995.

———. *The International Criminal Tribunal for Rwanda*. Irvington-on-Hudson, N.Y.: Transnational, 1998.

✎   International Criminal Tribunal for the Former Yugoslavia
Churchillplein 1
2517JW The Hague, Netherlands
Tel.: (31 70) 416 5343
Fax: (31 70) 416 5355

International Criminal Tribunal for Rwanda
PO Box 6016
Arusha, Tanzania
Tel. (in New York): (1) 212 963-2850
Fax (in New York): (1) 212 963-2848

@   International Criminal Tribunal for the Former Yugoslavia: www.un.org/icty/
     International Criminal Tribunal for Rwanda: www.un.org/ictr/

■ INTERNATIONAL FACT-FINDING COMMISSION

The International Fact-Finding Commission is an organ that investigates grave breaches of humanitarian law. Foreseen by Article 90 of the 1977 Additional Protocol I to the 1949 Geneva Conventions (Protocol I), it was to be an important addition to the Geneva Conventions, providing an independent mechanism to inquire into "any facts alleged to be a grave breach (. . .) or other serious violation of the Conventions or of this Protocol."

However, a minimum of twenty states had to accept the competence of the Commission before it could be established. This finally happened in 1991, in the wake of the Gulf War. As of March 2001, fifty-seven states had recognized ipso facto the Commission's competence.

1. Jurisdiction

The Commission's mandate is to investigate grave breaches and other serious violations of the Geneva Conventions and Protocol I. Most of these crimes come under the category of war crimes or crimes against humanity. While the Geneva Conventions and Protocol I are only applicable to international armed conflicts, the Commission announced (during its second session in 1996) that it was willing to inquire into alleged violations of humanitarian law committed in noninternational armed conflicts, particularly the violations enumerated in Article 3, common to the four Geneva Conventions, as long as the parties to the conflict agree.

Its role is also to "facilitate, through its good offices, the restoration of an attitude of respect for the Conventions and this Protocol" (PI Article 90.2.c.ii).

2. Composition

The Commission is made up of fifteen members "of high moral standing and acknowledged impartiality," elected for five years (GPI Article 90.1.a). After accepting the jurisdiction of the Commission, they are elected by the participating states, from a list drawn up by the states (each of which nominates one person). The first members were elected in January 1991; the second, in October 1996.

3. Functions

a. Exercise of Jurisdiction

The way in which cases may be referred to the Commission presents two innovations, compared with traditional mechanisms set up to investigate grave breaches of humanitarian law:

- Any state that has accepted the Commission's competence by acceding to Article 90 may request an inquiry, even if it is not directly concerned by the conflict. Thus, the investigation is not burdened with any suspicion of partiality—which might be implicit if the inquiry were requested by one of the parties to the conflict—and it becomes more of a collective control mechanism for states, based on the notion of public order and the respect for international law. However, for the Commission to be able to carry out its inquiry, the parties to the conflict under investigation must have accepted its competence.

- The states parties may also declare once and for all that they "recognize *ipso facto* and without special agreement" the competence of the Commission to inquire into allegations by any other state party that accepts the same obligation (PI Article 90.2.a). This means the Commission does not have to ask for any specific permission when it launches an investigation.

In other situations, in which the states have not explicitly recognized the Commission's competence, it can only begin an inquiry requested by one party to the conflict if the other party or parties concerned give their consent (PI Article 90.2.d).

b. Investigation

A chamber, consisting of seven of the Commission's members, undertakes the inquiries. These members are not nationals of any Party to the conflict, and are appointed with due regard to "equitable representation of the geographical areas." The Chamber can invite the parties to the conflict to assist it and to present evidence, but it may also seek other evidence itself, including through *in loco* investigations. It must fully disclose all evidence it finds to the parties involved, which have the right to comment on it or challenge it.

The result of the inquiry is a report submitted to the parties, with such recommendations as it may deem appropriate. The Commission does not report its findings publicly, unless all the parties to the conflict have requested that it do so, or if it finds that the state that was under investigation has not done anything to bring an end to the violations.

The party or parties requesting an inquiry must advance the necessary funds for expenses incurred by the Chamber. They are then reimbursed by the party or parties against which the allegations are made.

☞ Although states themselves created the International Fact-Finding Commission, they have not yet called on it to make any inquiries. States generally tend to avoid accusing other states of breaches of humanitarian law. When such violations are blatant, they prefer to establish ad hoc inquiry organs, which have a more diplomatic than judicial mission.

NGOs cannot refer cases directly to the Commission, but they may ask states to do so. This is important since this Commission, not the ad hoc Fact-Finding missions set up under other circumstances, is the only permanent international investigative body provided for under the Geneva Conventions.

The states that have currently recognized to competence of the International Fact-Finding Commission are Algeria, Argentina, Australia, Austria, Belgium, Belarus, Bolivia, Bosnia-Herzegovina, Brazil, Bulgaria, Canada, Cape Verde, Chili, Colombia, Croatia, Czech Republic, Denmark, Finland, Germany, Greece, Guinea, Hungary, Ireland, Iceland, Italy, Laos, Liechtenstein, Luxembourg, Macedonia, Madagascar, Malta, Mongolia, Namibia, Norway, the Netherlands, New Zealand, Paraguay, Poland, Portugal, Qatar, Romania, Russian Federation, Rwanda, Seychelles, Slovakia, Slovenia, Spain, Sweden, Switzerland, Tajikistan, Togo, Ukraine, United Arab Emirates, United Kingdom, and Uruguay.

Judicial Mechanisms to Punish Grave Breaches of Humanitarian Law

In addition to this mechanism to monitor and enforce the implementation of the Conventions, humanitarian law foresees various ways to investigate, prosecute, and punish

(*continues*)

(*continued*)

violations of its rules. These are based on states' obligations to punish the authors of grave breaches of humanitarian law, under the system of universal jurisdiction, which provides the possibility for victims to file complaints before national courts of any country.

Other nonpermanent mechanisms have been set up on an ad hoc basis to punish grave breaches of humanitarian law, such as the International Criminal Tribunals for the former Yugoslavia and for Rwanda.

On July 17, 1998, the statute of a permanent International Criminal Court was adopted. The ICC will be responsible for prosecuting individuals accused of crimes of genocide, war crimes, and crimes against humanity, as well as aggression at a later date. The Court will begin to operate only after sixty states have ratified the statute, which suggests that the Court will not begin to function for several years.

→ **International Criminal Court; International Criminal Tribunals; Universal jurisdiction**

→ **Individual recourse; International Criminal Court; International Criminal Tribunals; International humanitarian law; Penal sanctions in humanitarian law; Universal jurisdiction; War crimes/Crimes against humanity**
→ **List of states party to international human rights and humanitarian conventions (No. 2)**

✎ International Fact-Finding Commission
Palais Federal
CH-3003 Berne, Switzerland
Tel.: (41) 31 322 3082
Fax: (41) 31 324 9069

@ International Fact-Finding Commission: www.ihffc.org

📖 For Additional Information:

Krill, Françoise. "The International Fact-Finding Commission." *International Review of the Red Cross* 281 (March–April 1991): 190–207.
Roach, Ashley. "The International Fact-Finding Commission—Article 90 of Protocol Additional to the 1949 Geneva Conventions." *International Review of the Red Cross* 281 (March–April 1991): 167–89.

■ INTERNATIONAL HUMANITARIAN LAW

War is regulated by international humanitarian law, also called "the law of armed conflict." This ancient law was established progressively through the practice of states and codified through treaties they adopted. It seeks to govern the conduct of hostilities, mainly in an attempt to prevent conflicts from reaching a point of no return. One way that it does this is by restricting the choice of methods of warfare, so as to avoid unnecessary suffering and destruction. Humanitarian law also prohibits certain behavior and posits the right to relief for noncombatants, so as to alleviate the suffering engendered by war (GCIV Article 13).

The expression "international humanitarian law" is often preferred to "the law of armed conflict" because it emphasizes the humanitarian objectives of these rules. Although the word *humanitarian* is used in an increasing number of contexts, the term *humanitarian law* actually only describes law that is applicable to situations of armed conflict. Other branches of international law, however, may be relevant to humanitarian action—such as those relating to human rights, the rights of refugees, and the right to cooperation. This book refers to humanitarian law in the broad sense. Under international law, humanitarian activities can be undertaken both in times of peace and of war. → **Fundamental guarantees; Human rights; Refugees**

Nevertheless, it is important to consider the specificity of humanitarian law in the strict sense. It clearly establishes the various rights and duties of the actors in a conflict, and it relies on specific procedures both for the implementation of its provisions and for the punishment of violations thereof.

1. Sources of Humanitarian Law

The written rules of international humanitarian law can be found it the following treaties:

- The various declarations and conventions signed in The Hague, Netherlands (in 1899, 1907, 1954, 1957, 1970, and 1973). They establish the rules governing the conduct of hostilities.
- The four 1949 Geneva Conventions further codified the rules and customs of the law of armed conflict. They set limits to the methods of warfare that may be used, and they added rules relating to the protection and relief of noncombatants during hostilities. Today 188 states are party to these conventions.

  Each of the Conventions establishes the conditions for providing relief to a specific category of persons. The first three (GCI, GCII, GCIII) set forth the rules for the treatment of combatants who are wounded, shipwrecked, or prisoners of war, in international armed conflicts. The fourth Convention (GCIV) establishes provisions for the protection of the civilian population, also in international armed conflicts.
- Two Protocols additional to the Geneva Conventions were adopted in 1977 to consolidate and improve the rules of protection for victims of conflicts:
  —The first Protocol Additional to the Geneva Conventions, Relating to the Protection of Victims of International Armed Conflicts (PI), reinforces and completes the provisions foreseen by the Fourth Geneva Conventions. Currently 154 states are parties to Protocol I.
  —The second Protocol Additional, Relating to the Protection of Victims of Non-International Armed Conflicts (PII), completes the provisions for the protection of victims of noninternational armed conflicts, originally foreseen by Article 3, common to all four Geneva Conventions (known as common Article 3). Today 147 states are party to Protocol II.

Over time, the endurance and constancy of the rules of armed conflict have led to a number of them being considered "customary." This means that they are binding even on states or belligerents who have not formally adhered to these rules. This is specifically the case for the Geneva Conventions, but other guarantees come under the category of customary international law.

→ **Geneva Conventions; Hague Conventions**

2. Evolution of Humanitarian Law

The foundations of positive humanitarian law are rooted in a concept of war developed in the nineteenth century. Its laws were written by states and aimed, for the most part, to regulate interstate wars and to protect the rights of soldiers.

The conflicts that have taken place over the last fifty years do not fit clearly into that context. The two 1977 Protocols address the fact that civilians are increasingly exposed to, and therefore victims of, war, as well as the fact that a large number of conflicts are internal. Humanitarian law continues to evolve to meet these new challenges, in particular in granting increased importance to customary law.

Today, international humanitarian law is the only legal code regulating relief actions within the context of a conflict. Its rules, like any laws, must be interpreted in a manner that embraces the reality of conflicts, rather than in a manner aimed at avoiding responsibilities. Because war retains a pattern of more or less organized and institutionalized violence (although the level of organization varies), it is possible in all situations of conflict to identify the chains of command responsibility. This makes it possible to undertake negotiations that will include the application of, and respect for humanitarian law.

→ **Customary international law; Natural and positive law; Respect for international humanitarian law**

3. The Right to Violence and the Right to Relief

A distinction is sometimes made between the rules regulating the conduct of war and those governing the right to relief, with the Hague Conventions seen as governing the way war is waged and the Geneva Conventions regulating the rights of noncombatants in times of conflict. This distinction is artificial.

In practice, the provisions of the Geneva Conventions and Protocols are not confined to organizing the delivery of relief to civilians. They also codify and incorporate numerous rules relating to the conduct of hostilities. For instance, they restrict or prohibit certain methods of warfare and establish the responsibilities of all parties to the conflict with regard to war crimes.

The obligations of armed forces during hostilities are consolidated under the entries on → **methods (and means) of warfare, war,** and **weapons**. The issues relating to the punishment of violations of humanitarian law are addressed in the entries on → **penal sanctions in humanitarian law, universal jurisdiction,** and **war crimes/crimes against humanity**.

☞ Humanitarian organizations, citizens, and political authorities must know the provisions contained in the 1949 Geneva Conventions and the two 1977 Additional Protocols because they are the actors, by law and in practice, who organize and coordinate the responsibilities of civilian authorities and relief organizations in times of conflict.

Humanitarian law defends a right of action. Victims of conflicts are protected by the quality of relief actions carried out by humanitarian organizations. The quality of such actions depends on

- their speed and appropriateness (both the type and the quantity of aid provided);
- their conformity with the right to relief established by humanitarian law for the different categories of protected persons;
- the ability of relief organizations to account for any failures to address these rights.

→ **Humanitarian and relief personnel**

I. THE MEANS

To enable international humanitarian law to achieve its objective, rules and regulations have been developed that center around two axes: the responsibility of military commanders and the actions of humanitarian organizations.

1. The Responsibility of Military Commanders

Humanitarian law establishes certain rules, responsibilities, and requirements that must be respected.

- It presents a clear distinction between military and civilian objectives, between combatants and civilians, between strategic goods and objects essential to the survival of the civilian population. Fighting must only affect combatants and strategic objectives.
- It decrees that individuals and populations who are not taking part in the hostilities must not be targets and must be treated humanely at all times.
- It decrees that civilian objects and those indispensable to the survival of the population may not be targeted or destroyed.
- It requires that there be a clear chain of responsible command within the armed forces of all parties to the conflict. The hierarchy must ensure the discipline and respect for the rules of the law of armed conflict, both within the command structure and in the conduct of hostilities.
- It establishes a system of individual criminal responsibility for authors of war crimes (grave breaches of humanitarian law). All states commit to cooperate in searching for, prosecuting, and punishing the authors of such crimes, wherever they may be.

➔ **Civilian population; Combatants; Duty of commanders; Protected objects and property; Responsibility; Universal jurisdiction; War crimes/Crimes against humanity**

2. The Actions of Humanitarian Organizations

- Humanitarian law distinguishes between different kinds of situations and different categories of protected persons. It guarantees their right to the relief and protection that are best suited to their needs and the specific dangers they may face.
- It decrees the minimum guarantees that must be ensured in terms of relief and protection. These must be implemented in all situations, for all individuals.
- It clearly describes the relief and protection actions that the ICRC, relief organizations, and Protecting Powers are entitled to undertake for the benefit of the victims.
- It entrusts humanitarian organizations with a general right of initiative that allows them to conceive of and suggest any protection and assistance actions that may be necessary to protect the lives of the populations in danger.
- It specifies that activities of a humanitarian nature cannot be regarded as interference in the internal affairs of a state.

➔ **Intervention; Protected persons; Relief; Right of humanitarian initiative**

II. THE METHOD

Unlike human rights law, humanitarian law does not establish universal rights applicable to all individuals. Instead, the specificity of the four Geneva Conventions is that each one applies to a different category of protected persons, defining the minimum standard of treatment that must be respected for each category. Hence, the applicable law differs depending on whether the situation concerns an international or an internal armed conflict, an occupied territory or a besieged area. It also differs depending on whether it concerns persons who are wounded or sick, civilians, women, children, internees, prisoners of war, and so on. ➔ **International armed conflict; Noninternational armed conflict; Protected persons**

The strength of this approach is that it lists specific rights, carefully adapted to protect individuals in these categories from the specific risks they may incur as a result of their status or the nature of the situation.

The weakness of this method is that, if the Conventions are applied in bad faith, it can lead to a refusal or a delay in providing the necessary protection while the concerned parties debate the specific definition or status of the protected person or of the situation. Furthermore, this approach means that a number of persons and situations are not covered by the laws regulating armed conflict, since they do not fall into one of the specific categories. In such cases, the fundamental guarantees of humanitarian law and general international guarantees that remain applicable at all times must be applied to them.

☞ In humanitarian law, the legal qualification that persons or situations may be given represents important judicial and political stakes, since the rights of each individual depend on the definition of his or her status.

To limit the risks of having individuals not be protected because they do not come under one of the categories set forth, the law of armed conflict enumerates minimum rules, as well as fundamental guarantees, that must be implemented and defended at all times, in all circumstances, for all those who do not benefit from a more favorable regime of protection.

In the field of human rights, international conventions also enumerate certain rights that are considered "nonderogable." This means that states may never infringe on these rights, even in times of internal tension or of war. These peremptory norms are therefore also applicable to all individuals, no matter what their status is, in all circumstances and contexts, even during conflicts.

➔   **Fundamental guarantees; Situations and persons not expressly covered by humanitarian law**

III. THE CONTENTS OF INTERNATIONAL HUMANITARIAN LAW

The rules vary depending on the nature of the conflict. It is therefore important to distinguish between

- the law of international armed conflict, established by the Geneva Conventions and Protocol I, and
- the law of noninternational armed conflict, established by common Article 3 of the Geneva Conventions, completed by Protocol II.

Interpretation and Application of Humanitarian Law

While the law of armed conflict was written for specific situations and persons, nothing prevents it from being invoked and applied in other situations. In fact, many of its provisions can be found, in more or less detailed form, in a multitude of international texts. Furthermore, the provisions establishing the more detailed rules of protection can be used to interpret the more general clauses or to serve as a standard of reference for the provisions organizing relief operations.

   This is particularly important since the rules governing international armed conflicts are far more detailed than those governing internal conflicts. Hence, the provisions in the first set of rules can be used to give substance to the general principles referred to in other texts. Concretely, they are as follows:

- Although the 1977 Protocols have not been ratified by all states, their provisions can be used to illustrate and interpret the content of the Geneva Conventions that they complete or complement.
- The provisions set forth in the Geneva Conventions and Protocol I, relating to international armed conflicts, clarify the content of the general principles reaffirmed in Protocol II, which relates to internal armed conflicts.
- A certain number of articles are common to the four Geneva Conventions. This implies that they are applicable to virtually all situations. Such articles include, for instance, the right of humanitarian initiative, the treatment of the sick and wounded, and general guarantees of humane treatment.
- Humanitarian law encourages parties to the conflict to implement its provisions by signing special agreements. In so doing, they are not limited by legal qualifications of given situations and persons, from a legal standpoint, or by the general rules governing the application and implementation of international humanitarian conventions. NGOs may therefore always invoke this right in carrying out relief actions.

➔   **Fundamental guarantees; High Contracting Parties; International conventions; Legal status of parties to the conflict; Right of humanitarian initiative; Situations and persons not expressly covered by humanitarian law; Special agreement**

1. The law of international armed conflict

These rules are contained in the four Geneva Conventions of August 12, 1949, and the first 1977 Additional Protocol (Protocol I).

   The first three Conventions relate exclusively to the treatment of members of armed forces. We will only give a brief overview of their provisions because there is no lack of experts or means to uphold their content and implementation. We will go into more detail concerning the Fourth Convention, which relates to the treatment and protection of civilians, and Protocol I, which addresses the fate of all victims of armed conflict, without distinction.

a. Geneva Convention for the Amelioration of the Condition of the Wounded and Sick in Armed Forces in the Field (GCI)

- Articles 1 to 11: general provisions
- Articles 12 to 18: the wounded and sick
- Articles 19 to 23: medical units and establishments
- Articles 24 to 32: medical personnel
- Articles 33 to 34: buildings and material
- Articles 35 to 37: medical transports
- Articles 38 to 44: distinctive emblems
- Articles 45 to 48: execution of the Convention and unforeseen cases
- Articles 49 to 54: repression of abuses and infractions
- Articles 55 to 64: final provisions
- Annex I: draft agreement relating to hospital zones and localities
- Annex II: identity card for members of medical and religious personnel attached to the armed forces

b. Geneva Convention for the Amelioration of the Condition of the Wounded, Sick, and Shipwrecked Members of Armed Forces at Sea (GCII)

- Articles 1 to 11: general provisions
- Articles 12 to 21: the wounded, sick, and shipwrecked
- Articles 22 to 35: hospital ships
- Articles 36 to 37: medical personnel
- Articles 38 to 40: medical transports
- Articles 41 to 45: distinctive emblems
- Articles 46 to 49: execution of the Convention and unforeseen cases
- Articles 50 to 53: repression of abuses and infractions
- Articles 54 to 63: final provisions
- Annex: identity card for members of medical and religious personnel attached to the armed forces at sea

c. Geneva Convention Relative to the Treatment of Prisoners of War (GCIII)

- Part I (Articles 1–11): general provisions
- Part II (Articles 12–16): general protection of prisoners of war
- Part III: captivity
  —Articles 17 to 20 and 69 to 70: beginning of captivity and notification of capture
  —Articles 21 to 24: general observations regarding places and modalities of internment
  —Articles 25 to 29: quarters, food, and clothing of prisoners of war
  —Articles 30 to 33: hygiene and medical attention
  —Articles 34 to 38: religious, intellectual, and physical activities
  —Articles 39 to 45: discipline and rank
  —Articles 46 to 48: transfer of prisoners of war
  —Articles 49 to 68: labor and financial resources of prisoners of war
  —Articles 71 to 76: correspondence and relief shipments
  —Articles 78 to 81: prisoners of war representatives and the right of complaint
  —Articles 82 to 108: penal and disciplinary sanctions

- Part IV (Articles 109–121): termination of captivity, release, and repatriation
- Part V (Articles 122–125): information bureaus and relief societies for prisoners of war
- Part VI (Articles 126–143): execution of the Convention, general provisions, and final provisions
- Annex I: model agreement concerning direct repatriation and accommodation in neutral countries of wounded and sick prisoners of war
- Annex II: regulations concerning mixed medical commissions
- Annex III: regulations concerning collective relief
- Annex IV: identity card, capture card, correspondence card and letter, notification of death, and repatriation certificate
- Annex V: model regulations concerning payment sent by prisoners of war to their own country

d. Geneva Convention Relative to the Protection of Civilians in Time of War (GCIV)

- Part I: general provisions
  Articles 1 to 12 establish the general provisions relating to the implementation of the Convention—namely, the minimum guarantees applicable to situations not expressly covered by the Convention (Article 3); the definition of protected persons (Article 4); the possibility of negotiating special agreements (Article 7); the role of the Protecting Powers or their substitutes, the ICRC, or any other impartial humanitarian organization (Articles 9–11).
- Part II: general protection of populations against certain consequences of war
  Articles 13 to 26 address the creation of hospital and safety zones and localities (Articles 14 and 15); the protection of wounded persons and hospitals (Articles 16–20); the delivery of relief, medical supplies, food, and clothing to civilian populations (Article 23); the special protection of children and dispersed families (Articles 24–26).
- Part III: status and treatment of protected persons
  Articles 27 to 34 set forth the provisions common to occupied territories. These include the responsibility of the Occupying Power toward the population (Articles 27–29); prohibitions on using the population to serve as protection against military attacks and on taking hostages (Articles 29 and 34); the prohibition on coercion, certain forms of punishment, and intimidation of the population (Articles 31–33); the right of the population and of protected persons to apply to the Protecting Powers, the ICRC, or any other organization, for relief and protection (Article 30).
  Articles 35 to 46 protect foreigners in the territory of a party to the conflict.
  Articles 47 to 78 regulate the status of occupied territories—namely, the prohibition on individual or mass forcible transfers or deportations (Article 49); the protection of children (Article 50); the protection of workers and the limits on enlistment (Articles 51 and 52); the prohibited destruction and requisitions (Articles 53 and 57); the obligations of the Occupying Power in terms of the hygiene and public health of the populations, as well as the organization of relief (Articles 55–63); the guarantees concerning the applicable laws and the functions of courts of law (Articles 54, 64–75); the guarantees for detainees (Articles 76 and 77).
  Articles 79 to 135 regulate the status and treatment of internees.
  Article 136 to 141 regulate the provisions regarding the Central Tracing Agency, which centralizes the information concerning persons who are interned, detained, or have disappeared.
- Part IV: execution of the Convention
  Articles 142 to 159 regulate the general provisions and final provisions, namely the penal sanctions applicable to grave breaches of the Convention (Articles 146–149).

- Annex I: draft agreement relating to hospital and safety zones and localities
- Annex II: draft regulations concerning collective relief
- Annex III: internment card, letter, and correspondence card

e. Protocol Additional to the Geneva Conventions of 12 August 1949, and Relating to the Protection of Victims of International Armed Conflicts (PI)

- Part I: general provisions (Articles 1–7)—namely, general principles, scope of application, situations not expressly covered by the Convention, legal status of the parties to the conflict
- Part II: the wounded, sick, and shipwrecked
  —Articles 8 and 9: general protection and terminology
  —Articles 10 and 11: protection and care
  —Articles 12 to 16: general protection of medical services, units, and personnel, including protection against requisitions
  —Articles 17 and 18: role of relief societies and identification
  —Article 20: prohibition of reprisals against the wounded, sick, and medical installations
  —Articles 21 to 31: protection and regulation of different means of medical transportation
  —Articles 32 to 34: missing and dead persons
- Part III: methods and means of warfare, and the status of combatants and prisoners of war
  —Articles 35 to 37: basic rules, new weapons, and perfidy
  —Article 38: recognized emblems
  —Articles 43 to 47: status of combatants, prisoners of war, mercenaries, and spies
- Part IV: the civilian population
  General protection against effects of hostilities—namely:
  —Articles 48 and 49: basic rule and field of application
  —Articles 50 and 51: definition and protection of civilians and civilian population
  —Articles 52 to 56: definition and protection of civilian objects
  —Articles 49, 57, and 58: definition of attacks and precautions against the effects of attacks
  —Articles 59 and 60: localities and zones under special protection (nondefended and demilitarized)
  —Articles 61 to 67: definitions, organization, and identification of civil defense
  Relief in favor of the civilian population
  —Articles 68 to 71: definition of basic needs organization of relief actions and status of relief personnel
  Treatment of persons in the power of a party to the conflict
  —Article 73: refugees and stateless persons
  —Article 74: reunion of dispersed families
  —Article 75: fundamental guarantees
  —Article 76: protection of women
  —Articles 77 and 78: protection and evacuation of children
  —Article 79: measures or protection for journalists
- Part V: execution of the Conventions and of this Protocol
  —Articles 80 to 84: activities of the Red Cross and other humanitarian organizations (Article 81); legal advisers in armed forces (Article 82); dissemination and rules of application (Articles 83 and 84)
  —Articles 85 to 91: repression of breaches of the Conventions and this Protocol, namely: repression (Article 85); punishment of failures to act (Article 86); duty of commanders with regard to breaches (Article 87); mutual assistance in criminal matters and cooperation

International Humanitarian Law

> (Articles 88 and 89); International Fact-Finding Commission (Article 90); responsibility and compensation (Article 91)

- Part VI (Articles 92–102): final resolutions—namely, the restrictions imposed on the denunciation of the Conventions or Protocol
- Annex I: regulations concerning identification—namely, identity card for permanent civilian medical and religious personnel (Article 1); identity card for temporary civilian medical and religious personnel (Article 2); the distinctive emblem—its shape, nature, and use (Articles 3 and 4); distinctive signals—light signal, radio signal, electronic identification (Articles 5–8); communications—radio communications, use of international codes, other means of communication, flight plans, signals and procedures for the interception of medical aircraft (Articles 9–13); civil defense—identity card, international distinctive sign (Articles 14 and 15); works and installations containing dangerous forces—international special sign (Article 16).
- Annex II: identity card for journalists on dangerous professional missions

2. The Law of Noninternational Armed Conflict

These rules are contained in Article 3, common to the four Geneva Conventions of August 12, 1949, and the second 1977 Additional Protocol (Protocol II).

a. Article 3 Common to the Four Geneva Conventions

This article establishes the minimum level of protection that must be provided in times of noninternational armed conflict, as well as in the case of situations (or for persons) that are not expressly covered by the Conventions and that do not benefit from a more favorable regime of protection.

Common Article 3 begins by imposing an absolute prohibition on certain acts. This prohibition remains applicable at all times and in all circumstances with regard to noncombatants. This principle is therefore valid in situations of internal disturbances and tensions, to which the law of armed conflict does not otherwise apply.

> (1) The following acts are and shall remain prohibited at any time and in any place whatsoever with respect to [persons taking no active part in hostilities, including members of armed forces who have laid down their arms and those placed *hors de combat* by sickness, wounds, detention, or any other cause]:
>   (a) violence to life and person, in particular murder of all kinds, mutilation, cruel treatment and torture;
>   (b) taking of hostages;
>   (c) outrages upon personal dignity, in particular humiliating and degrading treatment;
>   (d) the passing of sentences and the carrying out of executions without previous judgment pronounced by a regularly constituted court, affording all the judicial guarantees which are recognized as indispensable by civilized peoples.
> (2) The wounded and sick shall be collected and cared for.
>
> An impartial humanitarian body, such as the International Committee of the Red Cross, may offer its services to the Parties to the conflict.
> The Parties to the conflict should further endeavour to bring into force, by means of special agreements, all or part of the other provisions of the present Convention.
> The application of the preceding provisions shall not affect the legal status of the Parties to the conflict. (GCI–IV Article 3)

b. Protocol Additional to the Geneva Conventions of August 12, 1949, and Relating to the Protection of Victims of Non-International Armed Conflicts (PII)

Protocol II concerns the victims of armed conflicts that "take place in the territory of a High Contracting Party between its armed forces and dissident armed forces or other organized armed groups which, under responsible command, exercise such control over a part of its territory as to enable them to carry out sustained and concerted military operations and to implement this Protocol" (Article 1.1).

It does not apply to situations of internal disturbances and tensions, such as riots, isolated and sporadic acts of violence, and other acts of a similar nature, which are not qualified as armed conflicts (Article 1.2).

The Protocol clearly specifies the protection that must be provided for victims of internal armed conflicts. It enumerates the guarantees that a state in the throes of such a conflict owes its citizens. Among other matters, it reinforces the fundamental rights of children and the protection against sexual violence and slavery. It also

- details the fundamental guarantees that must be ensured for all persons who are not or are no longer participating in the hostilities (Article 4);
- adds provisions, in addition to those of Article 4, that must be respected, as a minimum, with regard to persons deprived of their liberty for reasons related to the armed conflict, whether they are interned or detained (Article 5);
- establishes the judicial guarantees that are mandatory to ensure the respect for the fundamental guarantees (Article 6);
- sets forth the general measures of protection and care that must be provided for the wounded and sick (Articles 7–12); and
- enumerates the measures of protection and the right to relief from which the general civilian population must benefit (Articles 13–18).

→ **Customary international law; Detention; Fundamental guarantees; Humanitarian and relief personnel; Individual recourse; Internal disturbances and tensions; International conventions; International Criminal Court; Medical duties; Methods (and means) of warfare; Noninternational armed conflict; Penal sanctions in humanitarian law; Protected persons; Protecting Powers; Protection; Red Cross; Relief; Respect for international humanitarian law; Responsibility; Right of access; Right of humanitarian initiative; Situations and persons not expressly covered by humanitarian law; War; War crimes/Crimes against humanity**

For Additional Information:

Draper, G. I. A. D. "The Development of International Humanitarian Law." In *International Dimensions of Humanitarian Law*. Geneva: Henri Dupont Institute, 1988, 67–90.

Greenwood, Christopher. "Historical Development and Legal Basis: Scope of Application of Humanitarian Law." In *The Handbook of Humanitarian Law in Armed Conflicts*, ed. Dieter Fleck. Oxford: Oxford University Press, 1995, 1–64.

Nahlik, Stanislaw E. "A Brief Outline of International Humanitarian Law." *International Review of the Red Cross* 241 (July–August 1998): 187–226.

Preux, Jean de. *International Humanitarian Law: Synopses*. Geneva: ICRC, 1993.

Sandoz, Yves. "Implementing International Humanitarian Law." In *International Dimensions of Humanitarian Law*. Geneva: Henri Dupont Institute, 1988, 259–82.

■ INTERNATIONAL LAW

Law is the set of rules that organizes the lives of individuals in that society. Each society thus gives itself the means to organize its collective life and regulate its relations with other communities in a harmonious way, following preestablished "rules of the game," known to all. Law has both a normative role—to establish the standards of behavior—and a judicial one—to ensure the means to enforce respect for the rules.

In a system of law, the victim does not procure justice for him- or herself. The community condemns failures to respect the established public or social order and is in charge of compensating the victim.

- In a national society, the principle of the social contract, which inherently ties individuals to society, reflects the will of individuals to be governed by collective rules.
- In international society, states adopt agreements or conventions. Each state remains sovereign but may choose to limit its sovereignty by making commitments, through such conventions, that restrict their freedom of action in certain domains.

Thus, international law is the set of rules adopted by states to govern relations either among themselves (public international law) or between individuals or legal entities of different nationalities (private international law). The entire body and system of international law is complex, and, in this entry, we will simply indicate some of the key elements that may be useful when approaching questions of international law—in particular, the aspects with regard to which NGOs may have a role to play.

1. Sources

National and international law have three different sources:

- *Written texts:* These are drafted and adopted by legitimate authorities responsible for enforcing the rule of law. In domestic law they have different names, such as statutes, regulations, ordinances, or decrees. In some countries these texts may include religious writings. In international law, these rules are usually set forth in international conventions.
- *Judicial precedents* (stare decisis): This encompasses the judgments rendered by legally established courts and serves as a basis for interpreting legal texts in the future. International tribunals contribute to the creation of an international body of jurisprudence.
- *Custom:* This is a general and consistent practice accepted as law. Not all rules are written, and certain societies function mainly on the basis of customary law, which is defended in litigious cases before the courts and then becomes case law. International law leaves a great deal of room for customary law, basing itself on the repeated and accepted behavior of states (*opinio juris*).

International actors therefore have a great responsibility in defending international law and ensuring its evolution since, if a rule is not upheld in practice, it is weakened and may even disappear. On the other hand, if the behavior of international actors is regular and coherent, it contributes to the establishment of new standards and laws. International law gives NGOs a right of initiative in humanitarian matters, which gives them a share of the responsibility for the evolution of custom in this field.

☞ There are different legal systems in the world. Even within one system, such as that of common law, the procedure may vary. The main differences may be reflected in the sources of law on which the judiciary bases itself, the hierarchy of norms that must be respected, the rights given to each party to a dispute, and the procedure followed in each case.

The entry on → **hierarchy of norms** provides some examples of the different legal sources and their status as positive law—for instance, the different force of law that judicial precedents have in different systems. There are, however, certain peremptory norms of international law (*jus cogens* norms, explained later), which are considered binding on all states. Furthermore, international conventions, and particularly international courts, have incorporated various elements into their structure to take the different legal systems into account. Conventions, for instance, try to be of universal appeal and, once ratified, must be integrated into the domestic legal system.

In the case of international tribunals, it is all the more important to find a solution to any contradictions between the legal systems so that they, too, can strive for universal adherence. At the very least, most international courts posit that their members must represent "the principal legal systems of the world," as is enshrined in the statutes of the → **International Court of Justice,** the International Criminal Tribunals for the former Yugoslavia and Rwanda, and the International Criminal Court. In the case of recently established tribunals, in particular the → **International Criminal Court,** innovative efforts have been made to combine different legal systems of the world more concretely. The structure of the ICC and some of the rights accorded to victims, for instance, reflect a blend of systems—in particular, those of common law and civil law.

The entry on → **International Criminal Tribunals** explains some of the differences between these two systems—namely, in terms of the approach to criminal substantive law, trial procedures, rights of the victims and accused—under the section "Legal Basis of the Tribunals: International Law, Civil Law, and Common Law."

See also → **Customary international law; International conventions; Right of humanitarian initiative.**

2. Hierarchy of Norms

The many different rules and regulations that exist have a varying force or status of law, depending on the legal body and procedure by which they were adopted. In each situation, it is therefore important to compare the different applicable laws according to the official hierarchy of norms. If there is a contradiction between two principles of law, the one that has a higher legal authority prevails.

Nonetheless, certain rules—including unwritten ones—must prevail in all circumstances. Historically, this fact was reflected in the tension between the proponents of "natural law" and those of "positive law." Today, most states recognize the existence of peremptory norms, known as *jus cogens.*

Finally, all states, having adhered to the UN Charter, accept that their obligations under the UN Charter prevail over those under any other international agreement (Article 103 of UN Charter).

→ **Hierarchy of norms; Natural law and positive law**

Jus cogens

The notion of *jus cogens* was firmly established by the 1969 Vienna Convention on the Law of Treaties, which reaffirms the existence of certain norms of international law that are "accepted and recognized by the international community of states, as a whole, as a norm from which no derogation is permitted" (Article 53). These norms are binding on all states, without exception, and any convention or other international text that infringes on or violates these norms is void to the extent of the inconsistency. States have agreed that *jus cogens* norms prohibit acts such as genocide, slavery, and aggression. However, additional elements of this law have yet to be defined. That is one of the International Court of Justice's roles.

International human rights and humanitarian law conventions enumerate the rights and obligations from which no state can derogate, under any circumstance. These fundamental guarantees, or "nonderogable rights," represent the minimum standard of protection for individuals and are peremptory norms of international law

➜   **Fundamental guarantees**

---

3. Interpretation

Laws may be interpreted according to certain well-defined principles. These include the spirit of the law (meaning the intent of the legislator or drafter), the coherence between the interpretation of a law and its objectives, and good faith. Each rule of law is subject to different interpretations. In the context of international law, it may be that no court exists that can rule on such questions of law, although the International Court of Justice and regional human rights courts may do so for certain texts, if requested and with the consent of all states concerned. NGOs must monitor the implementation of international human rights and humanitarian law so as to ensure that they are not being interpreted in unilateral or abusive ways.

➜   **International conventions**

4. Implementation

International law may be implemented in different ways depending on the nature of the text itself (based on how it was adopted and how precise it is) and on the status given to international law domestically by the national legislation of each state. In addition to the rank accorded to international law, some treaties may be "self-executing," meaning they are precise enough to be implemented directly, without needing any additional interpretation.

In such cases, an individual can invoke these norms directly before domestic courts (once their government has ratified the treaty), even if there has been no implementing legislation. Many provisions, on the other hand, are "non-self-executing," meaning that the rules or procedures must be incorporated into national legislation before an individual may have recourse to such laws. This is particularly the case for issues of international criminal law, and even more so with regard to the prosecution of war crimes and crimes against humanity.

➜   **International conventions**

5. Sanctions

Courts impose sanctions for breaches of the law. The aim of punishment is to reestablish public order and to compensate victims.

In the international order, the role of the judiciary is very limited because there is no permanent international court with international jurisdiction. The International Court of Justice (ICJ) is responsible for prosecuting states if they violate their international obligations. However, it has no jurisdiction over criminal matters, cannot judge individuals, and can only judge states with their consent.

Nevertheless, states recently reached an agreement to define, prohibit, and punish certain criminal behavior that is considered particularly threatening to the international public order. In this context, they adopted the statute for a permanent International Criminal Court (ICC) on July 17, 1998. The ICC will be responsible for prosecuting individuals accused of crimes of genocide, war crimes, and crimes against humanity, as well as aggression, at a later date. The Court will only begin to operate once sixty states have ratified the statute, which may take several years given the time needed for most states to ratify an international convention.

The UN Security Council can decide to stigmatize or reprimand specific behavior that threatens international peace and security. The measures that may be implemented in such cases include embargoes, restricting or interrupting economic or diplomatic relations, as well as recourse to international armed force.

- In case of grave violations of humanitarian law (war crimes, crimes against humanity), the perpetrators may be prosecuted by the courts of any country—under the principle of universal jurisdiction—and, once in force, by the ICC (following certain preconditions). There are also two ad hoc International Criminal Tribunals set up to judge authors of crimes committed in the former Yugoslavia and in Rwanda. **➔ International Criminal Court; International Criminal Tribunals; Universal jurisdiction**
- In case of human rights violations, two regional courts can judge states: the European and the Inter-American Court of Human Rights. Certain human rights violations may come within the jurisdiction of the ICC if they are committed in the context of a policy of crimes against humanity, war crimes, or genocide. There are also nonjudicial bodies to which individuals or other entities may have recourse; these are explained in the entries on **➔ individual recourse** and **➔ human rights**.

6. Reparations

In general, international law does not provide mechanisms for victims of human rights and humanitarian law violations to receive reparation or compensation, except for the Inter-American Court of Human Rights, which has a relatively narrow jurisdiction, and the ICC, which is not yet operational. Victims and their families therefore continue to depend on the rulings of domestic courts or, for certain human rights violations, on ad hoc UN funds. Currently, there are only two such funds, set up by the UN General Assembly: the fund for victims of torture, created in 1982, and the fund for victims of contemporary forms of slavery, created in 1991.

➔ **Customary international law; Embargoes; European Court (and Commission) of Human Rights; Hierarchy of norms; Human rights; Individual recourse; Inter-American Court of (and Commission on) Human Rights; International** conventions; International Court of Justice; International Criminal Court; International Criminal Tribunals; Natural and positive law; Penal sanctions of humanitarian law; Sanctions (diplomatic, economic, or military); Security Council of the UN; Sanctions/Punishment; Soft law; Universal jurisdiction; War crimes/Crimes against humanity

📖 **For Additional Information:**

Brownlie, Ian. *Principles of Public International Law*, 4th ed. Oxford: Oxford University Press, 1990, 603–34.
Carter, Barry E., and Phillip R. Trimble. *International Law.* Boulder, Colo.: Aspen, 1999.
Shaw, Malcolm. *International Law,* 4th ed. Cambridge: Cambridge University Press, 1997.

■ INTERNMENT

In times of armed conflict, parties to a conflict may take measures of internment concerning civilians or prisoners of war. The difference between internment and detention is that decisions relating to internment are taken by administrative or military authorities, while those relating to detention generally come under the responsibility of judicial authorities.

- The rules regulating the internment and detention of combatants, during international armed conflicts, are covered under the precise and detailed rules of humanitarian law concerning the treatment of prisoners of war (GCIII Articles 21, 22, 30, 31, and 72). ➔ **Prisoners of war**
- Also in the case of international armed conflicts, humanitarian law sets forth specific guarantees for persons who are arrested, detained, or interned for reasons related to the armed conflict (PI Article 75.6). ➔ **Detention; Judicial guarantees**
- In the case of internal armed conflicts, humanitarian law does not explicitly set out measures for internment. However, Protocol II additional to the Geneva Conventions protects all persons who have been deprived of their liberty for reasons related to the armed conflict, whether they are interned or detained (PII Articles 4 and 5). The provisions relating to internment can always be used as a reference for comparable relief actions, because they are particularly detailed. ➔ **Detention**

1. Internment of Civilians

Internment is a security measure that a state may implement in times of armed conflict, concurrently with assigned residence. It targets civilian persons living in the territory of a party to the conflict who are of the nationality of the adverse party or other foreigners. It is also possible for foreigners residing in the territory of the state to request voluntary interment.

- The Occupying Power may intern or place in assigned residence certain members of the population of the occupied territories who are considered to be a threat. With regard to civilians, such measures may be ordered only if the security of the Detaining Power makes it absolutely necessary or if the civilians themselves request it (GCIV Articles 41, 42, 68, and 78).
- Any interned person is entitled to an internment decision being reconsidered as soon as possible by a court or administrative board designated by the Detaining Power for that purpose. If the internment or placing in assigned residence is maintained, this decision must be reviewed

periodically, at least twice a year (GCIV Article 43). Furthermore, if a civilian can no longer support him- or herself as a result of such measures, the party to the conflict that applied this decision is responsible for supporting this person and his or her dependents (GCIV Article 39).

The Fourth Geneva Convention provides the detailed rules and regulations concerning conditions of internment and the treatment of internees throughout seventy-two articles (Articles 79–141), the main elements of which are summarized later.

2. Places of Internment

Places of internment must be located away from the dangers of war, must be supplied with a system of identification and adequate shelter in case of attack, and must respect all norms of hygiene and health. They must be fully protected from dampness and adequately heated and lighted. The internees must have suitable bedding and sufficient blankets, taking into account the climate, as well as the age, sex, and state of health of the internees. They must have the use of sanitary conveniences that conform to the Geneva Conventions' rules of hygiene, both day and night. They must be given sufficient water, soap, and the necessary time for their personal hygiene and laundry (GCIV Articles 82, 83, 85, and 88).

3. Food and Clothing

Daily food rations for internees must be sufficient in quantity, quality, and variety to keep internees in a good state of health and prevent nutritional deficiencies. Their customary diet must be taken into account (GCIV Article 89). Internees must have clothing, footwear, and change of underwear that is adequate for the climate. Workers must receive suitable work outfits, including protective clothing. The clothing supplied by the Detaining Power to internees must not contain outward markings that are ignominious or expose them to ridicule (GCIV Article 90).

4. Hygiene and medical attention

Every place of internment shall have an adequate infirmary, under the direction of a qualified doctor, and must offer medical examinations every day. It is preferable that internees receive the attention of medical personnel of their own nationality. They may not be prevented from presenting themselves to the medical authorities for examination. Treatment shall be provided free of charge, including any apparatus necessary for the maintenance of internees in good health (e.g., dentures, eyeglasses, etc.). The medical authorities must, on request, issue an official medical report or certificate showing the nature of the illness or injury, and the duration and nature of the treatment given, to every internee who has undergone treatment.

In addition to voluntary medical examinations, when needed, medical inspections of internees must be carried out at least once a month to supervise the general state of health, nutrition, and cleanliness of internees and to detect contagious diseases. In particular, such inspections shall include checking the weight of each internee (GCIV Articles 91 and 92).

5. Religious, Intellectual, and Physical Activities

Internees shall enjoy complete latitude in the exercise of their religion and ministers of religion may visit them (GCIV Article 93).

Internees must be given opportunities for physical exercise, sports, and outdoor games (as well as educational and other intellectual exercises). For this purpose, sufficient open spaces must be allocated in all places of internment. Special playgrounds shall be reserved for children and young people (GCIV Article 94). The Detaining Power may employ internees as workers, if they so desire, separately from any work directly related to the lives of the internees. Such work must be neither degrading nor humiliating. The standards prescribed for the working conditions, compensation, and health coverage shall be in accordance with international labor rights and standards (GCIV Articles 95 and 96).

6. Personal Property and Financial Resources

Internees are allowed to retain articles of personal use, including identity documents. They must be given detailed receipts for any object or property withheld by the camp administrators (GCIV Article 97).

All internees must receive regular allowances, sufficient to enable them to purchase goods and articles, such as toilet requisites and tobacco. They may also receive allowances from the state of which they are a national, the Protecting Powers, any organizations that may assist them, or their families. Finally, they must also be able to send remittances to their families and other dependents (GVI Article 98).

7. Administration and Discipline

Every place of internment must be under the authority of a responsible officer or civil servant, who must possess a copy of the Fourth Geneva Convention in his or her language. This same Convention and the texts of any special agreements, regulations, orders, notices, and publications of every kind must be communicated to the internees and posted inside the places of internment, in a language they understand. In every place of internment, the internees may freely elect the members of a Committee empowered to represent them before the Detaining Power, the Protecting Powers, the ICRC, and any other organization that might assist them (GCIV Articles 99–104).

8. Relations with the Exterior

Within the week following his or her internment, each internee must be able to inform his or her family, as well as the Central Tracing Agency of the Red Cross. Internees must also be allowed to send and receive letters and cards, individual parcels, or collective shipments containing, in particular, foodstuffs, clothing, and medical supplies, as well as books and objects of a devotional, educational, or recreational character. Such relief shipments are exempt from import, customs, and other dues and may be transported by the ICRC or any other organization authorized by the parties to the conflict.

The censoring of correspondence shall be done as quickly as possible and may not be used as a pretext to delay the delivery of letters or parcels. Every internee is allowed to receive visitors, especially near relatives, at regular intervals and as frequently as possible (GCIV Articles 105–116).

9. Penal and Disciplinary Sanctions

The rules that regulate the penal and disciplinary sanctions that may be applied to interned persons for acts committed during their internment are established in Articles 117 to 126 of the

Fourth Geneva Convention. The laws in force in the territory on which they find themselves are applicable to internees who break the law during their internment. In passing sentences, the courts must take into account the fact that the defendant is not a national of the Detaining Power, and they may reduce the penalty prescribed. Disciplinary punishments may in no case be inhuman, brutal, or dangerous for the health of internees. Escape or attempted escape must be liable only to disciplinary punishment. Under no circumstances may internees undergo disciplinary punishment in penitentiary establishments. The premises in which the sanctions are undergone must be in conformity with sanitary requirements, including adequate sleeping quarters. Internees undergoing disciplinary punishment shall be allowed to exercise and to stay in the open air at least two hours each day. They can go to the medical examinations that are offered daily. They may read and write, and send and receive letters.

These rules are further explained in the entry on ➔ **judicial guarantees**.

10. Transfers of Internees

The transfer of internees must always be carried out humanely. As a general rule, the transfer must be conducted by rail or other means of transport, and under conditions at least equal to those enjoyed by the forces of the Detaining Power in their changes of station (GCIV Articles 127 and 128).

11. Deaths

Internees may give their wills to the responsible authorities for safekeeping. A doctor must certify the death of an internee, in every case, and must make out a death certificate, showing the causes of death and the conditions under which it occurred. Internees who die must be buried (or cremated, according to their religion or express request) honorably and, if possible, according to the rites of their religion. Every death the cause of which is suspect or unknown shall be immediately followed by an official inquiry by the Detaining Power (GCIV Articles 129–131).

12. Release, Repatriation, and Accommodation in Neutral Countries

Each interned person must be released by the Detaining Power as soon as the reasons that necessitated his or her internment no longer exist (GCIV Articles 132–135).

13. Information Bureaus and Central Agency

The Detaining Power must supply the Central Tracing Agency with all information concerning interned persons (GCIV Articles 136–141).

➔ **Central Tracing Agency; Detention; Judicial guarantees; Medical duties; Prisoners of war; Security**

📖 **For Additional Information:**

Fitzpatrick, Joan. "Temporary Protection of Refugees: Elements of a Formalized Regime." *American Journal of International Law* 94 (April 2000): 279.

ICRC. "Guiding Principles on Internal Displacement." *International Review of the Red Cross* 324 (September 1998): 545–56.

■ INTERVENTION

In international law, the concept of "intervention" is tied to the notion "interference" and is when a state intervenes in the internal affairs of another state, in violation of the latter's sovereignty. Such intervention is prohibited by the United Nations (UN) Charter (Article 2.7), under the principle of nonintervention, or noninterference, which posits that states should not "intervene in matters which are essentially within the domestic jurisdiction of any state." The purpose of this principle is to preserve the independence of weaker states against the interventions and pressures of more powerful ones. This concept is presented as the basis for international relations and therefore applies to interstate relations, not to relief activities carried out by impartial humanitarian organizations.

In fact, humanitarian law clearly states that aid activities may in no circumstances be regarded as interference in an armed conflict or as unfriendly acts (PI Articles 64 and 70).

In the past, states have used humanitarian arguments to justify direct and armed interventions that violated other states' sovereignty. Today, the UN Security Council holds the monopoly on the use of armed force in the international arena.

☞ International law recognizes only one "right of intervention" into a state's internal affairs; it is set forth and limited in Chapter VII of the UN Charter. This right is thus entrusted to the UN Security Council when a state's behavior can be construed as a threat to international peace and security. In such a case, the Council can undertake a series of measures, including diplomatic or economic sanctions. The Council is also authorized to use force and may decide that an international armed intervention is necessary to make the state in question stop its activities.

Several times, the Council has invoked humanitarian considerations when undertaking military or peacekeeping operations, yet peacekeeping operations obey broad imperatives linked to maintaining or reestablishing international peace and security, according to which humanitarian considerations remain secondary.

Thus, it is important not to confuse "humanitarian intervention" defended by states or the UN with humanitarian actions undertaken by impartial humanitarian organizations in situations of conflict.

---

1. Background and Definition

The "right of humanitarian intervention"—or the "right to intervene for humanitarian purposes"—is a notion that achieved widespread popularity thanks to its ambiguity. This concept was used to try to encourage and justify the use of force foreseen in the UN framework in order to protect populations threatened within their own country. This opened the way to armed operations within the framework of the UN, or with its authorization; however, it did not clarify the role that humanitarian considerations play in decisions to use force, nor did it succeed in clarifying UN soldiers' responsibility in terms of protecting populations in danger.

States have used noble motives for centuries to justify armed intervention into the domestic affairs of other states. Such justifications include the defense of human rights, minorities, and their own nationals. It began with the notion of the "just war," followed by the ideas of the European countries intervening to protect Christians in Islamic countries in the nineteenth century, and continued in the 1970s when, for instance, India intervened in Pakistan to protect the Bengali people from extortion by the army. The common point of all these interventions is the use of force to impose respect for the principles of humanity.

Contemporary international law does not recognize the legitimacy of such intervention when undertaken in a unilateral manner by one state. In the multilateral framework, the only justification for collective use of force against a state foreseen by the UN Charter rests on the threat that this state poses for international peace and security. Violations of humanitarian law are not explicitly mentioned. Furthermore, the UN Sub-Commission on Human Rights recently reaffirmed (August 20, 1999, Resolution E/CN.4/SUB.2/RES/1999/2) that the "duty" or "right" of certain states to carry out "humanitarian interventions" had no legal basis in international law—in particular, when it means the threat or use of force.

In most peacekeeping operations, agreements establishing the force's presence are signed with the "host state," under the aegis of the UN. The population's access to relief and its protection are rarely enforced, since the access and protection are negotiated with the very authorities who control the population. In practice, UN peacekeepers are rarely authorized to use force to enforce their mandate—even when it is to provide aid or to protect threatened populations—except in cases of self-defense. In other situations, the kind of equipment they carry (light weapons) and their relatively small numbers have explained their decision not to intervene—even in cases in which their enforcement mandate had been expanded to include use of force—specifically, when the populations they were meant to assist or protect were being attacked.

Today, "humanitarian intervention" is one of the mechanisms that the UN Security Council uses to explain and legitimize armed intervention, yet it is only one aspect of peacekeeping operations, alongside military, political, and diplomatic considerations. Impartial NGOs have no influence on the content of this concept, and the interventions carried out under the authority of (or approved by) the Security Council remain contingent on political choices that fluctuate under different outside constraints.

➙ **Peacekeeping; Protected areas and zones; Security Council; Self-defense**

☞ Actions undertaken in the name of the "right of humanitarian intervention" are the result of military and political compromises developed by the UN Security Council.

Chapter VI of the UN Charter establishes the possibility of undertaking noncoercive international operations, with the consent of the state concerned. Chapter VII, on the other hand, foresees the possibility of carrying out collective military operations without the consent of the state concerned, in cases when international peace and security are threatened. The UN's decisions to carry out a "humanitarian intervention" are taken sometimes under Chapter VI but more frequently under Chapter VII of the UN Charter, or at times under a combination of the two. In most cases, these decisions imply that

- the UN Security Council has not expressly or clearly recognized that the massive violations of humanitarian law or the persecution of civilian populations, against which it has decided to intervene, genuinely represent a threat to international peace and security; and
- the UN does not have the means for these operations to enforce the protection of these populations through force.

(continues)

(continued)

Such interventions are part of a new generation of peacekeeping operations. However, they can neither guarantee or enforce the respect for humanitarian law nor fully protect the vulnerable populations from violence.

International humanitarian law links individuals' right to assistance to impartial humanitarian organizations' right to undertake relief actions. It specifies that aid activities may in no circumstances be regarded as interference in an armed conflict or as unfriendly acts, and in fact parties to the conflict are under the obligation to facilitate such assistance (PI Articles 69 and 70). Humanitarian activities should thus be kept separate and independent from political and military initiatives.

2. Humanitarian Law and Intervention

International law, as codified by the UN Charter, gives priority to the notion of state sovereignty and all but forbids one state from intervening inside the borders of another without the latter's consent. However, certain exceptions do exist, tied mainly to the concept of collective security. The notion that noninternational conflicts, and particularly massive violations of humanitarian law, may threaten international peace and security, is a recent justification to place armed intervention in a UN framework. However, the UN has so far not given the intervention forces the legal mandate or the material means actually to protect civilians from massacres such as those that took place in Srebrenica or against extermination or genocide such as that which occurred in Rwanda. A report on UN peacekeeping operations released in August 2000 (by a panel chaired by Lakhdar Brahimi) is unlikely to change this. While insisting that the Security Council ensure that peacekeeping operations be given the resources necessary to carry out its mandate and arguing that ambiguous mandates can have disastrous consequences, it establishes quite clearly that "use of force only in self-defence should remain the bedrock principles of peacekeeping" (paragraph 48 of the report) and affirms that it is impossible for UN peacekeepers to protect the civilians in all the areas where they are deployed. ➔ **Collective security; Security Council; Sovereignty**

In 1977, when the Protocols additional to the Geneva Conventions were adopted, an important innovation was made with regard to actions undertaken by humanitarian and relief organizations for victims of conflicts or situations of tension. The states parties acknowledged that offers of relief that are "humanitarian and impartial in character and conducted without any adverse distinction . . . shall not be regarded as interference in the armed conflict or as unfriendly acts." Such acts must be undertaken if the civilian population of a state in conflict is not adequately provided with supplies, foodstuff, medicine, clothing, bedding, emergency shelter, and other supplies essential to the survival of the civilian population (PI Articles 69 and 70).

In the specific case of internal armed conflicts, the Additional Protocol II reiterates the UN Charter's nonintervention principle by stating that humanitarian law cannot be invoked as a "justification for intervening, directly or indirectly, for any reason whatever, in the armed conflict or in the internal or external affairs of the High Contracting Party in the territory of which that conflict occurs" (PII Article 3.2).

International law thus distinguishes between two kinds of missions: it confers on states and the UN the mission to prevent and punish war crimes and gives impartial humanitarian organizations the responsibility of organizing relief actions. States have clear obligations to prosecute and punish the authors of grave breaches of the Conventions (namely, war crimes and crimes against humanity), under the principle of universal jurisdiction. The system of prevention, however, is unclear. One international convention, the 1948 Convention on the Prevention and Punishment of the Crime of Genocide, clearly posits that states are under the obligation to intervene to stop acts of genocide. They must, at least, "call upon the competent organs of the UN to take such action as they consider appropriate for the prevention and suppression of acts of genocide" (Article 8 of the Genocide Convention).

It is therefore up to the UN Security Council and regional security organizations to define whether and how serious violations of humanitarian law threaten international or regional peace and security and can justify recourse to Chapter VII in order to launch a military intervention. It remains to be determined what form of protection the UN can offer to civilians in such situations.

→ **Collective security; Genocide; Humanitarian and relief personnel; International humanitarian law; Peacekeeping; Relief; Right of access; Right of humanitarian initiative; Sovereignty; Universal jurisdiction; War crimes/Crimes against humanity**

📖 **For Additional Information:**

Bettati, Mario. *Le Droit d'ingérence: Mutation de l'ordre international.* Paris: Odile Jacob, 1996.

Moore, Jonathan, ed. *Hard Choices: Moral Dilemmas in Humanitarian Intervention.* Lanham, Md.: Rowman & Littlefield, 1998.

Roberts, Adam, and Benedict Kingsbury, eds. *United Nations, Divided World: The UN's Roles in International Relations.* New York: Oxford University Press, 1993, 81–125.

Torrelli, Maurice. "From Humanitarian Assistance to 'Intervention on Humanitarian Grounds'?" *International Review of the Red Cross* (May–June 1992).

Weiss, Thomas G., David P. Forsythe, and Roger A. Coate. *The United Nations and Changing World Politics.* Boulder, Colo.: Westview, 1997.

■ INVIOLABILITY OF RIGHTS

Certain rights—namely, in the category of human rights—are inviolable. This means they may not be infringed on in any way and must be fully respected and defended.

> ☞ States may not, under any circumstance, adopt decisions that derogate from the most fundamental human rights (known as *nonderogable rights*) or limit them. Any national law or other legal document that limits or suspends such rights would be invalid.

Human rights conventions enumerate the list of nonderogable rights, also known as *jus cogens* norms. → **Fundamental guarantees; International law**

In times of conflict, humanitarian law completes these provisions. It specifically establishes that the rights established for civilians in occupied territories are also inviolable (GCIV Article 47). → **Occupied territory**

In addition to being inviolable, international law establishes that these rights are inalienable, or nonrenunciable, meaning that individuals may not renounce them, even voluntarily.

→ **Fundamental guarantees; Human rights; Inalienability of rights; International law**

J

■ JOURNALISTS

Humanitarian law establishes that war correspondents (journalists authorized directly by a party to the conflict to follow its troops) who are captured in the exercise of their functions in an area of conflict are considered prisoners of war. This puts them under the protection of the Third Geneva Convention, Relative to the Treatment of Prisoners of War (GCIII Article 4). In 1977, Additional Protocol I to the Geneva Conventions, Relating to the Protection of Victims of International Armed Conflicts (Protocol I), reiterated this.

Protocol I formally extends the protection of humanitarian law to other categories of journalists, who are not accredited with the armed forces. These journalists have the status of civilians and are to be protected as such (PI Article 79). Although Protocol I is meant to be applied to international armed conflicts, it is always possible to request that its provisions be defended in internal armed conflicts.

☞ Journalists engaged in professional missions in areas of armed conflict are considered civilians. As such, they may not be targeted. They are protected by their civilian status, on the condition that they refrain from any activity that might jeopardize their civilian status and character.

In its Annex II, Protocol I provides a model for an identity card for journalists. This card can be issued either by the state of which the journalist is a national, in whose territory he or she resides, or in which the news medium employing him or her is located. This card attests to his or her status as a journalist.

Journalists are not only at risk in situations of armed conflict. Many journalists are targeted because they are investigating matters of corruption or links between authorities and religious groups. Some of the countries most affected in recent years are Algeria, Bangladesh, Brazil, Colombia, Mexico, the Philippines, the Russian Federation, Serbia, Sierra Leone, and Thailand.

➔ **Civilians; Geneva Conventions; Prisoners of war**

📖 **For Additional Information:**

Gasser, Hans-Peter. "The Protection of Journalists Engaged in Dangerous Professional Missions." *International Review of the Red Cross* 232 (1983): 3–18.

Gutman, Roy W. "Spotlight on Violations of International Humanitarian Law: The Role of the Media." *International Review of the Red Cross* 325 (December 1998): 619–25.

Lee, Jennifer. "Peace and the Press: Media Rules during UN Peacekeeping Operations." *Vanderbilt Journal of Transnational Law* 30 (January 1997): 135.

■ JUDICIAL GUARANTEES

Judicial guarantees are among the fundamental rights accorded to individuals under the international conventions regulating humanitarian law and human rights. The aim of judicial guarantees is to ensure that

- no individual accused of a crime is convicted without having had a chance to defend him- or herself in a fair trial, and
- all persons are given the opportunity to contest or file a complaint against a measure or action that is prejudicial to them or jeopardizes their safety. There is no point in giving rights to individuals if those who are victims of violations cannot see justice done and obtain reparation for the injury incurred.

The specific due process rights that are guaranteed differ in times of peace and times of conflict.

☞ In the case of detention or internment, disciplinary measures may have dangerous consequences for the physical and mental health of an individual. Judicial guarantees protect individuals from unfair sentencing to penal sanctions. To protect detained or interned individuals, humanitarian law requires that judicial guarantees also be applied to disciplinary measures taken in such circumstances, for which it specifies certain precise guarantees.

I. DUE PROCESS RIGHTS ESTABLISHED IN HUMAN RIGHTS CONVENTIONS

The International Covenant on Civil and Political Rights (ICCPR), adopted December 16, 1966, by the General Assembly of the UN (GA Resolution 2200 A, XXI), sets out certain judicial guarantees from which no derogation is permitted. This means that these rights must be protected in all circumstances, including in times of conflict and during internal disturbances and tensions. The provisions of the ICCPR are reflected, almost verbatim, in two regional conventions: the American Convention on Human Rights (ACHR) and the European Convention for the Protection of Human Rights and Fundamental Freedoms (ECHR).

1. Nonderogable Due Process Rights

The judicial guarantees from which no derogation is permitted under the ICCPR are in its Articles 6, 15, and 16. These are as follows:

- The recognition that all persons have a juridical personality—in other words, they must be recognized as a person before the law. This means that a state may not limit a person's right to defend his or her rights in a system of justice (ICCPR Article 16; ACHR Article 3);

- The principle of nonretroactivity of punishment (freedom from *ex post facto* laws, or *nullum crimen sine lege*). This means that, under both national and international law, no one can be held guilty of a criminal offense on account of an act or omission that did not constitute a crime when it was committed (ICCPR Article 15.1, ACHR Article 9, and ECHR Article 7.1);
- Following the same reasoning, a heavier penalty may not be imposed than the one that was applicable at the time the act was committed. However, if a new provision has been adopted into law for the imposition of a lighter penalty, the offender must benefit from it (ICCPR Article 15.1, ACHR Article 9, and ECHR Article 7.1)

These are the same guarantees that are protected during situations of armed conflict by the Geneva Conventions.

➔   **Fundamental guarantees; Nonretroactivity**

Furthermore, the ICCPR regulates, in a nonderogable manner, the application of the death penalty (Articles 6.2–6.6). It restricts this sentence to only the most serious crimes and prohibits it for persons under the age of eighteen and pregnant women. These provisions are reflected in the ACHR (Articles 4.2–4.6), which goes one step further and prohibits states from reestablishing the death penalty once it has been abolished (Article 4.3).

2. A Fair and Impartial Trial

In all circumstances, including conflicts, no human being may be deprived of liberty, convicted, or punished outside the framework established by laws. This is part of the fundamental judicial guarantees applicable in all countries.

☞ The right to a fair trial rests on the following principles:

- the right to be judged by an impartial court established by law;
- the right to be judged on the basis of legislation enacted according to law and in force at the time of the events;
- the right to be informed of the nature and cause of the charges;
- the right to be judged for acts for which the accused is personally responsible; and
- the right to have the right to defend oneself, meaning at the very least having the opportunity to have one's defense heard.

International law establishes precise rules to protect the right to a fair trial, for all individuals, in all circumstances. Within that framework, there are specific sets of norms that regulate the judicial guarantees provided in times of peace or of conflict, for civilians or combatants. The rules reflect the general principles adopted by domestic courts and customary law.

Article 14 of the ICCPR details the rules that guarantee a fair and impartial hearing. These are now the recognized norms by which to regulate international judicial proceedings. However, the provisions of this article are not included in the list of nonderogable rights. This means that, under certain conditions, these rights may be limited if a government implements emergency measures in times of crisis or conflict. These rights are therefore not systematically protected in times of war or states of emergency.

The rules are as follows:

1. All persons shall be equal before the courts and tribunals. In the determination of any criminal charge against him, or of his rights and obligations in a suit at law, everyone shall be entitled to a fair and public hearing by a competent, independent and impartial tribunal established by law. [. . .]
2. Everyone charged with a criminal offence shall have the right to be presumed innocent until proven guilty according to law.
3. In the determination of any criminal charge against him, everyone shall be entitled to the following minimum guarantees, in full equality:
   (a) To be informed promptly and in detail, in a language which he understands, of the nature and cause of the charge against him;
   (b) To have adequate time and facilities for the preparation of his defence, and to communicate with counsel of his own choosing;
   (c) To be tried without undue delay;
   (d) To be tried in his presence, and to defend himself in person or through legal assistance of his own choosing . . . or to have legal assistance assigned to him [. . .]
   (e) To examine, or have examined, the witnesses against him, and to obtain the attendance and examination of witnesses on his behalf under the same conditions as witnesses against him;
   (f) To have the free assistance of an interpreter if he cannot understand or speak the language used in court;
   (g) Not to be compelled to testify against himself or to confess guilt.
4. In the case of juvenile persons, the procedure shall be such as will take account of their age and the desirability of promoting their rehabilitation.
5. Everyone convicted of a crime shall have the right to his conviction and sentence being reviewed by a higher tribunal according to law.
6. When a person has been convicted of a criminal offence by a final decision and when subsequently his conviction has been reversed or he has been pardoned on the ground that a new or newly discovered fact shows conclusively that there has been a miscarriage of justice, the person who has suffered punishment as a result of such conviction shall be compensated according to law [. . .]
7. No one shall be liable to be tried or punished again for an offence for which he has already been finally convicted or acquitted in accordance with the law and penal procedure of each country. (Article 14 of ICCPR.)

The rules guaranteeing a fair and impartial trial are also reflected in the ACHR (Article 8) and ECHR (Article 6).

II. JUDICIAL GUARANTEES OF HUMANITARIAN LAW

In times of armed conflict, the normal functioning of a system of justice may be severely hindered. The rules for controlling public order and the applicable criminal laws may be modified in different ways for a territory that is occupied or one that is not and for various categories of persons. Humanitarian law therefore establishes the minimum judicial guarantees that must be provided in such circumstances, paying particular heed to the protection of persons deprived of liberty or populations in occupied territories. These include provisions protecting a person's guarantees in cases in which disciplinary measures are adopted.

As will be explained later, specific minimum standards are established for international and noninternational armed conflicts. The judicial guarantees may be reinforced in situations of increased risk or for particularly vulnerable persons such as prisoners of war, persons deprived of liberty, populations in occupied territories, and children.

☞ The failure to respect the fundamental judicial guarantees applicable even in times of conflict is a grave violation of the four 1949 Geneva Conventions—in other words, it is considered a war crime. The third and fourth Conventions establish that willfully depriving a prisoner of war, or a person not directly taking part in hostilities, of his or her right to a fair and regular trial is a grave breach of those Conventions (GCIII Article 130; GCIV Article 147). As such, these crimes may be judged by the national courts of any state, even if the state has no significant links to the accused or to the acts committed, under the principle of universal jurisdiction.

→ **Universal jurisdiction; War crimes/Crimes against humanity**

1. Judicial Guarantees Applicable to All Persons in Times of Armed Conflict

Most due process rights protected by humanitarian law remain applicable in both international and internal armed conflict. There are certain differences, however.

a. Nonderogable Rights

The three nonderogable due process rights established by international human rights conventions (explained above) are reflected in specific humanitarian law provisions and therefore remain applicable in times of armed conflict.

- The recognition that all persons have a juridical personality: This means that individuals must always have access to a system of justice to defend their rights. Internees and prisoners of war, for instance, must always retain their "full civil capacity" and be able to exercise the rights this capacity confers on them (GCIII Article 14; GCIV Article 80).
- The principle of nonretroactivity of criminal laws and punishment: In humanitarian as in human rights law, no one may be prosecuted for an act or omission that did not constitute a criminal offense under the national or international law to which it was subject at the time it was committed (GCIII Article 99, GCIV Articles 65 and 67, PI Article 75, and PII Article 6).
- A heavier penalty may not be imposed than the one that was applicable at the time the act was committed. However, if a new law was adopted after the act was committed that provides for the imposition of a lighter penalty, the offender must benefit from it.

b. Judicial Guarantees in All Situations of Armed Conflict

The Geneva Conventions and Protocols have also set out certain specific judicial guarantees that must be applied broadly in all types of armed conflict. These are established in the following:

- Common Article 3 of the Geneva Conventions
- Article 75.4 of Protocol I and Article 6 of Protocol II
  These articles list the details of such "judicial guarantees which are recognized as indispensable by civilized peoples" (GCI–IV Article 3). They concern the prosecution and punishment of criminal offenses related to armed conflict and are applicable to persons who are not, or are no longer, taking part in hostilities.

Judicial Guarantees Applicable in All Situations of Armed Conflict

- "The following acts are and shall remain prohibited at any time and in any place whatsoever with respect to persons taking no active part in the hostilities [. . .]: the passing of sentences and the carrying out of executions without previous judgment pronounced by a regularly constituted court, affording all the judicial guarantees which are recognized as indispensable by civilized peoples" (GCI–IV Article 3.1.d → **Fundamental guarantees** [common Article 3]).

- "No sentence may be passed and no penalty may be executed on a person found guilty of a penal offence related to the armed conflict except pursuant to a conviction pronounced by an impartial and regularly constituted court respecting the generally recognized principles of regular judicial procedure, which include the following:
  - (a) the procedure shall provide for an accused to be informed without delay of the particulars of the offence alleged against him and shall afford the accused before and during his trial all necessary rights and means of defence;
  - (b) no one shall be convicted of an offence except on the basis of individual penal responsibility;
  - (c) no one shall be accused or convicted of a criminal offence on account of any act or omission which did not constitute a criminal offence under the national or international law to which he was subject at the time when it was committed; nor shall a heavier penalty be imposed than that which was applicable at the time when the criminal offence was committed; if, after the commission of the offence, provision is made by law for the imposition of a lighter penalty, the offender shall benefit thereby;
  - (d) anyone charged with an offence is presumed innocent until proved guilty according to law;
  - (e) anyone charged with an offence shall have the right to be tried in his presence;
  - (f) no one shall be compelled to testify against himself or to confess guilt"
  (PI Article 75.4; PII Article 6.2).

- "A convicted person shall be advised on conviction of his judicial and other remedies and of the time-limits within which they may be exercised" (PI Article 75.4.j; PII Article 6.3).

---

c. Additional Guarantees Applicable in Certain Situations of Armed Conflict

In the case of an international armed conflict, the first Protocol additional to the Geneva Conventions (Protocol I) guarantees additional due process rights. Some of these are also implicitly protected in internal armed conflicts:

- In international armed conflict, anyone charged with an offense "has the right to examine, or have examined, the witnesses against him and to obtain the attendance and examination of witnesses on his behalf under the same conditions as witnesses against him" (PI Article 75.4.g). This is reflected in the rights of the accused in noninternational armed conflict, in which he or she has the right be informed without delay of the particulars of the alleged offense and must be accorded all necessary rights and means of defense, before and during the trial (PII Article 6.2.a).

- No one may be prosecuted or punished by the same party for an offense for which he or she has already been finally convicted or acquitted under the same law and judicial procedure (PI Article 75.4.h). This is a firmly established principle of criminal law, known as protection from double jeopardy (or *ne bis in idem*), and is one of the main due process guarantees identified in the ICCPR (Article 14.7, quoted earlier). This guarantee is reflected in the statutes of the ICTY (Article 10), ICTR (Article 9), and the ICC (Article 20) and is therefore applicable in any internal armed conflict covered by these tribunals.
- Anyone prosecuted for an offense has the right to have the judgment pronounced publicly (PI Article 75.4.i).

d. Amnesties

Though international humanitarian law recommends granting amnesties for certain crimes committed in armed conflict, in particular at the end of an internal conflict, they may not be applied to grave breaches of the Geneva Conventions with regard to war crimes. → **Amnesties**

2. Specific Judicial Guarantees Provided by Humanitarian Law for Certain Categories of Persons

International humanitarian law establishes provisions to protect the due process rights of certain specific categories of persons. These guarantees are meant to be applied in times of international armed conflict, but they can serve as a framework when working in other types of conflicts.

These judicial guarantees—derived mainly from the Geneva Conventions—concern prisoners of war, internees, civilians in occupied territories, women, and children.

a. Prisoners of War (Third Geneva Convention, Chapter III)

Articles 82 to 107 provide the rules for penal and disciplinary sanctions that may be applied to prisoners of war.

- A prisoner of war shall be subject to the laws of the Detaining Power and its military tribunals. However, no proceedings or punishments contrary to the provisions of the Third Geneva Convention shall be allowed. If a prisoner of war is prosecuted for an act that would not normally be considered punishable by the Detaining Power, any resulting punishment may only be disciplinary, not penal (GCIII Article 82).
- The Detaining Power shall adopt disciplinary rather than judicial measures, wherever possible (GCIII Article 83).
- A court that tries a prisoner of war shall offer the essential guarantees of independence and impartiality and shall ensure that the procedure provides the accused with the rights and means of defense provided for in Article 105 (GCIII Article 84).
- Even if convicted, prisoners of war prosecuted for acts committed prior to capture shall remain under the protection of the Third Geneva Convention (which mainly establishes that the right to file complaints, and the rules regulating penal and disciplinary sanction, may never be infringed on, as established by Articles 78–126) (GCIII Articles 85 and 98).
- No prisoner of war may be punished more than once for the same act or on the same charge (GCIII Article 86).
- Prisoners of war may not be sentenced to any penalties except those provided for members of the armed forces of the Detaining Power who have committed the same acts. The courts or au-

thorities shall be at liberty to reduce the penalty prescribed and may even go below the minimal provision, given that the accused, not being a national of the Detaining Power, is not bound to it by any duty of allegiance (GCIII Article 87).

- Collective punishment for individual acts, corporal punishments, imprisonment in premises without daylight, and, in general, any form of torture or cruelty are forbidden (GCIII Article 87).
- A prisoner of war undergoing a disciplinary or judicial punishment shall not be subjected to more severe treatment than that applied to members of the armed forces of the Detaining Power of equivalent rank undergoing the same punishment. In particular, a woman prisoner of war shall not be sentenced to punishment more severe or undergo punishment in worse conditions than a woman member of the armed forces of the Detaining Power punished for a similar offense. Prisoners of war who have served disciplinary or judicial sentences shall not be treated differently from other internees (GCIII Article 88).
- The scale of applicable disciplinary punishments is clearly established by the Convention. Among other things, fatigue duties (military chores) may not exceed two hours per day and may not be applied to officers. In no case shall disciplinary punishments be inhuman, brutal, or dangerous to the health of prisoners of war (GCIII Article 89).
- In no case shall the duration of any single punishment exceed thirty days, even if the prisoner is answerable for several acts at the same time. If a prisoner of war is later sentenced to further disciplinary punishment, a period of at least three days shall separate the execution of the two punishments (GCIII Article 90).
- Attempting to escape, or aiding and abetting an escape, even if it is a repeated offense, shall occasion disciplinary punishment only (GCIII Articles 92 and 93).
- If a prisoner escapes, or is recaptured after an escape, the Detaining Power will notify the Power on which the prisoner depends, in the manner defined in Article 122 of the Convention (GCIII Article 94).
- A prisoner of war accused of a disciplinary infraction shall not be kept in confinement pending the hearing (preventive confinement). In no case shall preventive confinement exceed fourteen days (GCIII Article 95).
- Acts that constitute offenses against discipline shall be investigated immediately. The accused shall be given precise information regarding the offenses of which he or she is accused, and given an opportunity of explaining his or her conduct and of defending him- or herself. The prisoner shall be permitted to call witnesses and to have recourse to the services of a qualified interpreter. A record of disciplinary punishments shall be maintained by the camp commander and shall be open to inspection by representatives of the Protecting Power. The power to order disciplinary punishment may in no case be delegated to or exercised by a prisoner of war (GCIII Article 96).
- In no case shall prisoners of war be transferred to penitentiary establishments to undergo their disciplinary punishment. All premises in which disciplinary punishments are undergone shall conform to the sanitary requirements that are established for the living conditions of prisoners of war (Article 25). Separate disciplinary premises shall be provided for officers and persons of equivalent status, for noncommissioned officers or troops, as well as for women who must be under the immediate supervision of women (GCIII Article 97).
- Prisoners of war undergoing disciplinary punishment, shall continue to enjoy the protection of the Third Geneva Convention [. . .] . They shall be allowed to be present at the daily medical inspections and to receive the necessary medical attention, to exercise and stay in the open air at least two hours per day, to read and write, and to send and receive letters (GCIII Article 98).

- No prisoner of war may be tried or sentenced for an act that was not forbidden by the law of the Detaining Power or by international law at the time the said act was committed. No moral or physical coercion may be exerted on a prisoner of war in order to induce him or her to admit guilt. No prisoner of war may be convicted without having had an opportunity to present his or her defense (GCIII Article 99).
- Prisoners of war and the Protecting Powers shall be informed as soon as possible of the offenses which are punishable by the death sentence under the laws of the Detaining Power. Before pronouncing a death sentence, the court must take into consideration the fact that the accused, not being a national of the Detaining Power, is not bound to it by any duty of allegiance (GCIII Article 100).
- If the death penalty is pronounced on a prisoner of war, the sentence shall not be executed before at least six months after the date at which the Protecting Power was informed of this decision (GCIII Article 101).
- A sentence is valid only if it was pronounced by the same courts, and according to the same procedure, as in the case of members of the armed forces of the Detaining Power (GCIII Article 102).
- During periods of confinement awaiting trial, prisoners of war will benefit from the same rights and guarantees as those applicable to prisoners of war carrying out a disciplinary punishment (GCIII Article 103).
- The Protecting Power must be notified following precise rules every time judicial proceedings are begun against a prisoner of war; otherwise, the proceedings may have to be adjourned (GCIII Article 104).
- The prisoner of war is entitled to a qualified advocate or counsel, who will have at least two weeks to prepare for the trial. Particulars of the charges shall be communicated to the accused and his or her advocate, in a language that he or she understands, and in good time before the opening of the trial. Representatives of the Protecting Power may attend the trial (GCIII Article 105).
- Every prisoner of war has the right of appeal, petition, or revision of any sentence (GCIII Article 106).
- Any judgment and sentence pronounced shall be immediately reported to the Protecting Power (GCIII Article 107).
- Sentences shall be served in the same establishments and under the same conditions as provided for members of the armed forces of the Detaining Power (GCIII Article 108).

➜   **Prisoners of war**

b. Internees (Fourth Geneva Convention, Articles 42, 43, 78, and 117–126)

- A civilian may only be interned or placed in assigned residence by the Detaining Power when security concerns make it "absolutely necessary." The interned person must be able to appeal such a decision and the Detaining Power must create an appropriate court or administrative board for the specific purpose of reconsidering such decisions as quickly as possible (GCIV Articles 42, 43, and 78). This court or administrative board shall give consideration to these cases periodically, at least twice each year (GCIV Article 43).
- Articles 117 to 126 establish the judicial guarantees governing the rules for penal and disciplinary sanctions for acts committed by interned persons during their internment.
- Internees are subject to the laws of the territory on which they find themselves. If these laws establish that a given act is punishable when committed by an interned person—but not when committed by someone who is not—any resulting punishment may only be disciplinary, not penal (GCIV Article 117).

- In passing sentences, the courts must take into account the fact that the defendant is not a national of the Detaining Power. They are free to reduce the penalty prescribed, and may even go below the minimal provision. Internees who have served a sentence shall not be treated differently from other internees. The duration of preventive detention undergone by an internee shall be deducted from any disciplinary or judicial penalty involving confinement to which he or she may be sentenced. The appropriate Internee Committees shall be informed of all judicial proceedings instituted against internees (GCIV Article 118).

- Article 119 lists and limits the disciplinary punishments applicable to internees: the measures may in no case be inhuman, brutal or dangerous for the health of internees; they must take into account the internee's age, sex, and state of health; the duration of any single punishment may not exceed thirty consecutive days, even if the internee is answerable for several breaches of discipline (GCIV Article 119).

- Escape or attempted escape shall be liable only to disciplinary punishment, even if it is a repeated offense. Furthermore, it shall not be deemed an aggravating circumstance if an internee is being prosecuted for other offenses (GCIV Articles 120, 121).

- For all internees, confinement awaiting trial shall not exceed fourteen days and shall be deducted from the final sentence (GCIV Article 122).

- Only the commandant of the place of internment, or a responsible officer or official to whom the commandant has delegated the appropriate disciplinary powers, may order disciplinary punishment [. . .]. The commandant must maintain a record of disciplinary punishments which will be open to inspection by representatives of the Protecting Power (GCIV Article 123).

- Internees shall not, in any case, undergo disciplinary punishment in penitentiary establishments (prisons, penitentiaries, convict prisons, etc.). The premises in which such punishments are undergone must be in conformity with sanitary requirements. Internees shall in particular be provided with adequate bedding and will be able to wash themselves. Women internees undergoing disciplinary punishment shall be confined in separate quarters from males and be under the immediate supervision of women (GCIV Article 124).

- Internees undergoing disciplinary punishment shall be allowed to exercise and to stay in the open air at least two hours each day. They shall be allowed, at their request, to be present at the daily medical inspections and to receive the necessary medical attention. They shall have permission to read and write, likewise to send and receive letters (GCIV Article 125).

→ **Detention; Internment**

> ☞ Humanitarian law establishes similar guarantees to regulate the rules of penal and disciplinary sanctions for acts committed by persons deprived of liberty for reasons related to a conflict.

c. Civilian Persons in Occupied Territories (Fourth Geneva Convention, Articles 47, 54, 64, 66–75)

- The Occupying Power may subject the population of the occupied territory to provisions that it considers essential to ensure its own security and to "maintain the orderly government of the territory." To this effect, it may repeal or suspend the penal laws of the occupied territory that were in force. However, the new provisions shall have no retroactive effects and shall not come into force until they have been published and brought to the knowledge of the inhabitants in their own language (GCIV Articles 64 and 65).

- Furthermore, the Occupying Power cannot, in any case or in any manner, whether by passing laws or adopting regulations, deprive the persons in the occupied territory of the protection of the Fourth Geneva Convention (GCIV Article 47).
- It is also forbidden to alter the status of public officials or judges in the occupied territories, or to sanction them in any way, or to take any measures of coercion or pressure against them, if they abstain from fulfilling their functions for reasons of conscience (GCIV Article 54). They can still be requisitioned, however, in conformity with Article 51.
- In case a civilian in an occupied territory commits a breach of the penal provisions adopted by the Occupying Power, the latter may hand over the accused to its own military courts, to make up for the insufficiencies of local courts. However, in these cases, Article 66 requires that the military courts be "properly constituted and non-political." Furthermore, such courts must sit in the occupied country. It must take into consideration the fact that the accused is not a national of the Occupying Power, may apply only those provisions of law which were applicable prior to the offense, and must respect the principle that the penalty shall be proportional to the offense (GCIV Article 67).
- A protected person may only be sentenced to the death penalty in cases where the person is guilty of espionage, of serious acts of sabotage against the military installations of the Occupying Power, or of intentional offenses which caused the death of one or more persons. The death penalty may only be applied if such offenses were already punishable by death under the law of the territory in force before the occupation began. In any case, the death penalty may not be pronounced against a protected person who was under eighteen years of age at the time of the offense (GCIV Article 68).
- In all cases, the duration of the period during which an accused civilian was under arrest awaiting trial or punishment shall be deducted from any prison sentence (GCIV Article 69).
- Protected persons shall not be arrested, prosecuted or convicted by the Occupying Power for acts committed or for opinions expressed before the occupation. An exception is made in the case of breaches of the laws and customs of war. Nationals of the Occupying Power who, before the outbreak of hostilities, sought refuge in the territory of the occupied State, shall not be arrested, prosecuted, convicted, or deported from the occupied territory, unless they committed offenses after the outbreak of hostilities. They may also be arrested for ordinary criminal offenses committed before the outbreak of hostilities and which would have justified extradition in time of peace (GCIV Article 70).
- Sentences shall only be pronounced by the competent courts of the Occupying Power and only after a regular trial. Furthermore, the Protecting Power may request to be notified of the key elements concerning the trial, and shall have the right to attend the trial (GCIV Articles 71 and 74).
- Accused persons shall have the right to present evidence necessary for their defense and to be assisted by a qualified advocate or counsel (GCIV Article 72). They shall also have the right of appeal (GCIV Article 73).
- Persons condemned to death always have the right of petition for pardon or reprieve. No death sentence may be executed until at least six months after the date at which the Protecting Power was informed of the final judgment (GCIV Article 75).

→ **Occupied territories**

d. Women and Children

- Humanitarian law establishes many specific provisions for women and children in armed conflict, whether as civilians, prisoners of war, detainees, or internees.
→   **Children; Women**
- In particular, the Geneva Conventions and Protocols include in their judicial guarantees certain restrictions on the use of the death penalty: "it may not be pronounced against persons who were under eighteen years of age at the time of the offence, and shall not be carried out on pregnant women or mothers of young children" (GCIV Article 68; PII Article 6.4).
→ **Death penalty**

→   **Amnesties; Children; Collective punishment; Death penalty; Detention; Fundamental guarantees; International Criminal Tribunals; Internment; Nonretroactivity; Occupied territory; Penal sanctions in humanitarian law; Prisoners of war; Torture; War crimes/Crimes against humanity; Women**

📖 **For Additional Information:**

Gasser, Hans-Peter. "Respect for Fundamental Judicial Guarantees in Time of Armed Conflict—The Part Played by ICRC Delegates." *International Review of the Red Cross* 287 (March–April 1992): 121–43.

■ LEGAL STATUS OF THE PARTIES TO THE CONFLICT

The implementation of the rules of the law of armed conflict—and of special humanitarian agreements signed with or between parties to a conflict—has no bearing on the legal or political status of the parties to the conflict or of the territories concerned (GCI–IV common Article 3; PI Articles 4 and 5.5).

> ☞ The fact that belligerents implement humanitarian law need not result in any form of political recognition. Showing respect for the rules of armed conflict does not affect the legal definition or nature of the conflict, of the territories, or of the populations concerned. Humanitarian law is neutral. It is applicable when a specific situation exists: that of war. It can be implemented by parties that do not recognize one another and by nonstate entities that have not signed the Geneva Conventions. The ICRC and the humanitarian organizations act as neutral intermediaries between the parties.
>
> It is possible, therefore, to demand that the provisions of humanitarian law be enforced, without having to wait for the different parties to agree on the nature of the conflict and on their respective legal status.

- Humanitarian actors are not constrained by official legal definitions that describe the nature of a conflict or of the parties to the conflict. If the requirements for adequate protection call for provisions to be enforced that are not automatically applicable (e.g., because the provisions are mandatory only in certain circumstances), such provisions can be requested or negotiated and do not represent an infringement on a state's internal affairs. The possibility of signing special agreements was established specifically so as to enable the parties to a conflict to implement all relevant parts of the Geneva Convention, including in situations in which they would not automatically be applicable.
- Humanitarian organizations can sign agreements relating to the implementation of humanitarian law with any movement, faction, or unofficial government, without such act implying any

form of legal recognition. Special agreements must never weaken the protection provided for by the Geneva Conventions.

- Humanitarian law must be respected by states party to the Conventions even if the other party to the conflict is not party to the Conventions or is not a state entity. The obligation to respect humanitarian law is not, in fact, tied to reciprocal levels of commitment (GCI–IV common Articles 1 and 2).

→   **Belligerent; High Contracting Parties; International conventions; Parties to the conflict; Respect for international humanitarian law; Right of humanitarian initiative; Situations and persons not expressly covered by humanitarian law; Special agreement**

■ MANDATE

A *mandate* is the authority conferred on an individual or an organization to carry out certain tasks. The mandate thus links the one entrusted with the duties to the mandator, on whose behalf the actions are performed. The mandator always maintains a degree of control over the implementation of the mandate.

> ☞ The term *mandate* is frequently used by intergovernmental and nongovernmental organizations in reference to the goals of each organization. The mandate should also enable outsiders to identify on whose behalf and on what authority each organization acts and to which organization it is accountable.

1. Intergovernmental Organizations

In the international arena, states have entrusted intergovernmental organizations with the implementation of a number of missions of common interest. The mandate established in the charter or statute of an organization sets out the goals chosen by the founding states.

Such international organizations must report regularly on the implementation of their mandate, to a plenary organ where the member states are represented. In the realm of humanitarian action, states have officially mandated several agencies or organizations to carry out certain specific activities—namely, UNHCR, UNICEF, WFP, OCHA, ICRC, and so on.

2. Nongovernmental Organizations

In the private sphere, NGOs or humanitarian associations act on behalf of individuals. NGOs establish their own goals and set up the structure that will enable them to achieve their aim through concrete action. They must also report on their activities to their Board of Directors, the General Assembly of their members (in the case of an association), or any other body to which they are accountable. **➔ FAO; NGOs; UN; UNHCR; UNICEF; WFP; WHO**

■ MEDICAL DUTIES

The term *medical duties* (sometimes known as the "medical mission") describes the entire set of medical activities aimed at the civilian population in general, as well as wounded and sick persons, in times of conflict. They come under a specific protection regime within the framework of humanitarian law. Actually, the protection and care that must be granted to sick and wounded persons are the keys to treating individuals humanely in times of war and of peace.

Historically, these are the most ancient activities foreseen by humanitarian law. Henri Dunant created the first Red Cross Committee to regulate the fate and care of the sick and dead left on the battlefields of war.

The first two 1949 Geneva Conventions concern the protection of the wounded, sick, and shipwrecked members of armed forces, in the field or at sea. This special protection, foreseen for those who are no longer participating in the fighting because of wounds or illness, is extended to sick and wounded civilians, in the fourth 1949 Geneva Convention, and later to all noncombatants (civilians).

The two 1977 Additional Protocols consolidated the protection set forth by the Geneva Conventions for wounded and sick persons; medical personnel, units, and means of transportation; and civilian or military medical material. These provisions are generally known under the term *medical duties* (GCIV Articles 56 and 57, PI Articles 8–31, and PII Articles 7–12). The specific provisions are detailed in the entries on ➜ **medical ethics; medical personnel; medical services; and wounded and sick persons**.

The Basis of the International Protection for Wounded and Sick Persons

If a member of the armed forces is wounded or sick, he or she can no longer participate in the fighting and is exposed to acts of revenge and ill treatment. This individual is no longer a threat to the opponent and can no longer be considered an adversary. He or she therefore must benefit from the same protection as those who are not participating in the hostilities and must be treated humanely in all circumstances (GCI–IV common Article 3).

Civilians who are wounded or sick in a time of conflict are incapable of fleeing, protecting themselves, or providing for their own needs. They are vulnerable and threatened by their illness. They are entitled to reinforced protection against the effects of fighting and to the right to receive treatment.

The general principles regulating the protection of the medical duties are described in the following sections.

1. Ensuring the Protection of Wounded and Sick Persons in All Circumstances

The protection of wounded and sick persons must be ensured in all situations. Humanitarian law establishes that such persons are a separate category of protected persons, within which any distinction between combatant and civilian is abolished and all must be treated alike (GCI–IV common Article 3; PI Article 8).

This protection is established in Article 3, common to the four Geneva Conventions (known as common Article 3). This article establishes the minimum standards of protection that must be applied at all times, whether in international or internal armed conflicts, or even internal disturbances or tensions:

> Persons taking no active part in the hostilities, including members of armed forces who have laid down their arms and those placed hors de combat by sickness, wounds, detention, or any other cause, shall in all circumstances be treated humanely, without any adverse distinction founded on race, colour, religion or faith, sex, birth or wealth, or any other similar criteria. [. . .]
>
> The wounded and sick shall be collected and cared for. An impartial humanitarian body, such as the International Committee of the Red Cross, may offer its services to the Parties to the conflict. (common Article 3)

➔   **Wounded and sick persons**

2. Ensuring That the Medical Services Function

In practice, the wounded and sick are protected by the guarantees established by humanitarian law to ensure that medical services continue operating in times of conflict. The law grants special protection to medical units, personnel, and means of transportation and posits that medicine and medical relief must be guaranteed free passage. This means, specifically, that

- medical personnel and installations may not be the object of attacks,
- medical installations are authorized to carry the distinctive emblem of the Red Cross,
- medical personnel and material must be protected from requisition, and
- the delivery of medical supplies must always be ensured.

➔   **Medical personnel; Medical services; Requisition**

3. Searching and Caring for the Wounded and Sick

To ensure that the wounded and sick are searched for, transported, and cared for, humanitarian law establishes a special protection status for medical personnel and means of transportation. It authorizes them to wear a distinctive emblem and guarantees their freedom of movement:

- Medical personnel must always be respected and protected.
- Members of medical personnel may not be requisitioned.
- They can undertake activities to search for the wounded and sick members of the parties to the conflict and facilitate their transportation. Such activities can only be limited on a temporary basis and only because of imperious military necessity.
- They must always be granted access to the places where their services are needed.
- They may not be required to give priority to any one or group of persons.
- In providing care to the sick and wounded, no discrimination may be made on the basis of grounds other than medical ones.
- Medical personnel may not be compelled to carry out acts contrary to the rules of medical ethics.
- Members of medical personnel may not be punished for activities carried out, no matter what the circumstances may have been, as long as their actions were compatible with medical ethics.

➔   **Medical ethics; Medical personnel; Medical services; Requisition; Right of access**

4. In Occupied Territories, Detention, or Internment

In certain situations, such as occupied territories, detention, or internment, the guarantees granted to medical duties must be reinforced so as to avoid the specific risks incurred by both the sick person and the person providing the care. Humanitarian law decrees specific rules for the following:

- Wounded and sick prisoners of war (GCIII Articles 29–33): in certain cases, the patients must be cared for or hospitalized in a neutral country (GCIII Article 132).
- Detained or interned persons (GCIV Articles 91 and 92): the possibility of releasing certain categories of persons from the places of detention or arranging for their accommodation in a neutral country is also foreseen (GCIV Article 132).
- Occupied territories: the Occupying Power must not hinder the functions of medical services and must ensure that they are carried out in sufficient amount. The Protecting Powers of other humanitarian organizations are entitled to verify the condition of the food and medical supplies at all times (GCIV Articles 55–57 and 59–63).
- Finally, humanitarian law establishes specific rules for medical personnel and medical installations belonging to armed forces and for the wounded and sick persons in their care (GCI Articles 12–37).
→ **Detention; Internment; Occupied territories; Prisoners of war; Wounded and sick persons**

5. Medical Ethics in Times of War

Humanitarian law seeks to reinforce the strength and resilience power of medical ethics in situations of conflict. It raises medical ethics to the position of an international rule of law that is mandatory for all states. Without defining and codifying the entire content of medical ethics, the Geneva Conventions establish the framework of constant and consistent minimum rules within which the medical activities must take place.

The aim is to clarify the obligations and prohibitions that international law imposes on the practitioner to help him or her withstand the national context of pressure, constraint, and violence. Humanitarian law hence sets forth

- the medical behavior that is prohibited;
- the medical behavior that authorities may not prohibit;
- the principle that no person may be punished for medical activities they carried out, no matter what the circumstances may have been, as long as their actions were compatible with medical ethics; and
- it protects medical secrecy in times of conflict.
→ **Medical ethics**

6. The Obligation to Care for the Wounded and Sick

Humanitarian law endorses the obligation to care for the wounded and sick and to respect the medical ethics surrounding these acts. Any willful act or omission that seriously endangers the physical or mental health or integrity of any person is a grave breach of the Geneva Conventions and hence a war crime (GCI Article 50 and PI Article 11).

The Individual Medical Report

In situations in which illness, injury, or death, is the result of a misdemeanor or felony (e.g., rape, torture, or assault), the doctor is under the obligation to establish an individual medical report certifying the results of the medical examination. The report is for the benefit of the victim or his or her heirs. The doctor should also try to find out whether the crime was an isolated act or whether it was part of a broader plan or pattern of human rights violations.

In certain cases, the doctor has a legal obligation to transmit such documents to judicial authorities depending on the laws of the state. However, in situations of conflict or crisis, an automatic transmission of such information can endanger the victim's life. The doctor must therefore first defend the principle of medical secrecy and doctor–patient confidentiality and write the report with the best interests of the patient in mind. On the other hand, the report can be transmitted to the ICRC in the context of the protection activities it carries out on behalf of victims of violations of humanitarian law.

Medical reports may play an important role, since they may be the only evidence available for a victim to prove the violation suffered, and thus be able to defend his or her rights, whether claiming refugee status or disability or denouncing torture or rape in a criminal case. The report must thus always be given to the victim.

→ **Medical ethics; Medical personnel; Medical services; Wounded and sick persons**

📖 **For Additional Information:**

Baccino-Astrada, Alma. *Manual on the Rights and Duties of Medical Personnel in Armed Conflicts.* Geneva: ICRC, 1982.

Green, L. C. "War Law and the Medical Profession." In *Canadian Yearbook of International Law 1979.* Vancouver: University of British Columbia, 1979, 159–205.

Reyes, Hernan, and Remi Russbach. "The Role of the Doctor in ICRC Visits to Prisoners." *International Review of the Red Cross* 284 (September–October 1991): 469–82.

■ MEDICAL ETHICS

There is no international convention that regulates the content of medical ethics in times of peace. Medical ethics are established by national professional and public health regulations. The rules contained in these instruments do not vary greatly from one country to the next: the main principles of medical ethics are the same in all states. Doctors working "in the field," in a foreign country, remain subject to the ethics of the medical order to which they belong, as well as to the laws in force in the country where they are working.

Nevertheless, a large number of rules have been decreed by various international health associations. The World Medical Association (WMA, the international association of national medical associations), for instance, drafted and adopted an International Code of Medical Ethics, which is essentially based on the 1948 Physician's Oath (the Declaration of Geneva), the 1949 International Code of Medical Ethics (most recently amended in 1983 and applicable at all times), and specific rules governing times of armed conflict and cases of prisoners being tortured. However, these texts have no mandatory force of law, although they can serve as standards of reference for the work of nongovernmental organizations.

Given the power that doctors hold over the life and death of the sick, and over their physical and mental health, professional medical ethics developed in ancient times. It is distinct from professional ethics that exist in other fields because of the specific stakes and dilemmas involved.

The ethics include such fundamental obligations as

—doing no harm,
—not inflicting more suffering than is justified by the foreseeable benefits of the cure, and
—respecting the informed consent of the patient.

- In times of peace, failure to respect the principles of medical ethics can result in disciplinary sanctions imposed by professional organizations. It may also constitute a felony and be subject to a trial before national courts.
- In times of war, violations of the rules of medical ethics may constitute a war crime and be subject to punishment before international or national tribunals (under the principle of universal jurisdiction over such crimes, in the case of national courts). ➜ **Medical duties; Universal jurisdiction; War crimes/Crimes against humanity**
- In situations of detention, the UN has codified principles of medical ethics. They supplement those set out in the Geneva Conventions with regard to detention in a period of conflict. ➜ **Detention; Wounded and sick persons**

☞ In times of conflict, the overall protection that humanitarian law grants medical duties is tied to the respect for the principles of medical ethics.

The Geneva Conventions and their Additional Protocols defend these notions first and foremost by stipulating that no person may be punished for carrying out medical activities compatible with medical ethics, regardless of the circumstances and of the persons benefiting from their actions (PI Article 16.1 and PII Article 10.1).

Humanitarian law hence raises medical ethics to the position of an international rule of law that is mandatory for all states. Humanitarian law specifies which rules must be respected. This means that any national regulations or orders that are contrary to the principles of medical ethics cannot be imposed on "medical personnel," under any circumstances.

Furthermore, any act that is not in conformity with medical ethics or that endangers the physical or mental health of an individual, as well as any deliberate refusal to provide the necessary care to a wounded or sick person, is a war crime (GCI Article 50, GCII Article 51, GCIII Article 130, GCIV Article 147, and PI Article 11).

The Geneva Conventions do not give a precise definition of the entire content of medical ethics. However, several of their articles prohibit specific medical behavior, while others protect doctors' freedom of action. In return, it is the doctors' duty to defend the ethics of their medical actions.

I. PROHIBITED BEHAVIOR

1. Grave Breaches of Humanitarian Law

Willful killing, torture or inhuman treatment, including biological experiments, and willfully causing great suffering or serious injury to body or health, committed against persons protected by the Geneva Conventions, are grave breaches of humanitarian law and are therefore war crimes (GCI Article 50).

2. Withholding Care

Withholding assistance or discriminating in providing care are strictly prohibited by humanitarian law. Article 3 common to the four Geneva Conventions—an article that is applicable in all circumstances and at all times—establishes that wounded and sick persons must be collected and cared for.

Additional Protocol I of 1977 adds to this by stipulating that:

1. All the wounded, sick and shipwrecked, to whichever Party they belong, shall be respected and protected.
2. In all circumstances they shall be treated humanely and shall receive, to the fullest extent practicable and with the least possible delay, the medical care and attention required by their condition. There shall be no distinction among them founded on any grounds other than medical ones. (PI Article 10)

3. Protection

1. The physical or mental health and integrity of persons who are in the power of the adverse Party or who are interned, detained or otherwise deprived of liberty [for reasons related to the conflict] shall not be endangered by any unjustified act or omission. Accordingly, it is prohibited to subject the persons described in this Article to any medical procedure which is not indicated by the state of health of the person concerned and which is not consistent with generally accepted medical standards which would be applied under similar medical circumstances to persons who are nationals of the Party conducting the procedure and who are in no way deprived of liberty.
2. It is, in particular, prohibited to carry out on such persons, even with their consent:
   (a) physical mutilations;
   (b) medical or scientific experiments;
   (c) removal of tissue or organs for transplantation, except where these acts are justified in conformity with the conditions provided for in paragraph 1.
3. Exceptions to the prohibition in paragraph 2(c) may be made only in the case of donations of blood for transfusion or of skin for grafting, provided that they are given voluntarily and without any coercion or inducement, and then only for therapeutic purposes, under conditions consistent with generally accepted medical standards and controls designed for the benefit of both the donor and the recipient.
4. Any willful act or omission which seriously endangers the physical or mental health or integrity of any person who is in the power of a Party other than the one on which he depends and which either violates any of the prohibitions in paragraphs 1 and 2 or fails to comply with the requirements of paragraph 3 shall be a grave breach of this Protocol. (PI Article 11)
→ **War crimes/Crimes against humanity** (Section III, "Grave Breaches of International Humanitarian Law")

II. PROTECTING DOCTORS' INDEPENDENCE

Humanitarian law establishes certain clear rules within the framework of protecting the independence of medical personnel. This independence is important to their ability to defend their medical ethics.

- Medical and religious personnel must be respected and protected. They must be granted all available help for the performance of their duties and must not be compelled to carry out tasks that are not compatible with their humanitarian mission (PII Article 9.1).
- "In the performance of their duties medical personnel may not be required to give priority to any person except on medical grounds" (PII Article 9.2).
- "Under no circumstances shall any person be punished for having carried out medical activities compatible with medical ethics, regardless of the person benefiting therefrom" (PI Article 16.1; PII Article 10.1).
- Persons carrying out medical activities must not be compelled to perform acts or to carry out work contrary to the rules of medical ethics, other rules designed for the benefit of the wounded and sick, or other provisions of international humanitarian law, nor must they be compelled to refrain from acts required by such rules (PI Article 16.2; PII Article 10.2).
- The rules governing medical secrecy and the principle of doctor–patient confidentiality in times of international or internal conflict are explained in the next section.

III. PRESERVING MEDICAL CONFIDENTIALITY

☞ Medical secrecy is protected by international humanitarian law.

Any limitations on doctor–patient confidentiality and privileges must be set forth in the laws of the country. This means that a simple order or regulation issued by a military or administrative authority does not authorize a doctor to breach his or her obligation of medical secrecy. The medical secrecy is strengthened in situations of conflict.

1. In International Armed Conflicts

No person carrying out medical activities can be compelled to give out any information concerning the wounded and sick who are, or have been, under his or her care, as long as the medical person considers that such information might prove harmful to the patients concerned or to their families. This applies whether the person requesting the information belongs to the adverse party to the conflict or to the medical person's own party, except in cases foreseen by the person's domestic laws. However, regulations concerning the compulsory notification of communicable diseases must be respected (PI Article 16.3).

2. In Internal Armed Conflicts

The professional obligations of persons engaged in medical activities must be respected, subject to national legislation, with regard to information they may acquire concerning the wounded and sick under their care (PII Article 10.3).

"Subject to national law, no person engaged in medical activities may be penalized in any way for refusing or failing to give information concerning the wounded and sick who are, or who have been, under his care" (PII Article 10.4).

→ **Detention; Ill treatment; Medical duties; Medical personnel; Medical services; Torture; World Health Organization; Wounded and sick persons**

📖 **For Additional Information:**

Amnesty International. *Codes of Professional Ethics*. New York: Amnesty International Publications, 1984.
Baccino-Astrada, Alma. *Manual on the Rights and Duties of Medical Personnel in Armed Conflicts*. Geneva: ICRC, 1982.
Marange, Valerie. *Doctors and Torture: Resistance or Collaboration*. London: Bellew, 1991.

■ MEDICAL PERSONNEL

According to the Geneva Conventions and their Protocols, "medical personnel" designates persons assigned exclusively to medical duties, whether such assignments are permanent or temporary. Such medical purposes include

- the search for, collection, transportation, diagnosis, or treatment—including first aid treatment—of the wounded, sick, and shipwrecked;
- the prevention of disease;
- the management and administration of medical units or means of transportation.

The term also designates the persons assigned to medical units, which are structures such as hospitals and other similar units dedicated to the aforementioned medical purposes. Finally, it also covers the military and civilian medical personnel of a party to a conflict, the staff of international relief organizations, and those assigned to civil defense organizations (PI Article 8).

> ☞ Launching an intentional attack against medical personnel in the context of an international or internal armed conflict is a war crime, punishable under humanitarian law. It will also come under the jurisdiction of the new International Criminal Court (Articles 8.2.b.xxiv and 8.2.e.ii of the ICC statute).

In times of conflict, humanitarian law establishes a multitude of provisions aimed at protecting members of medical personnel in the exercise of their functions:

1. They must be respected and protected at all times, in all circumstances (GCI Article 24, GCII Article 36, GCIV Article 20, PI Article 15, and PII Article 9).
2. They are authorized to wear the distinctive emblem of the red cross and must take the necessary measures to be identifiable to the authorities (GCI Articles 40 and 41, GCII Article 42, GCIV Article 20, PI Article 18, and PII Article 12).
3. They come under the same protection regime as the civilian population (GCIV Articles 27–141) but have additional rights so as to be able to accomplish their mission despite the conflict.

4. Such personnel shall be given all necessary assistance in carrying out their functions and will not be compelled to carry out tasks that are not compatible with their missions (PI Article 15 and PII Article 9).

5. No one may require that they give priority to any one or group of persons, except on medical grounds (PI Article 15 and PII Article 9). Overall, the requisition of medical installations, personnel, material, and transport should be avoided. Specific rules, dispersed throughout the Geneva Conventions and Protocols, limit the times when it is allowed (GCI Article 33–35, GCIV Article 57, and PI Article 14). Such requisitions may only be carried out in temporary cases of emergency, by the Occupying Powers, and only after ensuring that the medical needs of the civilians, as well as those of the wounded and sick undergoing treatment who are affected by the requisition, continue to be met.

6. They must have freedom of movement so as to be able to collect the sick and wounded. Parties to a conflict have the obligation to facilitate medical missions and may not hinder the activities of such personnel (GCIV Article 56).

7. Civilian medical personnel must have access to any place where their services are essential, subject to supervisory and safety measures that the relevant party to the conflict may deem necessary (PI Article 15).

8. Parties to a conflict must give civilian medical personnel all available assistance in areas where their services are disrupted because of combat activity (PI Article 15).

9. Medical personnel must be allowed access to the scene of a combat to search for and collect the wounded and sick. This provision exists in the case of both international and internal conflicts: "Whenever circumstances permit and particularly after an engagement, all possible measures shall be taken, without delay, to search for and collect the wounded, sick and shipwrecked, to protect them against pillage and ill-treatment, to ensure their adequate care, and to search for the dead, prevent their being despoiled, and decently dispose of them" (PII Article 8 and GCI Article 15).

---

10. In any situation of armed conflict, members of medical personnel may not be punished for activities carried out, no matter what the circumstances may have been and regardless of the person benefiting from their actions, as long as these were compatible with medical ethics. No one may ever be harassed for having collected and given care to wounded or sick persons (GCI Article 18, PI Article 16, and PII Article 10). This protection extends to civilians who may have spontaneously collected and cared for wounded and sick, no matter what the nationality of such persons (PI Article 17 and PII Article 18). This applies in both international and internal armed conflict.

---

11. Medical personnel may not be compelled to carry out acts contrary to the rules of medical ethics or to breach doctor–patient privileged confidentiality (PI Article 16 and PII Article 10).

12. Members of such personnel will not be considered as prisoners of war if they fall in the hands of the adversary. They must be freed, unless the number of prisoners of war and their state of health require the contrary, in which case the medical personnel must be given the facilities and rights necessary to ensure the respect for medical ethics (GCI Articles 28 and 29, GCII Article 37, and GCIII Article 33). Furthermore, if prisoners of war have medical

expertise, they may be required to exercise medical function in the interest of other prisoners. In such cases, they have the same rights as the rest of the medical personnel (GCIII Article 32).

13. In occupied territory, the Occupying Power has the duty to ensure and maintain all medical activities, and must allow the medical personnel to accomplish their missions (GCIV Article 56).

14. Every place of internment must have an adequate infirmary. It is preferable for internees to have the attention of medical personnel of their own nationality (GCIV Article 91).

→   **Humanitarian and relief personnel; International Criminal Court; Medical duties; Medical ethics; Medical services; Right of Access; Wounded and sick**

📖 **For Additional Information:**

Baccino-Astrada, Alma. *Manual on the Rights and Duties of Medical Personnel in Armed Conflicts.* Geneva: ICRC, 1982.

■ MEDICAL SERVICES

The term *medical services* covers medical personnel, medical units, and medical transportation. It is a crucial element in bringing relief to the populations concerned. In situations of conflict, humanitarian law grants a special status and specific protection to medical services (GCIV Articles 56 and 57; PI Articles 8–31; PII Articles 7–12).

☞ The act of intentionally directing attacks against medical services in the context of an armed conflict, whether international or internal, is considered a war crime under humanitarian law. It also falls under the jurisdiction of the International Criminal Court (Article 8.2.b.xxiv and 8.2.e.ii of ICC statute).

I. MEDICAL UNITS

1. Definition

A *medical unit* describes a military or civilian establishment or other unit organized for medical purposes—namely, the search for, collection, transportation, or treatment (including first aid treatment) of the wounded, sick, and shipwrecked or for the prevention of disease.

In other words, medical units are hospitals, clinics, pharmacies, laboratories, and other medical centers. Humanitarian law tries to maintain continuity between all the medical services during a conflict and therefore applies the term *medical units* to such places to ensure that they are granted the protective status common to all such establishments.

- Medical units include
  —hospitals and other similar units,
  —blood transfusion centers,
  —centers and institutes for preventive medicine,
  —medical and pharmaceutical stores and materials, and
  —stocks of medical material and pharmaceutical products.

- These medical units can be fixed or mobile, permanent or temporary, and are protected under humanitarian law from destruction, attacks, and requisitions (GCI Articles 19–23, 33–35; GCIV Article 18; PI Articles 8, 12–14; PII Article 11). They are entitled to the protection provided through the use of the distinctive emblem of the red cross (GCI Articles 38 and 42; GCIV Article 18; PI Article 18; PII Article 12).

2. Protection

- Civilian hospitals that are organized to provide care for the wounded, the sick, the infirm, and maternity cases may in no circumstances be the object of attacks. They must be respected and protected, at all times, by the parties to the conflict (GCIV Article 18; PI Article 12; PII Article 11).

Medical Material and Medicine

Medical material designates all the equipment and supplies necessary for the functioning of medical units, which must also benefit from the protection granted to medical units.

- Medical material is not a strategic product or object. International law therefore forbids its destruction or requisition (GCIV Article 55; PI Article 14).
- Parties to the conflict must not prohibit any action that consists of supplying medicine and medical materials (GCIV Articles 23 and 55; PII Article 18).
- Humanitarian law further specifies that
  —an Occupying Power has the duty to ensure that food and medical supplies are provided for the population (GCIV Article 55);
  —each High Contracting Party is under the obligation to allow the free passage of all consignments of medicine and medical material that is intended solely for civilians of another party, even if the latter is its adversary (GCIV Article 23);
  —relief societies are authorized to undertake relief actions when a civilian population is suffering owing to a lack of supplies essential to its survival, such as foodstuff and medical supplies (PII Article 18);
  —the Protecting Power is always at liberty to verify the state of the food and medical material in occupied territories, "except where temporary restrictions are made necessary by imperative military necessity" (GCIV Article 55).
- → **Protected objects and property; Relief**

- Civilian hospitals shall be marked, if the state authorizes it, by means of the emblem provided for in Article 38 of the first Geneva Convention for the Amelioration of the Condition of the Wounded and Sick in Armed Forces in the Field of August 12, 1949, such as the red cross or red crescent (GCIV Article 18).
- Parties to a conflict shall, insofar as military considerations permit it, take the necessary steps to make the distinctive emblems indicating civilian hospitals clearly visible to the enemy forces—land, air, and naval—to obviate the possibility of any hostile action (GCIV Article 18).

- States parties to a conflict shall provide all civilian hospitals with certificates showing that they are civilian hospitals and that the buildings they occupy are not used for any purpose that would deprive these hospitals of protection (GCIV Article 18).
- In view of the dangers to which hospitals may be exposed by being close to military objectives, it is recommended that civilian hospitals be situated as far as possible from such objectives (GCIV Article 18).
- Under no circumstances may medical units be used in an attempt to shield military objectives from attack. Whenever possible, the parties to the conflict shall ensure that medical units are situated so that attacks against military objectives do not imperil their safety (PI Article 12).
- Fixed establishments and mobile medical units of the military medical services may in no circumstances be attacked, and they must at all times be respected and protected by the parties to the conflict. Should they fall into the hands of an adverse party, their personnel shall be free to pursue their duties, unless the capturing power itself has ensured the necessary care of the wounded and sick provided in such establishments and units. The responsible authorities shall ensure that these medical establishments and units are, as much as possible, situated in such a manner that attacks against military objectives cannot imperil their safety (PII Article 19).

3. Protection May Be Withdrawn in Certain Cases

The protection to which fixed medical establishments and mobile medical units are entitled shall not cease unless they are being used to commit acts, outside their humanitarian duties, that are harmful to the enemy. Even in such cases, protection can cease only after due warning has been given and this warning has remained unheeded. Such a warning must, in all appropriate cases, give a reasonable time limit after which the protection will cease (GCI Article 21, PI Article 13, and PII Article 11).

4. Cases in Which Protection May Not Be Withdrawn

The Geneva Conventions and their Additional Protocols consider that certain acts may not be defined as being of a nature that would permit a party to the conflict to deny protection to a medical unit or establishment. This includes situations in which

- the personnel of the unit or establishment is armed and uses the arms for its own defense or in defense of the wounded and sick in their charge;
- the unit or establishment is protected by a picket, by sentries, or by an escort, in the absence of armed orderlies;
- small arms and ammunition taken from the wounded and sick and not yet handed to the proper service are found in the unit or establishment;
- the humanitarian activities of medical units and establishments or their personnel extend to the care of civilian wounded or sick;
- members of the armed forces or other combatants are in the unit for medical reasons (GCI Article 22; PI Article 13).

II. MEDICAL TRANSPORTATION

Medical transportation means the act of conveying the wounded, sick, shipwrecked, medical personnel, religious personnel, medical equipment, or medical supplies protected by the Geneva

Conventions and their Additional Protocols, by land, water, or air. *Medical transports* refers to the means of transportation of such persons or supplies, whether military or civilian, permanent or temporary, assigned exclusively to medical transportation and under the control of a competent authority of a party to the conflict (PI Article 8).

- Means of transportation are protected by norms of international law and, under this status, may carry the emblem of the red cross (GCI Articles 35–38; GCII Articles 22–35, 38–41; GCIV Articles 21, 22; PI Articles 12, 21–31).
- Medical transportation—whether on land or sea or by air—must be respected and protected in the same way as mobile medical units. This means that such transportation may not be attacked and specific precautions identified by the Conventions must be taken to protect it (GCII Articles 35, 36; GCIV Articles 21, 22; PI Articles 12, 21). The precautions to be taken to protect such transportation include
  - identifying it as being entitled to such protection by bearing the appropriate protective emblem (e.g., the red cross or red crescent) and
  - informing the authorities of its presence.

1. Protection May Be Withdrawn Following Certain Acts

The Conventions specify which acts may lead to the withdrawal of such protection for medical transportation and which acts may not (GCII Articles 34, 35; PI Article 13):

- The protection to which means of medical transportation are entitled shall not cease unless they are being used to commit, outside their humanitarian duties, acts that are harmful to the enemy. Even in such cases, protection can cease only after due warning has been given (which gives, in all appropriate cases, a reasonable time limit) and after this warning has remained unheeded (GCII Article 34).
- The following acts may not be considered harmful to the enemy and may therefore not lead to the protection granted to medical transportation being discontinued: the fact that the personnel of a medical unit is equipped with light individual weapons for their own defense; the fact that the unit is guarded by an escort; the act of transporting members of the armed forces or other combatants for medical reasons (PI Article 13).

The Conventions set out the specific measures that must be taken for the identification and notification of movements. These measures are particularly detailed in the case of hospital ships, coastal rescue craft, and other ships (GCII Articles 22–36, 43; PI Articles 18, 22, 23) and medical aircraft (GCII Articles 39 and 40; PI Articles 18, 24–31), as well as medical units (GCI Articles 42 and 43; GCIV Article 22) and medical transports (GCI Articles 39 and 44; GCIV Article 21). → **Distinctive (or protective) emblems, signs, or signals**

2. Requisition

Precise rules also regulate the requisition of medical material and means of transportation (GCI Article 35; GCIV Article 57; PI Article 14). It is forbidden to requisition civilian medical units as long as these are needed to provide adequate medical services for the civilian population and to ensure the continuing medical care of any wounded and sick already undergoing treatment (PI Article 14.2).

If it is possible to carry out a requisition while respecting these principles, it is still subject to the following conditions (PI Article 14.3):

- The resources are being requisitioned because they are necessary for the adequate and immediate medical treatment of the wounded and sick members of the armed forces or of prisoners of war. Requisition may not be carried out for any other reason.
- The requisition must continue only as long as such necessity exists.
- Immediate arrangements must be made to ensure that the medical needs of the civilian population and those of any wounded and sick already under treatment continue to be satisfied.

➔ **Requisition**

Members of medical personnel are given a special status and protection by humanitarian law, as part of relief personnel. This protection is reinforced by the specific rights they are granted by virtue of their medical mission. This special status is addressed independently under the entry on ➔ **medical personnel.**

➔   **Distinctive (or protective) emblems, signs, or signals; Humanitarian and relief personnel; International Criminal Court; Medical duties; Medical personnel; Protected objects and property; Relief; Requisition; Wounded and sick persons**

📖 **For Additional Information:**

Baccino-Astrada, Alma. *Manual on the Rights and Duties of Medical Personnel in Armed Conflicts.* Geneva: ICRC, 1982.

■ MERCENARIES

As defined by Protocol I additional to the Geneva Conventions (Article 47), a mercenary is a person who is hired locally or abroad to fight in an armed conflict and who does, in fact, participate directly in the hostilities. A mercenary's primary motivation is the desire for private gain and material compensation that is substantially more than that promised or paid to combatants having similar rank and functions. Mercenaries are neither residents nor nationals of one of the parties to the conflict, nor are they members of the armed forces of a party to the conflict, nor have they been sent by a state which is not a party to the conflict on official duty as members of its armed forces.

> ☞ Mercenaries are not entitled to the status of combatant, prisoner of war (PI Article 47), or any of the categories of protected persons provided for by the Geneva Conventions, unless they are wounded or sick, although they must always benefit from humane treatment. In conformity with the Geneva Conventions, they are held criminally responsible if they commit war crimes or other grave breaches of humanitarian law. They are entitled to the fundamental guarantees established for all individuals.

➔   **Combatants; Fundamental guarantees; Penal sanctions in humanitarian law; Prisoners of war; War crimes/Crimes against humanity; Wounded and sick persons**

📖 **For Additional Information:**

Green, L. C. "The Status of Mercenaries in International Law." In *Israel Yearbook on Human Rights.* Tel Aviv: Faculty of Law, Tel Aviv University, 1978, vol. 8: 9–62.

Yusuf, A. A. "Mercenaries in the Law of Armed Conflicts." In *The New Humanitarian Law of Armed Conflict,* ed. A. Cassese. Naples: Editoriale Scientifica, 1979, vol. 1: 113–27.

■ METHODS (AND MEANS) OF WARFARE

Methods of warfare are the tactics or strategy used in hostilities against an enemy, in times of conflict. *Means of warfare* are the weapons or weapons systems used. The only legitimate objective of war is to weaken and overpower the opponent's military forces.

☞ War is a part of history and of international relations. It is a transitional phase and must be conducted in a way that will not make a return to peace impossible. Various international humanitarian law texts therefore establish the principles that limit the choice of methods of warfare.

- The 1899 and 1907 Hague Conventions, as well as the 1949 Geneva Conventions and their 1977 Protocols Additional, set forth the main rules, restrictions, and prohibitions concerning the use of violence and different methods of warfare.
- The endurance and repeated use of these rules over time has conferred the value of "customary norms" on a number of them. This means that they are binding on all parties to a conflict, even states or belligerents who have not formally adhered to such rules.
- The conventions define which acts are war crimes and establish sanctioning mechanisms to punish the authors of such crimes. Some of these crimes are defined as grave breaches of the Geneva Conventions and therefore come under the principle of universal jurisdiction, which allows any court of any country to prosecute perpetrators of grave violations of humanitarian law.
- → **Customary international law; International humanitarian law; Universal jurisdiction; War crimes/Crimes against humanity (Section III, "Grave Breaches of International Humanitarian Law")**

1. Regulating the Weapons of War

The right to choose the methods and means of warfare is not unlimited. International law imposes restrictions on the manufacture and use of certain weapons—namely, those that strike civilians and combatants indiscriminately or cause damage that is extensive or basically irreversible and is disproportionate to any specific military advantage. → **Military objectives; Mines; Weapons**

2. Regulating the Techniques of War

a. Humanitarian law prohibits gratuitous and wanton violence and destruction. It requires that any means of violence employed be proportionate to a real and direct military necessity.
→ **Military necessity; Proportionality**

b. International humanitarian law prohibits
- the use of means and methods of warfare of a nature to cause superfluous injury or unnecessary suffering (PI Article 35; Article 22 of the rules of the 1907 Hague Conventions; and the 1868 Saint Petersburg Declaration);
- carrying out attacks with the goal that there will be no survivors—in other words, giving no quarter (PI Articles 40 and 41; Article 35 of the 1907 Hague Convention on the laws and customs of war).

Prohibited methods of warfare include
- perfidy (PI Articles 37–39);
- terror (PI Article 51; PII Article 13);
- famine (starvation) of civilians (PI Article 54; PII Article 14);
- reprisals against nonmilitary objectives (GCI Article 46; GCII Article 47; GCIII Article 13; GCIV Article 33; PI Articles 20, 51–56; Article 46 of the 1954 Convention on the Protection of Cultural Property);
- attacks against protected persons and civilian objects;
- indiscriminate attacks (PI Articles 48 and 51),
- attacks aimed at causing damage to the natural environment (PI Articles 35, 52, and 55);
- attacks against works and installations containing dangerous forces (PI Articles 52 and 56; PII Article 15);
- pillage (GCIV Article 33; Article 4 of 1954 Convention on the Protection of Cultural Property; PII at 4);
- taking hostages (GCI–IV Article 3; GCIV Article 34; PI Article 75; principles of international law established by the statute and judgments of the Nuremberg Tribunals; Article 12 of the 1979 Convention against the Taking of Hostages);
- using the population movements to favor the conduct of hostilities (GCIV Article 49; PI Article 51; PII Article 17). ➜ **Attacks; Famine; Hostage; Human shields; Military objectives; Perfidy; Pillage; Population displacement; Protected objects and property; Protected persons; Reprisals; Terror**

c. Humanitarian law prohibits the use of prisoners of war, the civilian population, and resources in occupied territories for military purposes. It also limits the right of requisition. ➜ **Occupied territory; Prisoners of war; Requisition**

d. Military commanders are under the obligation to respect and enforce the respect for international humanitarian law, including the prohibitions listed above. They must
  —take certain precautions when attacking;
  —ensure that their subordinates know and understand humanitarian law;
  —punish any of their subordinates who have acted in violation of these rules.
  ➜ **Attacks; Duty of commanders**

e. The failure to respect these rules may constitute a war crime under international humanitarian law and according to the statute of the future International Criminal Court. ➜ **International Criminal Court; War crimes/Crimes against humanity**

➜ **Aggression; Annexation; Attacks; Blockade; Bombardment; Cease-fire; Duty of commanders; Evacuation; Extermination; Famine; Geneva Conventions and Protocols; The Hague Conventions; Hostage; Human shields; International Criminal Court; Military necessity; Military objectives; Mines; Population displacement; Proportionality; Reprisals; Requisition; Siege; War; War crimes/Crimes against humanity; Weapons**

📖 **For Additional Information:**

Mulinen, Frederic de. *Handbook on the Law of War for Armed Forces*. Geneva: ICRC, 1989.

■ MILITARY NECESSITY

In times of conflict, *military necessity* is the notion used to justify the recourse to violence. Any violence or destruction that is not justified by military necessity is prohibited by the law of armed conflict. The use of armed force is legitimate only when attempting to attain specific military objectives, and then only as long as it stays within the limits of the principle of proportionality.

Conversely, this notion can serve to contest the use of armed force if it seems that the violence or destruction were

- unnecessary—the target or victims were not linked to a specific military objective;
- disproportionate—the reprisal or attack was not proportionate to the original attack or threat;
- indiscriminate—the attack did not distinguish between military objectives and civilian objects;
- aimed at spreading terror among the civilian population.

→ **Attacks; Methods (and means) of warfare; Military objectives; Proportionality; Protected objects and property; War**

📖 **For Additional Information:**

Draper, G. I. A. D. "Military Necessity and Humanitarian Imperatives." *The Military Law and Law of War Review* (1973): 129–51.
MacCoubrey, Hilaire. "The Nature of the Modern Doctrine in Military Necessity." *The Military Law and Law of War Review* (1991): 215–52.
Mulinen, Frederic de. *Handbook on the Law of War for Armed Forces* Geneva: ICRC, 1989, 82–84.

■ MILITARY OBJECTIVES

Military objectives are objects that, by their nature, location, purpose, or use, make an effective contribution to military action, and whose total or partial destruction, capture, or neutralization offers a definite military advantage (PI Article 52).

The definition of a military objective is a crucial part of the mechanism for protecting civilians in times of conflict.

> ☞ In case of doubt concerning an object that is normally used for civilian purposes—such as a house or other dwelling, a place of worship, or a school—parties to a conflict must assume that the object in question is not being used for military purposes (PI Article 52.3).
>
> At all times, humanitarian law establishes that military commanders have the obligation to respect a number of precautions in the conduct of military operations, so as to ensure the protection of civilians. For instance, these precautions consist in doing "everything feasible to verify that the objectives to be attacked are neither civilians nor civilian objects" and in "minimizing incidental loss of civilian life, injury to civilians, and damage to civilian objects" (PI Article 57).

Attacks that are not directed at a specific military objective are prohibited, as are those employing methods or means of combat that cannot be directed at a specific military objective or are of a nature to strike military objectives and civilians or civilian objects without distinction (PI Article 51.4).

As a corollary to this, the presence or movements of the civilian population may not be used to render certain points or areas immune from military operations and, in particular, to shield military objectives from attacks (PI Article 51.7).

Furthermore, works or installations containing dangerous forces (namely, dams, dikes, and nuclear electricity-generating stations) must not be the target of attacks, even if they are military objectives (PI Article 56; PII Article 15).

→ **Attacks; Duty of commanders; Human shields; Methods (and means) of warfare; Military necessity; Protected objects and property**

📖 **For Additional Information:**

Mulinen, Frederic de. *Handbook on the Law of War for Armed Forces*. Geneva: ICRC, 1989, 13–14.

■ MINES

Mines are objects designed to be placed under, on, or near the ground and to explode due to the presence, proximity, or contact of a person (in the case of antipersonnel land mines) or a vehicle (in the case of antitank or antivehicle land mines). Mines can also be maritime.

From a strategic point of view, they are used to prevent the enemy from advancing or reaching a certain part of the territory.

I. REGULATIONS CONCERNING THE USE OF MINES

The use of mines is strictly limited by the general principles of the law of armed conflict, which were further codified and updated in the 1980 Convention on Conventional Weapons (explained later). In 1997, another convention banned mines and prohibited their use, however it is only applicable to the few states that have ratified the convention.

1. General Regulations in International Humanitarian Law

Certain rules of war forbid or limit the use of mines, booby traps, and other devices. These restrictions are based on two principles:

- Mines must always be used in a way that makes it possible to ensure that they are not having an indiscriminate effect, striking the civilian population as much as military objectives.
- The use of mines must be limited to the period of hostilities. One of the most basic principles of the laws of war is that a distinction must be made between times of peace and of war, meaning that the weapons used must be limited and controlled.

→ **Methods (and means) of warfare**

These principles are derived from the laws and customs of war, in particular the Geneva and Hague Conventions, which are binding on all states. The standards and rules set forth in these conventions reaffirm the principle that attacks must be proportionate to the goals sought and must distinguish between civilians and combatants. The purpose of these principles is to protect societies from the long-term material and psychological effects of war and to make a return to peace and reconciliation possible. These principles were reiterated and further codified in 1980.

→ **Attacks; Proportionality; War**

2. 1980 Protocol II on Prohibitions or Restrictions on the Use of Mines, Booby Traps, and Other Devices

On October 10, 1980, the Convention on Prohibitions of Restrictions on the Use of Certain Conventional Weapons Which May Be Deemed to Be Excessively Injurious or to Have Indiscriminate Effects (known as the Convention on Conventional Weapons) was adopted, under the auspices of the UN. It codified the rules governing the use of conventional weapons more precisely than earlier texts. Its second Protocol—on Prohibitions or Restrictions on the Use of Mines, Booby Traps and Other Devices—specifically addressed the use of mines and other such devices, in times of conflict. This protocol was amended in 1996 and entered into force on December 3, 1998. It is now known as "Protocol II as amended on 3 May 1996" and currently has fifty-eight states parties.

The Protocol, as a convention that regulates the law of armed conflict, establishes the rules for the use of mines but does not forbid their use. It is applicable to both international and internal armed conflicts.

a. General Prohibitions and Obligations

Some of the provisions of Protocol II as amended on May 3, 1996, prohibit certain specific uses and others set forth clear obligations, in an attempt to limit the use of mines to strictly military purposes and to protect civilians, both during and after a conflict:

- It is prohibited in all circumstances to use any mine, booby trap, or other device, which is designed or of a nature to cause superfluous injury or unnecessary suffering (Article 3.3);
- it is prohibited, in all circumstances, to direct these weapons against the civilian population or individual civilians or civilian objects (Article 3.7);
- the indiscriminate use of these weapons is prohibited (Article 3.8);
- all feasible precautions shall be taken to protect civilians from the effects of these weapons (Article 3.10);
- it is prohibited to use antipersonnel mines that are not detectable (Article 4);
- it is prohibited to use mines, booby traps, or remotely delivered mines that are not in compliance with the Protocol's precise provisions on self-destruction and self-deactivation (Articles 5 and 6);
- the states party to the Convention or parties to a conflict undertake to record all information concerning minefields, mined areas, mines, booby traps, and other devices, in accordance with the Protocol's Technical Annex (Article 9);
- each party to a conflict undertakes to clear, remove, destroy, or maintain all minefields, mined areas, mines, booby traps, and other devices in areas under their control, without delay after the cessation of active hostilities (Article 10);
- the international sign for minefields and mined areas (Article 4 of Technical Annex) are
  —*size and shape*: a triangle no smaller than 28 centimeters (11 inches) by 20 centimeters (7.9

inches) for a triangle, or a square no smaller than 25 centimeters by 25 centimeters (10 inches);

—*color*: red or orange with a yellow reflecting border;

—*content*: the recognized symbol for danger is the skull and crossbones, which must be on all Mine Danger signs. The Technical Annex also suggests other recognizable images.

b. Special Protection for International or Humanitarian Missions

Article 12 of Protocol II as amended on May 3, 1996, establishes that certain UN or humanitarian operations, carried out with the consent of the state concerned, must enjoy special protection from the effects of minefields, mined areas, mines, booby traps, and other devices. These operations include

- any UN force or mission performing peacekeeping, observation, or similar functions in any area in accordance with the Charter of the United Nations;
- any UN system humanitarian or fact-finding mission;
- any ICRC or national Red Cross or Red Crescent Society mission performing functions with the consent of the relevant states, as provided for by the Geneva Conventions;
- any humanitarian mission of an impartial humanitarian organization (including any impartial humanitarian demining mission);
- any mission of inquiry established pursuant to the Geneva Conventions.

These missions must be protected, as long as they are performing their functions with the consent of the High Contracting Party on whose territory they are acting. This requirement does not apply to the first category (UN peacekeeping missions).

With regard to all such missions, the states parties must

- take all necessary measures to protect the force or mission from the effects of mines, booby traps, and other devices in any area under its control;
- provide the personnel of the mission with safe passage to or through any place under its control that the mission needs to cross in order to perform its functions.

In the case of UN peacekeeping missions or forces, the party to the conflict must also, "if so requested by the head of a force or mission," remove or render harmless all mines, booby traps and other devices in the area in which it is performing its functions, as far as possible, and must inform the head of the force or mission of the location of all known minefields, mined areas, mines, booby traps, and other devices.

3. Continued Use of Mines

Originally, belligerents' respect for the obligations under the 1980 Convention on Conventional Weapons and Protocols, and other humanitarian law rules governing methods of warfare, was based on the principle of reciprocity rather than on punishment. The theory was that both sides had an interest in respecting these rules, in order to prepare for the return to peace.

Concrete reality and technological evolution upset the balance of reciprocity as a means of deterrence and control of the use of land mines: the invention of remotely delivered mines (dropped from aircraft or delivered by artillery) and nondetectable mines made the monitoring systems set up by humanitarian law useless.

Since humanitarian law does not strictly prohibit the use of mines, the debate on their conditions of use remained under the close control of military experts and mostly addressed complex technical issues.

The low cost of making mines makes them a popular weapon in many conflicts. Mines are generally used in a widespread manner to prevent access to entire territories or to spread terror among the population and, as such, have devastating effects on the civilian population. Civilians are the main victims of mines and they continue to suffer the consequences for years, even decades, after peace has been restored. The ICRC estimates that two thousand individuals, three-quarters of whom are civilians, are injured or killed each month. According to UNICEF, one million individuals have been victims of mines since 1975, one-third of whom are children under the age of fifteen.

II. PROHIBITION ON THE USE OF MINES: THE 1997 MINE BAN TREATY

Facing a dead end in terms of regulating the use of mines, the ICRC and numerous NGOs launched an International Campaign to Ban Landmines (ICBL). Its aim was to prohibit the production and use of antipersonnel mines. The ICBL failed in its initial effort to obtain binding state commitments to this effect at the revision conference on the 1980 Convention on Conventional Weapons. But states did finally adopt a Convention on the Prohibition of the Use, Stockpiling, Production and Transfer of Anti-personnel Mines and on Their Destruction (known as the Mine Ban Treaty)—under Canada's initiative and supported by the ICBL—in Oslo, Norway, on September 18, 1997. It was opened for signature in Ottawa, Canada, on December 3, 1997, and entered into force on March 1, 1999.

The Mine Ban Treaty currently has 111 states parties and a total of 139 have signed it, indicating their intent to ratify it. However, the main mine-producing states refuse to adhere to the Treaty. These include the United States, the Russian Federation, China, India, and Pakistan.

The Convention on the Prohibition of the Use, Stockpiling, Production, and Transfer of Anti-personnel Mines and on Their Destruction (the Mine Ban Treaty)

The Mine Ban Treaty, which entered into force on March 1, 1999, bans antipersonnel mines. These are mines "designed to be exploded by the presence, proximity or contact of a person and that will incapacitate, injure or kill one or more persons" (Article 2.1 of Mine Ban Treaty).

Each state party undertakes the following:

- never under any circumstances to use antipersonnel mines and to ensure that no one uses them in its territory (Article 1.1.a);
- never under any circumstances to "develop, produce, otherwise acquire, stockpile, retain or transfer to anyone, directly or indirectly, anti-personnel mines" (Article 1.1.b);
- to destroy all stockpiled antipersonnel mines it owns or that are under its jurisdiction or control, no later than four years after the Treaty enters into force for that state (Article 4);

(continues)

(*continued*)

- to destroy all "mined areas"—defined as an area that is dangerous due to the presence or suspected presence of mines—within ten years (Article 5.1); and
- to submit an annual report to the UN on the national implementation measures undertaken in conformity with the Treaty. In fact, states parties have the obligation to enact "all appropriate legal, administrative and other measures, including the imposition of penal sanctions, to prevent and suppress any activity prohibited [. . .] undertaken by persons or on territory under its jurisdiction or control" (Article 9).
- Finally, states have the option to authorize and send a fact-finding mission to verify a state's compliance with its obligations under the Treaty.

III. DEMINING

Demining is a costly and dangerous activity. In times of conflict, international humanitarian law clearly forbids prisoners of war from being employed at this task (GCIII Article 52). After the hostilities have ended, each party to the conflict may ask for technical and material assistance from other states and international organizations in their demining activities (Articles 9–11 of Protocol II as amended on May 3, 1996). The Mine Ban Treaty establishes that each state party "in a position to do so" is under the obligation to "provide assistance for mine clearance and related activities" (Article 6.4).

This is essential because the cost of demining programs is colossal, and states ravaged by a conflict cannot afford it. The UN does have a fund specifically for demining assistance, which was used in Afghanistan, Cambodia, Mozambique, and the former Yugoslavia. Formerly under the Department of Humanitarian Affairs (now the Office for the Coordination of Humanitarian Affairs), the fund is now in the Department of Peacekeeping Operations. At the current demining rate, it would take eleven centuries to get rid of all mines.

The term *humanitarian demining* only applies to activities carried out immediately following the cessation of hostilities. Although in recent conflicts it has become increasingly difficult to determine exactly when the conflict is over, the signing of a cease-fire or peace accords is often used as a point from which to begin demining operations. These operations are important in order to favor the return of displaced populations or to facilitate the organization of elections.

During a conflict, demining can be combined with humanitarian relief operations. However, such activities must be undertaken very carefully because they can be seen as a military threat and result in reprisals against humanitarian actors.

☞ Three-quarters of all mine victims are civilians, and one-third are children under the age of fifteen.

- Approximately 110 million land mines currently lie in wait in seventy countries. According to Handicap International, mines claim an average of one victim every twenty minutes (or more than twenty-six thousand per year).
- The average cost of a mine is between $3 and $30.
- The average cost to demine one is between $300 and $1,000.
- According to the ICBL, at the current demining rate, it would take more than a millennium and $33 billion to clear all of the existing mines in the world.

In theory, demining is the duty of the party that disseminated the mines in the first place. When peace accords are signed, parties to the conflict must exchange maps of the location of mines, and must transmit these to the Secretary-General of the UN. They must also establish who is responsible for the demining. Such provisions are set forth in Protocol II to the 1980 Convention on Conventional Weapons (Articles 9 and 10 of Protocol II on the Prohibitions or Restrictions on the Use of Mines, Booby-Traps and Other Devices, as amended on May 3, 1996).

To date, no international or national funds are set up for the compensation of mine victims, which may beg the question of how serious the international solidarity for victims of mines really is. The Mine Ban Treaty establishes that "each state party in a position to do so shall provide assistance for the care and rehabilitation, and social and economic reintegration, of mine victims and for mine awareness programs" (Article 6.3). Such assistance may be provided in cooperation with the UN or its agencies, the ICRC or national Red Cross and Red Crescent societies, NGOs, other states, and so on.

It is important that medical reports be established for victims of mines, so as to enable them to file later claims for compensation or a disability pension.

→ **Attacks; Methods (and means) of warfare; Proportionality; Weapons**
→ **List of states party to international human rights and humanitarian conventions (No. 26)**

📖 **For Additional Information:**

Cauderay, Gerald C. "Anti-personnel Mines." *International Review of the Red Cross* 295 (July–August 1993): 273–87.

Prokosch, Eric, and Robert O. Muller. *The Technology of Killing: A Military and Political History of Antipersonnel Weapons*. New York: St. Martin's, 1995.

Rogers, A. P. V. "Mines, Booby-Traps and Other Devices." *International Review of the Red Cross* 279 (November–December 1990): 521–34.

Russbach, Remi. "Anti-personnel Mines: A Disgrace for Humanity." *International Review of the Red Cross* 292 (January–February 1993): 57–58.

@ International Campaign to Ban Landmines: www.icbl.org

■ Minors

The age at which a person reaches legal majority varies from country to country—mostly between eighteen and twenty-one. The age of majority is when a person attains the full exercise of his or her rights. Below that age, the person is considered a minor and is entitled to special care and protection. In principle, minors are not regarded as legally responsible for their actions—they have not yet attained full juridical personality (full recognition as subjects of the law). This also means that they do not have obligations to society.

However, there are legal subcategories of minors, and these vary even more in different national laws. This is reflected in the fact that the Committee on the Rights of the Child (which monitors the implementation of the Convention on the Rights of the Child) requires that states provide the Committee with the definition of a child provided in their laws and regulations. It is this definition that determines the age at which a child may voluntarily and independently participate in the political and social life of society by exercising the right to vote, join the armed forces, testify in court, have sexual relations, get married, as well as the age at which they may be held criminally liable or may be deprived of their liberty.

Many judicial systems establish an age of criminal responsibility that is younger than that of legal majority (often around the age of thirteen). From this age until they reach legal majority, youths (sometimes also called *juveniles*) may be held responsible for their acts if they commit grave crimes, but they usually will be judged and sentenced under a different regime than adults.

☞ International law does not speak of *minors* since the age at which a child reaches legal majority varies from country to country, as do the possible criminal procedures that may exist for juveniles. Instead, it refers to *children*.

A regime of specialized protection is crucial since, for the most part, children depend on others to be able to exercise their rights, from having their voice heard to obtaining refugee status. Humanitarian law establishes rights and guarantees specifically for their protection. For instance, children must be given priority when receiving relief during international or internal armed conflicts. Furthermore, children under the age of fifteen may not be recruited into the armed forces.

In times of peace, there are additional norms regulating children's rights that must be respected, as established in international human rights conventions. For instance, these may concern their right to health and education; freedom from any form of maltreatment, sexual or other forms of abuse, exploitation, neglect, and traffic of children; and rules governing conditions of adoption and detention.

➔   **Children; Committee on the Rights of the Child; Detention; Judicial guarantees; UNICEF**

■ MUTUAL ASSISTANCE IN CRIMINAL MATTERS

States are under the obligation to collaborate with one another in punishing certain crimes that are defined by international criminal law.

☞ The aim of mutual assistance in criminal matters is to prevent criminals from escaping legal prosecution simply by leaving the territory of the state concerned. This principle is applicable to the pursuit of war crimes and crimes against humanity but also to other categories of crimes that threaten national security, such as terrorism.

The principle of *mutual assistance in criminal matters,* also referred to as *judicial assistance and cooperation,* centers around two obligations accepted by states: the obligation either to prosecute presumed criminals themselves or to extradite the accused to the state concerned by the crime committed or to the state that has an interest in pursuing the accused.

Extradition is the act of one state turning over a person who was on its territory to another state, upon the latter's request. The requesting state makes the entreaty with the aim of exercising its criminal jurisdiction over the accused. Such mutual cooperation takes place on a case-by-case basis, in the framework of bilateral or multilateral extradition treaties.

1. International Conventions Addressing Mutual Assistance in Criminal Matters

In 1949, the Geneva Conventions established a reinforced system of mutual assistance in criminal matters, which extends beyond making a choice between prosecution and extradition. The Conventions add the obligation to search actively for the alleged criminals, which precedes the sharing of responsibility in terms of trying the accused. They then hold each state accountable to its commitment to "bring such persons, regardless of their nationality, before its own courts," and impose guarantees to ensure that an extradition will not result in impunity for the accused (GVI Article 146; PI Article 88).

In terms of specific rules governing mutual assistance in criminal matters or extradition, however, there are no international conventions that bind all states. Obligations relating to these issues are regulated by bilateral or multilateral treaties, which, by default, create "judicial havens" in countries that have not ratified the treaties. The concrete application of judicial assistance must hence be examined on a case-by-case basis.

To implement this principle, technical agreements must regulate the cooperation between the different national police forces and judicial organs of the states concerned. This collaboration must hence be incorporated into the national criminal laws; otherwise, the international commitment remains a commitment in principle only and cannot be translated into practical judicial procedures.

The Convention on the Non-Applicability of Statutory Limitations to War Crimes and Crimes against Humanity, adopted by the General Assembly of the UN on November 26, 1968, tries to lift some of the obstacles to such cooperation. It entered into force in 1970 and now has forty-four states parties. It requires that states adopt all domestic measures, legislative or otherwise, that would be necessary to enable the extradition of the persons referred to in the Convention, in accordance with international law (Article 3). → **Nonapplicability of statutory limitations**

Finally, there is also a UN resolution on the Principles of International Cooperation in the Detection, Arrest, Extradition and Punishment of Persons Guilty of War Crimes and Crimes against Humanity (Resolution 3074 (XXVIII), adopted by the UN General Assembly on December 3, 1973).
→ **Universal jurisdiction**

2. Mutual Assistance under International Tribunal Statutes

The statutes of the two ad hoc International Criminal Tribunals created by the UN set forth an obligation to cooperate and to provide assistance on judicial matters (UN Security Council Resolution 827 of May 25, 1993, Annex S/25704; Article 29 of ICTY statute). Among other things, they establish a specific mechanism, different from extradition, aimed at alleviating the procedures surrounding the handover of arrested persons: the latter are "transferred" to the Tribunals, as opposed to "extradited."

The statute of the International Criminal Court (ICC), adopted on July 17, 1998, also lists the obligations in terms of cooperation and judicial assistance that states parties must provide to the Court, as well as the practical components of this cooperation (Articles 72, 86–111 of ICC statute).

As is the case for bilateral or multilateral agreements, states are under the obligation to incorporate the provisions and mechanisms of mutual assistance into their national judicial systems in order to cooperate with the ad hoc Tribunals or the ICC.

Interpol

Interpol is the international criminal police organization that intercedes in procedures of mutual assistance in criminal matters. Originally, to safeguard national sovereignty, Article 3 of Interpol's constitution stated that "it is strictly forbidden for the Organization to undertake any intervention or activities of a political, military, religious or racial character," meaning that no international cooperation was possible which related to political, military, religious, or racial crimes.

The restriction was lifted through various analogous provisions adopted so that Interpol could act in cases of genocide and in the fight against terrorism in Europe and could cooperate with the two ad hoc International Criminal Tribunals for the former Yugoslavia and Rwanda in cases of war crimes, crimes against humanity, and genocide (Interpol AGN/63/RAP, no. 13). Not all states are members of Interpol. There are 178 member states.

✎   Interpol
     200 Quai Charles-de-Gaulle
     69000 Lyon, France
     Tel.: (33) 04 72 44 70 00
     Fax: (33) 04 72 44 71 63
@   Interpol: www.interpol.com

➔   **Impunity; International Criminal Court; International Criminal Tribunals; Nonapplicability of statutory limitations; Terrorism; Universal jurisdiction; War crimes/ Crimes against humanity**

📖 **For Additional Information:**

Gilbert, Geoff. *Aspects of Extradition Law*. The Hague: Martinus Nijhoff, 1991.
United Nations. *Manual on the Model Treaty on Extradition and Manual on the Model Treaty on Mutual Assistance in Criminal Matters: An Implementation Guide, International Review of Criminal Policy*. Vienna: Author, 1995, nos. 45 and 46.

N

■ NATIONALITY

Nationality is the legal bond that ties a person to a state. It confers on this person a legal status as determined by national laws, such as those regulating the rights of persons and property.

Each state establishes its own legislation regulating nationality, which includes provisions concerning the acquisition or loss of such nationality, and its own laws regulating the personal status of individuals. There are different ways of acquiring a nationality, which vary greatly from country to country, and may depend on factors such as the place of birth, the territory of residence, and the nationality of one or both parents. It is the legal status derived from having a nationality that grants rights—both individual and collective—to individuals. Such rights include, among many others, the right to an identity, to get married and to work, the right of association, rights to physical security, rights to due process, and so on.

This status enables individuals to participate in the system of justice and claim respect for their rights before national courts. Such possibilities are almost nonexistent for individuals at an international level.

In fact, international law does not establish a comprehensive legal status for individuals. However, it does try to complete and reinforce the protection that exists based on a person's nationality.

☞ The protection of individuals occurs mainly at the national leval and depends on their national legal status. It is extremely difficult to offer adequate guarantees of protection to a person without a nationality. Serious problems therefore arise when a state revokes the nationality of a group of persons or when individuals can no longer benefit from the protection of their state of nationality. The latter may happen to individuals for a number of reasons—for instance, if they become refugees, stateless persons, populations in occupied territories, victims of a conflict, persons displaced within their own country, or victims of persecution by the authorities of the state of which they are nationals.

(continues)

(*continued*)

In such circumstances, international law attempts to fill the void left by national laws, by setting forth the foundation for an international legal status for individuals. This is based on numerous international conventions codifying and defending human rights and humanitarian law. They impose on states minimum international standards relating to the treatment of individuals, which in some cases include mechanisms for protection.

→　**International conventions; Protection**

1. Nationality in International Law

International law tries to ensure that each individual has a nationality and to limit cases of statelessness. The right to a nationality is actually one of the fundamental rights of individuals proclaimed by the Universal Declaration of Human Rights (Article 15 of UDHR).

International human rights conventions and declarations establish the standards for the treatment of the human person. Above all, these norms—which are not all directly binding on states—are references that are meant to inspire and guide the drafting of national laws relating to the status of individuals. In certain cases, if these international standards are violated in a country, a victim may invoke his or her rights under international law before domestic courts. There are also several international mechanisms, for claims or complaints filed by individuals, to which the victim may have recourse.

→　**Human rights; Individual recourse**

In certain situations of emergency, humanitarian law also tries to meet the protection needs of individuals who no longer have the protection of any state (in other words, stateless persons) or who temporarily cannot benefit from the full protection of their own state, such as populations living in a state of emergency, victims of a situation of conflict, populations in occupied territory, or refugees.

Finally, international law defines different categories of "protected persons" and establishes the fundamental rights and guarantees to which they are entitled. It puts this theory of protection into practice by explicitly authorizing humanitarian organizations—such as the ICRC, UNHCR, and certain NGOs—to carry out actions of relief and protection.

→　**Fundamental guarantees; Human rights; International humanitarian law; Protected persons; Protection; Refugees; Stateless persons**

→　**List of states party to international human rights and humanitarian conventions**

■ NATURAL LAW AND POSITIVE LAW

1. Positive Law

Law is a set of norms and standards that are usually established by the authorities who are in charge of representing the community that the laws are meant to serve. The laws may be in the form of constitutions, decrees, precedents, and so on. In the case of international law, it describes formal interstate agreements, international conventions, and other treaties that reflect the consent or will of states to be bound by such laws. *Positive law* describes the content of these texts. Lawyers analyze each word, each comma, to ascertain the intention of the drafters. They also evaluate the force or status of law held by each text. They determine this on the basis of the body that enacted it and the level of formality with which it was adopted. They are guided in their interpretation and application of laws by the hierarchy of legal norms. → **Hierarchy of norms; International conventions**

Customary international law is included in positivist thinking because, while it does not always reflect the express consent of states, it does reflect their implicit consent, as expressed through repeated and consistent practice. Hence, it represents the will of many nations, from which it receives its force of law: it is binding on all states. **➔ Customary international law**

2. Natural Law

Natural law is historically linked to the concept of moral law. It was developed on the basis of the notion that human beings have certain rights and entitlements that exist even if they are not enshrined in written texts and that these rights are natural, irrevocable. Though positive law took over as the principal and most effective means of regulating societal or interstate relations, the idea endured. The term *natural law* is rarely used in international law today; however, *jus cogens* occupies a similar place. Modern human rights principles are based on the concept that fundamental rights and freedoms are inherent and inalienable, and many of them are nonderogable.

☞ The proponents of the theory of natural law point out that rights may exist outside any formal codification, resulting from moral obligations inscribed in the conscience of individuals. They have used this concept to counter established rules of written law. An important historical example is the emphasis that was placed on moral law in the fight to abolish slavery.

International law has come to formally recognize the existence of such unwritten peremptory norms, against which no derogation is permitted. These are *jus cogens* norms.

By invoking *jus cogens*, it is possible to escape from rigid and stale laws that may be ill adapted to new situations or unjust, because they were enacted in one era and become controversial in the next. When the application of a written law clearly flouts human dignity, the reference to unwritten norms provides an opportunity to oppose such rules.

The key is not to succumb blindly to the formality of law. It is important, in all circumstances, to have the ability

- to determine the force or status of law of a given rule and to compare it to another rule that is superior to it in the hierarchy of norms and interpret it accordingly and
- to appraise the content of a law and compare it with another set of rules that may contradict or complement it.

Article 53 of the Vienna Convention on the Law of Treaties, adopted May 23, 1969, recognizes the existence of certain peremptory norms of general international law, or *jus cogens*, which are "accepted and recognized by the international community of states, as a whole, as a norm from which no derogation is permitted."
➔   Fundamental guarantees; International law

Today, these norms represent a sort of "international public order," which legally may not be infringed on. It is generally accepted that any law or treaty which violates *jus cogens* is void (Article 53 of the Vienna Convention on the Law of Treaties).

The exact content of *jus cogens* remains highly controversial. Nonetheless, certain rights, freedoms, and fundamental guarantees have been framed by international human rights and humanitarian law conventions. These texts specify that states are prohibited from infringing on, or in any way limiting or suspending, these fundamental rights. The list of the nonderogable human rights derived from these conventions is the first inclination toward a concrete definition of *jus cogens*. **➔ Fundamental guarantees**

→ **Customary international law; Fundamental guarantees; Hierarchy of norms; Human rights; Inalienability of rights; International conventions; International humanitarian law; International law; Inviolability of rights**

■ NONAPPLICABILITY OF STATUTORY LIMITATIONS

In international law, certain crimes are not subject to any statute of limitation. This means that, no matter how much time has lapsed, judicial proceedings can still be initiated against the perpetrators of these crimes.

This differs from certain domestic legal systems—in particular, civil law ones—that do have statutory limitations for some or all crimes. The limitation periods may vary from one year to thirty, depending on the gravity of the crime. Most domestic laws provide for this form of "prescription" for misdemeanors (usually defined as crimes punishable by one year in prison or less) and infractions (usually punishable only by fines; also known as summary or nonarrestable offenses in the United Kingdom). Thus, criminal law sets a time limit, which varies for different categories of crimes, after which all legal actions are stopped and judicial proceedings are no longer possible.

Common law systems usually do not establish a statute of limitations for serious felonies such as murder, while civil law systems apply extended limits for such felonies—more than twenty years.

☞ In the international arena, the nonapplicability of statutory limitations pertains to crimes that are extremely difficult to prosecute immediately after they were committed. This is particularly true of war crimes, crimes against humanity, or genocide. Given the context in which such crimes tend to be carried out, it is often necessary to wait for a change in the situation—an end to the conflict or a change in regime—for it to become possible, in practice, to initiate judicial proceedings. The nonapplicability of statutory limitations prevents the most serious crimes, and those most difficult to prosecute, from going unpunished.

An international Convention on the Non-Applicability of Statutory Limitations to War Crimes and Crimes against Humanity was adopted by the General Assembly of the UN on November 26, 1968 (GA Resolution 2391 [XXIII]). It entered into force on November 11, 1970, and currently has forty-four states parties.

It precisely defines the crimes to which statutory limitations are not applicable. These are war crimes and crimes against humanity, as defined in the charter of the Nuremberg Tribunal, as well as grave breaches of humanitarian law, as defined by the 1949 Geneva Conventions. → **War crimes/Crimes against humanity**

There is also a European Convention on the Non-Applicability of Statutory Limitations to Crimes against Humanity and War Crimes, adopted January 25, 1974. However, only the Netherlands has ratified this treaty, which is therefore not in force today.

1. Definition

No statutory limitation shall apply to the following crimes, irrespective of the date of their commission:

(a) War crimes as they are defined in the Charter of the International Military Tribunal, Nuremberg, of 8 August 1945 and confirmed by resolutions 3(1) of 13 February 1946 and 95(1) of 11 December 1946 of the General Assembly of the UN, particularly the "grave breaches" enumerated in the Geneva Conventions of 12 August 1949 for the protection of war victims;

(b) Crimes against humanity, whether committed in time of war or in time of peace, as they are defined in the Charter of the International Military Tribunal, Nuremberg, of 8 August 1945 and confirmed by resolutions 3(1) of 13 February 1946 and 95(1) of 11 December 1946 of the General Assembly of the UN, eviction by armed attack or occupation and inhuman acts resulting from the policy of apartheid, and the crime of genocide as defined in the 1948 Convention on the Prevention and Punishment of the Crime of Genocide, even if such acts do not constitute a violation of the domestic law of the country in which they were committed. (Article 1 of the Convention on the Non-Applicability of Statutory Limitations to War Crimes and Crimes against Humanity).

2. Implementation

To ensure the effectiveness of the Convention, the states parties undertake to incorporate into their domestic legislation such laws and other necessary measures as will enable the extradition of persons accused of these crimes, in accordance with their respective constitutional processes. They also undertake to adapt their laws so as to ensure that statutory or other limitations shall not apply to the prosecution and punishment of these crimes. If such limitations exist, they are to be abolished (Articles 3 and 4).

☞ In matters of criminal law, despite the existence of international conventions, most prosecutions take place before domestic courts, using national criminal legislation. It is therefore crucial that states bring their domestic laws into conformity with the relevant international conventions and that they refrain from hindering any proceedings undertaken by national courts with regard to these crimes.

   If the domestic laws of a country are not in conformity with its obligations under an international convention, it is possible to

- refer the situation to the domestic institution that is responsible for monitoring the legality or constitutionality of legislation (usually a specific court) and
- alert the authority with which the relevant convention is deposited (e.g., the UN, ICRC, EU, OAS, OAU).

The statute of the International Criminal Court, adopted in July 1998, in Rome, reaffirms the nonapplicability of statutory limitations to the crimes under its jurisdiction (Article 29 of ICC statute)—namely, genocide, crimes against humanity, and war crimes.

→ **International Criminal Court**

→ **Amnesties; Impunity; Mutual assistance in criminal matters; War crimes/Crimes against humanity**

📖 **For Additional Information:**

Meron, Theodor. "The Humanization of Humanitarian Law." *American Journal of International Law* 94 (April 2000): 239.

Zalaquett, José. "Moral Reconstruction in the Wake of Human Rights Violations and War Crimes." In *Hard Choices: Moral Dilemmas in Humanitarian Intervention*, ed. Jonathan Moore. Lanham, Md.: Rowman & Littlefield, 1998, 211–28.

■ NONCOMBATANTS

Under humanitarian law, all persons who are not, or are no longer, taking part in hostilities are protected. In the context of international armed conflicts, they are referred to as "protected persons," but they benefit from protection under humanitarian law in noninternational conflicts as well. The Geneva Conventions make a distinction between several categories of persons: the wounded and sick (whether military or civilian), prisoners of war, interned or detained civilians, and civilians in occupied or enemy territory. All individuals must be treated humanely. Each category of persons benefits from a general regime of protection, which is specifically adapted to their situation.

➔ **Civilians; Combatants; Protected persons**

■ NONGOVERNMENTAL ORGANIZATIONS

The term *nongovernmental organization* (NGO) does not define a precise legal category, either in international law or in domestic law. Instead, it is a convenient way to designate juridical persons under private international law, whose only common point is that they are not governmental structures and they are nonprofit. It also serves to differentiate them from intergovernmental organizations (sometimes referred to as international organizations) or for-profit companies. Although they are also sometimes known as *international nongovernmental organizations* (INGOs), the term *NGO* usually refers to organizations whose activities are not strictly national, while *nonprofit organization* is more frequently used to refer to domestic organizations with similar goals.

The status of these organizations is regulated by applicable domestic law. NGOs may be member-based associations, foundations, private volunteer organizations, or many other kinds of NGOs recognized by the domestic law of the relevant country. NGOs set their own mandate, establishing bylaws, charters, and missions statements, with the collaboration of the Board of Directors. Member-based associations join individuals around shared objectives that are set forth in the organization's statutes or constitution. Thus, they reflect the international solidarity of individuals, and they act as a complement to international political institutions and to the economic and trade laws of the global market.

The presence of NGOs in the international arena is not simply a product of their legal status. They take part in the life of the international community through the nonprofit activities that they undertake in various foreign states. The nature of these activities may vary greatly, depending on the organization. They may be humanitarian, cultural, educational, religious, economic, and so on.

☞ So as to protect freedom of association, the different countries' relevant laws usually do not include constraining mechanisms that monitor the different kinds of NGOs. The only strict obligation they face is that they must not carry out activities that profit any individual, and they must not conduct political activities. These organizations are mainly accountable to

(*continues*)

> (*continued*)
>
> their Board of Directors or the body that carries out that function (and that has obligations under domestic law), and where applicable, to the General Assembly of their members.
>
> This flexibility can also be a weakness. NGOs are often subject to various pressures, such as financial or political ones. For instance, some NGOs depend almost entirely on government funding to operate, which can jeopardize their independence and their nongovernmental nature.
>
> The checks and balances, as well as the vision, provided by an association's members or an organization's Board of Directors are the main guardians and guarantors of the independence and responsibility of NGOs' operations.

- NGOs can obtain consultative status with certain intergovernmental organizations, whose area of interest is close to the NGOs' field of action. This status allows them to be informed of the relevant international organization's work and to submit documents or participate in the debates with states over issues under their competence.
- When implementing international programs for public benefit, NGOs can sign operational partnership contracts with international organizations and financial contracts when accepting funds from international or national donors. They can also sign program agreements with the relevant ministries of the countries in which they are operating.
- In situations of conflict, the Geneva Conventions confer on impartial, humanitarian organizations the duty to provide relief and protection for victims. It is important that NGOs be aware of their responsibilities with regard to the mission of protection and assistance of civilians that humanitarian law confers on private organizations in such situations. Failing this, their actions can instead weaken the protection to which victims are entitled.

→ **Humanitarian principles; Protection; Relief; Responsibility; Right of humanitarian initiative**

📖 **For Additional Information:**

Beigbeder, Yves. *The Role and Status of International Humanitarian Volunteers and Organizations: The Right and Duty to Humanitarian Assistance*. Dordrecht: Martinus Nijhoff, 1991.

Brauman, Rony. "Refugee Camps, Population Transfers, and NGOs" In *Hard Choices: Moral Dilemmas in Humanitarian Intervention*, ed. Jonathan Moore. Lanham, Md.: Rowman & Littlefield, 1998, 177–94.

■ NONINTERNATIONAL ARMED CONFLICT

Often referred to as "civil war," a noninternational armed conflict is a conflict that takes place on the territory of one state, between its armed forces and dissident armed forces or other organized armed groups that, under responsible command, exercise such control over a part of the territory in a way which enables them to carry out sustained and concerted military operations.

The rule of law applicable in situations of noninternational armed conflict is based on

- the second 1977 Protocol additional to the Geneva Conventions and
- Article 3 common to the four Geneva Conventions of 1949.

Humanitarian law limits the means and methods of warfare during noninternational armed conflicts and establishes provisions for the relief and protection of civilian populations. It also codifies the right of initiative that allows any impartial humanitarian organization to carry out its relief activities (GCI–IV common Article 3; GCI, GCII, and GCIII common Article 9 and GCIV Article 10; PII Article 18.2).

☞ It is crucial to be able to qualify and define this kind of conflict so as to trigger the implementation and enforcement of the rules of humanitarian law foreseen for noninternational armed conflicts. The level of intensity of the fighting establishes the distinction between a situation of conflict and one of internal disturbance or tension.

Situations of internal disturbance and tension, such as riots, isolated and sporadic acts of violence, and other acts of a similar nature, are not considered to be armed conflicts (PII Article 1). However, even in such circumstances, the principles of Article 3 common to the Geneva Conventions, as well as the protection of nonderogable human rights, remain in force.

➜ **Fundamental guarantees (nonderogable rights, common Article 3)**

➜ **Fundamental guarantees; Geneva Conventions and Protocols; Internal disturbances and tensions; International humanitarian law; Legal status of the parties to the conflict; Right of humanitarian initiative; Situations and persons not expressly covered by humanitarian law; Special agreement; War crimes/Crimes against humanity**

📖 **For Additional Information:**

Abi-Saab, Georges. "Non-international Armed Conflicts." In *International Dimensions of Humanitarian Law*. Geneva: Henri Dupont Institute, 1988, 217–39.

"Rules of International Humanitarian Law Governing Conduct of Hostilities in Non-international Armed Conflict. Conclusions of the 14th Round Table at the International Institute of Humanitarian Law in San Remo." *International Review of the Red Cross* 278 (September–October 1990): 383–403.

■ NONRETROACTIVITY

A law can only be applied to an act that occurs after the law was adopted. This is a well-established legal principle, derived from the adage that ignorance of the law is no excuse.

In domestic criminal law, the principle of nonretroactivity is applicable to the definition or determination of both felonies and misdemeanors and to the scale of penalties and sentences incurred. This principle (also known as freedom from *ex post facto* laws, or *nullum crimen sine lege*) thus establishes that a law may not be applied to criminal acts that were committed before the law was enacted. It follows that a heavier penalty may not be imposed than the one that was applicable at the time the act was committed. However, if a new law was adopted after the act was committed, which provides for the imposition of a lighter penalty, the offender must benefit from it.

International law also recognizes the nonretroactivity of criminal laws and punishment for criminal acts as a fundamental judicial guarantee (Article 15 of the International Covenant on Civil and Political Rights). This principle is also integrated into the Geneva Conventions: a person may not be prosecuted for an act or omission that did not constitute a criminal offense under the national or international law to which he or she was subject at the time the act was committed (GCIII Article 99; GCIV Articles 65 and 67; PI Article 75; PII Article 6). ➔ **Judicial guarantees**

☞ In times of conflict, due to occupation of territory or capture, individuals may find themselves faced with the question of the applicability of laws that are unknown to them. The legal principle that is respected in this case derives from the general principle of nonretroactivity: the new law (in this case, the foreign law) may not impose higher penalties or establish offenses that were not foreseen in the domestic law of these persons.

In all situations, it is important to remember that a law that has not been officially enacted and published is not valid. The date before which nonretroactivity is applicable is the date at which the law was officially enacted—in other words, the date at which it was promulgated and published.

This principle is reflected in the recently adopted statute of the International Criminal Court (ICC). The Court will have jurisdiction only over crimes committed after its statute enters into force for the state concerned (Article 11 of ICC statute).

Until now, the only case in which an international tribunal could judge crimes committed before the tribunal was created is in the case of war tribunals, such as those set up in Nuremberg and Tokyo after World War II, and the ad hoc International Criminal Tribunals set up by the Security Council in 1993 and 1994 for the former Yugoslavia and Rwanda. Even in such situations, the tribunals can only judge acts that were already considered crimes when they were committed. At the time of the creation of the International Criminal Tribunal for the former Yugoslavia, the Secretary-General of the UN reaffirmed that the ICTY would "apply rules of international humanitarian law which are beyond any doubt part of customary law" (Report of the Secretary-General under Security Council Resolution 808, Doc. S/2504, May 3, 1993). ➔ **International Criminal Tribunals**

➔ **International Criminal Court; International Criminal Tribunals; Judicial guarantees; Occupied territories**

■ OCCUPIED TERRITORIES

In international law, a territory is considered "occupied" when it is under the authority of the hostile army.

Humanitarian law sets forth detailed rules establishing the rights and duties of the occupying forces and of the civilians in the occupied territories, as well as the rules governing the administration of these territories (GCIV Articles 47–78; PI Articles 63, 69, 72–79).

> ☞ Sometimes, occupying forces do not succeed in establishing or exercising authority over a certain territory—for instance, because of hostile acts committed against them by combatants of the occupied territory. In such cases, humanitarian law does not consider these areas as occupied territories but instead as invaded territories. In other words, they are battlefields, and the rules that apply to them are the general rules of armed conflict.
> → **International humanitarian law**

The basic obligations of the Occupying Power are to maintain law and order and public life. For the most part, it must follow the laws that were already in force in that territory before the occupiers arrived.

1. Relief Supplies and Actions

The Occupying Power has the duty to ensure that the adequate provision of food and medical supplies is provided, as well as clothing, bedding, means of shelter, other supplies essential to the survival of the civilian population of the occupied territory, and objects necessary for religious worship (GCIV Article 55; PI Article 69).

The Occupying Power must allow the Protecting Power, or the ICRC and other impartial humanitarian organizations, to verify the state of these supplies in occupied territories, and to visit protected persons so as to monitor their condition (GCIV Articles 30, 55, and 143). It is also under the obligation to allow the ICRC or any other impartial humanitarian organization to undertake their own strictly humanitarian relief actions aimed at this population. All states must allow and facilitate rapid and unimpeded passage of all relief supplies and must not divert them, in any way whatsoever, from their destination. The only restrictions that parties to the conflict may impose are technical ones, or they may ask for guarantees that the relief is destined to the population in need and will not be used by the adverse power.

The fact that humanitarian organizations are delivering relief in no way relieves the Occupying Power of any of its own responsibilities to ensure that the population is properly supplied (GCIV Articles 59–62 and 108–111; PI Articles 69–71).

→   **Relief; Right of access; Right of humanitarian initiative; Supplies**

2. Requisitions and Medical Duties

The Occupying Power may only requisition food, medical supplies, clothing, bedding, means of shelter, and other supplies essential to the survival of the civilian population of the occupied territory, for use by its forces and administration, if the needs of the civilian population in the occupied territory are covered (GCIV Article 55).

The Occupying Power may only requisition civilian hospitals temporarily, and then only if suitable arrangements are made in due time for both the care and treatment of the hospitals' patients. It must also ensure that the needs of the civilian population are met (GCIV Articles 56 and 57; GPI Article 14).

→   **Medical duties; Requisition**

3. Forced Population Displacement

The Occupying Power must not transfer or deport the population of occupied territories or transfer parts of its own civilian population into the territory it occupies (GCIV Article 49).

→   **Deportation; Population displacement**

4. Legal Status of the Population (in Particular Children), Forced Labor, and Enlistment

The Occupying Power must respect the personal status of children and must not hinder the proper working of all institutions devoted to their care and education. It may not enlist them in formations or organizations that are subordinate to it. It must also maintain any preferential measures that may have been adopted in favor of children and mothers (GCIV Article 50).

The Occupying Power may not compel persons protected by the Geneva Conventions to serve in its armed forces. It may not compel them to undertake any work that would involve them in military operations and any work they do must be carried out only in the occupied territory where they are. In no case shall requisition of labor lead to a mobilization of workers in an organization of a military or semimilitary character (GCIV Article 51).

→   **Children; Protected persons; Women**

5. Destruction

Any destruction by the Occupying Power of real estate or personal property is prohibited, unless such destruction is rendered absolutely necessary by military operations (GCIV Article 53).

6. Justice and Judicial Guarantees

The justice system for civilians in occupied territories must respect certain judicial guarantees established by the Geneva Conventions (GCIV Articles 47, 54, and 64–75). Additional details are given in the entry on ➔ **judicial guarantees** (Section II).

These provisions establish the following:

- The courts of occupied territories continue to operate and their impartiality must be respected. The Occupying Power may not alter the status of public officials or judges, or in any way apply sanctions to or take measures of coercion or discrimination against them (GCIV Article 54).
- The criminal law of the occupied territory remains in force. The Occupying Power may, however, adopt penal provisions aimed at ensuring the administration of the territory and the security of the Occupying Power, its members, property, and administration (GCIV Article 64). These penal provisions shall not come into force before they have been published and their effect shall not be retroactive (GCIV Article 65).
- In case of a breach of the penal provisions enacted by virtue of Article 64, the Occupying Power may hand over an accused to its military courts, as long as its courts are "properly constituted," "non-political," and sit in the occupied country (GCIV Article 66).
- Individuals must not be "arrested, prosecuted or convicted by the Occupying Power for acts committed or for opinions expressed before the occupation, or during a temporary interruption thereof, with the exception of breaches of the laws and customs of war" (GCIV Article 70).
- The trial procedure must respect fundamental international judicial principles and guarantees, including those concerning the notification of the accused, the right to legal representation, and the right to appeal (GCIV Articles 71–75).
- The death penalty may not be pronounced against a protected person unless the person is guilty of espionage, serious acts of sabotage against the military installations of the Occupying Power, or intentional offenses that caused the death of one or more persons. Furthermore, the death penalty can only be applied if such offenses were punishable by death under the law of the occupied territory in force before the occupation began. In any case, the death penalty may not be pronounced against an individual who was under eighteen years of age at the time of the offense (GCIV Article 68). A person sentenced to death shall always have the right to appeal such a ruling (GCIV Article 75).

7. Detention and Internment

Protected persons accused of offenses must be detained in the occupied country and, if convicted, serve their sentences therein (GCIV Article 76). ➔ **Detention**

The Geneva Conventions establish specific rights and guarantees for persons who are interned by the Occupying Power. ➔ **Internment**

8. Resistance

Members of militia and of organized resistance movements include those operating in occupied territory. They must be considered prisoners of war if they fall into the power of an adverse party, as long as they

- are commanded by a person responsible for his or her subordinates;
- have a fixed distinctive sign recognizable at a distance;

- carry arms openly;
- conduct their operations in accordance with the laws and customs of war (GCIII Article 4.2; PI Article 44).

→   **Combatants; Prisoners of war; Resistance movements**

→   **Annexation; Detention; International humanitarian law; Internment; Judicial guarantees; Prisoners of war; Protected persons; Protecting Powers; Relief; Responsibility; Right of humanitarian initiative; Right of access; Safety; Supplies**

📖 **For Additional Information:**

Benvenisti, Eyal. *The International Law of Occupation*. Princeton, N.J.: Princeton University Press, 1993.
ICRC. *Basic Rules of the Geneva Conventions and Their Additional Protocols*. Geneva: ICRC, 1988, 82–84.
Mulinen, Frederic de. *Handbook on the Law of War for Armed Forces*. Geneva: ICRC, 1989, 175–88.

■ OFFICE FOR THE COORDINATION OF HUMANITARIAN AFFAIRS (OCHA)

In 1992, following the UN General Assembly's request to the Secretary-General for a body to coordinate the different UN agencies carrying out humanitarian assistance in emergency situations, the UN Department for Humanitarian Affairs (DHA) was established, directly under the Secretary-General. In 1998, it was streamlined and renamed the Office for the Coordination of Humanitarian Affairs (OCHA).

1. Mandate

OCHA's mandate is still based on General Assembly Resolution 46/182 (April 14, 1992), which established DHA. Its mandate is to "mobilize and coordinate the collective efforts of the international community, in particular those of the UN system" in responding to "complex humanitarian emergencies" (political crises or conflicts), natural disasters, or technological disasters (e.g., nuclear disasters). It also focuses on policy development for all humanitarian issues, including examining any existing gaps in the protection and assistance mandates of the agencies. The operational activities that DHA used to carry out, however, were redistributed to other UN bodies or specialized agencies.

OCHA's mandate rests on the fact that the sovereignty, territorial integrity, and national unity of states must be respected, in conformity with the UN Charter. In this context, humanitarian assistance can only be provided with the consent of the state concerned. In principle and in practice, this means that the assistance should actually be provided on the basis of a formal request by the affected country.

OCHA's Emergency Relief Coordinator (discussed later) has three main responsibilities:

- helping the Secretary-General ensure that humanitarian questions are addressed, especially those that are not part of the specific mandates of UN bodies, such as assistance and protection of internally displaced persons;
- advocacy of humanitarian issues with political organs, in particular the UN Security Council; and
- coordination of the humanitarian response by ensuring that the appropriate response mechanisms are established on the ground.

OCHA is also responsible for

- monitoring and early warning of crises with humanitarian implications;
- advocacy of humanitarian and human rights principles, in collaboration with the UN High Commissioner for Human Rights (UNHCHR);
- centralizing information updates and analyses, through the Integrated Regional Information Network (IRIN), and an Internet web site;
- ensuring contingency planning and needs assessment, through operational agencies' field missions;
- issuing consolidated funding appeals;
- facilitating the access of operational organizations to the places where assistance is needed;
- managing the Central Emergency Revolving Funds, which allows for the immediate response to an emergency;
- ensuring the transition from emergency assistance to rehabilitation assistance by strengthening capacity for postconflict peace building, with the UN Department of Political Affairs.

2. Structure

Unlike the UN specialized agencies, OCHA is not autonomous. The head of OCHA and Emergency Relief Coordinator (currently Kenzo Oshima) has the rank of Undersecretary-General. OCHA is based in the UN's New York headquarters, and there is also an important liaison office in Geneva. There is currently a total of 151 international and 360 national staff worldwide, with a total annual budget of $63 million for 2001. It covers nineteen countries and three regions.

3. Means

- The Inter-Agency Standing Committee (IASC), coordinated by the ERC, is the main decision-making forum for emergencies. Its members are the heads of the UN operational agencies involved in humanitarian relief: UNDP, UNICEF, UNHCR, WFP, FAO, and WHO. Other international institutions, such as the International Organization for Migration (IOM) and the European Community Humanitarian Office (ECHO), and the Special Representative on Internally Displaced Persons, also participate. Finally, the International Committee of the Red Cross (ICRC) and the International Federation of Red Cross and Red Crescent Societies (IFRC) participate directly, as do certain NGOs.
- To coordinate the humanitarian response in a given country, OCHA works closely with the relevant UN Resident Coordinator (often the UNDP Resident Representative), who is designated to coordinate the other UN agencies on the ground.
- A Disaster Response System is operational twenty-four hours a day in Geneva, and it may benefit from personnel from other UN agencies or bodies, as well from military and civil defense personnel from various countries.
- The UN Disaster Assessment and Coordination Team, initially developed for natural disasters, is increasingly used for emergencies regarded as complex. This team consists of specially trained national emergency management experts.
- There is a warehouse of relief items in Pisa, Italy.
- Other standby arrangements exist for the mobilization of support networks—for instance in transport, telecommunications, and other infrastructure.

- The Consolidated Inter-Agency Appeals Process (CAP) sets clear goals to establish priorities for humanitarian organizations in given countries. Although most appeals are launched on an annual basis, OCHA also makes "flash" appeals for specific emergencies.
- The Central Emergency Revolving Funds is a mechanism of direct financing, which allows for rapid response, financed by voluntary state contributions and then reimbursed with the CAP.

4. Relationship with NGOs

The ICRC and IFRC participate fully in the Inter-Agency Standing Committee (IASC). Other NGOs may be invited to participate on an ad hoc basis, depending on the nature of the relief operation. Several NGO coalitions, including Interaction and the International Council for Voluntary Agencies (ICVA), are permanent IASC members.

OCHA also needs the collaboration of NGOs in assessing needs and in supplying information on available stocks of humanitarian materials.

➔ **Food and Agriculture Organization; International Committee of the Red Cross; Relief; UN Children's Fund; UN Development Fund; UN High Commissioner for Human Rights; UN High Commissioner for Refugees; World Food Program; World Health Organization**

✎ Office for the Coordination of Humanitarian Affairs (OCHA)
United Nations
New York, NY 10017 USA
Tel.: (1) 212 963-1234
Fax: (1) 212 963-1312
Office for the Coordination of Humanitarian Affairs (OCHA) in Geneva
Palais des Nations
CH 1211 Geneva 10, Switzerland
Tel.: (41) 22 917 1234
Fax: (41) 22 917 0023
@ www.reliefweb.int/ocha

P

■ PARTIES TO THE CONFLICT

So as to ensure the broadest possible application of international humanitarian law, the Geneva Conventions use the neutral term *parties to the conflict* to refer to both state and nonstate actors taking part in hostilities. This term replaces that of *belligerent,* which was dropped from modern international humanitarian law vocabulary because it reflected tenuous distinctions between state and nonstate entities that are not adapted to today's conflicts.

In reality, the actors in a conflict are not always the armed forces of two states that have recognized each other's existence. Furthermore, in the case of internal armed conflicts, one of the parties may be a group whose authority and existence have not been officially recognized, such as insurgents or liberation movements. It is crucial that the implementation of humanitarian law not be delayed by debates over the legal status of belligerents.

The Geneva Conventions therefore clearly state that the application of international humanitarian law does not affect the legal status of parties to the conflict (GCI–IV common Article 3; PI Article 4).

The Conventions do distinguish between parties to the conflict and the High Contracting Parties. The latter refers to states that have ratified the Conventions and therefore have given their commitment to respect them. The nonstate nature of a given party to a conflict (e.g., in the case of a rebellion), and the fact that it has not signed the Geneva Conventions, should not hinder the application of these laws. A party to the conflict, even if it is not a High Contracting Party, is also under the obligation to respect the provisions of the Conventions. The Conventions therefore set forth the provision that all parties to a conflict must endeavor to bring all or part of the Conventions into force, from the beginning of the conflict, by means of special agreements (GCI–IV common Article 3).

Many of the provisions of humanitarian law have the character of customary law. This means that they are binding on all states, even those that have not ratified the Conventions.

☞ The classic rules of reciprocity do not apply in the case of international humanitarian law. The fact that a party to a conflict has not ratified or has failed to respect the Geneva Conventions does not free the other party from its obligation to respect humanitarian law (GCI–IV common Articles 1 and 2). This is particularly important in the case of internal armed conflict, in which not all parties to the conflict are state entities.

→ **Belligerent; Combatants; Customary international law; High Contracting Parties; International conventions; Legal status of the parties to the conflict; Respect for international humanitarian law; Special agreement**

■ PEACE

Peace describes the state of society when differences are not solved through the threat or use of armed force and when public order is respected. Peace is sometimes defined as the absence of war. This does not mean that tensions and conflicts do not exist but that they may be solved through pacific means, through the UN or regional organizations, or by having recourse to arbitration or to the good offices of mediators. The UN Charter establishes a mechanism for collective security whose aim is the maintenance of international peace.

☞ In times of peace, both domestic and international law are applicable as foreseen, including international conventions for the protection of human rights. Humanitarian law is not applicable in such times.

→ **Cease-fire; Collective security; Human rights; Internal disturbances and tensions; Public order; Peacekeeping; Security Council of the UN; United Nations; War**

📖 **For Additional Information:**

Boutros-Ghali, Boutros. *An Agenda for Peace*. New York: United Nations, 1992.
Boutros-Ghali, Boutros. *Supplement to an Agenda for Peace*. New York: United Nations, 1995.
Dutli, Maria Teresa. "Implementation of International Humanitarian Law—Activities of Qualified Personnel in Peacetime." *International Review of the Red Cross* 292 (January–February 1993): 5–11.

■ PEACEKEEPING

I. ORIGINS

The UN Charter establishes that maintaining international peace and security is the primary goal of the UN (Article 1.1 of UN Charter). It entrust the UN Security Council with the main responsibility for achieving this goal (Article 24).

If an attempt to settle a dispute using pacific methods fails (Chapter VI of UN Charter—Pacific Settlement of Disputes), the Charter foresees a mechanism to defend the collective security, which authorizes the use of coercive actions (Chapter VII—Action with Respect to

Threats to the Peace, Breaches of the Peace, and Acts of Aggression). If need be, under Chapter VII, the Security Council can undertake military actions (Article 42). Originally, it was meant to have a permanent army at its disposal (Article 43), the strategic command of which was to be run by a Military Staff Committee (Articles 46 and 47). However, the Committee was never set up, and the Cold War paralyzed any attempts to set up the system as a whole.

Early on, the procedures to settle disputes pacifically, foreseen by Chapter VI, proved to be inadequate in open situations of conflict. Any application of Chapter VII, on the other hand, was blocked by the Cold War game of Security Council vetoes.

In 1956, during the Suez Canal crisis, the UN invented peacekeeping operations (PKOs). This was an ad hoc response to a situation not foreseen by the Charter, and a palliative measure to replace the use of force. Since there is no judicial basis for such measures, the justification for such operations is often referred to as the mythical "Chapter VI and a half."

II. STRUCTURE AND ORGANIZATION

Security Council resolutions create peacekeeping operations (PKOs) and establish their mandate. The PKOs are therefore under the authority of the Council. The UN Secretary-General is responsible for the organization and implementation of these operations. Several members and departments in the Secretariat support his efforts in this respect—in particular, the Department of Peace-Keeping Operations (DPKO). The Secretary-General is in charge of setting up the force: he solicits member states to get them to mobilize troops and selects the nationality of the contingents. An agreement is then signed between the UN and each country that contributes troops.

The Secretary General has reached an agreement with member states to set up a system with troops on stand-by, which will facilitate the rapid deployment of PKOs. Eighty-eight member states have accepted to put 147,900 troops at the UN's disposal. Thirty-three of these states have formalized their participation in this arrangement by signing a memorandum of understanding with the UN.

In most cases, PKOs can only be carried out with the consent of the government in the country where the operation is deployed and with the agreement of any other party involved. This consent is formalized through a written agreement covering all issues (administrative, legal, logistical, etc.) relating to the operation.

However, using its mandate under Chapter VII of the UN Charter, the Security Council can decide to proceed without this consent.

1. The Structure of Peacekeeping Forces

The Secretary-General nominates the Force Commander (or Chief Military Observer). In the case of large-scale operations, with an important civilian component, a Special Representative (or Chief of Mission) is also appointed. They are in charge of the operational command (military and political), on the ground. Their international status is meant to guarantee their independence from the states contributing personnel. The Force Commander selects the members of his military staff from the officers of the national contingents placed at his or her disposal.

The forces that are deployed are international and placed under the direct authority of the UN. The Commanders of the national contingents must hence exercise their authority in conformity with the orders given by the Force Commander of the entire force. However, they also remain subject to their national laws.

The Force Commander is responsible for the overall order and discipline of the troops. He or she sets up, nominates the members of, and runs, a military police office. This military police has the mandate to arrest any members of the force, and the Commander can impose transfers or assignments as sanctions. He or she can also request that a state recall all its military personnel. However, the real disciplinary power remains under the jurisdiction of the state providing the troops. To this effect, the state must name an officer within its contingent who acts as the national chief of the military police. The Force Commander is informed of any disciplinary measures, who may consult the commander of the national contingent, and even the authorities of the contributing state, if he or she considers that these measures were insufficient.

2. Scope and Cost of the Operations

Since the end of the Cold War, the UN has been increasingly solicited for this kind of operation. The Security Council has deployed three times as many PKOs since 1988 as in the preceding forty years. At the peak of this activity, at the end of 1995, seventeen operations were deployed, mobilizing more than seventy thousand troops. In 2001, there were fifteen peacekeeping operations deployed, involving 29,000 soldiers (not counting observers or police) from seventy-eight nations.

The increase of such operations has had financial repercussions: the special budget for PKOs took off, reaching a height of $3.6 billion in 1995, at the time of the operation in former Yugoslavia. The estimated budget for 2000 amounted to $2.6 billion. The budget is based on a specially scaled formula that establishes four categories of contributors, a modified version of the scale used for the regular UN budget, going from the permanent members of the Security Council to the poorest states. In reality, PKOs are funded almost exclusively by the most industrialized states, although many of these pay their contributions more than a year behind schedule; the unpaid peacekeeping dues are approximately $2.6 billion.

Because of these arrears, the UN has delayed its repayments to states that contribute troops by three or four years. The UN General Assembly created a Peacekeeping Reserve Fund worth $150 billion, in 1992, but this was not enough to cover the budget shortages, which are now beginning to affect the contingents' ability to accomplish their mission on the ground.

III. DIFFERENT KINDS OF OPERATIONS

The increase in the number of peacekeeping operations was paralleled by an evolution of the kind of the interventions carried out. In *An Agenda for Peace* (A/47/277-S/24111, June 17, 1992), then Secretary-General Boutros Boutros-Ghali made an attempt to rationalize the different kinds of PKOs, setting forth precise definitions for peacekeeping, peace making, and preventive diplomacy. In 1995, in *Supplement to An Agenda for Peace* (A/50/60-S/1995/1, January 3, 1995), he noted that the UN's "range of instruments for controlling and resolving conflicts between and within States [includes] preventive diplomacy and peacemaking; peace-keeping; peace-building; disarmament; sanctions; and peace enforcement," thereby demonstrating the different kinds of PKOs. Nonetheless, *peacekeeping* has remained a generic term that designates most different kinds of operations.

1. "Traditional" or First-Generation Peacekeeping Operations

Thirteen PKOs were set up from 1949 to 1988. They were established following strict limits both in their mandates and in their actions. Three main principles governed these interventions:

1. *Consent of the parties to the conflict:* a force could only be deployed with the agreement of the state on the territory of which it was going to operate.

2. *Impartiality:* the PKOs made no judgment on the rights, claims, or positions of the parties to the conflict. Their aim was not to determine who was the aggressor or the victim.
3. *Nonuse of force:* the peacekeepers were not authorized to use force, except in self-defense.

These operations played two main kinds of roles: acting as a buffer between the parties to the conflict and monitoring cease-fires. These straightforward, military monitoring missions were carried out in the context of interstate conflicts and reflected the weak maneuvering margin within which the UN operated during the Cold War.

2. Second-Generation Operations

At the end of the 1980s, peacekeeping operations acquired more ambitious goals. They were no longer meant only to stabilize a situation but actively to participate in the implementation of international political rules. The PKOs included very diverse tasks, such as election monitoring (sometimes including organizing and supervising them), national reconciliation activities (including demobilization and reintegration of former combatants, human rights monitoring and training), and mine clearance. The UN Transition Assistance Group in Namibia (UNTAG, 1989–90), the UN Advance and then Transitional Authority missions in Cambodia (UNAMIC and UNTAC, 1991–93), and the UN Observer Mission in El Salvador (ONUSAL, 1991–95), are examples of this kind of multifunctional operations, which take place directly within the states.

The three operational principles listed previously continue to be respected.

3. Third-Generation Operations

When the UN and states adopted the notion of the "right of intervention," the entire approach to peacekeeping was transformed. Three changes took place:

1. The UN's humanitarian mandate was broadened, because the qualification of a "threat to international peace and security" was extended to include "humanitarian crises." The result was that Chapter VII mechanisms resorting to the use of force were used increasingly to enforce humanitarian decisions.
2. The operations undertaken under Chapter VII began to have a more coercive and enforcing mandate. The force's authority to use force was extended beyond the prior restriction to cases of self-defense, particularly, in theory, to protect humanitarian operations or civilian population is "safe areas."
3. The UN increasingly delegated the use of force to national contingents under ad hoc international coalitions or in the context of regional organizations. These are not under the UN's direct command, although it is theoretically accountable for their actions.

These changes resulted in a new kind of operation, combining military and humanitarian components, which were deployed mostly in internal conflicts or other crises situations. Some refer to these as third-generation peacekeeping operations, while others make a distinction between the more traditional PKOs and a new form of peace enforcement or peace-making operations. Chapter VII of the UN Charter still does not foresee any of these kinds of operation, although it is invoked as the basis for the use of force by the UN resolutions authorizing such operations.

a. Operations under UN Command

Such operations are meant to be noncoercive, but their mandate is sometimes extended to include the use of force (other than for self-defense) under certain circumstances—to protect humanitarian convoys and/or civilian populations, for instance. In some cases, the troops deployed may consist only of UN peacekeepers (sometimes known as "blue helmets"), as was the case with the UN Protection Force in the former Yugoslavia (UNPROFOR) and the UN Operation in Somalia II (UNOSOM II). In other cases, the UN peacekeepers may be backed—either on the ground or by air—by national contingents (as was the case for the rapid reaction force in Bosnia) or regional military organizations (the NATO intervention in Bosnia). It was in this context that Boutros-Ghali's suggested replacing "peacekeeping" forces with "peacemaking" ones, in *An Agenda for Peace*, when the mandate was different.

b. Operations "Subcontracted" or Mandated by the UN

Such operations are not under the direct command of the UN, but their mandate was delegated by the UN Security Council, which thus confers on them the right to use force. Such operations are therefore always of a coercive nature and the troops deployed contain no UN peacekeepers. They consist of national contingents, under an ad hoc international coalition—Operation Restore Hope in Somalia, under U.S. command, and Operation Turquoise in Rwanda, under French command, for instance—or under an international coalition supervised by a regional organization—such as the Implementation Force (IFOR) and the Stabilization Force (SFOR) under NATO control in Bosnia and the Multilateral Protection Force in Albania.

This third generation of peacekeeping operations has strongly discredited the UN's ability in this respect, with the massacres in parts of Bosnia and Rwanda highlighting the inability of the troops to fulfill their protection mandate, despite the authorization to use force. In May 2000, several hundred UNAMSIL peacekeepers were taken hostage in Sierra Leone, despite the fact that UNAMSIL (established in October 1999 by SC Resolution 1270) has one of the strongest mandates in terms of self-defense, even including specific reference to protection of civilians, albeit with many caveats (the main one being to afford protection "within its capabilities and areas of deployment"). This raised further questions about the UN's ability to fulfill robust peacekeeping mandates. (See also ➔ **self-defense and protected areas and zones**.)

Peacekeeping Operations

Peacekeeping operations were not foreseen by the UN Charter. They began as an ad hoc mechanism created by the Security Council to respond to situations in which pacific methods for the settlement of disputes had failed but that did not call for full Chapter VII use of force. In theory, PKOs follow three main principles:

- they must have the consent of the parties to the conflict;
- they must be impartial;
- they must not use force except in self-defense.

(*continues*)

(*continued*)

Many of the peacekeeping operations carried out in the last ten years (three times as many as during the entire Cold War) have changed the notion of "peacekeeping." They now more closely resemble "peace making" or peace enforcement operations. Some of the main elements that changed stand in contradiction with the three principles listed earlier:

- in broadening the operations' mandate to include the enforcement of humanitarian operations, the operations sometimes by-passed, or seemed to forfeit, the consent of states or other parties to the conflict;
- the authorization to use force in situations other than self-defense—in particular, to protect civilian populations or humanitarian convoys—has sometimes defied attempts to remain impartial and of course goes against the principle of the nonuse of force.

However, there is no clear authorization to use force. This, combined with the fact that peacekeeping troops are generally not deployed in sufficient strength, has resulted in the UN missions' helplessness in the face of the massacres of civilians in former Yugoslavia or of the genocide in Rwanda.

A report on UN peacekeeping operations published in August 2000 (by a panel chaired by Lakhdar Brahimi) is unlikely to change this: while insisting that the Security Council ensure that peacekeeping operations be given the resources necessary to carry out their mandate and arguing that ambiguous mandates can have disastrous consequences, it establishes quite clearly that "use of force only in self-defence should remain the bedrock principles of peacekeeping" (paragraph 48 of the report) and affirms that it is impossible for UN peacekeepers to protect the civilians in all the areas where they are deployed.

→   **Collective security; Intervention; Self-defense; United Nations**

IV. Applicability of Humanitarian Law and Available Recourses in Case of Violations

The more "forceful" mandate that PKOs now enjoy begs the question more urgently than ever of how to apply humanitarian law and what the troops' responsibilities are in case there is a "slippage" while they carrying out their operations.

Article 2.2 of the Convention on the Safety of United Nations and Associated Personnel—adopted by the UN General Assembly on December 9, 1994 (A/RES/49/59), and which entered into force on January 15, 1999—confirms that humanitarian law applies to peacekeeping interventions.

The applicable laws and responsibilities of forces mandated by the UN but remaining under the authority of their national contingents is much clearer than for forces under UN command.

1. Operations "Subcontracted" or Mandated by the UN

The responsibilities of troops belonging to national or regional contingents, to which the UN has delegated peacekeeping or peace-making operations, are relatively clear. These are forces that already have coercive mandates and the UN Security Council simply gives them authorization to act.

Thus, they remain under the national authority of the contributing states. As a result, these forces become parties to the conflict in which they intervene, and they are therefore under the obligation to respect the international law of armed conflict. The states concerned are accountable for the actions of their armed forces and, in case of grave breaches of humanitarian law, not only the states but the individual authors of such crimes must be and can be held criminally responsible.

2. Applicability of Humanitarian Law to Operations under UN Command

For a long time, the UN refused to apply humanitarian law to its operations, explaining that, since it was not a signatory to the different conventions, and especially since the PKOs were of a noncoercive nature, it was not bound by these conventions. Once the PKOs were given the authority to use force, this justification became hard to defend.

The UN, as an international organization, has an "international legal personality." This means that it is granted certain rights and obligations—by humanitarian law, for instance—when it intervenes in situations of conflict. Of course, the UN itself is not a party to humanitarian law conventions, and the organization remains opposed to taking on such responsibility for technical reasons. For instance, it is impossible for an organization to implement certain provisions, such as those concerning the treatment of prisoners of war or those regulating the prosecution and punishment of grave breaches of the law.

Nevertheless, humanitarian law is applicable to the UN, *mutatis mutandis*. In other words, taking into consideration the specificity of the organization, the UN is bound to respect the general rules of humanitarian law, in particular those reflecting international custom and peremptory norms of international law. UN personnel—civil servants and experts, including the Secretary-General—hence have the obligation to respect international humanitarian law.

Operations under UN command have the status of subsidiary organs of the UN and therefore do not have their own international legal personality. Hence, their actions are under the UN's responsibility and must respect the same obligations as the UN, in particular the duties derived from humanitarian law.

In fact, humanitarian law has been applied to, and incorporated into, the practice of such operations. Different agreements are signed (among the UN, the states contributing forces, and, in principle, the host state) when a peacekeeping force is established under UN command, and they all reaffirm that the members of these forces must observe and respect the principles and spirit of the international conventions applicable to the conduct of military personnel. These provisions are contained, mainly, in the four 1949 Geneva Conventions and their two 1977 Additional Protocols, and the Convention for the Protection of Cultural Property in the Event of Armed Conflict, signed on May 14, 1954, under the aegis of UNESCO.

Thus, all members of UN forces, in particular the Force Commander, are under the obligation to respect humanitarian law.

→ **Duty of commanders; Respect for international humanitarian law**

☞ Humanitarian law does apply to peacekeeping operations when they use armed forces, despite a certain ambiguity to that effect.

▪ When a national force is mandated by the UN, but remains under national command, it in effect becomes a party to the conflict and must therefore respect international humanitarian

(continues)

(*continued*)

law. In case of a violation thereof, both the government itself and individual members of
the armed forces can be held accountable.

- When contingents come under UN command, as is meant to be the case for PKOs, the applicability of humanitarian law is more complex. Members of the UN do have an obligation to respect the duties derived from humanitarian law. The different agreements signed
  when PKOs are established (among the UN, the states contributing forces, and the host
  state) reaffirm this by declaring that such forces must observe and respect the principles
  and spirit of humanitarian law conventions.
- However, in case of violations of humanitarian law, the available recourses are rare. It is
  difficult to hold the UN itself accountable, because of the overall immunity it enjoys. By
  extension, the individual peacekeepers also benefit from immunity, but there are some possibilities, depending on the agreement signed at the time the force was created, and in particular depending on the gravity of the alleged crime. Certain crimes cannot be protected
  by any form of jurisdiction.
- → **Immunity; Penal sanctions in humanitarian law; Sanctions (diplomatic, economic,
  or military); Universal jurisdiction**

---

3. Available Recourses in Case of Violations of Humanitarian Law

It is important to note that the possibility of recourse against the UN itself, or against the members of its forces, is rare and haphazard—rare because the UN does not favor procedures that
might compel it to reveal information concerning the evolution of its operations, and haphazard
because the instruments are used and applied differently in each case. The controversy following tragic events such as the genocide in Rwanda or the fall of Srebrenica (when most of the
civilian population was massacred at the time the Bosnian Serb army took the city in July 1995)
highlights the fact that the states contributing troops do not easily tolerate having their actions
questioned. Hence, the ability to hold these forces accountable stumbles against the immunities
granted to the UN and peacekeeping forces.

a. Recourses against the UN Itself

The UN is directly responsible for all acts undertaken by its forces' commanders—in other
words, the Force Commander and his or her military staff. If an action is carried out by other
members of these forces, the UN is only responsible it was performed in the course of the individuals' official functions. In such cases, the UN is held responsible whether or not the individual acted pursuant to an order, since the individual was under the UN's authority. Conversely, if
the individual acted outside his or her official functions, the UN is technically not responsible,
since the acts were beyond its authority.

However, in cases where the person acted outside of official UN functions, the state of which
the individual is a national is accountable. To this effect, the agreements signed between the UN and
the contributing states set forth that the states concerned must ensure that the members of their national contingents know and understand the principles and spirit of humanitarian law. It has happened, however, that the UN was held responsible for violations of humanitarian law committed by
members of peacekeeping forces who acted outside their official functions.

In all cases, the UN's accountability does not exclude the state's since members of national
contingents remain subject to their national laws, whether or not they are under UN command.

This means that UN troops are responsible for respecting humanitarian law under a double mandate: under the regulations of the force to which they belong and under their national laws (since almost all states are parties to the Geneva Conventions, if not the Protocols as well).

In practice, however, it is difficult to hold the UN accountable, whether before international or national entities. At an international level, the available recourses only work if the victims are states or international organizations. Hence, individuals or juridical persons (e.g., NGOs) have no recourse before any international organ in case of injury caused by an international organization, unless the institutional system of the organization itself foresees such a possibility.

In almost all situations, individual victims can have recourse to national courts, either those in the state where the injury was suffered, or in their own. This does not apply with regard to the UN, which enjoys immunity from jurisdiction—that is, from legal process (Article 104 of UN Charter and Article 2 of the 1946 Convention on the Privileges and Immunities of the United Nations). Thus, domestic courts are deprived of their jurisdictional powers.

The mechanisms for recourse against the UN are the following:

The UN Administrative Tribunal, for Individuals or NGOs under Contract with the UN. The UN does have an Administrative Tribunal (UNAT), but it is reserved for UN staff and any other person who is under contract with the UN (Article 2.2 of UNAT's statute). On this basis, NGOs under contract with the UN can theoretically refer cases to UNAT. Furthermore, NGOs can qualify as "international agents," as defined in the 1949 International Court of Justice (ICJ) advisory opinion on Reparation for Injuries Suffered in the Service of the UN. This decision found that an agent is "any person who, whether a paid official or not, and whether permanently employed or not, has been charged by an organ of the Organization with carrying out, or helping to carry out, one of its functions—in short, any person through whom it acts."

Claims Commission. As for individuals, they have no judicial recourse before the UN and therefore none against it. Nonetheless, the organization is under the obligation to make provisions for "appropriate modes of settlement" of legal disputes "of a private law character" in which it is involved and for "disputes involving any official of the United Nations who by reason of his official position enjoys immunity, if immunity has not been waived by the Secretary-General" (section 29 of the 1946 Convention on the Privileges and Immunities of the UN).

For this reason, the UN has established a nonjudicial, ad hoc claims commission system for peacekeeping operations. This is the only recourse against the UN that is available to individuals. It is also available to juridical persons, therefore to NGOs. Hence, any agreement signed between the UN and a host state establishes that any dispute or complaint in the area of private law involving the UN must be submitted to this commission.

The commission has three members: two are designated by the UN Secretary-General and the government of the host state, respectively, and the third is nominated by common agreement between them or, failing that, by the president of the ICJ. The commission defines its own rules of procedure. Its decisions cannot be appealed and are binding. The procedures are not public, and the plaintiff cannot have access to the UN's files since its archives enjoy immunity. At the end of the process, the victims receive compensation.

Diplomatic Protection. One other recourse is available to individuals and NGOs, if their state of origin agrees to implement the procedure known as diplomatic protection. In such situations, the state endorses and takes on the victim's cause. The case must then be settled between the UN and the state in question through negotiation or arbitration. However, there are few entities before which this arbitration can take place since the ICJ cannot, under its statute, rule on cases between the UN and individuals or NGOs, even via diplomatic protection: since its jurisdiction over contentious cases only extends to states, international organizations can neither submit nor be subject to cases before the ICJ.

Finally, the diplomatic protection procedure remains a rare option, to be implemented by the victim's state on a discretionary basis. When this procedure does reach a conclusion, the UN and the state negotiate the amount of the compensation to be paid. The amount is then given to the state, which also distributes it on a discretionary basis.

b. Recourses against Members of Peacekeeping Forces

If a peacekeeper commits a criminal offense (whether a felony or a misdemeanor), the individual is under the exclusive jurisdiction of his or her state. This is part of the agreements signed between the UN and host states or between the UN and contributing states. In the case in which the crime constitutes a grave breach of humanitarian law, this provision is problematic because it is in contradiction with the principle of universal jurisdiction, which governs the punishment of such crimes.

The principle of universal jurisdiction, codified by the 1949 Geneva Conventions, establishes that all states have an obligation to search for and prosecute individuals accused of such crimes. By virtue of the hierarchy of norms, this obligation prevails over the different agreements signed at the time the forces were deployed. In practice, however, it is unlikely that a state would agree to see a member of its armed forced judged by any foreign jurisdiction.

The agreements signed between the UN and each host state also foresee that the government of the state in question can inform the Force Commander and give him or her any evidence in its possession, if it considers that a member of a PKO committed a criminal offense. This is an important part of the agreement since the Secretary-General must be able to obtain the assurance from contributing states that they are willing to exercise their jurisdiction over any crimes that may be committed by members of their contingent.

However, once again, the ability to hold individual peacekeepers accountable collides with the immunity from jurisdiction that peacekeeping forces enjoy, under their status as subsidiary organs of the UN (according to the 1946 Convention on the Privileges and Immunities of the UN). This immunity is cited in the different agreements signed when the force is created—an important part of the agreement for the contributing states. The members of PKOs thus enjoy immunity from jurisdiction for acts committed in the conduct of their duties. And they continue to benefit from this immunity even after they are no longer members of the operation.

The immunity granted by the 1946 Convention is not absolute, of course. The Convention establishes that the UN Secretary-General can waive an individual's immunity "in any case where, in his opinion, the immunity would impede the course of justice and can be waived without prejudice to the interests of the UN" (sections 20 and 23 of the 1946 Convention). It is therefore left to the Secretary-General's discretion as to whether to lift immunity.

The Belgian and French parliaments initiated investigations into their governments' responsibility during the PKO in Rwanda in 1994. Following these national investigations and based on their recommendations, the UN Secretary-General set up an independent panel of investigation into the UN's response to the genocide.

☞ International law establishes that individuals accused of war crimes or crimes against humanity cannot resort to immunity from jurisdiction or official status to avoid facing justice. This provision is codified in

- the 1948 Convention on the Prevention and Punishment of the Crime of Genocide (Article 4);
- the 1984 Convention against Torture and Other Cruel, Inhuman, or Degrading Treatment or Punishment (Article 1);
- the 1949 Geneva Conventions (GCI Article 59, GCII Article 50, GCIII Article 29, and GCIV Article 146)
- the statute of the international military tribunal of Nuremberg (Article 7);
- the statutes of the two International Criminal Tribunals (Article 7.2 of ICTY statute and Article 6.2 of ICTR statute); and
- the statute of the International Criminal Court (Article 27).

→ **Collective security; Duty of commanders; Hierarchy of norms; Immunity; International Criminal Court; International Criminal Tribunals; Intervention; Penal sanctions in humanitarian law; Public order; Respect for international humanitarian law; Sanctions (diplomatic, economic, or military); Secretariat of the UN; Security Council of the UN; Self-defense; United Nations; Universal jurisdiction**

📖 For Additional Information:

Annan, Kofi. "Peacekeeping, Military Intervention, and National Sovereignty in Internal Armed Conflict." In *Hard Choices: Moral Dilemmas in Humanitarian Intervention*, ed. Jonathan Moore. Lanham, Md.: Rowman & Littlefield, 1998, 55–71.

Dallaire, Romeo. "The End of Innocence: Rwanda 1994." In *Hard Choices: Moral Dilemmas in Humanitarian Intervention*, ed. Jonathan Moore. Lanham, Md.: Rowman & Littlefield, 1998, 71–86.

Durch, William J., ed. *The Evolution of UN Peacekeeping: Case Studies and Comparative Analysis*. New York: St. Martin's, 1993.

Palwankar, Umesh. "Applicability of International Humanitarian Law to UN Peacekeeping Forces." *International Review of the Red Cross* 294 (May–June 1993): 227–40.

Roberts, Adam, and Benedict Kingsbury, eds. *United Nations, Divided World: The UN's Roles in International Relations*. New York: Oxford University Press, 1993, 81–125.

■ PENAL SANCTIONS IN HUMANITARIAN LAW

1. The System of Sanctions Established by the Geneva Conventions

The penal and disciplinary sanctions that can be imposed by a Detaining Power or by an Occupying Power in times of conflict are regulated by the judicial guarantees determined by humanitarian law. → **Judicial guarantees**

The Geneva Conventions establish a specific system of penal sanctions to punish violations of international humanitarian law, whether committed by individuals, administrations, or organizations dependent on a government.

Violations of humanitarian law are acts carried out by combatants, acting either on orders or on their own volition. The rules balance the principle of authority against the principle of responsibility. Humanitarian law establishes provisions for the prevention and punishment of grave breaches of its rules by reaffirming the responsibility of states, military commanders, and individuals and by codifying a system of international jurisdiction for the prosecution of the authors of such violations.

- A party to a conflict may be held responsible for acts carried out by its members if it cannot prove that it took disciplinary measures against any of its soldiers who may have committed acts forbidden by humanitarian law on their own initiative.
- Combatants remain personally responsible for their acts, even if they acted on the order of a superior. In such a case, the superior will also be held accountable.
- Under the principle of universal jurisdiction, perpetrators of grave breaches of humanitarian law can be tried before any court of any country.
- States are not allowed to absolve themselves, or any other state, of their responsibilities to punish and demand reparations if grave breaches of the Geneva Conventions were committed by their nationals or in their name (GCI Article 51, GCII Article 52, GCIII Article 131, and GCIV Article 148).

2. Sanctions Imposed by International Tribunals

- There are currently two ad hoc International Criminal Tribunals in operation, set up in 1993 and 1994, to prosecute and sanction individuals accused of serious crimes (namely, violations of humanitarian law) committed in the former Yugoslavia and in Rwanda, respectively.
- The statute of a permanent International Criminal Court (ICC) was adopted in Rome, on July 17, 1998, as the result of a diplomatic conference organized under the aegis of the UN. Under certain conditions, it will be responsible for prosecuting individuals accused of crimes of genocide, war crimes, crimes against humanity, and aggression. Once it enters into force, it will function when states are unable or unwilling to carry out the investigation or prosecution on their own.

➔ **Amnesties; Duty of commanders; Individual recourse; International Criminal Court; International Criminal Tribunals; International Fact-Finding Commission; Respect for international humanitarian law; Responsibility; Sanctions; Universal jurisdiction; War crimes/Crimes against humanity (Section III)**

📖 **For Additional Information:**

Fernandez-Flores, José Luís. *Repression of Breaches of the Law of War Committed by Individuals*. Geneva: ICRC, 1996.
Roling, B. V. A. "Aspects of Criminal Responsibility for Violations of the Laws of War." In *The New Humanitarian Law of Armed Conflicts,* ed. A. Cassese. Naples: Editorale Scientifica, 1979, vol. 1: 199–231.
Verhaegen, Jacques. *Legal Obstacles to Prosecution of Breaches of Humanitarian Law*. Geneva: ICRC, 1989.

■ PERFIDY

An act of perfidy is committed when a person invokes the provisions of the Geneva Conventions that are meant for the protection of persons, with the intent to betray, kill, injure, or capture an adversary. For instance, the improper use of the emblem of the red cross or any other protective emblems, flags, or uniforms (used, e.g., to invite and then betray the adversary's trust) is forbidden, as is the act of feigning illness or pretending to be a civilian or other noncombatant (PI Articles 37–39 and 44).

☞ The international law of armed conflict makes a distinction between ruses of war, which are not prohibited, and perfidy, which is. The perfidious use of the distinctive emblem of the red cross or any other protective signs recognized by the Geneva Conventions or their Protocols is a grave violation of humanitarian law, and therefore a war crime (PI Article 85.3).

→ **Distinctive (or protective) emblems, signs, or signals; War crimes/Crimes against humanity**

📖 **For Additional Information:**

Mulinen, Frederic de. *Handbook on the Law of War for Armed Forces*. Geneva: ICRC, 1989.
Oeter, Stefan. "Methods and Means of Combat." In *The Handbook of Humanitarian Law in Armed Conflicts*, ed. Dieter Fleck. Oxford: Oxford University Press, 1995, 199–202.

■ PERSECUTION

1. Definitions

While the notion of "persecution" is often mentioned in international conventions, it was only recently given a legal definition, in the statute of the International Criminal Court (ICC), adopted on July 17, 1998. The ICC statute defines persecution as "the intentional and severe deprivation of fundamental rights contrary to international law by reason of the identity of the group or collectivity" (Article 7.2.g of ICC statute).

The statute of the ICC establishes that gender may be a ground for fearing persecution. It includes "persecution against any identifiable group or collectivity on political, racial, national, ethnic, cultural, religious, gender [. . .] or other grounds that are universally recognized as impermissible under international law" as a crime against humanity (Article 7.1.h of ICC statute). Once it enters into force, the ICC will have jurisdiction over individuals accused of genocide, war crimes, and crimes against humanity, after certain preconditions have been met.

Freedom from persecution is vital to the well-being of individuals in society and to their enjoyment of the rights to which they are entitled. Under international law, persecution is a crime against humanity. This was clearly established under the jurisdiction of the international military tribunals of Nuremberg and Tokyo and was reaffirmed most recently in the ICC statute.

Persecution is one of the main reasons that individuals flee their country of origin. It is recognized by the 1951 Convention relating to the Status of Refugees (Refugee Convention) as the principal justification for qualifying an individual as a refugee. This Convention—as well as the 1969 Convention Governing the Specific Aspects of Refugee Problems in Africa, adopted by the Organization of African Unity—defines a refugee as "every person who, owing to [a] well-founded fear of being persecuted for reasons of race, religion, nationality, membership of a particular social group or political opinion, is outside the country of his nationality and is unable or, owing to such fear, is unwilling to avail himself of the protection of that country" (Article 1 of both conventions). → **Refugees**

Fear of persecution is not only a valid reason for fleeing a country and requesting asylum in another, it is the basis of the principle of *nonrefoulement*, whereby states may not, under any circumstances, expel or return a person by force to a state where he or she fears persecution (cited in most conventions relating to the issue of refugees and in GCIV Article 45). ➔ **Asylum;** *Refoulement* **(forced return) and expulsion**

Since individuals are persecuted because of their membership in a specific group, behavior that reflects adverse discrimination is often considered an important indication of the risk of such persecution. Other much clearer indications include threats or attempts against the life of individuals—in particular violence to their person, extermination, torture, and other forms of ill treatment. UNHCR recently expressly added rape to the list of crimes that can constitute an element of persecution and that thus permit the recognition of refugee status as foreseen by the Refugee Convention. The ICC statute reaffirms that gender is a reason for fearing persecution (see the next section on sanctions). ➔ **Discrimination; Ill treatment; Rape; Torture**

2. Sanctions

In general, individuals who commit acts of persecution are subject to the penal sanctions foreseen for both violations of international humanitarian law—since it is a crime against humanity—and human rights violations. These are explained under ➔ **individual recourse; penal sanctions in humanitarian law; and war crimes/crimes against humanity**.

The two ad hoc International Criminal Tribunals, for the former Yugoslavia and Rwanda, may also prosecute individuals who commit acts of persecution, enumerated in the list of crimes against humanity (Article 5.h of ICTY statute; Article 3.h of ICTR statute).

➔ **Asylum; Discrimination; Human rights; Ill treatment; International Criminal Court; International Criminal Tribunals; Rape;** *Refoulement* **(forced return) and expulsion; Refugees; Torture; War crimes/crimes against humanity; Well-being**

■ PILLAGE

Pillage is the systematic and violent appropriation by members of the armed forces of movable public or private property that belongs either to persons protected by humanitarian conventions (civilians, wounded and sick, shipwrecked, and prisoners of war) or to the adverse state or party itself. Parties to the conflict are under obligation to take all necessary measures to protect the wounded, the dead, or any person exposed to grave danger from pillage and ill treatment (Article 4 of the Convention for the Protection of Cultural Property in the Event of Armed Conflict, signed in The Hague on May 14, 1954, under the aegis of UNESCO; GCI Article 15, GCII Article 18, GCIII Articles 16 and 33, and PII Article 4).

Pillage is a war crime, as established by the statutes and judgments of the Nuremberg and Tokyo military tribunals. Furthermore, it is a grave violation of the Geneva Conventions if it takes the form of "extensive destruction and appropriation of property, not justified by military necessity and carried out unlawfully and wantonly" (GCI Article 50, GCII Article 51, GCIII Article 130, GCIV Article 147, and PII Article 4). It is forbidden in both international and internal conflicts by the Geneva Conventions and their Protocols.

It is important to distinguish between pillage, which is always prohibited, and requisition, which is an authorized form of appropriating property. Other provisions of humanitarian law regulate the limited right to requisition during armed conflicts. ➔ **Requisition**

As for immovable property, its appropriation, even through force or violence, does not change its physical location. Such appropriation is therefore not considered pillage but rather stealing and may be prosecuted as such. The destruction of such immovable property is specifically forbidden by the Geneva Conventions if it belongs to the categories of persons it protects. These are civilian objects and property (including enemy civilian property), cultural property, and objects indispensable to the survival of the civilian population (PI Articles 52–54; PII Articles 13 and 14).

→ **Protected objects and property; Requisition; War crimes/Crimes against humanity**

■ POPULATION DISPLACEMENT

In situations of conflict, the fact that it is prohibited to attack civilians is not sufficient to ensure their safety. Population movements are a natural consequence of military operations, either spontaneously or as the result of a decision by armed forces.

In times of peace, the principle of freedom of movement applies to the entire population of a country. This liberty of movement can become a right to flee, which enables individuals to escape from danger.

In times of conflict, humanitarian law sets forth various provisions to limit or control the displacement of civilian populations. In particular, it prohibits forced population displacement (transfers or deportations). This provision is at the heart of the system of protection for civilians.

At all times and under all circumstances, it is forbidden to force individuals in flight back to a territory where they are in danger.

I. IN TIMES OF PEACE OR OF TENSION

International human rights conventions set forth various provisions relating to individuals' freedom of movement. Authorities are allowed to suspend or restrict certain of these rights for different reasons ranging from issues of public order to measures of urban planning. However, it is important to note that, if the motives invoked concern public order, the authorities must justify these measures and offer guarantees to the individuals concerned (Article 12 of ICCPR).

Furthermore, even when defending the public order, or at other times of unrest, certain provisions remain applicable: the peremptory human rights norms (those that may never be infringed on, no matter what the circumstance may be) must always be respected. If the level of violence reaches a certain intensity, even if it is one that cannot be described as a conflict, the fundamental guarantees enforced by humanitarian law can also be invoked. There are also certain political practices that may result in, or make use of, population displacement. These include acts such as apartheid or ethnic cleansing, which are strictly forbidden under international law.

Finally, as mentioned earlier, liberty of movement includes freedom to flee one's country and seek asylum in another. However, this right is limited by the fact that there is no reciprocal obligation on the part of states to offer asylum, beyond the principle of *nonrefoulement*, which clarifies that, even if individuals enter or finds themselves in a territory illegally, the state where they find themselves may not force them to return to a country where they fear for their safety.

→ **Fundamental guarantees; Public order; *Refoulement* (forced return) and expulsion**

Freedom of Movement and the Right to Flee

The Universal Declaration of Human Rights

Article 13:

- Everyone has the right to freedom of movement and residence within the borders of each State.
- Everyone has the right to leave any country, including his own, and to return to his country.

Article 14:

- Everyone has the right to seek and to enjoy in other countries asylum from persecution.
- This right may not be invoked in the case of prosecutions genuinely arising from non-political crimes or from acts contrary to the purposes and principles of the United Nations.

The International Covenant on Civil and Political Rights

Article 12:

1. Everyone lawfully within the territory of a State shall, within that territory, have the right to liberty of movement and freedom to choose his residence.
2. Everyone shall be free to leave any country, including his own.
3. The above-mentioned rights shall not be subject to any restrictions except those which are provided by law, are necessary to protect national security, public order (*ordre public*), public health or morals or the rights and freedoms of others, and are consistent with the other rights recognized in the present Covenant.
4. No one shall be arbitrarily deprived of the right to enter his own country.

II. IN TIMES OF CONFLICT

Humanitarian law distinguishes between spontaneous and forced population movements. Thus, it refers to

- "population movements," when describing spontaneous population movements that take place within or outside their country of origin;
- "displacement," "transfer," or "evacuation," when describing forced displacement of populations within a state in conflict;
- "deportation," when describing forced displacement of populations across a border.

1. Spontaneous Population Movements

A population may flee certain areas suddenly—for instance, because fighting is approaching. In such cases, the movement resembles an exodus, exile, or refugee flow, which may eventually involve crossing an international border.

To limit such displacement or to prevent the effects from being too harmful to the population, international humanitarian law establishes procedures of assistance and protection for the civilian population. It also forbids certain military practices that cause civilians to panic and flee:

- It is forbidden to make the civilian population the target of attacks (PI Article 51.2 and PII Article 13.2).
- Attacks or other "acts or threats of violence the primary purpose of which is to spread terror among the civilian population" are prohibited (PI Article 51.2 and PII Article 13.2).
- It is prohibited to deprive civilians of goods indispensable to their survival to "cause them to move away, or for any other motive" (PI Article 54.2 and PII Article 14),
- Civilians may not be used to shield military objectives from adverse attacks (GCIV Article 28, PI Article 51.7, and PII Article 13).
- It is forbidden to use population movements or to direct them toward specific destinations to attempt to protect or shield military objectives or military operations in general (GCIV Article 28 and PI Article 51.7).
- Individuals must not be expelled or returned (*refoulés*) to a territory where their life or freedom would be threatened (Article 33 of 1951 Refugee Convention and many other international conventions).

2. Forced Population Displacement, Transfer, or Deportation

Sometimes, population movements are caused by force or other forms of constraints being used against civilians. In such cases, humanitarian law uses the terms *forced displacement, forced transfer, evacuation,* or *deportation.*

Deportation, Evacuation, and Forced Transfer

- *Deportation* refers to the forced transfer of civilians (or other persons protected by the Geneva Conventions) from the territory where they reside to the territory of the Occupying Power, or to any other territory, whether occupied or not.
- *Population transfer* describes a forced movement of population that takes place within the national territory.
- *Evacuation* describes the temporary transfer of populations or individuals, due to imperative military reasons or if the safety of the population requires it.
- → **Deportation; Evacuation**

Humanitarian law prohibits any forced population displacement. There are legal exceptions to this principle, but they are strictly limited, and any violation of these provisions is a war crime.

The statute of the International Criminal Court (ICC), adopted in July 1998, reaffirms that such acts are war crimes, including it in the list of those over which the Court will have jurisdiction once it enters into force—after sixty states have ratified the statute (Articles 8.2.b.vii and 8.2.e.viii of ICC statute).

(continues)

(*continued*)

When committed as part of a widespread or systematic attack directed against any civilian population, deportation or forcible transfer of population are grave breaches of the Geneva Conventions. They can also be qualified as crimes against humanity (Article 7.1.d of ICC statute). Once the ICC is operational, it will be able to prosecute individuals accused of such crimes, under certain conditions regulating the exercise of its jurisdiction. Until then, such crimes come under universal jurisdiction.

→ **International Criminal Court; Universal jurisdiction; War crimes/Crimes against humanity**

a. International Armed Conflicts

In territories under military occupation, in the context of an international armed conflict, humanitarian law prohibits:

> individual or mass forcible transfers, as well as deportations of protected persons from occupied territory to the territory of the Occupying Power or to that of any other country, occupied or not [. . .], regardless of their motive.
>
> Nevertheless, the Occupying Power may undertake total or partial evacuation of a given area if the security of the population or imperative military reasons do demand. Such evacuations may not involve the displacement of protected persons outside the bounds of the occupied territory except when for material reasons it is impossible to avoid such displacement. [. . .]
>
> The Occupying Power shall not detain protected persons in an area particularly exposed to the dangers of war unless the security of the population or imperative military reasons so demand.
>
> The Occupying Power shall not deport or transfer parts of its own civilian population into the territory it occupies. (GCIV Article 49)

Any violation of these provisions is a war crime (GCIV Article 147; PI Article 85.4.a).

b. Noninternational Armed Conflicts

Humanitarian law establishes that the following acts are prohibited in the context of internal conflicts:

- "The displacement of the civilian population shall not be ordered for reasons related to the conflict unless the security of the civilians involved or imperative military reasons so demand.
  "Should such displacements have to be carried out, all possible measures shall be taken in order that the civilian population may be received under satisfactory conditions of shelter, hygiene, health, safety and nutrition" (PII Article 17).
- In addition to the general "prohibition of forced movement of civilians" (PII Article 17), humanitarian law establishes additional prohibitions to protect civilians from the effects of conflict: "the civilian population as such, as well as individual civilians, shall not be the object of attack. Acts or threats of violence the primary purpose of which is to spread terror among the civilian population are prohibited" (PII Article 13.2).

The Status of Displaced Persons

Population movements sometimes lead individuals outside their own country. In such cases, they are protected by international refugee law.

(*continues*)

(*continued*)

On the other hand, if they find refuge within their own country or are prevented from crossing borders because neighboring states have closed them, they are defined as "internally displaced persons" (IDPs) and remain under the authority of their own national authorities. If the country is at war, they are protected under humanitarian law as civilians. If the country is at peace, they are protected by international human rights norms.

→ **Asylum; Civilians; Displaced persons;** *Refoulement* **(forced return) and expulsion; Refugees**

→ **Apartheid; Asylum; Civilians; Deportation; Displaced persons; Ethnic cleansing; Evacuation; Internment; Protected areas and zones;** *Refoulement* **(forced return) and expulsion; Refugees; War**

📖 **For Additional Information:**

Brauman, Rony. "Refugee Camps, Population Transfers, and NGOs." In *Hard Choices: Moral Dilemmas in Humanitarian Intervention*, ed. Jonathan Moore. Lanham, Md.: Rowman & Littlefield, 1998, 177–94.

Kalin, Walter. "Protection in International Human Rights Law." In *Internally Displaced Persons Symposium, 23–25 October 1995,* ed. Jean-Philippe Lavoyer. Geneva: ICRC, 1996, 15–25.

Lavoyer, Jean-Philippe. "Protection under International Humanitarian Law." In *Internally Displaced Persons Symposium, 23–25 October 1995*, ed. Jean-Philippe Lavoyer. Geneva: ICRC, 1996, 26–36.

UNHCR. *The State of the World's Refugees, 1997–98: A Humanitarian Agenda*. New York: Oxford University Press, 1997.

■ PRISONERS OF WAR

A combatant who falls into the hands of an adverse party to a conflict in the course of an international armed conflict is a prisoner of war. The four sections that make up this entry explain the following:

I. The Third Geneva Convention of 1949 specifically regulates the treatment of prisoners of war, the definition of which is derived from the definition of combatants. → **Combatants**

II. The Additional Protocol to the Geneva Conventions Relating to the Protection of Victims of International Armed Conflicts (Protocol I), adopted in 1977, takes a different approach to the question of prisoners of war. It enumerates the categories of persons who must be protected under the status of prisoners of war if captured by an adverse party. The goal is to ensure that individuals are not denied this status if an authority chooses an excessively restrictive interpretation of the Third Geneva Convention definition. Protocol I also establishes guarantees to prevent the status from being denied to a person who is entitled to it.

III. These texts regulate the conditions for the detention of prisoners of war (housing, food, hygiene and medical care, religion, physical and intellectual activities, discipline, transfer, work, correspondence, money). Prisoner of war status entails certain fundamental guarantees in the case of disciplinary and penal sanctions.

IV. This status also takes into account the fact that combatants have a legitimate right to use violence, until they are captured. It tries to ascertain that capture and detention are

not used as an occasion for ill treatment or revenge against prisoners. Humanitarian law also provides fundamental guarantees for persons who are not entitled to this status.
→ **Fundamental guarantees**

☞ In 1977, the definition of a prisoner of war that had been established in 1949 was expanded to take into consideration the evolving notion of "combatants," tied to new military techniques. Under the new definition, prisoner of war status is no longer reserved exclusively for combatants who are members of the armed forces: it may also be granted to civilians who are members of resistance movements and to participants in popular uprisings.

Even if a combatant has committed grave violations of humanitarian law, he or she may not be deprived of prisoner of war status and the protections granted by this status.

The definition of a prisoner of war is rarely applicable to internal armed conflicts. However, the Additional Protocol to the Geneva Conventions Relating to the Protection of Victims of Non-International Armed Conflicts (Protocol II) establishes specific provisions and guarantees of treatment for persons detained for reasons related to a conflict (PII Article 5).

I. DEFINITION OF PRISONERS OF WAR (THIRD 1949 GENEVA CONVENTION)

The Third Geneva Convention defines the categories of persons who are entitled to prisoners of war status:

- Prisoners of war [. . .] are persons belonging to one of the following categories, who have fallen into the power of the enemy:
  —Members of the armed forces of a Party to the conflict as well as members of militias or volunteer corps forming part of such armed forces.
  —Members of other militias and members of other volunteer corps, including those of organized resistance movements, belonging to a Party to the conflict and operating in or outside their own territory, even if this territory is occupied, provided that [they] fulfill the following conditions:
    (a) that of being commanded by a person responsible for his subordinates;
    (b) that of having a fixed distinctive sign recognizable at a distance;
    (c) that of carrying arms openly;
    (d) that of conducting their operations in accordance with the laws and customs of war.
  —Members of regular armed forces who profess allegiance to a government or an authority not recognized by the Detaining Power.
  —Persons who accompany the armed forces without actually being members thereof, such as civilian members of military aircraft crews, war correspondents, supply contractors, members of labour units or of services responsible for the welfare of the armed forces, provided that they have received authorization from the armed forces which they accompany, who shall provide them for that purpose with an identity card. [. . .]
  —Members of crews, including masters, pilots and apprentices, of the merchant marine and the crews of civil aircraft of the Parties to the conflict, who do not benefit by more favourable treatment under any other provisions of international law.
  —Inhabitants of a non-occupied territory, who on the approach of the enemy spontaneously take up arms to resist the invading forces, without having had time to form themselves into regular armed units, provided they carry arms openly and respect the laws and customs of war. (GCIV Article 4.A)
- The following shall likewise be treated as prisoners of war under the present Convention:
  —Persons belonging, or having belonged, to the armed forces of the occupying country, if the Occupying Power considers it necessary by reason of such allegiance to intern them, even though it has originally liberated them while hostilities were going on outside the territory it occupies,

in particular where such persons have made an unsuccessful attempt to rejoin the armed forces to which they belong and which are engaged in combat, or where they fail to comply with a summons made to them with a view to internment.

— The persons belonging to one of the categories enumerated in the present Article, who have been received by neutral or non-belligerent Powers on their territory and whom these Powers are required to intern under international law, without prejudice to any more favourable treatment which these Powers may choose to give. [. . .] (GCIII Article 4.B)

In 1977, the definition of a combatant, and therefore that of a prisoner of war, was expanded to take into consideration the evolution of methods of warfare:

- The armed forces of a Party to a conflict consist of all organized armed forces, groups and units which are under a command responsible to that Party for the conduct or its subordinates, even if that Party is represented by a government or an authority not recognized by an adverse Party.
- Such armed forces shall be subject to an internal disciplinary system which, *inter alia*, shall enforce compliance with the rules of international law applicable in armed conflict.
- Members of the armed forces of a Party to a conflict (other than medical personnel and chaplains covered by Article 33 of the Third Convention) are combatants, that is to say, they have the right to participate directly in hostilities. (PI Article 43)

II. PROTECTION OF PRISONER OF WAR STATUS (PROTOCOL I)

A certain number of minimum guarantees are foreseen to regulate which persons are granted the status of prisoner of war and to protect individuals who are not entitled to this status.

- Any person who takes part in hostilities and falls into the power of an adverse party shall be presumed to be a prisoner of war (PI Article 45). This means that the Detaining Power must prove that an individual may not benefit from this status.
- Any member of the armed forces of a party to a conflict (other than medical and religious personnel) who falls into the power of the adverse party is a prisoner of war.
- A combatant's failure to respect the rules of international law applicable to armed conflicts may not deprive that person of his or her status of prisoner of war (PI Article 44.2).
- Children, even if they are combatants, remain protected by the special provisions foreseen for them by humanitarian law, whether or not they are prisoners of war.
- → **Children**
- However, a combatant who falls into the power of an adverse party after failing to distinguish him- or herself from the civilian population during a military operation forfeits his or her right to prisoner of war status. Nevertheless, that person shall benefit from protections equivalent to those granted to prisoners of war by the Third Geneva Convention and Protocol I (PI Article 44.4).

☞ In the case of combatants who fail to distinguish themselves from the civilian population during a military operation, the difference between granting them the "status" of a prisoner of war and granting them the "same treatment" as a prisoner of war is established because an individual who used force without acting openly in his or her capacity as combatant may be subject to criminal prosecution for their acts of violence, in conformity with the national laws of the Detaining Power. However, he or she continues to be entitled to the protection provided to prisoners of war by the Third Geneva Convention (discussed later).

→ **Judicial guarantees**

- Mercenaries are not entitled to prisoner of war status. The same applies to spies, if they act without wearing the uniform of their armed forces (PI Articles 46 and 47). They must be treated humanely, however, and are entitled at least to the fundamental guarantees. → **Fundamental guarantees**
- If a person who has fallen into the power of an adverse party is not being held as a prisoner of war and is to be tried by that party for an offense related to the hostilities, that person has the right to defend his or her right to prisoner of war status before a judicial tribunal and to have that question adjudicated. The representatives of the Protecting Power or of the ICRC are entitled to attend the proceedings in which the decision will be taken (PI Article 45.2).
- Civilians who participate directly in hostilities are not entitled to the protection granted to civilians by the law of armed conflict, for the duration of their direct participation in hostilities (PI Articles 45.3 and 51; PII Article 13.3). Nor are they entitled to the status of combatant or of prisoner of war, except in certain cases specified above. If they are detained, they remain protected by the fundamental guarantees established by humanitarian law. → **Detention; Fundamental guarantees**

III. THE STATUS OF PRISONER OF WAR (THIRD GENEVA CONVENTION)

Once prisoners of war are in the hands of the adversary, they are particularly vulnerable to acts of revenge, pressure, and humiliation. The status of prisoners of war is set out in detail throughout the 143 articles of the Third Geneva Convention, which regulates the protection of combatants fallen into the hands of the adverse power and the conditions of their detention.

This protection rests on the Convention's reaffirmation of certain rights and obligations, as well as on the mechanism of supervision embodied in the mandate of the Protecting Power. If the parties to a conflict fail to designate a Protecting Power, the ICRC will play this role with regard to the prisoners on both sides (GCIII Articles 8–10). In practice, this reciprocal principle is pivotal to convince the parties to the conflict to respect the rights established by the Third Convention. However, in certain situations—namely, in noninternational armed conflicts—the benefits of reciprocity are not always sufficient to prevent ill treatment. The role of the ICRC is even more important in such cases.

The rights and obligations set out by the Third Geneva Convention can be summarized as follows:

- Prisoners of war must be treated humanely at all times. Any unlawful act or omission by the Detaining Power causing death or seriously endangering the health of a prisoner of war in its custody is prohibited and will be considered a serious breach of humanitarian law (GCIII Article 13).
- Prisoners of war are entitled in all circumstances to respect for their person. Women must be treated with due regard to their specific needs and must benefit from treatment as favorable as that granted to men (GCIII Article 14). → **Women**
- The Detaining Power is bound to provide prisoners of war, free of charge, with the necessary maintenance and medical attention required by their state of health (Article 15).
- All prisoners of war must be treated alike by the Detaining Power (Article 16).
- No physical or mental torture, or any other form of coercion, may be inflicted on prisoners of war to secure from them information of any kind whatever. Prisoners are only under obligation to give their last and first names, rank, date of birth, and serial number. Each party to a conflict is required to furnish each prisoner of war under its jurisdiction with an identity card (Article 17).

- Prisoners of war may not be deprived of their personal belongings (Article 18).
- Prisoners of war must be evacuated, as soon as possible after their capture, to camps situated away from the combat zones. Such evacuation must be carried out humanely and in conditions similar to those for the forces of the Detaining Power in their changes of station. Prisoners of war must be given sufficient food and drinking water and the necessary clothing and medical attention (Articles 19 and 20).
- Premises of internment must provide every guarantee of hygiene and healthfulness and take into account the climate in the area (Article 22).
- Prisoner of war camps must be clearly marked by the letters *PW* or *PG* (for prisoners of war or *prisonniers de guerre*), whenever military considerations so permit (Article 23).
- Prisoners of war shall be quartered under conditions as favorable as those for the forces of the Detaining Power who are quartered in the same area. The said conditions must in no case be prejudicial to their health. The premises must be entirely protected from dampness and adequately heated and lighted (Article 25).
- The basic daily food rations must be sufficient in quantity, quality, and variety to keep prisoners of war in good health and to prevent weight loss or the development of nutritional deficiencies. The habitual diet of the prisoners must also be taken into account (Article 26).
- The Detaining Power is bound to take all necessary sanitary measures to ensure the cleanliness and healthfulness of camps and to prevent epidemics. In any camps in which female prisoners of war are accommodated, separate conveniences shall be provided for them (Article 29).
- Every camp must have a satisfactory infirmary. Prisoners of war shall receive medical attention, preferably from medical personnel of the Power on which they depend and, if possible, of their nationality. Prisoners of war suffering from serious diseases or whose condition necessitates special treatment must be admitted to any military or civilian medical unit where such treatment can be given. Medical inspections of prisoners of war are to be held at least once a month. They shall include checking and recording the weight of each prisoner and their general state of health, nutrition, and cleanliness (Articles 30 and 31).
- Members of the medical personnel and chaplains held by the Detaining Power with a view to assisting prisoners of war shall not be considered prisoners of war. They shall, however, receive as a minimum the benefits and protection of the Third Convention and shall be given all facilities necessary to carry out their work (Article 33).
- Prisoners of war shall enjoy complete latitude in the exercise of their religion, and in the practice of sports and intellectual activities (Articles 34–38).
- Every camp shall be put under the immediate authority of a responsible commissioned officer belonging to the regular armed forces of the Detaining Power. This officer must know and implement the provisions of the Third Geneva Convention. Any regulations relating to the conduct of prisoners—including the text of the Convention—shall be posted in the camp, in a language the prisoners of war understand (Articles 39–42).
- The Detaining Power may hire the prisoners of war as workers, taking into account their state of health, as well as their age, sex, and rank, and only for work that is not for military purposes. Noncommissioned officers shall only be required to do supervisory work. Prisoners of war may not be forced to do dangerous or humiliating work, and their labor must be paid (Articles 49–57).
- The management and transfer of prisoners of war's financial resources are precisely regulated by Articles 58 to 68.
- Prisoners' relations with the exterior are regulated by Articles 69 to 77. The provisions include the fact that the Detaining Power must notify the authorities on which the prisoners depend of

the capture, and it must allow the prisoners to receive and send letters—two to four per month, depending on the model card used. Prisoners are also allowed to receive individual parcels or collective shipments containing, in particular, foodstuffs, clothing, medical supplies, and articles of a religious, educational, or recreational character, under the ICRC's supervision.

- Prisoners of war have the right to make requests to the military authorities in whose power they are, regarding their conditions of captivity (Article 78).
- Articles 82 to 108 enumerate the penal and disciplinary sanctions.
  - As a rule, prisoners of war are subject to the laws of the Detaining Power and its military tribunals. Such tribunals must always offer guarantees of judicial independence and impartiality, and protect the means and rights of defense.
  - Even if convicted, prisoners of war continue to be protected by the provisions of the Convention (prisoners of war may never be deprived of the protection derived from Articles 78 to 126, concerning their right to file complaints and the judicial guarantees to which they were entitled).
  - Collective punishment imposed for individual acts, corporal punishment, imprisonment in premises without daylight, and, in general, any form of torture or cruelty, are forbidden.
  - The scale of applicable disciplinary punishments is clearly established by the Convention.
  - Escape may be punished only by disciplinary punishment. ➔ **Collective punishment; Corporal punishment; Judicial guarantees**
- Prisoners of war who are seriously wounded or suffer from specified diseases must be repatriated directly back to their own country or to a hospital in a neutral state (Articles 109–117). Article 110 sets forth the specific conditions governing such decisions.
  Those whose diseases or wounds warrant a direct repatriation are
  - the incurably wounded or sick whose mental or physical fitness seems to have been gravely diminished;
  - the wounded or sick who have recovered but whose mental or physical fitness seems to have been gravely and permanently diminished;
  - the wounded or sick who, according to medical opinion, are not likely to recover within one year.
  Those who may be accommodated in a neutral state are
  - the wounded and sick whose recovery may be expected within one year, or sooner if treated in a neutral country;
  - prisoners of war whose mental or physical health, according to medical opinion, is seriously threatened by continued captivity, but whose accommodation in a neutral country might remove such a threat.
  Certain prisoners of war accommodated in a neutral country can be directly repatriated following their treatment, under an agreement between the powers concerned, if
  - their state of health has deteriorated so as to fulfill the conditions laid down for direct repatriation;
  - their mental or physical powers remain considerably impaired, even after treatment.
- To address the needs of direct repatriation or hospitalization in a neutral state, the parties to a conflict must set up Mixed Medical Commissions from the beginning of the conflict, which examine the state of the wounded and sick (Annex I of the Third Geneva Convention, relating to Article 110, provides a model agreement concerning direct repatriation and accommodation in neutral countries of wounded and sick prisoners).
- Prisoners of war must be released and repatriated without delay after the cessation of active hostilities (Articles 118 and 119).

- Articles 120 and 121 address the death of prisoners of war. They regulate the validity of individual wills, notification of death certificates, the right to individual burial, and the obligation of the Detaining Power to investigate any death the cause of which is suspect.
- The parties to the conflict commit to setting up information bureaus that will gather information and organize relief actions relating to prisoners of war (Articles 122–125).
- The following acts, committed against prisoners of war, are grave breaches of the Geneva Conventions: "wilful killing, torture or inhuman treatment, including biological experiments, wilfully causing great suffering or serious injury to body or health, compelling a prisoner of war to serve in the forces of the hostile Power, or wilfully depriving a prisoner of war of the rights of fair and regular trial prescribed in this Convention" (Article 130).

➔ **War crimes/Crimes against humanity**

IV. FUNDAMENTAL GUARANTEES

Prisoner of war status is closely tied to the definition of combatants and hence to the status of members of the armed forces. However, combatant status does not automatically cover all persons who have participated in hostilities (which may include civilians, mercenaries, or child soldiers), especially in internal armed conflicts. A certain number of fundamental guarantees do remain applicable nonetheless in such situations. ➔ **Children; Combatants; Fundamental guarantees**

Individuals who are not, or are no longer, participating in hostilities hence remain entitled to certain fundamental protection guarantees, even if they cannot benefit from the status of prisoners of war.

1. International Armed Conflicts

- Any person who has taken part in hostilities but is not entitled to prisoner of war status and is not covered by more favorable provisions under the Fourth Geneva Convention (Relative to the Protection of Civilians) has a right, at all times, to the fundamental guarantees established by the Conventions (as detailed in PI Article 75).

2. Noninternational Armed Conflicts

Protocol II, relating to noninternational armed conflicts, does not directly refer to the definition of prisoners of war. However, the following provisions apply:

- All persons who are not covered by more favorable provisions are at least entitled to the fundamental guarantees and hence have the right to the respect for their person, their honor, their religious convictions and practices, and their right to be treated humanely, without any adverse distinction (common Article 3 of GCI–IV; PII Article 4).
- Persons deprived of their liberty for reasons related to the armed conflict benefit from specific guarantees (PII Article 5). These are detailed in the entry on detention. ➔ **Detention**
- Detained individuals who come under the category of combatants may be able to benefit from prisoner of war status and the guarantees attached to that status, according to the Third Geneva Convention (GCIII Articles 4.A.1–3 and 4.A.6), following specific conditions of reciprocity

and according to special agreements signed between the parties to the conflict. This status is thus not granted automatically but is the result of a reciprocal agreement signed between the parties to the internal conflict. ➔ **Detention**

➔ **Central Tracing Agency; Combatant; Detention; Evacuation; Fundamental guarantees; Judicial guarantees; Protecting Powers; Red Cross; Security**

📖 **For Additional Information:**

Hingorani, R. C. *Prisoners of War*. New Delhi: Oxford & IBH, 1982.
Pilloud, Claude. "Prisoners of War." In *International Dimensions of Humanitarian Law*. Geneva: Henri Dupont Institute; Paris: UNESCO; Dordrecht: Martinus Nijhoff, 1988, 167–86.
Rodley, Nigel. *The Treatment of Prisoners under International Law*. London: Clarendon, 1987.

■ PROPORTIONALITY

1. Proportionality in Attacks

The principle of proportionality states that the effect produced by the means and methods of warfare used in a given situation must not be disproportionate to the military advantage sought. Reprisals must also be proportionate to the attack that provoked them. Thus, it seeks to limit the damage caused by military operations to that which is strictly necessary or unavoidable.

International humanitarian law addresses this principle by prohibiting attacks that may cause "incidental loss of civilian life, injury to civilians, damage to civilian objects, or a combination thereof, which would be excessive in relation to the concrete and direct military advantage anticipated" (PI Articles 51, 57).

The statute of the International Criminal Court (ICC), adopted on July 17, 1998, also considers such acts as war crimes and includes them among the crimes over which it has jurisdiction. It adds to this definition the act of "intentionally launching an attack in the knowledge that such attack will cause [. . .] widespread, long-term and severe damage to the natural environment which would be clearly excessive in relation to the concrete and direct overall military advantage anticipated" (Article 8.2.b.iv of ICC statute).

☞ Proportionality is one of the key principles that enables and fosters a concrete debate on the limitations of military action and on the space that must be left for humanitarian operations within situations of conflict. This notion allows certain forms of suffering to be qualified as unnecessary. It does not mean that causing other kinds of harm is acceptable; rather, it reflects the fact that humanitarian law forbids suffering that is not caused in direct relation to a concrete military advantage.

The proportional nature of a reprisal in relation to the initial attack is the element that makes the distinction between a reprisal that is acceptable under the law of armed conflict and an act of revenge, which is always prohibited.

Humanitarian law clearly establishes the responsibility of military commanders with regard to the respect for this principle.

2. Judicial Proportionality

Proportionality is also used in reference to fundamental judicial guarantees, ensuring that the punishment is proportionate to the crime. This is reflected in the Geneva Conventions, which establish that "the courts [of the Occupying Power] shall apply [. . .] the principle that the penalty shall be proportioned to the offence" (GCIV Article 67).

→ **Attacks; Duty of commanders; International Criminal Court; Methods of warfare; Military necessity; Military objectives; Protected objects and property; Reprisals; War**

📖 **For Additional Information:**

Mulinen, Frederic de. *Handbook on the Law of War for Armed Forces*. Geneva: ICRC, 1989.
Oraa, Jaime. *Human Rights in States of Emergency in International Law*. Oxford: Clarendon, 1992, 140–70.

■ PROTECTED AREAS AND ZONES

Humanitarian law establishes different methods to define areas or zones within which special protection will be provided for populations in danger and in which no fighting may take place. The Geneva Conventions and the Protocols make a specific distinction between

- nondefended localities;
- hospital zones and localities;
- hospital and safety zones and localities;
- neutralized zones;
- demilitarized zones.

Each principle of humanitarian law bestows detailed rights and obligations. This includes a precise distribution of responsibilities for protecting the individuals gathered in the zones meant to ensure their safety.

The UN Security Council has added new concepts of safe havens meant to provide protection for civilians, known as "safe areas" or "secure humanitarian areas," for instance. These are based on the Geneva Convention notion of safety zones, but do not meet the criteria set by humanitarian law. In fact, these areas are protected by the presence of UN soldiers whose military capabilities and responsibilities with regard to protection of the civilian population are generally more symbolic than real.

☞ Gathering vulnerable populations into "protected" locations may actually result in increasing their vulnerability and the dangers they face. For instance, they may find themselves exposed—defenseless—to military operations. It is therefore crucial to establish, firmly and precisely, who has the legal and military responsibility to protect these zones and persons.

The "safe areas" created by the UN in the former Yugoslavia and the "secure humanitarian areas" set up in Rwanda did not meet the criteria set by humanitarian law for safety zones. Instead, they were the result of diplomatic and military compromises negotiated by the UN Security Council. The question of who was responsible for protecting the populations remained unclear, and the means to enforce such protection were inadequate. The tragic story

(continues)

> (*continued*)
> of the individuals gathered in these areas shows the necessity of critically examining the concept of such zones.
>
> In every case, relief organizations working in such areas must keep an eye on the protection guarantees given to the populations, as well as on the chain of responsibility and the different recourses available in such operations.

I. PROTECTED AREAS AND ZONES UNDER THE GENEVA CONVENTIONS AND PROTOCOLS

1. Nondefended Localities

These are any inhabited places situated near or in a zone where armed forces are in contact with one another and that are subject to enemy occupation, so as to avoid combat and destruction.

Humanitarian law establishes that certain zones can be specifically defined as "nondefended," so as to prevent fighting from taking place there. The aim is to spare the civilian population and civilian objects and property that are there. It follows that it is prohibited for the parties to the conflict to attack such localities, by any means whatsoever (PI Article 59.1).

The designation of a nondefended locality, and the distinctive sign that must mark it, are subject to detailed regulations (PI Articles 59.5–59.7). The parties to the conflict must agree on the signs that will mark such localities when they set them up.

Specific conditions must be met to ensure that a locality can be defined as nondefended:

- all combatants, as well as mobile weapons and mobile military equipment, must have been evacuated;
- no hostile use shall be made of fixed military installations or establishments;
- no acts of hostility shall be committed by the authorities or by the population; and
- no activities in support of military operations shall be undertaken (PI Article 59.2).

2. Hospital Zones and Localities

These are zones and localities organized on the territory of a party to the conflict or on occupied territory the aim of which is to protect wounded and sick members of the armed forces, as well as the medical personnel assigned to each zone, from the effects of war. The First Geneva Convention suggests that states establish such localities even in times of peace and that they sign ad hoc agreements with the adverse party in times of conflict. To this effect, the Convention provides a "Draft Agreement Relating to Hospital Zones and Localities" (Annex I).

The parties concerned must conclude agreements on mutual recognition of the hospital zones and localities they have created, which must be marked by the appropriate distinctive emblem. This emblem consists of a red cross, red crescent, or red lion and sun, on a white background placed on the outer precincts and on the buildings (GCI Article 23 and Annex I).

3. Hospital and Safety Zones and Localities

The Fourth Geneva Convention reiterates the notion of hospital zones and localities set forth in the First Convention (for the wounded and sick members of the armed forces). In this case, the localities must be set up to protect civilians from the effects of war. The hospital and safety zones and localities—also established on the territory of a party to the conflict or in occupied territory—are organized so as to protect the wounded, sick, and aged persons, children under fifteen, expectant mothers, and mothers of children under seven, as well as those meant to be protected by the hospital zones and localities listed above. Again, such localities should be foreseen in times of peace and agreed on between the adverse parties in times of war (GCIV Article 14 and Annex I).

This Convention also reiterates that the Protecting Powers and the International Committee of the Red Cross (ICRC) are "invited to lend their good offices in order to facilitate the institution and recognition of these hospital and safety zones and localities" (GCIV Article 14).

Hospital and safety zones must be marked by means of oblique red bands on a white ground, placed on the buildings and outer precincts. This is a distinctive emblem protected by the Geneva Conventions, and its perfidious use or failure to respect it are grave breaches of the Conventions, and are therefore war crimes (PI Article 85). Finally, zones reserved exclusively for the wounded and sick will be marked by a red cross (red crescent, red lion or sun) emblem on a white ground (GCIV Article 14 and Annex I).

4. Neutralized Zones

Neutralized zones may be established in regions where fighting is taking place. Such zones are intended to shelter the following persons, without distinction, from the effects of war: wounded and sick combatants or noncombatants, and civilian persons who take no part in hostilities and who perform no work of a military character while they reside in the zones. Parties to the conflict, neutral states, or humanitarian organizations may take the initiative to create a neutralized zone.

The parties to the conflict must conclude and sign a written agreement identifying the beginning and duration of the zone's neutralization, as well as the details of its geographic location, administration, food supply, and supervision (GCIV Article 15).

5. Demilitarized Zones

These are zones in which it is prohibited for the parties to the conflict to carry out military operations. Parties to the conflict are also prohibited from using these zones for any purpose related to the conduct of military operations.

These zones must be established by an express agreement, concluded either in peacetime or after the outbreak of hostilities. It can be verbal or written and concluded directly by the parties to the conflict or through the intermediary of a Protecting Power or an impartial humanitarian organization. The party that controls a demilitarized zone must clearly mark it, to the extent possible, with the signs agreed on with the other party.

To be qualified as "demilitarized," a zone must meet the following conditions:

- all combatants, as well as mobile weapons and mobile military equipment, must have been evacuated;
- no hostile use shall be made of fixed military installations or establishments;
- no acts of hostility shall be committed by the authorities or by the population; and
- any activity linked to the military effort must have ceased (PI Article 60).

No one party to the conflict may unilaterally revoke the status of a demilitarized zone, unless one of the parties to the conflict fails to respect these conditions or uses the zone for purposes related to the conduct of military operations. In such cases, the other party is released from its obligations under the initial agreement. In such an eventuality, the zone loses its status but continues to enjoy the protection provided by the other provisions of humanitarian law (PI Articles 60.6 and 60.7).

II. NEW SAFE AREAS ESTABLISHED BY THE UN SECURITY COUNCIL

It is important to note the terms of the agreements that must be the basis for any of the zones listed earlier. In Iraq, for instance, the UN Security Council established a demilitarized zone along the border with Kuwait, in consultation with both states concerned (S/RES/687 of April 3, 1991). This follows the regulations set forth by international humanitarian law. On the other hand, several other kinds of "zones" were set up by various states in Iraq, such as the U.S.-imposed "no-fly zones" in the north and south (covering about 60 percent of the territory), the aim of which is to protect the Kurdish and Shiite populations and which prohibits any flights as well as any antiaircraft activity; and a "safety zone" in the north (enforced by the United States, France, and the United Kingdom) meant to receive Kurdish refugees. These zones—though created on the basis of the UN Security Council Resolution 688, which condemned the "repression of the Iraqi civilian population [including] in Kurdish populated areas" (S/RES/688 of April 5, 1991)—are not recognized by Iraq and hence do not meet the legal criteria set by the Geneva Conventions and Protocol. They therefore do not make it possible to establish the responsibility of each actor with regard to the population.

1. Safe Areas

Safe area is the term that was given to the safety zones created by the UN in the Republic of Bosnia and Herzegovina. The UN Security Council first created the concept of "safe areas," also known as *safe havens,* for Srebrenica and its surroundings, by Resolution 819 of April 16, 1993 (S/RES/819), and then extended it to Tuzla, Zepa, Bihac, Gorazde, and Sarajevo, by Resolution 824 of May 6, 1993 (S/RES/824).

The aim of these resolutions was to prohibit any military activities inside and around these areas and to allow the deployment of UNPROFOR (the UN Protection Force), which was meant to ensure delivery of humanitarian assistance. Both resolutions were adopted on the basis of Chapter VII of the UN Charter, which makes them mandatory for all states, and were not subject to an ad hoc agreement between the parties to the conflict. Furthermore, in Resolution 836 of June 4, 1993 (S/RES/836), also adopted under its Chapter VII mandate, the Security Council authorized UNPROFOR to use force to "deter attacks against the safe areas."

This set of resolutions and military means failed to make the parties to the conflict respect the safe areas. When the Bosnian Serb army took Srebrenica in July 1995, they massacred a large part of the civilian population; more than seven thousand people were declared missing. The UN soldiers whose mission it was to protect this safe haven did not resort to force to protect the civilians, as their mandate authorized. Hence, this new concept of "safe areas" contains a major defect: it dilutes the responsibility for protecting the populations.

2. Secure Humanitarian Areas

In May 1994, the UN Security Council expanded the mandate of the UN Assistance Mission for Rwanda (UNAMIR, created by Resolution 912 of April 21, 1994) to allow it to establish and maintain secure humanitarian areas. It also recognized that UNAMIR might be required to use force to protect the populations at risk, UN and other humanitarian personnel, or the means of delivery and distribution of humanitarian relief (S/RES/918, May 17, 1994).

Yet the only "secure humanitarian area" that was created in Rwanda was not set up by UN-AMIR. Operation Turquoise, as it was known, was established on July 3, 1994, as a French initiative, backed by the UN Security Council. It covered the southwestern region of Rwanda, bordered by the districts of Cyangugu, Gikongoro, and the south of Kibuye. The authority of a foreign state to create this zone was based on Resolution 929—adopted on June 22, 1994, under Chapter VII of the UN Charter—which expressly authorized armed forces "under national command and control" to contribute to "the security and protection of displaced persons, refugees and civilians at risk" (S/RES/929). The French, Senegalese, and Mauritians who participated in this operation were hence authorized to use force to protect this zone.

When the French army withdrew and was replaced by UN peacekeepers, under a different mandate, the population that was still gathered in this area was subject to attacks and killings by the Rwandan army. Six thousand to eight thousand disappeared. Once again, the responsibilities of the UN force were not specific enough, with regard to the protection of the population, to prevent these massacres.

(Additional information concerning the authority of the Security Council under Chapter VII of the UN Charter and on the conditions governing the UNPROFOR's and UNAMIR's mandates to use force can be found in the entries on ➔ **peacekeeping; Security Council of the UN; self-defense.**)

➔ **Peacekeeping; Protection; Public order**

📖 **For Additional Information:**

ICRC. *ICRC's Response to the Dangers Resulting From the Conduct of Hostilities*. Geneva: Author, June 1995.
Roberts, Adam. "Humanitarian Issues and Agencies as Triggers for International Military Action." *International Review of the Red Cross* 839 (September 2000): 673–98.

■ PROTECTED OBJECTS AND PROPERTY

Humanitarian law establishes provisions for the general protection of civilian objects and property. It forbids attacks, reprisals, or other acts of violence against such objects, in both internal and international conflicts.

Humanitarian law also sets forth certain more specific rules to reinforce the protection of some of these objects. This specific protection is sometimes linked to the fact that the objects in question carry a distinctive emblem that is protected under humanitarian law. This strengthened protection concerns objects such as

- medical units, vehicles, and other transport (PI Articles 12 and 21; PII Article 11);
- cultural objects and places of worship (PI Article 53; PII Article 16);
- protection of objects indispensable to the survival of the civilian population (PI Article 54; PII Article 14);
- natural environment (PI Article 55);
- works and installations containing dangerous forces (PI Article 56; PII Article 15);
- nondefended localities (PI Article 59); and
- demilitarized zones (PI Article 60).

I. Civilian Objects

Civilian objects are defined as all objects that are not military objectives. Military objectives are limited to objects that, by their nature, location, purpose, or use, make an effective contribution to military action and whose total or partial destruction, capture, or neutralization offers a definite military advantage. In case of doubt concerning an object normally used for civilian purposes—such as a place of worship, a house or other dwelling, or a school—the parties to a conflict must presume that such object is not being used for military purposes (PI Article 52).

Humanitarian law prohibits acts of violence, attacks, and reprisals against civilian objects. Attacks that strike both military objectives and civilian objects indiscriminately are forbidden, as are those whose primary purpose is to spread terror among the civilian population (PI Article 51). Humanitarian law establishes specific precautions that must be taken to limit the effects of attacks on civilian objects and populations (PI Article 57 and 58). Military commanders have the obligation to ensure that these measures are implemented.

Whereas requisition is allowed under certain conditions, pillage is strictly prohibited (GCIV Article 33; PII Article 4.2.g). Furthermore, extensive destruction and appropriation of property that is not justified by military necessity is considered a grave breach of the Geneva Conventions (GCI Article 50, GCII Article 51, GCIII Article 130, and GCIV Article 147).

This protection is complemented by a corollary obligation, which imposes the obligation on armed forces not to use goods or persons in order to "render certain points or areas immune from military operations, in particular in attempts to shield military objectives from attacks or to shield, favor or impede military operations." The Conventions further specify that medical units must under no circumstances be used to shield military objectives from attacks (PI Articles 51.7 and 12).

This specific protection granted to medical units is further developed in the entry on ➔ **medical services**.

☞ Humanitarian and relief organizations have the duty to ensure that relief supplies are not diverted and used for military purposes. Otherwise, such organizations risk losing the protection to which they are entitled under the status of civilians and will be exposed to military operations.

➔ **Attacks; Methods of warfare; Military objectives; Pillage; Reprisals; Requisition; War; War crimes/Crimes against humanity**

II. Cultural Objects and Places of Worship

International law protects the cultural and spiritual heritage of all peoples (historic monuments, works of art, places of worship). In cases of armed conflict, these cultural objects and places of worship must be respected and safeguarded from the possible effects of war (PI Articles 53 and 85.4.d; PII Article 16). The Convention for the Protection of Cultural Property in the Event of Armed Conflict was adopted under the aegis of the UN Educational, Scientific and Cultural Organization (UNESCO) on May 14, 1954, specifically for that purpose. The Convention establishes precise rules for the protection of such objects and for the role to be played by UNESCO in this realm.

Cultural property should be marked with a special distinctive emblem: a shield consisting of a royal blue triangle above a royal blue square on a white background. ➔ **Distinctive (or protective) emblems, signs, and signals**

III. Enemy Property

This term describes military objectives and civilian objects belonging to the enemy. Civilian objects remain entitled to protection at all times. Such objects may not be used for military purposes or selected as a military objective and, furthermore, must be specifically protected in the case of an attack on nearby military objectives. ➔ **Attacks**

IV. Objects Indispensable to the Survival of the Civilian Population

Food products, agricultural areas for the production of foodstuffs, crops, livestock, drinking water installations and supplies, and irrigation works are considered by humanitarian law as goods that are essential to the survival of the civilian population, and are protected as such. This is tied to the fact that humanitarian law strictly prohibits the starvation of civilians as a method of warfare (PI Article 54; PII Article 14), as well as any use of terror against them. ➔ **Methods (and means) of warfare**

Two provisions are meant to ensure the protection of such goods:

- It is prohibited to attack, destroy, remove, or render such goods useless, for the specific purpose of depriving the civilian population of these objects (PI Article 54.2; PII Article 14).

    This prohibition does not apply if the objects are used by a party to the conflict as sustenance solely for the members of its armed forces, or in the case of imperative military necessity. If the objects are used in direct support of military action, they may be attacked, provided that in no event shall such actions result in the starvation of the civilian population or force its displacement (PI Article 54.3; PII Article 14).

- It is forbidden to prevent such goods from being supplied or to hinder relief operations delivering such supplies. Furthermore, these objects must not be made the object of reprisals (PI Article 54.4).

    International humanitarian law establishes that, if the civilian population is suffering undue hardship owing to a lack of supplies essential to its survival, such as foodstuff and medical supplies, relief societies are entitled to undertake relief actions for the civilian population (PII Article 18). It is prohibited to deprive the civilian population of such goods and to forbid or prevent relief actions from taking place. The list of essential supplies that must be provided is longer in the case of international armed conflicts than internal ones (PI Articles 69 and 70).

    The Occupying or Detaining Power has the obligation to ensure that such relief and supplies are provided to the persons who find themselves under its authority due to situations of occupation, detention, or internment (GCIV Articles 55, 60, and 81). Furthermore, such persons have the right to receive individual parcels or collective shipments containing relief or other supplies, whether they are in occupied territory or interned (GCIV Articles 62, 63, and 108–111).

☞ It is forbidden to prevent relief organizations from delivering supplies to civilian populations suffering from undue hardship caused by the lack of adequate food products and medical supplies, whether the hardship is due to the conflict in general (PI Article 70; PII Article 18) or because the civilians are in occupied or besieged territory (GCIV Articles 59, 17, and 23).

The parties to the conflict have the obligation to protect relief consignments and facilitate their rapid distribution. They only have the right to set the technical conditions under which such passage is permitted and to request guarantees of supervision over the distribution of the relief to the civilian population (PI Article 70.3).

The free passage of objects indispensable to the survival of the civilian population is thus guaranteed by international humanitarian law (GCIV Articles 59, 17, and 23; PI Article 70; PII Article 18) and is linked to the independent monitoring of distribution by the entity supplying the objects.

The list of supplies essential to the survival of the population includes not only food and medical supplies, but also clothing, bedding, means of shelter, objects necessary for religious worship, and any other indispensable objects (PI Article 69).

→   **Assistance; Relief; Supplies**

V. Natural Environment

Humanitarian law establishes specific provisions for the protection of the natural environment. Thus, it is prohibited to employ methods or means of warfare that are intended, or may be expected, to cause widespread, long-term, and severe damage to the natural environment and that may threaten the health or survival of the population (PI Articles 35.3 and 55). This comes from the principle that establishes that hostilities must not destroy objects that are indispensable to the survival of the civilian population (PII Article 14).

☞ The statute of the permanent International Criminal Court (ICC) was adopted on July 17, 1998. Article 8 of the statute defines the war crimes over which the Court will have jurisdiction, once the conditions required to trigger the exercise of its jurisdiction have been met. Whether committed during an international or internal armed conflict, these war crimes include

- deliberately launching attacks against civilian objects;
- intentionally directing attacks against installations, material, units, or vehicles involved in a humanitarian assistance or peacekeeping mission, as long as they are entitled to the protection given to civilians or civilian objects under the international law of armed conflict;
- deliberately directing attacks against medical installations and material;
- launching attacks in the knowledge that such attacks may cause widespread, long-term, and severe damage to the natural environment, and would be clearly excessive in relation to the concrete and direct overall military advantage anticipated;
- attacking or bombarding towns, villages, dwellings, or buildings that are undefended and are not military objectives;

(continues)

> (*continued*)
>
> ▪ intentionally directing attacks against buildings dedicated to religion, education, art, science or charitable purposes, as well as historic monuments, hospitals, and places where the sick and wounded are collected, provided that such buildings are not being used for military purposes.

Similarly, works or installations containing dangerous forces (namely, dams, dikes, and nuclear electricity-generating stations)—as well as other military objectives located at or in the vicinity of these works—must not be targets of attack. This applies "even where these objects are military objectives, if such attack may cause the release of dangerous forces and consequent severe losses among the civilian population" (PI Article 56; PII Article 15).

The few derogations that are allowed are strictly regulated:

The special protection against attack . . . shall cease:
   (a) for a dam or a dyke only if it is used for other than its normal function and in regular, significant and direct support of military operations and if such attack is the only feasible way to terminate such support;
   (b) for a nuclear electrical generating station only if it provides electric power in regular, significant and direct support of military operations and if such attack is the only feasible way to terminate such support;
   (c) for other military objectives located at or in the vicinity of these works or installations only if they are used in regular, significant and direct support of military operations and if such attack is the only feasible way to terminate such support (PI Article 56.2)

Furthermore, these works or installations should be marked with a distinctive emblem consisting of a group of three bright orange circles placed on the same axis (PI Article 56.7; PI Annex I, Article 16).

➔ **Attacks; Civilian population; Distinctive (or protective) emblems, signs, and signals; Famine; Food; International Criminal Court; Medical services; Methods (and means) of warfare; Military objectives; Population displacement; Proportionality; Protected Persons; Relief; Reprisals**

For Additional Information:

Antoine, Philippe. "International Humanitarian Law and the Protection of the Environment in Time of Armed Conflict." *International Review of the Red Cross* 291 (November–December 1992): 517–37.

Oeter, Stefan. "Protection of Civilian Objects." In *The Handbook of Humanitarian Law in Armed Conflicts*, ed. Dieter Fleck. Oxford: Oxford University Press, 1995, 169–93.

Partsch, Karl Josef. "Protection of Cultural Property." In *The Handbook of Humanitarian Law in Armed Conflicts*, ed. Dieter Fleck. Oxford: Oxford University Press, 1995, 377–404.

Toman, Jiri. *The Protection of Cultural Property in the Event of Armed Conflict.* Paris: UNESCO, 1996.

▪ PROTECTED PERSONS

Each of the four Geneva Conventions and their Additional Protocols applies to a specific category of person (with the Protocols applying more generally to "victims"). They define the rights and protections that must be respected and which each category is entitled to receive. The provisions vary slightly from one category to the next.

In theory, humanitarian law uses the term *protected persons* only in the context of international armed conflicts, since the exact term is not used in reference to internal armed conflicts. Nonetheless—for the sake of linguistic simplicity—we will use it in this entry to qualify the notion of protection to which individuals are entitled, including in noninternational conflicts. International humanitarian law identifies a total of fifteen categories of protected persons in the case of international armed conflicts and five in internal conflicts.

Unlike human rights law, humanitarian law does not establish universal rights applicable to all individuals. Instead, it defines categories of individuals to whom it grants specific rights and protection, either because these people are more exposed to the risks engendered by conflict or because they are naturally more vulnerable. The risk of this categorization is that certain individuals may not receive adequate protection if the actors in a conflict do not recognize them as belonging to one of the categories of protected persons. To counter this risk, humanitarian law also establishes certain fundamental guarantees that are applicable to all individuals in times of conflict.

Certain categories of protected persons have the right to additional protection, derived from their use of a distinctive emblem in a manner foreseen by the Conventions and Protocol I.

➜   **Distinctive (or protective) emblems, signs, and signals**

☞ An individual who has the status of a protected person under international humanitarian law has the right to special protection and reinforced relief.

- Individuals who cannot benefit from this status are nonetheless protected by the minimum rights and fundamental guarantees to which all individuals are entitled under the 1949 Geneva Conventions.
- Protocols I and II, of 1977, provide a more flexible definition of the different categories of protected persons, and consolidate the provisions that are meant to ensure a basic level of protection. The Protocols also list the fundamental guarantees that must be secured for all victims in a national or international situation of conflict who do not benefit from a specific preferential regime or categorization (PI Article 75 and 1.2; PII Article 4).
- Article 3 common to the four Geneva Conventions establishes a less comprehensive set of minimum guarantees applicable at all times to all persons.
- ➜   **Fundamental guarantees; Situations and persons not expressly covered by humanitarian law**

---

1. International Armed Conflict

In times of international armed conflict, humanitarian law provides for fifteen categories of protected persons—four related to combatants and eleven concerning civilians:

1. *The wounded and sick in armed forces in the field*
   Such persons are protected by the entire First Geneva Convention (in particular, Articles 12–18) and by Additional Protocol I (in particular, Articles 8–20).
2. *The wounded, sick and shipwrecked members of armed forces at sea*
   Such persons are protected by the entire Second Geneva Convention (in particular, Articles 12–21) and by Additional Protocol I (in particular, Articles 8–20).
3. *Medical and religious personnel attached to armed forces*
   Such persons are protected by the First and Second Geneva Conventions (GCI Articles 24 and 25; GCII Articles 36 and 37).
4. *Prisoners of war*
   Such persons are protected by the entire Third Geneva Convention (in particular, Articles 4 and 12–16) and by Additional Protocol I (Articles 43–47). ➔ **Prisoners of war**
5. *Wounded and sick civilians*
   Such persons are protected by the Fourth Geneva Convention (in particular, Articles 3 and 16–23) and by Additional Protocol I (Articles 10–16).
   Pregnant women, maternity cases, newborn infants, and infirm persons are included in the humanitarian law definition of "wounded and sick" (PI Article 8). ➔ **Wounded and sick**
6. *Medical and religious civilian personnel*
   This category is defined, and such persons are protected, by the Fourth Geneva Convention (Article 20) and by Additional Protocol I (Article 15). ➔ **Medical personnel**
7. *Parliamentarians*
   Such persons are protected by the Fourth 1907 Hague Convention, on the laws and customs of war.
8. *Personnel of civil defense organizations*
   Such persons are protected by Additional Protocol I (Articles 61–68).
9. *Relief personnel*
   Such persons are protected by Additional Protocol I (Article 71). ➔ **Humanitarian and relief personnel**
10. *The civilian population and civilian persons*
    Such persons are mainly protected by the Fourth Geneva Convention and by the Additional Protocol I (Articles 48–67). This category includes
    —the entire civilian population: all civilians must be protected against the effects of hostilities—in other words, they may not be the object of attack (Articles 48–51). They must also be able to receive all the necessary relief (GCIV Article 23; PI Articles 68–71). They also benefit from the fundamental guarantees protected by the conventions (Article 3 common to the four Geneva Conventions; PI Article 75);
    —civilians who find themselves in the hands of a party to a conflict or an Occupying Power of which they are not nationals benefit from the status of protected persons (GCIV Article 4). Civilian status in occupied territories is defined and protected by the Fourth Geneva Convention (Articles 27–141, which include the regulations applicable to internees).
    Nationals of a state not party to the 1949 Geneva Conventions are not protected by the Conventions' provisions.
    Nationals of a neutral state who find themselves in the territory of a belligerent state, as well as nationals of an ally of the belligerent state ("cobelligerent state"), shall not be regarded as protected persons as long as their state of nationality maintains normal diplomatic representation with the state in which they find themselves (GCIV Article 4).

Additional Protocol I has relaxed the strict definition of the categories of protected persons and consolidated the provisions ensuring a minimal level of protection. It also establishes the fundamental guarantees that remain applicable to all victims of a situation of conflict and who do not benefit from a specific, preferential regime or categorization (PI Article 75).

→ **Civilian populations; Fundamental guarantees**

11. *Persons detained, interned, or otherwise deprived of liberty* (GCIV Articles 41, 42, and 79–135; PI Article 75). → **Detention; Internment**

12. *The population of an occupied territory* (GCIV Articles 47–78; GPI Articles 63 and 69). → **Occupied territories**

13. *Women*
   Women are protected by Additional Protocol I (in particular, Article 76; GCIV Article 14). Women prisoners of war, internees, and detainees also benefit from specific protection under the Third and Fourth Geneva Conventions. → **Women**

14. *Children*
   Children are protected by Additional Protocol I (in particular, Articles 77 and 78). Children prisoners of war, internees, and detainees also benefit from specific protection under the Third and Fourth Geneva Conventions. → **Children**

15. *Foreigners, refugees, and stateless persons* (GCIV Articles 35–46; PI Article 73). → **Refugees; Stateless persons**

2. Internal Armed Conflict

In times of noninternational armed conflict, humanitarian law defines five categories of protected persons and specific guarantees:

1. All individuals must benefit from the minimum guarantees (Article 3 common to the four Geneva Conventions; PII Article 4). → **Fundamental guarantees**
2. The civilian population and objects indispensable to their survival (PII Articles 13 and 14) → **Civilians**
3. Persons deprived of their liberty for reasons related to the armed conflict (PII Article 5) → **Detention**
4. Wounded and sick civilians (GCIV Article 3; PII Articles 7, 8) → **Wounded and sick**
5. Medical and religious personnel (PII Article 9) → **Medical personnel**

3. The Rights of Protected Persons

The Geneva Conventions establish specific rights for protected persons in terms of protection and assistance, in times of international or internal armed conflict. The failure to respect the status of protected persons generally constitutes a war crime (GCIV Article 29).

The authorities that have power over the protected persons must treat them according to the rules and norms to which they committed under the Conventions and their Additional Protocols. The party to the conflict in whose hands protected persons find themselves is responsible for the treatment of such persons by its agents, irrespective of any individual responsibility that may be incurred.

→ **Family reunification; War crimes**

Representatives of Protecting Powers and of the ICRC are authorized to visit any place where protected persons are located (GCIV Article 130). This possibility is extended to other relief organizations.

Protected persons have the right to appeal decisions that affect them and address the Protecting Powers, the International Committee of the Red Cross, the National Red Cross, or the Red Crescent Society of the country where they find themselves, as well as to any organization that might assist them (GCIV Article 30). The local authorities may not refuse access to protected persons, except within the limits established by military necessity and security.

→ **Protecting Powers**

UN personnel can also benefit from specific provisions of humanitarian law. In situations in which UN personnel is involved, it is important to make a distinction between the humanitarian personnel—carrying out relief operations and protected under their status as civilians—and the military personnel—which, for instance, may be participating in peacekeeping operations.

→ **Humanitarian and relief personnel**

☞ The statute of a permanent International Criminal Court (ICC) was adopted on July 17, 1998, and will have jurisdiction over individuals accused of war crimes, crimes against humanity, and genocide. Its definition of war crimes includes intentionally directing attacks against medical personnel and units, personnel using the distinctive emblems protected by the Geneva Conventions, and personnel involved in humanitarian assistance or peacekeeping missions (as long as these persons are entitled to the protection granted to civilians under the law of armed conflict). Once established, the ICC will be able to prosecute the perpetrators of such attacks, whether committed in international or internal armed conflict (Articles 8.2.b.iii and 8.2.e.ii and iii of ICC statute).

→ **Children; Civilian population; Detention; Fundamental guarantees; Humanitarian and relief personnel; International humanitarian law; Internment; Journalists; Medical duties; Military objectives; Occupied territories; Prisoners of war; Protection; Relief; Security; Situations and persons not expressly covered by humanitarian law; Women; Wounded and sick**

📖 **For Additional Information:**

Blondel, Jean-Luc. "Assistance to Protected Persons." *International Review of the Red Cross* 260 (September–October 1987): 451–68.

Fleck, Dieter, ed. *The Handbook of Humanitarian Law in Armed Conflicts*. Oxford: Oxford University Press, 1995, 209–376.

■ PROTECTING POWERS

To ensure the protection of the general population in times of conflict, humanitarian law establishes a system of Protecting Powers, meant to safeguard the interests of the persons protected by the Geneva Conventions and their Protocols (GCI–III, Articles 8–11; GCIV Articles 9–12; PI Article 5).

I. FUNCTION AND MANDATE OF THE PROTECTING POWERS

1. Function

This system was set up to enable the adverse parties to a conflict to maintain a dialogue concerning the protection of their populations.

The Conventions provide that, from the beginning of a conflict, each party has the obligation to appoint a Protecting Power to ensure the implementation of the Conventions and Protocols. The delegates of the appointed Protecting Powers are subject to the approval of the adverse party with which they are to carry out their duties.

2. Mandate

The Protecting Powers' mandate is to monitor and safeguard the interests of the parties to the conflict and their nationals. To this end, they enjoy certain specific rights and duties (GIV Articles 30 and 143):

- the right to visit persons protected by the Geneva Conventions and their Additional Protocols;
- the right to evaluate their living conditions in cases of detention or in occupied territories;
- the right to supervise the distribution of relief supplies;
- the duty to ensure that relief operations are of a civilian and impartial nature and to prevent this relief from being diverted for military purposes;
- the right to supervise the concrete implementation of protective measures for protected persons, especially in cases of detention, internment, and occupied territory;
- the right to ensure that judicial guarantees are respected, in case of a trial, especially in cases possibly involving the death penalty;
- protected persons have the right to refer their cases to Protecting Powers.
- → **Detention; Internment; Occupied territory; Prisoners of war; Relief; Supplies**

II. WHO MAY TAKE ON THE RESPONSIBILITIES OF THE PROTECTING POWER?

1. States

In theory, Protecting Powers are representatives of states that are not involved in the conflict at hand and that accept to verify that humanitarian law is being respected on the territory of a given party to the conflict. In practice, since the Geneva Conventions were adopted in 1949, no state has ever accepted this role for any of the conflicts that have taken place. Through this refusal, states show their lack of concrete commitment to actually defending the implementation of humanitarian law. The Geneva Conventions had foreseen this diplomatic weakness and set up several provisions for substitution mechanisms. Also, the ICRC is formally under the obligation to offer its good offices so as to facilitate the designation of such Protecting Powers.

2. Substitute Protecting Powers: The ICRC and Humanitarian Organizations

The ICRC's mediation role is firmly established in the Conventions. It must ask each party to a conflict to provide it with a list of at least five states that it would consider acceptable as a Protecting Power in relation to an adverse party (GCI–III Article 8, GCIV Article 9, and PI Article 5).

If, despite this intervention, the parties to the conflict still do not succeed in designating a Protecting Power, the Conventions establish that the ICRC will act as substitute Protecting Power and take on its functions. Other impartial humanitarian organizations also have the possibility of taking on the role of Protecting Power if the relevant parties accept their offer of services.

In such cases, the substitutes are no longer states but organizations, presenting all guarantees of impartiality and effectiveness. After they have been accepted by the parties to the conflict, these organizations can take on the functions of the Protecting Powers: monitoring the application and defense of the rights and obligations set forth in the Geneva Conventions for protected persons (GCI–III Article 11, GCIV Article 12, and PI Article 5).

It is important to note that this system of substitution is subject to the reciprocal consent of the parties to the conflict, and therefore can fail. In such cases, the Geneva Conventions impose the presence and activities of humanitarian organizations on the parties to the conflict (GIV Articles 30 and 143).

☞ If the parties to a conflict fail to designate a Protecting Power or substitute of their own accord, they are nonetheless under the obligation to

- request that an organization such as the ICRC take on the humanitarian functions meant to be performed by Protecting Powers under the Geneva Conventions and
- accept offers of services of such an organization.

In practice, this role—which is central to the proper implementation of the Geneva Conventions—is fulfilled almost exclusively by the ICRC.

The provisions concerning a Protecting Power or substitute create a space for humanitarian protection that can be filled by international and nongovernmental organizations present in situations of conflict (GCI–III Article 10, GCIV Article 11, and PI Article 5.4).

→ **Death penalty; Detention; Judicial guarantees; Occupied territory; Prisoners of war; Protection; Red Cross; Relief**

📖 For Additional Information:

Aldrich, George H., and Christine M. Chinkin. "The Hague Peace Conferences: The Laws of War on Land." *American Journal of International Law* 94 (2000): 42.

Wolfrum, Rudiger. "Enforcement of International Humanitarian Law." In *The Handbook of Humanitarian Law in Armed Conflicts*, ed. Dieter Fleck. Oxford: Oxford University Press, 1995, 543–44.

■ PROTECTION

Individuals have a legal status that is defined by national and international laws. This status is the basis on which their protection is ensured, in the context of society.

The protection of individuals stands at the crossroads between defense of individual rights and constraints relating to public safety. The national legal status of individuals is reinforced by various elements contained in international law that grant specific rights to individuals in times of disturbance or conflict.

It is important not to confuse the notion of protection with that of physical safety. The only entities that can assure the safety of individuals are those which control the use of public force. Law offers only legal protection: it limits the way in which force or restraint may be used against individuals, and it sets forth the concrete means to uphold and defend these laws and rights. Humanitarian organizations cannot physically interpose themselves between individuals and a source of danger to ensure their safety. They can, however, monitor the respect for the rules of protection established by international humanitarian law for the benefit of populations in danger.

➔   **Human rights; Individual recourse; Respect for international humanitarian law; Responsibility; Safety**

☞ Protecting means recognizing that individuals have rights and that the authorities who exercise power over them have obligations. It means defending the legal existence of individuals, alongside their physical existence. It means attaching the juridical link of responsibility to the chain of assistance measures that guarantee the survival of individuals.

The notion of "protection" therefore reflects all the concrete measures that enable individuals at risk to enjoy the rights and assistance foreseen for them by international conventions.

In each case, relief actions are based on laws established for the benefit of protected persons. Relief organizations must both know and advocate these laws concretely. If these laws are not used, relief action risks weakening the framework of international legal protection set up for individuals in danger.

When providing relief in times of conflict, humanitarian organizations therefore must not separate the provision of assistance from protection. These organizations must respect the rights that are guaranteed for victims and for relief organizations by humanitarian law and must report any violations encountered in the exercise of their work.

I. Protection in Times of Peace or of Tension

In times of peace, the nationality of an individual establishes his or her personal legal status. The status itself is defined by national laws. These, for the most part, center around the concept of a "social contract," whereby society confers certain rights and obligations on its members, in exchange for which it ensures their safety and respect for public order. This means that the state has the responsibility for

- determining, through laws, the rights and obligations of individual members of the national community;
- watching over the physical safety of individuals by defending the public order;
- setting up the legal institutions to which victims can have recourse in case their rights are violated, as well as the appropriate legal procedures to punish breaches of the public order.

The national laws that determine the legal status of individuals must be in conformity with the general principles and rights set forth in international human rights conventions. ➔ **Human rights; Nationality**

In exceptional circumstances, however, such as situations of internal disturbances or tension, states may suspend the normal application of certain individual rights, to ensure the defense of the country. In such cases, the authorities usually declare a state of emergency or a state of siege, if applicable.

Nevertheless, even under such conditions, there are certain rights that the state may not suspend or infringe on in any way. These are the fundamental guarantees that remain applicable at all times, for all individuals. These rights, which include judicial guarantees, are enumerated in international human rights conventions. They are "nonderogable," inviolable, and inalienable.

The numerous conventions set forth various mechanisms to which individuals or states may have recourse in case individuals' human rights or fundamental freedoms are violated.

International Legal Status of Individuals

Although the legal status of individuals is defined mainly by national laws, there are various elements in international law that confer an international legal status on individuals. These elements come from both human rights conventions, applicable in times of peace or of tension, and the 1949 Geneva Conventions on humanitarian law applicable in times of armed conflict.

The manifestations of this international legal status for individuals are as follows:

- Mandatory and peremptory international human rights norms and, in particular, international standards regulating the treatment of individuals who are specifically protected by international law. These norms enforce a limited number of objective rights for individuals.
- Recourse for individuals or states before international organs, judicial or not, in case of violations of the rules of international law relating to the treatment of individuals.
- ➔ **Fundamental guarantees; Human rights; Individual recourse; Judicial guarantees; Nationality; Protected persons; Public order; Siege**

II. PROTECTION IN TIMES OF CONFLICT

In times of armed conflict, the protection provided by an individual's own state may no longer be sufficient to protect individuals, either because they are exposed to an adverse party or because their own state authorities have adopted restrictive measures that affect them. These restrictions may concern individual human rights and the operation of the justice system, for instance.

Humanitarian law therefore sets forth the principle guarantees that states involved in a conflict must grant individuals (whether of their own nationality or that of the adverse party). It develops a protection mechanism based on two complementary aspects of its rules and regulations:

- provisions that grant an international legal status to individuals in danger;
- international regulations addressing relief actions.

1. International Legal Status of Individuals under Humanitarian Law

International humanitarian law establishes categories of protected persons and goods, to which it grants a specific legal status. This status has rights and guarantees attached to it, which states undertake to protect.

These rights and guarantees are different for each category of persons, since the needs differ depending on the individuals and situations. For instance, individuals who are interned or detained by the adverse party, prisoners of war, wounded and sick persons, a hospital, or a hydraulic dam will all require different protective measures.

Humanitarian law also establishes the responsibilities of the authority that has control over the protected persons. The failure to respect the status of protected persons, by this authority or its agents, can be considered a war crime.

There are mechanisms, also established by humanitarian law, that monitor the respect for these rights, through the system of Protecting Powers. This system establishes that individuals may address or file claims directly with representatives of these Protecting Powers and that the Protecting Powers must always have access to protected persons so as to monitor their condition. In practice, the ICRC or other humanitarian organizations fulfill the mission of the Protecting Power.

Other branches of international law also provide recourse for individuals in case their rights, established by human rights conventions (in particular, those concerning torture), are violated.

→ **Humanitarian and relief personnel; Individual recourse; Protected objects and property; Protected persons; Protecting Powers; Universal jurisdiction; War crimes/ Crimes against humanity**

2. Protection for Refugees

Refugees are individuals who no longer benefit from the protection of their state of origin. The 1951 Convention Relating to the Status of Refugees grants them international protection, through the intermediary of UNHCR. UNHCR is responsible for making sure that refugees, recognized as such, obtain individual, legal refugee status from another state. To this effect, it ensures that people who have fled their state due to fear of persecution and who can no longer benefit from the protection of their own state can make a request for asylum in another country.

While the refugees wait for their official asylum status, UNHCR has no means of ensuring their physical safety. However, it remains responsible for monitoring the fairness of procedures that grant refugee status, and for making sure that appropriate measures are taken to secure refugee camps, and that the refugees are not subjected to forced repatriation or expulsion (*refoulement*) toward a source of danger.

Finally, UNHCR is also responsible for coordinating the relief that will guarantee at least humane living conditions for the refugees while they wait to obtain their official status.

→ **Refugees**

3. Regulations Concerning Relief Action

International humanitarian law authorizes and regulates concrete relief actions undertaken by the ICRC or impartial humanitarian organizations for the benefit of protected persons. Nonetheless, the parties to the conflict remain responsible for the fate of the protected populations. Hence, they are not allowed to prevent relief actions. At the same time, they are not allowed to depend exclusively on outside initiatives to ensure the survival of the populations and individuals over whom they exercise control.

Relief actions take place in a broader framework of responsibility toward humanity. Humanitarian organizations must understand and fulfill their share of this responsibility. They must also remind the political and military authorities involved of their responsibilities.

➔ **Relief**

4. Protection of Medical Secrecy

No person carrying out medical activities can be compelled to give out any information concerning the wounded and sick who are, or have been, under his or her care, as long as the medical person considers that such information might prove harmful to the patients concerned or to their families. This applies whether the person requesting the information belongs to the adverse party to the conflict or to the medical person's own party, except in cases foreseen by the person's domestic laws. However, regulations concerning the compulsory notification of communicable diseases must be respected (PI Article 16.3).

➔ **Medical ethics**

➔ **Children; Civilians; Detention; Displaced persons; Duty of commanders; Human rights; Humanitarian and relief personnel; Individual recourse; International humanitarian law; Military objectives; Occupied territories; Prisoners of war; Protected objects and property; Protected persons; Protecting Powers; Refugees; Safety; Stateless persons; Women; Wounded and sick persons**

📖 **For Additional Information:**

Blondel, Jean-Luc. "Assistance to Protected Persons." *International Review of the Red Cross* 260 (September–October 1987): 451–68.

■ PUBLIC ORDER

In humanitarian law, the terms *public order* or *law and order* describe the general conditions that must exist so that individuals can enjoy their rights and freedoms.

States are responsible for defending public safety. However, in all circumstances, even when taking measures to defend the public order, governments must always respect certain fundamental human rights. ➔ **Fundamental guarantees**

There is no specific definition to explain the contents of the notion of "public order." It is generally understood to include both legal and physical guarantees of freedom, security, and peace of mind, which are necessary for individuals to live together in society.

The basic rules that govern public order in society and are agreed on by almost all states are codified in various international treaties. Beyond this common foundation, each society must decide for itself what framework to apply to law and order, depending on the goals of its population (or government), the country's political choices, and its material constraints.

1. National Measures to Protect Public Order

It is up to the government to prevent disturbances of public order that may threaten the collective security of individuals. To defend the public order from such threats, states may limit some individual rights, if their exercise presents a real and concrete risk of disturbing law and order.

International law recognizes the importance of safeguarding public order by allowing governments—to the extent strictly required by the urgency of a given situation—to take measures derogating from their obligations to safeguard and defend the human rights of its citizens.

☞ The government has the duty to maintain or reestablish law and order through legitimate means. The obligation to respect these "legitimate means" denotes the fact that, even during efforts to restore public order in situations of unrest or conflict, the state must protect the fundamental guarantees to which individuals are entitled under international human rights instruments and, when applicable, the Geneva Conventions and their Protocols (PI Article 75; PII Article 3.1; Article 29 of the Universal Declaration of Human Rights; Article 4 of the International Covenant on Civil and Political Rights; Article 15 of the European Convention for the Protection of Human Rights and Fundamental Freedoms; Article 27 of the American Convention on Human Rights; Article 8 of the UNESCO Convention for the Protection of Cultural Property in the Event of Armed Conflict).

→ **Fundamental guarantees**

2. Measures to Protect the International Public Order

The Security Council of the UN is responsible for defending the international public order from acts of states that threaten international peace and security. According to Chapter VII of the UN Charter (concerning Action with Respect to Threats to the Peace, Breaches of the Peace, and Acts of Aggression), responses to breaches of international public order can derogate from the principle of state sovereignty and serve to justify the UN resorting to the use of force.

The Protection of International Public Order

A reading of the decisions taken by the Security Council to date will not lead to a definition of all the acts that may endanger international law and order. Furthermore, the definition of such acts is evolving rapidly. For decades, the only acts considered "criminal" were those threatening international peace and security. Within the UN structure, only the Security Council has the authority to determine if a given situation constitutes a breach of, or threat to, peace (Article 39 of the UN Charter). According to the UN Charter, the Security Council is not responsible for enforcing the respect for law per se; however, recent conflicts have led the Council to recognize that certain grave and massive violations of humanitarian law could endanger international peace and security.

In Resolution 808 of February 22, 1993, the Security Council reaffirmed that the grave and widespread violations of international humanitarian law committed in the territory of the former Yugoslavia, in particular mass killings and the continued practice of ethnic cleansing, constituted a "threat to international peace and security" and therefore a

(continues)

(continued)

breach of the international public order. Later resolutions concerning the situations in the former Yugoslavia and Rwanda also qualified such grave violations of humanitarian law as threats to international peace and security (Resolution 827, of May 15, 1993, and Resolution 955, of November 8, 1994).

On July 17, 1998, at the outcome of a diplomatic conference in Rome organized under the aegis of the UN, states adopted the statute of a permanent International Criminal Court (ICC). Once operational, the ICC will be responsible for prosecuting individuals accused of crimes that "threaten the peace, security, and well-being of the world" (preamble of ICC statute): genocide, war crimes, and crimes against humanity. Eventually, the Court will also have jurisdiction over the crime of aggression, once states reach a common definition of the term.

The Security Council will have the authority to refer situations to the Court for investigation and prosecution. Subject to certain preconditions, the ICC may also investigate cases when a state party has referred a situation to the Prosecutor or on the Prosecutor's own initiative.

→ **International Criminal Court**

→ **Collective Security; Fundamental guarantees; Internal disturbances and tensions; International armed conflict; Intervention; Noninternational armed conflict; Peacekeeping; Safety; Sanctions (diplomatic, economic, or military); Security Council of the UN; State of emergency; UN**

📖 **For Additional Information:**

Hadden, Tom, and Colin Harvey. "The Law of Internal Crisis and Conflict." *International Review of the Red Cross* 833 (March 1999): 119–33.

R

■ RAPE

Rape is the act of obliging an individual to have sexual intercourse against his or her will, using force, violence, or any other form of coercion. It is considered a felony in the criminal laws of most countries. Rape may occur between people of the same sex, as well as of opposite sexes.

In many legislative systems, if there is insufficient evidence to prove that there was penetration or that the individual was coerced, the crime may no longer be prosecuted as "rape," and therefore a felony, but as "sexual assault" or even "sexual misconduct." In such a case, the act may not be prosecuted as a felony but perhaps as a misdemeanor. It is sometimes difficult to prove that such an act was not consensual. The victims must prove that they did not freely consent to the act. The submission may have been obtained by force, threat, abuse of authority or of trust, or other forms of coercion. Some countries have particularly high burdens of proof, such as the requirement of physical proof or even witnesses.

When this grave crime occurs between an adult and a minor, it is generally called *statutory rape.* Some countries have specific national laws that expand the possibilities for prosecuting such acts, whether they qualify as felonies or misdemeanors. These laws enable individuals who committed sexual offenses against minors to be prosecuted even if they are in a different country. Trials in such cases can also be conducted before the courts of the state of which the accused is a national, as well as before the courts of the state where the acts were committed. Such laws, prevalent mostly in Europe, were often adopted in the context of the fight against pedophilia and sex tourism.

☞ In addition to the victim's testimony, the results of a medical examination may be used to reinforce the proof that a person was raped, when the medical report certifies that there were lesions caused by the violent or forced nature of the sexual act. It is also possible to carry out psychological examinations to determine the consequences to the victim's mental state. A doctor faced with such a situation has the duty, in all circumstances, to establish such a report for the victim, as soon as possible after the events.

(continues)

> (*continued*)
>
> Many difficulties may result from making a victim testify, particularly in court, both because of the humiliation that may be suffered in the cross-examination during the trial—especially in accusatory legal systems—and because of the personal risks that may be incurred by testifying—especially if the sexual violence took place in the context of an armed conflict. This makes it all the more important for doctors—whether national doctors or foreign humanitarian doctors—to establish a medical report. It is therefore important to give victims access to doctors so that they can be examined without too much delay.
>
> ➔ **Medical duties**

Rape is a violation of international law, although it is not explicitly mentioned in most international humanitarian law texts, and in few human rights treaties. Since it can be categorized under other crimes, which are explicit violations of international law—such as violence to life and person, outrages on personal dignity, torture, or cruel, inhuman, or degrading treatment or punishment—it is forbidden under all clauses prohibiting such acts. Certain conventions and authorities that have explicitly recognized rape as a form of torture include the 1994 Inter-American Convention on the Prevention, Punishment and Eradication of Violence against Women; the 1993 UN Declaration on the Elimination of Violence against Women; the Inter-American Commission on Human Rights; the statute of the International Criminal Court (ICC); and—as will be further detailed later—the International Criminal Tribunals for the Former Yugoslavia and for Rwanda (ICTY and ICTR). ➔ **Torture**

Rape and sexual violence were long considered inevitable "collateral damage" of war. It was not distinguished from other crimes committed against civilians. Among recent examples, it appeared in Bosnia and Rwanda as a mass occurence and as a weapon of war linked to the policy of ethnic cleansing.

This crime is now formally recognized under international law as a crime against humanity and, when committed in the context of a conflict, as a war crime.

- Specific provisions of the 1949 Geneva Conventions and their Protocols are meant to protect women from attacks on their honor, outrages on personal dignity, humiliating and degrading treatment, and, in particular, rape, enforced prostitution, or any form of indecent assault, in both internal and international conflicts (GCIV Article 27; PI Article 76; PII Article 4). States parties are also under the obligation, at any time and in any place, to ensure that women are granted the fundamental guarantees provided by the Conventions, which prohibit violence to life and person, in particular murder of all kinds, mutilation, cruel treatment, and torture (GCI–GCIV common Article 3). ➔ **Detention; Fundamental guarantees; Women**
- Since rape may be categorized as torture or cruel and inhuman treatment, it is also a grave breach of the Geneva Conventions, whether the victim is male or female (GCI Article 50, GCII Article 51, GCII Article 130, and GCIV Article 147). ➔ **War crimes/Crimes against humanity**
- Rape is sometimes carried out on a systematic or massive scale, as part of a policy aimed at ethnic cleansing or as a means of terrorizing the population. According to the UN, twenty-five thousand women were raped in Rwanda during the 1994 genocide. Today, UNHCR acknowledges that rape can constitute an element of persecution and permits the recognition of the status of refugee as foreseen by the 1951 Convention Relating to the Status of Refugees. UNHCR

further recommends that, during the procedure to determine the status of a refugee, asylum seekers who may have been victims of sexual violence be treated with due regard to their suffering.

- More recently, the ICTY raised the legal status of the crime of rape, as such, to that of a crime against humanity and a war crime. The Tribunal has jurisdiction over individuals who perpetrated such crimes during the conflict. Furthermore, its Rules of Procedure and Evidence provide measures requiring a lighter burden of proof in cases of sexual assault (Article 5.g of ICTY statute and Rule 96 of its Rules of Procedure and Evidence). One-quarter of the indictments issued by the ICTY include accusations of sexual violence, which is an important legal step. However, it applies only in the specific context of this ad hoc tribunal, whose jurisdiction is restricted to crimes committed in the former Yugoslavia.

- The ICTR also has jurisdiction over rape as a crime against humanity and a war crime, in addition to which it extends the notion of grave breaches of the 1949 Geneva Conventions to include situations of internal armed conflict. It bases accusations on violations of Article 3 of Protocol II of 1977 (Article 4 of ICTR statute).

For the first time under international law, the ICTR determined that rape and sexual violence can constitute acts of genocide when committed with the intent to destroy, in whole or in part, a national, ethnic, racial, or religious group.

Rape, as Defined by the International Criminal Tribunal for Rwanda

The Akayesu judgment (ICTR-96-4-T, September 2, 1998), which found Jean-Paul Akayesu guilty of rape as a crime against humanity, among other crimes, was the first international sentence to define rape, thereby setting an important legal precedent:

The Chamber defined rape as "a physical invasion of a sexual nature, committed on a person under circumstances which are coercive. Sexual violence, including rape, is not limited to physical invasion of the human body and may include acts which do not involve penetration or even physical contact. The Chamber notes in this context that coercive circumstances need not be evidenced by a show of physical force. Threats, intimidation, extortion and other forms of duress which prey on fear or desperation may constitute coercion."

The ICTR also noted that such acts cannot be "captured in a mechanical description of objects and body parts." The Tribunal also raised the question of "cultural sensitivities involved in public discussion of intimate matters and recall[ed] the painful reluctance and inability of witnesses to disclose graphic anatomical details of the sexual violence they endured."

It also underscored that rape and sexual violence "constitute genocide in the same way as any other act as long as they were committed with the specific intent to destroy, in whole or in part, a particular group, targeted as such."

→ **Ethnic cleansing; Genocide; Torture**

- The newly adopted statute of the International Criminal Court (ICC), approved in Rome on July 17, 1998, includes sexual violence in its definition of both the crimes against humanity and war crimes over which it has jurisdiction, in international and noninternational armed conflicts (Articles 7.1.g, 8.2.b.xxii, and 8.2.e.vi of ICC statute). It defines these acts as "rape, sexual slavery, enforced prostitution, forced pregnancy, enforced sterilization, and any other form of sexual violence also constituting a grave breach of the Geneva Conventions." *Forced pregnancy* is defined as "the unlawful confinement of a woman forcibly made pregnant, with the intent of affecting the ethnic composition of any population or carrying out other grave violations of international law" (Article 7.2.f of ICC statute). ➔ **War crimes/Crimes against humanity**

■ Cases in which the crime of rape is aggravated by voluntary (or involuntary) contamination by the AIDS virus have not yet been addressed by international law.

➔ **Ethnic cleansing; Genocide; Inter-American Court and Commission on Human Rights; International Criminal Court; International Criminal Tribunals; Medical duties; Persecution; Refugees; Torture; War crimes/Crimes against humanity; Women**

📖 **For Additional Information:**

Allen, B. *Rape Warfare: The Hidden Genocide in Bosnia-Herzegovina and Croatia*. Minneapolis: University of Minnesota Press, 1996.
Fédération Internationale des Ligues des Droit de l'Homme and Human Rights Watch. *Shattered Lives: Sexual Violence during the Rwandan Genocide and Its Aftermath*. New York: Human Rights Watch, 1996.
Gardam, Judith. "Women, Human Rights and International Humanitarian Law." *International Review of the Red Cross* 324 (September 1998): 421–32.
Meron, T. "Rape as a Crime under International Humanitarian Law." *American Journal of International Law* (1993): 424–28.

■ THE RED CROSS

The Red Cross is an international movement, consisting of three types of independent institutions: the National Red Cross and Red Crescent Societies, the International Federation of Red Cross and Red Crescent Societies, and the International Committee of the Red Cross (ICRC).

The three components of the Movement meet every four years, at the International Conference of the Red Cross and Red Crescent, with representatives of the states party to the Geneva Conventions (as per Article 1.3 of the statute of the Movement). The International Red Cross and Red Crescent Movement (also known as the International Red Cross) is organized according to its statute, adopted by the Twenty-fifth International Conference of the Red Cross and Red Crescent in Geneva, in 1986. The ICRC and the Federation have their own statutes.

Within the Movement, each institution is autonomous, with independent administrative bodies and separate programs. But each branch must respect the Movement's seven Fundamental Principles of action: humanity, impartiality, neutrality, independence, voluntary service, unity, and universality.
➔ **Humanitarian principles**

I. THE NATIONAL RED CROSS AND RED CRESCENT SOCIETIES

These Societies are mentioned several times in the Geneva Conventions. They are responsible for promoting and disseminating the principles of humanitarian law and the ideals of the Movement, and for organizing relief operations, even in times of peace.

They are established in the territory of states party to the Geneva Conventions and serve as medical auxiliaries to the authorities. In times of peace, the National Societies make up a civilian health network (particularly in times of natural disasters, but also while carrying out activities such as first aid or humanitarian law training, blood banks, etc.). In situations of conflict, they serve as auxiliaries to the military medical services. Hence, their personnel is subject to military laws and regulations (Article 2 of a standard statute of a National Society; GCI Article 26).

☞ International humanitarian law makes a distinction between the role of impartial humanitarian organizations and that of National Relief Societies, which belong to one of the parties to the conflict. Humanitarian law does not recognize the National Societies of the Red Cross and Red Crescent as neutral and independent humanitarian actors in times of conflict. It thus limits their authorized use of the red cross and other relevant protective emblems in times of war (GCI Article 44).

Currently 175 National Societies are recognized by the ICRC. Although the National Societies have the function of medical auxiliaries to government authorities in general, their aim is to retain sufficient independence of action from their own government to ensure that they always respect the seven fundamental principles of the Movement, listed earlier.

II. THE INTERNATIONAL FEDERATION OF RED CROSS AND RED CRESCENT SOCIETIES (FORMERLY THE LEAGUE OF RED CROSS AND RED CRESCENT SOCIETIES)

The International Federation (often referred to as the Federation) is the umbrella organization of the National Societies (Article 6 of statute of the Movement). It promotes the establishment and assists the activities of National Societies in each country. It also has the function of permanent body of liaison, coordination, and study between the National Societies, to which it should give any assistance they might request (Article 6.4 of statute of the Movement).

☞ The Federation implements the principles of the Red Cross and Red Crescent in situations that are not specifically addressed or covered by humanitarian law and hence are missing from the ICRC mandate. For instance, in times of peace, the Federation is in charge of responding to natural disasters.

In recent years, it has intervened increasingly in situations involving refugees, although the ICRC ensures that its own prerogatives established under humanitarian law are respected. An agreement concerning the organization of the Movement's international activities was adopted by the Council of Delegates, in Seville in 1997.

The Federation coordinates the projects of National Societies and provides them with operational support, such as financing expertise (Article 5.1.a of statute of the League). It coordinates emergency activities (e.g., in cases of earthquakes or epidemics) in which several Societies participate. The Federation may also directly carry out certain relief projects for victims of disasters (Article 5.1.c of statute of the League).

The Fundamental Principles of the Red Cross and Red Crescent Movement

The Red Cross's humanitarian action rests on seven principles that were proclaimed in 1965 and further clarified in 1986 to be incorporated into the Movement's statute when the latter was revised.

Humanity

International Red Cross and Red Crescent Movement, born of a desire to bring assistance without discrimination to the wounded on the battlefield, endeavors to prevent and alleviate human suffering wherever it may be found. Its purpose is to protect life and health and to ensure respect for the human being. It promotes mutual understanding, friendship, cooperation, and lasting peace among all peoples.

Impartiality

It makes no discrimination as to nationality, race, religious beliefs, class, or political opinions. It endeavors to relieve the suffering of individuals, being guided solely by their needs, and to give priority to the most urgent cases of distress.

Neutrality

In order to continue to enjoy the confidence of all, the Movement may not take sides in hostilities or engage at any time in controversies of a political, racial, religious, or ideological nature.

Independence

The Movement is independent. The National Societies, while auxiliaries in the humanitarian services of their governments and subject to the laws of their respective countries, must always maintain their autonomy so that they may be able at all times to act in accordance with the principles of the Movement.

Voluntary service

It is a voluntary relief movement not prompted in any manner by desire for gain.

Unity

There can be only one Red Cross or one Red Crescent Society in any one country. It must be open to all. It must carry on its humanitarian work throughout its territory.

Universality

The International Red Cross and Red Crescent Movement, in which all Societies have equal status and share equal responsibilities and duties in helping each other, is worldwide.

III. THE INTERNATIONAL COMMITTEE OF THE RED CROSS (ICRC)

After witnessing a battle in Solferino, Italy, in 1859, Henry Dunant wrote *A Memory of Solferino*, published in 1863. That year, Dunant created the International Committee for Relief to the Wounded, with four other members. In 1876, it was renamed the International Committee of the Red Cross.

The ICRC still operates on the basis of the original structure. The Red Cross Movement succeeded in linking private initiatives, in terms of relief and humanity, with the necessary support of states.

Legally, the ICRC is a Swiss organization. Its mandate was conferred on it by the states party to the Geneva Conventions, for the implementation of humanitarian law.

The supreme policymaking body of the ICRC is the Assembly, which consists of fifteen to twenty-five members, co-opted from among Swiss citizens. The Assembly sets the principles and general policy of the ICRC and supervises all ICRC activities.

Approximately 50 percent of the regular budget is covered by the Swiss government. The extraordinary budget (for emergencies) is financed by states, National Societies, and private donations resulting from calls for funds for specific programs. It is thus a hybrid institution and unique in that it affirms its independence by establishing firm links with states. Furthermore, it benefits from means of operation that no other private organization enjoys, such as its seat as Observer at the UN, since 1990, and an international radio station frequency allotted by the International Telecommunication Union.

☞ Within the Red Cross Movement, the ICRC remains independent, as guaranteed by its separate statute. Although it is a private organization, its mission is explicitly defined by the Geneva Conventions. It is therefore recognized and accepted by the states party to these conventions (statute of June 21, 1973, most recently revised on July 20, 1998).

- Of its own initiative, or basing itself on the Geneva Conventions and their Protocols, the ICRC strives to provide protection and assistance to victims of international and noninternational armed conflicts or internal disturbances and tensions.
- It is also the guardian of these Conventions. This means that it promotes the understanding and dissemination of humanitarian law, and prepares eventual developments thereof.
- It enjoys the status of Observer at the UN, in the sessions and work of the General Assembly. It maintains a permanent office at UN headquarters.

The ICRC has received the Nobel Peace Prize four times: through Henry Dunant, in 1901, and in 1917, 1944, and 1963. Its current President is Dr. Jakob Kellenberger.

The ICRC was the driving factor in the drafting of international humanitarian law. It has retained a privileged relationship with governments since after adopting the statute of the Committee and the Conventions regulating the rules of war, states formally recognized it as a neutral and impartial actor and put it in charge of striving to ensure the rights of military and civilian victims in conflicts. The ICRC hence may intervene in all situations of armed conflict to ensure the protection of, and assistance to, victims of war.

☞ The Geneva Conventions and Protocols establish a number of rights and obligations to ensure the relief for, and protection of, victims of war. Some of these rights are reserved for the ICRC's activities (exclusive mandate), while others are foreseen for the ICRC and all other impartial humanitarian organizations (general humanitarian mandate).

---

1. Exclusive Mandate

The Geneva Conventions and the ICRC's statute give the organization an exclusive mandate for certain interventions.

a. Visiting Places of Internment

ICRC delegates have "permission to go to all places where protected persons are, particularly to places of internment, detention and work. They shall have access to all premises occupied by protected persons and shall be able to interview them without witnesses" (GCIV Article 143). The same applies to prisoners of war (GCIII Article 126).

→   **Prisoners of war**

b. Monitoring the Implementation of Conventions

The ICRC has the mandate to receive any complaints based on alleged breaches of international humanitarian law applicable in armed conflicts (Article 4.1.c of ICRC statute).

Furthermore, it promotes the development and dissemination of humanitarian law. It publishes commentaries on the Conventions and their Protocols and other reference texts concerning humanitarian law, to contribute to a better understanding of the issues by states, which act as legislators in such matters. The ICRC also defines the general principles of such law. In cases in which the texts are not clear, its role is not necessarily to defend an interpretation that favors the victims. However, it does strive for an improvement of the texts, and regularly presents resolutions to be voted on by the International Diplomatic Conference (Article 4.1.g of ICRC statute).

c. Restoring Family Links: Searching for Missing Persons, Exchanging Correspondence

Families have a right to know the fate of their relatives. The Geneva Conventions therefore provide for a system through which information is received and transmitted to dispersed families. The ICRC arranges for this exchange of correspondence and traces individuals who have disappeared. This is carried out under a strict guarantee of confidentiality of information (e.g., other than that the visits are carried out with the knowledge of the Detaining Power), since it is crucial to prevent those who are threatening the protected persons from carrying out reprisals or other exaction against them (GCIV Articles 136–141). Such activities are carried out by a separate entity: the Central Tracing Agency (CTA).

→   **Central Tracing Agency**

2. De Facto Exclusive "Humanitarian" Mandate

The Geneva Conventions state that any impartial humanitarian organization may act as a substitute Protecting Power. In practice, however, only the ICRC has the diplomatic and effective potential to take on this role. Thus, it frequently participates in negotiations—for instance, concerning the freeing of prisoners of war.

→   **Protecting Powers**

3. General Humanitarian Mandate

International humanitarian law clearly recognizes the right of the ICRC and any other impartial humanitarian body to undertake relief and protection operations, in conformity with the applicable conventions. This right is established in the articles concerning the right of humanitarian initiative (GCI–GCIII Article 9; GCIV Article 10; Article 4.2 of ICRC statute). It is reinforced by certain specific provisions, for instance concerning the sick and wounded (Article 3 common to the four Geneva Conventions), protected persons (GCIV Article 30), and relief for populations (GCIV Article 59).

→   **Central Tracing Agency; European Committee for the Prevention of Torture; Humanitarian law; Humanitarian Principles; Protecting Powers; Protection; Relief; Right of humanitarian initiative**

📖 **For Additional Information:**

Haug, Hans. *Humanity for All*. Geneva: ICRC, 1993.

ICRC. *Handbook of the International Red Cross and Red Crescent Movement,* 13th ed. Geneva: ICRC and Federation, 1994.

✎   International Federation of Red Cross and Red Crescent Societies
    17, Chemin des Crêts
    CH 1211 Geneva 19, Switzerland
    Tel.: (41) 22 730 4222
    Fax: (41) 22 733 0395
    International Committee of the Red Cross (ICRC)
    19, avenue de la Paix
    CH 1202 Geneva, Switzerland
    Tel.: (41) 22 734 6001
    Fax: (41) 22 733 2057
@   International Federation of Red Cross and Red Crescent Societies: www.ifrc.org
    International Committee of the Red Cross: www.icrc.org

■ *REFOULEMENT* (FORCED RETURN) AND EXPULSION

Refoulement (forced return) is when a state adopts measures, at its border, that prohibit and actively prevent a foreign person who is not already a legal resident of its territory from entering its national territory.

Expulsion is a measure by which the authorities of a state forbid an individual present on its territory to continue his or her stay there and proceed to escort the individual back to the border, or send him or her back to the state of origin.

To ensure the protection of refugees and avoid endangering them by sending them back to a country where their life is threatened, the 1951 Convention Relating to the Status of Refugees (Refugee Convention) and other international texts establish guarantees with regard to the expulsion or *refoulement* of refugees.

1. Guarantees in Case of Expulsion

States are forbidden from expelling or returning (*refouler*) a refugee to a territory where his or her life or freedom would be threatened. The only derogation allowed concerns individuals who represent a danger for the national security of the state in question or who, "having been convicted by a final judgment of a particularly serious crime, constitute a danger to the community of that country" (Article 33 of Refugee Convention). The expulsion of such a refugee shall be carried out only following a decision reached in accordance with due process of law. The refugee has the right to submit evidence to clear him- or herself, to appeal the decision, and to be represented before the competent authority. If the decision to expel the person is upheld, he or she must be granted a reasonable period of time within which to seek legal admission into another country.

These provisions, set forth in Articles 32 and 33 of the Refugee Convention, are echoed in the 1966 International Covenant on Civil and Political Rights (Article 13). However, in the Covenant, the provisions only concern aliens who are lawfully in the territory of a state party.

2. The Principle of *Nonrefoulement*

The principle of *nonrefoulement* represents the practical defense of an individual's right not to be sent back by force toward a source of danger. It provides a sense of concrete reality to the right of asylum, which gives individuals the right to flee from persecution in their country but does not establish obligations on the part of states to give them asylum. Hence, the only guarantee left is the prohibition to send individuals back once they have fled their country of origin and entered the territory of another state. A refugee may not be returned to a state where he or she fears persecution. → **Persecution; Refugees**

The principle of *nonrefoulement* provides double protection:

- It establishes that any individual who enters the territory of another, even illegally, has the right to submit a request for asylum and have his or her case heard.
- Even if the request for asylum is denied, authorities are still prohibited from returning him or her to a territory where his or her life or liberty are threatened. In order to force an individual to leave the territory of first asylum, there must be a country of second asylum (known as the "safe third country") that is willing to receive the refugee.

The principle of *nonrefoulement* is increasingly threatened by an administrative practice carried out by governments, according to which they establish a list of countries declared to be "safe." This practice does not give due consideration to the diversity of personal situations. The principle is also threatened by a general trend toward hastening the return of refugees to their country as soon as certain peace accords have been signed and before security has been reestablished. → **Human rights; Ill treatment; Refugees; Stateless persons; Torture**

However, it has become very difficult to find countries of second asylum, the tendency being to send asylum seekers back to their state of first asylum. The result is that more and more public authorities are closing their borders to avoid being the first safe state that a refugee reaches. In practice, this means that the right to asylum is increasingly threatened. → **Asylum**

The Principle of *Nonrefoulement*

This principle is clearly set forth in most international and regional texts on relevant issues, including the following:

- 1967 UN Declaration on Territorial Asylum (Article 3.1)
- Final Act of the 1954 UN Conference Relating to the Status of Stateless Persons (Article 4)
- 1969 OAU Convention on Refugees (Article 2.3)
- 1969 American Convention on Human Rights (Article 22.8)
- 1984 Convention against Torture and Other Cruel, Inhuman, or Degrading Treatment or Punishment (Article 3). This article clearly forbids returning an individual to a state where there is reason to believe that he or she might be at risk of torture; other forms of cruel, inhuman, or degrading treatment or punishment; or ill treatment (including rape

(continues)

(*continued*)

- 1951 Convention Relating to the Status of Refugees (Article 33), which states:

> No Contracting State shall expel or return ("*refouler*") a refugee in any manner whatsoever to the frontiers of territories where his life or freedom would be threatened on account of his race, religion, nationality, membership of a particular social group or political opinion.
>
> The benefit of the present provision may not, however, be claimed by a refugee whom there are reasonable grounds for regarding as a danger to the security of the country in which he is, or who, having been convicted by a final judgement of a particularly serious crime, constitutes a danger to the community of that country.

➔   **Human rights; Ill treatment; Refugees; Stateless persons; Torture**

---

3. Repatriation

Under the right conditions, it is possible to repatriate refugees. One of the most important conditions is that repatriation must be voluntary (Article 5.1 of OAU Convention): it must be up to the refugees to decide whether or not to return to their country of origin. Involuntary repatriation can be considered *refoulement*. ➔ **Repatriation**

➔   **Asylum; Persecution; Refugees; Repatriation; UNHCR**

📖 **For Additional Information:**

Hathaway, James C. *Reconceiving International Refugee Law*. The Hague: Martinus Nijhoff, 1997, 171.
Zieck, Marjoleine. *UNHCR and Voluntary Repatriation of Refugees: A Legal Analysis*. The Hague: Martinus Nijhoff, 1997.

■ REFUGEES

I. Definitions

1. Definition from 1951 Refugee Convention

The Convention Relating to the Status of Refugees was adopted on July 28, 1951, by the United Nations Conference of Plenipotentiaries on the Status of Refugees and Stateless Persons convened under General Assembly Resolution 429 (V), entering into force on April 22, 1954. The Convention and the 1967 Protocol relating to the Status of Refugees serve as the basis for international refugee law. They define a refugee as

> any person who, [. . .] owing to well-founded fear of being persecuted for reasons of race, religion, nationality, membership of a particular social group or political opinion, is outside the country of his nationality and is unable or, owing to such fear, is unwilling to avail himself of the protection of that country [. . .].

The provisions of this Convention shall not apply to any person with respect to whom there are serious reasons for considering that:

(a) he has committed a crime against peace, a war crime, or a crime against humanity, as defined in the international instruments drawn up to make provision in respect of such crimes;

(b) he has committed a serious non-political crime outside the country of refuge prior to his admission to that country as a refugee;

(c) he has been guilty of acts contrary to the purposes and principles of the United Nations. (Article 1 of Refugee Convention)

The Refugee Convention was adopted at the same time as the UN High Commissioner for Refugees (UNHCR) was created to govern the legal status of refugees. It is dependent on states and UNHCR for its implementation. As of March 2001, it has 137 states parties and is the main reference text on this issue.

The way in which states have interpreted this definition only includes individuals fleeing a serious risk of persecution that is committed or tolerated by national authorities. The strictest interpretation applied by certain states thus does not include people fleeing in small groups or en masse from a collective danger, such as insecurity or war. It also excludes people fleeing acts of persecution that are not committed by national authorities, such as those committed by terrorist, rebel, or other groups, unless such persecution is tolerated or caused by national authorities.

In 1997, the European Court of Human Rights broadened this interpretation to include persecution inflicted by groups that do not depend on public authorities as a basis for granting refugee status.

It is important to note that UNHCR has added rape to the list of crimes that can constitute an element of persecution and may hence result in the recognition of the refugee status, as foreseen by the Refugee Convention, for individuals who fear or were victims of rape. UNHCR further recommends that, during the procedure to determine refugee status, asylum seekers who may have been victims of sexual violence be treated with special compassion.

The recently adopted statute of the permanent International Criminal Court reaffirms that gender may be a ground for fearing persecution. It includes "persecution against any identifiable group or collectivity on political, racial, national, ethnic, cultural, religious, gender [. . .] or other grounds that are universally recognized as impermissible under international law" as a crime against humanity (Article 7.1.h of ICC statute).

→ **Persecution; Rape; Women**

2. Definition from OAU Convention on Refugees

To this day, only one regional convention completes the international definition of a refugee set forth by the 1951 Refugee Convention. It is the Convention Governing the Specific Aspects of Refugee Problems in Africa, adopted by the Organization of African Unity (OAU) on September 10, 1969 (1001 UNTS 45), and which entered into force June 20, 1974. As of March 2001, it has forty-five states parties.

Its definition of refugees extends to "every person who, owing to external aggression, occupation, foreign domination or events seriously disturbing public order in either part or the whole of his country of origin or nationality, is compelled to leave his place of habitual residence in order to seek refuge in another place outside his country of origin or nationality" (Article 1.2 of OAU Convention).

This interpretation thus includes people fleeing war or collective persecutions en masse, whether the acts were committed by national authorities or not.

3. Humanitarian Law Definition

Above all, refugees are civilians who no longer receive protection from their government. Thus, international humanitarian law interprets the notion of refugees more widely, also taking into consideration population displacements caused by conflicts. This definition does not mean that refugees must automatically be granted that status under national laws, but it does establish their right to receive international protection and assistance while the conflict lasts.

These guarantees include provisions, for instance, that individuals may not be considered enemies simply because of their nationality, even if their nationality is that of an adverse party to the conflict (GCIV Article 40). If they find themselves in territory that is suddenly occupied by the state they originally fled, the Occupying Power may not arrest, prosecute, convict, or deport them for acts committed before the outbreak of hostilities (GCIV Article 70). They must be granted the same protection as civilians (PI Article 73; PII Article 4).

☞ International human rights law establishes that "everyone has the right [to flee his own country,] to seek and to enjoy in other countries asylum from persecution" (Article 14 of Universal Declaration of Human Rights).

States are not under the obligation to accord asylum to all individuals who request it, but all individuals who are threatened in their own country have the right to flee and seek asylum elsewhere. Thus, there is a gap between the rights of individuals and those of states, a gap populated by individuals seeking asylum.

Many refugees do not meet the requirements to qualify as a refugee under the 1951 Refugee Convention and therefore to not receive the guarantees provided by the refugee status established by the Convention. For these nonstatutory refugees, there are minimum standards of treatment that states must respect (see Section II.4, later).

Definitions are important because of the rights they confer on or open up for individuals. During the transitional steps and stages that a refugee must take to obtain formally the refugee status, as defined by the Refugee Convention, each refugee nevertheless is entitled to a set of minimum rights and guarantees.

II. RIGHTS OF INDIVIDUALS IN DIFFERENT SITUATIONS

1. Transitional Statuses

Before obtaining formal refugee status, individuals usually fall into other juridical categories:

- *Persons in search of asylum:* These individuals have fled their country but have not yet made a formal request for refugee status to the relevant authorities of the country where they are located.
- *Asylum seekers:* These individuals have submitted a formal request for refugee status with the competent national authorities and are awaiting the results from the examination of their file.
- *De facto refugees:* These individuals have entered the territory of another state in the course of a large-scale influx of people from their state of origin because of a conflict or other disaster. They cannot, however, justify their flight for reasons of individual persecution and therefore do not come under the strict definition of a refugee.

Although the individuals mentioned here do not enjoy official refugee status, they are entitled to the minimum guarantees set forth by the Refugee Convention. The aim of these guarantees is to protect the right—and enable the possibility—of individuals to flee their own country and request asylum in another without encountering insurmountable administrative obstacles. They also protect the individuals' right not to be expelled or sent back to a source of danger (*refoulement*).

Internally displaced persons (IDPs) are individuals who have fled their home but have not crossed any international border. They therefore remain under the jurisdiction of their national authorities and thus are not refugees. They are protected by general human rights conventions and, in case of conflict, by humanitarian law.

→ **Displaced persons**

2. Basic Rights Granted to Individuals Fleeing Their Country

To ensure that a person fleeing his or her country can submit a request for asylum to the authorities of a foreign state, the 1951 Refugee Convention reaffirms certain fundamental rights of individuals whose life or freedom is threatened.

a. The Right to Seek Asylum in Another Country

This reflects the fact that individuals have the right to flee their country by any means, and to enter the territory of another state, even illegally. States party to the Convention may not impose penalties on refugees on account of their illegal entry or presence, if, having come directly from a territory where their life or freedom was threatened, they enter or are present in that state's territory without authorization. This provision applies as long as the refugees present themselves without delay to the authorities and show good cause for their illegal entry or presence (Article 31 of Refugee Convention).

The right to flee one's own country does not mean that a refugee has the right to choose his or her country of asylum. Current laws favor the jurisdiction of the country of first asylum, which is the country through which the refugee first passed, in which he or she could have made a request for asylum.

b. The Right to Submit a Request for Asylum before the Appropriate Authorities

This means that states must not impede refugees' access to the competent national authorities and, in fact, must facilitate this access. Furthermore, UNHCR must be allowed to assist individuals with these formalities. Hence, refugees no longer receive administrative assistance from their state of origin to validate their rights. Other states are therefore under the obligation to provide the necessary administrative services, either directly or through an international authority—namely, UNHCR. As a result, UNHCR or the state in whose territory a refugee is residing commit to delivering or ensuring the delivery of documents or certifications that would normally be delivered to aliens by or through their national authorities (Article 25 of Refugee Convention).

c. The Right of Refugees to Have Their Request Examined by the Appropriate National Authorities

The examination of their file must be in conformity with the rules established by the Refugee Convention and must be carried out under the supervision of UNHCR (Article 8.a of UNHCR Statute).

d. The Right Not to Be Expelled or Returned to Their State of Origin as Long as There is a Threat to Their Safety (Nonrefoulement)

No state is permitted to expel or return (*refouler*) a refugee, in any manner whatsoever, toward the frontiers of territories where his or her life or freedom would be threatened on account of his or her race, religion, nationality, membership in a particular social group, or political opinion (Article 33 of Refugee Convention). Hence, individuals whose request has been dismissed may nevertheless benefit from temporary asylum since they cannot be sent back to their state of origin because of the dangers they would incur. They must also benefit from the minimum standards of protection attached to this temporary asylum.

3. The Rights of Individuals Who Have Obtained Official Refugee Status

Once their case has been examined, the individuals who come under the definition of the 1951 Refugee Convention obtain a juridical status that usually gives them rights similar to those of the citizens of the state in question. The legal status thus obtained—a recognition of the person's refugee status in a territory of asylum—is defined by the national laws of the country in question.

Nevertheless, the Refugee Convention enumerates the main rights that must be granted to refugees by the national laws of each country (Articles 12–34):

- Article 12: The personal status of a refugee shall be recognized and governed by the law of the country of asylum.
- Article 13: Refugees shall have the right to movable and immovable property.
- Article 14: They shall enjoy the right to the protection of industrial and intellectual (artistic) property.
- Article 15: They shall enjoy the right of association.
- Article 16: They shall have free access to, and rights before, courts.
- Articles 17 to 19: States shall grant refugees the most favorable treatment granted to nationals of a foreign country, with regard to the right to engage in wage-earning employment, self-employment, or liberal professions.
- Article 20: Where a rationing system exists, refugees shall receive the same treatment as nationals.
- Article 21: With regard to housing, states shall treat refugees as favorably as possible.
- Articles 22 and 23: With regard to public education and public assistance, states shall treat refugees in the same way as nationals.
- Article 24: In terms of labor laws and social security, refugees shall enjoy the same treatment as nationals.
- Article 25: As explained earlier (section 2.b), refugees have the right to submit a request for asylum to the competent national authorities that, under the supervision of UNHCR, must deliver or ensure the delivery of "such documents or certifications as would normally be delivered to aliens by or through their national authorities." Such documents replace the official instruments delivered by the national authorities and shall be given credence in the absence of proof to the contrary.
- Article 26: Refugees shall have the right to choose their place of residence and to move freely within the territory where it has obtained refugee status.
- Article 27: States must issue identity papers to any refugee in their territory who does not possess a valid travel document.
- Article 28: States must issue travel documents for the purpose of travel outside the territory to refugees who are lawfully staying in their territory. States may also issue such travel docu-

ments to any other refugee who finds him- or herself in their territory, who are unable to obtain a travel document from the country of their lawful residence.

- Article 29: Refugees must not be subject to higher taxes than nationals.
- Article 30: States must allow refugees to transfer assets that they have brought into its—no discrimination on the grounds of race, religion, political opinion, nationality, country of origin, or physical incapacity;territory, to another country where they have been admitted for the purposes of resettlement.
- Article 31: States shall not impose penalties on refugees who entered or are present illegally on its territory if they arrive directly from a territory where their life or freedom was threatened.
- Articles 32 and 33: States shall not expel or return (*refouler*) a refugee toward territories where his or her life or freedom would be threatened. The only derogation that is allowed concerns individuals who represent a danger for the national security of the state in question, or who, "having been convicted by a final judgment of a particularly serious crime, constitute a danger to the community of that country."

    The expulsion of such a refugee shall be carried out only following a decision reached in accordance with due process of law. The refugee shall have the right to submit evidence to clear him- or herself, to appeal the decision, and to be represented before the competent authority. If the decision to expel the person is maintained, he or she shall be accorded a reasonable period within which to seek legal admission into another country.
- Article 34: States must facilitate the assimilation and naturalization of refugees.

4. Minimum Standards of Protection Established by UNHCR for Individuals Who Have Not Received the Formal Status of Refugees

Only states can grant refugee status. However, UNHCR can use its good offices to help states find durable solutions to refugee problems. UNHCR's Executive Committee has set forth the minimum rights that must be granted by all states, until a durable solution can be found, to refugees who do not come under the definition of the 1951 Refugee Convention and therefore cannot benefit from the status it provides.

Protection of Asylum Seekers in Situations of Large-Scale Influx

Conclusion 22 (Session XXXII) of April 24, 1981, adopted by the UNHCR Executive Committee on International Protection of Refugees

Individuals who cannot benefit from formal refugee status nonetheless must be treated in conformity with certain minimum standards of protection:

- The right to flee persecution does not automatically entail the right to receive asylum. In case of a mass exodus of people, states' priority must be to provide temporary refuge for them.
- States shall not expel or return (*refouler*) such people toward a territory where they risk persecution.
- Until durable solutions are found, states must respect the following minimum rights:
    - —no penal sanctions because of illegal entry or presence in a state;
    - —respect for their fundamental rights and guarantees;
    - —material assistance (food, shelter, medical assistance, etc.);
    - —prohibition on cruel, inhuman, or degrading treatment;

(continues)

(*continued*)

    —no discrimination on the grounds of race, religion, political opinion, nationality, country of origin, or physical incapacity;

    —access to courts and other due process rights;

    —the settlement must be located in a safe area; in other words, it must not be too near the border of the country of origin;

    —respect for family unity;

    —assistance in searching for family members;

    —protection of minors and unaccompanied children;

    —possibility of sending and receiving correspondence;

    —registration of any births, deaths, or marriages;

    —permission to transfer assets;

    —favorable conditions for voluntary repatriation;

    —obligation of states to search for a durable solution.

➔ **Camps; Children; Discrimination; Fundamental guarantees; Internment; Judicial guarantees; *Refoulement* (forced return) and expulsion; Repatriation; Women**

III. Means for the Protection of Refugees

1. UNHCR

UNHCR was created as the international organ responsible for coordinating the regulations and actions taken by different states with regard to the right of asylum and protection of refugees.

It has taken on the responsibility of trying to harmonize national laws concerning this issue and makes sure that the laws defend the right of asylum efficiently. It also helps ensure joint responsibility and solidarity by coordinating states' efforts to meet the financial burden that must be borne to welcome refugees.

It also provides material assistance and protection, in coordination with NGOs. In fact, UNHCR can sign official operational partnership contracts with NGOs for assistance and protection actions (Articles 8 and 10 of UNHCR statute).

2. NGOs

NGOs are thus formally associated with UNHCR's actions of assistance, which defend the rights of refugees.

Through their very presence at the refugees' side, NGOs are in a privileged position to evaluate, for instance, the refugees' physical safety, the quality of assistance they receive, and the different pressures they face in making certain decisions—namely, in cases of repatriation—and to report this to UNHCR.

3. States

States are held to international solidarity and accountability to manage refugee flows, especially in the case of large-scale influxes of refugees who must be granted temporary asylum. All states must provide host states with immediate assistance, in conformity with the "principle of equitable burden-sharing" (preamble of Refugee Convention, paragraph 4; UNHCR Executive Committee Conclusion 15, on Refugees without an asylum state, Session XXX, 1979).

The cost of hosting refugees cannot be borne solely by the state to which people flee because of its geographic proximity. If this were the case, potential host states would soon shut down their borders to any person seeking refuge, thereby denying the right of persecuted persons to flee their country. Hence, all states have the duty to contribute to assisting refugees. One of the principal ways in which they do this is by financing UNHCR, which protects and assists refugees.

This international solidarity is not founded only on altruism. It comes from desire of states party to the Convention to "do everything within their power to prevent this problem from becoming a cause of tension between States" (preamble of Refugee Convention, paragraph 5).

→ **Asylum; Camps; Displaced persons; NGOs; Protection;** *Refoulement* **(forced return) and expulsion; Relief; Repatriation; Stateless persons; UNHCR**

→ **List of states party to international human rights and humanitarian conventions (Nos. 15, 16, 17)**

📖 **For Additional Information:**

Amnesty International. *Refugees: Human Rights Have No Borders*. London: Author, 1997.

Brauman, Rony. "Refugee Camps, Population Transfers, and NGOs." In *Hard Choices: Moral Dilemmas in Humanitarian Intervention*, ed. Jonathan Moore. Lanham, Md.: Rowman & Littlefield, 1998, 177–94.

Médecins sans Frontières. *Refugee Health*. London: Macmillan, 1997.

UNHCR. *The State of the World's Refugees, 1997–98: A Humanitarian Agenda*. New York: Oxford University Press, 1997.

■ RELIEF

The Geneva Conventions and their Additional Protocols establish the rules for ensuring the relief to which victims of conflicts are entitled. In so doing, they pursue two pragmatic and complementary objectives:

- In general, they aim to lessen the suffering caused by hostilities to those who are not, or are no longer, participating in hostilities. This includes, for instance, preventing shortages of goods essential to the survival of the population.
- More specifically, they aim to ensure that the basic protection needs (centered around the right to life) of different categories of persons threatened by the logic of destruction and violence are recognized.

In situations of conflict, scarcity is always relative. Violence, on the other hand, always threatens the most vulnerable categories of the population with direct or indirect destruction. The relief operations foreseen by humanitarian law link the notions of assistance and protection: material assistance should be provided in tandem with the recognition of a minimum legal status for populations in danger. The different elements that make up these notions are set forth most clearly in Articles 70 and 71 of Protocol I additional to the Geneva Conventions (Protocol I). They are explained later here, as the different aspects of relief actions are introduced.

→ **Assistance; Protected persons; Protection**

1. The Contents of Relief Actions

Humanitarian law foresees and regulates relief actions, based on the concept of goods and needs that are essential to the survival of the population in a situation of conflict.

The main principle governing the right to provide and receive relief is that starving the population is forbidden as a method of warfare. Parties to a conflict therefore must not destroy essential goods or prevent civilians from obtaining such goods. This is emphasized in situations when the civilians find themselves in the power of the adverse party, which might be a result of the territory being occupied, the area being under siege, or the individuals being interned or detained.

"Objects indispensable to the survival of the civilian population" include

- foodstuff, whether in the form of food supplies or crops and livestock, as well as drinking water installations and supplies, and irrigation works;
- medicine and medical supplies;
- objects necessary for religious worship;
- essential foodstuffs, clothing, and tonics intended for children under fifteen, expectant mothers and maternity cases (GCIV Article 23, PI Article 54, and PII Articles 14 and 18).

In international armed conflicts, this list is lengthened in the case of occupied territories and besieged areas, which must more specifically receive

- clothing, bedding, means of shelter, other supplies essential to the survival of the civilian population of the occupied territory, and objects necessary for religious worship (PI Article 69);
- if necessary, relief personnel may form part of the assistance provided in any relief action, which must be authorized by the party in whose territory they will carry out their duties (PI Articles 70 and 71).■

➜ **Famine; Medical duties; Protected objects and property (objects indispensable to the survival of the civilian population); Supplies**

2. Aid Recipients

Humanitarian law establishes that the civilian population as a whole is entitled to benefit from relief. It also establishes specific provisions regulating the relief intended for specific categories of persons, such as detainees, internees, prisoners of war, wounded and sick persons, populations of occupied territories, women, and children. These more specifically targeted relief activities are presented in the following specific entries.

➜ **Children; Civilians; Detention; Internment; Prisoners of war; Protected persons; Women; Wounded and sick persons**

3. The Right of Protected Persons to Receive Relief

If the population of any territory is not adequately provided with the supplies essential to its survival, relief operations can be undertaken. The parties to the conflict are under the obligation to allow and facilitate the free passage of these supplies and may not forbid or hinder them. They only have the right to stipulate technical conditions or to require that the relief organizations monitor the distribution of supplies. This is to guarantee that supplies are not diverted from the intended civilian population. Thus, international humanitarian law guarantees the right to receive aid (GCIV Articles 17, 23, and 59; PI Article 70; PII Article 18).

This principle is spelled out in different legal texts, depending on whether the shortage suffered by the population is a result of the conflict in general (PI Article 70 and PII Article 18), the territory being occupied (GCIV Articles 55 and 59) or besieged (GCIV Articles 17 and 23), or an internal conflict (PII Article 18).

The Detaining or Occupying Power is under the obligation to provide the necessary supplies to the individuals who are in their power as a result of internment, detention, or occupation (GCIV Articles 81, 55, and 60). They must also allow independent humanitarian evaluations of the situation and of the needs of the population (GCIV Articles 30 and 143), by the protecting powers or, failing that, by the ICRC or the humanitarian organizations.

Furthermore, individuals in such situations have the right to receive individual or collective relief, whether they are interned (GCIV Articles 108–111), wounded or sick (GCIV Articles 16, 17, and 23; PII Article 7), prisoners of war (GCIII Articles 15, 72, and 73), deprived of liberty for other reasons (PII Article 5.1.c), or in occupied territory (GCIV Articles 59, 62, and 63).

☞ Persons protected by humanitarian law have the right to apply to the Protecting Powers, the ICRC, or any other qualified organization, for assistance. The authorities in power must facilitate their application to such organizations, who must be allowed to carry out independent evaluations of the population's needs (GCIV Article 30).

→ **Detention; Occupied territories; Prisoners of war; Protected persons; Protecting Powers; Right of access**

---

4. The Obligation to Allow Free Passage of Supplies That Are Essential to the Survival of the Population

As established by Protocol I, "the Parties to the conflict and each High Contracting Party shall allow and facilitate rapid and unimpeded passage of all relief consignments, equipment and personnel provided [. . .] even if such assistance is destined for the civilian population of the adverse Party" (PI Article 70.2). They must not, in any way whatsoever, divert or delay the relief supplies (PI Article 70.3.c).

Furthermore, the parties to the conflict must ensure the protection of relief supplies and facilitate their rapid distribution (PI Articles 70.4 and 70.5).

These obligations—which are also set forth in the Fourth Geneva Convention (Articles 23, 55, and 59–62)—assume that the goods being supplied are indispensable to the survival of the population, and that the relief actions undertaken are impartial and humanitarian. The relief actions must therefore be carried out without any adverse distinction. In the distribution of supplies, priority must be given to the most vulnerable persons, such as children, expectant mothers, maternity cases, and nursing mothers (PI Article 70.1).

Parties to the conflict are prohibited from refusing relief actions. They only have the right to

- prescribe the technical arrangements under which such passage is permitted, including searches;
- make such permission conditional on the distribution of this assistance being made under the local supervision of a Protecting Power, or its substitute, to ensure that it is not being used for military purposes (PI Article 70.3.a, b; GCIV Article 59).

☞ In practice, the system of Protecting Powers is not used; therefore, relief organizations bear the responsibility of evaluating needs and supervising the distribution of aid to ensure that it offers the guarantees required by law—namely, the assurance that the aid cannot be diverted or used for military purposes—to the parties to the conflict. Otherwise, there is a risk that the belligerents might refuse the free passage of supplies.

If the UN Security Council or a regional organization decides to impose a sanction on a member state, such as an embargo, humanitarian relief cannot be subject to it.

→ **Blockade; Embargo; Protected objects and property; Right of access; Sanctions Committees; Siege; Supplies**

5. The Right of Humanitarian Organizations to Offer Assistance

Offers of humanitarian and impartial relief, conducted without any adverse distinction "shall not be regarded as interference in the armed conflict or as unfriendly acts" (PI Article 70.1).

Furthermore, the Geneva Conventions establish that the ICRC and other impartial humanitarian organizations may always offer their services to the parties to the conflict and, with their agreement, may undertake relief and protection activities for the civilian population (GCI–IV common Article 3; GCIV Article 10).

Besides the missions entrusted to Protecting Powers, humanitarian law invites the parties to the conflict to provide the best possible reception to religious or relief organizations or any other whose aim is to provide assistance to protected persons (GCIV Article 142). States party to the Conventions also undertake to provide the ICRC and other humanitarian organizations with all the facilities within their power that these organizations need to carry out the protection and assistance functions assigned to them by the Conventions and Protocols (PI Article 81).

In internal armed conflicts, states also undertake to allow relief societies to "offer their services for the performance of their traditional functions in relation to the victims of the armed conflict" (PII Article 18.1).

Humanitarian law thus entrusts relief organizations with a double responsibility:

- they must offer their services to care for and protect the victims of conflicts;
- they must know the requirements of humanitarian law so as to ensure that they are not weakening the protection to which the victims are entitled;
- namely, they shall make sure that the relief is not diverted for military purposes, so as to prevent parties to the conflict from refusing aid under the pretext that it is being used by the adverse party.

→ **Humanitarian principles; Protecting Powers; Responsibility; Right of humanitarian initiative**

6. The Protection of Relief Personnel

The personnel participating in relief action must be respected and protected (PI Article 71.2).

Different persons can undertake relief operations. They may be representatives of Protecting Powers, Red Cross or Red Crescent societies, civil defense organizations, neutral states or ones that are not parties to the conflict, humanitarian organizations, or the UN. The population itself can undertake relief operations.

Members of humanitarian personnel may benefit from various statuses, which may grant them more or less extensive rights, depending on what organization they represent.

Article 71 of Protocol I establishes the minimum protection framework covering relief personnel. It reaffirms that, in certain situations, such personnel is necessary as a part of the assistance provided, in particular for the transportation and distribution of relief supplies. This personnel must have the approval of the party to the conflict in whose territory they carry out their duties. However, the authorities must respect and protect relief personnel, must cooperate with them, and may only limit their activities in case of imperative military necessity.

The members of relief personnel must not exceed the mandate of their mission. In particular, they must take into account the security requirements of the party in whose territory they are carrying out their duties. This is of particular importance, for instance, when considering how to communicate information concerning the military situation of a territory. The assignment of any person who fails to respect these conditions can be terminated.

➔ **Humanitarian and relief personnel; Medical personnel; Protecting Powers**

7. Medical Relief Comes under a Special Regime

➔ **Medical duties; Medical services**

➔ **Detention; Famine; Humanitarian and relief personnel; Internment; Medical duties; Occupied territories; Prisoners of war; Protected persons; Protection; Right of access; Right of humanitarian initiative; Siege; Supplies**

📖 **For Additional Information:**

Anderson, Mary B. "'You Save My Life Today, but for What Tomorrow?' Some Moral Dilemmas of Humanitarian Aid." In *Hard Choices: Moral Dilemmas in Humanitarian Intervention*, ed. Jonathan Moore. Lanham, Md.: Rowman & Littlefield, 1998, 137–56.

Brauman, Rony. *L'Action humanitaire*. Paris: Dominos-Flammarion, 1995.

Macalister-Smith, Peter. *International Humanitarian Assistance: Disaster Relief Actions in International Law and Organizations*. The Hague: Martinus Nijhoff; Geneva: Henri Dunant Institute, 1985.

■ REPATRIATION

Being a refugee is meant to be a temporary condition, which ends when the individuals concerned return to their country of origin. Hence, the statute of the United Nations High Commissioner for Refugees (UNHCR) entrusts UNHCR with the responsibility of "assisting governmental and private efforts to promote voluntary repatriation or assimilation within new national communities" (Article 8.c of UNHCR statute, adopted by the UN General Assembly on December 14, 1950, Resolution 428 [V]).

The 1969 Organization of African Unity (OAU) Convention Governing the Specific Aspects of Refugee Problems in Africa also notes the importance of repatriation and emphasizes that it must be voluntary (Article 5.1 of OAU Convention on Refugees).

Refugees may be repatriated for several reasons:

- if the prevailing conditions change in the country they fled (since refugees flee their country to escape individual persecution, their status may be reexamined if the situation changes);

- the host state may encourage repatriation if it can no longer afford the burden that the refugees represent;
- refugees may be forced to return to their country of origin because of various kinds of pressure.

One of UNHCR's responsibilities is to guarantee that all repatriations are voluntary.

☞ International refugee law has no provisions aimed at protecting individuals within their own country, since, by definition, refugees must have crossed an international border. If they remain in their own country, they are considered internally displaced persons, and their government is entirely responsible for them. Nevertheless, international human rights conventions and international humanitarian law set certain limits to states' sovereignty over their residents.

The 1951 Convention Relating to the Status of Refugees (known as the Refugee Convention) only gives UNHCR a mandate to protect individuals who have crossed a border. Hence, this mandate can only be exercised in the state of exile, and the protection it provides stops at the border of the state of origin. This means that, in principle, refugees lose UNHCR's protection once they decide to return home.

In terms of repatriation, the only protection guarantee for individuals is the fact that repatriation to their country of origin must be voluntary. The 1969 OAU Refugee Convention reaffirms and emphasizes this principle by stating that the "voluntary character of repatriation shall be respected in all cases and no refugee shall be repatriated against his will" (Article 5.1 of OAU Convention on Refugees.). Refugees must therefore be able to freely evaluate the advisability of a return.

I. UNHCR's Role and Obligations in Repatriation Operations

1. UNHCR's Mandate and Role

UNHCR's mandate in terms of repatriation can be summarized by the following actions:

- to monitor the voluntary character of refugees' repatriation;
- to promote the creation of conditions that facilitate voluntary repatriation, in safety and dignity;
- to encourage the voluntary repatriation of refugees, once certain preconditions have been met (explained later);
- to facilitate spontaneous voluntary repatriation of refugees, should it occur without the preconditions having been met that enable UNHCR to organize such an event;
- to monitor the status of persons who have been repatriated to their country and the fulfillment of any obligations toward them and intercede on their behalf, if necessary;
- to undertake activities in support of states' judicial systems, to help them solve problems at the root of refugee movements;
- to collect funds to support governments' repatriation or reintegration programs;
- to coordinate NGO assistance in this domain, with short and long-term needs in mind.

In 1980, the UNHCR Executive Committee examined the issue of repatriation in detail and codified what UNHCR's role should be in such operations (Conclusion 18, Session XXXI). Its mandate translates into the obligation to

- ensure that the voluntary character of repatriation is respected;
- cooperate with governments to assist refugees who wish to be repatriated;
- obtain formal guarantees for the safety of returning refugees;
- advise refugees on these guarantees and on the prevailing conditions in their country;
- monitor the situation of returning refugees to their countries of origin;
- receive the returning refugees and establish projects for their reintegration in their country of origin.

In 1985, the Executive Committee reinforced this framework of responsibilities for UNHCR by reaffirming its mandate over repatriation. It ranges "from the outset in assessing the feasibility and, thereafter, in both the planning and implementation stages of repatriation" (Conclusion 40, Session XXXVI). States must recognize that UNHCR has a legitimate concern for the consequences of the return on individuals, and they should therefore have direct and unhindered access to returnees.

Conclusion 40 also noted that the system of tripartite agreements—among UNHCR, the country of origin, and the country of asylum—is well adapted to facilitate voluntary repatriation. Unfortunately, there is nothing to prevent governments from organizing repatriation without involving UNHCR. If no agreement is reached between UNHCR and the governments concerned or between the two governments involved in the repatriation, the Executive Committee's conclusions remain simple declarations of intent without any practical effect other than giving permission to UNHCR to hold a dialogue with the authorities.

The most important aspect of UNHCR's role is that it must choose whether to promote or simply facilitate repatriation, based on the circumstances. Depending on the approach it chooses, its specific obligations toward the refugees are different.

2. UNHCR's Obligations When Actively Promoting Repatriation

a. Preconditions to UNHCR Promoting Repatriation

Certain preconditions must be met before UNHCR will actively promote repatriation:

- the conditions in the country of origin must show an overall and significant improvement, so as to enable a return in safety and dignity for the majority of the refugees;
- all the parties concerned must undertake to respect the voluntary nature of the return;
- the country of origin must have supplied adequate guarantees concerning the refugees' safety, including, if possible, formal legal or legislative guarantees;
- UNHCR must have free and unhindered access to the refugees and returnees;
- the terms and conditions of the return must be set forth in a formal, written repatriation agreement, signed by UNHCR and the concerned parties.

b. UNHCR's Concrete Obligations

When these conditions have been met, UNHCR can promote a return. This means it may encourage refugees to return and may participate in the entire operation. In such cases, its practical contributions consist of

- obtaining access to the entire refugee population and ensuring the voluntary character of their decision to return to their country of origin;

- undertaking an information campaign to enable the refugees to make their decision with full knowledge of the relevant facts;
- interviewing, advising, and registering candidates for repatriation, and organizing a safe environment for the return;
- developing and implementing (directly or through partners) rehabilitation and reintegration programs;
- monitoring the legal, physical, and material safety of the returnees.

3. UNHCR's Obligations When Facilitating Repatriation

When UNHCR considers that the conditions under which it would actively promote a repatriation have not been met, but the refugees wish to return anyway and are undertaking their own spontaneous repatriation, it can decide to facilitate such repatriation in an attempt to improve the safety of the returnees and to offer them material assistance.

a. Conditions to UNHCR Facilitating a Spontaneous Repatriation

The only condition on which UNHCR bases its decision to participate in this form of repatriation is the fact that refugees have requested to be repatriated voluntarily. UNHCR must therefore be able to determine whether the decision was strictly voluntary or if any form of pressure was applied to force or influence the decision.

This form of intervention takes place without an agreement between UNHCR and the government authorities establishing the terms and conditions of the return and without the country of origin's formal guarantees ensuring the safety of the returnees.

In such circumstances UNHCR's role is clearly more ambiguous than in other situations, and its support for such operations is based on respect for refugees' decision to return home and not on UNHCR's legal and material ability to protect them.

b. UNHCR's Role in Spontaneous Repatriations

In such circumstances, UNHCR's role is to do the following:

- Supply information concerning the conditions in the country of origin, in general, and in the areas to which the refugees will return, in particular. This information must be complete and reliable.
- Provide material assistance to those returning
- Inform the returnees of the limits of the protection and assistance that UNHCR is able to supply in this situation (e.g., the fact that UNHCR will not be present in the reinstallation zones, that there is no written agreement between UNHCR and the country of origin setting forth clear guarantees, etc.).
- Inform the refugees of the obstacles they may encounter during their return or reinstallation.
- Whenever possible, UNHCR must seek to improve the safety of the returnees in their country of origin. Once the return has taken place, UNHCR must try to negotiate amnesties and guarantees, as well as agreements concerning its own presence in the area to which the refugees will return.
- If UNHCR succeeds in obtaining permission to be present in the area to which the refugees are returning, it must exercise its monitoring responsibilities as much as possible, in agreement with the local authorities.

Repatriation in Times of Conflict

If a conflict is under way, UNHCR cannot promote repatriation but can facilitate such a movement if it occurs spontaneously. In such cases, its role is restricted to making sure that

- the repatriation is genuinely voluntary;
- the refugees have all the necessary information to make an informed decision;
- the country of origin is not opposed to the return; and
- the refugees' reasons for returning are pacific, not military.

UNHCR always has the authority to request direct and unhindered access to the returnees, so as to monitor the conditions of their return, by insisting that the protection of returnees is always of legitimate concern to UNHCR (Conclusion 40, Session XXXVI, 1985). However, if the country of origin has no previous agreement with the organization, it has no obligations in this respect.

In times of conflict, UNHCR's legal instruments do not enable it to protect refugees efficiently. If a refugee camp is bombarded or attacked, for instance, it is difficult to say that the population movement that results is of a voluntary nature. The relevant rules of international humanitarian law are therefore more appropriate in such situations than the rules of refugee law: the former ensure the protection of refugees as civilians. The entire Fourth Geneva Convention Relative to the Protection of Civilians in Time of War, Article 3 common to the four Geneva Conventions, and Additional Protocol II to these Conventions, Relating to the Protection of Victims of Non-International Armed Conflicts, can always be invoked to protect refugees, returnees, or persons displaced inside their own country.

→ **Civilians; Population displacement; Protected persons; Protection**

II. OPERATIONAL PRINCIPLES GOVERNING REPATRIATION

1. The Voluntary Character of Repatriation

The principle safeguarding the voluntary character of any repatriation is the cornerstone of the international protection of refugees. Although it is not expressly set forth in the 1951 Refugee Convention, it is derived directly from the principle of *nonrefoulement*, which is set forth in the Convention: it is forbidden to send individuals back to countries where they fear for their safety.

The 1969 OAU Refugee Convention does establish explicitly that the "voluntary character of repatriation shall be respected in all cases" and that no refugee shall be repatriated against his or her will (Article 5 of the OAU Convention).

In practice, given that the protection offered by UNHCR stops at the border of the country of origin, any involuntary repatriation is equivalent to *refoulement* (forced return).

UNHCR must monitor the voluntary character of repatriation with regard to

- the conditions in the country of origin (the refugees must have access to reliable information before leaving) and
- the situation in the country of asylum (which must allow freedom of choice).

It must also make sure that the factors that draw the refugees to return to their country of origin are the driving force, not the constraints compelling them to leave the country of asylum.

a. How to Determine Whether a Repatriation Is Voluntary

- UNHCR must have free, direct, and unhindered access to the refugees.
- It must be able to evaluate any changes in the refugees' situation in the camps or other installations that might be influencing their decision to return.
- It must be able to ensure that the individual choices of refugees are independent of any collective decision to return.
- UNHCR representatives must make sure that they do not speak only to the refugees' representatives. They must consult the refugees themselves and, in particular, groups of women refugees to verify that the leaders genuinely represent the will and interest of the refugees as whole.

b. A Repatriation Is Not Voluntary When

- the authorities of the "host" country remove any possibility for the refugees to have freedom of choice by imposing coercive measures such as decreasing the refugees' vital supplies, housing them in hostile or dangerous areas, or encouraging xenophobia among the local population;
- the different factions among the refugee population, or political organizations in exile, influence the refugees' decisions—this may take place directly, using physical pressure, or indirectly, through actions such as misinformation campaigns;
- certain interest groups in the host state discourage repatriation by disseminating false information.

2. Defining a "Safe Return"

A safe return has the following characteristics:

- There are judicial conditions that will make it safer for the returnees (e.g., amnesties, public guarantees of individual security, nondiscrimination laws, no risk of reprisals or persecution as a result of the return).
- Physical security is guaranteed (from protection against armed attacks to protection from the threat of land mines).
- Material safety is ensured (access to land, to means of general subsistence, etc.).

These elements can be integrated into any tripartite agreements among UNHCR, the country of origin, and the country of asylum.

3. Returning in Dignity

This principle is more vague than the previous two. It implies that the honor and human dignity of individuals must be respected. Refugees must be able to return home unconditionally, and, if they decide to do so spontaneously, they must be able to do so at their own speed and not in convoys where they are forced to march. They must not be separated from their families, must be treated with respect, and must be accepted by national authorities who commit to grant them their universal human rights.

In practice, to monitor that the principles of safety and dignity are being respected, UNHCR must evaluate the following elements:

- the physical safety of the refugees at every stage in their return (on the road, during and after their return, when they are received, at their final destination);
- the respect for family unity;
- the attention granted to vulnerable groups (e.g., the sick and wounded, the elderly, pregnant women, children, etc.);
- the alleviation of formalities at the border;
- the authorization given to the refugees to bring all their transportable belongings with them;
- the respect for the school year and agricultural calendars throughout the course of these events;
- freedom of movement;
- the respect for human rights.

→ **Asylum; Camps; Discrimination; Family; Internally displaced persons; Persecution; Population displacement; Protection;** *Refoulement* **(forced return) and expulsion; Refugees; UNHCR**

📖 **For Additional Information:**

Lawyers Committee for Human Rights. *General Principles Relating to the Promotion of Refugee Repatriation.* Geneva: UNHCR Documentation Center, 1992.

UNHCR. *The State of the World's Refugees, 1997–98: A Humanitarian Agenda.* New York: Oxford University Press, 1997.

■ REPRISALS

Reprisals are measures of pressure that derogate from the normal rules of international law: they are carried out by a state in response to unlawful acts committed against it by another state, and are intended to force that state to respect the law. Reprisals may also be carried out in response to an attack. The question of the legality of reprisals has been in debate since conventional (positive) international law—which includes the UN Charter—posited that states are prohibited from using force, except as a defense against aggression.

In times of conflict, reprisals are considered legal under certain conditions: they must be carried out in response to a previous attack, they must be proportionate to that attack, and they must be aimed only at combatants and military objectives.

Humanitarian law hence forbids all reprisals against civilian persons and objects protected by the Geneva Conventions and their Protocols. These include wounded, sick, or shipwrecked persons; medical or religious personnel, units, transports, or material; prisoners of war; civilian persons or civilian objects; cultural property or places of worship; objects indispensable to the survival of the civilian population; the natural environment; works and installations containing dangerous forces; and buildings and material used for the protection of the civilian population (GCI Article 46; GCII Article 47; GCIII Article 13; GCIV Article 33; PI Articles 20 and 51–56).

☞ It is important to distinguish between reprisals, acts of revenge, and retaliation. Acts of revenge are never authorized under international law, while retaliation and reprisals are foreseen by humanitarian law.

Measures of retaliation are acts by which a state responds to unfriendly, but lawful, acts by another state (for instance, reciprocal expulsion of diplomats).

Reprisals must always be proportionate to the attacks to which they are responding and must never aim at civilians or protected objects. If these conditions are not respected, then it is an act of revenge.

In case of reprisals, military commanders have the duty to implement the precautionary measures foreseen by international law with regard to methods of warfare. Humanitarian law specifies the individual responsibility of each member of the armed forces with regard to such actions.

→ **Attacks; Duty of commanders; Methods of warfare; Protected objects and property; Protected persons; Proportionality; Responsibility**

📖 **For Additional Information:**

Nahlik, Stanislaw-Edward. "From Reprisals to Individual Penal Responsibility." *Humanitarian Law of Armed Conflict—Challenges Ahead: Essays in Honor of Frits Kalshoven*, ed. A. J. M. Delissen and G. J. Tania. The Hague: Martinus Nijhoff, 1991, 165–76.

Obradovic, Konstantin. "Prohibition of Reprisals in Protocol I: Greater Protection for War Victims." *International Review of the Red Cross* 320 (September–October 1997): 524–28.

■ REQUISITION

A requisition is a demand, made by a belligerent or a government representative, for the temporary or permanent use of certain objects (movable or immovable) or services. In principle, requisition is carried out in exchange for compensation. To prevent requisitions from causing excessive deprivation within the population, humanitarian law specifically regulates the right of requisition in numerous cases, especially in occupied territories.

1. Requisition of Medical Material and Personnel

Specific rules limit the requisition of medical installations, personnel, material, and transport. These rules are dispersed throughout the Geneva Conventions and their Protocols (GCI Articles 33–35; GCIV Article 57; PI Article 14).

- Real and personal property belonging to aid societies is considered private property. The right of requisition recognized for belligerents by the laws and customs of war must only be exercised in cases of urgent necessity, and only after the welfare of the wounded and sick has been ensured (GCI Article 34).
- Humanitarian law also establishes rules to protect medical buildings and material belonging to armed forces. These may not be diverted from their purpose as long as they are required for the care of wounded and sick and must not be intentionally destroyed (GCI Article 33). Transports of wounded and sick persons or of medical equipment must be respected and protected.

"Should such transports or vehicles fall into the hands of the adverse Party, they shall be subject to the laws of war, on condition that the Party to the conflict who captures them shall, in all cases, ensure the care of the wounded and sick they contain" (GCI Article 35).

▪ In occupied territories:

—"[A]n Occupying Power may requisition civilian hospitals only temporarily and only in cases of urgent necessity for the care of military wounded and sick, and then on condition that suitable arrangements are made in due time for the care and treatment of the patients and for the needs of the civilian population for hospital accommodation. The material and stores of civilian hospitals cannot be requisitioned so long as they are necessary for the needs of the civilian population" (GCIV Article 57).

—The first 1977 Protocol Optional to the Geneva Conventions (Protocol I) further enumerates the details of the measures to be taken with regard to medical requisition. These provisions (see PI Article 14, later) may serve as a reference in situations other than occupied territories.

2. Occupied Territory

▪ In an occupied territory, requisitions must be proportionate to the resources of the state, to make sure that objects indispensable to the survival of the population are spared (GCIV Article 55; PI Article 63).

▪ Article 14 of Protocol I unifies and clarifies the existing rules concerning the requisition of medical material and personnel. It makes them equally applicable to all hospitals, as well as temporary or mobile medical units, and includes medical personnel, medical objects, and the means of medical transportation, among the objects or services that can be requisitioned only under very specific circumstance and conditions:

1. The Occupying Power has the duty to ensure that the medical needs of the civilian population in occupied territory continue to be satisfied.
2. The Occupying Power shall not, therefore, requisition civilian medical units, their equipment, their material or the services of their personnel, so long as these resources are necessary for the provision of adequate medical services for the civilian population and for the continuing medical care of any wounded and sick already under treatment.
3. Provided that the general rule in paragraph 2 continues to be observed, the Occupying Power may requisition the said resources, subject to the following particular conditions:
   (a) that the resources are necessary for the adequate and immediate medical treatment of the wounded and sick members of the armed forces of the Occupying Power or of prisoners of war;
   (b) that the requisition continues only while such necessity exists; and
   (c) that immediate arrangements are made to ensure that the medical needs of the civilian population, as well as those of any wounded and sick under treatment who are affected by the requisition, continue to be satisfied. (PI Article 14)

▪ When persons are being requisitioned, individuals must not be forced to take part in military operations against their own country (GCIV Article 51).

➔   **Medical duties; Medical personnel; Medical services; Occupied Territory; Pillage**

■ RESISTANCE MOVEMENTS

In 1949, the Geneva Conventions had already established that members of organized resistance movements could benefit from the status of prisoner of war (GCIII Article 4.A.2). These provisions can thus be extended to members of such groups. In 1977, the Protocol Additional to the Geneva Conventions, Relating to the Protection of Victims of International Armed Conflicts (Protocol I), extended the protection provided by its provisions to other types of armed movements.

Among the legitimate categories of combatants in a conflict, Protocol I identifies the members of "all organized armed forces, groups and units which are under a command responsible to a party [to the conflict] for the conduct of its subordinates." This applies even to parties represented by a government or authority that is not recognized by an adverse party (PI Article 43.1). This provision introduces the possibility of applying Protocol I to conflicts in which government forces are opposed to resistance or national liberation movements.

The conditions set forth by Protocol I are based on the fact that "such armed forces shall be subject to an internal disciplinary system which, *inter alia*, shall enforce compliance with the rules of international law applicable in armed conflict" (PI Article 43.1). These conditions were established to draw the line between a private and anarchic use of violence and a structured, hierarchic, and controlled use of violence by a military group.

Humanitarian law further takes into account the specificity of certain methods of warfare. It acknowledges that in some situations in armed conflicts, owing to the nature of hostilities, armed combatants cannot distinguish themselves from the civilian population in the required manner. In such cases, they can retain their status as combatants as long as they carry their weapons openly during each military engagement (PI Article 44.3).

The Additional Protocol II, relating to Non-International Armed Conflicts, provides for guarantees in the case of individuals detained in connection with the conflict, without referring to the individuals as prisoners of war.

→   **Combatants; Duty of commanders; Prisoners of war**

📖 **For Additional Information:**

Abi-Saab, Georges. "War of National Liberation in the Geneva Conventions and Protocols." *Receuil des Cours de l'Académie de droit international* 4, no. 165 (1979): 353–445.

Cassese, Antonio. "Resistance Movements." In *Encyclopedia of Public International Law,* ed. R. Bernhardt. Amsterdam: North-Holland, 1982, vol. 4: 188–90.

■ RESPECT FOR INTERNATIONAL HUMANITARIAN LAW

States party to the Geneva Conventions are under the obligation to respect and to ensure respect for humanitarian law, in all circumstances (GCI–IV Article 1; PI Articles 1 and 80.2). The fact that humanitarian law reaffirms states' obligation to respect its provisions—though this duty exists for all treaties (Article 26 of the Vienna Convention on the Law of Treaties)—reflects the binding nature of these texts. → **International Conventions**

The duty to enforce this respect exists on two levels. On a national level, states must incorporate the provisions of international humanitarian law into their domestic legislation and ensure that national penal sanctions exist, in case someone commits a violation. On the international level, states must take action if another state commits a violation, because the respect for humanitarian law is crucial to maintaining the international public order that all states must defend.

This respect and accountability are not based only on mechanisms for punishing violations. Because the damage caused by such violations is irreparable, this respect must be implemented before the need for punishment arises. The enforcement of humanitarian law therefore also rests on the creation of distinct spheres of responsibility for all participants in situations of tension or conflict, whether they are states, organizations, or individuals. These may include, in particular, states party to the Conventions, parties to the conflict, combatants, and relief organizations. ➔ **Responsibility**

Furthermore, it is important to note that all states or parties to a conflict are held accountable under humanitarian law, even if an adverse state or party violates its rules. The obligation to respect humanitarian law is not, in fact, tied to reciprocal levels of commitment (GCI–IV common Articles 1 and 2). It remains applicable even in situations in which one or more parties to a conflict are not party to the Conventions, for instance, or in cases in which they represent non-state entities or authorities that the adversary does not recognize. ➔ **International conventions; Legal status of the parties to the conflict**

Governments are still the main entities held accountable under humanitarian law, since they have the means to protect, apply, and enforce respect for it. The obligations of states in this regard can be divided into several specific duties:

- Parties to a conflict, and in general states party to the Geneva Conventions, must give orders and instructions to ensure that the provisions of the Conventions and Protocol I are observed and must supervise their implementation.
- States undertake to incorporate the provisions of humanitarian law into their national laws, especially in matters of criminal law (GCI Article 49, GCII Article 50, GCIII Article 129, and GCIV Article 146).
- They have the duty to disseminate the norms and rules of humanitarian law as widely as possible throughout their countries and, in particular, to the members of their armed forces (GCI Article 47, GCII Article 48, GCIII Article 127, GCIV Article 144, PI Articles 83.1 and 87.2, and PII Article 19).
- They are under the obligation to establish effective penal sanctions for persons who commit or order any acts that violate humanitarian law (GCI Articles 49 and 52, GCII Articles 50 and 53, GCIII Article 129 and 132, GCIV Articles 146 and 149, and PI Article 86.1). If such a crime is committed, states are under the obligation to search for the authors of these acts and bring them before their own courts, regardless of their nationality. They may also—if they prefer, and in accordance with the provisions of their own legislation—hand such persons over for trial to another state party concerned, provided this party has made out a *prima facie* case.
- States undertake to act jointly or individually, in cooperation with the United Nations and in conformity with the UN Charter, in situations of grave violations of the Conventions or of Protocol I (PI Article 89).

☞ The obligation to respect humanitarian law creates responsibilities for the different national authorities. However, if they fail to meet these obligations, the possibility of judicial recourse is not automatic. In case of grave breaches of the Geneva Conventions, international humanitarian law foresees penal sanctions based on the principle of universal jurisdiction and, once it is operational, through the International Criminal Court.

In case of other violations of the Conventions, judicial recourse may exist at national levels, but these are not specified in the Conventions and the recourse will therefore depend on each different national system of justice.

(continues)

> (*continued*)
>
> As a general rule, it is always possible to inform the International Committee of the Red Cross (ICRC) of any violations that have been noted, since the ICRC is the guardian of humanitarian law and the organ carrying out the role of Protecting Power.
>
> States may also refer to an independent fact-finding commission to investigate violations of humanitarian law that occurred in the context of a specific conflict (PI Article 90).
>
> Violations of humanitarian law often qualify as violations of other international conventions—namely, human rights conventions. In each case, the entire range of recourses offered by these treaties must be taken into consideration.
>
> ➔ **Individual recourse; Penal sanctions in humanitarian law**

➔ **Individual recourse; International conventions; International Criminal Court; International Fact-Finding Commission; Legal status of the parties to the conflict; Mutual assistance in criminal matters; Penal sanctions of humanitarian law; Protecting Powers; Protection; Responsibility; Universal jurisdiction; War crimes/Crimes against humanity**

📖 **For Additional Information:**

ICRC. "Respect for International Humanitarian Law: ICRC Review of Five Years Activity (1987–1991)." *International Review of the Red Cross* 286 (January–February 1992): 74–93.

Palwankar, Umesh. "Measures Available to States for Fulfilling Their Obligations to Ensure Respect of International Humanitarian Law." *International Review of the Red Cross* 298 (January–February 1994): 9–26.

■ RESPONSIBILITY

The notion of responsibility is an essential part of the implementation and respect for laws. A right is most often tied to a reciprocal obligation. If this obligation is violated, the individual who has committed such an act may be held accountable to his or her civil or criminal responsibilities. To enforce this responsibility, international law has established different mechanisms to defend the rights and freedoms it establishes.

Respect for human rights is upheld by a number of instruments allowing various forms of individual or state recourse, either judicial or not, by different international institutions.

➔ **Human rights; Individual recourse**

Respect for the law of armed conflict, on the other hand, rests on the enumeration of the specific obligations for which states, commanders, and combatants are responsible. International humanitarian law reaffirms the criminal responsibility of the different hierarchical actors. In case of grave breaches of humanitarian law, it also sets forth the recourses that can be used.

International humanitarian law does not set forth obligations for humanitarian organizations and their personnel in terms of penal responsibility and sanctions. However, it does establish their responsibility to respect humanitarian law in the context of their relief actions. Their responsibility as witnesses is also engaged when they confront massive crimes or coercion committed against the populations that they take in charge.

➔ **Humanitarian principles; Individual recourse; International Criminal Court; International Criminal Tribunals; Penal sanctions in humanitarian law; Respect for international humanitarian law; War crimes/Crimes against humanity**

1. The Responsibility of States

States party to the Geneva Conventions "undertake to respect and to ensure respect for the [Geneva] Conventions in all circumstances" (GCI–IV Article 1; PI Articles 1 and 80.2). This general commitment translates into several concrete responsibilities:

- States are responsible for all acts committed by members of their armed forces. Furthermore, if a state violates humanitarian law, it may be held accountable and have to pay compensation (PI Article 91).
- States are under the obligation to disseminate the text of humanitarian law conventions widely among their armed forces and civilians (GCI Article 47, GCII Article 48, GCIII Article 127, GCIV Article 144, PI Articles 83.1 and 87.2, and PII Article 19). For instance, they should include the rules and regulations of humanitarian law in their military regulations, instructions for armed forces, and code of military discipline, and they must ensure that their commanders know the rules.
- The political and military authorities have the obligation to take all necessary measures to ensure that the obligations foreseen by humanitarian law are respected (GCI Article 49; GCII Article 50; GCIII Article 129; GCIV Article 146; and PI Articles 80.1, 86, and 87).
- States are under the obligation to search for persons alleged to have committed, or to have ordered to be committed, such grave breaches and shall bring such persons before its own courts (GCI Article 49, GCII Article 50, GCIII Article 129, GCIV Article 146, and PI Article 86). This is regardless of the nationality of the accused, who may be a member of their own armed forces.
- States undertake to enact any legislation necessary to provide effective penal sanctions for persons committing, or ordering to be committed, any of the grave breaches to humanitarian law (GCI Article 49, GCII Article 50, GCIII Article 129, and GCIV Article 146).
- A state may not absolve itself or any other state of any liability incurred with regard to breaches of the Geneva Conventions, which were committed by their authorities, their nationals, or in their name (GCI Article 51, GCII Article 52, GCIII Article 131, and GCIV Article 148).

In the near future, failure to uphold the respect for humanitarian law, and particularly failure to search for and prosecute perpetrators of war crimes and other grave breaches, will be punishable by the International Criminal Court (ICC). Its statute was adopted on July 17, 1998. Once it enters into force, the Court will have jurisdiction over individuals accused of genocide, war crimes, and crimes against humanity, when no concerned state has launched such pursuits themselves (Article 17 of ICC statute).

2. Responsibility of Commanders

The law of armed conflict takes into account the hierarchical nature of armed forces and the discipline imposed by commanders. It therefore confers certain specific obligations on commanders and, in certain situations, holds them individually criminally accountable.

☞ The principle of authority must always be coupled with that of responsibility. This responsibility concerns both acts and omissions.

(*continues*)

(*continued*)

Humanitarian law holds commanders criminally accountable when they:

- give orders to their subordinates that violate humanitarian law;
- allow their subordinates to commit such violations;
- fail to punish subordinates who violate humanitarian law of their own initiative;
- do not prevent such a violation if they knew, or had information that should have enabled them to conclude, that such a breach was being committed or was going to be committed (GCI Article 49, GCII Article 50, GCIII Article 129, GCIV Article 146, and PI Article 86.2).

The commanders may be held accountable before competent national courts, before foreign courts (by virtue of universal jurisdiction) or before existing International Criminal Tribunals.

Commanders are also responsible for ensuring that members of the armed forces under their command are aware of their obligations under humanitarian law (PI Article 87.2).

The statute of the ICC reinforces these elements of responsibility (Article 25 of ICC statute), extending them to crimes against humanity, committed in times of peace or of war, and war crimes, whether committed in internal or international armed conflicts. It holds military commanders accountable, as well as other superiors, including civilians (Article 28 of ICC statute).

3. Responsibility of Individuals

All individuals having reached the age of legal majority are individually criminally responsible for any grave breaches of humanitarian law they commit, no matter what the circumstances may be. Combatants are held accountable even if the are carrying out the orders of a superior.

Superior Orders

International humanitarian law takes into account the fact that combatants generally act in the framework of a hierarchical organization or unit. It therefore first imposes specific responsibilities on commanders. However, the fact that a combatant acted pursuant to superior orders will not shield him or her from individual criminal responsibility incurred for grave breaches of humanitarian law. Individuals hence remain personally accountable, even when following orders. Thus, war criminals are individually criminally responsible for their acts (Article 3 of 1907 Hague Convention on the laws and custom of war; GCI Article 49; GCII Article 50; GCIII Article 129; GCIV Article 146; PI Articles 75.4.b, 86, 87).

The statute of the ICC also posits that "the fact that a crime within the jurisdiction of the Court has been committed by a person pursuant to an order of a Government or of a superior, whether military or civilian, shall not relieve that person of criminal responsibility." While some grounds for excluding criminal responsibility exist in the case of war crimes, there are no exceptions in the case of genocide or crimes against humanity (Article 33 of ICC statute).

The statute of the ICC clearly sets forth the elements that make up individual responsibility in terms of genocide, crimes against humanity, and war crimes:

a person shall be criminally responsible and liable for punishment for a crime within the jurisdiction of the Court if that person:

(a) Commits such a crime, whether as an individual, jointly with another or through another person, regardless of whether that other person is criminally responsible;

(b) Orders, solicits or induces the commission of such a crime which in fact occurs or is attempted;

(c) For the purpose of facilitating the commission of such a crime, aids, abets or otherwise assists in its commission or its attempted commission, including providing the means for its commission;

(d) In any other way contributes to the commission or attempted commission of such a crime by a group of persons acting with a common purpose.
Such contribution shall be intentional and shall either:

   (i) Be made with the aim of furthering the criminal activity or criminal purpose of the group, where such activity or purpose involves the commission of a crime within the jurisdiction of the Court; or

   (ii) Be made in the knowledge of the intention of the group to commit the crime;

(e) In respect of the crime of genocide, directly and publicly incites others to commit genocide;

(f) Attempts to commit such a crime by taking action that commences its execution by means of a substantial step, but the crime does not occur because of circumstances independent of the person's intentions. However, a person who abandons the effort to commit the crime or otherwise prevents the completion of the crime shall not be liable for punishment under this Statute for the attempt to commit that crime if that person completely and voluntarily gave up the criminal purpose. (Article 25 of ICC statute)

Certain limited grounds for excluding criminal responsibility are foreseen in the statute (Articles 26, 30, and 31). For instance, these provisions protect individuals who were under the age of eighteen at the time the acts were allegedly committed, as well as individuals who suffered from a mental disease or defect or who acted in the context of legitimate—and proportionate—self-defense, under threat of imminent death, or under threat of continuing or imminent serious bodily harm.

4. The Responsibility of Relief Organizations

The implementation of international humanitarian law depends on two features of the law: the definition of the violations committed and the mechanisms for penal sanctions established by the Geneva Conventions for belligerents. It is important to note that humanitarian law is particularly creative in this area, since the basis on which it establishes individual responsibility for both subordinates and superiors is whether or not illegal orders were obeyed. It was also innovative in establishing that the courts of all states can have jurisdiction over cases of grave breaches (under the principle of universal jurisdiction).

However, the respect for humanitarian law does not rest only on its punishment mechanisms. In situations of conflict, humanitarian law seeks above all to prevent civilians from being the object of direct attacks or other kinds of violence or from being subject to living conditions that result in the death of the most vulnerable. Humanitarian law's first concern is to prevent violence from occurring, not relying on postmortem justice. For this reason, the Geneva Conventions and Protocols have conferred an essential role on impartial humanitarian organizations.

Of course, humanitarian law imposes specific obligations on belligerents to spare civilian populations in times of conflict, and it enumerates the rights that belligerents must grant the civilians. But, in the end, it entrusts impartial humanitarian organizations with the responsibility, the burden, of defending the protection guarantees for the civilian population, through their relief actions.

Humanitarian law effectively establishes that impartial humanitarian organizations have (*inter alia*) the right to

- offer their assistance to parties to the conflict, at any time, without this being construed as interference in the domestic affairs of the state concerned;
- verify that a population is not suffering undue hardship due to a scarcity of supplies essential for its survival, such as food and medical supplies;
- undertake relief actions for the benefit of the population when it does suffer from severe shortages of essential supplies and monitor the distribution to the most vulnerable;
- collect and care for the wounded and sick and ensure that their treatment is in conformity with medical ethics and does not involve any form of adverse discrimination;
- guarantee that persons who are displaced or detained as a result of a conflict receive the protection and assistance to which they are entitled;
- provide all categories of protected persons with assistance in conformity with the rights and protections that humanitarian law grants them.

→   **Protecting Powers**

The Geneva Conventions do not impose strict legal obligations on humanitarian organizations that potentially could make them subject to penal sanctions. However, it is inconceivable that the rights they are granted do not, in exchange, create specific responsibilities for such organizations.

Such responsibility falls broadly under two categories: responsibility as potential witnesses to crimes committed against the population and responsibility as actors undertaking relief actions.

a. Responsibility as Potential Witnesses to Crimes against the Population

Through their presence on the ground, members of humanitarian organizations may be direct witnesses of crimes and coercion committed against civilians in situations of conflict.

Humanitarian organizations are not responsible for the general promotion or defense of human rights. However, their responsibility directly covers grave violations of humanitarian law (e.g., war crimes and crimes against humanity). They must report grave violations of humanitarian law that they witness and protest to the relevant national or international authorities that the violations must cease. When a humanitarian organization makes such a denunciation, it does not do so based on moral or legal imperatives: its aim is to secure the immediate improvement of the conditions for assistance and protection for the population in danger, through dialogue or confrontation.

The quality and effectiveness of the dialogue or confrontation that takes place between the authorities responsible for the population concerned and the relief organizations flows from the organizations' ability to speak out directly and to raise these violations to public debate at a local or international level.

Humanitarian organizations encounter various problems in trying to determine what attitude to adopt in such situations.

- The first dilemma is based on the fact that any public action undertaken with regard to a crime may jeopardize the safety, and therefore the presence and actions of the organizations on the ground. For a long time, humanitarian organizations adopted an absolutist interpretation of the principle of neutrality with regard to solving such problems. Neutrality prohibits organizations from taking a position vis-à-vis belligerents and their methods of warfare. However, in the case of genocide or acts of extermination, for instance, arguments that favor ensuring the continuation of relief operations for the population rather than risk jeopardizing aid operations no longer makes sense. Silence can no longer be the dogma for humanitarian organizations, since an authority might permit humanitarian activities to cover up crimes committed against part or all of the population. It is also possible that the suffering and deprivation experienced by the population is in fact deliberately organized by a given authority to attract and then divert aid. Such behavior challenges the responsibility and practices of humanitarian organizations.

  Therefore, the issue of neutrality must be viewed from the perspective of the real impact that protection and assistance effectively gives the populations concerned. It must be noted that in the conflict in the former Yugoslavia, for instance, the International Red Cross decided that denouncing grave violations of humanitarian law was not a breach of the principle of neutrality.

  Some organizations prefer to transmit the information they possess concerning grave violations, confidentially, to human rights organizations, which can make such information public without jeopardizing the safety of their own relief operations on the ground (since they do not carry them out). There are also various United Nations mechanisms that make it possible to render such information public, while maintaining the anonymity of the source. One danger of such an approach is that these procedures cannot ensure a 100 percent guarantee of a source's anonymity, and therefore the source's safety. Furthermore, such solutions also risk diluting each organization's responsibility, since they have different objectives and act under different time constraints. As a general rule, humanitarian organizations should act pursuant to a logic of immediate prevention, rather than follow a logic of after-the-fact condemnation and legal documentation.

- The second obstacle to denouncing crimes comes from the impression that their perpetrators will never be punished, whether because of the failures of the local justice system or law enforcement body. Under international humanitarian law, this is not a relevant concern, since perpetrators of grave violations can be tried by a variety of other courts: any criminal court in any country (under the principle of universal jurisdiction), potentially by an ad hoc International Criminal Tribunal (if one has been set up), and soon by the International Criminal Court—once its statute enters into force.

  Furthermore, it is important to note that many of the crimes in question are not subject to a statute of limitations (meaning there is no time limit within which legal proceedings must be initiated). This makes it possible to wait until political and military conditions have evolved to a point in which it is feasible to pursue such trials. In the meantime, it is important that humanitarian organizations contribute to the efforts to spread awareness of these crimes, in order to get them to stop. They can also document what is taking place before the evidence disappears. Finally, they can also provide medical reports and other documents to the victims, so as to enable them to assert their claims and their rights, wherever possible.

- In all cases, humanitarian organizations must be capable of qualifying the situations in which they are acting. This enables them to be in a position to negotiate their relief activities with regard for the rights that international humanitarian law grants to victims and humanitarian organizations in each specific case and to insist on the application of the relevant provisions of humanitarian law. This ability to qualify a given situation rests on the assumption that organizations have an understanding and knowledge of the fate of the populations and the crimes committed against them. It is the first stage of responsible relief action. Thus, fact finding and documentation of humanitarian law violations are an integral part of any responsible relief action.

- These organizations are under the obligation to signal these crimes to the relevant civilian or military authorities, to the ICRC, or to the members states of the UN Security Council in the most serious cases.

b. Responsibility as Relief Actors

Humanitarian law establishes specific rules governing assistance and protection of civilians in times of conflict. Humanitarian organizations involved in such situations bear the responsibility of negotiating their working conditions with the belligerents. These conditions must conform with the guarantees set forth by humanitarian law. Humanitarian organizations also carry the responsibility of reporting on the degree to which they succeed in or are prevented from ensuring the protection and survival of the populations concerned. This responsibility is not limited to simply exercising proper financial control over the use of the funds allocated to them in the name of international solidarity and compassion for the populations in danger.

Humanitarian organizations cannot delegate their responsibilities as relief actors to other organizations, including those specialized in human rights. Their responsibilities can be divided into several categories:

- They have the duty to negotiate working conditions with the authorities, in conformity with the guarantees set forth by humanitarian law to benefit the populations.
- They are responsible for identifying and reporting any obstacles, impediments, or prohibitions imposed on their relief activities. This action must be carried out at the local, national, and international levels. It is crucial, because it draws attention to any failures in the application of humanitarian law, and therefore to the dangers that a given population continues to face, despite the presence of organizations on the ground and the volume of aid being brought in.
- They are responsible for denouncing situations in which aid activities are diverted from their objectives or used to endanger the populations they are meant to protect. Sometimes, the very presence of humanitarian organizations and their actions are used against the populations they are trying to help.

For instance, this is the case when relief organizations are used to locate and attack the places where the vulnerable members of a population are gathered or when the distribution of aid is used to gather together populations who will then be attacked, sorted, or displaced by force. Sometimes, a party to a conflict has deliberately deprived a population of essential supplies to attract and divert aid. Finally, relief organizations are sometimes authorized to deliver material assistance so as to provide an appearance of normalcy to places where, despite the aid, the populations are subject to violence and coercion.

It is important that, in such situations, relief organizations be capable of analyzing the true nature of their action. They must not, through their silence and their presence, condone situations in which, despite the distribution of aid, the safety and the lives of populations continue to be threatened.

Many humanitarian organizations are still in an embryonic phase when it comes to taking these responsibilities into consideration. Too often, they are addressed through general debates surrounding the moral dilemmas faced by humanitarian action. These responsibilities should be an integral part of the evaluation of the impact and effectiveness of relief action at the heart of each organization, and should be subject to greater public transparency.

→ **Amnesties; Duty of commanders; Humanitarian principles; Immunity; Individual recourse; International Criminal Court; International Criminal Tribunals; Peacekeeping; Penal sanctions in humanitarian law; Respect for international humanitarian law; Universal jurisdiction; War crimes/Crimes against humanity**

📖 **For Additional Information:**

Aubert, Maurice. "The Question of Superior Orders and the Responsibility of Commanding Officers in the Protocol Additional to the Geneva Conventions of 12 August 1949, and Relating to the Protection of Victims of International Armed Conflicts (Protocol I), of 8 June 1977." *International Review of the Red Cross* 263 (March–April 1988): 105–20.

Blishenko, Igor P. "Responsibility in Breaches of Humanitarian Law." In *International Dimensions of Humanitarian Law*. Geneva: Henri Dupont Institute; Paris: UNESCO; Dordrecht: Martinus Nijhoff, 1988, 283–96.

Brownlie, Ian. *Principles of Public International Law*, 4th ed. Oxford: Clarendon, Oxford, 1990, 432–76.

Graditzky, Thomas. "Individual Criminal Responsibility for Violations of International Humanitarian Law Committed in Non-international Armed Conflicts." *International Review of the Red Cross* 322 (March–April 1998): 29–56.

Moore, Jonathan, ed. *Hard Choices: Moral Dilemmas in Humanitarian Intervention*. Lanham, Md.: Rowman & Littlefield, 1998.

■ RIGHT OF ACCESS

In situations of conflict, humanitarian law establishes that relief organizations have the right of access to victims and regulates the conditions governing this access. This right is a central element of humanitarian action because it enables humanitarian organizations to carry out their work based on independent evaluations of the needs of the populations, to ensure the efficiency of their activities, and to control the delivery and fair distribution of aid.

Various rules organize this right of access for different categories of persons protected by humanitarian law. Relief actions of a medical nature are entitled to a broader right of access than more general forms of relief. As we will explain later, the rules are more detailed for international armed conflicts (Section I) than internal ones (Section II). In addition to the 1949 Geneva Conventions and their Additional Protocols of 1977, certain UN resolutions invoke the right of access (Section III). However, these are not mandatory for states, unlike the Conventions.

> ☞ Humanitarian law posits and defends a right of access for the ICRC, impartial humanitarian organizations, and Protecting Powers, depending on the situation. This right is linked to the duties and responsibilities entrusted to relief organizations, which, in turn, are based on the rights of the different categories of victims.
>
> *(continues)*

> (*continued*)
>
> The duties of humanitarian organizations are never limited to delivering relief supplies. They also incur certain obligations with regard to protection of the populations they are assisting, by virtue of their very presence on the ground, and they must know these duties and take them on.
> → **Protection; Responsibility**

I. Access to Victims in International Armed Conflicts

1. Access to Wounded and Sick Persons

To provide relief to wounded and sick persons efficiently, medical personnel must have access to any place where their services are essential. This right is set forth expressly. It is only subject to supervisory and safety measures that the relevant party to the conflict might deem necessary (PI Article 15.4).

More generally, humanitarian law defends the right of access through the provisions that enforce the respect for and protection of medical personnel, vehicles, and installations and by establishing that no person can be punished for carrying out medical activities. It also provides for the evacuation or exchange of wounded and sick persons in besieged or encircled areas and for the free passage of medical and religious personnel, and medical supplies and equipment destined to this area (GCI Article 15, GCII Article 18, and GCIV Article 20).

→ **Medical and relief personnel; Medical duties; Wounded and sick persons**

2. Access to Prisoners of War

Humanitarian law also establishes provisions that ensure the right of access to prisoners of war for relief societies or any other organization assisting prisoners of war (GCIII Article 125). Detaining Powers may not prohibit such access. They can only limit the number of relief organizations authorized to visit and assist the prisoners. When making decisions restricting access, they must respect the special role entrusted to the ICRC by the Conventions with regard to access to and visits of prisoners of war (GCIII Article 126).

→ **Prisoners of war; Red Cross**

3. Access to Protected Persons

Persons protected by humanitarian law include those who are interned or detained, living in occupied territories, wounded or sick, and nationals of an enemy power residing in the territory of the adverse party.

The Geneva Conventions establish clear provisions for their protection. In particular, the Fourth Geneva Convention, Relative to the Protection of Civilians in Time of War, defends a right of access to, and relief for, all the persons protected by its provisions. These include civilians in occupied territories or gathered in places of internment, detention, or work, as well as wounded and sick persons. The Convention posits that relief societies and organizations (GCIV Article 142) and representatives of Protecting Powers or their substitutes, such as the ICRC (Article 143), must have access to these people.

States party to a conflict may never forbid such access. If they choose to limit it, they must respect certain minimum guarantees. In other words, subject to measures that they may consider essential to ensure their security or to meet other reasonable needs, the Detaining Powers must provide all religious organizations, relief societies, or any other organizations assisting the protected persons—and their accredited representatives—with all necessary facilities for visiting the protected persons and distributing relief supplies and other material needed for their work (GCIV Article 142).

As with prisoners of war, the restriction that the Detaining Power may impose is a limit on the number of societies and organizations allowed to carry out their activities in its territory and under its supervision. However, this limitation must not hinder the supply of effective and adequate relief to all protected persons (GCIV Article 142).

☞ The ICRC and Protecting Powers have a special right of access to, and specific protection duties toward, protected persons. This role must not be jeopardized by the actions of other relief organizations.

Humanitarian organizations are authorized to take on the role of substitute Protecting Power. In such cases, they must fulfill the protective functions foreseen by humanitarian law for the benefit of the individuals concerned.

→ **Detention; Internment; Protected persons; Protecting Powers; Red Cross**

4. Access to Civilians

In addition to the provisions governing the access to persons expressly protected by the Geneva Conventions, humanitarian law posits that relief supplies must be granted free passage to civilians in general.

All parties to the 1949 Geneva Conventions must allow the free passage of shipments of medicine and material, as well as objects necessary for religious worship intended only for the civilian population of another party, even if the latter is its adversary. It must also permit the free passage of all supplies of essential foodstuffs, clothing, and tonics intended for children under fifteen, expectant mothers, and maternity cases.

> The obligation of a High Contracting Party to allow the free passage of the consignments indicated in the preceding paragraph is subject to the condition that this Party is satisfied that there are no serious reasons for fearing:
> (a) that the consignments may be diverted from their destination;
> (b) that the control may not be effective; or
> (c) that a definite advantage may accrue to the military efforts or economy of the enemy. [. . .]
> (GCIV Article 23)

The power allowing the passage of these shipments is authorized to make its permission conditional on the distribution to beneficiaries being made under the local supervision of the Protecting Power. If there is no Protecting Power, this control is usually carried out by humanitarian organizations.

☞ The quality and efficiency with which humanitarian organizations exercise control over the distribution and use of relief supplies are essential elements to the provision of aid. Humanitarian operations must meet these obligations in order to invoke the right of access and free passage of such supplies.

Provisions for allowing the free passage of relief are also established for the populations in occupied territories. If all or part of such a population is inadequately supplied, the Occupying Power must agree to have relief operations carried out on behalf of this population "and shall facilitate them by all the means at its disposal" (GCIV Article 59).

The only limitation it may impose is to require that the humanitarian organization or the Protecting Power control the delivery of supplies, so as to ascertain that they are to be used for the population in need (GCIV Article 59).

Specific Provisions Governing Humanitarian Organizations' Right of Access to Civilians

In 1977, Additional Protocol I to the Geneva Conventions, Relating to the Protection of Victims of International Armed Conflicts, widened the scope and added details to the Geneva Conventions' provisions governing the right of access. Even if relief organizations find themselves in situations in which parties to the conflict have not ratified the Protocol, they can use this text to interpret, refine, and complete the rules set forth in the Fourth Geneva Convention.

- If the civilian population of any territory under the control of a Party to the conflict, other than occupied territory, is not adequately provided with [food, medical supplies, and other necessary materials], relief actions which are humanitarian and impartial in character and conducted without any adverse distinction shall be undertaken, subject to the agreement of the Parties concerned in such relief actions. Offers of such relief shall not be regarded as interference in the armed conflict or as unfriendly acts. In the distribution of relief consignments, priority shall be given to those persons, such as children, expectant mothers, maternity cases and nursing mothers, who, under the Fourth Convention or under this Protocol, are to be accorded privileged treatment or special protection [PI Article 70.1].
- The Parties to the conflict and each High Contracting Party shall allow and facilitate rapid and unimpeded passage of all relief consignments, equipment and personnel provided in accordance with this Section, even if such assistance is destined for the civilian population of the adverse Party [PI Article 70.2].
- The Parties to the conflict and each High Contracting Party which allow the passage of relief consignments, equipment and personnel in accordance with paragraph 2:

  (a) shall have the right to prescribe the technical arrangements, including search, under which such passage is permitted;
  (b) may make such permission conditional on the distribution of this assistance being made under the local supervision of a Protecting Power;
  (c) shall, in no way whatsoever, divert relief consignments from the purpose for which they are intended nor delay their forwarding, except in cases of urgent necessity in the interest of the civilian population concerned [PI Article 70.3].

- The Parties to the conflict shall protect relief consignments and facilitate their rapid distribution [PI Article 70.4].

- The free passage of relief supplies includes the right of access to the population in need and the free passage for the relief personnel participating in the operation (PI Article 71). This is tied to the provisions establishing the following:
  —the freedom of movement of medical personnel must also be guaranteed (PI Article 71).

(continues)

(*continued*)
> —"The Parties to the conflict and each High Contracting Party concerned shall encourage and facilitate effective international co-ordination of the relief actions referred to in paragraph 1" (PI Article 70.5).
➔ **Civilians; Humanitarian and relief personnel; Relief; Right of humanitarian initiative; Supplies**

II. ACCESS TO VICTIMS IN NONINTERNATIONAL ARMED CONFLICTS

If the civilian population is suffering undue hardship owing to a lack of supplies essential for its survival, such as foodstuff and medical supplies, Additional Protocol II to the Geneva Conventions, Relating to the Protection of Victims of Non-International Armed Conflicts, reaffirms the principle of free passage of supplies that are of an exclusively humanitarian and impartial nature (PII Article 18).

It also reaffirms that medical personnel must enjoy freedom of movement: whenever circumstances permit, and particularly after an engagement, all possible measures must be taken, without delay, to search for and collect the wounded and sick and to protect them and ensure their adequate care (PII Article 8).

Although this Protocol does not give additional details, the principles it reaffirms can be interpreted using the more specific provisions set forth in the context of international armed conflicts (see above).
➔ **Civilians; Humanitarian and relief personnel; Wounded and sick persons**

III. THE RIGHT OF ACCESS ESTABLISHED BY UN RESOLUTIONS

The rules of humanitarian law concerning the right of access to victims of conflicts have been reaffirmed by a number of UN resolutions, adopted during natural disasters or similar emergencies or disasters caused by humankind. Humanitarian law only applies to situations of armed conflict.

> ☞ UN resolutions reaffirming the right of access to victims of disasters fill a juridical void when they concern events that occur in times of peace. But in times of war, such resolutions risk weakening existing law if they are used to avoid officially recognizing a situation of conflict at a diplomatic level, or if they set forth requirements that are inferior to those imposed by humanitarian law, they risk weakening existing law.
>
> These resolutions' force of law does not make them mandatory for all states, unless they are adopted by the Security Council under Chapter VII of the UN Charter.

The resolutions do not establish a "right of humanitarian intervention." In fact, they reaffirm the sovereignty, territorial integrity, and national unity of states and recognize that it is the responsibility of each state to take care of the victims of natural disasters and similar emergency situations that take place in its territory.

The resolutions account for the fact that, in such situations, massive relief must be delivered rapidly to limit the number of dead, and that international organizations and NGOs may be able to play a major and positive role in such relief actions. For this reason, the resolutions invite all states who need such assistance to facilitate the implementation of humanitarian assistance operations by international organizations and NGOs. In particular, this applies to "the supply of food, medicine or health care, for which access to victims is essential" (General Assembly Resolution A/RES/43/131 of December 8, 1988).

Sometimes, to facilitate such access, the UN General Assembly suggests creating "relief corridors." In such cases, it asks for the cooperation of neighboring states (General Assembly Resolution A/RES/45/100 of December 14, 1990). The Security Council has used many variations on the notion of "relief corridors"—for instance, for the conflicts in the Sudan, Iraq, Liberia, Angola, Somalia, and the former Yugoslavia. The terms used in the resolutions vary depending on the level of political pressure applied. In Resolution 688 (S/RES/688 of April 5, 1991), for instance, the Security Council "insists that Iraq allow immediate access by international humanitarian organizations to all those in need of assistance in all parts of Iraq" and that the Iraqi government "make available all necessary facilities for their operations."

Relief Corridors

The creation of, and respect for, relief corridors established by UN resolutions do not impose any concrete legal obligations on states. Furthermore, the relevant resolutions are not always adopted on the basis of Chapter VII of the UN Charter, which means that their provisions are not mandatory for states. Also, when they apply to situations where there is a conflict that is more or less recognized, they do not systematically refer to the real obligations set forth by humanitarian law.

In general, such resolutions have been adopted in the context of larger peacekeeping operations, supported by the use of international force, as was the case in Iraqi Kurdistan or Somalia. Hence, they gave the impression of imposing mandatory access to victims, without taking on any of the protection obligations that are foreseen by humanitarian law for the benefit of victims.

➔ **Peacekeeping; Protected areas and zones**

➔ **Humanitarian and relief personnel; International humanitarian law; Intervention; Medical duties; Protected objects and property; Protected persons; Protecting Powers; Relief; Right of humanitarian initiative**

📖 **For Additional Information:**

Law in Humanitarian Crises—Access to Victims: Right to Intervene or Right to Receive Humanitarian Assistance? Luxembourg: European Commission, 1995.

■ RIGHT OF HUMANITARIAN INITIATIVE

Humanitarian law in general, and the Geneva Conventions in particular, establish obligations for belligerents and rights for persons who may be victims of the violence engendered by situations of conflict. The main obligations undertaken by the parties to a conflict are to refrain from committing acts that are prohibited and to fulfill their responsibilities toward civilians and other persons protected by the law of armed conflict.

To further protect or assist these persons, humanitarian law confers a right of initiative on the ICRC and other impartial humanitarian organizations, entitling them to offer their services. The Conventions forbid parties to the conflict to refuse such services, unless the parties can demonstrate that they are not needed, and also forbid parties to regard offers of services as interference in their internal affairs.

The laws also establish punishment that can be imposed in case humanitarian law is violated.

Unfortunately, these obligations and sanctions are not enough to guarantee the daily protection and survival of populations at risk, which is the main objective of humanitarian law. Hence, it is very important that humanitarian and relief organizations know their rights and obligations under international law and are able to provide aid and protection to the populations in danger.

> ☞ Humanitarian law does not rely only on justice and tribunals to enforce the respect for its provisions and punish violations thereof. It is a law of action that seeks to preserve life in situations of emergency. To this effect, it entrusts impartial humanitarian organizations with the responsibility of intervening to help protect the individuals and populations in danger.
>
> In addition to the specific provisions defending relief and protection actions and duties, the Geneva Conventions entitle the ICRC and other impartial humanitarian organizations to a general right of initiative (Article 3 common to the four Geneva Conventions). Concretely, the ICRC and NGOs can conceive of and initiate the kinds of actions that will best ensure the protection for and assistance to the victims. The Conventions specify that such activities may in no circumstances be regarded as interference in the internal affairs of a state. Parties to the conflict must facilitate rapid and unimpeded passage of all relief supplies, equipment, and personnel (PI Article 70).
>
> Humanitarian law thus reinforces the rights of humanitarian organizations in situations of conflict. If these organizations have poor knowledge of these laws, they risk weakening not only their own rights but also those of the individuals they seek to assist.

Humanitarian law thus creates a balance between judicial protection and immediate concrete initiatives to safeguard the lives and interests of the persons protected by humanitarian law.

1. Protecting Powers

The drafters of, and parties to, the Geneva Conventions recognized the value of having neutral intermediaries (e.g., humanitarian organizations) play a role in situations of conflict.

Impartial humanitarian organizations have several advantages over other actors: they have the trust of the belligerents (having negotiated their presence with them), their objective is to protect noncombatants, and they have the means to provide relief directly and efficiently to populations threatened by shortages or violence. Thus, they already play an official role in the system of protection foreseen by the law of armed conflict. The Conventions make direct reference to Protecting Powers or their substitutes, neutral and impartial intermediaries, the ICRC and any other impartial humanitarian organization, relief societies, and so on.

Such organizations have rights detailed explicitly in the Conventions. Their general right of initiative extends to any humanitarian activity or issue, which means that they also can offer their services for activities and in situations that are not expressly provided for in the Geneva Conventions or their Additional Protocols.

2. The Right of Initiative

The "right of initiative" itself is clearly established in Article 3 common to the four Geneva Conventions (known as common Article 3) and is reiterated in other articles of humanitarian law (GCI–III Article 9, GCIV Article 10, PI Article 81, and PII Article 18).

This right entitles any impartial humanitarian organization (the ICRC is mentioned explicitly as being such an organization) to offer its services in the context of a conflict. States party to the Conventions undertake not to regard such acts as interference in their internal affairs or as "unfriendly acts," and, in fact, they must facilitate rapid and unimpeded passage of all relief supplies, equipment, and personnel (PI Article 70). They may not refuse such offers for political motives or reasons related to the conflict.

The provisions establishing this right are aimed at ensuring that states do not interpret and apply the rules set forth by the Conventions in ways that limit or infringe on the protection to which the victims of conflicts are entitled. Thus, one of the Conventions' goals is to free humanitarian organizations from unnecessarily restrictive interpretations of humanitarian law's provisions. For this reason, they posit that states must not use or interpret any of the Conventions' provisions in a way that constitutes an "obstacle to the humanitarian activities which the International Committee of the Red Cross or any other impartial humanitarian organization may, subject to the consent of the Parties to the conflict concerned, undertake for the protection of civilian persons and for their relief" (GCI–III Article 9; GCIV Article 10).

Hence, humanitarian law—and in particular, the Geneva Conventions—grants a right of initiative—known as the "right of humanitarian initiative"—to the ICRC and any other impartial humanitarian organization. This seems to exclude other actors wishing to undertake humanitarian actions, such as states.

The ICRC reinforces its own right of initiative in its statute, which authorizes it to "take any humanitarian initiative which comes within its role as a specifically neutral and independent institution and intermediary, and may consider any question requiring examination by such an institution" (Article 4.2 of the ICRC statute).

→   **International humanitarian law; NGOs; Protecting Powers; Protection; Red Cross; Relief**

📖 **For Additional Information:**

ICRC. *Human Rights and the ICRC: International Humanitarian Law.* Geneva: Author, 1993.

S

■ Safety

Respect for national and international public order is meant to ensure the security of individuals. In times of peace, systems of justice exist to enforce the protection of individuals.

Situations of conflict, on the other hand, inherently result in diminished security both for individuals and for the state itself. In such precarious circumstances, the justice system cannot, in of itself, hinder immediate threats of physical violence. For this reason, humanitarian law foresees different kinds of safety provisions.

The Geneva Conventions and their Additional Protocols enumerate certain specific prohibitions regarding military and civilian authorities, aimed at protecting the physical security of the most vulnerable groups within each population. To achieve respect for such provisions, humanitarian law tries to take into account the specific stakes and dangers at play for each category of persons. Hence, it establishes levels of responsibility for the different official authorities, so as to ensure the safety of the following groups or entities:

- *Prisoners of war:* The evacuation and transfer of prisoners must be carried out humanely and in adequate conditions of safety (GCIII Articles 20, 46, and 47). It is forbidden to expose prisoners of war to a source of danger with the aim of using their presence to render certain areas immune from attacks (GCIII Article 23).
- *Foreigners:* Foreigners present on the territory of a party to a conflict are entitled to leave that territory under adequate conditions of safety, which are the responsibility of the national authorities (GCIV Articles 35 and 36).
- *Civilian internees:* A party to a conflict may intern protected persons only if its security makes it absolutely necessary to do so. Precise limits are set to protect places of internment against attacks, and guarantees are established to ensure adequate conditions of safety in case of transfer (GCIV Articles 42, 78, 88, and 127).
- *The civilian population:* To ensure the safety of the civilian population, parties to a conflict may not prevent civilians from means of subsistence. For instance, measures of security adopted by a party to a conflict may not prevent civilians from having paid employment

(GCIV Articles 39 and 51). In case of imperative military necessity, the population of an occupied territory may be evacuated (GCIV Article 49).

- *The state:* If a protected person carries out activities that are hostile to the security of a state (e.g., espionage or sabotage), that person loses his or her status of protected person but continues to benefit from the fundamental guarantees accorded to all individuals (GCIV Article 5).
- *Parties to a conflict:* Members of relief personnel may not exceed the terms of their mission and must therefore take into consideration the security requirements of the party on whose territory they are carrying out their duties (PI Articles 71, 74, and 75). If need be, the Occupying Power may disarm the members of civil defense personnel to ensure its own security (PI Articles 63 and 64). The Occupying Power may modify the criminal laws of an occupied territory so as to be able to ensure its own safety; however, there are established limits to protect the population from abuses. For instance, if a protected person must stand trial, a representative of the Protecting Power has the right to be present for the trial (GCIV Articles 64 and 74).
- *Protected persons or installations:* The Occupying Power cannot compel protected persons to ensure, by force, the security of the installations where they are forced to work (GCIV Article 51).
- *Relief organizations:* The principle of inviolability guarantees the safety of relief personnel, the free passage of humanitarian supplies, and the safety of other relief operations carried out by such organizations (PI Article 71). Parties to a conflict commit to providing relief societies with all facilities necessary to accomplishing their mission. States may take measures to limit the activities of these organizations; however, such limitation must not hinder the supply of effective and adequate relief to all protected persons (GCIV Article 142).
- *Medical transportation (land, sea, air):* All medical vehicles, ships, craft, and aircraft shall be respected and protected, subject to the relevant provisions such as those governing the conditions for flights and the notifications and agreements concerning medical aircraft (PI Articles 23–29).
- *Refugees:* The state on the territory of which refugees have sought refuge is responsible for their safety. To speak of "refuge," the territory in question must be safe; therefore, refugee camps must be established at a reasonable distance from the border.

Unfortunately, the safety of refugee settlements has not always been ensured. They have sometimes been used as buffer zones to protect a border from attacks. At other times, such "protected zones" have been militarized and used as a base from which to launch attacks. Yet, international law sets forth among the responsibilities of the territorial state that

— it must not use the presence of refugees as reason or a base from which to carry out hostile activities against another state, and

— it must ensure the safety of refugees.

UNHCR, and NGOs working in partnership with it, are responsible for monitoring the quality and level of safety and protection enjoyed by refugees.

➔   **Duty of commanders; Humanitarian and relief personnel; Medical services; Protected objects; Protected persons; Protection; Public order; Responsibility**

■ SANCTIONS (DIPLOMATIC, ECONOMIC, OR MILITARY)

Sanctions may be imposed against a state that does not respect its international commitments or when its behavior infringes on or threatens the international public order.

Sanctions are a means of coercion that may be political, economic, or military, ranging from arms embargoes to import quotas or interruption of diplomatic relations. They may be imposed by one state against another (unilateral sanctions) or by a group of states in the framework of an international organization such as the UN (collective sanctions).

1. Unilateral Sanctions

States may try to resolve their differences by resorting to diplomatic or economic sanctions. However, they can also submit their disputes to the International Court of Justice (ICJ) for arbitration or to regional bodies, such as the European Court of Justice. Although these judgments represent a legal ruling and are binding on the states concerned, they do not involve any criminal sanctions, as such. The only consequence of a failure to perform the obligations under an ICJ judgment is if the UN Security Council decides to use force to enforce the ruling (Article 94.2 of the UN Charter).

2. Collective Sanctions

The UN Charter establishes a system of collective security that regulates the pacific settlement of disputes among states. If these mechanisms fail, the Charter's Chapter VII (Articles 39–51) foresees the possibility of imposing collective sanctions on individual states, in case of "threats to the peace, breaches of the peace, and acts of aggression." The aim is to pressure the state in question into changing its behavior.

In such cases, the Security Council may adopt certain coercive measures, which must be respected by all UN member states. Before resorting to military sanctions, which are to be used only in exceptional circumstances, the Charter sets forth measures that do not involve armed force. The Security Council can hence adopt mandatory measures to implement selective or limited economic sanctions (e.g., an embargo on weapons exports) or full economic embargoes (an embargo on all economic trade), as well as diverse diplomatic sanctions.

The sanctions foreseen by the UN Charter are, in the order of increasing gravity: the complete or partial interruption of economic relations and of rail, sea, air, postal, radio, or other means of communication; the interruption of diplomatic relations; and armed intervention.

Humanitarian Exemptions

In the case of a "total embargo" on all forms of economic trade, humanitarian relief is always exempt from such restriction.

The UN, or the regional organization that imposed the embargo, sets up a Sanctions Committee to monitor the implementation and effects of the embargo or sanctions and to rule on exemptions.

→ **Collective security; Embargo; International Court of Justice; Peacekeeping; Public order; Sanctions Committees; UN Security Council**

📖 For Additional Information:

Minear, Larry. "The Morality of Sanctions." In *Hard Choices: Moral Dilemmas in Humanitarian Intervention*, ed. Jonathan Moore. Lanham, Md.: Rowman & Littlefield, 1998, 229–50.

Segall, Anna. "Economic Sanctions: Legal and Policy Constraints." *International Review of the Red Cross* 836 (December 1999): 763–84.

Weiss, Thomas G., David Cortright, George A. Lopez, and Larry Minear. *Political Gain and Civilian Pain: Humanitarian Impacts of Economic Sanctions*. Lanham, Md.: Rowman & Littlefield, 1997.

■ SANCTIONS COMMITTEES

The UN Security Council establishes Sanctions Committees to monitor the implementation and effects of embargoes or sanctions it has decided to impose against states for various reasons. Embargoes can be imposed against certain items only, such as weapons, or they can be "total," blocking all forms of economic trade.

☞ Even in the case of a "total embargo," humanitarian supplies, foreseen by humanitarian law to benefit populations in danger, can never be blocked from reaching their destination. Sanctions Committees decide whether a product can be exempt from the embargo, taking into consideration the commercial or humanitarian nature of the transaction or of the goods in question.

→   **Embargo; Sanctions (diplomatic, economic, or military)**

I. HUMANITARIAN GOODS EXCLUDED FROM EMBARGOES

Food and supplies intended for strictly medical purposes—in other words, medicine, medical supplies, and so on—are considered goods that are humanitarian by nature. They must be exempt from any embargo, and they are subject only to the notification procedure.

Merchandise the purpose of which is to enable certain institutions considered "indispensable to the survival of the civilian population" to operate, such as schools and hospitals (known as goods that are humanitarian by destination), may also be excluded from embargoes. However, they are subject to the more burdensome nonobjection procedure.

II. ROLE AND STRUCTURE

Each Sanctions Committee is generally referred to by the number of the UN resolution that imposed the embargo and thereby (e.g., Committee 661 monitors the total embargo against Iraq that was adopted on August 6, 1990, by Security Council Resolution 661 [1990]).

Each Committee is made up of the fifteen members of the Security Council, who elect a one-year chairperson from among the nonpermanent Security Council members. The chairperson has a secretariat (a secretary and five to six staff members) and is part of the UN's Department of Political Affairs.

Each Committee adopts its own rules of procedure, but they are generally the same for all the Committees. The decisions are taken by consensus (meaning all the members have veto power), and in the presence of all the members (meaning that any one absence blocks the decision).

Regional state organizations (e.g., the OAU, OAS, etc.) can also create Sanctions Committees, if they initiated the embargo. Their Committees' composition and their exemptions procedures may differ.

II. EXEMPTIONS PROCEDURES

The Sanctions Committees follow one of two decision-making procedures, which vary depending on the nature of the humanitarian goods under discussion.

1. Notification

When shipping certain goods (namely, goods that are humanitarian by nature), humanitarian organizations simply need to send a letter of notification to the Sanctions Committee. The acknowledgment of the letter's receipt that is then sent out by the president of the Committee is the authorization allowing the goods to be imported.

2. Nonobjection Procedure

For all other goods, each exemption request must be sent to the secretariat of the Sanctions Committee on a standard form.

Sanctions Committees examine requests for exemption and authorize imports of relief products that are of a humanitarian nature, on a case-by-case basis. Only states, intergovernmental humanitarian organizations (e.g., UN agencies) and the ICRC can make such requests. Nongovernmental organizations (NGOs) have to go through the government of the state where their headquarters are located. Concretely, this means that they transmit their request to the appropriate ministry, which then transmits the request to its ambassador to the UN, who finally submits the request to the relevant Committee.

The request is then transmitted to all the members and a deadline is chosen by which date the members must express any objection. If none has done so when the deadline expires, the president considers that the request has been accepted and informs the requesting organization by letter.

This exemption authorization is granted for a predetermined length of time (three months in the case of Committee 724, e.g., which monitors the "general and complete embargo on all deliveries of weapons and military equipment" to the former Yugoslavia, imposed on December 15, 1991, by Security Council Resolution 724). However, if one or more members of the Committee contest the request, it is subject to one, or possibly two, examinations. The final decisions of the Committees cannot be appealed.

NGOs have often criticized Sanctions Committees for a lack of transparency in their decisions. The decisions are taken behind closed doors and do not have to be justified, and no record of the meetings are held.

The criticisms also refer to delays that occur in giving responses to requests for exemptions. Any kind of delay is, of course, incompatible with emergency situations.

Finally, the embargo procedures and the Sanctions Committees are meant to apply political pressure on a government, a constraint that often weighs against the independence of humanitarian actions undertaken in such circumstances.

→ **Embargo; Protected objects and property; Relief; Sanctions (diplomatic, economic, or military)**

■ SANCTIONS/PUNISHMENT

Penal sanctions or punishment is imposed when a rule of national or international law is violated. The goals vary: to punish a guilty person, to protect the public order, or to solemnly reaffirm that the rule of law will survive violations thereof. Compensation or reparation for the victims are other kinds of mechanisms aimed at rectifying an injury. Reparation is rarely foreseen under international law, which usually refers the victims to the jurisdiction of national courts. Rare exceptions include the Inter-American Court of Human Rights, which has a relatively narrow jurisdiction, and the future International Criminal Court, the statute of which was adopted in July 1998.

1. The Method for Punishment

The method according to which sanctions are imposed varies depending on the nature of the crime and on whether the perpetrator was an individual, an organization, or a state.

Normal rules of criminal law apply to punish "classic" crimes. Special rules must be applied to prosecute and punish crimes of particular gravity, such as war crimes, crimes against humanity, genocide, torture, terrorism, and so on.

Penal sanctions are pronounced against individuals. Governments, states, and organizations cannot be found guilty in the criminal law sense of the term. Hence, they do not incur penal or criminal sanctions, as such, although they can be held responsible for damages caused by their activities and obliged to pay reparations. Only their leaders can be held individually criminally responsible and prosecuted as individuals.

Certain international judicial or nonjudicial organs can "judge" the behavior of states and even rule on disputes. Such rulings and decisions are mandatory, but the disputes are only submitted if the states themselves agree to do so. Furthermore, most of these organs are not mandated to issue sanctions. Certain political bodies, such as the UN Security Council, can impose diplomatic, economic, or military sanctions against states.

➔ **Human rights; Individual recourse; International Court of Justice; International Criminal Court; International Criminal Tribunals; Mutual assistance in criminal matters; Nonapplicability of statutory limitations; Penal sanctions in humanitarian law; Universal jurisdiction; War crimes/Crimes against humanity**

2. The Nature of Sanctions

The kind of punishment that can be incurred varies depending on the entity that imposes the sanction. The two main kinds are penal sanctions and disciplinary ones.

a. Penal Sanctions

Penal or criminal sanctions are pronounced by national courts in conformity with the rules of due process of the law. Individuals are subject to criminal sanctions when they commit a felony or misdemeanor defined by law. International law and humanitarian law establish rules and standards to ensure a fair and equitable trial and other judicial guarantees.

Humanitarian law sets forth precise rules regulating the administration of justice and punishment in times of conflict (mainly for prisoners of war and interned or detained persons) and in territories under foreign occupation. Sanctions must be imposed by an impartial and "regularly constituted" court, respecting the accepted norms of judicial guarantees (Article 3 common to the four Geneva Conventions). These guarantees include the following principles: an individual cannot be punished for an act that was not considered a crime at the time it was committed (this is the principle of nonretroactivity of criminal laws, or *nullum crimen sine lege*); an individual cannot incur a heavier penalty than the one that was applicable at the time the act was committed; and sanctions must be individual and applied only to the guilty person—collective punishment is always prohibited. → **Judicial guarantees**

b. Disciplinary Sanctions

Disciplinary sanctions are imposed by a superior against a subordinate under his or her authority who violated an internal regulation.

> ☞ Disciplinary sanctions are not surrounded by the same procedural guarantees as penal sanctions, although they can have serious consequences for individuals who (especially in times of conflict) are deprived of liberty, detained, or interned. Humanitarian law establishes precise rules and guarantees in terms of disciplinary sanctions that can be imposed on such persons.
>
> Humanitarian law also establishes precise limits on the disciplinary punishment that can be imposed on detainees, internees, and prisoners of war.
>
> → **Detention; Internment; Prisoners of war**

3. The Scale of Applicable Punishment

The kind of sanctions imposed, and their degree of gravity, depends on the crime committed but also on the judicial system under which the trial takes place. They also vary depending on whether the accused is an individual or a state.

Sanctions taken against individuals are defined by domestic laws and are scaled according to the gravity of the offense. They include the following:

- The death penalty
- Deprivation of liberty (prison sentences)
- Fines
- Corporal punishment: this form of punishment is abolished in many states that have adopted the principle of *habeus corpus* and focus their sanctions on different lengths of prison terms. Such punishment does continue to exist, however, namely in Islamic law. → **Corporal punishment; Death penalty; Detention; Internment; Judicial guarantees; Prisoners of war**
- Punishment by compensation: this kind of sanction combines punishment of the guilty person with compensation for the injury suffered by the victim. It is the basis of most civil suits, for instance, and is also common in more traditional legal systems. It includes the system of "blood money," for example, according to which the criminal's family pays the victim a lump sum equivalent to the harm incurred.
- Some communities punish individuals by banishing them from their society.

Sanctions may also be taken against states, either unilaterally or in the context of mechanisms enforcing collective security. In such cases, the sanctions are diplomatic, economic, or military.

→   **Sanctions (diplomatic, economic, or military)**

→   **Collective punishment; Collective security; Corporal punishment; Death penalty; International Court of Justice; International Criminal Court; International Criminal Tribunals; Judicial guarantees; Penal sanctions in humanitarian law; Sanctions (diplomatic, economic, or military); War crimes/Crimes against humanity**

📖 **For Additional Information:**

Orentlicher, Diane F. "Settling Accounts: The Duty to Prosecute Human Rights Violations of a Prior Regime." *Yale Law Journal* 2537 (1991).

Zalaquett, José. "Moral Reconstruction in the Wake of Human Rights Violations and War Crimes." In *Hard Choices: Moral Dilemmas in Humanitarian Intervention*, ed. Jonathan Moore. Lanham, Md.: Rowman & Littlefield, 1998, 211–28.

■ SECRETARIAT OF THE UN

1. Responsibilities and Powers of the Secretariat and the Secretary-General

Established under Chapter XV of the UN Charter, the Secretariat of the UN is at the service of all the other organs of the UN to implement their programs (Article 98 of the Charter). The Secretary-General represents the organization as its highest officer (Article 97). He (so far only men have held this office) oversees all of the employees of the UN. In addition to his administrative responsibilities, he may be entrusted with any other function, including political duties, by the organs of the UN (Article 98). He can also recommend actions to states, an important responsibility.

All actions undertaken by the Secretary-General must be guided by the highest concern for impartiality, and he must act in the broadest international interest. As the chief administrative officer of the UN, he reflects the independence enjoyed by international civil servants as opposed to representatives of governments who are appointed to different UN organs to represent their country. "In the performance of their duties, the Secretary-General and the staff shall not seek or receive instructions from any government or from any other authority external to the Organization." Furthermore, each member state undertakes to respect the exclusively international character of the Secretary-General and the staff and "not to seek to influence them in the discharge of their responsibilities" (Article 100).

The Secretary-General is appointed by the General Assembly of the UN, on recommendation of the Security Council, for a renewable period of five years (Article 97). Kofi Annan currently holds this position (1997–2002). He is assisted by a Deputy Secretary General, Louise Fréchette, a position added under recent UN reforms.

2. Structure of the Secretariat

The Secretariat is divided into nineteen departments or offices, headed by Assistant Secretary-Generals and by Undersecretary-Generals:

- Executive Office of the Secretary-General
- Office of Internal Oversight Services
- Office of Legal Affairs
- Department of Political Affairs

- Department for Disarmament Affairs
- Department of Peace-keeping Operations
- Office for the Coordination of Humanitarian Affairs
- Department of Economic and Social Affairs
- Department of General Assembly Affairs and Conference Services
- Department of Public Information
- Department of Management
- Office of Program Planning, Budget and Accounts
- Office of Human Resources Management
- Office of Central Support Services
- Office of the Iraq Program
- Office of the Special Representative of the Secretary-General for Children and Armed Conflict
- United Nations Fund for International Partnerships
- United Nations Joint Staff Pension Fund
- Office of the United Nations Security Coordinator

When the Security Council is examining a crisis situation in a given country, the Secretary-General is in charge of implementing the measures adopted by the Council. He must also report regularly on the evolution of the situation. The position of Secretary-General must not be confused with the UN's permanent representatives or Special Rapporteurs, who are also entrusted with monitoring specific country or thematic situations on behalf of different UN Agencies.

→ **Economic and Social Council of the UN; General Assembly of the UN; International Court of Justice; Security Council of the UN; Special Rapporteurs; United Nations**

■ SECURITY COUNCIL OF THE UN

Established under Chapter V of the UN Charter, the Security Council is the UN organ responsible for making decisions on issues concerning the maintenance of international peace and security, through a system of resolutions and votes.

1. Composition

The Council is composed of fifteen members, five of which have a permanent seat (China, France, the Russian Federation, the United Kingdom, the United States—collectively known as the P-5), and ten of which are elected by the General Assembly every two years, with specific regard to equitable geographic distribution (Article 23 of the UN Charter). The specific geographic allocation of seats was defined in a 1963 General Assembly resolution: three seats for African states, two for Asia, one for eastern Europe, two for Latin America, and two for western Europe and the rest of the world.

Some countries that have gained international influence are calling for a revision of the Charter and claiming the right to a permanent seat on the Security Council (Brazil, Germany, India, Japan). They emphasize the fact that the world order has changed since 1945 and that the UN must adapt. To be adopted, however, such an amendment to the Charter must be approved by the current permanent five members.

2. Voting Procedure

Security Council resolutions are adopted by an affirmative vote of nine members, which must include the concurring votes of all five permanent members. The effective result is to give veto power to the P-5, since no resolution can be adopted if one of them is opposed to it (Article 27.3 of the Charter).

This veto power can be avoided in two cases:

- a decision on procedural matters can be adopted with any nine votes (Article 27.2);
- if a vote is the result of a decision taken under Chapter VI of the UN Charter (on Pacific Settlement of Disputes), any state party to the dispute in question must abstain from voting (Article 27.3).

3. Functions and Powers

The Security Council exists "in order to ensure prompt and effective action by the UN."

The member states have entrusted it with the "primary responsibility for the maintenance of international peace and security" (Article 24.1).

To carry out its mandate, the Council may intervene in several different ways, as defined in Chapters VI, VII, VIII, and XII of the Charter.

a. Chapter VI: Pacific Settlement of Disputes

The Council acts as political mediator between states to help find peaceful solutions to disputes. A situation may be brought before the Council by a state involved in the dispute or by any other state, or the Council may decide on its own to examine a situation (Articles 33–35, 37). It can then make recommendations and suggest appropriate procedures. It may also carry out investigations.

In practice, most peacekeeping operations have been set up as a result of decisions taken under this Chapter. These operations are carried out with the agreement of the parties to the conflict, and their aim is to guarantee the compliance with a cease-fire or other type of accord reached by the parties. Such operations may be implemented by sending in observers, positioning peacekeeping forces, or through other methods to monitor the agreement in question. These are all acts, therefore, which are carried out with the consent of the states involved.

b. Chapter VII: Action with Respect to Threats to the Peace, Breaches of the Peace, and Acts of Aggression

In cases that fall under the Council's Chapter VII mandate, the Council disposes of increased powers. The decisions it takes in these situations are mandatory and binding on all member states of the UN, including those involved in the conflict, and do not need any agreement on their part. The Council can choose different measures to maintain or enforce peace and security:

- It can decide to adopt measures that do not involve the use of armed force, such as complete or partial interruption of economic or diplomatic relations, or of rail, sea, air, postal, radio, or other means of communication (Article 41 of UN Charter). It may even establish ad hoc International Criminal Tribunals, as it did for the former Yugoslavia and Rwanda.
- It may choose to employ forceful measures to maintain or restore peace (Article 42).

In the case of armed intervention, the UN Charter includes a provision whereby the Council's plan for the use of force would be implemented with the assistance of a Military Staff Committee (Article 47); however, this Committee has never been functional.

> ☞ The Security Council has the power—quite considerable from a legal standpoint—to qualify an act or determine its existence (Article 39 of the UN Charter). There is no precise definition of a breach or threat to international peace and security, and the Council alone determines whether a given act constitutes such a threat or violation. The Council also determines whether an effort to achieve a pacific settlement of disputes has succeeded or failed and whether a threat to the international public order exists. It can then enact the necessary measures to end the crisis or threat, which may or may not involve the use of force.
>
> ### The Security Council and the International Criminal Court (ICC)
>
> The statute of the new International Criminal Court (ICC) responsible for prosecuting individuals accused of genocide, crimes against humanity, war crimes, and—once defined—aggression, preserves the Council's prerogatives in situations reflecting a threat to, or breach of, the peace. The ICC also provides the Council with a new instrument of judicial pressure that can be applied to states in dealing with crises.
>
> The ICC statute includes a provision allowing the Council to suspend a prosecution or investigation undertaken by the Court for a renewable period of twelve months (Article 16 of the ICC statute).
>
> The Security Council can also refer a case to the Prosecutor under Chapter VII of the UN Charter, thereby making compliance with the ICC binding on states. Hence, it can impose the ICC jurisdiction on states that may not have ratified the ICC statute (Article 13 of the ICC statute).

c. Chapter VIII: Regional Arrangements

The Security Council encourages the pacific settlement of local disputes to be undertaken through regional agreements or agencies, provided that their goals and activities are "consistent with the Purposes and Principles of the United Nations" (Article 52).

The Council can therefore utilize regional arrangements to enforce decisions it has taken relating to the maintenance or restoration of peace (Article 53). In this manner, several peacekeeping operations have been "subcontracted by the UN to regional organizations such as the North-Atlantic Treaty Organization (NATO) in former Yugoslavia, the Organization of African Unity (OAU) in Liberia, and the Organization for Security and Cooperation in Europe (OSCE) in Chechnya.

> ☞ The Security Council takes on the legal responsibility for the way in which force is used (Article 47.3 of the UN Charter). Any claims or complaints concerning failure to respect humanitarian law in implementing embargoes or in the use of international forces must be submitted to the Council.
>
> *(continues)*

> (continued)
>
> In cases in which peacekeeping activities are delegated to regional organizations (e.g., NATO, OSCE, OAU, WEU), those entities take on the legal responsibility for the use of force. However, the Council remains responsible, and therefore retains authority over these actions (Articles 53 and 54).

Chapter XII, which concerns the International Trusteeship System for nonautonomous territories, has fallen into disuse.

Finally, the Council is also theoretically responsible for establishing a system to regulate armaments (Article 26), a prerogative it has never exercised.

4. Method of Operation

The Security Council is organized so as "to be able to function continuously" (Article 28.1). If necessary, it can meet in an emergency and in places other than the UN headquarters (Article 28.3). A situation can be brought to the attention of the Council by any member state of the UN (Article 35.1), as well as nonmember states (Article 35.2), the General Assembly (Article 11.3), or the Secretary-General (Article 99), or of its own initiative (Article 34).

The Council adopts decisions (generally referred to as resolutions), which are binding on states (Article 25), or recommendations, which are not. Norms of international law adopted by international organizations pertain to the body of "soft law." The force or status of law ascribed to such resolutions varies.

→   **Aggression; Collective security; International armed conflicts; International Criminal Court; International Criminal Tribunals; Intervention; Noninternational armed conflicts; Peacekeeping; Public order; Sanctions (diplomatic, economic, or military); Self-defense; Soft law; United Nations; Veto**

📖 **For Additional Information:**

Bailey, Sydney. *The UN Security Council and Human Rights*. New York: St. Martin's, 1994.

Roberts, Adam, and Benedict Kingsbury, eds. *United Nations, Divided World: The UN's Roles in International Relations*. New York: Oxford University Press, 1993, 63–103.

Weiss, Thomas G., David P. Forsythe, and Roger A. Coate. *The United Nations and Changing World Politics*. Boulder, Colo.: Westview, 1997, 21–122.

■ SELF-DEFENSE

One of the foundations of life in society is the principle that individuals must not use force to carry out justice themselves. The domestic laws of most states legislate that the only exception to this rule is the case of self-defense, when an individual uses force in response to an aggression that threatens his or her life or person. This notion does not include the use of force in response to aggression against material goods.

In relations between states, Article 51 of the UN Charter establishes the "inherent right of individual or collective self-defense if an armed attack occurs against a Member of the United Nations, until the Security Council has taken measures necessary to maintain international peace and security."

Peacekeeping forces, in fact, may only have recourse to force in cases of personal self-defense or under very specific conditions, unless they have a mandate that expressly provides otherwise. However, in theory at least, this notion has been extended in recent UN operations, which have been more forceful than previous ones, to include the authorization to use force if the mission's mandate itself is threatened, not just the persons of the peacekeepers. The resolutions allowing such extension refer to "extended" or "functional" self-defense.

In certain cases, members of the military have interpreted their mandate in humanitarian missions to include such forms of self-defense. Hence, in Bosnia, to ensure that the humanitarian convoys could be protected by force, the troops of the UN Protection Force (UNPROFOR) were authorized (under UN Security Council Resolution 776, of September 14, 1992) to use force in self-defense if armed persons attempted to prevent them from carrying out their mandate by force (Report S/24540 of the Secretary-General, September 10, 1992, and UN Security Council Resolution 776, September 14, 1992).

Similarly, in June 4, 1993, the Security Council adopted Resolution 836, which authorized UNPROFOR to use force to protect the civilians located in "safe areas." It thus extended the definition of the situations in which UNPROFOR could fire to include responses to "bombardments against safe areas by any of the parties or to armed incursion into them, or in the event of any deliberate obstruction in or around those areas to the freedom of movement of UNPROFOR or of protected humanitarian convoys."

In practice, however, the rules governing the use of force in such situations are often interpreted restrictively by the field commanders, mainly because of the shortage of military resources at their disposal that are necessary to implement such decisions. When a gap exists between the mandate and the means, experience has shown that officers privilege the security of the peacekeepers over the respect for the mandate. At other times, the mandates' definitions already set forth the PKO's limitations. For instance, the United Nations Mission in Sierra Leone (UNAMSIL), established in October 1999 under Resolution 1270, has one of the stronger mandates granted by the UN Security Council, in terms of both self-defense and protection of civilians. It is authorized to "take the necessary action to ensure the security and freedom of movement of its personnel and, within its capabilities and areas of deployment, to afford protection to civilians under imminent threat of physical violence, taking into account the responsibilities of the Government of Sierra Leone." When several hundred peacekeepers were taken hostage in May 2000, it became clear that UNAMSIL's ability to protect civilians was severely limited.

In fact, until today, the rare trials initiated against field commanders were based on the failure to protect peacekeepers and not on the basis of the failure to accomplish a mission. For instance, the Belgian Colonel Marchall was court-marshaled for lack of foresight because he risked the lives of ten peacekeepers from the UN Assistance Mission for Rwanda (UNAMIR), on April 6, 1994, at the beginning of the genocide in Rwanda. Only in May 1994 did the UN Security Council recognize that UNAMIR's mandate empowered it to "take action in self-defense against persons or groups who threaten protected sites and populations, UN and other humanitarian personnel, or the means of delivery and distribution of humanitarian relief" (Resolution 918 of May 17, 1994).

→ **Collective security; Peacekeeping; Public order**

📖 **For Additional Information:**

Doswald-Beck, Louise. "International Humanitarian Law and the Advisory Opinion of the International Court of Justice on the Legality of the Threat or Use of Nuclear Weapons." *International Review of the Red Cross* 316 (February 1997): 35–55.

Greenwood, C. "Self-defence and the Conduct of International Armed Conflict." In *International Law at a Time of Perplexity,* ed. Y. Dinstein. Dordrecht: Martinus Nijhoff, 1988, 273–88.

■ SIEGE

This is a method of warfare characterized by the encirclement of a locality or area, leading to its isolation and followed by attacks to crush its resistance. In the event of an attack on a besieged locality, medical units and cultural property must be spared. Pillage of the locality after its conquest is forbidden (GCI article 15, GCII article 18, GCIV article 16):

The rights of the besieged populations (non-combatants) are as follows:

- diplomatic agents and citizens of neutral states must be granted the right to leave, unless fighting is in progress;
- regarding the general civilian population, the parties to the conflict must endeavor to conclude local agreements to remove wounded, sick, and infirm persons and pregnant women from besieged areas;
- such agreements must also provide for the safe passage of medical and religious personnel and medical material within, and on their way to, such areas (GCI article 15, GCII article 18, GCIV article 17). These texts make no reference to food supplies.

Two additional provisions are specified in the case of internal armed conflict:

- starvation of civilians as a method of combat is prohibited (PII article 14);
- if the civilian population is suffering undue hardship because of a lack of supplies essential to its survival (such as foodstuff and medical supplies), relief actions of an exclusively humanitarian and impartial nature can be undertaken for the civilian population (PII article 18.2).

→ **Blockade; Evacuation; Famine; Methods of warfare; Protected Persons; Protecting Powers; Relief**

📖 For additional information:

Dinstein, S. "Siege Warfare and the Starvation of Civilians," *Humanitarian Law of Armed Conflict—Challenges Ahead: Essays in Honour of Fritz Kalshoven*, ed. Delissen, A. J. M., and Tanja, G. J. Martinus Nijhoff, The Hague, 1991, 145–152.

■ SITUATIONS AND PERSONS NOT EXPRESSLY COVERED BY HUMANITARIAN LAW

Legal approaches to the question of protecting individuals get caught in a dilemma. To offer the most effective protection, it is important to provide a precise definition of each situation and of the persons involved in it, to establish the specific protection to which they may be entitled. At the same time, the fortified protection granted to these persons may result in a weakening of the more general provisions meant to protect other persons or situations. Another risk is that searching for such precise definitions may cause arguments between those trying to determine the correct qualification for a given case. This may delay or hinder the application of protection needed for victims of a conflict. It is important to keep this issue in mind when examining the rights that remain applicable to situations and persons not expressly covered by humanitarian law.

Within this context, it is useful to remember that human rights conventions are applicable to all individuals, in all states that have ratified them. However, states have the authority to suspend a great number of human rights and liberties in times of conflict, internal disturbances, or tension. Only a small number of rights and freedoms remain enforceable at all times: these are the rights that may never be infringed on or suspended, known as nonderogable rights, and that continue to protect the fundamental guarantees to which individuals are entitled. → **Fundamental guarantees**

The 1949 Geneva Conventions and their 1977 Additional Protocols have a limited scope of application. To protect individuals better, these texts proceed by category: categories of conflicts and categories of persons.

The four Geneva Conventions and the Additional Protocol I are only applicable to international armed conflicts, except for Article 3 common to the Geneva Conventions (known as common Article 3), which covers noninternational armed conflicts and is complemented by the Additional Protocol II. However, in situations of internal disturbances or tension—when the violence has not reached a level of intensity high enough to qualify a given situation as a conflict— for instance, in the case of riots or sporadic acts of violence—humanitarian law does not apply, except for the principles set forth in common Article 3.

Humanitarian law sets forth the distinct rights of civilians, combatants, wounded and sick persons, women, children, detained or interned persons, prisoners of war, and populations of occupied territories or besieged areas. The strength of this approach is that it lists specific rights, carefully adapted to protect individuals in these categories from the specific risks that they may incur as a result of their status or the nature of the situation. The weakness of this method is that the more precise a definition is, the greater chance there is that a person or situation will be excluded from the protection that the definition is meant to engender.

To prevent the specialized protection that the Conventions provide from weakening the general protection they offer, several of their articles establish that

1. provisions of international humanitarian law are applicable to situations in which the Geneva Conventions might not otherwise or automatically be applicable (see section 1, later);
2. there is a minimum standard of protection that must be ensured for all individuals. It can be supplemented with additional but specific measures of protection meant to benefit certain specific categories of persons or situations (see section 2, later).

1. The Ad Hoc Application of the Geneva Conventions

The extensive rules set forth in the four Geneva Conventions only regulate international armed conflicts, except for common Article 3, which establishes the minimum protection that must be enforced in other situations, including internal conflicts. The article also establishes that parties to a conflict should "endeavor to bring into force, by means of special agreements, all or part of the other provisions of the present Convention." This mechanism allows the Conventions' scope of application to be enlarged on an ad hoc basis. It also helps to break any judicial reflexes that may exist and to emphasize belligerents' goodwill, or lack thereof, in terms of their willingness to protect the populations that are victims of the conflict.

In practice, this is facilitated because common Article 3 further states that the application of this provision "shall not affect the legal status of the parties to the conflict." Thus, one party to a conflict cannot use the recognition and application of the international law of armed conflict, or the signature of special agreements to that effect, to try to obtain formal recognition from the adverse or opposing political or military authorities.

This ad hoc approach to law does have an important safeguard: no special agreement may weaken the protection established by the Conventions (GCI–III Article 6; GIV Article 7).
➔ **Special agreement**

The Conventions further establish that "each party to the conflict, acting through its commanders-in-chief, shall ensure the detailed execution of the [Convention's provisions], and provide for unforeseen cases," in conformity with the general principles of the Conventions (GCI Article 45; GCII Article 46).

2. Minimum Protection

Common Article 3 establishes the minimum standards of protection applicable in times of conflict, whether international or internal. The principles it enumerates remain applicable at all times, including situations not covered by humanitarian law, such as internal disturbances and tensions.

This article, which defines the acts that are strictly prohibited in all circumstances, with regard to all non-combatants without adverse distinction, is explained in the entries on ➔ **international humanitarian law** (Section II.2) and **fundamental guarantees** (Section II). It also posits that "the wounded and sick shall be collected and cared for" and that "an impartial humanitarian body, such as the International Committee of the Red Cross, may offer its services to the parties to the conflict." The Additional Protocols provide further detail to these fundamental guarantees.

Humanitarian law also establishes that "in cases not covered by [the Geneva Conventions and Protocols] or by other international agreements, civilians and combatants remain under the protection and authority of the principles of international law derived from established custom, from the principles of humanity and from dictates of public conscience" (PI Article 1.2, GCI Article 63, GCII Article 62, GCIII Article 142, and GCIV Article 158).

This formulation is almost identical to the Martens clause that is part of the preamble to the 1899 Hague Convention (II) with Respect to the Laws and Customs of War on Land. This clause—named after Frédéric de Martens, the Russian delegate to the Peace Conferences held in The Hague in 1899, who introduced this language into the convention—was retained by contemporary humanitarian law. It reaffirms the duties and obligations toward humanity that states must uphold with regard to situations and persons not expressly covered by humanitarian law.

Finally, for situations in which fighting is not intense enough to trigger the application of humanitarian law, or for individuals who might not come under one of the categories of protected persons established by the Conventions, it is always possible to invoke the fundamental guarantees enumerated by human rights conventions. The "nonderogable" rights that they set forth are rights that can never be suspended or in any way infringed on. These rights are applicable to all persons, in all circumstances, no matter what their status may be.

Humanitarian law also depends on relief organizations to fill the void in situations in which no specific laws are enforceable.
➔ **Right of humanitarian initiative**

➔ **Customary international law; Fundamental guarantees; Human rights; Internal disturbances and tensions; International armed conflict; International humanitarian law; Noninternational armed conflict; Protected persons; Special agreement; Siege**

📖 **For Additional Information:**

ICRC. "Protection and Assistance Activities in Situations Not Covered by International Humanitarian Law." *International Review of the Red Cross* 262 (January–February 1988): 9–37.

Miyazaki, S. "The Martens Clause and International Humanitarian Law." In *Etudes et éssais sur le droit international humanitaire et les principes de la Croix-Rouge,* ed. C. Swinaski. Geneva: ICRC–Martinus Nijhoff, 1984, 433–44.

■ SOFT LAW

All resolutions adopted by organs of international or intergovernmental organizations (whether of a legal or nonlegal nature) pertain to the body of "soft law." Terms such as *resolution, declaration,* or *decision* are used almost interchangeably by international organizations.

The concept of soft law is used to distinguish its rules of law (sometimes drawn up unilaterally) from those considered to be the classic rules of international law, known as "hard law." Hard law is based on rules and regulations developed and adopted with the participation and explicit consent of the states or other actors who will be bound by these rules. International treaties and conventions fall under this category of law, for instance.

→ **International conventions**

I. DEFINITIONS

The legal definitions of the words *resolution, declaration, recommendation,* and *decision* are not strict. Nevertheless, it is possible to try to clarify the actual meaning of each of these terms, although their practical use may not reflect these variations.

Resolutions, Decisions, and Declarations

- *Resolution:* This term is used to designate the entire set of norms which make up soft law, whether binding or not, and is used most frequently. Both decisions and declarations are resolutions.
- *Decision:* This term is sometimes used to define a resolution that is legally binding. Hence, a Security Council resolution adopted under Chapter VII of the UN Charter is considered to be a decision (Article 25 of the Charter).
- *Declaration* or *recommendation:* These terms describe resolutions that can be qualified as expressing a statement of intent. They do not entail any binding legal obligations.

It is important to make a distinction between the following types of regulations or resolutions, adopted by international organs:

- *Self-regulating resolutions* are rules that directly affect the organ that adopts them, such as regulations on internal operations. In this case, the texts are automatically binding.
- *Non-self-regulating resolutions* are rules aimed at regulating international relations. Theoretically, these texts are not of a binding nature, but they may have a status of law.

II. Legal Obligations

The force or status of law ascribed to soft law norms varies. Most resolutions are not of a legally binding nature. In other words, their implementation is not mandatory. However, depending on the entity that adopts these texts, and their form and content, the resolutions may create obligations for states and may have a certain status of law.

Most resolutions adopted by UN entities do not entail mandatory legal obligations. This is even the case for Security Council resolutions, except those adopted under Chapter VII of the UN Charter, and for most resolutions and declarations adopted by the General Assembly. It is often the vague terminology used by international organizations to achieve consensus among the states that results in the absence of legal obligations, whereas precise recommendations can have an impact even if the resolution adopted does not carry mandatory force of law.

1. Legally Binding Resolutions

Some resolutions are legally binding. This depends on the organ that adopted them and the powers it exercises. Taking the UN as an example (in a simplified version), a strict interpretation of Article 25 of the UN Charter provides that only Security Council resolutions adopted under Chapter VII (which regulates actions undertaken with respect to threats to the peace, breaches of the peace, and acts of aggression) are binding. In 1971, the International Court of Justice gave a much broader interpretation of the scope of this article; however, doubts persist on the binding nature of Security Council resolutions adopted under chapters other than Chapter VII.

2. UN General Assembly Resolutions

As for resolutions adopted by the UN General Assembly, there has been extensive debate over whether they are binding. Though they are not a formal source of law, General Assembly resolutions do retain strength and authority since they reflect the opinion, or "general will," of states on a specific subject. If member states specifically give their consent to be bound by a decision, that can make it legally binding.

In other words, one must not underestimate the legal impact of a resolution that all or a majority of states declare is a legally binding norm: this reflects "general practice accepted as law," or *opinio juris*. In this case, the resolution can be said to have codified a customary norm that states had already recognized in daily practice, and it could be used as one of the sources of law applied by the International Court of Justice (Article 38.1 of the statute of the ICJ). Hence, the authority and weight of a legal obligation are not derived from the kind of entity that produces the norm but rather from its own customary nature. The fact that a resolution may not include any enforcement mechanism does not mean that it does not imply any obligations.

Often, if a resolution is formulated precisely enough to allow its application without any further interpretation, and it was adopted unanimously by the member states, it may have significant legal impact. A General Assembly resolution, adopted by a large majority, using precise language, and reflecting the opinion of the international community, may be considered as being of a legally binding nature, although it may not be enforceable.

3. The Legal Status of Soft Law Norms

The force of law that a norm of soft law may have—and hence its potentially binding nature—must first be determined on a case-by-case basis, by

- possible customary nature,
- the precision and specificity of its content, and
- the manner in which it was adopted (e.g., whether by consensus or not).

The force of law must then also be determined in conformity with the general principles of the hierarchy and interpretation of norms of international law.

→ **Hierarchy of norms; International conventions; International law**

■ SOVEREIGNTY

A state's sovereignty is based on the exclusive power that it exercises over its territory and its nationals. In international law, states themselves (i.e., governments) write the rules that they will be required to follow.

The principle of sovereignty regulates interstate relations. It is a fundamental rule that promotes pacific coexistence. It was sanctified by the Charter of the UN, which states that the organization is based on the "sovereign equality" of all member states (Article 2.1 of the UN Charter). Hence, all states must respect the prerogatives of all other states in their policies over their own population and their own territory.

It follows from this principle that no state may "intervene in matters which are essentially within the domestic jurisdiction of any other state" (Article 2.7 of the UN Charter).

However, nothing prevents states from voluntarily limiting their sovereignty. This is the case, for instance, when they ratify international conventions. When they do so, they bind themselves to the provisions of the conventions, thereby agreeing to restrict or set aside their sovereignty on the issues addressed in such texts—for instance, human rights or humanitarian law conventions. A large majority of states have signed international conventions that establish

- rules and standards of behavior that are applicable to state activities, within their own territories;
- international mechanisms and systems to monitor and control the implementation of these norms; and
- international organs that rule on complaints and provide recourses against national acts that violate or contradict international standards.

Many such international organs or control mechanisms were set up to monitor and control human rights and humanitarian law. In ratifying the conventions, states agree to submit to their decisions.

☞ With regard to relations between a state and individuals, the principle of sovereignty is no longer the golden rule. By ratifying conventions that establish international standards for the treatment of individuals, states have voluntarily renounced part of their sovereignty. In theory, individuals can have recourse against their government in front of international organs, whether judicial or not, without the rulings of such institutions being considered interference. However, these mechanisms are not easily implemented.

In times of conflict, states entrust impartial humanitarian organizations with the official responsibility for the protection of victims through the Geneva Conventions and other humanitarian texts.

States often criticize other states when they divert these institutions' goals by using them to weaken a government, diplomatically, instead of in defense of human rights.

➔ **Fundamental guarantees; High Contracting Parties; Human rights; Individual recourse; International conventions; International humanitarian law; International law; Intervention; Legal status of parties to the conflict; Nationality; Protecting Powers; Respect for international humanitarian law**

📖 **For Additional Information:**

Annan, Kofi. "Peacekeeping, Military Intervention, and National Sovereignty in Internal Armed Conflict." In *Hard Choices: Moral Dilemmas in Humanitarian Intervention*, ed. Jonathan Moore. Lanham, Md.: Rowman & Littlefield, 1998, 55–71.

Hehir, J. Bryan. "Military Intervention and National Sovereignty: Recasting the Relationship." In *Hard Choices: Moral Dilemmas in Humanitarian Intervention*, ed. Jonathan Moore. Lanham, Md.: Rowman & Littlefield, 1998, 29–54.

■ SPECIAL AGREEMENT

A special agreement offers the possibility of applying all or part of the Geneva Conventions to a specific situation of conflict. It is an agreement that is signed on an ad hoc basis by the parties to the conflict. Its aim is to make the provisions of the Conventions applicable in situations in which one or more of the parties to the conflict might not have ratified the Conventions or in which such provisions might not be automatically applicable for other reasons.

The 1949 Geneva Conventions and their two Additional Protocols, adopted in 1977, have a limited scope of application, which depends on two criteria—the nature of the conflict and the nature of the persons involved:

- The protection foreseen by humanitarian law is different in international and internal armed conflicts.
- Humanitarian law also distinguishes between various categories of protected persons (civilians, combatants, prisoners of war, the wounded or sick, relief personnel, and so on). It grants them different rights and establishes different measures of protection.

To prevent these distinctions from weakening the overall protection, Article 3 common to the four Geneva Conventions (known as common Article 3), sets the minimum rules that remain applicable at all times, in all circumstances. Furthermore, in situations where the Conventions are not automatically applicable, common Article 3 states that the parties to the conflict should endeavor to bring into force all or part of the Conventions' provisions, by means of special agreements. Article 6, common to GCI, GCII, and GCIII, and Article 7 of GCIV establish the framework for these agreements.

☞ Thanks to the mechanism of special agreements, it is possible to apply the most protective provisions of the Geneva Conventions or their Protocols, in all situations of tension or conflict, in a way that is binding.

A special agreement must never weaken the protection established by the Conventions. Humanitarian organizations can use this system of special agreements when drawing up contracts that regulate their work in a given country and that are concluded with the relevant authorities of that state.

➔ **Fundamental guarantees; High Contracting Parties; International humanitarian law; Legal status of the parties to the conflict; Situations and persons not expressly covered by humanitarian law**

■ SPECIAL RAPPORTEURS

Special Rapporteurs are experts who are responsible for monitoring specific human rights. This monitoring system was established by the UN Commission on Human Rights. The Commission's mandate to establish such mechanisms was firmly recognized in the Economic and Social Council's Resolution 1235 (XLII) of June 6, 1967, which states that "The Commission on Human Rights may, in appropriate cases [. . .] make a thorough study of situations which reveal a consistent pattern of violations of human rights [. . .] and report, with recommendations thereon, to the Economic and Social Council."

Special Rapporteurs are appointed to examine the general human rights situation of a specific country or to study a specific thematic aspect of human rights at an international level.

They are nominated pursuant to resolutions adopted by the Commission, which must then be confirmed by another resolution adopted by the Economic and Social Council. Their mandate is officially granted for one year, renewable each year. However, the Special Rapporteurs with thematic mandates are nominated on the basis of a three-year mandate, on average.

1. Mission

Their mission is to report to the UN General Assembly and to the Commission on the theme or country for which they are responsible. They therefore have no protection mandate.

The main method used by Special Rapporteurs consists of gathering all relevant information from all available sources, including NGOs. They may also visit the countries in question. The Commission or General Assembly may request that they issue several successive reports on the same subject.

Through practice, Special Rapporteurs, representatives, independent experts, working groups, and other such bodies that monitor and report on specific countries or issues have progressively established practical rules that states must respect to guarantee the independence, objectivity, and integrity of their mission on the ground.

These rules are

- freedom and ease of movement throughout the entire country being examined, in particular any zones where access is restricted;
- freedom of investigation, in particular with regard to: access to prisons, detention centers, and places of interrogation; contact with members of the government and decentralized authorities; confidential contact with witnesses and any individual, including persons deprived of their liberty, whom the Rapporteur wishes to see, without the presence of any representatives of authorities; full access to all written information that is relevant to the Rapporteur's mandate;
- the guarantee on the part of the government that no representative of the authorities or any other individual who has had contact with the Special Rapporteur will be subject to threats, pressure, punishment, or judicial procedures, as a result of this contact;
- the government's guarantee of safety for the Rapporteur, but without restricting his or her freedom of movement and investigation;
- UN personnel assisting the Rapporteur must be granted the same guarantees and ease of movement, before, during, and after the visit.

☞ Special Rapporteurs can use information transmitted by NGOs in a confidential manner. They do not have an obligation to cite the nature of their sources, which ensures that NGOs can safely and efficiently transmit relevant information, once they have reached an agreement with the Special Rapporteur.

Special Rapporteurs present detailed reports to the UN General Assembly, sometimes referring to specific cases, based on information received from many sources. This can free their reports from a number of diplomatic constraints. These reports can be useful instruments to pressure states to respect human rights and humanitarian law.

The relevance and legitimacy of the reports often depend on the personality and level of competence of the Special Rapporteur.

2. Country and Thematic Mandates

Special Rapporteurs currently have the following country and thematic mandates:

Country Mandates

- Afghanistan
- Burundi
- Democratic Republic of Congo
- Former Yugoslavia
- Iraq
- Myanmar
- Occupied Arab Territories
- Sudan

Thematic Mandates

- Adequate housing
- Contemporary forms of racism, racial discrimination, and xenophobia
- Education
- Extrajudicial, summary, or arbitrary executions
- Food
- Freedom of opinion and expression
- Human rights of migrants
- Illicit movement and dumping of toxic waste
- Independence of judges and lawyers
- Mercenaries
- Religious intolerance
- Sale of children, child prostitution, and child pornography
- Toxic waste
- Torture and other cruel, inhuman, or degrading treatment or punishment
- Violence against women, its causes and consequences

3. Special Representatives and Experts

Special Rapporteurs are among the many UN human rights–monitoring instruments. Their mission should not be confused with that of other individuals, such as Special Representatives and

Experts, nominated directly by the UN Secretary-General or by other UN bodies, as well as working groups, to monitor the situation in a country or to carry out a study on a specific topic, including human rights issues.

These individuals are nominated without the broader consent of the member states of the Commission on Human Rights; however, their role is of growing importance within the UN human rights monitoring system. The current country mandates include Cambodia, Equatorial Guinea, Haiti, Iran, Rwanda, and Somalia. The Secretary-General himself has a mandate on human rights issues in Cyprus, East Timor, and Kosovo. The thematic mandates of the Experts and Representatives cover issues such as the impact of armed conflict on children; internally displaced persons; the restitution and compensation of victims of grave violations of human rights; extreme poverty; human rights defenders; structural adjustment policies and foreign debt; and the right to development. The Secretary-General has been entrusted with a mandate on human rights issues, HIV/AIDS, mass exoduses, and reprisals (states' cooperation with representatives of UN human rights bodies). There are also two working groups, one on arbitrary detention and one on enforced or involuntary disappearances.

→ **Commission on Human Rights; Human rights; Individual recourse; Women**

✎ Special Rapporteurs
c/o Office of the High Commissioner for Human Rights (OHCHR)
52 rue Paquis 1202
Geneva, Switzerland
Tel.: (00 41) 22 917 91 59
Fax: (00 41) 22 917 90 12

■ STATE OF EMERGENCY/STATE OF SIEGE

In the case of serious threats to the public order or of dangers threatening the existence of a country, the government of that country may declare a state of emergency or a state of siege (depending on the circumstances). The legislative branch of a government may then vote to adopt—or the executive branch may enact—exceptional measures necessary to face the threat.

The measures implemented in such situations—for instance, internal disturbances and tensions—may limit or suspend certain rights. There are, however, fundamental human rights and freedoms that may not be infringed on: these are the nonderogable rights set forth in international human rights conventions.

Humanitarian law may only be invoked if the violence reaches the level of an actual armed conflict. Nonetheless, the principles protected by common Article 3 of the Geneva Conventions are applicable.

→ **Fundamental guarantees; Noninternational armed conflict**

1. State of Siege

When faced with a situation of particular gravity within a state, caused by a state of war or other exceptional circumstances (generally relating to the dangers prevailing in a besieged or encircled locality), a state of siege may be proclaimed. Exceptional measures may be adopted to ensure or restore law and order. Such measures may extend to the delegation of civilian powers to the military authority.

2. State of Emergency

This is a judicial situation that resembles a state of siege but gives rise to less severe restrictions on civil liberties. It is generally declared because of a present or imminent danger arising from natural disaster or because of serious disturbances to law and order.

→   **Fundamental guarantees; Internal disturbances and tensions; International humanitarian law; Public order; Siege; Situations and persons not expressly covered by humanitarian law**

📖 **For Additional Information:**

Gasser, Hans-Peter. "Humanitarian Standards for Internal Strife—A Brief Review of New Developments." *International Review of the Red Cross* 294 (May–June 1993): 221–26.
Herczegh, Geza. "State of Emergency and Humanitarian Law—On Article 75 of Additional Protocol I." *International Review of the Red Cross* 242 (September–October 1984): 251–62.

■ STATELESS PERSONS

A stateless person is someone who is not considered to be a citizen by any state on the basis of its national laws. There are ways of acquiring a nationality, which vary greatly from country to country. These may depend on the place of birth, the territory of residence, the nationality of the parents, or of only the father or the mother, and so on.

It is possible to lose a nationality, even one legally acquired, or to have it revoked by law. This may happen, for instance, through a marriage or a birth outside the country of which the parents are a national, which can result in the loss of that nationality but without the certainty that the person in question will acquire a different one. Events such as territorial transfers, decolonization, or the disintegration, breakup, or creation of a state may engender statelessness if the new laws do not grant the nationality of the state in question to all persons residing on the territory concerned.

☞ Stateless persons pose a serious problem to an international society that is organized around the concept of nationality. Individuals are protected as a result of their national legal status, since they do not have an autonomous international legal personality.

In times of conflict, a party to a conflict is forbidden from considering stateless persons as enemies and must grant them the protection provided to all civilians under humanitarian law (PI Article 73). Stateless persons must also be granted the rights granted to foreign nationals who find themselves on the territory of a party to a conflict (GCIV Articles 35–46).

Two international conventions are currently in force that try to establish minimum guarantees for stateless persons and aim to reduce the effects that may cause statelessness.

1. Convention on the Reduction of Statelessness

This Convention was adopted on August 30, 1961 (pursuant to GA Resolution 896/IX), and entered into force on December 13, 1975. It establishes that each state party must grant its nationality to persons who are born in its territory and would otherwise be stateless. It also requires that each state grant its nationality to any individual whose father or mother had the nationality of the state in question, if the individual would otherwise be stateless.

The main goal of the Convention is hence to make sure that all individuals who would otherwise be stateless—despite existing links with a state, such as birth, descent, or residence—can acquire or keep a nationality. The Convention does not establish any specific rights for stateless persons. Its text recommends the creation of an entity, within the framework of the United Nations, "to which a person claiming the benefit of this Convention may apply for the examination of his claim and for assistance in presenting it to the appropriate authority" (Article 11). This organ was never set up, and its functions were turned over to UNHCR.

2. Convention Relating to the Status of Stateless Persons

This Convention was adopted on September 28, 1954 (360 UNTS 117), and entered into force on June 6, 1960. It sets a minimum international status that must be granted to stateless persons. The Convention itself does not create rights for them; however, it does reaffirm the rights that must be granted to them by the laws of the state on whose territory they legally reside. States party to the Convention must treat stateless persons as favorably as possible and no less favorably than other foreign persons in the same circumstances. In particular, these provisions apply to the following rights:

- family rights, respect for personal status, freedom of conscience and religion (Articles 4 and 12);
- right to property (Articles 13 and 14);
- right of association (Article 15);
- right of access to courts (Article 16);
- right to engage in different professions (Articles 17–19);
- right to benefit from various social, administrative, and other public services (Articles 20–25);
- right to freedom of movement, travel documents, and transfer of assets (Articles 26–30);
- respect for rights in terms of expulsion and naturalization (Articles 31 and 32).

→ **Nationality; Refugees; UNHCR**

For Additional Information:

UNHCR. *The State of the World's Refugees, 1997–1998: A Humanitarian Agenda.* Oxford: Oxford University Press, 1997, 225–62.

■ SUPPLIES

Various provisions of humanitarian law address the issue of providing food and medical supplies to populations in times of conflict. The main principle guiding these rules is the fact that the parties to a conflict are responsible for ensuring the well-being and, at very least, the survival of the populations under their control, whether these populations are civilians in occupied or besieged territories or prisoners of war (GCIV Article 66; PI Article 69).

By requiring parties to a conflict to fulfill this responsibility, international law seeks to prevent the fact that relief is being brought in from outside the conflict to allow the belligerents to dispose of additional financial resources to sustain their war efforts. However, the law of armed conflict does set forth a number of exceptions to this principle, and gives humanitarian organizations the right to provide supplies to civilians.

☞ Civilians have the right to receive relief in situations of conflict. Humanitarian law establishes that relief operations must be undertaken by impartial relief organizations if the population is not adequately provided with supplies essential to its survival, such as foodstuffs and medical supplies, or is suffering undue hardship owing to a lack thereof (PI Article 70; PII Article 18.2).

The delivery of such supplies is subject to an agreement with the parties concerned. This is an "agreement in principle," established by humanitarian law, since it is forbidden for the parties to a conflict to refuse such supplies for political or military reasons. The agreement is only necessary for the practical implementation of relief operations. Parties to the conflict may only request guarantees that the supplies are not diverted for military purposes and that humanitarian organizations control the distribution.

The parties must allow the free passage of relief supplies or shipments. This obligation only concerns goods indispensable to the population's survival, such as food and medical supplies. This applies to besieged areas as well as any other area where there are civilians.

→ **Protected objects and property**

Humanitarian law posits that Protecting Powers or humanitarian organizations must always be at liberty to evaluate the needs of the affected populations (especially in terms of food and medical supplies) to ensure that they are not suffering from unnecessary or excessive shortages or deprivations (GCIV Article 55).

The law of armed conflict establishes that starvation must not be used as a weapon of war against civilian populations (PI Article 54.1; PII Article 14). It is permitted, however, against the adverse armed forces (PI Article 54.3). To justify and defend free passage of relief supplies, humanitarian law posits that humanitarian organizations must supervise the distribution of relief destined for the civilian population.

→ **Assistance; Detention; Famine; Food; Internment; Protected objects and property; Prisoners of war; Relief; Siege; Right of access**

📖 **For Additional Information:**

Macalister-Smith, Peter. "Protection of the Civilian Population and the Prohibition of Starvation as a Method of Warfare." *International Review of the Red Cross* 284 (September–October 1991): 440–59.

T

■ TERROR

Methods of warfare, and acts or threats of violence, the primary purpose of which is to spread terror among the civilian population, are prohibited by humanitarian law. Such acts include indiscriminate bombardment (PI Article 51; PII Article 13).

→ **Attacks; Duty of commanders; Ethnic cleansing; International humanitarian law; Methods (and means) of warfare; Population displacement; Responsibility; Terrorism; War; War crimes/Crimes against humanity**

■ TERRORISM

International law provides no clear definition for the term *terrorism*. An ad hoc UN Committee has been trying to reach one that would be acceptable to all states for several years. It is important to make a clear distinction between terrorist acts and activities carried out in the context of an internal armed conflict by belligerents who may not have been formally recognized by national authorities (such as guerrilla and other resistance movements). This step is crucial to determine the applicable law in each situation. In the case of terrorism, the state generally responds by increasing the police force's authority and activities, and by restricting certain human rights. In the case of an internal armed conflict, the state has the obligation to apply humanitarian law in the means and methods of warfare it selects, with regard to both the combatants and the civilian population.

→ **Noninternational armed conflicts**

The effort to reach a universal consensus in condemning terrorism has grown in recent years, with the UN and regional organizations adopting declarations suggesting measures to combat terrorism. In 1992, the UN Security Council adopted a resolution stating that international terrorism is a threat to international peace and security (Resolution S/RES/748). In times of peace, various international conventions that regulate mutual assistance in criminal matters address some of the measures to be taken. Those specifically related to terrorism are the following:

- The Convention to Prevent and Punish the Acts of Terrorism Taking the Form of Crimes against Persons and Related Extortion That Are of International Significance, adopted under the aegis of the Organization of American States on February 2, 1971 (it enters into force for each state as it ratifies the convention). As of March 2001, it has thirteen participant states.

- The European Convention on the Suppression of Terrorism, adopted under the aegis of the Council of Europe on January 27, 1977, and entered into force on August 4, 1978. As of July 1999, it has thirty-one participant states.
- The International Convention for the Suppression of Terrorist Bombings (Doc. A/RES/52/164.), adopted by the UN General Assembly on December 15, 1997, is not yet in force.

In times of conflict, humanitarian law prohibits acts of terrorism, such as attacks against the civilian population, and civilian objects and property. It also prohibits any acts the primary purpose of which is to spread terror among the civilian population. This applies to both international and internal armed conflicts (GCIV Article 33, PI Article 51, and PII Articles 4 and 13).

☞ The international law of armed conflict takes into consideration the specificity of guerrilla methods of warfare. It seeks to prevent such acts from being labeled as terrorism so as to limit the way in which states are authorized to use force in such situations. Protocol II additional to the Geneva Conventions, relating to the protection of victims of noninternational armed conflicts, is meant to apply in situations that go beyond riots or isolated and sporadic acts of violence. These are defined as all armed conflicts between a state party's armed forces and "dissident armed forces or other organized armed groups which, under responsible command, exercise such control over a part of its territory as to enable them to carry out sustained and concerted military operations" and to implement discipline (PII Article 1).

Minimum rules also exist that members of guerrilla movements must follow. For instance, they must act within the framework of an organized hierarchy, carry their weapons openly when engaged in a military operation, and not use terror against civilian populations (PI Article 44).

→　**Attacks; Methods (and means) of warfare; Mutual assistance in judicial matters; Prisoners of war; Resistance movements; Terror**

📖 **For Additional Information:**

Gasser, Hans-Peter. "Prohibition of Terrorist Acts in International Humanitarian Law." *International Review of the Red Cross* 253 (July–August 1986): 189–99.

Green, L. C. "Terrorism and Armed Conflict: the Plea and the Verdict." *Israel Yearbook of Human Rights*. Tel Aviv: Tel Aviv University, 1989, 131–66.

Witten, Samuel M. "The International Convention for the Suppression of Terrorist Bombings." *American Journal of International Law* 92 (October 1998): 774.

■ TORTURE

I. DEFINITION

According to Article 1 of the Convention Against Torture and Other Cruel, Inhuman, or Degrading Treatment or Punishment (known as the Torture Convention), adopted on December 10,

1984, torture is "any act by which severe pain or suffering, whether physical or mental, is intentionally inflicted on a person," for purposes such as

- obtaining information or a confession from the individual or a third person;
- punishing an individual for an act he or she, or a third person, committed or is suspected of having committed;
- intimidating or coercing the individual or a third person;
- any reason based on discrimination of any kind.

Such pain and suffering is inflicted by, at the instigation of, or with the express or implicit consent or acquiescence of a public official or other person acting in an official capacity. When individuals who are not officials commit such an act, it is not seen as an international crime. Instead, it should be judged as a violation of domestic laws and judged before the national courts of the country where the crime occurred.

Torture is a grave and deliberate form of cruel, inhuman, or degrading punishment or treatment, and no state may authorize or tolerate such acts, even in the most exceptional circumstances, including a state or threat of war, internal political instability, or any other public emergency (Article 2.2 of Torture Convention).

II. LEGAL BASIS FOR THE ABSOLUTE PROHIBITION ON TORTURE

Both human rights and humanitarian law texts establish that protection from torture is a "nonderogable" human right and a fundamental guarantee that must be protected at all times, both in times of peace and of war. ➔ **Fundamental guarantees**

States have the obligation to take all necessary legislative, administrative, judicial, or other measures to prevent torture and other cruel, inhuman, or degrading treatment or punishment from taking place in any territory under their jurisdiction, and to punish the authors of such crimes. It is important to note that the Torture Convention is one of very few conventions that has incorporated the notion of universal jurisdiction into its provisions, allowing any court of any state to prosecute perpetrators of crimes of torture, if they are found on their territory (Article 5.2 of the Torture Convention). ➔ **Universal jurisdiction**

1. Humanitarian Law Prohibits Torture at All Times and under All Circumstances

The 1949 Geneva Conventions clearly establish that torture is a grave breach of humanitarian law, that is, a war crime, if committed in times of conflict (GCI Articles 12 and 50; GCII Articles 12 and 51; GCIII Articles 17, 87, and 130; GCIV Articles 31, 32, and 147).

Furthermore, the Geneva Conventions strictly prohibit torture, at all times and in all circumstances. Article 3, common to the four Geneva Conventions, clarifies that "violence to life and person, in particular murder of all kinds, mutilation, cruel treatment and torture, [and] outrages on personal dignity, in particular humiliating and degrading treatment [carried out against any individuals who are not or are no longer fighting] are and shall remain prohibited at any time and in any place whatsoever."

In 1977, the Protocols additional to the Geneva Conventions reinforced this prohibition, reaffirming that such acts could be physical or mental (PI Article 75) and specifying that these provisions also applied to noninternational conflicts (PII Article 4). This has recently been reaffirmed by the statute of a permanent International Criminal Court (ICC), adopted in 1998, which includes physical and psychological torture in the definition of both the war crimes and crimes against humanity over which it will have jurisdiction once it enters into force.

→ **War crimes/Crimes against humanity** (Section III, "Grave Breaches")

2. Refugee Law: Torture as a Legitimate Ground for Seeking Asylum

Fleeing from torture or fear thereof is a legitimate ground for refugees to seek asylum in another state. In laying out the principle of *nonrefoulement*, the 1951 Convention Relating to the Status of Refugees clearly posits that "no Contracting State shall expel or return (*refouler*) a refugee in any manner whatsoever to the frontiers of territories where his life or freedom would be threatened on account of his race, religion, nationality, membership of a particular social group or political opinion" (Article 33 of Refugee Convention).

The Torture Convention reaffirms this by establishing that "no State Party shall expel, return ("*refouler*") or extradite a person to another State where there are substantial grounds for believing that he would be in danger of being subjected to torture" (Article 3.1 of Torture Convention). It also notes that torture must be included among the extraditable offenses in any extradition treaty between states.

→ *Refoulement* **(forced return) and expulsion**

3. Human Rights Provisions

Human rights conventions clearly establish that freedom from torture is a "nonderogable" right, meaning that states cannot infringe on or restrict this right, no matter what the circumstances may be. As mentioned earlier, the Torture Convention reaffirms that "no exceptional circumstances whatsoever" can be invoked to justify torture.

Three conventions (one international and two regional ones) specifically address the crime of torture:

- The Convention against Torture and Other Cruel, Inhuman, or Degrading Treatment or Punishment (known as the Torture Convention), adopted on December 10, 1984, and entered into force on June 26, 1987. It currently has 123 states parties.

   This convention, as explained earlier, created the → **Committee against Torture** (Articles 17–24).
- The European Convention for the Prevention of Torture and Inhuman or Degrading Treatment or Punishment, adopted by the Council of Europe on November 26, 1987, and entered into force on February 1, 1989. It currently has forty states parties.

   This convention mainly serves to establish the → **European Committee for the Prevention Torture**.
- The Inter-American Convention to Prevent and Punish Torture, adopted on December 9, 1985, under the aegis of the Organization of American States (OAS), and entered into force on February 28, 1987. It currently has sixteen states parties.

   For the most part, this convention mirrors the provisions of the international Torture Convention, with regard to states' judicial and extradition obligations, universal jurisdiction, and so on, adding the duty to incorporate national regulations guaranteeing suitable compensation for victims of torture into domestic laws (Article 9). It does not create a Committee, since the

Inter-American Court and Commission on Human Rights have jurisdiction over crimes of torture.

Finally, its definition of torture further clarifies the notion of mental or psychological torture: it adds "the use of methods on a person intended to obliterate the personality of the victim or to diminish his physical or mental capacities, even if they do not cause physical pain or mental anguish" to the international definition.

Other international conventions that prohibit torture include

- the 1948 Universal Declaration of Human Rights (Article 5),
- the 1966 International Covenant on Civil and Political Rights (Article 7),
- the 1950 European Convention for the Protection of Human Rights and Fundamental Freedoms (Article 3),
- the 1978 American Convention on Human Rights (Article 5), and
- the 1981 African Charter on Human and Peoples' Rights (Article 5).

Although human rights conventions mainly apply in times of peace, they list these articles among those from which no derogation is ever allowed, even in times of public emergency or war. Moreover, as already explained, since humanitarian law also lists protection from torture among the fundamental guarantees that must be upheld under all circumstances, the prohibition on such acts is upheld by a diversity of international norms, no matter what the circumstances may be.

Recourse in Case of Torture

In addition to the theoretical recourse before the courts of all states that have ratified the Torture Convention, torture victims can have recourse to international judicial or nonjudicial entities, under certain conditions.

a. Judicial Recourse

- Individuals can file a complaint before any court, of any state, under the principle of universal jurisdiction, whether the crimes were committed in times of peace or of conflict, provided that the perpetrator is found in the territory of that state (Article 5.2 of the Torture Convention, GCI Article 49, GCII Article 50, GCIII Article 129, and GCIV Article 146).
- If they reside in Europe, they can file complaints before the European Court of Human Rights (Article 34 of the European Convention on Human Rights).
- Once the International Criminal Court (ICC) begins operating, they will be able to refer cases to the ICC Prosecutor, under certain conditions. These are as follows: The state where the crime was allegedly committed or the state of which the accused is a national must have ratified the ICC statute, the acts must have been committed as part of war crimes or crimes against humanity, and these crimes must not be the object of any domestic judicial investigation or prosecution.
- The ICC statute excludes "pain or suffering arising only from, inherent in or incidental to, lawful sanctions" from its definition of torture (Article 7.2.e of ICC statute).

(continues)

(*continued*)

b. Nonjudicial Recourse

Automatic recognition of individual complaints: If the state in question has ratified the relevant treaty, individuals may automatically send communications or file complaints with the following entities:

- the Human Rights Committee (established pursuant to the First Optional Protocol to the International Covenant on Civil and Political Rights of 1966);
- the African Commission on Human Rights (African Charter on Human and People's Rights);
- the Inter-American Commission on Human Rights (American Convention on Human Rights).

Optional recognition of individual complaints: If their state has ratified the treaty in question and explicitly accepted the optional mechanisms that allow individual recourse, individuals may send communications or petitions to the following entity:

- the Committee against Torture (Article 22 of the Convention against Torture);
- The European Committee for the Prevention of Torture and Inhuman or Degrading Treatment or Punishment, established pursuant to Article 1 of the European Torture Convention, is not competent to receive communications from individuals. It is responsible for carrying out surprise visits to any place where persons are deprived of their liberty by a state that has ratified the Convention, and it can be alerted to intervene to prevent torture in cases of emergency. Nothing prevents victims from sending information to the Committee.

➜   **Individual recourse**

➜   **African Commission on Human and People's Rights; Commission on Human Rights; Committee against Torture; Corporal punishment; European Committee for the Prevention of Torture; European Court (and Commission) of Human Rights; Fundamental guarantees; Human Rights Committee; Individual recourse; Inter-American Court of (and Commission on) Human Rights; International Criminal Court; Ill treatment; Universal jurisdiction; War crimes/Crimes against humanity**

➜   **List of states party to international human rights and humanitarian conventions (Nos. 12, 13, 14)**

📖 **For Additional Information:**

Amnesty International. *Torture in the Eighties*. New York: Dodd Mead, 1984.

Haug, Hans. "Efforts to Eliminate Torture through International Law." *International Review of the Red Cross* 268 (January–February 1989): 9–25.

The International Fight against Torture. Paris: Nomos, 1991.

■ UNICEF (United Nations Children's Fund)

I. Structure and Functions

UNICEF (the UN Children's Fund) is one of the main subsidiary bodies of the UN. Originally founded by the General Assembly as the UN International Children's Emergency Fund in 1946, UNICEF became a permanent UN Agency in 1953. It now employs 5,600 people, with headquarters in New York.

The thirty-six members of its Executive Board, which meets once a year, are elected to three-year terms by the UN Economic and Social Council (ECOSOC), following a specific regional allocation of seats. The main contributing and beneficiary countries are represented. UNICEF submits its annual reports to the General Assembly and to ECOSOC.

The Executive Director is nominated for a period of five years by the Secretary-General of the UN in consultation with the Executive Board. Carol Bellamy currently holds this position. Her first mandate expired in May 2000, but it was renewed in September 1999 for an additional five years by the Secretary-General.

All contributions to the organization's budget are voluntary. States contribute approximately 61 percent. UNICEF also receives funds from private individuals—mostly through the sale of greeting cards—through the support of the national committees for UNICEF in industrialized states. In 1998, the total budget amounted to $1.1 billion.

The Executive Board allocates its budget to specific populations based on three criteria: the infant mortality rate for children under the age of five, the gross domestic product (GDP) per capita, and the number of children in the population.

II. Mandate

UNICEF's mission is to help governments meet children's basic needs and to help children reach their full potential. In 1996, the Executive Board adopted a new statement on the organization's mandate, incorporating into its mission the commitment to the protection of children's rights and the goal to establish these rights as "enduring ethical principles and international standards of behavior toward children."

1. Programs

UNICEF works with governments on their long-term programs aimed at improving the quality of life of children. These programs cover health, vaccination and nutrition, medical prevention, primary education, and "children in especially difficult circumstances" (e.g., street children, orphans, and children in areas of armed conflict).

    As is the case for all UN bodies and agencies, UNICEF may not carry out any activities in a state without first consulting the government in question and receiving its permission.

- In emergencies, UNICEF responds to the urgent needs of children and their mothers by offering assistance programs to the government, including healthcare, nutrition, and sanitation, as well as basic education and psychosocial rehabilitation. It collaborates with the relevant bodies in the UN system, for instance, in ensuring coordination in the humanitarian domain. It is one of the lead agencies in the Inter-Agency Standing Committee (IASC), run by the Office for the Coordination of Humanitarian Affairs (OCHA).
- UNICEF also develops research and evaluation activities so as to "be alert to the different circumstances that affect children's well being in different countries around the world" and thus improve the efficiency of its programs.
- It works in close collaboration with the Committee on the Rights of the Child, the treaty body set up as a result of the 1989 Convention on the Rights of the Child (CRC) to monitor its implementation. The Convention establishes that the Committee may call on specialized agencies and other UN bodies—namely, UNICEF—to give recommendations on the implementation of the Convention (Article 45, paragraphs a and b, of the CRC). In 1991, UNICEF's Executive Board decided to contribute actively to the implementation of the Convention and hence set a new orientation for the organization. UNICEF is now guided by this international instrument that falls under its mandate—the protection of childhood. Before the Committee on the Rights of the Child, it had formally committed to promoting children's rights and to monitor the implementation of the Convention in the different countries where it works. → **Children**
- Since the Convention was adopted in 1989, UNICEF has carried out awareness and sensitivity campaigns. It has also lobbied in favor of children's rights, in particular, pressuring governments to adhere to the Convention, which has now been ratified by every state in the world, except Somalia and the United States. UNICEF works in association with celebrities, who are "roving ambassadors" for its causes.
- Finally, UNICEF acts as the center for information concerning the situation of children around the world, through publications, conferences, and documentation centers.

2. Cooperation with NGOs

In emergencies, UNICEF works in coordination with UN bodies, humanitarian agencies, and other operational partners to develop programs rapidly to bring relief to children. It also cooperates with NGOs who already have a consultative status with ECOSOC. The NGOs can disseminate documents, may assist the Executive Board in writing its reports, and even—with the agreement of the President of the Executive Board—make verbal interventions.

→ **Children; Committee on the Rights of the Child; ECOSOC; Minors; Office for the Coordination of Humanitarian Affairs (OCHA)**

✎ UNICEF
Three UN Plaza
New York, NY 10017 U.S.A.
Tel.: (1) 212 326-7000
Fax: (1) 212 888-7465
@ UNICEF: www.unicef.org

■ UNITED NATIONS (UN)

With 189 member states and 8,700 employees in the New York Secretariat, the UN is the largest international organization in the world. Its membership is open to all states that accept the obligations established in the Charter, and its aim is to achieve universal adherence.

1. The Charter of the UN

The Charter of the UN is the treaty that founded the organization. It was signed in San Francisco in 1945. The states that participated in the San Francisco Conference chose to give this treaty a higher status than all other treaties (Article 103 of the UN Charter). This means that, in case a contradiction or conflict arises, states' obligations to the Charter must prevail over those under other conventions. Hence, no other Convention may derogate from the Charter's principles. → **Hierarchy of norms; International conventions**

The Charter defines the goals of the worldwide organization. To "save succeeding generations from the scourge of war" (preamble), the Charter sets out two main objectives for the UN:

- the maintenance of international peace and security through a system of collective security: member states commit to renounce the use of force as a means of settling their disputes, and the UN commits to protect the international public order;
- the promotion of the economic and social advancement of all peoples, through respect for human rights and the development of technical cooperation among states.

These two pillars of the UN are entrusted to different organs of the organization. Its principal organs and their commissions make up the UN per se; these organs, their subsidiary bodies, the programs, funds, and specialized agencies of the UN form the entire "UN system" or "UN family."

2. The UN Organs

The five principal organs provided for in the Charter are

- the General Assembly (Chapter IV of the Charter),
- the Security Council (Chapter V),
- the Economic and Social Council (Chapter X),
- the International Court of Justice (Chapter XIV), and
- the Secretariat (Chapter XV).

Chapter XIII of the Charter established a Trusteeship Council to oversee the transition of nonindependent territories to self-government. It has fallen into disuse. **→ Economic and Social Council; General Assembly; International Court of Justice; Secretariat of the UN; Security Council**

These organs have mandates that enable them to create subsidiary bodies. The principal organ delegates the relevant duties to such a body, but retains the overall control and responsibilities. The subsidiary bodies are not international organizations in the legal sense; that is, they do not have an independent international legal personality. This means that they continue to depend legally on the principal organ that created them. Examples of such bodies include the World Food Program (WFP), the UN High Commissioner for Refugees (UNHCR), the UN Children's Fund (UNICEF), the UN Development Program (UNDP), the ad hoc international criminal tribunals for the former Yugoslavia and Rwanda, and peacekeeping operations. **→ International Criminal Tribunals; Peacekeeping; UNDP; UNHCR; UNICEF; World Food Program**

3. Specialized Agencies of the UN

In certain cases, states may want to be more independent from the UN than the principal organs can be, particularly in areas of technical cooperation. They then set up a new entity—with its own membership, rules, and mandate—through an international convention. These are called Specialized Agencies of the UN, but they are legally independent from it. This is the case for the World Health Organization (WHO), the Food and Agriculture Organization (FAO), and sixteen other agencies.

→ FAO; WHO

4. The UN and Humanitarian Affairs

The head of the Office for the Coordination of Humanitarian Affairs (OCHA) is an Undersecretary-General and coordinates an Inter-Agency Standing Committee (IASC), which is the main decision-making forum for emergencies. Its members are the heads of the UN bodies and specialized agencies involved directly in humanitarian relief: UNDP, UNICEF, UNHCR, WFP, FAO, and WHO. The International Committee of the Red Cross (ICRC) participates directly, and NGOs may also be invited to do so.

→ Office for the Coordination of Humanitarian Affairs (OCHA)

→ Collective Security; Commission on Human Rights; Economic and Social Council of the UN; Food and Agriculture Organization; General Assembly of the UN; International Court of Justice; International Criminal Tribunals; Office for the Coordination of Humanitarian Affairs (OCHA); Peacekeeping; Public order; Secretariat of the UN; Security Council of the UN; UN High Commissioner for Refugees; UNICEF; World Food Program; World Health Organization

✎   United Nations (headquarters)
    One UN Plaza
    New York, NY 10017 U.S.A.
    Tel.: (1) 212 963-1234
    Fax: (1) 212 963-4879
    Office of the United Nations in Geneva
    Palais des Nations

CH 1211 Geneva, Switzerland
Tel.: (41) 22 917 1234
Fax: (41) 22 917 0023

📖 **For Additional Information:**

Alston, Philip, ed. *The United Nations and Human Rights: A Critical Appraisal*. New York: Oxford University Press, 1992.
Roberts, Adam, and Benedict Kingsbury, eds. *United Nations, Divided World: The UN's Roles in International Relations*. New York: Oxford University Press, 1993.
United Nations. *Basic Facts about the United Nations*. New York: Author, 1999.
———. *Yearbook of the United Nations.* New York: Author, published annually.
Weiss, Thomas G., David P. Forsythe, and Roger A. Coate. *The United Nations and Changing World Politics*. Boulder, Colo.: Westview, 1997.

@   United Nations: www.un.org
      United Nations System: www.unsystem.org

■ UNITED NATIONS DEVELOPMENT PROGRAM (UNDP)

The UN Development Program (UNDP) was founded in 1965 by the General Assembly of the UN. It is a subsidiary organ of the UN with its headquarters in New York.

1. Mandate

UNDP is "committed to the principle that development is inseparable from the quest for peace and human security and that the UN must be a strong force for development as well as peace" (UNDP mission statement). UNDP's main goal is to help countries develop the capacity to achieve "sustainable human development" and build "good governance" in an attempt to eradicate poverty. UNDP often coordinates with other UN organs and agencies: its Resident Representatives usually serve as Resident Coordinators of the operational activities of the UN system, coordinating development and humanitarian assistance.

It also "strives to be an effective development partner for the UN relief agencies. [. . .] It acts to help countries to prepare for, avoid and manage complex emergencies and disasters." To this effect, it is one of the lead organs in the UN Inter-Agency Standing Committee (IASC), which aims to ensure coordination in humanitarian emergencies.

2. Structure

UNDP is controlled by an Executive Board consisting of thirty-six member states, elected to three-year renewable terms. The Administrator is elected by the Secretary-General of the UN, with the consent of the General Assembly. Eighty-five percent of the UNDP staff is based in the field.

UNDP has 132 country offices, with programs in more than 170 countries. In 1996, it received over $2 billion in voluntary contributions; $23.5 million was for emergency humanitarian assistance. In addition to its regular programs, it administers certain special-purpose funds, such as the UN Development Fund for Women (UNIFEM), the Office to Combat Desertification and Drought (UNSO), and the UN Volunteers, and it cofunds the Global Environment Facility as well as a global program on HIV/AIDS.

3. Means

- Its programs around the world focus on themes such as poverty eradication, environmental regeneration, job creation, and the advancement of women. In administering its programs, it draws on the expertise of national NGOs and individuals, as well as the UN specialized agencies.
- In 1997, UNDP launched a Human Development Report, which offers a new "multidimensional" way to measure poverty. The report suggests developing actions around six main axes: economic empowerment of the poor, promotion of gender equality, proactive economic growth for the poor, managing globalization with a greater concern for global equity, good governance, and "special actions for special situations." This last policy suggestion includes establishing special measures of international support for countries facing extreme poverty for various reasons—for instance, social disintegration or conflict.
- In terms of emergency situations, the Resident Representatives can organize relief efforts in direct cooperation with the Emergency Relief Coordinator for the UN Office for the Coordination of Humanitarian Affairs (OCHA). UNDP also tries to integrate rehabilitation projects into relief operations to alleviate the poverty that often further fuels tension. Finally, it also runs a Disaster Management Training Program in coordination with OCHA.

➔ **Office for the Coordination of Humanitarian Affairs (OCHA); Relief; United Nations; Women**

✎ UN Development Program (UNDP)
One UN Plaza
New York, NY 10017 U.S.A.
Tel.: (1) 212 906-5315
Fax: (1) 212 906-5364
@ UN Development Program: www.undp.org

■ UNITED NATIONS HIGH COMMISSIONER FOR HUMAN RIGHTS (UNHCHR)

The position of a UN High Commissioner for Human Rights (UNHCHR) was established pursuant to UN General Assembly Resolution 48/181 of December 20, 1993, which followed the recommendations of the Vienna Declaration and Program of Action adopted on June 25, 1993, at the UN World Conference on Human Rights. In 1997, the Office of the UNHCHR and the pre-existing UN Center for Human Rights were consolidated into one office, located in Geneva.

1. Mandate

The UNHCHR's mission is to "ensure the universal enjoyment of all human rights by giving practical effect to the will and resolve of the world community as expressed by the UN." Its mandate is based on several of the UN Charter's articles, including Article 55, which reaffirms the organization's aim to create the "conditions of stability and well-being which are necessary for peaceful and friendly relations among nations based on respect for the principles of equal rights and self-determination of peoples," and its commitment to promote universal respect for human rights and fundamental freedoms for all, without distinction.

2. Structure

The Office is divided into organizational units, headed by the High Commissioner who holds the rank of UN Undersecretary-General, a four-year mandate. (Mary Robinson has held this position since 1997.) She is assisted by a Deputy High Commissioner, a staff, and an administrative section. A small New York office represents the High Commissioner at UN headquarters.

The Office of the UNHCHR has several branches: the Research and Right to Development branch, the Support Services branch, and an Activities and Programs branch. Its budget for 2001 was $75.3 million.

3. Means

UNHCHR promotes international cooperation for human rights, in particular, coordinating actions and stimulating policies throughout the UN system. Its functions to this effect include the following:

- Promoting universal ratification and implementation of international conventions and other standards, and assisting in the development of new norms → **Human rights; International law**
- Managing the information services of the UN human rights program, including the documentation center and library, and providing policy analysis, studies, and advice, on issues including the practice of UN Organs and other substantive procedures
- Promoting the establishment of national human rights infrastructures, including through field activities and operations. It undertakes field activities and operations and provides education, information advisory services, and technical assistance on the issue of human rights, at the request of governments, and manages voluntary funds for human rights field missions.
- It currently runs field operations (technical cooperation and monitoring) in Abkhazia (Georgia), Angola, Armenia, Azerbaijan, Bhutan, Burundi, Cambodia, Central African Republic, Chad, Colombia, Croatia, the Democratic Republic of Congo, El Salvador, Gabon, Gaza (Palestine), Guatemala, Guinea-Bissau, Indonesia, Latvia, Moldova, Liberia, Madagascar, Malawi, Mongolia, Morocco, Namibia, Russian Federation, Rwanda, Sierra Leone, Somalia, South Africa, Togo, Uganda, and the former Yugoslavia.
- Providing support to human rights fact-finding and investigative mechanisms, such as Special Rapporteurs and working groups mandated by the Commission on Human Rights or other UN bodies → **Special Rapporteurs**
- Supporting international human rights organs and treaty-monitoring bodies. It plans, prepares, and runs the meetings of the UN Commission on Human Rights, the Sub-Commission on the Prevention of Discrimination and Protection of Minorities, related Working Groups, and the Committees established by human rights treaty bodies. UNHCHR also processes the communications submitted by individuals, organizations, or states to treaty bodies under optional procedures and under the "1503" procedure. → **Children; Commission on Human Rights; Committee against Torture; Committee on Economic, Social, and Cultural Rights; Committee on the Elimination of Discrimination against Women; Committee on the**

Elimination of Racial Discrimination; Committee on the Rights of the Child; Discrimination; Human rights; Human Rights Committee; Individual recourse; Women

In situations of emergency, UNHCHR works with the relevant organs in the UN system. It participates in the Inter-Agency Standing Committee (IASC), run by the Office for the Coordination of Humanitarian Affairs (OCHA). It especially works with OCHA to develop approaches within the UN system (namely, with regard to humanitarian action), which take human rights issues into consideration, especially during the postconflict peace-building phase.

➜   **Children; Commission on Human Rights; Committee against Torture; Committee on Economic, Social, and Cultural Rights; Committee on the Elimination of Discrimination against Women; Committee on the Elimination of Racial Discrimination; Committee on the Rights of the Child; Discrimination; Economic and Social Council of the UN; Human rights; Human Rights Committee; Individual recourse; United Nations; Well-being; Women**

✎   Office of the High Commissioner for Human Rights (OHCHR)
      52 rue Paquis
      1202 Geneva, Switzerland
      Tel.: (00 41) 22 917 92 39
      Fax: (00 41) 22 917 90 12
@   UN High Commissioner for Human Rights: www.unhchr.ch

■ UNITED NATIONS HIGH COMMISSIONER FOR REFUGEES (UNHCR)

I. STRUCTURE

The United Nations High Commissioner for Refugees (UNHCR) is a subsidiary organ of the UN General Assembly, which created it in 1949. It began operating in 1951, and its headquarters are in Geneva. It currently employs approximately 5,100 people.

The High Commissioner (currently Ruud Lubbers, who assumed this post in January 2001, following Sadako Ogata's nine-year tenure) is elected by the UN General Assembly to a five-year term, on nomination by the UN Secretary-General (Article 13 of UNHCR statute). Each year, the High Commissioner reports to the General Assembly, which usually adopts a resolution in support of UNHCR.

The Executive Committee (ExCom) is composed of representatives of the fifty-four states that are members of the UN Economic and Social Council (ECOSOC). It meets every year in October and produces "conclusions" that establish the framework for UNHCR's activities.

Since the ExCom (elected by the UN General Assembly) represents the community of states in the exercise of its functions, states that are not party to the 1951 Convention Relating to the Status of Refugees (known as the Refugee Convention) are hence not excluded from UNHCR. For instance, India is a member of the ExCom but is not a party to the Refugee Convention. In fact, it is acknowledged that all member states of the UN recognize and accept UNHCR's mandate.

The organization is divided into several departments (international protection, operational support, finances, inspection and evaluation, human resources), as well as regional divisions.

II. MANDATE

UNHCR's goal is to guarantee the fundamental rules accepted by all states concerning the right of individuals to flee their country and seek asylum in another. To this end, it helps states face the administrative, legal, diplomatic, financial, and human problems that are caused by the refugee phenomenon.

UNHCR has several functions:

- To promote the rights of refugees and to monitor the implementation of the Refugee Convention by its states parties;
- To protect refugees by working with states on the examination of administrative and legal problems related to the granting of refugee status and to the defense of the right of asylum.

UNHCR also works with governments to search for durable solutions for refugees. Being a refugee is a transitory condition for an individual. To protect such individuals or groups of individuals, states must grant them a stable and lasting legal status. To this effect, UNHCR favors various forms of voluntary repatriation, integration into the state of asylum, and third country resettlement.

- To provide material assistance: international solidarity—in the form of interstate cooperation and support, but also with the support of intergovernmental and nongovernmental organizations—is necessary so as to allow for a sharing of the financial and other burdens that refugees may represent for the host state. Concretely, this support translates into assistance programs for refugees that are run by UNHCR. States contribute financially to these programs on a voluntary basis.
- To provide "good offices" services to governments to help them solve problems resulting from population movements that are slightly outside UNHCR's mandate and especially to provide assistance to groups outside its mandate (e.g., internally displaced persons), when requested to do so by the UN Secretary-General or the General Assembly.

Legal Basis of UNHCR's Mandate

UNHCR's mandate is based on

- the statute of the Office of the United Nations High Commissioner for Refugees, adopted by the UN General Assembly on December 14, 1950 (Resolution 428 [V]), creating UNHCR;
- the 1951 Refugee Convention, which entered into force in 1954, currently has 133 member states (as of July 1999), and establishes UNHCR's mandate to monitor the implementation of the Convention (under Article 35 of the Refugee Convention);
- specific requests made by the UN General Assembly (Article 9 of UNHCR statute) or by the Secretary-General (General Assembly Resolution 48/116 of December 20, 1993), on the basis of which UNHCR's mandate may be extended on an ad hoc basis to help states face specific refugee problems.

III. MEANS OF ACTION

The legal mechanisms at UNHCR's disposal vary depending on whether a given mission comes under the framework of its statute, the Refugee Convention, or an ad hoc extension of its mandate.

During the first years of its existence, UNHCR was not an operational agency. It did not carry out material relief actions directly for refugees—its contribution was limited to giving financial support to private organizations that carried out such tasks. Thus, its contribution to the protection of refugees focused on negotiating and obtaining legal guarantees to their benefit and facilitating administrative formalities. With the growth in the number of refugees, UNHCR turned into an operational agency that is now present in more than 120 countries.

1. Legal Means Provided by UNHCR's Statute

UNHCR has a double mission: it is accountable to both states and individual refugees.

a. UNHCR's Mission with Regard to States

It must ensure and coordinate states' defense of the right of asylum and their financial burden sharing aimed at alleviating the problems of refugees.

Resolution 428 (V), adopted by the General Assembly on December 14, 1950, established UNHCR's statute and set forth the commitments undertaken by governments to cooperate with the organization on refugee issues. Governments are invited to

- participate in the drafting of international conventions relating to the protection of refugees, ratify them, and adopt the appropriate measures to implement them;
- implement measures aimed at improving the situation of refugees and reducing the number of those who require protection, by concluding special agreements with UNHCR;
- encourage the admission of refugees onto their territory, without excluding those in the most destitute categories;
- support the efforts of UNHCR to assist in the voluntary repatriation of refugees;
- favor the integration of refugees within new national communities, namely by facilitating their naturalization;
- deliver travel and other documents that would normally be provided by the refugees' national authorities;
- authorize refugees to transfer their assets, especially those necessary for their resettlement;
- provide UNHCR with information concerning the number and conditions of refugees in their territories and the laws and regulations concerning them.

b. UNHCR's Mission with Regard to the Protection of Refugees

Article 8 of UNHCR's statute states that "the High Commissioner shall provide for the protection of refugees falling under the competence of his Office." Originally, UNHCR's mandate only extended to individuals who met the definition of a refugee contained in the statute and repeated in the 1951 Refugee Convention (detailed under the entry on ➜ **refugees**). It was progressively expanded to include other persons (in particular war refugees) by successive UN General Assembly resolutions. The organization's mandate over internally displaced persons (IDPs) remains ad hoc, meaning that it is subject to a vote by the General Assembly, or at the request of the Secretary General, and to the approval of state concerned.

UNHCR can ensure the protection of refugees by

(a) Promoting the conclusion and ratification of international conventions for the protection of refugees, supervising their application and proposing amendments thereto;
(b) promoting through special agreements with governments the execution of any measures calculated to improve the situation of refugees and to reduce the number requiring protection;
(c) assisting governmental and private efforts to promote voluntary repatriation or assimilation within new national communities;
(d) promoting the admission of refugees, not excluding those in the most destitute categories, to the territories of States;
(e) endeavouring to obtain permission for refugees to transfer their assets and especially those necessary for their resettlement;
(f) obtaining from governments information concerning the number and conditions of refugees in their territories and the laws and regulations concerning them;
(g) keeping in close touch with the governments and inter-governmental organizations concerned;
(h) establishing contact in such manner as [it] may think best with private organizations dealing with refugee questions;
(i) facilitating the co-ordination of the efforts of private organizations concerned with the welfare of refugees. (Article 8 of UNHCR statute)

2. Legal Means Provided by the 1951 Refugee Convention

UNHCR's mandate is limited to individuals who meet the definition of *refugees* set forth by the Refugee Convention. "The High Contracting Parties . . . [note] that the United Nations High Commissioner for Refugees is charged with the task of supervising international conventions providing for the protection of refugees, and recogniz[e] that the effective coordination of measures taken to deal with this problem will depend on the cooperation of States with the High Commissioner" (preamble, paragraph 6).

UNHCR is entrusted with the responsibility of monitoring the application and implementation of the Convention's provisions. States undertake to cooperate with UNHCR and to provide it with all the necessary information and statistical data, especially concerning refugees, the implementation of the Convention, and any other laws enacted that relate to refugees (Article 35 of Refugee Convention).

The Convention does not offer UNHCR any additional means of action to those conferred by its statute. It does mention, however, that national authorities, or "an international authority" (UNHCR), are under the obligation to issue to refugees any administrative documents that they can no longer obtain from their own national authorities but that are indispensable for the exercise of their individual rights. This function is crucial in order to lift administrative obstacles that refugees often face. These documents include identification papers or temporary travel documents (Article 25 of Refugee Convention).

3. Legal Means Provided by the UN General Assembly

The General Assembly may request, on a case-by-case basis, that UNHCR take charge of specific refugee problems that do not come under the strict definitions established by the Refugee Convention and UNHCR's statute (issues concerning internally displaced persons, for instance). In such situations, UNHCR has no means of action beyond those negotiated and included in the bilateral or trilateral agreements signed with the governments of the concerned states.

The General Assembly has already broadened the organization's mandate in three different directions, with the aim of

- providing material assistance to refugees, and therefore of making an appeal for funds (Resolution 538B of 1952);
- using its "good offices" in case of large-scale flows of people seeking asylum (Resolution 1388 of 1959); and
- extending its activities to cover the case of internally displaced persons (Resolution 2958 of 1972).

4. Financial Means

UNHCR administers the funds it receives from both public and private sources for assistance to refugees. It first distributes them to the privates agencies that it deems best qualified to provide such assistance. It may also, as appropriate, distribute part of the funds to public agencies. It may reject any offers that it does not consider appropriate or which cannot be utilized—for instance, because of conditions attached to the funds (Article 10 of UNHCR statute).

A small part of the administrative overhead costs (about 3 percent) is covered by the regular budget of the UN. The programs are financed by voluntary state contributions. UNHCR may not appeal to governments for funds without the prior approval of the General Assembly (Article 10 of UNHCR statute).

Until 1999, the program budget was divided into General Programs (33 percent) and Special Programs (66 percent). The Special Programs were all those not strictly covered by the UNHCR mandate, such as support for internally displaced persons (IDPs), "good offices" missions, special training, and so on. Since January 1, 2000, these were merged into one Annual Program Budget. It presents the budget for all operations in each country, including the ongoing refugee protection and assistance programs, emergency operations, voluntary repatriation, and assistance to nonrefugees such as IDPs. The projected total budget for 2000 was $913.2 million.

Nevertheless, in case of an unforeseen large-scale emergency, the High Commissioner has the authority to create Supplementary Program Budgets. These are to be approved, after the fact, by the Executive Committee, at its regular sessions, and absorbed into the following year's Annual Program Budget. Some of the programs adopted for 2000 were for refugees and IDPs from Chechnya, Eritrea, East Timor, and Sierra Leone.

☞ Despite its humanitarian mandate, UNHCR is an organ within the UN system. This means, for instance:

- Its actions depend on the content of agreements it negotiates with the governments concerned in each situation. They also depend on the voluntary financial contributions from states.
- It is directly subject to the consequences of national asylum policies, which have become increasingly restrictive in recent years, and of budgetary limitations.
- It is also subject to practical constraints tied to the growing number of people in need of international protection. Today, there are an estimated thirteen million refugees throughout

(continues)

(continued)

the world and approximately twenty to twenty-five million displaced persons, according to the Special Representative of the UN Secretary-General on internally displaced persons.

UNHCR's activities are founded on very diverse legal bases. Some of the operations it carries out—its good offices actions for instance—include almost no rules governing the protection of individuals. UNHCR's legal capacity to protect individuals must be examined closely in each of its interventions.

It is not UNHCR but the governments concerned that choose whether to grant refugee status to an individual or a group. UNHCR monitors and participates in the proceedings, and individuals may submit their cases to it.

When a state refuses to provide refugee status to individuals who have fled *en masse*, UNHCR makes sure that they are not forced to return (*refouler*) to a country where their life would be threatened and that they at least benefit from temporary asylum. UNHCR can appeal to governments to allow temporary asylum in such cases, which is separate from providing refugee status.

5. Relations with NGOs

UNHCR's primary role is not an operational one. In addition to its function as legal counsel (pressuring and assisting governments in their admission of refugees), UNHCR has undertaken increasingly concrete assistance and protection operations for refugees, often in partnership with NGOs. UNHCR can sign operational partnership contracts with NGOs (Articles 8 and 10 of UNHCR statute) so as to coordinate the funding of such actions.

NGOs thus defend the rights of refugees through their assistance activities, and they therefore carry a share of the responsibilities in protecting these populations. Through their very presence at the refugees' side, NGOs are in a privileged position to evaluate, for instance, the refugees' physical safety, the quality of assistance they receive, and the different pressures they face in making certain decisions—namely, in cases of repatriation—and to report this to UNHCR.

→ **Asylum; Boat people; Camps; Displaced persons; NGOs; Protection;** *Refoulement* **(forced return) and expulsion; Refugees; Relief; Repatriation; Stateless persons**

✎ UNHCR
94, rue de Montbrillant
CH-1202 Geneva, Switzerland
Tel.: (41) 22 739 8111
Fax: (41) 22 739 7377
@ UNHCR: www.unhcr.ch

■ UNIVERSAL DECLARATION OF HUMAN RIGHTS

1. Background

The Universal Declaration of Human Rights (UDHR) was adopted by the General Assembly of the UN (Resolution 217 A [III]), on December 10, 1948. The Declaration, prepared by the UN Commission on Human Rights—and inspired by people such as René Cassin, of France; Charles

Malik, of Lebanon; and Eleanor Roosevelt, of the United States—was adopted by forty-eight votes in favor, eight abstentions, and no votes against.

The UDHR contains thirty articles that enumerate the civil and political rights of individuals, as well as their economic and social rights. It is the first international text to address the issue of human rights. General Assembly resolutions are not legally binding treaties, in the way that international conventions are, and the UDHR was adopted as a Declaration because it is meant to be more an ideal that all states should strive to achieve than a list of precise and constraining engagements. The UDHR was first a crucial point of reference in the development of national and international tools concerning human rights, which entail mandatory obligations. Today, however, it is binding on all states, because it has become part of international customary law. ➜ **Customary law; International conventions; International law**

The Declaration served as the basis for the drafting of the International Covenant on Civil and Political Rights (and its first Optional Protocol), and the International Covenant on Economic, Social, and Cultural Rights. These two Covenants were adopted in 1966 and are binding on states parties. The UDHR and the two Covenants make up what is known today as the international bill of rights. The UDHR is also quoted in several regional and international conventions, such as the founding documents for the Organization of African Unity (OAU), the Organization for Security and Cooperation in Europe (OCSE), and a dozen national constitutions, and it is often invoked by UN organs.

It also serves as one of the bases for identifying a likely "consistent pattern of gross and reliably attested violations of human rights and fundamental freedoms" that may trigger a confidential procedure before the UN Commission on Human Rights (1503 Procedure; ECOSOC Resolution 1503 [XLVIII], 1970). The 1503 Procedure was set up to hear communications and complaints from individuals or groups who claim to be victims of human rights violations and from any person or group of people who have direct, reliable knowledge of violations (e.g., NGOs), in accordance with recognized principles of human rights. If the complaints are retained, an envoy may be sent to the country in question, a confidential investigation may be launched, or the issue may be adopted for public discussion (1235 Procedure; ECOSOC Resolution 1235 [XLII], 1967). It is important not to confuse these international human rights instruments with the French Declaration of the Rights of Man and of the Citizen (of 1789).
➜   **Custom; Human Rights Commission; International conventions; International law**

2. The Rights Established by the UDHR

Article 1:   Equality of human beings in dignity and in rights
Article 2:   Nondiscrimination between human beings, on any basis such as race, color, sex, language, religion, political or other opinion, national or social origin—including the political, legal, or international status of the territory of which they are a national—property, birth or other status
Article 3:   Right to life, liberty, and security of person
Article 4:   Prohibition on slavery
Article 5:   Prohibition on torture or cruel, inhuman, or degrading treatment or punishment
Article 6:   Right to recognition everywhere as a person before the law (juridical personality)
Article 7:   Equal protection before the law
Article 8:   Right to an effective judicial remedy before a court against violations of fundamental rights
Article 9:   Prohibition on arbitrary arrest, detention, or exile
Article 10:   Right to legal recourse before an independent and competent court

Article 11: Judicial and due process guarantees for individuals

Article 12: Respect for privacy, family, and home

Article 13: Freedom of movement and residence within each country, and right to leave and return to one's country

Article 14: Right to flee from persecution and to seek asylum

Article 15: Right to a nationality

Article 16: Right to marriage and protection of marriage

Article 17: Right to property

Article 18: Freedom of thought, conscience and religion

Article 19: Freedom of expression and opinion, including the right to receive and impart information and ideas, regardless of frontiers

Article 20: Right to freedom of peaceful assembly and association

Article 21: Right to take part in the government of one's country, directly or through freely chosen representatives, based on universal and equal suffrage

Article 22: Right to social security

Article 23: Right to work and to free choice of employment, with equal pay for equal work

Article 24: Right to rest and leisure

Article 25: Right to a standard of living adequate for the health and well-being and to special care and assistance for the most vulnerable

Article 26: Right to education

Article 27: Right to participate freely in the cultural life of the community and to the protection of scientific, literary, or artistic production

Article 28: Right to a social and international order in which human rights and freedoms can be fully realized

Article 29: Duties of individuals toward the community: any limitations determined by law must be solely for the purpose of securing due recognition and respect for the rights and freedoms of others and of meeting the just requirements of morality, public order, and the general welfare in a democratic society. Rights and freedoms may in no case be exercised contrary to the purposes and principles of the United Nations.

Article 30: Nothing in the Universal Declaration of Human Rights may be interpreted as allowing any activity aimed at the destruction of any of the rights and freedoms set forth therein.

→ **Discrimination; Human rights; Individual recourse; Judicial guarantees; Nationality; Public order; Refugees; Safety**

📖 **For Additional Information:**

Morsink, Johannes. *The Universal Declaration of Human Rights: Origins, Drafting, and Intent*. Philadelphia: University of Pennsylvania Press, 1999.

■ UNIVERSAL JURISDICTION

The principle of universal jurisdiction is an exceptional measure of criminal justice. It gives states the authority to prosecute the authors of certain serious crimes, even if the states have no significant links to the accused or to the acts committed. In other words, an individual accused of a grave violation of humanitarian law can be prosecuted before any court, in any country.

The principle—meant to fill the void in international law left by the absence of a competent and efficient form of international jurisdiction—was codified by the 1949 Geneva Conventions. Universal jurisdiction is applicable to all grave breaches of the Geneva Conventions, most of which fall under the category of "war crimes" or "crimes against humanity." The definition of these crimes can be found under the entry on ➔ **war crimes/crimes against humanity** (Section III). Other specific crimes over which states may exercise universal jurisdiction include genocide (committed in times of war), torture, slave trade, attacks on or hijacking of aircraft, and certain acts of terrorism.

Most principles of criminal law limit the jurisdiction of domestic courts to the prosecution of crimes that took place on the territory of the country in question, or whose perpetrators or victims are nationals of that country. The very nature of war crimes and crimes against humanity, and the context in which they tend to be committed, makes it difficult to prosecute them in the courts of the country where they were perpetrated.

On July 17, 1998, the statute of a permanent International Criminal Court (ICC) was adopted, which will have jurisdiction over the most serious crimes of international concern— genocide, war crimes, and crimes against humanity (and aggression, at a later date). But the ICC will still not completely fill the void in the international legal response to the numerous grave violations of humanitarian law that take place today: when the ICC statute enters into force, the Court's jurisdiction will be constrained by many limitations, especially a set of conditions requiring the consent of certain states. ➔ **International Criminal Court**

Historically, the fact that there has never been a permanent international criminal tribunal increased the chance that the individuals who have committed such crimes could act with impunity. To prevent this, the states party to the Geneva Conventions commit to participating in the search, prosecution, and punishment of the perpetrators of war crimes and crimes against humanity. Hence, the Geneva Conventions impose on each state party the following obligations:

- to search for persons alleged to have committed, or to have ordered to be committed, grave breaches of the Conventions;
- to bring such persons, regardless of their nationality, before its own courts;
- possibly also to hand over such persons for trial to another High Contracting Party concerned by the case, provided such state party has made out a valid case (GCI Article 49, GCII Article 50, GCIII Article 129, and GCIV Article 146).

The provisions of the Geneva Conventions go well beyond the bonds of traditional mutual assistance that is carried out between states to prevent criminals from escaping prosecution simply by crossing borders. States' duties in terms of mutual assistance in criminal matters usually requires that they choose between the obligation to prosecute and the obligation to extradite. Humanitarian law has added the obligation to search actively for the alleged criminals, and it imposes guarantees meant to ensure that an extradition will not result in impunity for the accused.

The exercise of universal jurisdiction is the most effective recourse that exists at an international level today for penalizing the most serious crimes. It has been incorporated into several international conventions, such as the Convention Against Torture and Other Cruel, Inhuman, or Degrading Treatment or Punishment (known as the Torture Convention), adopted in New York on December 10, 1984. A victim of torture can file a complaint before any domestic court of a foreign country, on condition that the alleged offender is present on a territory under that country's jurisdiction and that the state in question has incorporated the provisions of the convention into its domestic laws. ➔ **Torture**

In addition to this procedure, international law provides various tools, in terms of mutual assistance in criminal matters and the duty to extradite, that are meant to facilitate the punishment of these crimes. ➔ **Mutual assistance in criminal matters**

The Importance of Universal Jurisdiction

In theory, the victims of war crimes, torture, or crimes against humanity committed in times of war, can file complaints before foreign domestic courts on the basis of universal jurisdiction, as established in the 1949 Geneva Conventions and the 1984 Torture Convention. Exercising this jurisdiction is currently the most effective international recourse for penalizing the most serious crimes.

These complaints may be thwarted, however, if the countries in question have not brought their domestic legislation into conformity with this international obligation. Special provisions must be incorporated into national criminal legislation and rules of procedure, so that the jurisdiction of domestic courts can take effect.

In 1999, the UN Security Council requested that states amend their domestic legislation to incorporate the principle of universal jurisdiction into their laws and be able to punish perpetrators of humanitarian law violations (SC presidential statement of February 12, 1999). The UN Secretary General formulated the same request in his report on the protection of civilians in armed conflict (September 8, 1999).

Some countries, mostly members of the European Union (and a few others—e.g., Switzerland and Canada), have harmonized their laws with this obligation. Other states are more reticent—in particular, the United States and France—and base themselves on specific national regulations regarding such crimes.

Most domestic legislation holds that the accused must be present on the territory of the country in question in order to trigger the jurisdiction of its courts.

➔ **Immunity; Impunity; Individual recourse; International Criminal Court; Mutual assistance in criminal matters; Torture; War crimes/Crimes against humanity**

📖 **For Additional Information:**

Dinstein, Yoram. "International Criminal Law." In *Israel Yearbook on Human Rights,* ed. Yoram Dinstein. The Hague: Martinus Nijhoff, 1975, vol. 5.

Graditzky, Thomas. "Individual Criminal Responsibility for Violations of International Humanitarian Law Committed in Non-international Armed Conflicts." *International Review of the Red Cross* 322 (March–April 1998): 29–56.

ICRC. "National Enforcement of International Humanitarian Law: Universal Jurisdiction over War Crimes." Geneva: Author, February 1999.

——. "State Consent Regime vs. Universal Jurisdiction." Geneva: Author, December 1997.

■ Veto

Individual veto power enables a single voter to prevent a decision from being taken or implemented, even though the majority may be in favor of the decision. Having "veto power" means being able to oppose the majority rule at the time of a vote.

This form of decision making is common among international governmental organizations. It allows states to defend their interests against decisions that could hurt them. Many actions are hence blocked within such organizations as a result of vetoes.

At the UN Security Council, the five permanent members have veto power (Article 27.3 of the UN Charter): China, France, the Russian Federation, the United Kingdom, and the United States. During the Cold War, this system froze all decision making within the Council, especially in terms of managing conflicts and of peacekeeping. There are no rules that specify the conditions and limits to states' use of the veto power at the Council. This leads to a lack of transparency—for instance, with regard to decisions taken on peacekeeping matters.

Intergovernmental organizations often prefer to adopt texts by consensus so as to avoid the risk of a veto. These texts are the result of compromise and are adopted without a vote, as long as no state openly objects.

→   **Security Council of the UN**

■ WAR

War is a phenomenon of organized collective violence that affects either the relations between two or more societies or the power relations within a society. War is governed by the law of armed conflict, also called "international humanitarian law." Throughout the ages, rules have been written and accepted by states to limit the use of force to protect societies from the long-term effects of war, by attempting to prevent conflicts from reaching a point of no return.

International law does this by regulating war and prohibiting specific acts and behavior, such as gratuitous massacres and the extermination of civilian populations, which may make a return to peace and reconciliation difficult. It also stresses the importance of distinguishing between civilians and combatants. This is meant for the protection of civilians, as well as to clarify that the use of force that is permitted is not granted to all individuals, but must be carried out within a collective and structured organization, under a clear chain of command.

According to experts, approximately fifty international and internal wars have taken place around the world since the end of the Cold War. According to the Stockholm International Peace Research Institute, approximately twenty-five major conflicts were under way in 2000.

The law of international armed conflict was codified progressively over the course of hundreds of years. The endurance and constancy of these rules over time means that a number of them are considered "customary," meaning they are internationally accepted. In other words, they are binding even on states or belligerents that have not formally adhered to such rules. The roots of positive international law come from a concept of war developed in the nineteenth century. The laws were written by states, and their aim, for the most part, was to regulate interstate wars and to protect the rights of soldiers. The conflicts that took place over the past fifty years no longer clearly fit into that context. Furthermore, humanitarian law has continued to evolve to improve the protection of civilians and reinforce the rules applicable to internal armed conflicts. This is most clearly expressed in the Fourth Geneva Convention of 1949 and the two 1977 Protocols additional to these Conventions. Humanitarian law adapts to respond to these fluctuating challenges by according increasing importance to custom—to the practices of states and combatants, as well as humanitarian organizations.

→   **Customary international law; International conventions; International humanitarian law**

1. Different Kinds of Conflicts

The word *war* is no longer used in international law. The term *international armed conflict* is used when referring to a war between two or more states and *noninternational armed conflict* when referring to a civil war. A certain level and intensity of violence must be reached before a situation is qualified as one of "armed conflict." Beneath that threshold, violent situations are called "internal disturbances" or "tensions." Riots, isolated and sporadic acts of violence, and other acts of a similar nature are not considered armed conflicts (PII Article 1.2).

Humanitarian law only applies to situations of armed conflict. Nonetheless, in cases of internal disturbances and tensions, both human rights and humanitarian law establish certain fundamental guarantees that must be enforced.

→   **Fundamental guarantees; Internal disturbances and tensions; International armed conflict; Noninternational armed conflict; Siege**

2. The Parties to a Conflict

In situations of conflict, armed forces use methods of mass violence, in an organized and united manner. The fact that rules exist makes it possible to differentiate between armed conflict and chaos. Combatants must be organized into groups and units that respond to a hierarchy of command, which in turn is responsible for giving orders and ensuring discipline, including compliance with humanitarian law.

Combatants confronting one another may belong to official and recognized political authorities, such as governments, or they may make up the armed forces of a political authority that has not been recognized by the adverse party to the conflict or by other states. This is often the case in wars of national liberation and civil wars, for instance. The law of armed conflict applies to all belligerents, no matter what political authority commands them.

→   **Belligerents; Combatants; High Contracting Party; Parties to the conflict; Resistance movements; Situations and persons not expressly covered by humanitarian law; Special agreement**

3. Conflict Prevention

In 1928, states rejected the option of resorting to war in international relations, under the Kellog-Briand Pact. This renunciation was short-lived. The UN Charter limits the right to use force in relations between states but does not forbid it completely (states may only use armed force for self-defense, in response to aggression). Instead, they should settle their international disputes through pacific means, with the help of the international community and various mechanisms set up within the UN system to this effect.

In fact, states are under the express obligation to seek peaceful solutions. If pacific attempts fail and international peace and security are threatened, the Charter foresees the possibility of using international armed forces to restore peace. In the last fifty years, such mechanisms have operated in a partial and ad hoc manner, through the different peacekeeping operations that have taken place.

Despite all these restrictions, war remains a component of international relations, as it has since ancient times.

→ **Collective security; Peacekeeping; Security Council of the UN; United Nations**

4. Rules of War

☞ The international law of armed conflict was codified progressively over the course of hundreds of years. The philosophy behind such regulation is the same on all continents:

- War is a transitional phase; therefore, it must be conducted in a way that will not make a return to peace impossible, both for society as a whole and for soldiers who must be able to readapt to civilian life.
- The spirit of the rules is consistent: it aims to avoid unnecessary suffering and destruction, and it prohibits acts that are disproportionate to the specific military advantage that is sought. It emphasizes the importance of distinguishing between military and civilian objects.

States have been regulating and limiting the means and methods of warfare since long before the existence of the UN—in the framework of which additional rules governing the use of force have been adopted.

The basic principle is that a military operation is only legitimate if it is a means of attaining a specific military objective. The weapons used must be proportionate and coherent with this objective and must avoid unnecessary destruction and suffering. The method of combat must enable the combatants to distinguish between civilian and military targets. The methods used must also allow aid to be brought to the civilian victims during the fighting.

The four 1949 Geneva Conventions and their Additional Protocols of 1977 are the most recent example of the codification of these principles. They regulate the methods of warfare and reaffirm the right to relief for civilians and other noncombatants.

a. The Right to Violence

Violence, destruction, and killing are regulated by the 1949 Geneva Conventions and the 1899 Hague Conventions through the provisions concerning weapons and methods of warfare.

➔ **Attacks; Geneva Conventions and Protocols; Hague Conventions; International humanitarian law; Methods (and means) of warfare; Weapons**

b. The Right to Assistance

The Geneva Conventions and their Protocols establish the details of the protection that must be provided to civilians and the relief to which victims of conflicts are entitled.

➔ **Geneva Conventions and Protocols; International humanitarian law; Medical duties; Protected objects and property; Protected persons; Protection; Relief**

Fundamental Guarantees

The Geneva Conventions also ensure a minimum standard of protection, applicable in any kind of conflict. In particular, these concern the essential rules governing relief and protection for civilians.

➔ **Fundamental guarantees; Special Agreement**

5. Responsibilities

The Geneva Conventions also establish states' specific responsibilities, as well as those of the commanders of armed forces and of individuals, in terms of the implementation and respect for the rules of the law of armed conflict. They also establish the different penal sanctions that can be applied to punish war crimes or other crimes against humanity.

➔ **Attacks; Duty of commanders; Penal sanctions in humanitarian law; Proportionality; Respect for international humanitarian law; Responsibility; War crimes/Crimes against humanity**

➔ **International humanitarian law; Methods (and means) of warfare**

📖 **For Additional Information:**

Hassner, Pierre. "From War and Peace to Violence and Intervention: Permanent Moral Dilemmas under Changing Political and Technological Conditions." In *Hard Choices: Moral Dilemmas in Humanitarian Intervention*, ed. Jonathan Moore. Lanham, Md.: Rowman & Littlefield, 1998, 9–28.

———. *Violence and Peace: From the Atomic Bomb to Ethnic Cleansing.* Budapest: Central European University Press, 1997.

Shawcross, William. *Deliver Us from Evil: Warlords and a World of Endless Conflict.* New York: Simon & Schuster, 2000.

■ WAR CRIMES/CRIMES AGAINST HUMANITY

There are different definitions of war crimes and crimes against humanity, each of which refers to a different system of law and punishment. As we will explain in this entry, these crimes were codified clearly after World War II, at an international level, in the statutes of the international military tribunals set up in Nuremberg and Tokyo by the Allies; in the 1949 Geneva Conventions and their 1977 Additional Protocols (the grave breaches to these Conventions); and, more recently, in the statutes of the ad hoc International Criminal Tribunals for the former Yugoslavia and Rwanda. The statute for a permanent International Criminal Court (ICC), adopted in July 1998 and not yet in force, sets forth the most comprehensive list of crimes punishable by an international judicial body. This entry will present the penal sanctions and the definitions of crimes set forth in

- the statutes of international ad hoc tribunals (I),
- the statute of the ICC (II), and
- the Geneva Conventions (III).

1. Domestic Legislation

Crimes against peace, war crimes, crimes against humanity, and crimes of genocide are defined in, and punishable by, the criminal laws of each country, although the precise name given to such crimes and the elements that define them may vary. However, attempting to punish such crimes through national legal venues may be risky since, in practice, they are most often committed in the context of a conflict and frequently involve representatives of public authorities. The national judicial systems on which the accused or the victim depends will in such cases most likely no longer be capable of independence or impartiality, nor will they have the necessary means to prosecute adequately.

In practice, therefore, the possibility of punishing war crimes and crimes against humanity rests on international judicial action and cooperation or on the creation of international criminal tribunals. So as to avoid complete impunity for these crimes, international law has established that they are not subject to statutory limitations. This means that there is no time limit within which these crimes must be judged and that criminal pursuits may always be initiated, even decades after the events, when the political or military climate has evolved sufficiently to enable such prosecutions. → **Impunity; Nonapplicability of statutory limitations**

The 1949 Geneva Conventions broadened the jurisdiction of domestic courts to prosecute such crimes, even if committed in another country, by codifying the principle of universal jurisdiction into its provisions. This principle establishes that all states undertake to search for and prosecute the authors of certain serious crimes, including war crimes and crimes against humanity, even if the state has no significant links to the accused or to the acts committed. To be able to implement this form of jurisdiction, states must incorporate this concept into their national laws. → **Universal jurisdiction**

Furthermore, military laws—which exist for the armed forces in each country—establish codes of discipline and set up instruments to penalize acts that violate military regulations. These mechanisms are under the responsibility of the military or civilian judicial system in each country.

2. International Laws

There are different international punishment mechanisms. The definitions of war crimes and crimes against humanity are different for the institutions administering these mechanisms.

☞ It has taken the UN fifty years to draw up an official list of acts that are considered crimes against the peace and security of humanity. The list has grown continually, incorporating internationally recognized crimes, from genocide to terrorism, and many more. However, the UN never succeeded in getting this list formally adopted by its members (although it is still trying) or in setting up a permanent international tribunal that would have jurisdiction over these crimes (until 1998). Such crimes have been punished only on an ad hoc basis, by the Nuremberg and Tokyo Tribunals and, nearly fifty years later, the International Criminal Tribunals for the former Yugoslavia and Rwanda.

The statute of a permanent International Criminal Court (ICC) was finally adopted in Rome on July 17, 1998. Under certain conditions, the ICC will have jurisdiction over the crimes of genocide, war crimes, and crimes against humanity in cases in which states are unwilling or unable to carry out the investigation or prosecution. It will take several years before the Court begins to operate.

I. THE INTERNATIONAL AD HOC TRIBUNALS

1. The International Military Tribunals of Nuremberg and Tokyo

War crimes and crimes against humanity committed during World War II were punished by the international military tribunals in Nuremberg and Tokyo. These two tribunals—set up on an ad hoc basis by the Allies on August 8, 1945, and January 18, 1946, respectively—judged members of the armed forces of the defeated countries who had committed such crimes.

The statute of the Nuremberg tribunal makes a distinction between different kinds of crimes committed in times of war: crimes against peace, war crimes, and crimes against humanity. Article 6 of the statute defines these crimes in the following manner:

- Crimes against peace are those aimed at the "planning, preparation, initiation or waging of a war of aggression, or a war in violation of international treaties." Crimes against peace are not subject to any statute of limitations.
- War crimes include
  —murder, ill treatment, or deportation as slave labor or for any other purpose, of the civilian population in occupied territory;
  —murder or ill treatment of prisoners of war or persons on the seas;
  —killing of hostages and plunder of public or private property;
  —wanton destruction of cities, towns, or villages;
  —devastation not justified by military necessity.
  War crimes are committed in times of war and are not subject to any statute of limitations.
- Crimes against humanity concern the "murder, extermination, enslavement, deportation, and other inhumane acts committed against any civilian population, before or during the war, or persecutions on political, racial or religious grounds in execution of or in connection with any crime within the jurisdiction of the Tribunal." This definition applies to crimes committed in times of war or in relation to war.

☞ The absence of a permanent international tribunal at times allows impunity for perpetrators of war crimes and crimes against humanity. On November 26, 1968, to counter this, the member states of the UN adopted the Convention on the Non-Applicability of Statutory Limitations to War Crimes and Crimes against Humanity (GA Resolution 2391 [XXIII]), clearly establishing that such crimes are not subject to any statute of limitations. This means that criminal pursuits may be initiated against the authors of such crimes at any time, even years after the events. Only forty-four states have thus far ratified this convention.

→ **Nonapplicability of statutory limitations**

---

2. The Ad Hoc International Criminal Tribunals for the Former Yugoslavia and Rwanda

Two ad hoc International Criminal Tribunals were set up in 1993 and 1994 by the UN to prosecute crimes committed in the former Yugoslavia and in Rwanda. Unlike the Nuremberg and Tokyo tribunals, these are civilian institutions. In their statutes, new definitions of war crimes and crimes against humanity were adopted. Namely, these refer to grave breaches of the 1949 Geneva Conventions.

Furthermore, the Tribunals incorporate violations of Article 3, common to the four Geneva Conventions (known as common Article 3), and of Additional Protocol II, which refer to internal conflicts such as Rwanda's into their definition of crimes. This represents an important step toward punishing serious violations of humanitarian law committed in the context of internal conflicts.

→ **International Criminal Tribunals**

The power of these Tribunals is restricted by their ad hoc nature, which means that their jurisdiction is strictly limited to certain specified crimes, committed during a limited time frame on a specific territory.

II. THE INTERNATIONAL CRIMINAL COURT

The statute of a permanent International Criminal Court (ICC) was adopted in Rome, on July 17, 1998. Following certain preconditions, the ICC will be responsible for prosecuting individuals accused of crimes of genocide, war crimes, and crimes against humanity, when no state is willing or able to carry out the investigation or prosecution itself. The statute will enter into force only once sixty states have ratified it. → **International Criminal Court**

After setting up the military tribunal for Nuremberg, states had not succeeded in creating a permanent international tribunal or in reaching agreement on a list of clearly defined crimes of concern to the international community. The ICC will not be a centralized instrument of justice. Rather, it will complement national instruments of justice—since it will operate only when states fail to prosecute the crimes over which it has jurisdiction—and thus it will be an additional link in the chain of existing mechanisms created by humanitarian law to punish such crimes.

→ **Penal sanctions in humanitarian law; Universal jurisdiction**

1. Exercise of Jurisdiction

States parties, the UN Security Council, and the Prosecutor can refer cases to the ICC (Articles 13–15 of ICC statute). The Prosecutor may initiate investigations on the basis of information received from victims, NGOs, or any other reliable source, subject to approval by a Pre-Trial Chamber.

If a situation is referred to the Court by a state party or the Prosecutor, the ICC's ability to exercise its jurisdiction is subject to certain constraining preconditions that depend on the consent of specific states:

- The ICC may exercise its jurisdiction only if either the state of which the person accused of the crime is a national or the state on the territory of which the crime was committed is a party to the statute or has otherwise accepted the jurisdiction of the Court (Article 12 or the ICC statute).
- On ratifying the statute, states have the possibility of refusing the ICC's jurisdiction over war crimes for seven years (Article 124).
- If a state concerned by the situation in question undertakes an investigation or prosecution at a national level, the ICC may not exercise its jurisdiction. However, there are two situations in which the Court may proceed with its investigation and prosecution (Article 17):
  —it may do so if it considers that the national legal proceedings were undertaken for the purpose of shielding the accused from having to face his or her criminal responsibility before the ICC, that there was an unjustified delay in the proceedings, or that these were not conducted in an independent and impartial manner;
  —it may also consider a case admissible if it finds the relevant state unable to carry out the proceedings for a particular case due to a total or substantial collapse, or unavailability, of its national judicial system.
- None of these restrictions on the Court's jurisdiction applies if a situation is referred by the UN

Security Council acting under Chapter VII of the UN Charter (Article 12). Furthermore, the Security Council may, at any time, prevent or interrupt the activities of the ICC, by adopting a resolution to this effect under Chapter VII of the UN Charter. This deferral concerns both the investigation and prosecution stages. It lasts one year and may be renewed indefinitely under the same conditions (Article 16).

☞ Articles 7 and 8 of the ICC statute provide the definitions of war crimes and crimes against humanity over which the ICC will have jurisdiction. These definitions—presented in detail in this entry—represent a certain evolution in the codification of international law.

- Article 7 concerns crimes against humanity. It clearly specifies that the definition of such crimes applies to acts committed both in times of conflict and at other times, including times of peace. It adds the practice of enforced disappearances to this category.
- The definition of war crimes provided in Article 8 is not derived directly or exclusively from the 1949 Geneva Conventions and their 1977 Additional Protocols. In fact, since the Protocols have not been ratified by all states, the drafters considered that the prohibitions they contain and the crimes they define cannot be considered as being of a internationally recognized or customary nature, as is the case for the Geneva Conventions. The statute therefore only mentions the Conventions explicitly and then adds a precise definition of other crimes that it considers part of the customary rules of the law of armed conflict and over which it will have jurisdiction. This does not change the fact that the provisions of the Protocols remain binding on all the states that have ratified them.
  → **International humanitarian law**
- Article 8 adds two new elements to the crimes punishable in both international and internal armed conflicts:
  —rape, sexual slavery, enforced prostitution, forced pregnancy, enforced sterilization, or any other form of sexual violence are explicitly listed as grave breaches of the Geneva Conventions;
  —conscripting or enlisting children under the age of fifteen years into the national armed forces or using them to participate actively in hostilities.
  → **Children; International Criminal Tribunals; Rape; Women**
- Furthermore, Articles 8.2.c to 8.2.f provide a precise definition of the war crimes applicable in internal armed conflicts. It summarizes the prohibitions established in Article 3 common to the Geneva Conventions and the "other serious violations of the laws and customs applicable in armed conflicts not of an international character."
- However, certain acts prohibited by Additional Protocol II of 1977, relating to the protection of victims of noninternational armed conflicts (Protocol II), are not included in the ICC definition. For instance, the intentional starvation of civilians, the deprivation of any indispensable supplies, the use of civilians as human shields, and the act of launching deliberate attacks in the knowledge that they will cause incidental loss of lives, and the use of prohibited weapons are not in the list of war crimes established for noninternational conflicts. Nevertheless, these prohibitions continue to be binding on states that have ratified Protocol II.

2. The Definition of War Crimes and Crimes against Humanity in the Statute of the International Criminal Court

a. Crimes against humanity (Article 7 of ICC statute)

1. For the purpose of this Statute, "crime against humanity" means any of the following acts when committed as part of a widespread or systematic attack directed against any civilian population, with knowledge of the attack:
   (a) Murder;
   (b) Extermination;
   (c) Enslavement;
   (d) Deportation or forcible transfer of population;
   (e) Imprisonment or other severe deprivation of physical liberty in violation of fundamental rules of international law;
   (f) Torture;
   (g) Rape, sexual slavery, enforced prostitution, forced pregnancy, enforced sterilization, or any other form of sexual violence of comparable gravity;
   (h) Persecution against any identifiable group or collectivity on political, racial, national, ethnic, cultural, religious, gender as defined in paragraph 3, or other grounds that are universally recognized as impermissible under international law, in connection with any act referred to in this paragraph or any crime within the jurisdiction of the Court;
   (i) Enforced disappearance of persons;
   (j) The crime of apartheid;
   (k) Other inhumane acts of a similar character intentionally causing great suffering, or serious injury to body or to mental or physical health.
2. For the purpose of paragraph 1:
   (a) "Attack directed against any civilian population" means a course of conduct involving the multiple commission of acts referred to in paragraph 1 against any civilian population, pursuant to or in furtherance of a State or organizational policy to commit such attack;
   (b) "Extermination" includes the intentional infliction of conditions of life, inter alia the deprivation of access to food and medicine, calculated to bring about the destruction of part of a population;
   (c) "Enslavement" means the exercise of any or all of the powers attaching to the right of ownership over a person and includes the exercise of such power in the course of trafficking in persons, in particular women and children;
   (d) "Deportation or forcible transfer of population" means forced displacement of the persons concerned by expulsion or other coercive acts from the area in which they are lawfully present, without grounds permitted under international law;
   (e) "Torture" means the intentional infliction of severe pain or suffering, whether physical or mental, on a person in the custody or under the control of the accused; except that torture shall not include pain or suffering arising only from, inherent in or incidental to, lawful sanctions;
   (f) "Forced pregnancy" means the unlawful confinement of a woman forcibly made pregnant, with the intent of affecting the ethnic composition of any population or carrying out other grave violations of international law. This definition shall not in any way be interpreted as affecting national laws relating to pregnancy;
   (g) "Persecution" means the intentional and severe deprivation of fundamental rights contrary to international law by reason of the identity of the group or collectivity;
   (h) "The crime of apartheid" means inhumane acts of a character similar to those referred to in paragraph 1, committed in the context of an institutionalized regime of systematic oppression and domination by one racial group over any other racial group or groups and committed with the intention of maintaining that regime;

(i) "Enforced disappearance of persons" means the arrest, detention or abduction of persons by, or with the authorization, support or acquiescence of, a State or a political organization, followed by a refusal to acknowledge that deprivation of freedom or to give information on the fate or whereabouts of those persons, with the intention of removing them from the protection of the law for a prolonged period of time.

3. For the purpose of this Statute, it is understood that the term "gender" refers to the two sexes, male and female, within the context of society. The term "gender" does not indicate any meaning different from the above.

b. War Crimes (Article 8 of ICC Statute)

1. The Court shall have jurisdiction in respect of war crimes in particular when committed as a part of a plan or policy or as part of a large-scale commission of such crimes.
2. For the purpose of this Statute, "war crimes" means:
   (a) Grave breaches of the Geneva Conventions of 12 August 1949, namely, any of the following acts against persons or property protected under the provisions of the relevant Geneva Convention:
       (i)   Willful killing;
       (ii)   Torture or inhuman treatment, including biological experiments;
       (iii) Willfully causing great suffering, or serious injury to body or health;
       (iv)   Extensive destruction and appropriation of property, not justified by military necessity and carried out unlawfully and wantonly;
       (v)   Compelling a prisoner of war or other protected person to serve in the forces of a hostile Power;
       (vi)   Willfully depriving a prisoner of war or other protected person of the rights of fair and regular trial;
       (vii) Unlawful deportation or transfer or unlawful confinement;
       (viii) Taking of hostages.
   (b) Other serious violations of the laws and customs applicable in international armed conflict, within the established framework of international law, namely, any of the following acts:
       (i)   Intentionally directing attacks against the civilian population as such or against individual civilians not taking direct part in hostilities;
       (ii)   Intentionally directing attacks against civilian objects, that is, objects which are not military objectives;
       (iii) Intentionally directing attacks against personnel, installations, material, units or vehicles involved in a humanitarian assistance or peacekeeping mission in accordance with the Charter of the United Nations, as long as they are entitled to the protection given to civilians or civilian objects under the international law of armed conflict;
       (iv)   Intentionally launching an attack in the knowledge that such attack will cause incidental loss of life or injury to civilians or damage to civilian objects or widespread, long-term and severe damage to the natural environment which would be clearly excessive in relation to the concrete and direct overall military advantage anticipated;
       (v)   Attacking or bombarding, by whatever means, towns, villages, dwellings or buildings which are undefended and which are not military objectives;
       (vi)   Killing or wounding a combatant who, having laid down his arms or having no longer means of defence, has surrendered at discretion;
       (vii) Making improper use of a flag of truce, of the flag or of the military insignia and uniform of the enemy or of the United Nations, as well as of the distinctive emblems of the Geneva Conventions, resulting in death or serious personal injury;
       (viii) The transfer, directly or indirectly, by the Occupying Power of parts of its own civilian population into the territory it occupies, or the deportation or transfer of all or parts of the population of the occupied territory within or outside this territory;

(ix)   Intentionally directing attacks against buildings dedicated to religion, education, art, science or charitable purposes, historic monuments, hospitals and places where the sick and wounded are collected, provided they are not military objectives;

(x)   Subjecting persons who are in the power of an adverse party to physical mutilation or to medical or scientific experiments of any kind which are neither justified by the medical, dental or hospital treatment of the person concerned nor carried out in his or her interest, and which cause death to or seriously endanger the health of such person or persons;

(xi)   Killing or wounding treacherously individuals belonging to the hostile nation or army;

(xii) Declaring that no quarter will be given;

(xiii) Destroying or seizing the enemy's property unless such destruction or seizure be imperatively demanded by the necessities of war;

(xiv) Declaring abolished, suspended or inadmissible in a court of law the rights and actions of the nationals of the hostile party;

(xv)   Compelling the nationals of the hostile party to take part in the operations of war directed against their own country, even if they were in the belligerent's service before the commencement of the war;

(xvi) Pillaging a town or place, even when taken by assault;

(xvii) Employing poison or poisoned weapons;

(xviii) Employing asphyxiating, poisonous or other gases, and all analogous liquids, materials or devices;

(xix) Employing bullets which expand or flatten easily in the human body, such as bullets with a hard envelope which does not entirely cover the core or is pierced with incisions;

(xx)   Employing weapons, projectiles and material and methods of warfare which are of a nature to cause superfluous injury or unnecessary suffering or which are inherently indiscriminate in violation of the international law of armed conflict, provided that such weapons, projectiles and material and methods of warfare are the subject of a comprehensive prohibition and are included in an annex to this Statute, by an amendment in accordance with the relevant provisions set forth in Articles 121 and 123;

(xxi) Committing outrages on personal dignity, in particular humiliating and degrading treatment;

(xxii) Committing rape, sexual slavery, enforced prostitution, forced pregnancy, as defined in article 7 [on crimes against humanity], paragraph 2 (f), enforced sterilization, or any other form of sexual violence also a grave breach of the Geneva Conventions;

(xxiii) Utilizing the presence of a civilian or other protected person to render certain points, areas or military forces immune from military operations;

(xxiv) Intentionally directing attacks against buildings, material, medical units and transport, and personnel using the distinctive emblems of the Geneva Conventions in conformity with international law;

(xxv) Intentionally using starvation of civilians as a method of warfare by depriving them of objects indispensable to their survival, including willfully impeding relief supplies as provided for under the Geneva Conventions;

(xxvi) Conscripting or enlisting children under the age of fifteen years into the national armed forces or using them to participate actively in hostilities.

(c) In the case of an armed conflict not of an international character, serious violations of article 3 common to the four Geneva Conventions of 12 August 1949, namely, any of the following acts committed against persons taking no active part in the hostilities, including members of armed forces who have laid down their arms and those placed hors de combat by sickness, wounds, detention or any other cause:

(i)   Violence to life and person, in particular murder of all kinds, mutilation, cruel treatment and torture;

(ii) Committing outrages on personal dignity, in particular humiliating and degrading treatment;

(iii) Taking of hostages;

(iv) The passing of sentences and the carrying out of executions without previous judgement pronounced by a regularly constituted court, affording all judicial guarantees which are generally recognized as indispensable.

(d) Paragraph 2 (c) applies to armed conflicts not of an international character and thus does not apply to situations of internal disturbances and tensions, such as riots, isolated and sporadic acts of violence or other acts of a similar nature.

(e) Other serious violations of the laws and customs applicable in armed conflicts not of an international character, within the established framework of international law, namely, any of the following acts:

(i)   Intentionally directing attacks against the civilian population as such or against individual civilians not taking direct part in hostilities;

(ii) Intentionally directing attacks against buildings, material, medical units and transport, and personnel using the distinctive emblems of the Geneva Conventions in conformity with international law;

(iii) Intentionally directing attacks against personnel, installations, material, units or vehicles involved in a humanitarian assistance or peacekeeping mission in accordance with the Charter of the United Nations, as long as they are entitled to the protection given to civilians or civilian objects under the law of armed conflict;

(iv) Intentionally directing attacks against buildings dedicated to religion, education, art, science or charitable purposes, historic monuments, hospitals and places where the sick and wounded are collected, provided they are not military objectives;

(v)   Pillaging a town or place, even when taken by assault;

(vi) Committing rape, sexual slavery, enforced prostitution, forced pregnancy, as defined in article 7, paragraph 2 (f), enforced sterilization, and any other form of sexual violence also constituting a serious violation of article 3 common to the four Geneva Conventions;

(vii) Conscripting or enlisting children under the age of fifteen years into armed forces or groups or using them to participate actively in hostilities;

(viii) Ordering the displacement of the civilian population for reasons related to the conflict, unless the security of the civilians involved or imperative military reasons so demand;

(ix) Killing or wounding treacherously a combatant adversary;

(x)   Declaring that no quarter will be given;

(xi) Subjecting persons who are in the power of another party to the conflict to physical mutilation or to medical or scientific experiments of any kind which are neither justified by the medical, dental or hospital treatment of the person concerned nor carried out in his or her interest, and which cause death to or seriously endanger the health of such person or persons;

(xii) Destroying or seizing the property of an adversary unless such destruction or seizure be imperatively demanded by the necessities of the conflict.

(f) Paragraph 2 (e) applies to armed conflicts not of an international character and thus does not apply to situations of internal disturbances and tensions, such as riots, isolated and sporadic acts of violence or other acts of a similar nature. It applies to armed conflicts that take place in the territory of a State when there is protracted armed conflict between governmental authorities and organized armed groups or between such groups. (Article 8 of ICC statute)

☞ It is important to note that the definition of the war crimes over which the ICC will have jurisdiction in cases of noninternational armed conflict, while similar to many of the provi-

(continues)

(*continued*)

sions in the definition of war crimes committed in international conflicts, is much more restrictive than those. For instance, attacks causing incidental loss of civilian lives, the starvation of civilians, the use of human shields, or the use of prohibited weapons are not included.

→ **International Criminal Court; Responsibility**

III. GRAVE BREACHES OF INTERNATIONAL HUMANITARIAN LAW

The requirements of justice and the battle against impunity are the central elements of humanitarian law, along with the protection of relief actions.

Humanitarian law, in the internationally recognized form of the Geneva Conventions and their Protocols, defines both violations and grave breaches of its rules, both of which are qualified as war crimes. These elements and more recently codified humanitarian law provide a different definition of these crimes from that established by the Nuremberg tribunal. The complexity and divergence of these elements may lead to confusion and require a close reading. The sanctions that can be incurred differ depending on whether the act committed was a violation or a grave breach.

In the absence of a permanent standing international criminal court, the Geneva Conventions establish the obligation of all states to judge the perpetrators of grave breaches before their national courts, regardless of their nationality. This is called the "principle of universal jurisdiction."

→ **Universal jurisdiction**

1. Violations of Humanitarian Law

Violations are the transgressions of humanitarian law that are not defined as grave breaches (discussed later). Humanitarian law does not provide a detailed, comprehensive definition of these breaches, the punishment of which is left up to the competent national authorities. The punishment of these crimes is carried out by the normal judicial and disciplinary control mechanisms—in other words, the civilian or military tribunals.

These crimes may be the subject of amnesties within the framework of a national law adopted following a conflict. They may benefit from a statute of limitations, unlike the war crimes and crimes against humanity defined by the Nuremberg tribunals and the grave breaches of the Geneva Conventions for which there is no time limit for initiating proceedings. Violations must be examined in the context of a framework determining the scale of responsibility of national authorities, military commanders, and individuals.

→ **Penal Sanctions in humanitarian law; Responsibility**

2. Grave Breaches of Humanitarian Law

The Geneva Conventions and the Additional Protocol I of 1977, relating to the protection of victims of international armed conflicts (Protocol I), clearly define a limited number of crimes that fall into the category of grave breaches. No statute of limitations can apply to these crimes, and humanitarian law has established a specific system for penal sanctions.

The definition of these grave breaches varies depending on whether they were committed in international or internal armed conflicts. The 1949 Geneva Conventions provide a first definition in the context of international armed conflicts (GCI Article 50, GCII Article 51, GCIII Article 130, and GCIV Article 147), which has been expanded and further detailed in Protocol I (Article 85).

The Geneva Conventions prohibit states from absolving themselves, or any other state, of any liability incurred with regard to grave breaches to the Conventions (GCI Article 51, GCII Article 52, GCIII Article 131, and GCIV Article 148). Since states have undertaken to punish such violations, they may not grant amnesties for such crimes, whether by enacting national legislation or in the context of peace accords.

a. Grave Breaches in International Conflicts

1949 Geneva Conventions

Grave breaches are specific violations of the laws of armed conflict, which states are under the obligation to prevent and sanction. They involve any of the following acts, if committed against persons or property protected by the four Geneva Conventions:

- willful killing, torture, or inhuman treatment, including biological experiments;
- deliberately causing great suffering or serious injury to body or health;
- unlawfully deporting, transferring, or confining a protected person or taking hostages;
- compelling a person protected by the Conventions (whether civilian or prisoner of war) to serve in the forces of an enemy power;
- depriving a protected person of his or her right to a fair and regular trial, as established by international humanitarian law;
- causing extensive destruction and appropriation of property, not justified by military necessity and carried out unlawfully and wantonly.

These acts are hence forbidden when carried out against

- civilians, the sick, and wounded (GCIV Article 147);
- prisoners of war (GCIII Article 130);
- the wounded, sick, and shipwrecked members of armed forces at sea (GCII Article 51); and
- the wounded and sick in armed forces in the field (GCI Article 50).

> ☞ The 1977 Protocol I additional to the Geneva Conventions (Protocol I) expands and details the crimes that are considered grave breaches of the Geneva Conventions. Notably, it adds acts such as the failure to respect relief personnel or supplies (PI Article 85) or to respect medical duties (PI Article 11) to the list of war crimes punishable under the Protocol.

1977 Protocol I (PI Article 85)

Acts described as grave breaches in the Conventions are grave breaches of Protocol I if committed against

- persons in the power of an adverse Party protected by the Geneva Conventions and Protocol I (as defined in Articles 44, 45, and 73 of Protocol I or in the entry on ➔ **protected persons**);
- the wounded, sick, or shipwrecked of the adverse party;

- the medical or religious personnel, medical units, or medical transports which are under the control of the adverse Party and are protected by Protocol I (PI Article 85.2).

Furthermore, the following acts, in violation of Protocol I, are considered grave breaches when they are committed willfully and cause death or serious injury to body or health (PI Article 85.3):

(a) making the civilian population or individual civilians the object of attack;
(b) launching an indiscriminate attack affecting the civilian population or civilian objects in the knowledge that such attack will cause excessive loss of life, injury to civilians or damage to civilian objects;
(c) launching an attack against works or installations containing dangerous forces in the knowledge that such attack will cause excessive loss of life, injury to civilians or damage to civilian objects;
(d) making non-defended localities and demilitarized zones the object of attack;
(e) making a person the object of attack in the knowledge that he is hors de combat;
(f) the perfidious use, in violation of Article 37, of the distinctive emblem of the red cross, red crescent or red lion and sun or of other protective signs recognized by the Conventions or this Protocol.

→ **Attacks**

The following acts are also regarded as grave breaches of humanitarian law when committed willfully and in violation of the Conventions or Protocol I, even if they do not result in death or serious injury to body or health (PI Article 85.4)

(a) the transfer by the Occupying Power of parts of its own civilian population into the territory it occupies, or the deportation or transfer of all or parts of the population of the occupied territory within or outside this territory, in violation of Article 49 of the Fourth Convention;
(b) unjustifiable delay in the repatriation of prisoners of war or civilians;
(c) practices of apartheid and other inhuman and degrading practices involving outrages on personal dignity, based on racial discrimination;
(d) making the clearly-recognized historic monuments, works of art or places of worship which constitute the cultural or spiritual heritage of peoples and to which special protection has been given by special arrangement, for example, within the framework of a competent international organization, the object of attack, causing as a result extensive destruction thereof, where there is no evidence of the violation by the adverse Party of Article 53(b), and when such historic monuments, works of art and places of worship are not located in the immediate proximity of military objectives;
(e) depriving a person protected by the Conventions . . . of the rights of fair and regular trial.

1977 Protocol I (PI Article 11)

The physical or mental health and integrity of persons who are in the power of the adverse party—or who are interned, detained, or otherwise deprived of liberty—must not be endangered by any unjustified act or omission. Accordingly, it is prohibited to subject these persons to any medical procedure that is not indicated by their state of health and is inconsistent with generally accepted medical standards that normally would be applied under similar medical circumstances to nationals of the party conducting the procedure and who are not deprived of liberty (PI Article 11.1). In particular, it is prohibited to carry out on such persons, even with their consent:

- physical mutilations;
- medical or scientific experiments;
- removal of tissue or organs for transplant, except where these acts are justified in conformity with generally accepted medical standards which would be applied under similar medical

circumstances to nationals of the party conducting the procedure and who are in no way deprived of liberty (PI Article 11.2).

Hence, any such willful act or omission against a person under the control of a party other than the one on which he or she depends—which either violates any of the prohibitions enumerated above or fails to comply with the requirements governing such acts—is a grave breach of Protocol I (PI Article 11.4).

The only possible derogations that can be made from these prohibitions are "in the case of donations of blood for transfusion, or of skin for grafting, provided that they are given voluntarily and without any coercion or inducement, and then only for therapeutic purposes, under conditions consistent with generally accepted medical standards and controls designed for the benefit of both the donor and the recipient" (PI Article 11.3).

b. Grave Breaches Applicable to Internal Armed Conflicts

No definition of grave breaches to the Geneva Conventions was included in Protocol II, which relates to the protection of victims of noninternational armed conflicts. The question of which definition to apply and what punishment mechanisms are available in such situations has yet to be solved in a clear and unquestionable manner. The current tendency of conflicts—more frequently internal than international—as well as the recent developments in international law, require that the existing definitions and systems of sanctions for war crimes and crimes against humanity in international armed conflicts be used more consistently.

- The statute of the ad hoc International Criminal Tribunal for Rwanda establishes the Tribunal's jurisdiction over crimes of genocide, war crimes, and crimes against humanity, as well as grave breaches of Article 3 common to the four Geneva Conventions (explained earlier) and of Protocol II, which codifies the protection that must be provided for victims of internal conflicts. The statute of the International Criminal Court provides a detailed definition of the crimes committed in internal conflicts over which it will have jurisdiction (also detailed earlier).
- The International Fact-Finding Commission, established pursuant to the Geneva Conventions (PI Article 90), has formally recognized its competence to investigate grave violations of common Article 3 (which refers explicitly to noninternational armed conflicts). Inquiries concerning such violations must follow the general conditions regulating the procedure and rules of request specific to the Commission.

    Article 3 common to the four Geneva Conventions forbids

    (a) violence to life and person, in particular murder of all kinds, mutilation, cruel treatment and torture;
    (b) taking of hostages;
    (c) outrages on personal dignity, in particular humiliating and degrading treatment;
    (d) the passing of sentences and the carrying out of executions without previous judgment pronounced by a regularly constituted court, affording all the judicial guarantees which are recognized as indispensable by civilized peoples. (GCI–IV Article 3)

☞ On ratifying the Geneva Conventions, states commit to respect and ensure respect for humanitarian law (GCI–IV Article 1). They must do everything possible—jointly, individually,

(continues)

> (*continued*)
>
> or in cooperation with the United Nations—to put an end to grave breaches of the law (PI Article 89).
>
> Grave breaches of the Geneva Conventions are defined as war crimes. In some cases, such acts may also come under the category of crimes against humanity. This means that all states are under the obligation to search for persons alleged to have committed or ordered such crimes, and to bring them, regardless of their nationality, before their own courts. This is known as the principle of universal jurisdiction.
>
> States, NGOs, and individuals may transmit to the ICRC any complaint concerning grave violations of the Conventions (Article 4.1.c of ICRC statute).
>
> The Conventions also establish a procedure of inquiry and establish provisions for an International Fact-Finding Commission to investigate such grave breaches.
>
> Hence, testimony relating to violations of humanitarian law may be transmitted to the court of any of the states concerned, to the UN, to the ICRC, to the International Fact-Finding Commission, and to the Prosecutor of the new International Criminal Court (once it is operating).
>
> → **Human rights; Individual recourse; Respect for international humanitarian law; Universal jurisdiction**

c. Existing Structures for the Punishment of Grave Breaches

Several principles, definitions, and restrictions set the framework within which grave breaches can be punished.

- Humanitarian law limits the possibility of granting amnesties, whether in the context of negotiating peace accords or in any other circumstances. As mentioned, the Geneva Conventions provide that no state may absolve itself or any other state of any liability incurred with regard to violations of international humanitarian law (GCI Article 51, GCII Article 52, GCIII Article 131, and GCIV Article 148). → **Amnesties**
- Grave breaches are defined as war crimes (PI Article 85.5). In certain cases, they may also be qualified as crimes against humanity. As such they are not subject to any statute of limitations, as per Article 1 of the International Convention on the Non-Applicability of Statutory Limitations to War Crimes and Crimes Against Humanity adopted at the UN on November 26, 1968. → **Nonapplicability of statutory limitations**
- The principle of universal jurisdiction, touched on earlier in this entry, reflects the international obligation of all states party to the Conventions to punish grave breaches of humanitarian law. It represents a genuine system of collective security on a judicial level. States are under the obligation to search for persons suspected of having committed or ordered such grave breaches. In ratifying the Conventions, they have also undertaken to bring such persons, regardless of their nationality, before their own courts. States may also transfer such persons to another state party, provided that this state has already initiated proceedings and that the accused would face appropriate punishment.

  To this effect, a system of mutual assistance in criminal matters between states parties is established by the Geneva Conventions (GCI Article 49; GCII Article 50; GCIII Article 129; GCIV Article 146; PI Articles 86 and 88).

☞ In the absence of a permanent and truly universal international criminal tribunal, which would be responsible for judging grave breaches of humanitarian law, states bear the responsibility of searching for and punishing authors of such crimes.

The statute for the International Criminal Court (ICC) maintains this balance. It posits that the Court will only exercise its jurisdiction if states are unwilling or unable to carry out the necessary investigations or prosecution of the accused. Furthermore, the ICC's statute has not yet entered into force: sixty states must first ratify it, which means that it will be several years before the Court begins to operate.

In the meantime, the courts of all states party to the Geneva Conventions (i.e., virtually every single state in the world) have jurisdiction over authors of grave breach of the Conventions. On ratifying the Conventions, they undertook to modify their domestic legislation so as to enable their courts to rule on such cases. However, very few states have fulfilled this obligation.

It is crucial that states incorporate these provisions into their laws, so as to be in conformity with their obligations, and that they not impede the action of domestic courts that might eventually be seized of cases concerning such crimes (GCI Articles 49 and 51; GCII Articles 50 and 52; GCIII Articles 129 and 131; GCIV Articles 146 and 148; PI Articles 85–87).

→ **Mutual assistance in criminal matters; Universal jurisdiction**

- Provisions for a system of inquiry aimed at establishing the existence of violations are set up by the Geneva Conventions (GCI Article 52, GCII Article 53, GCIII Article 132, and GCIV Article 149). Such inquiries may be carried out only with the agreement of the concerned parties to the conflict.
- An International Fact-Finding Commission was created, as per Article 90 of Protocol I. It is a permanent independent organ in charge of investigating possible grave breaches and serious violations of humanitarian law. Article 90 is optional, meaning that the Commission may only act with regard to countries that have recognized its competence.

→ **International Fact-Finding Commission**

Available Recourses in Case of Grave Breaches of Humanitarian Law

- Victims of war crimes and crimes against humanity may in principle bring cases before foreign national courts on the basis of universal jurisdiction, as established by the four 1949 Geneva Conventions. However, such complaints are likely to fail if the state in question has not brought its legislation into conformity with this international obligation.
- The victims of events that took place in the former Yugoslavia or in Rwanda cannot file a complaint directly with the two ad hoc International Criminal Tribunals, but they may submit information to the Prosecutor. They do not benefit from the status of "victim" before these Tribunals but from that of "witness."
- Victims may not directly seize the International Fact-Finding Commission, which is responsible for investigating alleged grave breaches and serious violations of humanitarian law. They must address themselves to states parties, which alone may request that the Commission initiate an inquiry.

(continues)

(*continued*)

- Victims of genocide, war crimes, and crimes against humanity will be able to transmit information to the Prosecutor of the International Criminal Court, once it is operational.
- The principle of universal jurisdiction may also apply to certain grave human rights violations, such as torture. For other such violations, other recourses are available at an international level, which can be used by individuals, NGOs, and states.

→ **Human rights; Individual recourse**

→ **Amnesties; Duty of commanders; Immunity; Impunity; Individual recourse; International Criminal Court; International Criminal Tribunals; International Fact-Finding Commission; Mutual assistance in criminal matters; Nonapplicability of statutory limitations; Penal sanctions of humanitarian law; Responsibility; Universal jurisdiction**

📖 **For Additional Information:**

Bassiouni, Cherif. *Crimes against Humanity in International Criminal Law*. The Hague: Martinus Nijhoff, 1992.

Goldstone, Richard J. "Bringing War Criminals to Justice during an Ongoing War." In *Hard Choices: Moral Dilemmas in Humanitarian Intervention,* ed. Jonathan Moore. Lanham, Md.: Rowman & Littlefield, 1998, 195–228.

Meron, Theodor. "War Crimes Law Comes of Age." *American Journal of International Law* (July 1998): 92.

Zalaquett, José. "Moral Reconstruction in the Wake of Human Rights Violations and War Crimes." In *Hard Choices: Moral Dilemmas in Humanitarian Intervention*, ed. Jonathan Moore. Lanham, Md.: Rowman & Littlefield, 1998, 211–28.

■ WEAPONS

A large variety of weapons exist, and they can be used in many different ways.

☞ International humanitarian law regulates the use of weapons:

- Some weapons are simply prohibited, as such: not only is their use strictly prohibited, but so is their production, transfer, and stockpiling.
- Other weapons are authorized, but their use is regulated by prohibiting certain forms of use; for instance, any use that is indiscriminate or disproportionate is prohibited.
- States must examine whether any new weapon is compatible with the principles of international humanitarian law, in consultation with the ICRC.

I. HUMANITARIAN LAW LIMITS THE CHOICE OF WEAPONS

In general, humanitarian law prohibits any weapon "of a nature to cause superfluous injury or unnecessary suffering" and any that may have indiscriminate or excessively injurious effects.

This is an ancient principle, linked to the axiom that "the right of the parties to the conflict to choose methods or means of warfare is not unlimited" (PI Article 35).

Humanitarian law may therefore prohibit the use, production, stockpiling, or selling of certain kinds of weapons. This is now the case for biological and chemical weapons, for instance, and to some extent for landmines. Since 1977 (when Protocol I additional to the 1949 Geneva Conventions was adopted), humanitarian law has also codified that it is forbidden to employ methods or means of warfare that are intended, or may be expected, to cause widespread, long-term, and severe damage to the natural environment (PI Article 35).

For the most part, the rules governing the use of such weapons are set forth in international conventions that address these issues specifically and therefore only apply to the states party to these conventions. The main exceptions are the Geneva Conventions, whose rules apply to all states—having the status of customary international law—and which go a long way toward regulating means and methods of warfare. ➔ **Methods (and means) of warfare**

Furthermore, in the study, development, acquisition, or adoption of a new weapon, states are under the obligation to determine whether the use of this weapon would be prohibited by humanitarian law, in some or all circumstances (PI Article 36). The International Committee of the Red Cross (ICRC) has a consultative role to play with regard to this question.

II. Humanitarian Law Limits the Way in Which Weapons Are Used

The four 1949 Geneva Conventions and their two 1977 Protocols set forth the restrictions on the use of weapons. Today, these rules are mandatory for all states. Some of the main rules are as follows:

- Parties to the conflict must distinguish between civilian and military objects. The weapons they use must always allow them to respect this distinction.
- Weapons must not be used in a way that would not be justified by a genuine military requirement or that would be disproportionate to the military advantage sought or to the supposed military threat. The aim of these provisions is to limit superfluous, gratuitous, or unnecessary damage or suffering.
- During attacks, parties to the conflict (in particular, their commanders) are under the obligation to take certain precautions to limit their possible effects on civilians and civilian objects.
➔   **Attacks; Duty of commanders**

Another important landmark in restricting the use of weapons, in a more general way, was the adoption of the Convention on Prohibitions or Restrictions on the Use of Certain Conventional Weapons Which May be Deemed to Be Excessively Injurious or Have Indiscriminate Effects (known as the Convention on Conventional Weapons), in Geneva on October 10, 1980.

III. Categories of Weapons

Different kinds of weapons are available. Some weapons are authorized, except certain uses thereof (edge weapons and firearms), while others are strictly prohibited (incendiary, biological, and chemical weapons). The general rule that prohibits attacks against civilians is applicable to the use of all weapons.

1. Edge Weapons

These are any offensive or cutting blades or other weapons made of metal or steel, such as knives, swords, machetes, daggers, or bayonets. Their use is restricted by the general rules of humanitarian law, which prohibit attacking noncombatants, killing or wounding treacherously, and causing superfluous injury or unnecessary suffering (Article 23 of Hague Convention IV; PI Articles 35–37).

2. Firearms

This is a very broad category of weapons, including all those that shoot cartridges or explosive projectiles, such as shotguns, cannons, bombs, missiles, and so on. Only some of these weapons are prohibited:

- explosive projectiles that weigh less than four hundred grams (fourteen ounces), as established by the 1868 St. Petersburg Declaration Renouncing the Use, in Time of War, of Certain Explosive Projectiles;
- bullets that expand or flatten easily in the human body, as set forth in the 1899 Hague Peace Declarations;
- any weapon the main effect of which is to injure by fragments that are not detectable by X-rays once inside the human body, as established by Protocol I to the 1980 Convention on Conventional Weapons (Protocol on Non-Detectable Fragments).

3. Incendiary Weapons

These weapons come under the category of firearms. Their aim is to set fire to objects or to cause burn injuries to humans. As with all weapons, it is prohibited to use them against individuals and objects protected by humanitarian law (e.g., civilians and civilian goods, including forests, etc.). It is also prohibited to use them against combatants and military objectives that are located "within a concentration of civilians," as per Protocol III to the 1980 Convention on Conventional Weapons (Protocol on Incendiary Weapons).

4. Weapons of Mass Destruction

This denomination includes three categories of weapons: biological, chemical, and nuclear. Since these are indiscriminate, by nature, their use is hard to reconcile with the spirit of humanitarian law, which is based on the military ability to distinguish between civilian and military objectives, and between civilians and members of armed forces.

5. Bacteriological (or Biological) Weapons

Bacteriological weapons (commonly known as biological weapons) are those that aim to spread disease that threaten the health of human beings, animals, and plants. Their use, production, and stockpiling are prohibited by two main international texts:

- the Protocol for the Prohibition of the Use of Asphyxiating, Poisonous or Other Gases, and of Bacteriological Methods of Warfare, adopted in Geneva on June 17, 1925—this convention has 132 states parties;

- the Convention on the Prohibition of the Development, Production and Stockpiling of Bacteriological (Biological) and Toxin Weapons and on Their Destruction, opened for signature on April 10, 1972—it has 143 states parties. The fact that this Convention is relatively recent, and its prohibitions are very broad, has made it the point of reference in terms of regulating biological weapons.

   The main prohibitions are enumerated in Article 1: each state party undertakes "never in any circumstance to develop, produce, stockpile, or otherwise acquire or retain microbial or other biological agents, or toxins [. . .], or weapons, equipment or means of delivery designed to use such agents or toxins." The convention offers no further definition, which is problematic because the meaning of "weapons, equipment or means of delivery" is now a subject of controversy among states.

6. Chemical Weapons

Chemical weapons—the clearest definition of which is offered in the 1993 Convention listed later—cause death, temporary incapacitation, or permanent harm to humans or animals. Mainly, they include the munitions and devices that release toxic chemicals. Various conventions prohibit their use, production, and stockpiling:

- The Hague declarations prohibiting the launching of projectiles, the aim of which is to spread asphyxiating or poisonous gases, adopted July 29, 1899.
- The Protocol for the Prohibition of the Use of Asphyxiating, Poisonous or Other Gases, and of Bacteriological Methods of Warfare, adopted in Geneva on June 17, 1925—this convention has 132 states parties. This convention does not include any enforcement or verification mechanisms. It prohibits the use of chemical and biological weapons in times of conflict but does not prohibit their stockpiling or production. Furthermore, it authorizes the use of these weapons in reprisals against states that make use of such weapons first, or against states that are not parties to the Protocol.
- The Convention on the Prohibition of the Development, Production, Stockpiling and Use of Chemical Weapons and on Their Destruction, adopted in Paris on January 13, 1993—it entered into force in April 1997 and had 144 states parties as of March 2001.
   This convention created the Organization for the Prohibition of Chemical Weapons (OPCW). Based in The Hague, this monitoring body is made up of a secretariat and teams of inspectors. It analyzes the reports that states parties are under the obligation to submit to it, concerning their activities relating to chemical agents; it carries out routine or surprise inspections to production sites; and it monitors the destruction operations of existing stockpiles.

✎ OPCW
    Johan de Wittlaan 32
    NL-2517 AR The Hague, Netherlands
    Tel.: (31) 70 416 3300
    Fax: (31) 70 306 3535
@ OPCW: www.opcw.nl

7. Nuclear Weapons

There is no general prohibition on the use of nuclear weapons. Today's doctrine holds that nuclear weapons are weapons of mass destruction and, as such, have indiscriminate effects. From this perspective, and for both reasons, they should be prohibited by the provisions of Protocol I additional to the Geneva Conventions that forbid indiscriminate or excessively injurious weapons (see Section I of this entry). Most of the states that possess nuclear weapons have not ratified Protocol I for this very reason, except for the Russian Federation, which did so in 1989, and the United Kingdom, which did so in 1998.

On July 8, 1996, the International Court of Justice (ICJ) rendered an advisory opinion on the legality of the threat or use of nuclear weapons, on the United Nations General Assembly's request. The opinion, which is very ambiguous, reaches four main conclusions: (1) the use of nuclear weapons is neither formally prohibited nor formally authorized; (2) the threat or use of nuclear weapons is contrary to the fundamental rules of humanitarian law; (3) the use of nuclear weapons in a conflict, during actions or combats in which tactical weapons would be permitted, is strictly forbidden; and (4) it was not possible to conclude definitely whether the threat or use of nuclear weapons would be lawful or unlawful in a case of self-defense, if a state were to face an extreme circumstance that threatened its very survival.

Officially, five nuclear powers exist: the five members of the UN Security Council (China, France, the Russian Federation, the United Kingdom, and the United States). However, in 1998, both India and Pakistan conducted several nuclear tests. These two states, as well as Israel, are considered "threshold" states, meaning they have the necessary resources to produce nuclear weapons but are not officially declared as possessing them.

The International Atomic Energy Agency (IAEA), based in Vienna, Austria, monitors the use of nuclear energy, including weapons. There are two main international conventions that aim to control nuclear weapons:

- The Treaty on the Non-Proliferation of Nuclear Weapons (known as the Nuclear Non-Proliferation Treaty, or NPT), which was adopted under the aegis of the UN in 1968. It entered into force on March 5, 1970, but was suspended indefinitely in 1995. As of March 2001, it had 187 participating states, including the five Security Council nuclear powers. Israel, India, and Pakistan have not ratified it.
- The Comprehensive Nuclear Test Ban Treaty (CTBT), which was adopted at the UN Conference on Disarmament. It has not yet entered into force. It has to be ratified by forty-four nuclear-capable states, including the three threshold states, before it can enter into force. As of September 1999, 160 states had signed it, but only 76 had actually ratified it (of which only 20 are among the nuclear-capable states, and the threshold states have declared that they will not ratify it). This treaty completes an earlier treaty, the 1963 Moscow Treaty (Treaty Banning Nuclear Weapon Tests in the Atmosphere, in Outer Space and Under Water), which foresaw a partial prohibition on nuclear weapons.

✎ IAEA
PO Box 100
Wagrammer Strasse 5
A-1400 Vienna, Austria
Tel.: (43) 12 60 00
Fax: (43) 12 60 07
@ IAEA: www.iaea.org

8. Mines

For details on mines, refer to the entry on ➜ **mines.**

According to the Stockholm International Peace Research Institute, based in Stockholm, Sweden, international arms trade grew by 24 percent between 1994 and 1997. In 1998, arms trade decreased slightly to $22 billion, from $25 billion in 1997.

The arms market is dominated by five exporters: the United States, the Russian Federation, France, the United Kingdom, and Germany. The main purchasing regions are Asia (39 percent of arms imports) and the Near East (31 percent). Worldwide military and arms spending have decreased continuously since 1987, except in these two regions. In 1998, the total value of the arms market was $745 billion.

According to a report published by UN experts in August 1999, internal conflicts (which represent 90 percent of today's conflicts) are fueled by small arms and light weapons. Five hundred million such weapons are in circulation around the world, and 40 percent of their trade is illegal, often in violation of embargoes.

➜ **Attacks; International humanitarian law; Methods (and means) of warfare; Mines; War**

📖 **For Additional Information:**

Aubert, Maurice. "The International Red Cross and the Problem of Excessively Injurious or Indiscriminate Weapons." *International Review of the Red Cross* 279 (November–December 1990): 477–97.

Mulinen, Frederic de. *Handbook on the Law of War for Armed Forces.* Geneva: ICRC, 1989, appendix 1.

Oeter, Stefan. "Methods and Means of Combat." In *The Handbook of Humanitarian Law in Armed Conflicts,* ed. Dieter Fleck. Oxford University Press, 1995, 121–52.

■ WELL-BEING

There is no legal definition of *well-being*. Nevertheless, the well-being of individuals is protected by law through

- the prohibition against ill treatment and torture or any other form of cruel or degrading treatment or punishment;
- the provisions of humanitarian law for the protection of objects that are indispensable to the survival of the civilian population;
- the prohibition of any form of violence to the physical or mental well-being of civilians, wounded or sick, prisoners of war, or persons under the responsibility of a party to an armed conflict (as defined in GI Article 13, GII Article 13, GIII Article 4, and PI Article 75);
- the provisions for the relief and protection foreseen for civilian and protected persons in situations of conflict.

Outside periods of conflict, the main international human rights conventions confirm the responsibility of states to ensure and protect the well-being of their citizens. This is the very foundation of the social contract that ties individuals to society, and any action that violates this norm may be subject to a complaint. These conventions also establish the fundamental right of all persons to have a standard of living adequate for their health and well-being and that of their family (Articles 25 and 29.2 of the 1948 Universal Declaration of Human Rights; Article 4 of the International Covenant on Economic, Social, and Cultural Rights).

➜ **Ill treatment; Persecution; Protected property Protection; Relief;**

■ WOMEN

In times of conflict, international humanitarian law gives women both general protection, as civilians, and special protection, which takes into account the fact that women may be particularly vulnerable to certain kinds of violence. This need for special protection focuses in particular on women's needs as mothers and on the necessity to protect them more specifically from sexual violence.

At other times, including during internal disturbances and tensions, women's rights are protected under international law by various conventions, starting with human rights conventions, which strive to guarantee equal rights for women by prohibiting all forms of adverse discrimination (including on the basis of sex), and set up mechanisms to monitor and condemn such acts. The one aimed specifically at defending women's rights is the 1979 Convention on the Elimination of All Forms of Discrimination against Women, which has 167 participating states.

General Protection

In times of armed conflict, women are entitled to the guarantees that must be granted to all protected persons—namely, the respect for their person, honor, family rights, and religious convictions and practices, as well as the right to humane treatment at all times and to protection from all acts of violence or threats thereof. In addition to these rights, humanitarian law states that "women shall be especially protected against any attack on their honor, in particular against rape, enforced prostitution, or any form of indecent assault" (GCIV Article 27; GPI Article 76.1).
➔ **Protected persons**

At all times, whether during armed conflict or not, women—and all protected persons—must be protected from "violence to life and person, in particular murder of all kinds, mutilation, cruel treatment and torture [. . .], outrages on personal dignity, in particular humiliating and degrading treatment" (common Article 3.1 of Geneva Conventions). ➔ **Fundamental guarantees; Torture**

As mentioned, women are also protected by the nonadverse discrimination clauses that exist in most international human rights conventions. For instance, the statute of the International Criminal Court (ICC), adopted on July 17, 1998, states that "the application and interpretation of law [. . .] must be consistent with internationally recognized human rights, and be without any adverse distinction founded on grounds such as gender" (Article 21 of ICC statute). ➔ **Discrimination**

Furthermore, the ICC statute defines persecution on the basis of gender (among other grounds) as a crime against humanity (Article 7.1.h of ICC statute). ➔ **Ill treatment; Persecution; Well-being**

☞ Rape, enforced prostitution, and any form of indecent assault are forbidden under international humanitarian law in both international and internal conflicts (GCIV Article 27, PI Article 76.1, and PII Article 4.2.e). Nevertheless, rape has become truly accepted as a grave breach of humanitarian law only in recent years—in particular, since its massive occurrence in the former Yugoslavia and in Rwanda. The two ad hoc international criminal tribunals set up to judge serious crimes committed in these conflicts have specifically qualified rape and other acts of sexual violence committed in the former Yugoslavia and in Rwanda as war crimes and crimes against humanity. In the International Criminal Tribunal for Rwanda, rape is explicitly cited as a grave breach of the 1949 Geneva Conventions, which are extended to include situations of internal armed conflict.

In 1995, the Beijing Declaration and Platform for Action reinforced the obligation of governments to pursue and punish perpetrators of rape and other forms of sexual violence against women and girls in situations of conflict, and to define such acts as war crimes.

(continues)

(*continued*)

The statute of the International Criminal Court was adopted on July 17, 1998. It includes rape, sexual slavery, enforced prostitution, forced pregnancy (defined in Article 7.2.f of ICC statute), enforced sterilization, and any other form of sexual violence of comparable gravity, in its definition of both crimes against humanity and war crimes over which it has jurisdiction, in both international and noninternational armed conflicts (Articles 7.1.g, 8.2.b.xxii, 8.2.e.vi of ICC statute).

→ **International Criminal Court; International Criminal Tribunals; Rape; War crimes/ Crimes against humanity**

I. THE PROTECTION OF WOMEN IN TIMES OF CONFLICT: THE GENEVA CONVENTIONS AND THEIR PROTOCOLS

In addition to the general protection described earlier, the Geneva Conventions set forth specific provisions for the protection of women.

1. Pregnant Women and Maternity Cases

Pregnant women and women in labor come under the category of "wounded persons" and hence benefit from the same "particular protection and respect" to which the wounded and sick are entitled under humanitarian law (GCIV Article 16; PI Article 8).

→ **Wounded and sick persons**

- Parties to a conflict must endeavor to evacuate expectant mothers to hospitals or safety zones and out of besieged and encircled areas (GCIV Articles 14, 16, 17, 21, and 22). Whether or not they are evacuated, they must receive the necessary aid: states are under the obligation to "permit the free passage of all consignments of essential foodstuffs, clothing and tonics intended for children under fifteen, expectant mothers and maternity cases" (GCIV Article 23).
- In case pregnant women and mothers of children under seven—as well as children under fifteen—find themselves on the territory of a party to the conflict of which they are not nationals, they must benefit from any preferential treatment that is granted to the women and children who are nationals of the state concerned (GCIV Article 38.5).
- An Occupying Power may not hinder the application of preferential measures in favor of women and children, which were adopted prior to its occupation (GCIV Article 50).

→ **Evacuation; Occupied territories**

2. Civilian Internees and Prisoners of War

- "Women shall be treated with all the regard due to their sex and shall in all cases benefit by treatment as favourable as that granted to men" (GCIII Article 14 and also Articles 16, 49, and 88; GCI–III Article 12).
- A woman prisoner of war shall not be sentenced to punishment more severe or undergo punishment in worse conditions than a woman member of the armed forces of the Detaining Power punished for a similar offense (GCIII Article 88).

- Women must be held or confined in quarters separate from men (except for civilian internees who are accommodated with their families) and under the immediate supervision of women (GCIII Articles 25, 97, and 108; GCIV Articles 76, 85, and 124).
- "Expectant and nursing mothers and children under fifteen years of age shall be given additional food, in proportion to their physiological needs" (GCIV Article 89). They must also receive treatment and care which must not be inferior to that provided for the general population (GCIV Article 91). Additional Protocol I to the Geneva Conventions further states that "pregnant women and mothers having dependent infants who are arrested, detained or interned for reasons related to the armed conflict, shall have their cases considered with the utmost priority" (PI Article 76.2).
- A woman internee may be searched only by a woman (GCIV Article 97).
- Disciplinary punishment must take into account the internee's age, sex, and state of health (GCIV Article 119).
- Parties to a conflict must try to reach an agreement for the release, repatriation, or return, or the accommodation in a neutral country, of certain internees, in particular children, pregnant women, and mothers with infants and young children (GCIV Article 132).

→ **Detention; Internment; Prisoners of war**

3. Judicial Guarantees and the Death Penalty

In times of armed conflict, women benefit from the same judicial guarantees as other protected persons. Furthermore, the death penalty may not be carried out against pregnant women or mothers of young or dependent children (PI Article 76.3; PII Article 6.4).

4. Internal Armed Conflict

During noninternational conflicts, the specific clauses that apply to women, under the 1977 Additional Protocol II to the Geneva Conventions, are as follows:

- The protection of all fundamental guarantees, including "violence to life and person, in particular murder of all kinds, mutilation, cruel treatment and torture [. . .], outrages on personal dignity, in particular humiliating and degrading treatment" (common Article 3.1 of Geneva Conventions and PII Article 4) and "rape, enforced prostitution, and any form of indecent assault" (PII Article 4.2.e).
- Women must be held in quarters separate from those of men and be under direct supervision of women, except when accommodated with their family (PII Article 5.2.a).
- The death penalty shall not be pronounced on pregnant women or mothers of young children (PII Article 6.4).

5. Refugees

The increased attention and recognition given to crimes such as rape, to which women are more particularly vulnerable, have led to specific measures being taken in the case of women refugees. The UNHCR Executive Committee issued several conclusions addressing the need to provide reinforced protection for women refugees, both legally (in terms of including sexual violence among the main grounds for persecution, which will help enable women fleeing persecution to receive refugee status) and in practice, once they have reached a destination. It thus acknowledges and adapts assistance to the fact that "refugees and asylum-seekers, including children, in many instances have been subjected to rape or other forms of sexual violence during their flight or following their arrival" (UNHCR ExCom Conclusion 73 [XLIV], 1993).

In the case of repatriation, the UNHCR representatives must make sure that they do not speak only to the refugees' representatives when deciding whether a group wants to return to their home state. They must consult the refugees themselves and, in particular, groups of women refugees to verify that the leaders genuinely represent the will and interest of the refugees as whole.

→ **Refugees; Repatriation**

II. PROTECTION OF WOMEN IN TIMES OF PEACE OR TENSION

In times other than armed conflicts (either peace or internal disturbances), the Convention on the Elimination of All Forms of Discrimination against Women (CEDAW— adopted by the UN General Assembly, on December 18, 1979, and entered into force on September 3, 1981) establishes the provisions that states must implement to protect women against the negative effects of discrimination. The Convention currently has 167 participating states, which commit to "pursue by all appropriate means and without delay a policy of eliminating discrimination against women" (Article 2 of CEDAW).

States therefore undertake to establish legislative provisions to prevent, prohibit, or punish any acts, customs, or regulations that discriminate against women. This includes the obligations to embody the principle of equality between men and women into national constitutions and to adopt appropriate legislative and other measures to ensure the practical implementation of this principle, including sanctions to punish discrimination against women.

The articles in the Convention specify that appropriate measures must be adopted, laws adapted, or social and cultural patterns modified, so as to prevent trafficking of women and girls and to ensure equality in terms of men and women's rights to political participation, nationality, education, employment, health care and other social benefits, due process before the law, and marriage and family relations.

Attempts have been made to identify a more comprehensive set of rights and protections to which women are specifically entitled, in particular in times of conflict. In 1993, the UN General Assembly adopted the Declaration on the Elimination of Violence against Women (Resolution 48/104, December 20, 1993), which notes that "women in situations of armed conflict are especially vulnerable to violence." Though adopted by consensus, this is not a binding treaty under international law. Relief organizations may, however, use it as a frame of reference for their operations.

The only convention to date which directly addresses violence against women is the Inter-American Convention on the Prevention, Punishment and Eradication of Violence Against Women, adopted by the Organization of American States in June 1994 and which has thirty states parties. Specific duties of states are enumerated, including to "pursue, by all appropriate means and without delay, policies to prevent, punish and eradicate such violence" (Article 7) and to adopt the necessary domestic legal procedures to investigate and punish such crimes.

Human rights conventions apply to every individual—women as well as men—and protect them as equal human beings. This is particularly important because these conventions define a core set of rights against which states cannot derogate, no matter what the circumstances are. These nonderogable human rights and fundamental guarantees remain applicable at all times, including times of conflict. → **Fundamental guarantees**

III. Recourses Available in Case of Violations of Women's Rights

1. Individual Recourse

According to Articles 17 to 22 of CEDAW, a Committee on the Elimination of Discrimination against Women was created. It is made up of twenty-three experts who monitor and make recommendations concerning the implementation of CEDAW. The participant states must submit reports at least every four years on the legislative, judicial, and other measures they have taken to incorporate the provisions of the Convention into their laws. → **Committee on the Elimination of Discrimination against Women**

On October 6, 1999, the UN General Assembly, acting without a vote, adopted a twenty-one-article Optional Protocol to the Convention on the Elimination of All Forms of Discrimination against Women, drafted with the collaboration of the Committee on the Elimination of Discrimination against Women and the UN Commission on the Status of Women. The Protocol entered into force on December 22, 2000, following the ratification of the tenth state party to the Convention. Currently, sixty-six states have signed the Protocol and nineteen have ratified it.

When a state ratifies the Optional Protocol, it recognizes the competence of the Committee on the Elimination of Discrimination against Women to receive and consider complaints from individuals or groups within its jurisdiction. There are two possible procedures: consider petitions from individual women or groups of women who have exhausted all national remedies; or the Committee itself can initiate inquiries into situations of grave or systematic violations, although states may opt out of the inquiry procedure. No other reservations are permitted to the Protocol's terms.

Until the Protocol came into force—and still today in most countries—the only international recourse that existed to file individual complaints specifically concerning violations of women's rights was through the Commission on the Status of Women, a UN body established by the Economic and Social Council (ECOSOC) in 1946. Today, its function is to monitor and review the implementation of the Nairobi Forward-Looking Strategies for the Advancement of Women, adopted in 1985 at the third UN World Conference on Women. This includes developing recommendations on urgent problems concerning women's rights.

The Commission may receive communications from individuals and groups; however, it takes no action based on individual complaints. Its aim is to develop policy recommendations to try to solve widespread problems. Women can, for example, refer to international bodies that allow individual complaints, such as the Human Rights Committee, the Committee against Torture, and more.

Women may also have recourse before the Human Rights Committee, which monitors the implementation of the 1966 International Covenant on Civil and Political Rights (ICCPR) and can receive individuals complaints, including violations of the gender equality provisions of the ICCPR. This procedure is available to individuals in the countries that have ratified the Optional Protocol to the ICCPR. Women in these countries can file complaints concerning violations of the provisions of the ICCPR, as well as of the International Covenant on Economic, Social, and Cultural Rights and other international human rights conventions to which their country is a party.
→ **Human Rights Committee; Individual Recourse**

2. UN Special Rapporteurs

Several UN Special Rapporteurs cover women's issues—namely, the Special Rapporteur on Violence against Women, Its Causes and Consequences, as well as certain others such as the

Special Rapporteur on Contemporary Forms of Racism, Racial Discrimination, and Xenophobia who examines issues such as systematic rape, sexual slavery, and slavery-like practices during armed conflict.

➔   **Special Rapporteurs**

3. UN Development Fund for Women (UNIFEM)

UNIFEM is one of the subsidiary bodies of the UN. It was created in 1976 to promote the participation of women at all stages of development, to support activities benefiting women at all levels, and to promote women's use of human rights instruments, particularly CEDAW. Its headquarters are in New York.

UNIFEM carries out programs mainly in countries of relative political stability, since its focus is to strengthen women's economic capacity and political participation. It promotes women's rights as a goal toward achieving sustainable development; therefore, it generally does not have programs in situations of conflict. In such cases, UNIFEM generally works with both children and women and offers its participation through the UN's Resident Coordinator system, whereby one of the principal bodies is designated to coordinate the others.

UNIFEM initiated a campaign for a Trust Fund in Support of Actions to Eliminate Violence against Women, which was established by the UN General Assembly in 1996. This includes active campaigns to address war crimes committed against women, such as rape and other forms of sexual violence. This campaign is partly a result of UNIFEM's work with refugees, during the conflict resolution and postconflict phases, when it strives to strengthen women's roles in the peace process and to empower local NGOs trying to rebuild society.

➔   **Children; Committee on the Elimination of Discrimination against Women; Detention; Family; Family reunification; Fundamental guarantees; Individual recourse; International Criminal Court; International Criminal Tribunals; Internment; Judicial guarantees; Prisoners of war; Protected persons; Rape**

📖 For Additional Information:

Amnesty International. *Human Rights Are Women's Rights*. London: Author, 1995.
Gardam, Judith G. "Women, Human Rights and International Humanitarian Law." *International Review of the Red Cross* 324 (September–October 1998): 421–32.
International Committee of the Red Cross. *Women and War*. Geneva: Author, 1995.
Krill, Françoise. "The Protection of Women in International Humanitarian Law." *International Review of the Red Cross* 249 (November–December 1985): 337–63.

✎   UNIFEM
      304 E. 45th Street, 6th Floor
      New York, NY 10017 U.S.A.
      Tel: (1) 212 906-6400
      Fax: (1) 212 906-6705
@   UN Development Fund for Women: www.unifem.undp.org

✎   Commission on the Status of Women
      c/o Division for the Advancement of Women
      PO Box 20
      One United Nations Plaza, Room DC2-1220
      New York, NY 10017 U.S.A.
      Tel.: (1) 212 963-1234
      Fax: (1) 212 963-3463

■ WORLD FOOD PROGRAM (WFP)

The World Food Program (WFP) was founded in 1963 by the General Assembly of the UN and the Food and Agriculture Organization (FAO). It is a subsidiary body of the UN and its headquarters are in Rome.

1. Mandate

Within the UN system, WFP is the body in charge of food aid, with the goal of combating hunger and improving food safety in the poorest countries. WFP's mandate is

- to save the lives of people caught in humanitarian crises, through its Food for Life program;
- to improve the nutrition and quality of life of the most vulnerable people at critical times in their lives, through its Food for Growth program; and
- to help build assets and promote self-reliance of individuals in the poorest communities, through its Food for Work program.

Both when promoting economic and social development and when responding to emergency situations, WFP's aim is to reinforce self-reliance of populations. WFP makes sure that its assistance programs are designed and implemented on the basis of the broadest participation possible—in particular, of women. In 1999, it provided 3.4 million tons of food aid to eighty-nine million people, including fifty-nine million victims of conflicts and natural disasters.

2. Structure

WFP is controlled by an Executive Board consisting of thirty-six member states (and the European Union, as observer), elected to three-year, renewable terms. The Executive Director is elected by both the Secretary-General of the UN and by the Director-General of the FAO, in consultation with the Executive Board.

WFP's headquarters have eight departments: the Office of the Executive Director; Operations; Transport and Logistics; Resources and External Relations; Finance and Information Systems; Strategy and Policy; Management Services; and Human Resources. In 1996, WFP launched a process of decentralization that established regional offices, each of which enjoys considerable decision-making autonomy. WFP employs approximately five thousand people, 70 percent of whom work directly in the field.

3. Means

- WFP intervenes at the request of governments. It carries out its own evaluation and then negotiates and signs a Letter of Understanding concerning the programs with the authorities.
- WFP's expenditures amounted to $1.4 billion in 1998. Thirty percent of WFP's resources go toward development projects. Through the Food for Work program, it participates in the development of agricultural and other kinds of infrastructure, such as road construction. WFP also promotes human development through its school nutrition, health, and food programs.
- In the case of relief operations (emergency interventions and protracted relief operations, representing 70 percent of its resources), WFP is in charge of ensuring the supply of basic food products and their international and internal transportation to the distribution points.

To this effect, it has access to the International Emergency Food Reserve. This program was set up in 1976 following a request by the General Assembly. The minimum annual reserve is set at half a million tons of food. WFP is also responsible for the Immediate Response Account (IRA), which ensures that emergency operations are launched immediately, without having to wait for donors' funds to become available. Its minimum annual reserve is set at $35 million. Nevertheless, the mobilization of resources for relief operations mainly comes from special calls and appeals for funding, issued throughout the year as emergencies arise.

- The work of WFP also contains an important logistics component. As stated, this means first international transportation, then transit within the destination country to the actual point of distribution. WFP is responsible for finding a solution to any "missing link" in a chain of transportation, and it must replace this link and gain access to the populations in need of assistance. This is the rationale for its work on air, water, and road infrastructures. The International Maritime Organization has recognized WFP's logistics needs, and has given it the rights to its own transportation document, the Worldfood Waybill Charter. This certifies that the products being transported are for humanitarian use and normally facilitates the administrative procedures of customs clearance and transit of merchandise. Approximately twenty cargo containers permanently roam the Earth, ready to be diverted to the site of a crisis.

- The weakness of this system is that its funding depends entirely on voluntary contributions by states ($1.7 billion in 1998). The funds are distributed based on the type of operation:
  —regular budget for development projects and protracted relief operations for refugees or displaced persons,
  —emergency operations for refugees and displace persons,
  —contributions to the International Emergency Food Reserve,
  —contributions to the Immediate Response Account, and
  —nonfood contributions (e.g., assistance by technical and administrative personnel, tools, material).

  Contributions are provided half in nature and half in cash. Since 1996, such funding is based on the principle of "full costs recovery," recovering all administrative costs and needs in cash. WFP has therefore developed a policy of purchasing food products locally, which reduces the cost of transportation, ensures the distribution of food suited to the nutritional habits of the beneficiaries of the programs, and stimulates local economies.

- To improve the efficiency of its activities, WFP collaborates with the relevant bodies in the UN system. For issues concerning food aid to refugees, displaced or stateless persons, the cooperation with UNHCR was solidified through the signing of a Memorandum of Understanding (MOU) in 1985, setting out the framework of their partnership. This MOU was updated in 1991, 1994, and 1997. An MOU was signed with UNICEF in 1998. WFP also works closely with the UN departments that ensure coordination in the humanitarian domain. For instance, it is one of the lead agencies in the Inter-Agency Standing Committee (IASC), run by the Office for the Coordination of Humanitarian Affairs (OCHA), and the Executive Committee for Humanitarian Affairs (ECHA).

- Over the past several years, WFP has greatly developed its cooperation with NGOs: it has now signed formal agreements with fifteen partners, and a mechanism for annual consultations was set up in 1995. WFP collaborates with more than a thousand NGOs in the field. These operations generally rest on ad hoc partnerships, established in tripartite Letters of Understanding signed by WFP, the NGO, and the government of the host country. In addition to this, the headquarters of an NGO Liaison Unit were established in Rome in 1987.

→ **Famine; Food and Agriculture Organization; Nutrition; Relief**

✎ World Food Program
    Via Cesare Giulio Viola. 68, Parco dei Medici
    I 00148 Rome, Italy

Tel.: (39) 06 57 051
Fax: (39) 06 57 0531 or 06 57 0551/55
@ World Food Program: www.wfp.org

■ WORLD HEALTH ORGANIZATION (WHO)

The World Health Organization (WHO) was founded in 1946 and currently has 191 member states and two associate members (observers). It is one of the Specialized Agencies of the UN, and its headquarters are in Geneva.

1. Mandate

WHO's objective is "the attainment by all peoples of the highest possible level of health." To achieve this aim, it acts as "the directing and coordinating authority on international health work." In 1978, the organization set the goal of Health for All by 2000.

Its mission statement defines health as "a state of complete physical, mental and social well-being, and not merely the absence of disease or infirmity." WHO follows a guiding principle, which is that "the enjoyment of the highest attainable standard of health is one of the fundamental human rights of every human being." Furthermore, governments are responsible for the health of their people and must therefore take the appropriate medical and social measures.

2. Structure

The World Health Assembly is WHO's plenary organ. Its members are highly qualified experts in the field of health, preferably representing the relevant national body, usually the health ministry. The Assembly meets once per year and elects the thirty-two members of its Executive Board, which meets every six months. The member states are elected for three years, and the representatives they designate act in their capacity as individual experts and not as government representatives. The Director-General is nominated for a five-year term (currently Dr. Gro Harlem Brundtland, 1998–2003).

WHO is regionally organized, with each section containing a Regional Committee (member states and associates), and a Regional Office (the administrative body). The six regions are: Africa, the Americas, Eastern Mediterranean, Europe, Southeast Asia, and Western Pacific. WHO employs 3,800 people.

3. Means

- *Cooperation with states:* Member states must submit annual reports to WHO on new measures they have adopted and progress they have achieved in improving the health of their populations. On an operational level, the Secretariat and Offices work directly with the relevant ministries in the member states.
- *Cooperation with NGOs:* The organization can establish "official relations" with NGOs, based on a procedure giving them consultative status. However, any contact with a national NGO is subject to approval by the member state concerned.
- *International health legislation:* The Assembly develops and adopts international conventions that are then open to ratification by member states. Each state commits to declaring, within six months, whether or not it will ratify. If a state refuses, it must justify its reasons.

The Assembly is mandated to make recommendations to member states on their health policies. It also has the authority to regulate certain issues directly within the member states, unless a state formally opposes it, on a case-by-case basis. This authority relates to measures concerning quarantine, listing of diseases, methods of public hygiene, diagnosis, and pharmaceutical norms.

- *International medical action:* The role of WHO is not restricted to the elaboration of international health legislation. The organization also implements activities favoring the improvement of a country's health conditions (e.g., through vaccination campaigns). These activities are financed by special, extrabudgetary contributions.

In situations of emergency it also collaborates with the relevant organs in the UN system, participating in the Inter-Agency Standing Committee (IASC), for instance, through its Division of Emergency and Humanitarian Action. WHO provides epidemiological monitoring and health emergency training, run by the Office for the Coordination of Humanitarian Affairs (OCHA).

→   **Medical duties; Medical services; Wounded and sick persons**.

✎   World Health Organization
20, avenue Appia
CH 1211 Geneva 27, Switzerland
Tel.: (41) 22 791 2111
Fax: (41) 22 791 0746

@   World Health Organization: www.who.org

■ WOUNDED AND SICK PERSONS

The *wounded and sick,* as defined in humanitarian law, are individuals, either military or civilian, who are in need of medical care (whether because of trauma, disease, or other physical or mental disorder or disability) and who refrain from any act of hostility (PI Article 8). Humanitarian law forbids any adverse distinction between them for reasons other than medical ones. If the individual in question is a combatant, his or her status as a wounded or sick person takes precedence over that of combatant. This lasts as long as the wound or disease keeps the person out of combat (*hors de combat*). A combatant who recovers while in the hands of an adverse party then becomes a prisoner of war, at which point he or she comes under the provisions protecting such persons.

☞ The general principle concerning the wounded and sick of any party to a conflict is that they must be treated humanely in all circumstances, and given the medical care required by their condition, to the fullest extent practicable and with the least possible delay. No distinction may be made among them, except ones founded on medical grounds (common Article 3 of GCI–IV; PI Articles 8 and 10; PII Articles 7 and 8).

---

1. Protection of, and Obligations of, Medical Personnel

Humanitarian law protects the independence and integrity of doctors by reaffirming the rules of medical ethics. It specifies which medical acts are permitted and which are not—namely, when the wounded and sick persons are at the mercy of an authority of which they are not a national, due to a situation of occupation or detention (common Article 3 of GCI–IV; PI Articles 10, 11, 16; PII Articles 9 and 10). ➔ **Medical ethics**

Humanitarian law also protects medical installations from attacks (GCIV Article 18; PI Article 12; PII Article 11) and requisitions (GCIV Article 57; PI Article 14) and allows the use of the distinctive emblem of the red cross to protect such installations (GCI Articles 38–44; GCIV Article 18; PI Article 18; PII Article 12). Finally, it authorizes the free passage and delivery of medicine and medical supplies, including to besieged areas (GCIV Article 23). ➔ **Distinctive (or protective) emblems, signs, and signals; Medical services; Requisition; Siege**

Humanitarian law imposes the obligation to search for, collect, and care for the wounded and sick (common Article 3 of GCI–IV, GCIV Article 16, and PII Article 8). Members of medical personnel are entitled to special protection in order to facilitate their movement and access to any place where their services are needed (GCI Article 15; PI Articles 15 and 23). ➔ **Medical personnel; Right of access**

☞ Pregnant women, maternity cases, newborn infants, and infirm persons are included in the humanitarian law definition of *wounded and sick*, for the purpose of increasing the protection to which they are entitled (PI Article 8). This provision reinforces the responsibility of humanitarian and medical organizations with respect to these members of the civilian population.

---

2. Wounded or Sick Prisoners of War

Wounded or sick prisoners of war who are suffering from certain serious injuries or diseases are entitled to special measures of protection under humanitarian law. These provisions take into account the vulnerability and the risks of abuse faced by such seriously ill or injured persons, and the advantages that may be gained by treating them in a peaceful and safe environment (GCIII Articles 109–117). The Geneva Conventions and their Protocols establish the conditions under which seriously sick or wounded prisoners of war may be evacuated or hospitalized in a neutral state, rather than continuing to treat them in the hospitals of the Detaining Power and continuing to consider them prisoners of war.

Article 110 of the Third Geneva Convention sets forth the list of diseases and illnesses that require a prisoner of war to be repatriated directly or accommodated in a neutral country. Those whose diseases or wounds warrant a direct repatriation are

- the incurably wounded or sick whose mental or physical fitness seems to have been gravely diminished;
- the wounded or sick who have recovered but whose mental or physical fitness seems to have been gravely and permanently diminished;
- the wounded or sick who, according to medical opinion, are not likely to recover within one year.

Those who may be accommodated in a neutral state are

- wounded and sick whose recovery may be expected within one year, or sooner if treated in a neutral country;

- prisoners of war whose mental or physical health, according to medical opinion, is seriously threatened by continued captivity but whose accommodation in a neutral country might remove such a threat.

Certain prisoners of war accommodated in a neutral country can be directly repatriated following their treatment, under an agreement between the powers concerned, if

—their state of health has deteriorated so as to fulfill the conditions laid down for direct repatriation;

—their mental or physical powers remain considerably impaired, even after treatment.

→ **Prisoners of war**

Such measures may also be implemented for civilian internees who are seriously ill or injured (GCIV Article 132).

☞ The authorities are responsible for the health and physical integrity of the persons in their power. If they refuse to provide the necessary care to a person under their authority, or if they deliberately endanger the person's health, they are guilty of war crimes.

Both Additional Protocols of the Geneva Conventions reinforce the protection that must be provided to victims of conflict, in general, and the wounded and sick, in particular. "The physical or mental health and integrity of persons who are in the power of the adverse Party or who are interned, detained or otherwise deprived of liberty as a result of a [conflict] shall not be endangered by any unjustified act or omission." Any such act or omission constitutes a war crime (PI Article 11; PII Article 5).

This provision emphasizes the responsibility of humanitarian and medical organizations in terms of monitoring the state of health of the civilian population and the fate of the wounded and sick.

→ **Detention; Medical duties; Medical ethics; Medical personnel; Medical services; Prisoners of war; Relief**

📖 **For Additional Information:**

Rezek, Jose-Francisco. "Wounded, Sick and Shipwrecked Persons." In *International Dimensions of Humanitarian Law*. Geneva: Henri Dupont Institute; Paris: UNESCO; Dordrecht: Martinus Nijhoff, 1988, 153–66.

Appendix A

State of Ratification
of Humanitarian Law
and Human Rights Conventions

In the following pages, the state of ratification of each of the conventions numbered hereunder is shown by country.

KEY TO CONVENTIONS

International Humanitarian Law Conventions (IHL) (1–3)

1. The Geneva Conventions of August 12, 1949; 189 states parties
   - Geneva Convention for the Amelioration of the Condition of the Wounded and Sick in Armed Forces in the Field
   - Geneva Convention for the Amelioration of the Condition of Wounded, Sick and Shipwrecked Members of Armed Forces at Sea
   - Geneva Convention Relative to the Treatment of Prisoners of War
   - Geneva Convention Relative to the Protection of Civilian Persons in Time of War
2. Protocol Additional to the Geneva Conventions of August 12, 1949, and Relating to the Protection of Victims of International Armed Conflicts (Protocol I), June 8, 1977; 157 states parties
   2a. Declaration Article 90 (acceptance of competence of the International Fact-Finding Commission); fifty-eight states
3. Protocol Additional to the Geneva Conventions of August 12, 1949, and Relating to the Protection of Victims of Non-International Armed Conflicts (Protocol II), June 8, 1977; 150 states parties

International Human Rights Conventions (International HR) (4–7)

4. International Covenant on Economic, Social and Cultural Rights, December 16, 1966; 143 states parties
5. International Covenant on Civil and Political Rights, December 16, 1966; 148 states parties
   5a. Declaration Article 41 (acceptance of Human Rights Committee's competence to receive state communications); 47 states parties
6. Optional Protocol to the International Covenant on Civil and Political Rights, December 16, 1966; 98 states parties
7. Second Optional Protocol to the International Covenant on Civil and Political Rights, aiming at the abolition of the death penalty, December 15, 1989; 43 states parties

Regional Human Rights Conventions (Regional HR) (8–10)

8. The European Convention for the Protection of Human Rights and Fundamental Freedoms was adopted on November 4, 1950; 41 states parties
   8a. Protocol 11, of May 11, 1994, amending the control mechanisms established by the Convention for the Protection of Human Rights and Fundamental Freedoms
9. The American Convention on Human Rights was adopted on November 22, 1969; 25 states parties
   9a. Declaration Article 45 (acceptance of Inter-American Commission on Human Rights' competence to receive state communications); 10 states
   9b. Declaration Article 62 (acceptance of the jurisdiction of the Inter-American Court of Human Rights); 20 states
10. The African Charter on Human and Peoples' Rights was adopted on June 27, 1981; 49 states parties

Children (11)

11. Convention on the Rights of the Child, November 20, 1989; 193 states parties

Torture (12–14)

12. Convention against Torture and Other Cruel, Inhuman, or Degrading Treatment or Punishment, December 10, 1984; 123 states parties
    12a. Declaration Article 21 (acceptance of Committee against Torture's competence to receive state communications); 46 states
    12b. Declaration Article 22 (acceptance of Committee against Torture's competence to receive individual communications); 43 states
13. European Convention for the Prevention of Torture and Inhuman or Degrading Treatment or Punishment, November 26, 1987; 41 states parties
14. Inter-American Convention to Prevent and Punish Torture, December 9, 1985; 16 states parties

Refugees and Stateless Persons (15–19)

15. Convention Relating to the Status of Refugees, July 28, 1951; 137 states parties
16. Protocol relating to the Status of Refugees, January 31, 1967; 136 states parties
17. The Organization of African Unity Convention Governing the Specific Aspects of Refugee Problems in Africa, September 10, 1969; 45 states parties
18. Convention Relating to the Status of Stateless Persons, September 28, 1954; 53 states parties
19. Convention on the Reduction of Statelessness, August 30, 1961; 23 states parties

Genocide (20)

20. Convention on the Prevention and Punishment of the Crime of Genocide, December 9, 1948; 132 states parties

War Crimes and Crimes against Humanity (21–22)

21. Convention on the Non-Applicability of Statutory Limitations to War Crimes and Crimes against Humanity, November 26, 1968; 44 states parties
22. European Convention on the Non-Applicability of Statutory Limitations to War Crimes and Crimes against Humanity, January 25, 1974; 1 state party

Discrimination (23–25)

23. International Convention on the Elimination of All Forms of Racial Discrimination, December 21, 1965; 157 states parties
    23a. Declaration Article 14 (accepting Committee on the Elimination of Racial Discrimination's competence to receive individual communications); 27 states
24. Convention on the Elimination of All Forms of Discrimination against Women; December 18, 1979; 167 states parties
25. International Convention on the Suppression and Punishment of the Crime of Apartheid, November 30, 1973; 101 states parties

Land Mines (26) (icbl.org)

26. Convention on the Prohibition of the Use, Stockpiling, Production, and Transfer of Anti-Personnel Mines and on their Destruction, September 18, 1997; 111 states parties

International Criminal Court (27)

27. Statute of the International Criminal Court, July 17, 1998; 29 states parties

Appendix B

List of States Party to International Humanitarian Law and Human Rights Conventions (as of October 2000)

Dates shown are those of ratification, accession, or succession. Conventions that were signed but not ratified are marked with an *S* following the date.

Afghanistan
IHL: 1 (1956); 2 (no); 2a (no); 3 (no); **International HR:** 4 (1983); 5 (1983); 5a (no); 6 (no); 7 (no); **Children:** 11 (1994); **Torture:** 12 (1987); 12a (no); 12b (no); **Refugees and Stateless persons:** 15 (no); 16 (no); 18 (no); 19 (no); **Genocide:** 20 (1956); **War crimes and Crimes against humanity:** 21 (1983); **Discrimination**: 23 (1983); 23a (no); 24 (1980 S); 25 (1983); **Land mines**: 26 (no); **International Criminal Court**: 27 (no)

Albania
IHL: 1 (1957); 2 (1993); 2a (no); 3 (1993); **International HR:** 4 (1991); 5 (1991); 5a (no); 6 (no); 7 (no); **Regional HR:** 8 (1996); 8a (1996); **Children:** 11 (1992); **Torture:** 12 (1994); 12a (no); 12b (no); 13 (1996); **Refugees and Stateless persons:** 15 (1992); 16 (1992); 18 (no); 19 (no); **Genocide:** 20 (1955); **War crimes and Crimes against humanity:** 21 (1971); 22 (no); **Discrimination**: 23 (1994); 23a (no); 24 (1994); 25 (no); **Land mines**: 26 (2000); **International Criminal Court**: 27 (1998 S)

Algeria
IHL: 1 (1960); 2 (1989); 2a (yes); 3 (1989); **International HR:** 4 (1989); 5 (1989); 5a (yes); 6 (1989); 7 (no); **Regional HR:** 10 (1987); **Children:** 11 (1993); **Torture:** 12 (1985); 12a (yes); 12b (yes); **Refugees and Stateless persons:** 15 (1963); 16 (1967); 17 (1974); 18 (1964); 19 (no); **Genocide:** 20 (1963); **War crimes and Crimes against humanity:** 21 (no); **Discrimination**: 23 (1972); 23a (yes); 24 (1996); 25 (1982); **Land mines**: 26 (1997 S); **International Criminal Court**: 27 (2000 S)

Andorra
IHL: 1 (1993); 2 (no); 2a (no); 3 (no); **International HR:** 4 (no); 5 (no); 5a (no); 6 (no); 7 (no); **Regional HR:** 8 (1996); 8a (1996); **Children:** 11 (1996); **Torture:** 12 (no); 12a (no); 12b (no); 13 (1997); **Refugees and Stateless persons:** 15 (no); 16 (no); 18 (no); 19 (no); **Genocide:** 20 (no); **War crimes and Crimes against humanity:** 21 (no); 22 (no); **Discrimination:**: 23 (no); 23a (no); 24 (1997); 25 (no); **Land mines:** 26 (1998); **International Criminal Court:** 27 (1998 S)

Angola
IHL: 1 (1984); 2 (1984); 2a (no); 3 (no); **International HR:** 4 (1992); 5 (1992); 5a (no); 6 (1992); 7 (no); **Regional HR:** 10 (1990); **Children:** 11 (1990); **Torture:** 12 (no); 12a (no); 12b (no); **Refugees and Stateless persons:** 15 (1981); 16 (1981); 17 (1981); 18 (no); 19 (no); **Genocide:** 20 (no); **War crimes and Crimes against humanity:** 21 (no); **Discrimination**: 23 (no); 23a (no); 24 (1986); 25 (no); **Land mines**: 26 (1997 S); **International Criminal Court**: 27 (1998 S)

450

Antigua and Barbuda
IHL: 1 (1986); 2 (1986); 2a (no); 3 (1986); **International HR:** 4 (no); 5 (no); 5a (no); 6 (no); 7 (no); **Regional HR:** 9 (no); 9a (no); 9b (no); **Children:** 11 (1993); **Torture:** 12 (1993); 12a (no); 12b (no); 14 (no); **Refugees and Stateless persons:** 15 (1995); 16 (1995); 18 (1988); 19 (no); **Genocide:** 20 (1988); **War crimes and Crimes against humanity:** 21 (no); **Discrimination**: 23 (1988); 23a (no); 24 (1989); 25 (1982) **Land mines**: 26 (1999); **International Criminal Court**: 27 (1998 S)

Argentina
IHL: 1 (1956); 2 (1986); 2a (yes); 3 (1986); **International HR:** 4 (1986); 5 (1986); 5a (yes); 6 (1986); 7 (no); **Regional HR:** 9 (1984); 9a (yes); 9b (yes); **Children:** 11 (1990); **Torture:** 12 (1986); 12a (yes); 12b (yes); 14 (1988); **Refugees and Stateless persons:** 15 (1961); 16 (1967); 18 (1972); 19 (no); **Genocide:** 20 (1956); **War crimes and Crimes against humanity:** 21 (no); **Discrimination**: 23 (1968); 23a (no); 24 (1985); 25 (1985); **Land mines**: 26 (1999); **International Criminal Court**: 27 (2001)

Armenia
IHL: 1 (1993); 2 (1993); 2a (no); 3 (1993); **International HR:** 4 (1993); 5 (1993); 5a (no); 6 (1993); 7 (no); **Children:** 11 (1993); **Torture:** 12 (1993); 12a (no); 12b (no); **Refugees and Stateless persons:** 15 (1993); 16 (1993); 18 (1994); 19 (1994); **Genocide:** 20 (1993); **War crimes and Crimes against humanity:** 21 (1993); **Discrimination**: 23 (1993); 23a (no); 24 (1993); 25 (1993); **Land mines**: 26 (no); **International Criminal Court**: 27 (1999 S)

Australia
IHL: 1 (1958); 2 (1991); 2a (yes); 3 (1991); **International HR:** 4 (1975); 5 (1980); 5a (yes); 6 (1991); 7 (1990); **Children:** 11 (1990); **Torture:** 12 (1989); 12a (yes); 12b (yes); **Refugees and Stateless persons:** 15 (1954); 16 (1973); 18 (1973); 19 (1973); **Genocide:** 20 (1949); **War crimes and Crimes against humanity:** 21 (no); **Discrimination**: 23 (1975); 23a (yes); 24 (1983); 25 (no); **Land mines**: 26 (1999); **International Criminal Court**: 27 (1998 S)

Austria
IHL: 1 (1953); 2 (1982); 2a (yes); 3 (1982); **International HR:** 4 (1978); 5 (1978); 5a (yes); 6 (1987); 7 (1993); **Regional HR:** 8 (1958); 8a (1995); **Children:** 11 (1992); **Torture:** 12 (1987); 12a (yes); 12b (yes); 13 (1989); **Refugees and Stateless persons:** 15 (1954); 16 (1973); 18 (no); 19 (1972); **Genocide:** 20 (1958); **War crimes and Crimes against humanity:** 21 (no); 22 (no); **Discrimination**: 23 (1972); 23a (no); 24 (1982); 25 (no); **Land mines**: 26 (1998); **International Criminal Court**: 27 (2000)

Azerbaijan
IHL: 1 (1993); 2 (no); 2a (no); 3 (no); **International HR:** 4 (1992); 5 (1992); 5a (no); 6 (no); 7 (**1999**); **Children:** 11 (1992); **Torture:** 12 (**1996**); 12a (no); 12b (no); **Refugees and Stateless persons:** 15 (1993); 16 (1993); 18 (1996); 19 (1996); **Genocide:** 20 (1996); **War crimes and Crimes against humanity:** 21 (1996); **Discrimination**: 23 (1996); 23a (no); 24 (1995); 25 (1996); **Land mines**: 26 (no); **International Criminal Court**: 27 (no)

Bahamas
IHL: 1 (1975); 2 (1980); 2a (no); 3 (1980); **International HR:** 4 (no); 5 (no); 5a (no); 6 (no); 7 (no); **Regional HR:** 9 (no); 9a (no); 9b (no); **Children:** 11 (1991); **Torture:** 12 (no); 12a (no); 12b (no); 14 (no); **Refugees and Stateless persons:** 15 (1993); 16 (1993); 18 (no); 19 (no); **Genocide:** 20 (1975); **War crimes and Crimes against humanity:** 21 (no); **Discrimination**: 23 (1975); 23a (no); 24 (1993); 25 (1981)**Land mines**: 26 (1998); **International Criminal Court**: 27 (2000)

Bahrain
IHL: 1 (1971); 2 (1986); 2a (no); 3 (1986); **International HR:** 4 (no); 5 (no); 5a (no); 6 (no); 7 (no); **Children:** 11 (1992); **Torture:** 12 (**1998**); 12a (no); 12b (no); **Refugees and Stateless persons:** 15 (no); 16 (no); 17 (no); 19 (no); **Genocide:** 20 (1990); **War crimes and Crimes against humanity:** 21 (no); **Discrimination**: 23 (1990); 23a (no); 24 (no); 25 (1990); **Land mines**: 26 (no); **International Criminal Court**: 27 (2000)

Bangladesh
IHL: 1 (1972); 2 (1980); 2a (no); 3 (1980); **International HR:** 4 (1998); 5 (2000); 5a (no); 6 (no); 7 (no); **Children:** 11 (1990); **Torture:** 12 (1998); 12a (no); 12b (no); **Refugees and Stateless persons:** 15 (no); 16 (no); 18

(no); 19 (no); **Genocide:** 20 (**1998**); **War crimes and Crimes against humanity:** 21 (no); **Discrimination**: 23 (1979); 23a (no); 24 (1984); 25 (1985); **Land mines**: 26 (2000); **International Criminal Court**: 27 (1999 S)

Barbados
IHL: 1 (1968); 2 (1990); 2a (no); 3 (1990); **International HR:** 4 (1973); 5 (1973); 5a (no); 6 (1973); 7 (no); **Regional HR:** 9 (1981); 9a (no); 9b (no); **Children:** 11 (1990); **Torture:** 12 (no); 12a (no); 12b (no); 14 (no); **Refugees and Stateless persons:** 15 (no); 16 (no); 18 (1972); 19 (no); **Genocide:** 20 (1980); **War crimes and Crimes against humanity:** 21 (no); **Discrimination**: 23 (1972); 23a (no); 24 (1980); 25 (1979); **Land mines**: 26 (1999); **International Criminal Court**: 27 (2000 S)

Belarus
IHL: 1 (1954); 2 (1989); 2a (no); 3 (1989); **International HR:** 4 (1973); 5 (1973); 5a (yes); 6 (1992); 7 (no); **Children:** 11 (1990); **Torture:** 12 (1987); 12a (no); 12b (no); **Refugees and Stateless persons:** 15 (no); 16 (no); 18 (no); 19 (no); **Genocide:** 20 (1954); **War crimes and Crimes against humanity:** 21 (1969); **Discrimination**: 23 (1969); 23a (no); 24 (1981); 25 (1975); **Land mines**: 26 (no); **International Criminal Court**: 27 (no)

Belgium
IHL: 1 (1952); 2 (1986); 2a (yes); 3 (1986); **International HR:** 4 (1983); 5 (1983); 5a (yes); 6 (1994); 7 (1990); **Regional HR:** 8 (1955); 8a (1997); **Children:** 11 (1991); **Torture:** 12 (1999); 12a (yes); 12b (no); 13 (1991); **Refugees and Stateless persons:** 15 (1953); 16 (1969); 18 (1960); 19 (no); **Genocide:** 20 (1951); **War crimes and Crimes against humanity:** 21 (no); 22 (1984 S); **Discrimination**: 23 (1975); 23a (no); 24 (1985); 25 (no); **Land mines**: 26 (1998); **International Criminal Court**: 27 (2000)

Belize
IHL: 1 (1984); 2 (1984); 2a (no); 3 (1984); **International HR:** 4 (1976); 5 (1996); 5a (no); 6 (no); 7 (no); **Regional HR:** 9 (no); 9a (no); 9b (no); **Children:** 11 (1990); **Torture:** 12 (1986); 12a (no); 12b (no); 14 (no); **Refugees and Stateless persons:** 15 (1990); 16 (1990); 18 (no); 19 (no); **Genocide:** 20 (1998); **War crimes and Crimes against humanity:** 21 (no); **Discrimination**: 23 (2000); 23a (no); 24 (1990); 25 (no); **Land mines**: 26 (1998); **International Criminal Court**: 27 (2000)

Benin
IHL: 1 (1961); 2 (1986); 2a (no); 3 (1986); **International HR:** 4 (1993); 5 (1992); 5a (no); 6 (1992); 7 (no); **Regional HR:** 10 (1986); **Children:** 11 (1990); **Torture:** 12 (1992); 12a (no); 12b (no); **Refugees and Stateless persons:** 15 (1962); 16 (1970); 17 (1973); 18 (no); 19 (no); **Genocide:** 20 (no); **War crimes and Crimes against humanity:** 21 (no); **Discrimination**: 23 (1967 S); 23a (no); 24 (1992); 25 (1974); **Land mines**: 26 (1998); **International Criminal Court**: 27 (1999 S)

Bhutan
IHL: 1 (1991); 2 (no); 2a (no); 3 (no); **International HR:** 4 (no); 5 (no); 5a (no); 6 (no); 7 (no); **Children:** 11 (1990); **Torture:** 12 (no); 12a (no); 12b (no); **Refugees and Stateless persons:** 15 (no); 16 (no); 18 (no); 19 (no); **Genocide:** 20 (no); **War crimes and Crimes against humanity:** 21 (no); **Discrimination**: 23 (1973 S); 23a (no); 24 (1981); 25 (no); **Land mines**: 26 (no); **International Criminal Court**: 27 (no)

Bolivia
IHL: 1 (1976); 2 (1983); 2a (yes); 3 (1983); **International HR:** 4 (1982); 5 (1982); 5a (no); 6 (1982); 7 (no); **Regional HR:** 9 (1979); 9a (yes); 9b (yes); **Children:** 11 (1990); **Torture:** 12 (**1999**); 12a (no); 12b (no); 14 (1985 S); **Refugees and Stateless persons:** 15 (1982); 16 (1982); 18 (1983); 19 (1983); **Genocide:** 20 (1948 S); **War crimes and Crimes against humanity:** 21 (1983); **Discrimination**: 23 (1970); 23a (no); 24 (1990); 25 (1983); **Land mines**: 26 (1998); **International Criminal Court**: 27 (1998 S)

Bosnia
IHL: 1 (1992); 2 (1992); 2a (yes); 3 (1992); **International HR:** 4 (1993); 5 (1993); 5a (yes); 6 (1995); 7 (2000); **Children:** 11 (1993); **Torture:** 12 (1993); 12a (no); 12b (no); **Refugees and Stateless persons:** 15 (1993); 16 (1993); 18 (1993); 19 (1996); **Genocide:** 20 (1992); **War crimes and Crimes against humanity:** 21 (1993); **Discrimination**: 23 (1993); 23a (no); 24 (1993); 25 (1993); **Land mines**: 26 (1998); **International Criminal Court**: 27 (2000 S)

Botswana
IHL: 1 (1968); 2 (1979); 2a (no); 3 (1979); **International HR:** 4 (no); 5 (2000); 5a (no); 6 (no); 7 (no); **Regional HR:** 10 (1986); **Children:** 11 (1995); **Torture:** 12 (2000); 12a (no); 12b (no); **Refugees and Stateless persons:** 15 (1969); 16 (1969); 17 (1995); 18 (1969); 19 (no); **Genocide:** 20 (no); **War crimes and Crimes against humanity:** 21 (no); **Discrimination**: 23 (1974); 23a (no); 24 (1996); 25 (no); **Land mines:** 26 (2000); **International Criminal Court**: 27 (2000)

Brazil
IHL: 1 (1957); 2 (1992); 2a (yes); 3 (1992); **International HR:** 4 (1992); 5 (1992); 5a (no); 6 (no); 7 (no); **Regional HR:** 9 (1992); 9a (no); 9b (no); **Children:** 11 (1990); **Torture:** 12 (1989); 12a (no); 12b (no); 14 (1989); **Refugees and Stateless persons:** 15 (1960); 16 (1972); 18 (1996); 19 (no); **Genocide:** 20 (1952); **War crimes and Crimes against humanity:** 21 (no); **Discrimination**: 23 (1968); 23a (no); 24 (1984); 25 (no); **Land mines:** 26 (1999); **International Criminal Court**: 27 (2000 S)

Brunei
IHL: 1 (1991); 2 (1991); 2a (no); 3 (1991); **International HR:** 4 (no); 5 (no); 5a (no); 6 (no); 7 (no); **Children:** 11 (1995); **Torture:** 12 (no); 12a (no); 12b (no); **Refugees and Stateless persons:** 15 (no); 16 (no); 18 (no); 19 (no); **Genocide:** 20 (no); **War crimes and Crimes against humanity:** 21 (no); **Discrimination**: 23 (no); 23a (no); 24 (no); 25 (no); **Land mines:** 26 (1997 S); **International Criminal Court**: 27 (no)

Bulgaria
IHL: 1 (1954); 2 (1989); 2a (yes); 3 (1989); **International HR:** 4 (1970); 5 (1970); 5a (yes); 6 (1992); 7 (no); **Regional HR:** 8 (1992); 8a (1994); **Children:** 11 (1991); **Torture:** 12 (1986); 12a (yes); 12b (yes); 13 (1994); **Refugees and Stateless persons:** 15 (1993); 16 (1993); 18 (no); 19 (no); **Genocide:** 20 (1950); **War crimes and Crimes against humanity:** 21 (1969); 22 (no); **Discrimination**: 23 (1966); 23a (yes); 24 (1982); 25 (1974); **Land mines:** 26 (1998); **International Criminal Court**: 27 (1999 S)

Burkina Faso
IHL: 1 (1961); 2 (1987); 2a (no); 3 (1987); **International HR:** 4 (1999); 5 (1999); 5a (no); 6 (1999); 7 (no); **Regional HR:** 10 (1989); **Children:** 11 (1990); **Torture:** 12 (1999); 12a (no); 12b (no); **Refugees and Stateless persons:** 15 (1980); 16 (1980); 17 (1974); 18 (no); 19 (no); **Genocide:** 20 (1965); **War crimes and Crimes against humanity:** 21 (no); **Discrimination**: 23 (1974); 23a (no); 24 (1987); 25 (1978); **Land mines:** 26 (1998); **International Criminal Court**: 27 (1998 S)

Burundi
IHL: 1 (1971); 2 (1993); 2a (no); 3 (1993); **International HR:** 4 (1990); 5 (1990); 5a (no); 6 (no); 7 (no); **Regional HR:** 10 (1984); **Children:** 11 (1990); **Torture:** 12 (1993); 12a (no); 12b (no); **Refugees and Stateless persons:** 15 (1963); 16 (1971); 17 (1975); 18 (no); 19 (no); **Genocide:** 20 (1997); **War crimes and Crimes against humanity:** 21 (no); **Discrimination**: 23 (1977); 23a (no); 24 (1992); 25 (1978); **Land mines:** 26 (1997 S); **International Criminal Court**: 27 (1999 S)

Cambodia
IHL: 1 (1958); 2 (1998); 2a (no); 3 (1998); **International HR:** 4 (1992); 5 (1992); 5a (no); 6 (no); 7 (no); **Children:** 11 (1992); **Torture:** 12 (1992); 12a (no); 12b (no); **Refugees and Stateless persons:** 15 (1992); 16 (1992); 18 (no); 19 (no); **Genocide:** 20 (1950); **War crimes and Crimes against humanity:** 21 (no); **Discrimination**: 23 (1983); 23a (no); 24 (1992); 25 (1981); **Land mines:** 26 (1999); **International Criminal Court**: 27 (2000 S)

Cameroon
IHL: 1 (1963); 2 (1984); 2a (no); 3 (1984); **International HR:** 4 (1984); 5 (1984); 5a (no); 6 (1984); 7 (no); **Regional HR:** 10 (1989); **Children:** 11 (1993); **Torture:** 12 (1986); 12a (no); 12b (no); **Refugees and Stateless persons:** 15 (1961); 16 (1967); 17 (1985); 18 (no); 19 (no); **Genocide:** 20 (no); **War crimes and Crimes against humanity:** 21 (1972); **Discrimination**: 23 (1971); 23a (no); 24 (1994); 25 (1976); **Land mines:** 26 (1997 S); **International Criminal Court**: 27 (1998 S)

Canada
IHL: 1 (1965); 2 (1990); 2a (yes); 3 (1990); **International HR:** 4 (1976); 5 (1976); 5a (yes); 6 (1976); 7 (no); **Regional HR:** 9 (no); 9a (no); 9b (no); **Children:** 11 (1991); **Torture:** 12 (1987); 12a (yes); 12b (yes); 14 (no); **Refugees and Stateless persons:** 15 (1969); 16 (1969); 18 (no); 19 (1978); **Genocide:** 20 (1952); **War crimes and Crimes against humanity:** 21 (no); **Discrimination**: 23 (1970); 23a (no); 24 (1981); 25 (no); **Land mines**: 26 (1997); **International Criminal Court**: 27 (2000)

Cape Verde
IHL: 1 (1984); 2 (1995); 2a (yes); 3 (1995); **International HR:** 4 (1993); 5 (1993); 5a (no); 6 (no); 7 (no); **Regional HR:** 10 (1987); **Children:** 11 (1992); **Torture:** 12 (1992); 12a (no); 12b (no); **Refugees and Stateless persons:** 15 (no); 16 (1987); 17 (1989); 18 (no); 19 (no); **Genocide:** 20 (no); **War crimes and Crimes against humanity:** 21 (no); **Discrimination**: 23 (1979); 23a (no); 24 (1980); 25 (1979); **Land mines**: 26 (1997 S); **International Criminal Court**: 27 (no)

Central African Republic
IHL: 1 (1966); 2 (1984); 2a (no); 3 (1984); **International HR:** 4 (1981); 5 (1981); 5a (no); 6 (1981); 7 (no); **Regional HR:** 10 (1986); **Children:** 11 (1992); **Torture:** 12 (no); 12a (no); 12b (no); **Refugees and Stateless persons:** 15 (1962); 16 (1967); 17 (1970); 18 (no); 19 (no); **Genocide:** 20 (no); **War crimes and Crimes against humanity:** 21 (no); **Discrimination**: 23 (1971); 23a (no); 24 (1991); 25 (1981); **Land mines**: 26 (no); **International Criminal Court**: 27 (1999 S)

Chad
IHL: 1 (1970); 2 (1997); 2a (no); 3 (1997); **International HR:** 4 (1995); 5 (1995); 5a (no); 6 (1995); 7 (no); **Regional HR:** 10 (1986); **Children:** 11 (1990); **Torture:** 12 (1995); 12a (no); 12b (no); **Refugees and Stateless persons:** 15 (1981); 16 (1981); 17 (1981); 18 (1999); 19 (1999); **Genocide:** 20 (no); **War crimes and Crimes against humanity:** 21 (no); **Discrimination**: 23 (1977); 23a (no); 24 (1995); 25 (1974); **Land mines**: 26 (1999); **International Criminal Court**: 27 (1999 S)

Chile
IHL: 1 (1950); 2 (1991); 2a (yes); 3 (1991); **International HR:** 4 (1972); 5 (1972); 5a (yes); 6 (1992); 7 (no); **Regional HR:** 9 (1990); 9a (yes); 9b (yes); **Children:** 11 (1990); **Torture:** 12 (1988); 12a (no); 12b (no); 14 (1988); **Refugees and Stateless persons:** 15 (1972); 16 (1972); 18 (no); 19 (no); **Genocide:** 20 (1953); **War crimes and Crimes against humanity:** 21 (no); **Discrimination**: 23 (1971); 23a (yes); 24 (1989); 25 (no); **Land mines**: 26 (1997 S); **International Criminal Court**: 27 (1998 S)

China
IHL: 1 (1956); 2 (1983); 2a (no); 3 (1989); **International HR:** 4 (1997 S); 5 (1998 S); 5a (no); 6 (no); 7 (no); **Children:** 11 (1992); **Torture:** 12 (1988); 12a (no); 12b (no); **Refugees and Stateless persons:** 15 (1982); 16 (1982); 18 (no); 19 (no); **Genocide:** 20 (1983); **War crimes and Crimes against humanity:** 21 (no); **Discrimination**: 23 (1981); 23a (no); 24 (1980); 25 (1983); **Land mines**: 26 (no); **International Criminal Court**: 27 (no)

Colombia
IHL: 1 (1961); 2 (1993); 2a (yes); 3 (1995); **International HR:** 4 (1969); 5 (1969); 5a (no); 6 (1969); 7 (1997); **Regional HR:** 9 (1973); 9a (yes); 9b (yes); **Children:** 11 (1991); **Torture:** 12 (1987); 12a (no); 12b (no); 14 (1985 S); **Refugees and Stateless persons:** 15 (1961); 16 (1980); 18 (1954 S); 19 (no); **Genocide:** 20 (1959); **War crimes and Crimes against humanity:** 21 (no); **Discrimination**: 23 (1981); 23a (no); 24 (1982); 25 (1988); **Land mines**: 26 (2000); **International Criminal Court**: 27 (1998 S)

Comoros
IHL: 1 (1985); 2 (1985); 2a (no); 3 (1985); **International HR:** 4 (no); 5 (no); 5a (no); 6 (no); 7 (no); **Regional HR:** 10 (1986); **Children:** 11 (1993); **Torture:** 12 (no); 12a (no); 12b (no); **Refugees and Stateless persons:** 15 (no); 16 (no); 17 (no); 18 (no); 19 (no); **Genocide:** 20 (no); **War crimes and Crimes against humanity:** 21 (no); **Discrimination**: 23 (2000 S); 23a (no); 24 (1994); 25 (no); **Land mines**: 26 (no); **International Criminal Court**: 27 (2000 S)

Congo (Brazzaville)
IHL: 1 (1967); 2 (1983); 2a (no); 3 (1983); **International HR:** 4 (1983); 5 (1983); 5a (yes); 6 (1983); 7 (no); **Regional HR:** 10 (1982); **Children:** 11 (1993); **Torture:** 12 (no); 12a (no); 12b (no); **Refugees and Stateless persons:** 15 (1962); 16 (1970); 17 (1971); 18 (no); 19 (no); **Genocide:** 20 (no); **War crimes and Crimes against humanity:** 21 (no); **Discrimination:** 23 (1988); 23a (no); 24 (1982); 25 (1983); **Land mines:** 26 (no); **International Criminal Court:** 27 (1998 S)

Congo (Democratic Republic of)
IHL: 1 (1961); 2 (1982); 2a (no); 3 (no); **International HR:** 4 (1976); 5 (1976); 5a (no); 6 (1976); 7 (no); **Regional HR:** 10 (1987); **Children:** 11 (1990); **Torture:** 12 (1996); 12a (no); 12b (no); **Refugees and Stateless persons:** 15 (1965); 16 (1975); 17 (1973); 18 (no); 19 (no); **Genocide:** 20 (1962); **War crimes and Crimes against humanity:** 21 (no); **Discrimination:** 23 (1976); 23a (no); 24 (1986); 25 (1978); **Land mines:** 26 (no); **International Criminal Court:** 27 (2000 S)

Costa Rica
IHL: 1 (1969); 2 (1983); 2a (no); 3 (1983); **International HR:** 4 (1968); 5 (1968); 5a (no); 6 (1968); 7 (1998); **Regional HR:** 9 (1970); 9a (yes); 9b (yes); **Children:** 11 (1990); **Torture:** 12 (1993); 12a (no); 12b (no); 14 (1999); **Refugees and Stateless persons:** 15 (1978); 16 (1978); 18 (1977); 19 (1977); **Genocide:** 20 (1950); **War crimes and Crimes against humanity:** 21 (no); **Discrimination:** 23 (1967); 23a (yes); 24 (1986); 25 (1986); **Land mines:** 26 (1999); **International Criminal Court:** 27 (1998 S)

Croatia
IHL: 1 (1992); 2 (1992); 2a (yes); 3 (1992); **International HR:** 4 (1992); 5 (1992); 5a (yes); 6 (1995); 7 (1995); **Regional HR:** 8 (1997); 8a (1997); **Children:** 11 (1992); **Torture:** 12 (1992); 12a (yes); 12b (yes); 13 (1997); **Refugees and Stateless persons:** 15 (1992); 16 (1992); 18 (1992); 19 (no); **Genocide:** 20 (1992); **War crimes and Crimes against humanity:** 21 (1992); **Discrimination:** 23 (1992); 23a (no); 24 (1992); 25 (1992); **Land mines:** 26 (1998); **International Criminal Court:** 27 (1998 S)

Cuba
IHL: 1 (1954); 2 (1982); 2a (no); 3 (1999); **International HR:** 4 (no); 5 (no); 5a (no); 6 (no); 7 (no); **Regional HR:** 9 (no); 9a (no); 9b (no); **Children:** 11 (1991); **Torture:** 12 (1995); 12a (no); 12b (no); 14 (no); **Refugees and Stateless persons:** 15 (no); 16 (no); 18 (no); 19 (no); **Genocide:** 20 (1953); **War crimes and Crimes against humanity:** 21 (1972); **Discrimination:** 23 (1972); 23a no); 24 (1980); 25 (1977); **Land mines:** 26 (no); **International Criminal Court:** 27 (no)

Cyprus
IHL: 1 (1962); 2 (1979); 2a (no); 3 (1996); **International HR:** 4 (1969); 5 (1969); 5a (no); 6 (1992); 7 (no); **Regional HR:** 8 (1962); 8a (1995); **Children:** 11 (1991); **Torture:** 12 (1991); 12a (yes); 12b (yes); 13 (1989); **Refugees and Stateless persons:** 15 (1963); 16 (1968); 18 (no); 19 (no); **Genocide:** 20 (1982); **War crimes and Crimes against humanity:** 21 (no); 22 (no); **Discrimination:** 23 (1967); 23a (yes); 24 (1985); 25 (no); **Land mines:** 26 (1997); **International Criminal Court:** 27 (1998 S)

Czech Republic
IHL: 1 (1993); 2 (1993); 2a (yes); 3 (1993); **International HR:** 4 (1993); 5 (1993); 5a (yes); 6 (1993); 7 (no); **Regional HR:** 8 (1992); 8a (1995); **Children:** 11 (1993); **Torture:** 12 (1993); 12a (yes); 12b (yes); 13 (1995); **Refugees and Stateless persons:** 15 (1993); 16 (1993); 18 (no); 19 (no); **Genocide:** 20 (1993); **War crimes and Crimes against humanity:** 21 (1993); 22 (no); **Discrimination:** 23 (1993); 23a (no); 24 (1993); 25 (1993); **Land mines:** 26 (1999); **International Criminal Court:** 27 (1999 S)

Denmark
IHL: 1 (1951); 2 (1982); 2a (yes); 3 (1982); **International HR:** 4 (1972); 5 (1972); 5a (yes); 6 (1972); 7 (1994); **Regional HR:** 8 (1953); 8a (1996); **Children:** 11 (1991); **Torture:** 12 (1987); 12a (yes); 12b (yes); 13 (1989); **Refugees and Stateless persons:** 15 (1952); 16 (1968); 18 (1956); 19 (1977); **Genocide:** 20 (1951); **War crimes and Crimes against humanity:** 21 (no); 22 (no); **Discrimination:** 23 (1971); 23a (yes); 24 (1983); 25 (no); **Land mines:** 26 (1998); **International Criminal Court:** 27 (1998 S)

Djibouti
IHL: 1 (1978); 2 (1991); 2a (no); 3 (1991); **International HR:** 4 (no); 5 (no); 5a (no); 6 (no); 7 (no); **Regional HR:** 10 (1991); **Children:** 11 (1990); **Torture:** 12 (no); 12a (no); 12b (no); **Refugees and Stateless persons:** 15 (1977); 16 (1977); 17 (no); 18 (no); 19 (no); **Genocide:** 20 (no); **War crimes and Crimes against humanity:** 21 (no); **Discrimination**: 23 (no); 23a (no); 24 (1998); 25 (no); **Land mines**: 26 (1998); **International Criminal Court**: 27 (1998 S)

Dominica
IHL: 1 (1981); 2 (1996); 2a (no); 3 (1996); **International HR:** 4 (1993); 5 (1993); 5a (no); 6 (no); 7 (no); **Regional HR:** 9 (**1993**); 9a (no); 9b (no); **Children:** 11 (1991); **Torture:** 12 (no); 12a (no); 12b (no); 14 (no); **Refugees and Stateless persons:** 15 (1994); 16 (1994); 18 (no); 19 (no); **Genocide:** 20 (no); **War crimes and Crimes against humanity:** 21 (no); **Discrimination**: 23 (no); 23a (no); 24 (1980); 25 (no); **Land mines**: 26 (1999); **International Criminal Court**: 27 (2001 S)

Dominican Republic
IHL: 1 (1958); 2 (1994); 2a (no); 3 (1994); **International HR:** 4 (1978); 5 (1978); 5a (no); 6 (1978); 7 (no); **Regional HR:** 9 (1978); 9a (no); 9b (no); **Children:** 11 (1991); **Torture:** 12 (1985 S); 12a (no); 12b (no); 14 (1986); **Refugees and Stateless persons:** 15 (1978); 16 (1978); 18 (no); 19 (1961 S); **Genocide:** 20 (1948 S); **War crimes and Crimes against humanity:** 21 (no); **Discrimination**: 23 (1983); 23a (no); 24 (1982); 25 (no); **Land mines**: 26 (2000); **International Criminal Court**: 27 (2000 S)

Ecuador
IHL: 1 (1954); 2 (1979); 2a (no); 3 (1979); **International HR:** 4 (1969); 5 (1969); 5a (yes); 6 (1969); 7 (1993); **Regional HR:** 9 (1977); 9a (yes); 9b (yes); **Children:** 11 (1990); **Torture:** 12 (1988); 12a (yes); 12b (yes); 14 (1999); **Refugees and Stateless persons:** 15 (1955); 16 (1969); 18 (1970); 19 (no); **Genocide:** 20 (1949); **War crimes and Crimes against humanity:** 21 (no); **Discrimination**: 23 (1966); 23a (yes); 24 (1981); 25 (1975); **Land mines**: 26 (1999); **International Criminal Court**: 27 (1998 S)

Egypt
IHL: 1 (1952); 2 (1992); 2a (no); 3 (1992); **International HR:** 4 (1982); 5 (1982); 5a (no); 6 (no); 7 (no); **Regional HR:** 10 (1984); **Children:** 11 (1990); **Torture:** 12 (1986); 12a (no); 12b (no); **Refugees and Stateless persons:** 15 (1981); 16 (1981); 17 (1980); 18 (no); 19 (no); **Genocide:** 20 (1952); **War crimes and Crimes against humanity:** 21 (no); **Discrimination**: 23 (1967); 23a (no); 24 (1981); 25 (1977); **Land mines**: 26 (no); **International Criminal Court**: 27 (2000 S)

El Salvador
IHL: 1 (1953); 2 (1978); 2a (no); 3 (1978); **International HR:** 4 (1979); 5 (1979); 5a (no); 6 (1995); 7 (no); **Regional HR:** 9 (1978); 9a (no); 9b (yes); **Children:** 11 (1990); **Torture:** 12 (1996); 12a (no); 12b (no); 14 (1994); **Refugees and Stateless persons:** 15 (1983); 16 (1983); 18 (no); 19 (no); **Genocide:** 20 (1950); **War crimes and Crimes against humanity:** 21 (no); **Discrimination**: 23 (1979); 23a (no); 24 (1981); 25 (1979); **Land mines**: 26 (1999); **International Criminal Court**: 27 (no)

Equatorial Guinea
IHL: 1 (1986); 2 (1986); 2a (no); 3 (1986); **International HR:** 4 (1987); 5 (1987); 5a (no); 6 (1987); 7 (no); **Regional HR:** 10 (1986); **Children:** 11 (1992); **Torture:** 12 (no); 12a (no); 12b (no); **Refugees and Stateless persons:** 15 (1986); 16 (1986); 17 (1980); 18 (no); 19 (no); **Genocide:** 20 (no); **War crimes and Crimes against humanity:** 21 (no); **Discrimination**: 23 (no); 23a (no); 24 (1984); 25 (no); **Land mines**: 26 (1998); **International Criminal Court**: 27 (no)

Eritrea
IHL: 1 (2000); 2 (no); 2a (no); 3 (no); **International HR:** 4 (no); 5 (no); 5a (no); 6 (no); 7 (no); **Regional HR:** 10 (no); **Children:** 11 (1994); **Torture:** 12 (no); 12a (no); 12b (no); **Refugees and Stateless persons:** 15 (no); 16 (no); 17 (no); 18 (no); 19 (no); **Genocide:** 20 (no); **War crimes and Crimes against humanity:** 21 (no); **Discrimination**: 23 (no); 23a (no); 24 (1995); 25 (no); **Land mines**: 26 (no); **International Criminal Court**: 27 (1998 S)

Estonia
IHL: 1 (1993); 2 (1993); 2a (no); 3 (1993); **International HR:** 4 (1991); 5 (1991); 5a (no); 6 (1991); 7 (no); **Regional HR:** 8 (1996); 8a (1996); **Children:** 11 (1991); **Torture:** 12 (1991); 12a (no); 12b (no); 13 (1996); **Refugees and Stateless persons:** 15 (1997); 16 (1997); 18 (no); 19 (no); **Genocide:** 20 (1991); **War crimes and Crimes against humanity:** 21 (1991); 22 (no); **Discrimination:** 23 (1991); 23a (no); 24 (1991); 25 (1991); **Land mines:** 26 (no); **International Criminal Court:** 27 (1999 S)

Ethiopia
IHL: 1 (1969); 2 (1994); 2a (no); 3 (1994); **International HR:** 4 (1993); 5 (1993); 5a (no); 6 (no); 7 (no); **Regional HR:** 10 (no); **Children:** 11 (1991); **Torture:** 12 (1994); 12a (no); 12b (no); **Refugees and Stateless persons:** 15 (1969); 16 (1969); 17 (1973); 18 (no); 19 (no); **Genocide:** 20 (1949); **War crimes and Crimes against humanity:** 21 (no); **Discrimination:** 23 (1976); 23a (no); 24 (1981); 25 (1978); **Land mines:** 26 (1997 S); **International Criminal Court:** 27 (no)

Fiji
IHL: 1 (1971); 2 (no); 2a (no); 3 (no); **International HR:** 4 (no); 5 (no); 5a (no); 6 (no); 7 (no); **Children:** 11 (1993); **Torture:** 12 (no); 12a (no); 12b (no); **Refugees and Stateless persons:** 15 (1972); 16 (1972); 18 (1972); 19 (no); **Genocide:** 20 (1973); **War crimes and Crimes against humanity:** 21 (no); **Discrimination:** 23 (1973); 23a (no); 24 (1995); 25 (no); **Land mines:** 26 (1998); **International Criminal Court:** 27 (1999)

Finland
IHL: 1 (1955); 2 (1980); 2a (yes); 3 (1980); **International HR:** 4 (1975); 5 (1975); 5a (yes); 6 (1975); 7 (1991); **Regional HR:** 8 (1990); 8a (1996); **Children:** 11 (1991); **Torture:** 12 (1989); 12a (yes); 12b (yes); 13 (1990); **Refugees and Stateless persons:** 15 (1968); 16 (1968); 18 (1968); 19 (no); **Genocide:** 20 (1959); **War crimes and Crimes against humanity:** 21 (no); 22 (no); **Discrimination:** 23 (1970); 23a (yes); 24 (1986); 25 (no); **Land mines:** 26 (no); **International Criminal Court:** 27 (2000)

France
IHL: 1 (1951); 2 (no); 2a (no); 3 (1984); **International HR:** 4 (1980); 5 (1980); 5a (no); 6 (1984); 7 (no); **Regional HR:** 8 (1974); 8a (1996); **Children:** 11 (1990); **Torture:** 12 (1986); 12a (yes); 12b (yes); 13 (1989); **Refugees and Stateless persons:** 15 (1954); 16 (1971); 18 (1960); 19 (1962 S); **Genocide:** 20 (1950); **War crimes and Crimes against humanity:** 21 (no); 22 (1974 S); **Discrimination:** 23 (1971); 23a (yes); 24 (1983); 25 (no); **Land mines:** 26 (1998); **International Criminal Court:** 27 (2000)

Gabon
IHL: 1 (1965); 2 (1980); 2a (no); 3 (1980); **International HR:** 4 (1983); 5 (1983); 5a (no); 6 (no); 7 (no); **Regional HR:** 10 (1986); **Children:** 11 (1994); **Torture:** 12 (2000); 12a (no); 12b (no); **Refugees and Stateless persons:** 15 (1964); 16 (1973); 17 (1986); 18 (no); 19 (no); **Genocide:** 20 (1983); **War crimes and Crimes against humanity:** 21 (no); **Discrimination:** 23 (1980); 23a (no); 24 (1983); 25 (1980); **Land mines:** 26 (2000); **International Criminal Court:** 27 (2000)

Gambia
IHL: 1 (1966); 2 (1989); 2a (no); 3 (1989); **International HR:** 4 (1978); 5 (1979); 5a (yes); 6 (1988); 7 (no); **Regional HR:** 10 (1983); **Children:** 11 (1990); **Torture:** 12 (1985 S); 12a (no); 12b (no); **Refugees and Stateless persons:** 15 (1966); 16 (1967); 17 (1980); 18 (no); 19 (no); **Genocide:** 20 (1978); **War crimes and Crimes against humanity:** 21 (1978); **Discrimination:** 23 (1978); 23a (no); 24 (1993); 25 (1978); **Land mines:** 26 (1997 S); **International Criminal Court:** 27 (1998 S)

Georgia
IHL: 1 (1993); 2 (1993); 2a (no); 3 (1993); **International HR:** 4 (1994); 5 (1994); 5a (no); 6 (1994); 7 (1999); **Regional HR:** 8 (1999); 8a (1999); **Children:** 11 (1994); **Torture:** 12 (1994); 12a (no); 12b (no); 13 (2000); **Refugees and Stateless persons:** 15 (1999); 16 (1999); 18 (no); 19 (no); **Genocide:** 20 (1993); **War crimes and Crimes against humanity:** 21 (1995); 22 (no); **Discrimination:** 23 (1999); 23a (no); 24 (1994); 25 (no); **Land mines:** 26 (no); **International Criminal Court:** 27 (1998 S)

Germany
IHL: 1 (1954); 2 (1991); 2a (yes); 3 (1991); **International HR:** 4 (1973); 5 (1973); 5a (yes); 6 (1993); 7 (1992); **Regional HR:** 8 (1952); 8a (1995); **Children:** 11 (1992); **Torture:** 12 (1990); 12a (no); 12b (no); 13 (1990); **Refugees and Stateless persons:** 15 (1953); 16 (1969); 18 (1976); 19 (1977); **Genocide:** 20 (1954); **War crimes and Crimes against humanity:** 21 (no); 22 (no); **Discrimination:** 23 (1969); 23a (no); 24 (1985); 25 (no); **Land mines:** 26 (1998); **International Criminal Court:** 27 (2000)

Ghana
IHL: 1 (1958); 2 (1978); 2a (no); 3 (1978); **International HR:** 4 (2000); 5 (2000); 5a (no); 6 (2000); 7 (no); **Regional HR:** 10 (1989); **Children:** 11 (1990); **Torture:** 12 (2000); 12a (no); 12b (no); **Refugees and Stateless persons:** 15 (1963); 16 (1968); 17 (1975); 18 (no); 19 (no); **Genocide:** 20 (1958); **War crimes and Crimes against humanity:** 21 (2000); **Discrimination:** 23 (1966); 23a (no); 24 (1986); 25 (1978); **Land mines:** 26 (2000); **International Criminal Court:** 27 (1999)

Greece
IHL: 1 (1956); 2 (1989); 2a (1998); 3 (1993); **International HR:** 4 (1985); 5 (1997); 5a (no); 6 (1997); 7 (1997); **Regional HR:** 8 (1974); 8a (1997); **Children:** 11 (1993); **Torture:** 12 (1988); 12a (yes); 12b (yes); 13 (1991); **Refugees and Stateless persons:** 15 (1960); 16 (1968); 18 (1975); 19 (no); **Genocide:** 20 (1954); **War crimes and Crimes against humanity:** 21 (no); 22 (no); **Discrimination:** 23 (1970); 23a (no); 24 (1983); 25 (no); **Land mines:** 26 (1997 S); **International Criminal Court:** 27 (1998 S)

Grenada
IHL: 1 (1981); 2 (1998); 2a (no); 3 (1998); **International HR:** 4 (1981); 5 (1991); 5a (no); 6 (no); 7 (no); **Regional HR:** 9 (1978); 9a (no); 9b (no); **Children:** 11 (1990); **Torture:** 12 (no); 12a (no); 12b (no); 14 (no); **Refugees and Stateless persons:** 15 (no); 16 (no); 18 (no); 19 (no); **Genocide:** 20 (no); **War crimes and Crimes against humanity:** 21 (no); **Discrimination:** 23 (1981 S); 23a (no); 24 (1990); 25 (no); **Land mines:** 26 (1998); **International Criminal Court:** 27 (no)

Guatemala
IHL: 1 (1952); 2 (1987); 2a (no); 3 (1987); **International HR:** 4 (1988); 5 (1992); 5a (no); 6 (2000); 7 (no); **Regional HR:** 9 (1978); 9a (no); 9b (yes); **Children:** 11 (1990); **Torture:** 12 (1990); 12a (no); 12b (no); 14 (1986); **Refugees and Stateless persons:** 15 (1983); 16 (1983); 18 (2000); 19 (no); **Genocide:** 20 (1950); **War crimes and Crimes against humanity:** 21 (no); **Discrimination:** 23 (1983); 23a (no); 24 (1982); 25 (no); **Land mines:** 26 (1999); **International Criminal Court:** 27 (no)

Guinea
IHL: 1 (1984); 2 (1984); 2a (yes); 3 (1984); **International HR:** 4 (1978); 5 (1978); 5a (no); 6 (1993); 7 (no); **Regional HR:** 10 (1982); **Children:** 11 (1990); **Torture:** 12 (1989); 12a (no); 12b (no); **Refugees and Stateless persons:** 15 (1965); 16 (1968); 17 (1972); 18 (1962); 19 (no); **Genocide:** 20 (2000); **War crimes and Crimes against humanity:** 21 (1971); **Discrimination:** 23 (1977); 23a (no); 24 (1982); 25 (1975); **Land mines:** 26 (1998); **International Criminal Court:** 27 (2000 S)

Guinea-Bissau
IHL: 1 (1974); 2 (1986); 2a (no); 3 (1986); **International HR:** 4 (1992); 5 (2000 S); 5a (no); 6 (2000 S); 7 (2000 S); **Regional HR:** 10 (1985); **Children:** 11 (1990); **Torture:** 12 (2000 S); 12a (no); 12b (no); **Refugees and Stateless persons:** 15 (1976); 16 (1976); 17 (1989); 18 (no); 19 (no); **Genocide:** 20 (no); **War crimes and Crimes against humanity:** 21 (no); **Discrimination:** 23 (2000 S); 23a (no); 24 (1985); 25 (no); **Land mines:** 26 (1997 S); **International Criminal Court:** 27 (2000 S)

Guyana
IHL: 1 (1968); 2 (1988); 2a (no); 3 (1988); **International HR:** 4 (1977); 5 (1977); 5a (yes); 6 (1993); 7 (no); **Regional HR:** 9 (no); 9a (no); 9b (no); **Children:** 11 (1991); **Torture:** 12 (1988); 12a (no); 12b (no); 14 (no); **Refugees and Stateless persons:** 15 (no); 16 (no); 18 (no); 19 (no); **Genocide:** 20 (no); **War crimes and Crimes against humanity:** 21 (no); **Discrimination:** 23 (1977); 23a (no); 24 (1980); 25 (1977); **Land mines:** 26 (1997 S); **International Criminal Court:** 27 (2000 S)

Haiti
IHL: 1 (1957); 2 (no); 2a (no); 3 (no); **International HR:** 4 (no); 5 (1991); 5a (no); 6 (no); 7 (no); **Regional HR:** 9 (1977); 9a (no); 9b (no); **Children:** 11 (1995); **Torture:** 12 (no); 12a (no); 12b (no); 14 (1986 S); **Refugees and Stateless persons:** 15 (1984); 16 (1984); 18 (no); 19 (no); **Genocide:** 20 (1950); **War crimes and Crimes against humanity:** 21 (no); **Discrimination**: 23 (1972); 23a (no); 24 (1981); 25 (1977); **Land mines**: 26 (1997 S); **International Criminal Court**: 27 (1999 S)

Holy See
IHL: 1 (1951); 2 (1985); 2a (no); 3 (1985); **International HR:** 4 (no); 5 (no); 5a (no); 6 (no); 7 (no); **Children:** 11 (**1990**); **Torture:** 12 (no); 12a (no); 12b (no); **Refugees and Stateless persons:** 15 (1956); 16 (1967); 18 (1954 S); 19 (no); **Genocide:** 20 (no); **War crimes and Crimes against humanity:** 21 (no); **Discrimination**: 23 (1969); 23a (no); 24 (no); 25 (no); **Land mines**: 26 (1998); **International Criminal Court**: 27 (no)

Honduras
IHL: 1 (1965); 2 (1995); 2a (no); 3 (1995); **International HR:** 4 (1981); 5 (1966); 5a (no); 6 (1966 S); 7 (1990 S); **Regional HR:** 9 (1977); 9a (no); 9b (yes); **Children:** 11 (1990); **Torture:** 12 (1996); 12a (no); 12b (no); 14 (1986 S); **Refugees and Stateless persons:** 15 (1992); 16 (1992); 18 (1954 S); 19 (no); **Genocide:** 20 (1952); **War crimes and Crimes against humanity:** 21 (no); **Discrimination**: 23 (no); 23a (no); 24 (1983); 25 (no); **Land mines**: 26 (1998); **International Criminal Court**: 27 (1998 S)

Hungary
IHL: 1 (1954); 2 (1989); 2a (yes); 3 (1989); **International HR:** 4 (1974); 5 (1974); 5a (yes); 6 (1988); 7 (1994); **Regional HR:** 8 (1992); 8a (1995); **Children:** 11 (1991); **Torture:** 12 (1987); 12a (yes); 12b (yes); 13 (1993); **Refugees and Stateless persons:** 15 (1989); 16 (1989); 18 (no); 19 (no); **Genocide:** 20 (1952); **War crimes and Crimes against humanity:** 21 (1969); 22 (no); **Discrimination**: 23 (1967); 23a (yes); 24 (1980); 25 (1974); **Land mines**: 26 (1998); **International Criminal Court**: 27 (1998 S)

Iceland
IHL: 1 (1965); 2 (1987); 2a (yes); 3 (1987); **International HR:** 4 (1979); 5 (1989); 5a (yes); 6 (1979); 7 (1991); **Regional HR:** 8 (1953); 8a (1995); **Children:** 11 (1992); **Torture:** 12 (1996); 12a (yes); 12b (yes); 13 (1990); **Refugees and Stateless persons:** 15 (1955); 16 (1968); 18 (no); 19 (no); **Genocide:** 20 (1949); **War crimes and Crimes against humanity:** 21 (no); 22 (no); **Discrimination**: 23 (1967); 23a (yes); 24 (1985); 25 (no); **Land mines**: 26 (1999); **International Criminal Court**: 27 (2000)

India
IHL: 1 (1950); 2 (no); 2a (no); 3 (no); **International HR:** 4 (1979); 5 (1979); 5a (no); 6 (no); 7 (no); **Children:** 11 (1992); **Torture:** 12 (no); 12a (no); 12b (no); **Refugees and Stateless persons:** 15 (no); 16 (no); 18 (no); 19 (no); **Genocide:** 20 (1959); **War crimes and Crimes against humanity:** 21 (1971); **Discrimination**: 23 (1968); 23a (no); 24 (1993); 25 (1977); **Land mines**: 26 (no); **International Criminal Court**: 27 (no)

Indonesia
IHL: 1 (1958); 2 (no); 2a (no); 3 (no); **International HR:** 4 (no); 5 (no); 5a (no); 6 (no); 7 (no); **Children:** 11 (1990); **Torture:** 12 (1998); 12a (no); 12b (no); **Refugees and Stateless persons:** 15 (no); 16 (no); 18 (no); 19 (no); **Genocide:** 20 (no); **War crimes and Crimes against humanity:** 21 (no); **Discrimination**: 23 (1999); 23a (no); 24 (1984); 25 (no); **Land mines**: 26 (1997 S); **International Criminal Court**: 27 (no)

Iran
IHL: 1 (1957); 2 (1977 S); 2a (no); 3 (1977 S); **International HR:** 4 (1975); 5 (1975); 5a (no); 6 (no); 7 (no); **Children:** 11 (1994); **Torture:** 12 (no); 12a (no); 12b (no); **Refugees and Stateless persons:** 15 (1976); 16 (1976); 18 (no); 19 (no); **Genocide:** 20 (1956); **War crimes and Crimes against humanity:** 21 (no); **Discrimination**: 23 (1968); 23a (no); 24 (no); 25 (1985); **Land mines**: 26 (no); **International Criminal Court**: 27 (2000 S)

Iraq

IHL: 1 (1956); 2 (no); 2a (no); 3 (no); **International HR:** 4 (1971); 5 (1971); 5a (no); 6 (no); 7 (no); **Children:** 11 (1994); **Torture:** 12 (no); 12a (no); 12b (no); **Refugees and Stateless persons:** 15 (no); 16 (no); 18 (no); 19 (no); **Genocide:** 20 (1959); **War crimes and Crimes against humanity:** 21 (no); **Discrimination**: 23 (1970); 23a (no); 24 (1986); 25 (1975); **Land mines**: 26 (no); **International Criminal Court**: 27 (no)

Ireland

IHL: 1 (1962); 2 (1999); 2a (1999); 3 (1999); **International HR:** 4 (1989); 5 (1989); 5a (yes); 6 (1989); 7 (1993); **Regional HR:** 8 (1953); 8a (1996); **Children:** 11 (1992); **Torture:** 12 (1992 S); 12a (no); 12b (no); 13 (1988); **Refugees and Stateless persons:** 15 (1956); 16 (1968); 18 (1962); 19 (1973); **Genocide:** 20 (1976); **War crimes and Crimes against humanity:** 21 (no); 22 (no); **Discrimination**: 23 (2000); 23a (no); 24 (1985); 25 (no); **Land mines**: 26 (1997); **International Criminal Court**: 27 (1998 S)

Israel

IHL: 1 (1951); 2 (no); 2a (no); 3 (no); **International HR:** 4 (1991); 5 (1991); 5a (no); 6 (no); 7 (no); **Children:** 11 (1991); **Torture:** 12 (1991); 12a (no); 12b (no); **Refugees and Stateless persons:** 15 (1954); 16 (1968); 18 (1958); 19 (1961 S); **Genocide:** 20 (1950); **War crimes and Crimes against humanity:** 21 (no); **Discrimination**: 23 (1979); 23a (no); 24 (1991); 25 (no); **Land mines**: 26 (no); **International Criminal Court**: 27 (2000 S)

Italy

IHL: 1 (1951); 2 (1986); 2a (yes); 3 (1986); **International HR:** 4 (1978); 5 (1978); 5a (yes); 6 (1978); 7 (1995); **Regional HR:** 8 (1955); 8a (1997); **Children:** 11 (1991); **Torture:** 12 (1989); 12a (yes); 12b (yes); 13 (1988); **Refugees and Stateless persons:** 15 (1954); 16 (1972); 18 (1962); 19 (no); **Genocide:** 20 (1952); **War crimes and Crimes against humanity:** 21 (no); 22 (no); **Discrimination**: 23 (1976); 23a (yes); 24 (1985); 25 (no); **Land mines**: 26 (1999); **International Criminal Court**: 27 (1999)

Ivory Coast

IHL: 1 (1961); 2 (1989); 2a (no); 3 (1989); **International HR:** 4 (1992); 5 (1992); 5a (no); 6 (1997); 7 (no); **Regional HR:** 10 (1992); **Children:** 11 (1991); **Torture:** 12 (1995); 12a (no); 12b (no); **Refugees and Stateless persons:** 15 (1961); 16 (1970); 17 (1998); 18 (no); 19 (no); **Genocide:** 20 (1995); **War crimes and Crimes against humanity:** 21 (no); **Discrimination**: 23 (1973); 23a (no); 24 (1995); 25 (no); **Land mines**: 26 (2000); **International Criminal Court**: 27 (1998 S)

Jamaica

IHL: 1 (1964); 2 (1986); 2a (no); 3 (1986); **International HR:** 4 (1975); 5 (1975); 5a (no); 6 (no; withdrawal in 1997); 7 (no); **Regional HR:** 9 (1978); 9a (yes); 9b (no); **Children:** 11 (1991); **Torture:** 12 (no); 12a (no); 12b (no); 14 (no); **Refugees and Stateless persons:** 15 (1964); 16 (1980); 18 (no); 19 (no); **Genocide:** 20 (1968); **War crimes and Crimes against humanity:** 21 (no); **Discrimination**: 23 (1971); 23a (no); 24 (1984); 25 (1977); **Land mines**: 26 (1998); **International Criminal Court**: 27 (2000 S)

Japan

IHL: 1 (1953); 2 (no); 2a (no); 3 (no); **International HR:** 4 (1979); 5 (1979); 5a (no); 6 (no); 7 (no); **Children:** 11 (1994); **Torture:** 12 (1999); 12a (2000); 12b (no); **Refugees and Stateless persons:** 15 (1981); 16 (1982); 18 (no); 19 (no); **Genocide:** 20 (no); **War crimes and Crimes against humanity:** 21 (no); **Discrimination**: 23 (1995); 23a (no); 24 (1985); 25 (no); **Land mines**: 26 (1998); **International Criminal Court**: 27 (no)

Jordan

IHL: 1 (1951); 2 (1979); 2a (no); 3 (1979); **International HR:** 4 (1975); 5 (1975); 5a (no); 6 (no); 7 (no); **Children:** 11 (1991); **Torture:** 12 (1992); 12a (no); 12b (no); **Refugees and Stateless persons:** 15 (no); 16 (no); 18 (no); 19 (no); **Genocide:** 20 (1950); **War crimes and Crimes against humanity:** 21 (no); **Discrimination**: 23 (1974); 23a (no); 24 (1992); 25 (1992); **Land mines**: 26 (1998); **International Criminal Court**: 27 (1998 S)

Kazakhstan
IHL: 1 (1992); 2 (1992); 2a (no); 3 (1992); **International HR:** 4 (no); 5 (no); 5a (no); 6 (no); 7 (no); **Children:** 11 (1994); **Torture:** 12 (1998); 12a (no); 12b (no); **Refugees and Stateless persons:** 15 (1999); 16 (1999); 18 (no); 19 (no); **Genocide:** 20 (1998); **War crimes and Crimes against humanity:** 21 (no); Discrimination: 23 (1998); 23a (no); 24 (1998); 25 (no); **Land mines**: 26 (no); **International Criminal Court**: 27 (no)

Kenya
IHL: 1 (1966); 2 (1999); 2a (no); 3 (1999); **International HR:** 4 (1972); 5 (1972); 5a (no); 6 (no); 7 (no); **Regional HR:** 10 (1992); **Children:** 11 (1990); **Torture:** 12 (1997); 12a (no); 12b (no); **Refugees and Stateless persons:** 15 (1966); 16 (1981); 17 (1992); 18 (no); 19 (no); **Genocide:** 20 (no); **War crimes and Crimes against humanity:** 21 (1972); **Discrimination**: 23 (no); 23a (no); 24 (1984); 25 (1974); **Land mines**: 26 (2001); **International Criminal Court**: 27 (1999 S)

Kiribati
IHL: 1 (1989); 2 (no); 2a (no); 3 (no); **International HR:** 4 (no); 5 (no); 5a (no); 6 (no); 7 (no); **Children:** 11 (1995); **Torture:** 12 (no); 12a (no); 12b (no); **Refugees and Stateless persons:** 15 (no); 16 (no); 18 (1983); 19 (1983); **Genocide:** 20 (no); **War crimes and Crimes against humanity:** 21 (no); **Discrimination**: 23 (no); 23a (no); 24 (no); 25 (no); **Land mines**: 26 (2000); **International Criminal Court**: 27 (no)

Korea (Democratic People's Republic of)
IHL: 1 (1957); 2 (1988); 2a (no); 3 (no); **International HR:** 4 (1981); 5 (1981); 5a (no); 6 (no); 7 (no); **Children:** 11 (1990); **Torture:** 12 (no); 12a (no); 12b (no); **Refugees and Stateless persons:** 15 (no); 16 (no); 18 (no); 19 (no); **Genocide:** 20 (1989); **War crimes and Crimes against humanity:** 21 (1984); **Discrimination**: 23 (no); 23a (no); 24 (2001); 25 (no); **Land mines**: 26 (no); **International Criminal Court**: 27 (no)

Korea (Republic of)
IHL: 1 (1966); 2 (1982); 2a (no); 3 (1982); **International HR:** 4 (1990); 5 (1990); 5a (yes); 6 (1990); 7 (no); **Children:** 11 (1991); **Torture:** 12 (1995); 12a (no); 12b (no); **Refugees and Stateless persons:** 15 (1992); 16 (1992); 18 (1962); 19 (no); **Genocide:** 20 (1950); **War crimes and Crimes against humanity:** 21 (no); **Discrimination**: 23 (1978); 23a (yes); 24 (1984); 25 (no); **Land mines**: 26 (no); **International Criminal Court**: 27 (2000 S)

Kuwait
IHL: 1 (1967); 2 (1985); 2a (no); 3 (1985); **International HR:** 4 (1996); 5 (1996); 5a (no); 6 (no); 7 (no); **Children:** 11 (1991); **Torture:** 12 (1996); 12a (no); 12b (no); **Refugees and Stateless persons:** 15 (no); 16 (no); 18 (no); 19 (no); **Genocide:** 20 (1995); **War crimes and Crimes against humanity:** 21 (1995); **Discrimination**: 23 (1968); 23a (no); 24 (1994); 25 (1977); **Land mines**: 26 (no); **International Criminal Court**: 27 (2000 S)

Kyrgyzstan
IHL: 1 (1992); 2 (1992); 2a (no); 3 (1992); **International HR:** 4 (1994); 5 (1994); 5a (no); 6 (1994); 7 (no); **Children:** 11 (1994); **Torture:** 12 (1997); 12a (no); 12b (no); **Refugees and Stateless persons:** 15 (1996); 16 (1996); 18 (no); 19 (no); **Genocide:** 20 (**1997**); **War crimes and Crimes against humanity:** 21 (no); **Discrimination**: 23 (1997); 23a (no); 24 (1997); 25 (1997); **Land mines**: 26 (no); **International Criminal Court**: 27 (1998 S)

Laos
IHL: 1 (1956); 2 (1980); 2a (1998); 3 (1980); **International HR:** 4 (no); 5 (no); 5a (no); 6 (no); 7 (no); **Children:** 11 (1991); **Torture:** 12 (no); 12a (no); 12b (no); **Refugees and Stateless persons:** 15 (no); 16 (no); 18 (no); 19 (no); **Genocide:** 20 (1950); **War crimes and Crimes against humanity:** 21 (1984); Discrimination: 23 (1974); 23a (no); 24 (1981); 25 (1981); **Land mines**: 26 (no); **International Criminal Court**: 27 (no)

Latvia

IHL: 1 (1991); 2 (1991); 2a (no); 3 (1991); **International HR:** 4 (1992); 5 (1992); 5a (no); 6 (1994); 7 (no); **Regional HR:** 8 (1997); 8a (1997); **Children:** 11 (1992); **Torture:** 12 (1992); 12a (no); 12b (no); 13 (**1998**); **Refugees and Stateless persons:** 15 (1997); 16 (1997); 18 (1999); 19 (1992); **Genocide:** 20 (1992); **War crimes and Crimes against humanity:** 21 (1992); 22 (no); **Discrimination**: 23 (1992); 23a (no); 24 (1992); 25 (1992); **Land mines:** 26 (no); **International Criminal Court**: 27 (1999 S)

Lebanon

IHL: 1 (1951); 2 (1997); 2a (no); 3 (1997); **International HR:** 4 (1972); 5 (1972); 5a (no); 6 (no); 7 (no); **Children:** 11 (1991); **Torture:** 12 (2000); 12a (no); 12b (no); **Refugees and Stateless persons:** 15 (no); 16 (no); 18 (no); 19 (no); **Genocide:** 20 (1953); **War crimes and Crimes against humanity:** 21 (no); **Discrimination**: 23 (1971); 23a (no); 24 (1997); 25 (no); **Land mines**: 26 (no); **International Criminal Court**: 27 (no)

Lesotho

IHL: 1 (1968); 2 (1994); 2a (no); 3 (1994); **International HR:** 4 (1992); 5 (1992); 5a (no); 6 (2000); 7 (no); **Regional HR:** 10 (1992); **Children:** 11 (1992); **Torture:** 12 (no); 12a (no); 12b (no); **Refugees and Stateless persons:** 15 (1981); 16 (1981); 17 (1988); 18 (1974); 19 (no); **Genocide:** 20 (1974); **War crimes and Crimes against humanity:** 21 (no); **Discrimination**: 23 (1971); 23a (no); 24 (1995); 25 (1983); **Land mines**: 26 (1998); **International Criminal Court**: 27 (2000)

Liberia

IHL: 1 (1954); 2 (1988); 2a (no); 3 (1988); **International HR:** 4 (1967 S); 5 (1967 S); 5a (no); 6 (no); 7 (no); **Regional HR:** 10 (1982); **Children:** 11 (1993); **Torture:** 12 (no); 12a (no); 12b (no); **Refugees and Stateless persons:** 15 (1964); 16 (1980); 17 (1971); 18 (1964); 19 (no); **Genocide:** 20 (1950); **War crimes and Crimes against humanity:** 21 (no); **Discrimination**: 23 (1976); 23a (no); 24 (1984); 25 (1976); **Land mines**: 26 (1999); **International Criminal Court**: 27 (1998 S)

Libya

IHL: 1 (1956); 2 (1978); 2a (no); 3 (1978); **International HR:** 4 (1970); 5 (1970); 5a (no); 6 (1989); 7 (no); **Regional HR:** 10 (1986); **Children:** 11 (1993); **Torture:** 12 (1989); 12a (no); 12b (no); **Refugees and Stateless persons:** 15 (no); 16 (no); 17 (1981); 18 (1989); 19 (1989); **Genocide:** 20 (1989); **War crimes and Crimes against humanity:** 21 (1989); **Discrimination**: 23 (1968); 23a (no); 24 (1989); 25 (1976); **Land mines**: 26 (no); **International Criminal Court**: 27 (no)

Liechtenstein

IHL: 1 (1950); 2 (1989); 2a (yes); 3 (1989); **International HR:** 4 (1998); 5 (1998); 5a (yes); 6 (1998); 7 (1998); **Regional HR:** 8 (1982); 8a (1995); **Children:** 11 (1995); **Torture:** 12 (1990); 12a (yes); 12b (yes); 13 (1991); **Refugees and Stateless persons:** 15 (1957); 16 (1968); 18 (1954 S); 19 (no); **Genocide:** 20 (1994); **War crimes and Crimes against humanity:** 21 (no); 22 (no); **Discrimination**: 23 (2000); 23a (no); 24 (1995); 25 (no); **Land mines**: 26 (1999); **International Criminal Court**: 27 (1998 S)

Lithuania

IHL: 1 (1996); 2 (2000); 2a (2000); 3 (2000); **International HR:** 4 (1991); 5 (1991); 5a (no); 6 (1991); 7 (2000 S); **Regional HR:** 8 (1995); 8a (1995); **Children:** 11 (1992); **Torture:** 12 (1996); 12a (no); 12b (no); 13 (1998); **Refugees and Stateless persons:** 15 (1997); 16 (1997); 18 (2000); 19 (no); **Genocide:** 20 (1996); **War crimes and Crimes against humanity:** 21 (1996); 22 (no); **Discrimination**: 23 (1998); 23a (no); 24 (1994); 25 (no); **Land mines**: 26 (1999 S); **International Criminal Court**: 27 (1998 S)

Luxembourg

IHL: 1 (1953); 2 (1989); 2a (yes); 3 (1989); **International HR:** 4 (1983); 5 (1983); 5a (yes); 6 (1983); 7 (1990); **Regional HR:** 8 (1953); 8a (1996); **Children:** 11 (1994); **Torture:** 12 (1987); 12a (yes); 12b (yes); 13 (1988); **Refugees and Stateless persons:** 15 (1953); 16 (1971); 18 (1960); 19 (no); **Genocide:** 20 (1981); **War crimes and Crimes against humanity:** 21 (no); 22 (no); **Discrimination**: 23 (1978); 23a (yes); 24 (1989); 25 (no); **Land mines**: 26 (1999); **International Criminal Court**: 27 (2000)

Macedonia
IHL: 1 (1993); 2 (1993); 2a (yes); 3 (1993); **International HR:** 4 (1994); 5 (1994); 5a (no); 6 (1994); 7 (1995); **Regional HR:** 8 (1997); 8a (1997); **Children:** 11 (1993); **Torture:** 12 (1994); 12a (no); 12b (no); 13 (1997); **Refugees and Stateless persons:** 15 (1994); 16 (1994); 18 (1994); 19 (no); **Genocide:** 20 (1994); **War crimes and Crimes against humanity:** 21 (1994); 22 (no); **Discrimination**: 23 (1994); 23a (no); 24 (1994); 25 (1994); **Land mines**: 26 (1998); **International Criminal Court**: 27 (1998 S)

Madagascar
IHL: 1 (1963); 2 (1992); 2a (yes); 3 (1992); **International HR:** 4 (1971); 5 (1971); 5a (no); 6 (1971); 7 (no); **Regional HR:** 10 (1992); **Children:** 11 (1991); **Torture:** 12 (no); 12a (no); 12b (no); **Refugees and Stateless persons:** 15 (1967); 16 (no); 17 (1969 S); 18 (1962); 19 (no); **Genocide:** 20 (no); **War crimes and Crimes against humanity:** 21 (no); **Discrimination**: 23 (1969); 23a (no); 24 (1989); 25 (1977); **Land mines**: 26 (1999); **International Criminal Court**: 27 (1998 S)

Malawi
IHL: 1 (1968); 2 (1991); 2a (no); 3 (1991); **International HR:** 4 (1993); 5 (1993); 5a (no); 6 (1996); 7 (no); **Regional HR:** 10 (1989); **Children:** 11 (1991); **Torture:** 12 (1996); 12a (no); 12b (no); **Refugees and Stateless persons:** 15 (1987); 16 (1987); 17 (1987); 18 (no); 19 (no); **Genocide:** 20 (no); **War crimes and Crimes against humanity:** 21 (no); **Discrimination**: 23 (1996); 23a (no); 24 (1987); 25 (no); **Land mines**: 26 (1998); **International Criminal Court**: 27 (1999 S)

Malaysia
IHL: 1 (1962); 2 (no); 2a (no); 3 (no); **International HR:** 4 (no); 5 (no); 5a (no); 6 (no); 7 (no); **Children:** 11 (1995); **Torture:** 12 (no); 12a (no); 12b (no); **Refugees and Stateless persons:** 15 (no); 16 (no); 18 (no); 19 (no); **Genocide:** 20 (1994); **War crimes and Crimes against humanity:** 21 (no); **Discrimination**: 23 (no); 23a (no); 24 (1995); 25 (no); **Land mines**: 26 (1999); **International Criminal Court**: 27 (no)

Maldives
IHL: 1 (1991); 2 (1991); 2a (no); 3 (1991); **International HR:** 4 (no); 5 (no); 5a (no); 6 (no); 7 (no); **Children:** 11 (1991); **Torture:** 12 (no); 12a (no); 12b (no); **Refugees and Stateless persons:** 15 (no); 16 (no); 18 (no); 19 (no); **Genocide:** 20 (1984); **War crimes and Crimes against humanity:** 21 (no); **Discrimination**: 23 (1984); 23a (no); 24 (1993); 25 (1984); **Land mines**: 26 (2000); **International Criminal Court**: 27 (no)

Mali
IHL: 1 (1965); 2 (1989); 2a (no); 3 (1989); **International HR:** 4 (1974); 5 (1974); 5a (no); 6 (no); 7 (no); **Regional HR:** 10 (1981); **Children:** 11 (1990); **Torture:** 12 (1999); 12a (no); 12b (no); **Refugees and Stateless persons:** 15 (1973); 16 (1973); 17 (1981); 18 (no); 19 (no); **Genocide:** 20 (1974); **War crimes and Crimes against humanity:** 21 (no); **Discrimination**: 23 (1974); 23a (no); 24 (1985); 25 (1977); **Land mines**: 26 (1998); **International Criminal Court**: 27 (2000)

Malta
IHL: 1 (1968); 2 (1989); 2a (yes); 3 (1989); **International HR:** 4 (1990); 5 (1990); 5a (yes); 6 (1990); 7 (1994); **Regional HR:** 8 (1967); 8a (1995); **Children:** 11 (1990); **Torture:** 12 (1990); 12a (yes); 12b (yes); 13 (1988); **Refugees and Stateless persons:** 15 (1971); 16 (1971); 18 (no); 19 (no); **Genocide:** 20 (no); **War crimes and Crimes against humanity:** 21 (no); 22 (no); **Discrimination**: 23 (1971); 23a (yes); 24 (1991); 25 (no); **Land mines**: 26 (1997 S); **International Criminal Court**: 27 (1998 S)

Marshall Islands
IHL: 1 (no); 2 (no); 2a (no); 3 (no); **International HR:** 4 (no); 5 (no); 5a (no); 6 (no); 7 (no); **Children:** 11 (1993); **Torture:** 12 (no); 12a (no); 12b (no); **Refugees and Stateless persons:** 15 (no); 16 (no); 18 (no); 19 (no); **Genocide:** 20 (no); **War crimes and Crimes against humanity:** 21 (no); **Discrimination**: 23 (no); 23a (no); 24 (no); 25 (no); **Land mines**: 26 (1997 S); **International Criminal Court**: 27 (2000)

Mauritania
IHL: 1 (1962); 2 (1980); 2a (no); 3 (1980); **International HR:** 4 (no); 5 (no); 5a (no); 6 (no); 7 (no); **Regional HR:** 10 (1986); **Children:** 11 (1991); **Torture:** 12 (no); 12a (no); 12b (no); **Refugees and Stateless persons:** 15 (1987); 16 (1987); 17 (1972); 18 (no); 19 (no); **Genocide:** 20 (no); **War crimes and Crimes against humanity:** 21 (no); **Discrimination:** 23 (1988); 23a (no); 24 (no); 25 (1988); **Land mines:** 26 (2000); **International Criminal Court:** 27 (no)

Mauritius
IHL: 1 (1970); 2 (1982); 2a (no); 3 (1982); **International HR:** 4 (1973); 5 (1973); 5a (no); 6 (1973); 7 (no); **Regional HR:** 10 (1992); **Children:** 11 (1990); **Torture:** 12 (1992); 12a (no); 12b (no); **Refugees and Stateless persons:** 15 (no); 16 (no); 17 (no); 18 (no); 19 (no); **Genocide:** 20 (no); **War crimes and Crimes against humanity:** 21 (no); **Discrimination:** 23 (1972); 23a (no); 24 (1984); 25 (no); **Land mines:** 26 (1997); **International Criminal Court:** 27 (1998 S)

Mexico
IHL: 1 (1952); 2 (1983); 2a (no); 3 (no); **International HR:** 4 (1981); 5 (1981); 5a (no); 6 (no); 7 (no); **Regional HR:** 9 (1981); 9a (no); 9b (no); **Children:** 11 (1990); **Torture:** 12 (1986); 12a (no); 12b (no); 14 (1987); **Refugees and Stateless persons:** 15 (2000); 16 (2000); 18 (2000); 19 (no); **Genocide:** 20 (1952); **War crimes and Crimes against humanity:** 21 (1969 S); **Discrimination:** 23 (1975); 23a (no); 24 (1981); 25 (1980); **Land mines:** 26 (1998); **International Criminal Court:** 27 (2000 S)

Micronesia
IHL: 1 (1995); 2 (1995); 2a (no); 3 (1995); **International HR:** 4 (no); 5 (no); 5a (no); 6 (no); 7 (no); **Children:** 11 (1993); **Torture:** 12 (no); 12a (no); 12b (no); **Refugees and Stateless persons:** 15 (no); 16 (no); 18 (no); 19 (no); **Genocide:** 20 (no); **War crimes and Crimes against humanity:** 21 (no); **Discrimination:** 23 (no); 23a (no); 24 (no); 25 (no); **Land mines:** 26 (no); **International Criminal Court:** 27 (no)

Moldova (Republic of)
IHL: 1 (1993); 2 (1993); 2a (no); 3 (1993); **International HR:** 4 (1993); 5 (1993); 5a (no); 6 (no); 7 (no); **Regional HR:** 8 (1997); 8a (1997); **Children:** 11 (1993); **Torture:** 12 (1995); 12a (no); 12b (no); 13 (1997); **Refugees and Stateless persons:** 15 (no); 16 (no); 18 (no); 19 (no); **Genocide:** 20 (1993); **War crimes and Crimes against humanity:** 21 (1993); 22 (no); **Discrimination:** 23 (1993); 23a (no); 24 (1994); 25 (no); **Land mines:** 26 (2000); **International Criminal Court:** 27 (2000 S)

Monaco
IHL: 1 (1950); 2 (2000); 2a (no); 3 (2000); **International HR:** 4 (1997); 5 (1997); 5a (no); 6 (no); 7 (2000); **Children:** 11 (1993); **Torture:** 12 (1991); 12a (yes); 12b (yes); **Refugees and Stateless persons:** 15 (1954); 16 (no); 18 (no); 19 (no); **Genocide:** 20 (1950); **War crimes and Crimes against humanity:** 21 (no); **Discrimination:** 23 (1995); 23a (no); 24 (no); 25 (no); **Land mines:** 26 (1998); **International Criminal Court:** 27 (1998 S)

Mongolia
IHL: 1 (1958); 2 (1995); 2a (yes); 3 (1995); **International HR:** 4 (1974); 5 (1974); 5a (no); 6 (1991); 7 (1993); **Children:** 11 (1990); **Torture:** 12 (no); 12a (no); 12b (no); **Refugees and Stateless persons:** 15 (no); 16 (no); 18 (no); 19 (no); **Genocide:** 20 (1967); **War crimes and Crimes against humanity:** 21 (1969); **Discrimination:** 23 (1969); 23a (no); 24 (1981); 25 (1975); **Land mines:** 26 (no); **International Criminal Court:** 27 (2000 S)

Morocco
IHL: 1 (1956); 2 (1977 S); 2a (no); 3 (1977 S); **International HR:** 4 (1979); 5 (1979); 5a (no); 6 (no); 7 (no); **Regional HR:** 10 (no); **Children:** 11 (1993); **Torture:** 12 (1993); 12a (no); 12b (no); **Refugees and Stateless persons:** 15 (1956); 16 (1971); 17 (1974); 18 (no); 19 (no); **Genocide:** 20 (1958); **War crimes and Crimes against humanity:** 21 (no); **Discrimination:** 23 (1970); 23a (no); 24 (1993); 25 (no); **Land mines:** 26 (no); **International Criminal Court:** 27 (2000 S)

Mozambique
IHL: 1 (1983); 2 (1983); 2a (no); 3 (no); **International HR:** 4 (no); 5 (1993); 5a (no); 6 (no); 7 (1993); **Regional HR:** 10 (1989); **Children:** 11 (1994); **Torture:** 12 (no); 12a (no); 12b (no); **Refugees and State-**

less persons: 15 (1983); 16 (1989); 17 (1989); 18 (no); 19 (no); **Genocide:** 20 (1983); **War crimes and Crimes against humanity:** 21 (no); **Discrimination**: 23 (1983); 23a (no); 24 (1997); 25 (1983); **Land mines**: 26 (1998); **International Criminal Court**: 27 (2000 S)

Myanmar
IHL: 1 (1992); 2 (no); 2a (no); 3 (no); **International HR:** 4 (no); 5 (no); 5a (no); 6 (no); 7 (no); **Children:** 11 (1991); **Torture:** 12 (no); 12a (no); 12b (no); **Refugees and Stateless persons:** 15 (no); 16 (no); 18 (no); 19 (no); **Genocide:** 20 (1956); **War crimes and Crimes against humanity:** 21 (no); **Discrimination**: 23 (no); 23a (); 24 (1997); 25 (no); **Land mines**: 26 (no); **International Criminal Court**: 27 (no)

Namibia
IHL: 1 (1991); 2 (1994); 2a (yes); 3 (1994); **International HR:** 4 (1994); 5 (1994); 5a (no); 6 (1994); 7 (1994); **Regional HR:** 10 (1992); **Children:** 11 (1990); **Torture:** 12 (1994); 12a (no); 12b (no); **Refugees and Stateless persons:** 15 (1995); 16 (no); 17 (no); 18 (no); 19 (no); **Genocide:** 20 (1994); **War crimes and Crimes against humanity:** 21 (no); **Discrimination**: 23 (1982); 23a (no); 24 (1992); 25 (1982); **Land mines**: 26 (1998); **International Criminal Court**: 27 (1998 S)

Nepal
IHL: 1 (1964); 2 (no); 2a (no); 3 (no); **International HR:** 4 (1991); 5 (1991); 5a (no); 6 (1991); 7 (1998); **Children:** 11 (1990); **Torture:** 12 (1991); 12a (no); 12b (no); **Refugees and Stateless persons:** 15 (no); 16 (no); 18 (no); 19 (no); **Genocide:** 20 (1969); **War crimes and Crimes against humanity:** 21 (no); **Discrimination**: 23 (1971); 23a (no); 24 (1991); 25 (1977); **Land mines**: 26 (no); **International Criminal Court**: 27 (no)

Netherlands
IHL: 1 (1954); 2 (1987); 2a (yes); 3 (1987); **International HR:** 4 (1978); 5 (1978); 5a (yes); 6 (1978); 7 (1991); **Regional HR:** 8 (1954); 8a (1997); **Children:** 11 (1995); **Torture:** 12 (1988); 12a (yes); 12b (yes); 13 (1988); **Refugees and Stateless persons:** 15 (1956); 16 (1968); 18 (1962); 19 (1985); **Genocide:** 20 (1966); **War crimes and Crimes against humanity:** 21 (no); 22 (1981); **Discrimination**: 23 (1971); 23a (yes); 24 (1991); 25 (no); **Land mines**: 26 (1999); **International Criminal Court**: 27 (1998 S)

New Zealand
IHL: 1 (1959); 2 (1988); 2a (yes); 3 (1988); **International HR:** 4 (1978); 5 (1978); 5a (yes); 6 (1989); 7 (1990); **Children:** 11 (1993); **Torture:** 12 (1989); 12a (yes); 12b (yes); **Refugees and Stateless persons:** 15 (1960); 16 (1973); 18 (no); 19 (no); **Genocide:** 20 (1978); **War crimes and Crimes against humanity:** 21 (no); **Discrimination**: 23 (1972); 23a (no); 24 (1985); 25 (no); **Land mines**: 26 (1999); **International Criminal Court**: 27 (2000)

Nicaragua
IHL: 1 (1953); 2 (1977 S); 2a (no); 3 (1977 S); **International HR:** 4 (1980); 5 (1980); 5a (no); 6 (1980); 7 (**1990 S**); **Regional HR:** 9 (1979); 9a (no); 9b (yes); **Children:** 11 (1990); **Torture:** 12 (1985 S); 12a (no); 12b (no); 14 (1987 S); **Refugees and Stateless persons:** 15 (1980); 16 (1980); 18 (no); 19 (no); **Genocide:** 20 (1952); **War crimes and Crimes against humanity:** 21 (1986); **Discrimination**: 23 (1978); 23a (no); 24 (1981); 25 (1980); **Land mines**: 26 (1998); **International Criminal Court**: 27 (no)

Niger
IHL: 1 (1964); 2 (1979); 2a (no); 3 (1979); **International HR:** 4 (1986); 5 (1986); 5a (no); 6 (1986); 7 (no); **Regional HR:** 10 (1986); **Children:** 11 (1990); **Torture:** 12 (1998); 12a (no); 12b (no); **Refugees and Stateless persons:** 15 (1961); 16 (1970); 17 (1971); 18 (no); 19 (1985); **Genocide:** 20 (no); **War crimes and Crimes against humanity:** 21 (no); **Discrimination**: 23 (1967); 23a (no); 24 (no); 25 (1978); **Land mines**: 26 (1999); **International Criminal Court**: 27 (1998 S)

Nigeria
IHL: 1 (1961); 2 (1988); 2a (no); 3 (1988); **International HR:** 4 (1993); 5 (1993); 5a (no); 6 (no); 7 (no); **Regional HR:** 10 (1983); **Children:** 11 (1991); **Torture:** 12 (1988 S); 12a (no); 12b (no); **Refugees and Stateless persons:** 15 (1967); 16 (1968); 17 (1986); 18 (no); 19 (no); **Genocide:** 20 (no); **War crimes and Crimes against humanity:** 21 (1970); **Discrimination**: 23 (1967); 23a (no); 24 (1985); 25 (1977); **Land mines**: 26 (no); **International Criminal Court**: 27 (2000 S)

Norway
IHL: 1 (1951); 2 (1981); 2a (yes); 3 (1981); **International HR:** 4 (1972); 5 (1972); 5a (yes); 6 (1972); 7 (1991); **Regional HR:** 8 (1952); 8a (1995); **Children:** 11 (1991); **Torture:** 12 (1986); 12a (yes); 12b (yes); 13 (1989); **Refugees and Stateless persons:** 15 (1953); 16 (1967); 18 (1956); 19 (1971); **Genocide:** 20 (1949); **War crimes and Crimes against humanity:** 21 (no), 22 (no); **Discrimination**: 23 (1970); 23a (yes); 24 (1981); 25 (no); **Land mines**: 26 (1998); **International Criminal Court**: 27 (2000)

Oman
IHL: 1 (1974); 2 (1984); 2a (no); 3 (1984); **International HR:** 4 (no); 5 (no); 5a (no); 6 (no); 7 (no); **Children:** 11 (1996); **Torture:** 12 (no); 12a (no); 12b (no); **Refugees and Stateless persons:** 15 (no); 16 (no); 18 (no); 19 (no); **Genocide:** 20 (no); **War crimes and Crimes against humanity:** 21 (no); **Discrimination**: 23 (no); 23a (no); 24 (no); 25 (1991); **Land mines**: 26 (no); **International Criminal Court**: 27 (2000 S)

Pakistan
IHL: 1 (1951); 2 (1977 S); 2a (no); 3 (1977 S); **International HR:** 4 (no); 5 (no); 5a (no); 6 (no); 7 (no); **Children:** 11 (1990); **Torture:** 12 (no); 12a (no); 12b (no); **Refugees and Stateless persons:** 15 (no); 16 (no); 18 (no); 19 (no); **Genocide:** 20 (1957); **War crimes and Crimes against humanity:** 21 (no); **Discrimination**: 23 (1966); 23a (no); 24 (1996); 25 (1986); **Land mines**: 26 (no); **International Criminal Court**: 27 (no)

Palau
IHL: 1 (1996); 2 (1996); 2a (no); 3 (1996); **International HR:** 4 (no); 5 (no); 5a (no); 6 (no); 7 (no); **Children:** 11 (1995); **Torture:** 12 (no); 12a (no); 12b (no); **Refugees and Stateless persons:** 15 (no); 16 (no); 18 (no); 19 (no); **Genocide:** 20 (no); **War crimes and Crimes against humanity:** 21 (no); **Discrimination**: 23 (no); 23a (no); 24 (no); 25 (no); **Land mines**: 26 (no); **International Criminal Court**: 27 (no)

Panama
IHL: 1 (1956); 2 (1995); 2a (no); 3 (1995); **International HR:** 4 (1977); 5 (1977); 5a (no); 6 (1977); 7 (1993); **Regional HR:** 9 (1978); 9a (no); 9b (yes); **Children:** 11 (1990); **Torture:** 12 (1987); 12a (no); 12b (no); 14 (1991); **Refugees and Stateless persons:** 15 (1978); 16 (1978); 18 (no); 19 (no); **Genocide:** 20 (1950); **War crimes and Crimes against humanity:** 21 (no); **Discrimination**: 23 (1967); 23a (no); 24 (1981); 25 (1977); **Land mines**: 26 (1998); **International Criminal Court**: 27 (1998 S)

Papua New Guinea
IHL: 1 (1976); 2 (no); 2a (no); 3 (no); **International HR:** 4 (no); 5 (no); 5a (no); 6 (no); 7 (no); **Children:** 11 (1993); **Torture:** 12 (no); 12a (no); 12b (no); **Refugees and Stateless persons:** 15 (1986); 16 (1986); 18 (no); 19 (no); **Genocide:** 20 (1982); **War crimes and Crimes against humanity:** 21 (no); **Discrimination**: 23 (1982); 23a (no); 24 (1995); 25 (no); **Land mines**: 26 (no); **International Criminal Court**: 27 (no)

Paraguay
IHL: 1 (1961); 2 (1990); 2a (1998); 3 (1990); **International HR:** 4 (1992); 5 (1992); 5a (no); 6 (1995); 7 (no); **Regional HR:** 9 (1989); 9a (no); 9b (yes); **Children:** 11 (1990); **Torture:** 12 (1990); 12a (no); 12b (no); 14 (1990); **Refugees and Stateless persons:** 15 (1970); 16 (1970); 18 (no); 19 (no); **Genocide:** 20 (1948); **War crimes and Crimes against humanity:** 21 (no); **Discrimination**: 23 (2000); 23a (no); 24 (1987); 25 (no); **Land mines**: 26 (1998); **International Criminal Court**: 27 (1998 S)

Peru
IHL: 1 (1956); 2 (1989); 2a (no); 3 (1989); **International HR:** 4 (1978); 5 (1978); 5a (yes); 6 (1980); 7 (no); **Regional HR:** 9 (1978); 9a (yes); 9b (yes); **Children:** 11 (1990); **Torture:** 12 (1988); 12a (no); 12b (no); 14 (1986); **Refugees and Stateless persons:** 15 (1964); 16 (1983); 18 (no); 19 (no); **Genocide:** 20 (1960); **War crimes and Crimes against humanity:** 21 (no); **Discrimination**: 23 (1971); 23a (yes); 24 (1982); 25 (1978); **Land mines**: 26 (1998); **International Criminal Court**: 27 (2000 S)

Philippines
IHL: 1 (1952); 2 (1977 S); 2a (no); 3 (1986); **International HR:** 4 (1974); 5 (1986); 5a (yes); 6 (1989); 7 (no); **Children:** 11 (1990); **Torture:** 12 (1986); 12a (no); 12b (no); **Refugees and Stateless persons:** 15

(1981); 16 (1981); 18 (1955 S); 19 (no); **Genocide:** 20 (1950); **War crimes and Crimes against humanity:** 21 (1973); **Discrimination**: 23 (1967); 23a (no); 24 (1981); 25 (1978); **Land mines**: 26 (2000); **International Criminal Court**: 27 (2000 S)

Poland
IHL: 1 (1954); 2 (1991); 2a (yes); 3 (1991); **International HR:** 4 (1977); 5 (1977); 5a (yes); 6 (1991); 7 (2000 S); **Regional HR:** 8 (1993); 8a (1997); **Children:** 11 (1991); **Torture:** 12 (1989); 12a (yes); 12b (yes); 13 (1994); **Refugees and Stateless persons:** 15 (1991); 16 (1991); 18 (no); 19 (no); **Genocide:** 20 (1950); **War crimes and Crimes against humanity:** 21 (1969); 22 (no); **Discrimination**: 23 (1968); 23a (no); 24 (1980); 25 (1976); **Land mines**: 26 (1997 S); **International Criminal Court**: 27 (1999 S)

Portugal
IHL: 1 (1961); 2 (1992); 2a (yes); 3 (1992); **International HR:** 4 (1978); 5 (1978); 5a (no); 6 (1983); 7 (1990); **Regional HR:** 8 (1978); 8a (1997); **Children:** 11 (1990); **Torture:** 12 (1989); 12a (yes); 12b (yes); 13 (1990); **Refugees and Stateless persons:** 15 (1960); 16 (1976); 18 (no); 19 (no); **Genocide:** 20 (**1999**); **War crimes and Crimes against humanity:** 21 (no); 22 (no); **Discrimination**: 23 (1982); 23a (no); 24 (1980); 25 (no); **Land mines**: 26 (1999); **International Criminal Court**: 27 (1998 S)

Qatar
IHL: 1 (1975); 2 (1988); 2a (yes); 3 (no); **International HR:** 4 (no); 5 (no); 5a (no); 6 (no); 7 (no); **Children:** 11 (1995); **Torture:** 12 (2000); 12a (no); 12b (no); **Refugees and Stateless persons:** 15 (no); 16 (no); 18 (no); 19 (no); **Genocide:** 20 (no); **War crimes and Crimes against humanity:** 21 (no); **Discrimination**: 23 (1976); 23a (no); 24 (no); 25 (1975); **Land mines**: 26 (1998); **International Criminal Court**: 27 (no)

Romania
IHL: 1 (1954); 2 (1990); 2a (yes); 3 (1990); **International HR:** 4 (1974); 5 (1974); 5a (no); 6 (1993); 7 (1991); **Regional HR:** 8 (1994); 8a (1995); **Children:** 11 (1990); **Torture:** 12 (1990); 12a (no); 12b (no); 13 (1994); **Refugees and Stateless persons:** 15 (1991); 16 (1991); 18 (no); 19 (no); **Genocide:** 20 (1950); **War crimes and Crimes against humanity:** 21 (1969); 22 (1997 S); **Discrimination**: 23 (1970); 23a (no); 24 (1982); 25 (1978); **Land mines**: 26 (2000); **International Criminal Court**: 27 (1999 S)

Russian Federation
IHL: 1 (1954); 2 (1989); 2a (yes); 3 (1989); **International HR:** 4 (1973); 5 (1973); 5a (yes); 6 (1991); 7 (no); **Regional HR:** 8 (1998); 8a (1998); **Children:** 11 (1990); **Torture:** 12 (1987); 12a (yes); 12b (yes); 13 (1998); **Refugees and Stateless persons:** 15 (1993); 16 (1993); 18 (no); 19 (no); **Genocide:** 20 (1954); **War crimes and Crimes against humanity:** 21 (1969); 22 (no); **Discrimination**: 23 (1969); 23a (yes); 24 (1981); 25 (1975); **Land mines**: 26 (no); **International Criminal Court**: 27 (2000 S)

Rwanda
IHL: 1 (1964); 2 (1984); 2a (yes); 3 (1984); **International HR:** 4 (1975); 5 (1975); 5a (no); 6 (no); 7 (no); **Regional HR:** 10 (1983); **Children:** 11 (1991); **Torture:** 12 (no); 12a (no); 12b (no); **Refugees and Stateless persons:** 15 (1980); 16 (1980); 17 (1979); 18 (no); 19 (no); **Genocide:** 20 (1975); **War crimes and Crimes against humanity:** 21 (1975); **Discrimination**: 23 (1975); 23a (no); 24 (1981); 25 (1981); **Land mines**: 26 (2000); **International Criminal Court**: 27 (no)

Saint Kitts and Nevis
IHL: 1 (1986); 2 (1986); 2a (no); 3 (1986); **International HR:** 4 (no); 5 (no); 5a (no); 6 (no); 7 (no); **Children:** 11 (1990); **Torture:** 12 (no); 12a (no); 12b (no); **Refugees and Stateless persons:** 15 (no); 16 (no); 18 (no); 19 (no); **Genocide:** 20 (no); **War crimes and Crimes against humanity:** 21 (no); **Discrimination**: 23 (no); 23a (no); 24 (1985); 25 (no); **Land mines**: 26 (1998); **International Criminal Court**: 27 (no)

Saint Lucia
IHL: 1 (1981); 2 (1982); 2a (no); 3 (1982); **International HR:** 4 (no); 5 (no); 5a (no); 6 (no); 7 (no); **Regional HR:** 9 (no); 9a (no); 9b (no); **Children:** 11 (1993); **Torture:** 12 (no); 12a (no); 12b (no); 14 (no); **Refugees and Stateless persons:** 15 (no); 16 (no); 18 (no); 19 (no); **Genocide:** 20 (no); **War crimes**

and Crimes against humanity: 21 (no); **Discrimination**: 23 (1990); 23a (no); 24 (1982); 25 (no); **Land mines**: 26 (1999); **International Criminal Court**: 27 (1999 S)

Saint Vincent and the Grenadines

IHL: 1 (1981); 2 (1983); 2a (no); 3 (1983); **International HR:** 4 (1981); 5 (1981); 5a (no); 6 (1981); 7 (no); **Regional HR:** 9 (no); 9a (no); 9b (no); **Children:** 11 (1993); **Torture:** 12 (no); 12a (no); 12b (no); 14 (no); **Refugees and Stateless persons:** 15 (1993); 16 (no); 18 (1999); 19 (no); **Genocide:** 20 (1981); **War crimes and Crimes against humanity:** 21 (1981); **Discrimination**: 23 (1981); 23a (no); 24 (1981); 25 (1981); **Land mines**: 26 (1997 S); **International Criminal Court**: 27 (no)

San Marino

IHL: 1 (1953); 2 (1994); 2a (no); 3 (1994); **International HR:** 4 (1985); 5 (1985); 5a (no); 6 (1985); 7 (no); **Regional HR:** 8 (1989); 8a (1996); **Children:** 11 (1991); **Torture:** 12 (no); 12a (no); 12b (no); 13 (1990); **Refugees and Stateless persons:** 15 (no); 16 (no); 18 (no); 19 (no); **Genocide:** 20 (no); **War crimes and Crimes against humanity:** 21 (no); 22 (no); **Discrimination**: 23 (no); 23a (no); 24 (no); 25 (no); **Land mines**: 26 (1998); **International Criminal Court**: 27 (1999)

Sao Tomé and Principe

IHL: 1 (1976); 2 (1996); 2a (no); 3 (1996); **International HR:** 4 (1995 S); 5 (1995 S); 5a (no); 6 (2000 S); 7 (no); **Regional HR:** 10 (1986); **Children:** 11 (1991); **Torture:** 12 (2000 S); 12a (no); 12b (no); **Refugees and Stateless persons:** 15 (1978); 16 (1978); 17 (no); 18 (no); 19 (no); **Genocide:** 20 (no); **War crimes and Crimes against humanity:** 21 (no); **Discrimination**: 23 (2000 S); 23a (no); 24 (1995 S); 25 (1979); **Land mines**: 26 (1998 S); **International Criminal Court:** 27 (2000 S)

Saudi Arabia

IHL: 1 (1963); 2 (1987); 2a (no); 3 (no); **International HR:** 4 (no); 5 (no); 5a (no); 6 (no); 7 (no); **Children:** 11 (1996); **Torture:** 12 (**1997**); 12a (no); 12b (no); **Refugees and Stateless persons:** 15 (no); 16 (no); 18 (no); 19 (no); **Genocide:** 20 (1950); **War crimes and Crimes against humanity:** 21 (no); **Discrimination**: 23 (1997); 23a (no); 24 (2000); 25 (no); **Land mines**: 26 (no); **International Criminal Court**: 27 (no)

Senegal

IHL: 1 (1963); 2 (1985); 2a (no); 3 (1985); **International HR:** 4 (1978); 5 (1978); 5a (yes); 6 (1978); 7 (no); **Regional HR:** 10 (1982); **Children:** 11 (1990); **Torture:** 12 (1986); 12a (yes); 12b (yes); **Refugees and Stateless persons:** 15 (1963); 16 (1967); 17 (1971); 18 (no); 19 (no); **Genocide:** 20 (1983); **War crimes and Crimes against humanity:** 21 (no); **Discrimination**: 23 (1972); 23a (yes); 24 (1985); 25 (1977); **Land mines**: 26 (1998); **International Criminal Court**: 27 (1999)

Seychelles

IHL: 1 (1984); 2 (1984); 2a (yes); 3 (1984); **International HR:** 4 (1992); 5 (1992); 5a (no); 6 (1992); 7 (1994); **Regional HR:** 10 (1992); **Children:** 11 (1990); **Torture:** 12 (1992); 12a (no); 12b (no); **Refugees and Stateless persons:** 15 (1980); 16 (1980); 17 (1980); 18 (no); 19 (no); **Genocide:** 20 (1992); **War crimes and Crimes against humanity:** 21 (no); **Discrimination**: 23 (1978); 23a (no); 24 (1992); 25 (1978); **Land mines**: 26 (2000); **International Criminal Court**: 27 (2000 S)

Sierra Leone

IHL: 1 (1965); 2 (1986); 2a (no); 3 (1986); **International HR:** 4 (1996); 5 (1996); 5a (no); 6 (1996); 7 (no); **Regional HR:** 10 (1983); **Children:** 11 (1990); **Torture:** 12 (1985 S); 12a (no); 12b (no); **Refugees and Stateless persons:** 15 (1981); 16 (1981); 17 (1987); 18 (no); 19 (no); **Genocide:** 20 (no); **War crimes and Crimes against humanity:** 21 (no); **Discrimination**: 23 (1967); 23a (no); 24 (1988); 25 (no); **Land mines**: 26 (1998 S); **International Criminal Court**: 27 (2000)

Singapore

IHL: 1 (1973); 2 (no); 2a (no); 3 (no); **International HR:** 4 (no); 5 (no); 5a (no); 6 (no); 7 (no); **Children:** 11 (1995); **Torture:** 12 (no); 12a (no); 12b (no); **Refugees and Stateless persons:** 15 (no); 16 (no); 18 (no); 19 (no); **Genocide:** 20 (1995); **War crimes and Crimes against humanity:** 21 (no); **Discrimination**: 23 (no); 23a (no); 24 (1995); 25 (no); **Land mines**: 26 (no); **International Criminal Court**: 27 (no)

Slovakia
IHL: 1 (1993); 2 (1993); 2a (yes); 3 (1993); **International HR:** 4 (1993); 5 (1993); 5a (yes); 6 (1993); 7 (1999); **Regional HR:** 8 (1992); 8a (1994); **Children:** 11 (1993); **Torture:** 12 (1993); 12a (yes); 12b (yes); 13 (1994); **Refugees and Stateless persons:** 15 (1993); 16 (1993); 18 (2000); 19 (2000); **Genocide:** 20 (1993); **War crimes and Crimes against humanity:** 21 (1993); 22 (no); **Discrimination**: 23 (1993); 23a (yes); 24 (1993); 25 (1993); **Land mines**: 26 (1999); **International Criminal Court**: 27 (1998 S)

Slovenia
IHL: 1 (1992); 2 (1992); 2a (yes); 3 (1992); **International HR:** 4 (1992); 5 (1992); 5a (yes); 6 (1993); 7 (1994); **Regional HR:** 8 (1994); 8a (1994); **Children:** 11 (1992); **Torture:** 12 (1993); 12a (yes); 12b (yes); 13 (1994); **Refugees and Stateless persons:** 15 (1992); 16 (1992); 18 (1992); 19 (no); **Genocide:** 20 (1992); **War crimes and Crimes against humanity:** 21 (1992); 22 (no); **Discrimination**: 23 (1992); 23a (no); 24 (1992); 25 (1992); **Land mines**: 26 (1998); **International Criminal Court**: 27 (1998 S)

Solomon Islands
IHL: 1 (1981); 2 (1988); 2a (no); 3 (1988); **International HR:** 4 (1982); 5 (no); 5a (no); 6 (no); 7 (no); **Children:** 11 (1995); **Torture:** 12 (no); 12a (no); 12b (no); **Refugees and Stateless persons:** 15 (1995); 16 (1995); 18 (no); 19 (no); **Genocide:** 20 (no); **War crimes and Crimes against humanity:** 21 (no); **Discrimination**: 23 (1982); 23a (no); 24 (no); 25 (no); **Land mines**: 26 (1999); **International Criminal Court**: 27 (1998 S)

Somalia
IHL: 1 (1962); 2 (no); 2a (no); 3 (no); **International HR:** 4 (1990); 5 (1990); 5a (no); 6 (1990); 7 (no); **Regional HR:** 10 (1985); **Children:** 11 (no); **Torture:** 12 (1990); 12a (no); 12b (no); **Refugees and Stateless persons:** 15 (1978); 16 (1978); 17 (1969 S); 18 (no); 19 (no); **Genocide:** 20 (no); **War crimes and Crimes against humanity:** 21 (no); **Discrimination**: 23 (1975); 23a (no); 24 (no); 25 (1975); **Land mines**: 26 (no); **International Criminal Court**: 27 (no)

South Africa
IHL: 1 (1952); 2 (1995); 2a (no); 3 (1995); **International HR:** 4 (1994 S); 5 (1998); 5a (yes); 6 (no); 7 (no); **Regional HR:** 10 (1996); **Children:** 11 (1995); **Torture:** 12 (1998); 12a (yes); 12b (yes); **Refugees and Stateless persons:** 15 (1996); 16 (1996); 17 (1995); 18 (no); 19 (no); **Genocide:** 20 (1998); **War crimes and Crimes against humanity:** 21 (no); **Discrimination**: 23 (1998); 23a (yes); 24 (1995); 25 (no); **Land mines**: 26 (1998); **International Criminal Court**: 27 (2000)

Spain
IHL: 1 (1952); 2 (1989); 2a (yes); 3 (1989); **International HR:** 4 (1977); 5 (1977); 5a (yes); 6 (1985); 7 (1991); **Regional HR:** 8 (1979); 8a (1996); **Children:** 11 (1990); **Torture:** 12 (1987); 12a (yes); 12b (yes); 13 (1989); **Refugees and Stateless persons:** 15 (1978); 16 (1978); 18 (1997); 19 (no); **Genocide:** 20 (1968); **War crimes and Crimes against humanity:** 21 (no); 22 (no); **Discrimination**: 23 (1968); 23a (yes); 24 (1984); 25 (no); **Land mines**: 26 (1999); **International Criminal Court**: 27 (2000)

Sri Lanka
IHL: 1 (1959); 2 (no); 2a (no); 3 (no); **International HR:** 4 (1980); 5 (1980); 5a (yes); 6 (1997); 7 (no); **Children:** 11 (1991); **Torture:** 12 (1994); 12a (no); 12b (no); **Refugees and Stateless persons:** 15 (no); 16 (no); 18 (no); 19 (no); **Genocide:** 20 (1950); **War crimes and Crimes against humanity:** 21 (no); **Discrimination**: 23 (1982); 23a (no); 24 (1981); 25 (1982); **Land mines**: 26 (no); **International Criminal Court**: 27 (no)

Sudan
IHL: 1 (1957); 2 (no); 2a (no); 3 (no); **International HR:** 4 (1986); 5 (1986); 5a (no); 6 (no); 7 (no); **Regional HR:** 10 (1986); **Children:** 11 (1990); **Torture:** 12 (1986 S); 12a (no); 12b (no); **Refugees and Stateless persons:** 15 (1974); 16 (1974); 17 (1972); 18 (no); 19 (no); **Genocide:** 20 (no); **War crimes and Crimes against humanity:** 21 (no); **Discrimination**: 23 (1977); 23a (no); 24 (no); 25 (1977); **Land mines**: 26 (1997 S); **International Criminal Court**: 27 (2000 S)

Suriname

IHL: 1 (1976); 2 (1985); 2a (no); 3 (1985); **International HR:** 4 (1976); 5 (1976); 5a (no); 6 (1976); 7 (no); **Regional HR:** 9 (1987); 9a (no); 9b (yes); **Children:** 11 (1993); **Torture:** 12 (no); 12a (no); 12b (no); 14 (1987); **Refugees and Stateless persons:** 15 (1978); 16 (1978); 18 (no); 19 (no); **Genocide:** 20 (no); **War crimes and Crimes against humanity:** 21 (no); **Discrimination**: 23 (1984); 23a (no); 24 (1993); 25 (1980); **Land mines**: 26 (1997 S); **International Criminal Court**: 27 (no)

Swaziland

IHL: 1 (1973); 2 (1995); 2a (no); 3 (1995); **International HR:** 4 (no); 5 (no); 5a (no); 6 (no); 7 (no); **Regional HR:** 10 (1995); **Children:** 11 (1995); **Torture:** 12 (no); 12a (no); 12b (no); **Refugees and Stateless persons:** 15 (2000); 16 (1969); 17 (1989); 18 (no); 19 (1999); **Genocide:** 20 (no); **War crimes and Crimes against humanity:** 21 (no); **Discrimination**: 23 (1969); 23a (no); 24 (no); 25 (no); **Land mines**: 26 (1998); **International Criminal Court**: 27 (no)

Sweden

IHL: 1 (1953); 2 (1979); 2a (yes); 3 (1979); **International HR:** 4 (1971); 5 (1971); 5a (yes); 6 (1971); 7 (1990); **Regional HR:** 8 (1952); 8a (1995); **Children:** 11 (1990); **Torture:** 12 (1986); 12a (yes); 12b (yes); 13 (1988); **Refugees and Stateless persons:** 15 (1954); 16 (1967); 18 (1965); 19 (1969); **Genocide:** 20 (1952); **War crimes and Crimes against humanity:** 21 (no); 22 (no); **Discrimination**: 23 (1971); 23a (yes); 24 (1980); 25 (no); **Land mines**: 26 (1998); **International Criminal Court**: 27 (1998 S)

Switzerland

IHL: 1 (1950); 2 (1982); 2a (yes); 3 (1982); **International HR:** 4 (1992); 5 (1992); 5a (yes); 6 (no); 7 (1994); **Regional HR:** 8 (1974); 8a (1995); **Children:** 11 (1997); **Torture:** 12 (1986); 12a (yes); 12b (yes); 13 (1988); **Refugees and Stateless persons:** 15 (1955); 16 (1968); 18 (1972); 19 (no); **Genocide:** 20 (2000); **War crimes and Crimes against humanity:** 21 (no); 22 (no); **Discrimination**: 23 (1994); 23a (no); 24 (1997); 25 (no); **Land mines**: 26 (1998); **International Criminal Court**: 27 (1998 S)

Syria

IHL: 1 (1953); 2 (1983); 2a (no); 3 (no); **International HR:** 4 (1969); 5 (1969); 5a (no); 6 (no); 7 (no); **Children:** 11 (1993); **Torture:** 12 (no); 12a (no); 12b (no); **Refugees and Stateless persons:** 15 (no); 16 (no); 18 (no); 19 (no); **Genocide:** 20 (1955); **War crimes and Crimes against humanity:** 21 (no); **Discrimination**: 23 (1969); 23a (no); 24 (no); 25 (1976); **Land mines**: 26 (no); **International Criminal Court**: 27 (2000)

Tajikistan

IHL: 1 (1993); 2 (1993); 2a (yes); 3 (1993); **International HR:** 4 (1999); 5 (1999); 5a (no); 6 (1999); 7 (no); **Children:** 11 (1993); **Torture:** 12 (1995); 12a (no); 12b (no); **Refugees and Stateless persons:** 15 (1993); 16 (1993); 18 (no); 19 (no); **Genocide:** 20 (no); **War crimes and Crimes against humanity:** 21 (no); **Discrimination**: 23 (1995); 23a (no); 24 (1993); 25 (no); **Land mines**: 26 (1999); **International Criminal Court**: 27 (2000)

Tanzania

IHL: 1 (1962); 2 (1983); 2a (no); 3 (1983); **International HR:** 4 (1976); 5 (1976); 5a (no); 6 (no); 7 (no); **Regional HR:** 10 (1984); **Children:** 11 (1991); **Torture:** 12 (no); 12a (no); 12b (no); **Refugees and Stateless persons:** 15 (1964); 16 (1968); 17 (1975); 18 (no); 19 (no); **Genocide:** 20 (1984); **War crimes and Crimes against humanity:** 21 (no); **Discrimination**: 23 (no); 23a (no); 24 (no); 25 (1976); **Land mines**: 26 (1997 S); **International Criminal Court**: 27 (2000 S)

Thailand

IHL: 1 (1954); 2 (no); 2a (no); 3 (no); **International HR:** 4 (no); 5 (1996); 5a (no); 6 (no); 7 (no); **Children:** 11 (1992); **Torture:** 12 (no); 12a (no); 12b (no); **Refugees and Stateless persons:** 15 (no); 16 (no); 18 (no); 19 (no); **Genocide:** 20 (no); **War crimes and Crimes against humanity:** 21 (no); **Discrimination**: 23 (no); 23a (no); 24 (1985); 25 (no); **Land mines**: 26 (1998); **International Criminal Court**: 27 (2000 S)

Togo
IHL: 1 (1962); 2 (1984); 2a (yes); 3 (1984); **International HR:** 4 (1984); 5 (1984); 5a (no); 6 (1988); 7 (no); **Regional HR:** 10 (1982); **Children:** 11 (1990); **Torture:** 12 (1987); 12a (yes); 12b (yes); **Refugees and Stateless persons:** 15 (1962); 16 (1969); 17 (1970); 18 (no); 19 (no); **Genocide:** 20 (1984); **War crimes and Crimes against humanity:** 21 (no); **Discrimination:** 23 (1972); 23a (no); 24 (1983); 25 (1984); **Land mines:** 26 (2000); **International Criminal Court:** 27 (no)

Tonga
IHL: 1 (1978); 2 (no); 2a (no); 3 (no); **International HR:** 4 (no); 5 (no); 5a (no); 6 (no); 7 (no); **Children:** 11 (1995); **Torture:** 12 (no); 12a (no); 12b (no); **Refugees and Stateless persons:** 15 (2000); 16 (2000); 18 (no); 19 (no); **Genocide:** 20 (1972); **War crimes and Crimes against humanity:** 21 (no); **Discrimination:** 23 (1972); 23a (no); 24 (no); 25 (no); **Land mines:** 26 (no); **International Criminal Court:** 27 (no)

Trinidad and Tobago
IHL: 1 (1963); 2 (no); 2a (no); 3 (no); **International HR:** 4 (1978); 5 (1978); 5a (no); 6 (1980); 7 (no); **Regional HR:** 9 (1991); 9a (no); 9b (yes); **Children:** 11 (1991); **Torture:** 12 (no); 12a (no); 12b (no); 14 (no); **Refugees and Stateless persons:** 15 (2000); 16 (2000); 18 (1966); 19 (no); **Genocide:** 20 (no); **War crimes and Crimes against humanity:** 21 (no); **Discrimination:** 23 (1973); 23a (no); 24 (1990); 25 (1979); **Land mines:** 26 (1998); **International Criminal Court:** 27 (1999)

Tunisia
IHL: 1 (1957); 2 (1979); 2a (no); 3 (1979); **International HR:** 4 (1969); 5 (1969); 5a (yes); 6 (no); 7 (no); **Regional HR:** 10 (1983); **Children:** 11 (1992); **Torture:** 12 (1988); 12a (yes); 12b (yes); **Refugees and Stateless persons:** 15 (1957); 16 (1968); 17 (1989); 18 (1969); 19 (2000); **Genocide:** 20 (1956); **War crimes and Crimes against humanity:** 21 (1972); **Discrimination:** 23 (1967); 23a (no); 24 (1985); 25 (1977); **Land mines:** 26 (1999); **International Criminal Court:** 27 (no)

Turkey
IHL: 1 (1954); 2 (no); 2a (no); 3 (no); **International HR:** 4 (2000 S); 5 (2000 S); 5a (no); 6 (no); 7 (no); **Regional HR:** 8 (1954); 8a (1997); **Children:** 11 (1995); **Torture:** 12 (1988); 12a (yes); 12b (yes); 13 (1988); **Refugees and Stateless persons:** 15 (1962); 16 (1968); 18 (no); 19 (no); **Genocide:** 20 (1950); **War crimes and Crimes against humanity:** 21 (no); 22 (no); **Discrimination:** 23 (1972 S); 23a (no); 24 (1985); 25 (no); **Land mines:** 26 (no); **International Criminal Court:** 27 (no)

Turkmenistan
IHL: 1 (1992); 2 (1992); 2a (no); 3 (1992); **International HR:** 4 (1997); 5 (1997); 5a (no); 6 (1997); 7 (2000); **Children:** 11 (1993); **Torture:** 12 (1999); 12a (no); 12b (no); **Refugees and Stateless persons:** 15 (1998); 16 (1998); 18 (no); 19 (no); **Genocide:** 20 (no); **War crimes and Crimes against humanity:** 21 (no); **Discrimination:** 23 (1994); 23a (no); 24 (1997); 25 (no); **Land mines:** 26 (1998); **International Criminal Court:** 27 (no)

Tuvalu
IHL: 1 (1981); 2 (no); 2a (no); 3 (no); **International HR:** 4 (no); 5 (no); 5a (no); 6 (no); 7 (no); **Children:** 11 (1995); **Torture:** 12 (no); 12a (no); 12b (no); **Refugees and Stateless persons:** 15 (1986); 16 (1986); 18 (no); 19 (no); **Genocide:** 20 (no); **War crimes and Crimes against humanity:** 21 (no); **Discrimination:** 23 (no); 23a (no); 24 (1999); 25 (no); **Land mines:** 26 (no); **International Criminal Court:** 27 (no)

Uganda
IHL: 1 (1964); 2 (1991); 2a (no); 3 (1991); **International HR:** 4 (1987); 5 (1995); 5a (no); 6 (1995); 7 (no); **Regional HR:** 10 (1986); **Children:** 11 (1990); **Torture:** 12 (1986); 12a (no); 12b (no); **Refugees and Stateless persons:** 15 (1976); 16 (1976); 17 (1987); 18 (1965); 19 (no); **Genocide:** 20 (1995); **War crimes and Crimes against humanity:** 21 (no); **Discrimination:** 23 (1980); 23a (no); 24 (1985); 25 (1986); **Land mines:** 26 (1999); **International Criminal Court:** 27 (1999 S)

Ukraine

IHL: 1 (1954); 2 (1990); 2a (yes); 3 (1990); **International HR:** 4 (1973); 5 (1973); 5a (yes); 6 (1991); 7 (no); **Regional HR:** 8 (**1997**); 8a (**1997**); **Children:** 11 (1991); **Torture:** 12 (1987); 12a (no); 12b (no); 13 (1997); **Refugees and Stateless persons:** 15 (no); 16 (no); 18 (no); 19 (no); **Genocide:** 20 (1954); **War crimes and Crimes against humanity:** 21 (1969); 22 (no); **Discrimination**: 23 (1969); 23a (yes); 24 (1981); 25 (1975); **Land mines**: 26 (1999 S); **International Criminal Court**: 27 (2000 S)

United Arab Emirates

IHL: 1 (1972); 2 (1983); 2a (yes); 3 (1983); **International HR:** 4 (no); 5 (no); 5a (no); 6 (no); 7 (no); **Children:** 11 (1997); **Torture:** 12 (1996); 12a (no); 12b (no); **Refugees and Stateless persons:** 15 (1983); 16 (1983); 18 (1954 S); 19 (no); **Genocide:** 20 (1950); **War crimes and Crimes against humanity:** 21 (no); **Discrimination**: 23 (1974); 23a (no); 24 (no); 25 (1975); **Land mines**: 26 (no); **International Criminal Court**: 27 (2000 S)

United Kingdom

IHL: 1 (1957); 2 (1998); 2a (1999); 3 (1998); **International HR:** 4 (1976); 5 (1976); 5a (yes); 6 (no); 7 (no); **Regional HR:** 8 (1951); 8a (1994); **Children:** 11 (1991); **Torture:** 12 (1988); 12a (yes); 12b (no); 13 (1988); **Refugees and Stateless persons:** 15 (1954); 16 (1968); 18 (1959); 19 (1966); **Genocide:** 20 (1970); **War crimes and Crimes against humanity:** 21 (no); 22 (no); **Discrimination**: 23 (1969); 23a (no); 24 (1986); 25 (no); **Land mines**: 26 (1998); **International Criminal Court**: 27 (1998 S)

United States

IHL: 1 (1955); 2 (1977 S); 2a (no); 3 (1977 S); **International HR:** 4 (1977 S); 5 (1992); 5a (yes); 6 (no); 7 (no); **Regional HR:** 9 (1977 S); 9a (no); 9b (no); **Children:** 11 (1995 S); **Torture:** 12 (1994); 12a (yes); 12b (no); 14 (no); **Refugees and Stateless persons:** 15 (no); 16 (1968); 18 (no); 19 (no); **Genocide:** 20 (1988); **War crimes and Crimes against humanity:** 21 (no); **Discrimination**: 23 (1994); 23a (no); 24 (1980 S); 25 (no); **Land mines**: 26 (no); **International Criminal Court**: 27 (2000 S)

Uruguay

IHL: 1 (1969); 2 (1985); 2a (yes); 3 (1985); **International HR:** 4 (1970); 5 (1970); 5a (no); 6 (1970); 7 (1993); **Regional HR:** 9 (1985); 9a (yes); 9b (yes); **Children:** 11 (1990); **Torture:** 12 (1986); 12a (yes); 12b (yes); 14 (1992); **Refugees and Stateless persons:** 15 (1970); 16 (1970); 18 (no); 19 (no); **Genocide:** 20 (1967); **War crimes and Crimes against humanity:** 21 (no); **Discrimination**: 23 (1968); 23a (yes); 24 (1981); 25 (no); **Land mines**: 26 (1997 S); **International Criminal Court**: 27 (2000 S)

Uzbekistan

IHL: 1 (1993); 2 (1993); 2a (no); 3 (1993); **International HR:** 4 (1995); 5 (1995); 5a (no); 6 (1995); 7 (no); **Children:** 11 (1994); **Torture:** 12 (1995); 12a (no); 12b (no); **Refugees and Stateless persons:** 15 (no); 16 (no); 18 (no); 19 (no); **Genocide:** 20 (1999); **War crimes and Crimes against humanity:** 21 (no); **Discrimination**: 23 (1995); 23a (no); 24 (1995); 25 (no); **Land mines**: 26 (no); **International Criminal Court**: 27 (2000 S)

Vanuatu

IHL: 1 (1982); 2 (1985); 2a (no); 3 (1985); **International HR:** 4 (no); 5 (no); 5a (no); 6 (no); 7 (no); **Children:** 11 (1993); **Torture:** 12 (no); 12a (no); 12b (no); **Refugees and Stateless persons:** 15 (no); 16 (no); 18 (no); 19 (no); **Genocide:** 20 (no); **War crimes and Crimes against humanity:** 21 (no); **Discrimination**: 23 (no); 23a (no); 24 (1995); 25 (no); **Land mines**: 26 (1997 S); **International Criminal Court**: 27 (no)

Venezuela

IHL: 1 (1956); 2 (1998); 2a (no); 3 (1998); **International HR:** 4 (1978); 5 (1978); 5a (no); 6 (1978); 7 (1993); **Regional HR:** 9 (1977); 9a (yes); 9b (yes); **Children:** 11 (1990); **Torture:** 12 (1991); 12a (yes); 12b (yes); 14 (1991); **Refugees and Stateless persons:** 15 (no); 16 (1986); 18 (no); 19 (no); **Genocide:** 20 (1960); **War crimes and Crimes against humanity:** 21 (no); **Discrimination**: 23 (1967); 23a (no); 24 (1983); 25 (1983); **Land mines**: 26 (1999); **International Criminal Court**: 27 (2000)

Vietnam
IHL: 1 (1957); 2 (1981); 2a (no); 3 (no); **International HR:** 4 (1982); 5 (1984); 5a (no); 6 (no); 7 (no); **Children:** 11 (1990); **Torture:** 12 (no); 12a (no); 12b (no); **Refugees and Stateless persons:** 15 (no); 16 (no); 18 (no); 19 (no); **Genocide:** 20 (1981); **War crimes and Crimes against humanity:** 21 (1983); **Discrimination**: 23 (1982); 23a (no); 24 (1982); 25 (1981); **Land mines**: 26 (no); **International Criminal Court**: 27 (no)

Western Samoa
IHL: 1 (1984); 2 (1984); 2a (no); 3 (1984); **International HR:** 4 (no); 5 (no); 5a (no); 6 (no); 7 (no); **Children:** 11 (1994); **Torture:** 12 (no); 12a (no); 12b (no); **Refugees and Stateless persons:** 15 (1988); 16 (1994); 18 (no); 19 (no); **Genocide:** 20 (no); **War crimes and Crimes against humanity:** 21 (no); **Discrimination**: 23 (no); 23a (no); 24 (1992); 25 (no); **Land mines**: 26 (1998); **International Criminal Court**: 27 (1998 S)

Yemen
IHL: 1 (1970); 2 (1990); 2a (no); 3 (1990); **International HR:** 4 (1987); 5 (1987); 5a (no); 6 (no); 7 (no); **Children:** 11 (1991); **Torture:** 12 (1991); 12a (no); 12b (no); **Refugees and Stateless persons:** 15 (1980); 16 (1980); 18 (no); 19 (no); **Genocide:** 20 (1987); **War crimes and Crimes against humanity:** 21 (1987); **Discrimination**: 23 (1972); 23a (no); 24 (1984); 25 (1987); **Land mines**: 26 (1998); **International Criminal Court**: 27 (2000 S)

Yugoslavia
IHL: 1 (1950); 2 (1979); 2a (no); 3 (1979); **International HR:** 4 (1971); 5 (1971); 5a (no); 6 (1990); 7 (no); **Children:** 11 (1991); **Torture:** 12 (1991); 12a (yes); 12b (yes); **Refugees and Stateless persons:** 15 (1959); 16 (1968); 18 (1959); 19 (no); **Genocide:** 20 (1950); **War crimes and Crimes against humanity:** 21 (1970); **Discrimination**: 23 (1967); 23a (no); 24 (1982); 25 (1975); **Land mines**: 26 (no); **International Criminal Court**: 27 (2000 S)

Zambia
IHL: 1 (1966); 2 (1995); 2a (no); 3 (1995); **International HR:** 4 (1984); 5 (1984); 5a (no); 6 (1984); 7 (no); **Regional HR:** 10 (1984); **Children:** 11 (1991); **Torture:** 12 (1998); 12a (no); 12b (no); **Refugees and Stateless persons:** 15 (1969); 16 (1969); 17 (1973); 18 (1974); 19 (no); **Genocide:** 20 (no); **War crimes and Crimes against humanity:** 21 (no); **Discrimination**: 23 (1972); 23a (no); 24 (1985); 25 (1983); **Land mines**: 26 (2001); **International Criminal Court**: 27 (1998 S)

Zimbabwe
IHL: 1 (1983); 2 (1992); 2a (no); 3 (1992); **International HR:** 4 (1991); 5 (1991); 5a (yes); 6 (no); 7 (no); **Regional HR:** 10 (1986); **Children:** 11 (1990); **Torture:** 12 (no); 12a (no); 12b (no); **Refugees and Stateless persons:** 15 (1981); 16 (1981); 17 (1985); 18 (1998); 19 (no); **Genocide:** 20 (1991); **War crimes and Crimes against humanity:** 21 (no); **Discrimination**: 23 (1991); 23a (no); 24 (1991); 25 (1991); **Land mines**: 26 (1998); **International Criminal Court**: 27 (1998 S)

Term Index

Bold is used to indicate when the term is also a subject entry in the main text.

Humanitarian Law Themes:
A Guide to Key Entries by Subject

CHILDREN
Adoption; Children; Committee on the Rights of the Child (CRC); Detention; Evacuation; Family; Family reunification; Food; Minors; Rape; Relief; Supplies; UNICEF

COLLECTIVE SECURITY
Aggression; Arbitration; Collective security; Embargo; International Court of Justice (ICJ); Peace; Peacekeeping; Public order; Safety; Sanctions (diplomatic, economic, or military); Sanctions committees; Security Council of the UN; Self-defense; Sovereignty; Veto → **Protection; War**

DETENTION
Camps; Children; Collective Punishment; Corporal punishment; Death penalty; Detention; Family; Internment; Judicial guarantees; Prisoners of war; Sanctions (diplomatic, economic, or military); Women

FAMILY
Adoption; Central Tracing Agency (CTA); Children; Evacuation; Family; Family reunification; Red Cross; Women

FOOD
General: Blockade; Embargo; Famine; Food; Food and Agricultural Organization (FAO); Protected objects and property; Relief; Supplies; World Food Program (WFP)
Specific statuses: Children; Detention; Prisoners of war; Women

HEALTH
General: Medical duties; Medical ethics; Medical personnel; Medical services; Protected areas and zones; Well-being; World Health Organization (WHO); Wounded and sick persons
Specific health regulations: Detention; Internment; Prisoners of war

HUMAN RIGHTS
Application: Disasters (natural or humanitarian); *Force majeure;* Fundamental guarantees; Human rights; Internal disturbances and tensions; International conventions; International law; Judicial guarantees; Nonretroactivity; Siege; Situations and persons not expressly covered by humanitarian law; Sovereignty; State of emergency/State of siege
Recourse: African Commission on Human and People's Rights; Committee against Torture (CAT); Committee on the Elimination of Discrimination against Women; Committee on the Elimination of Racial Discrimination; Committee on the Rights of the Child (CRC); European Committee for the Prevention of Torture (CPT); European Court of Human Rights; Human rights; Individual Recourse; Inter-American Court of, and Commission on, Human Rights; International Criminal Court (ICC); Special Rapporteurs; UN Commission (and Sub-Commission) on Human Rights; UN High Commissioner for Human Rights (UNHCHR)

Sources and content: Apartheid; Children
(Convention on the Rights of the Child);
Discrimination; Genocide (Convention on the
Prevention and Punishment of the Crime of
Genocide); Human rights (African Charter on
Human and Peoples' Rights; American
Convention on Human Rights; European
Convention for the Protection of Human Rights
and Fundamental Freedoms; International
Covenant on Civil and Political Rights;
International Covenant on Economic, Social,
and Cultural Rights); Inalienability of rights;
Inviolability of rights; Nationality;
Nonapplicability of statutory limitations;
Persecution; *Refoulement* (forced return) and
expulsion; Torture (Convention against Torture
and Other Cruel, Inhuman, or Degrading
Treatment or Punishment; European
Convention for the Prevention of Torture and
Inhuman or Degrading Treatment or
Punishment; Inter-American Convention to
Prevent and Punish Torture); Universal
Declaration of Human Rights; War
crimes/Crimes against humanity → **List of
states party to international human rights
and humanitarian conventions**

HUMAN RIGHTS AND FUNDAMENTAL FREEDOMS

Collective Punishment; Corporal Punishment;
Death penalty; Fundamental guarantees; Human
rights; Inalienability of rights; Internal
disturbances and tensions; International
humanitarian law; International law; Judicial
guarantees; Nonapplicability of statutory
limitations; Nonretroactivity; Siege; Sovereignty;
State of emergency/State of siege

HUMANITARIAN AND RELIEF PERSONNEL

Humanitarian and relief personnel; Immunity;
Intervention; Medical personnel; Protection;
Relief; Responsibility; Right of humanitarian
initiative

HUMANITARIAN LAW

Application: High Contracting Parties; Internal
disturbances and tensions; International armed
conflict; International conventions;
Noninternational armed conflict; Parties to the
conflict; Peace; Situations and persons not

expressly covered by humanitarian law;
Sovereignty; Special Agreement
Recourse: Amnesties; Humanitarian principles;
Impunity; Inalienability; Individual recourse;
International Criminal Court (ICC);
International Criminal Tribunals for the former
Yugoslavia (ICTY) and Rwanda (ICTR);
International Fact-Finding Commission (IFFC);
Inviolability of rights; Universal jurisdiction;
War crimes/Crimes against humanity
Source and content: Duty of commanders; Geneva
Conventions and Additional Protocols;
Genocide; (The) Hague Conventions;
Humanitarian and relief personnel;
Humanitarian principles; International
humanitarian law; Medical duties;
Noncombatants; Protected objects and
property; Protected persons; Protecting Powers;
Protection; Red Cross; Relief; Respect for
international humanitarian law; Responsibility;
Right of access; Right of humanitarian
initiative; Supplies; Weapons → **List of states
party to international human rights and
humanitarian conventions**

INTERNATIONAL LAW

Application of law: Fundamental guarantees;
Internal disturbances and tensions;
International conventions; International law;
Judicial guarantees; Legal status of parties to
the conflict; Siege; Situations and persons not
expressly covered by humanitarian law;
Special Agreement; State of emergency/State
of siege
Legal sanctions/Punishment: Arbitration;
International Court of Justice (ICJ);
International Criminal Court (ICC);
International Criminal Tribunals for the former
Yugoslavia (ICTY) and Rwanda (ICTR); Penal
sanctions in humanitarian law; Responsibility;
Sanctions (diplomatic, economic, or military)
Sources of law: Customary international law;
Hierarchy of norms; International conventions;
International law; Mandate; Natural law and
positive law; Soft law; Special Agreement
→ **Humanitarian law; Human rights; War
crimes/Crimes against humanity**

MISSING OR DISAPPEARED PERSONS

Central Tracing Agency (CTA); Family
reunification; Red Cross; Special Rapporteurs

NONGOVERNMENTAL ORGANIZATIONS (NGOS)

Human rights; Humanitarian principles; International humanitarian law; Nongovernmental organizations (NGOs); Protecting Powers; Protection; Relief; Responsibility; Right of access; Right of humanitarian initiative

OCCUPATION

Annexation; Civil defense; International humanitarian law; Internment; Judicial guarantees; Occupied territories; Prisoners of war; Protecting Powers; Relief

POPULATION DISPLACEMENT

Camps; Deportation; Evacuation; Internally displaced persons; Population displacement; Refugees; UN High Commissioner for Refugees (UNHCR)

PROTECTION

General: Civil defense; Humanitarian principles; Nongovernmental Organizations (NGOs); Protecting Powers; Protection; Public order; Red Cross; Responsibility; Safety

Protected areas: Distinctive (or protective) emblems, signs, or signals; Medical services; Protected areas and zones (demilitarized zones; hospital and safety zones and localities; hospital zones and localities; neutralized zones; nondefended localities; safe areas; secure humanitarian areas); Protected objects and property; Requisition

Protected objects and property: Medical services; Military objectives; Protected objects and property (civilian; cultural; enemy; essential; natural); Requisition

Protected persons: Children; Civilians; Detention; Hostages; Humanitarian and relief personnel; Human shields; Journalists; Medical personnel; Noncombatants; Prisoners of war; Protected persons; Refugees; Requisition; Women; Wounded and sick persons

REFUGEES

Asylum; Boat people; Camps; Central Tracing Agency (CTA); Family reunification; *Refoulement* (forced return) and expulsion; Refugees; Repatriation; Return (of refugees); Stateless persons; UN High Commissioner for Refugees (UNHCR)

RELIEF

Assistance; Disasters (natural or humanitarian); Distinctive (or protective) emblems, signs, or signals; Food; Humanitarian and relief personnel; Humanitarian principles; Internally displaced persons; Intervention; Medical personnel; Nongovernmental organizations (NGOs); Protected areas and zones; Red Cross; Refugees; Relief; Responsibility; Right of access; Right of humanitarian initiative; Supplies → **Health; Protected persons; Protection**

UNITED NATIONS

Economic and Social Council (ECOSOC); Food and Agricultural Organization (FAO); General Assembly of the UN; International Court of Justice (ICJ); International Criminal Court (ICC); Intervention; Mandate; Office for Coordination of Humanitarian Affairs of the UN (OCHA); Peace; Peacekeeping; Refugees; Secretariat of the UN; Security Council; Self-defense; UN Development Program (UNDP); **UN High Commissioner for Human Rights (UNHCHR); UN High Commissioner for Refugees (UNHCR);** UNICEF; United Nations (UN); World Food Program (WFP); World Health Organization (WHO)

VIOLATIONS OF LAW

Definitions: Apartheid; Deportation; Discrimination; Ethnic cleansing; Extermination; Genocide; Hostages; Ill treatment; Perfidy; Persecution; Pillage; Population displacement; Rape; Terror; Terrorism; Torture; War crimes/Crimes against humanity

Recourse: African Commission on Human and People's Rights; Committee against Torture (CAT); Committee on the Elimination of Discrimination against Women; Committee on the Elimination of Racial Discrimination; Committee on the Rights of the Child (CRC); European Committee for the Prevention of Torture (CPT); European Court of Human Rights; Human Rights Committee (HRC); Individual Recourse; Inter-American Court of, and Commission on, Human Rights; International Court of Justice; International Fact-Finding Commission; Special Rapporteurs; UN Commission (and Sub-Commission) on Human Rights

Responsibility: Amnesties; Duty of commanders; Immunity; Impunity; Peacekeeping; Responsibility

Sanctions/Punishment: Amnesties; Embargo; Impunity; International Criminal Court; International Criminal Tribunals for the former Yuogoslavia (ICTY) and Rwanda (ICTR); Mutual assistance in criminal matters; Nonapplicability of statutory limitations; Penal sanctions in humanitarian law; Respect for international humanitarian law; Sanctions (diplomatic, economic, or military); Universal jurisdiction

WAR

Definitions: Belligerent; Combatant; Espionage; High Contracting Parties; Insurgents; Internal disturbances and tensions; International armed conflict; Mercenaries; Noncombatants; Noninternational armed conflict; Parties to the conflict; Resistance movements; War

Methods (and means) of warfare: Aggression; Annexation; Attacks; Blockade; Bombardment; Cease-fire; Civilians; Combatants; Distinctive (or protective) emblems, signs or signal; Duty of commanders; Evacuation; Hostages; Human shields; Methods (and means) of warfare; Military necessity; Military objectives; Prisoners of war; Proportionality; Protected objects and property; Protected persons; Reprisals; Requisition; Responsibility; Siege

Weapons: Methods (and means) of warfare; Mines; Weapons

WOMEN

Committee on the Elimination of Discrimination against Women; Detention; Evacuation; Family; Relief; Rape; Supplies; Women

About the Author

Françoise Bouchet-Saulnier, an expert in the field of humanitarian law, has been legal director of the international humanitarian aid organization Médecins Sans Frontières/Doctors Without Borders (MSF) in Paris since 1991 and research director of the Médecins Sans Frontières Foundation since 1995. Bouchet-Saulnier has been pivotal in shaping MSF responses to conflict situations such as Rwanda, Somalia, and Kosovo and educating MSF aid workers on humanitarian law issues. She has also worked on various urban poverty initiatives, advocating for the legal protection of children in Madagascar, Armenia, and Guatemala. She is frequently in the field to support negotiations and international advocacy campaigns.

In addition to her work with MSF, Bouchet-Saulnier has been teaching law at the University of Paris since 1992 and is engaged in research on international justice. She is the coauthor of a book focusing on the Rwandan genocide and has written numerous articles on humanitarian law. Before joining MSF, Bouchet-Saulnier acted as a consultant for several organizations, including the United Nations Disaster Relief Office and Amnesty International. She holds a doctorate in international law from the University of Nice.